Acadamh Ríoga na hÉireann   An Roinn Gnóthaí Eachtracha

Cáipéisí ar Pholasaí Eachtrach na hÉireann

Imleabhar II

1923 ~ 1926

EAGARTHÓIRÍ
Ronan Fanning
Michael Kennedy
Dermot Keogh
Eunan O'Halpin

Royal Irish Academy Department of Foreign Affairs

Documents on Irish Foreign Policy

Volume II

1923 ~ 1926

EDITORS
Ronan Fanning
Michael Kennedy
Dermot Keogh
Eunan O'Halpin

First published in 2000 by the
Royal Irish Academy
19 Dawson Street
Dublin, Ireland

A catalogue record for this title is available from the British Library

ISBN 1 874045 83 6

Publishing consultants
Institute of Public Administration, Dublin

Design by Jan de Fouw
Typeset by Wendy A. Commins
Printed by Betaprint, Dublin

Contents

Editors

Professor Ronan Fanning MRIA
(Professor of Modern History, University College Dublin)

Dr Michael Kennedy
(Executive Editor, Documents on Irish Foreign Policy Series,
Royal Irish Academy)

Professor Dermot Keogh
(Professor of History, University College Cork)

Professor Eunan O'Halpin
(Professor of Contemporary Irish History, University of Dublin,
Trinity College)

Editorial Advisory Board

(In addition to the Editors)

Mr Gary Ansbro (Department of Foreign Affairs)
(June 1997-May 1999)

Mr Patrick Buckley (Royal Irish Academy)

Ms Catriona Crowe (National Archives of Ireland)

Dr Gerard Keown (Department of Foreign Affairs)
(June 1997-May 1999)

Mr Noel Kilkenny (Department of Foreign Affairs)
(from May 1999)

Ms Orla McBreen (Department of Foreign Affairs)
(from July 2000)

Ms Alma ní Choighligh (Department of Foreign Affairs)
(May 1999-July 2000)

Abbreviations

The following is a list of the most commonly used abbreviated terms and phrases in the volume, covering both documents and editorial matter. Other abbreviations have been spelt out in the text.

DE	Dáil Éireann series files, National Archives, Dublin
DFA	Department of Foreign Affairs collection, National Archives, Dublin
DFIN	Department of Finance collection, National Archives, Dublin
DT S	Department of the Taoiseach, S series files, National Archives, Dublin
ES	Early Series files, Department of Foreign Affairs collection, National Archives, Dublin
ILO	International Labour Organisation
SdN	Société des Nations
TD	Teachta Dála (Member of Dáil Éireann)
UCDA	University College Dublin, Archives Department

Preface

The National Archives Act, 1986, provides for the transfer of departmental records more than thirty years old to the National Archives of Ireland for inspection by the public, unless they are certified to be in regular use by a Department for administrative purposes, or unless they are certified as withheld from public inspection on one of the grounds specified in the Act. The bulk of the material consulted for this volume comes from the records of the Department of Foreign Affairs (previously the Department of External Affairs) and the Department of the Taoiseach, all of which are available for inspection at the National Archives of Ireland at Bishop Street in Dublin. Other material from personal collections comes from the holdings of the University College Dublin Archives Department. The Department of Foreign Affairs documents in the National Archives of Ireland have been made available to researchers since January 1991.[1]

The concept of a multi-volume series of documents on Irish foreign policy was put forward in 1994 by the Department of Foreign Affairs. Mr Ted Barrington, then the Political Director of the Department of Foreign Affairs and now the Irish Ambassador in London, brought the proposal to a meeting of the Royal Irish Academy's National Committee for the Study of International Affairs of which he was then a member. The then Tánaiste and Minister for Foreign Affairs, Mr Dick Spring, sanctioned the proposal which was also welcomed by the Director of the National Archives of Ireland, Dr David Craig, whose permission was necessary for the publication of material in his care. The Royal Irish Academy agreed to become a partner in the project when Council approved its foundation document on 3 April 1995.

The main provisions of the foundation document are:

- that the project's 'basic aim is to make available, in an organised and accessible way, to people who may not be in a position easily to consult the National Archives, documents from the files of the Department which are considered important or useful for an understanding of Irish foreign policy';
- that an Editorial Advisory Board, comprising representatives of the Department, of the Academy and of the National Archives, in addition to senior Irish academics working in the fields of modern

[1] The Department of Foreign Affairs was known as the Department of External Affairs from December 1922 to 1971. From January 1919 to December 1922 the Department was known as the Department of Foreign Affairs or the Ministry of Foreign Affairs (see DIFP volume I for further details).

history and international relations, would oversee decisions on publication;
- that the series would 'begin at the foundation of the State and publish volumes in chronological order' and that the basic criterion for the selection of documents would be their 'use or importance in understanding the evolution of policies and decisions'.

These arrangements found public expression in the 1996 White Paper on foreign policy, *Challenges and Opportunities Abroad* (16.48), which provided that –

> As part of the Government's desire to encourage a greater interest in Irish foreign policy, it has been agreed that the Department of Foreign Affairs, in association with the Royal Irish Academy, will publish a series of foreign policy documents of historic interest. It is hoped that this initiative will encourage and assist greater academic interest in the study of Irish foreign policy.

Provision for the project was first included in the Department's estimates for 1997 and a preliminary meeting of what became the Editorial Advisory Board, in Iveagh House on 10 April 1997, agreed that an assistant editor should be appointed to support the editors nominated by the National Committee for the Study of International Affairs: Professors Ronan Fanning, MRIA, Dermot Keogh and Eunan O'Halpin. Dr Michael Kennedy was appointed in June 1997 when work began on the selection of documents. Dr Kennedy has since been designated as executive editor, and is responsible for the direction and day-to-day running of the Documents on Irish Foreign Policy Project.

The first volume, *Documents on Irish Foreign Policy Volume I*, covering the period 1919 to 1922, was published in November 1998 in the run-up to the eightieth anniversary of the founding of the Department of Foreign Affairs in January 1919. Subsequent volumes are to be published at two-yearly intervals, with Volume II appearing in November 2000 and Volume III, covering the period from March 1926 to March 1932, planned for publication in the winter of 2002.

Introduction

This volume of selected documents, the second in the Documents on Irish Foreign Policy series, covers the development of Irish foreign policy and the Irish diplomatic service from 6 December 1922 to 19 March 1926.[1]

December 6, 1922, marks the date that the Irish Free State, created by the Anglo-Irish Treaty of 6 December 1921, was officially established, following a period of provisional government. The closing date, that of the Ultimate Financial Settlement between the Irish Free State and Britain, which completed the restructuring of Anglo-Irish financial relations after the 1921 Treaty, marks a suitable focal point in the middle years of the term of office of the Cumann na nGaedheal government of William T. Cosgrave (which held power until March 1932). Volume III of the Documents on Irish Foreign Policy series will run from March 1926 to March 1932.

***

The unifying theme of this volume is the establishment of the Irish Free State as a sovereign independent state in the international system. Through membership of the Commonwealth and the League of Nations and through limited bilateral relations, particularly with the USA and Britain, the Irish Free State's small diplomatic service, headed by the Minister for External Affairs, Desmond FitzGerald and the Secretary of the Department, Joseph P. Walshe, sought to protect and enhance the international identity of the new Irish state.

The split in the government of Dáil Éireann over the December 1921 Treaty, which had resulted in civil war breaking out in the Irish Free State in June 1922, continued to resonate through the Irish foreign service in the early twenties. Anti-Treatyite representatives, including a number of former members of the diplomatic service, based in Britain, France and, particularly, the United States, sought, through press and public speaking campaigns, to undermine the international standing of the Irish Free State. However, international support for the anti-Treaty side dwindled as the Irish government consolidated its domestic and international position in the latter months of the civil war in the spring of 1923.

Timothy A. Smiddy represented the Irish Free State in Washington from early 1922. His first policy priority was countering propaganda against the Irish government. The Irish-American community had become even more highly politicised between 1919 and 1921 and was deeply divided over the Treaty and a wide range of national and international issues, particularly

[1] To ensure complete coverage of Boundary Commission policy in a single volume, four documents pre-dating December 1922 were held back from Volume I and are included here as documents 1 to 4.

United States membership of the League of Nations. Securing Smiddy's recognition as the Minister Plenipotentiary and Envoy Extraordinary of the Irish Free State to the United States was the immediate objective of the Minister for External Affairs and the Secretary of the Department. Following protracted discussions with London and Washington, Smiddy was eventually accredited on 7 October 1924. This made the Irish Free State the first dominion to appoint a diplomatic representative independent of Britain. The appointment was a major success for the Irish Free State in its goal of pursuing an independent foreign policy.

The Irish Free State also sought to demonstrate its independent foreign policy through membership of the League of Nations. Ireland joined the League of Nations on 10 September 1923 and played a full role in League assemblies through the 1920s, being elected to the Council of the League in 1930. The Irish Free State representative to the League from 1923 to 1928, Michael MacWhite, became a well-known figure at Geneva. With the help of another Irishman, Edward J. Phelan, a senior official of the International Labour Organisation, MacWhite represented the Irish Free State's views on foreign policy issues in co-operation with the representatives of the other fifty member states; states in the main with which Ireland would otherwise have had no diplomatic exchanges, but with many of which she had much in common as a new, small and weak member of the post-Versailles international system.

Edward J. Phelan's role in Irish diplomacy was so important – at times his views were specifically sought by FitzGerald and Walshe in Dublin – that we have included a number of his letters which, although they are not strictly Irish diplomatic documents, had an important bearing on the course of Irish policy at the League of Nations.

The Irish Free State also used the League to further distinct foreign policy goals such as the registration of the 1921 Treaty as an international treaty at Geneva, a goal achieved on 11 July 1924. Registering the Treaty had a two-fold purpose: it demonstrated how the state could use the League to achieve its foreign policy objectives, and it confirmed that the Cosgrave government intended to promote the redefinition of dominion status away from an imperial relationship and towards a commonwealth of independent states.

Attendance at Commonwealth conferences from 1923 was as much a hallmark of Cumann na nGaedheal foreign policy as was yearly attendance at sessions of the League of Nations assembly. At the 1923 Imperial Conference, the first since the signing of the Anglo-Irish Treaty, Irish diplomats learnt how the Commonwealth worked and began developing their plans to change the structure and theory of dominion status. Their intention to bring about radical change was dramatically illustrated at the 1926 Imperial Conference (to be dealt with in DIFP volume III).

In the first half of the 1920s, Anglo-Irish relations, as distinct from

Commonwealth relations, were dominated by the Boundary Commission and its remit to redraw the frontier between the Irish Free State and Northern Ireland. Established under article 12 of the 1921 Anglo-Irish Treaty, the Boundary Commission did not meet until 1924. From 1922 to 1924 the Irish Free State developed its case for presentation at the Commission through the North-Eastern Boundary Bureau. Eoin MacNeill, the Minister for Education and a brother of James McNeill, the Irish High Commissioner in London, was appointed as the Irish Free State's Boundary Commissioner on 20 July 1923.[1] Between 1923 and 1925, William T. Cosgrave, assisted by James McNeill, took responsibility for most of the direct Anglo-Irish contact relating to the Commission and its actions.

A leak of the proposed alterations to the Irish Free State / Northern Ireland boundary, which appeared in the *Morning Post* newspaper on 7 November 1925, precipitated Eoin MacNeill's resignation from the Boundary Commission (MacNeill's letter of resignation is reproduced in facsimile as document No. 340 below) and later from his post as Minister for Education. As the ensuing political crisis deepened in the Irish Free State, Cosgrave and his ministers entered into emergency talks with the British government. These negotiations led to an agreement on 3 December 1925 to suppress the report of the Boundary Commission, to retain the existing boundary between the Irish Free State and Northern Ireland, and to cancel certain debt repayments by the Irish Free State to Britain arising from the provisions of the 1921 Treaty.

The minutes of the Anglo-Irish talks of November and early December 1925 are reproduced in full in this volume. It should be noted that the British, as hosts, wrote these minutes and that this was consonant with a convention in diplomatic practice 'whereby the principal secretary at a conference is usually an official of the country in which it is held ... and other members of the secretariat are also furnished by it, supplemented ... by others drawn from among the suites of the various representatives'.[2] The minutes are accompanied by the only known Irish record of these meetings: handwritten notes made by the Irish Cabinet Secretary, Diarmuid O'Hegarty (reproduced in facsimile as document No. 351 below).

The volume also covers some less central areas in Irish foreign relations. These include early moves towards the promotion of Ireland as a tourist destination, Irish efforts to develop transatlantic air travel, and the state's role in facilitating the installation of transatlantic telegraph cable links running through Ireland and on to continental Europe. The documents also reveal an early awareness of the need to develop Ireland's international

[1] Though Eoin MacNeill and James McNeill were brothers, they spelt their surnames differently.

[2] See Lord Gore-Booth (ed), *Satow's guide to diplomatic practice* (fifth edition), p. 235 for further details.

trade position and to do so using branded Irish speciality goods in niche markets. The involvement of Irish diplomats in these areas demonstrates that the Irish Free State saw its foreign relations embracing trade and economic questions as well as the political and inter-state issues which were its main concerns.

Although the scope of Irish foreign policy interests and activities was widening in the 1920s, the same could not be said for the resources at the disposal of the small Department of External Affairs. Joseph Walshe, with his second in command, Seán Murphy, could do nothing to prevent the closing down of the Irish missions in Rome and Berlin in 1923 and 1924 respectively. The Paris mission was reduced to an essentially consular role. The Irish Free State's main diplomatic posts abroad in the early 1920s were Washington, London and Geneva. After the Rome and Berlin closures, these three posts, together with two trade and general offices in Paris and Brussels, were Ireland's only foreign missions.

The Department of External Affairs itself, situated in Government Buildings in Dublin, suffered from being regarded in many sections of the administration and government as virtually an extension of the Department of the President of the Executive Council. Until 1927 Walshe was its 'Acting Secretary', whereas his equivalents in all other departments had full status. While 'Acting Secretary' Walshe successfully fended off attempts by the Department of the President and the Department of Finance to close External Affairs down as a cost cutting measure and merge it with the Department of the President. The threat of merger remained a constant backdrop to External Affairs' management of Ireland's foreign relations from 1922 to 1929 when a small expansion of the Department and of missions abroad took place.

Despite the many positive developments and achievements, including membership of the League of Nations, the future administrative independence of the Department of External Affairs remained as uncertain in 1926 as it had been at the foundation of the Irish Free State in 1922. Nonetheless, the actions of Ireland's small and efficient diplomatic service had, by 1926, ensured that the young state was growing increasingly confident of its international sovereignty and was prepared to take a more active role on the world stage.

Records of the Department of Foreign Affairs, and other archival sources

Until the passage of the National Archives Act (1986), government departments in Ireland were under no compulsion to release their archival sources. The Department of the Taoiseach, however, has voluntarily released material since the mid-1970s. The records of the Department of Foreign Affairs have been released on an annual basis since 1991.

The Early Series files of the Department of Foreign Affairs, from which many of the documents in this volume have been selected, were initially thought to be quite disparate and fragmented. They were listed in 1992, making access to them considerably easier. The research and selection process engaged in for this volume, and for volume I of the series, has shown that the files form a much more coherent collection than hitherto believed. It has been possible for the Executive Editor to track movements within the diplomatic service from archival sources on an almost day-to-day basis. This seems to indicate that there was very little destruction of documents in this series.

An early form of departmental registry was established in the Department of External Affairs in 1923 using an alpha-numeric system (the so-called D/EA/GR/LN/P/PP Series). In addition to the Early Series files, the External Affairs documents reproduced in this volume come mainly from this early alpha-numeric system. This system contains copies of many of the documents in the files of the Early Series and it would seem that the two systems may have initially operated side-by-side.

In the late 1920s a numerical system was developed with individual subject categories being assigned a number (e.g. 26 was allocated to the League of Nations) and each file within a category being assigned a further number (e.g. 26/95 deals with the Irish Free State's candidature for the League of Nations Council in 1930). This system was further developed, and remained in use until recently. A relatively small number of documents from this series have been reproduced in this volume.

The main files from the Department of the Taoiseach (known from 1922 to 1937 as the Department of the President of the Executive Council, or simply 'the Department of the President'), the third of the major collections of documents represented in this collection, are known as the 'S-Files' series; they begin at S1 and progress numerically (S1, S2, S3 etc.) in a roughly chronological order. These files reflect the fact that foreign policy matters appeared regularly on the agenda of the Executive Council (as the Irish Free State Cabinet was known from 1922 to 1937) in the 1920s. They further reveal that, contrary to received wisdom, W.T. Cosgrave, as President of the Executive Council, took a great interest in foreign policy, at times directing policy over the head of his Minister for External Affairs, Desmond FitzGerald.

Editorial policy and the selection of documents

The Executive Editor was responsible for the initial wide choice of documents. These documents were then assessed by the four Editors, meeting once a month, to select the most appropriate for publication. Documents were prioritised in terms of importance on a one to five scale and were processed by the Editors in geographical and thematic tranches.

Documents are presented in chronological order based on date of despatch. The text of documents has been reproduced as exactly as possible. Marginal notes and annotations have been reproduced in footnotes. Where possible the authors of marginal notes have been identified. There have been no alterations to the text of documents nor have there been any deletions without indication being given of where changes occur. Nothing was omitted that might conceal or gloss over defects in policymaking and policy execution. All material reproduced was already open to the public at the relevant repository.[1]

At some points in the text the footnotes refer to documents that were either 'not located' or 'not printed'. Either the document referred to could not be found, or it was routine or repeated information found elsewhere in the material selected and so was not printed.

Where it was impossible to decipher a word or series of words, an ellipsis has been inserted or the assumed word inserted with an explanatory footnote. Spelling mistakes have been silently corrected, but capitalisation, punctuation, signatures and contemporary spelling have in the main been left as found in the originals and have been changed only where the sense is affected. Additions to the text appear in square brackets. Original abbreviations have been preserved and either spelled out between square brackets or explained in the list of abbreviations.

Where a sender has signed a document, either in original or copy form, the word 'signed', in square brackets, has been inserted. A similar practice has been followed with initialled or stamped documents, with the word 'initialled' or 'stamped' inserted in square brackets as appropriate. In all cases without an insertion in square brackets, the signature or initials were typed on the original document and are reproduced as found. Where an unsigned copy of a letter is reproduced, the words 'copy letter unsigned' have been inserted in square brackets. The Editors have at all times tried to confirm the identity of the senders and recipients of unsigned letters, and in cases where identity is impossible to establish footnotes have been inserted to that effect.

In correspondence, English was the working language of Irish diplomats. It is evident from the archives that Irish was only used in documents of symbolic national importance, although it was the spoken language of a number of diplomats, particularly Joseph Walshe, and many officials were bilingual. In correspondence, the Irish language was more commonly used

[1] The guidelines of the Department of Foreign Affairs state that

> There may be no alteration of the text, no deletions without indicating the place in the text where the deletion is made, and no omission of the facts which were of major importance in reaching a decision. Nothing may be omitted for the purpose of concealing or glossing over what might be regarded by some as a defect of policy.
>
> However, certain omissions of documents are permissible to avoid publication of matters that would tend to impede current diplomatic negotiations or other business.
>
> In addition, the above guidelines are to be interpreted in conjunction with the obligations laid out in the National Archives Act (1986) and the Freedom of Information Act (1997), the provisions contained in which are to be regarded as taking precedence.

None of the documents in Volume II of the Documents on Irish Foreign Policy series had matter omitted for such reasons. Nor were any documents so omitted.

for salutations and in signatures. In many cases there was no consistent spelling of Gaelicised names and in the volume many different spellings of the same name and salutation in Irish occur. These have not been standardised and are reproduced as found.

The authors of the documents reproduced tended to refer to Britain as 'England' or made no distinction between the two geographical entities and the Editors have not thought it necessary to insert (sic) at all relevant points throughout the volume.

Acknowledgements

Documents on Irish Foreign Policy is a project of the Department of Foreign Affairs in association with the Royal Irish Academy. The editors would like to thank all those who were involved in the production of the second volume of the series. The assistance of the following is particularly acknowledged.

At the Department of Foreign Affairs: Pádraic MacKernan, Secretary General; Gary Ansbro; Noel Kilkenny; Dr Gerard Keown; Alma Ní Choighligh and Orla McBreen.

At the Royal Irish Academy: Patrick Buckley, Executive Secretary of the Academy; Professor Eda Sagarra and Professor Mary Daly (successively Secretary of the Academy); Sara Whelan; Hugh Shiels; Trevor Mullins, and Dr Eamon O hÓgain, Stiúrthóir of the Academy's Foclóir na nua-Ghaeilge project.

At the National Archives: Dr David Craig, Director, for his generosity in providing access to the facilities and collections; Catriona Crowe, for her continuing advice and support for the DIFP project; and Paddy Sarsfield for photocopying the very large number of documents from which the initial selection for publication was made.

At the University College Dublin Archives Department: Professor Thomas Bartlett, Director; Ailsa Holland, and Seamus Helferty.

At the Institute of Public Administration: Tony McNamara; Kathleen Harte; Jan de Fouw and Tom Turley.

At the Public Record Office, London: Sara Tyacke CB (Keeper of Public Records); Dr Elizabeth Hallam Smith, and Michael Leydon.

We would also like to thank Wendy Commins; Dr Diarmuid Ferriter; the late Commandant Peter Young; Commandant Victor Laing; Helen Litton; Dr Garret FitzGerald; Maurice O'Brien, and James McGuire of the Royal Irish Academy's Dictionary of Irish Biography.

Ronan Fanning
Michael Kennedy
Dermot Keogh
Eunan O'Halpin

17 July 2000

List of archival sources

National Archives

Dáil Éireann
Dáil Éireann secretariat files
Cabinet Minutes

Department of Finance
Early files (1922-1924) (FIN)

Department of Foreign Affairs
D Series (1920s)
EA Series (1920s)
Early Series (ES)
Embassies Series
GR Series (1920s)
Letter Books
LN Series (1920s)
Minister's Office Files
Number Series
- Pre-100 Series
- 100 Series
- 400 Series

P Series (1920s)
Secretaries' Files (S Series)
Unregistered papers

Department of the Taoiseach
S Files
Cabinet Minutes

University College Dublin Archives

Ernest Blythe papers	(P24)
Desmond FitzGerald papers	(P80)
Hugh Kennedy papers	(P4)
Eoin MacNeill papers	(LAI)

Biographical Notes

This list gives priority to the main Irish ministerial, diplomatic and administrative figures who appear in the text. Key foreign figures have also been identified, but generally in less detail. Minor figures, or people who receive only an occasional mention, have been identified in the text in footnotes.

Amery, Leopold (1873-1955) British politician (Conservative); Parliamentary Secretary, Colonial Office (1919-21); First Lord of the Admiralty (1922-24); Secretary of State for the Colonies (1924-29); Secretary of State for Dominion Affairs (1925-29); Secretary of State for India (1940-45).

Anderson, Sir John (1882-1958) Head of the British administration in Dublin Castle as Joint Under-Secretary for Ireland (1920-22); Permanent Under-Secretary, Home Office, London (1922-32).

Baldwin, Stanley (1867-1947) British Prime Minister (Conservative 1923-24, 1924-29, 1935-37).

Belcourt, Senator Napoleon Antoine (1860-1932) Canadian MP and Senator, Minister Plenipotentiary at the Inter-Allied Conference in London (1924).

Bewley, Charles Henry (1888-1969) Educated at Winchester and New College, Oxford; called to the Irish Bar in 1914; Irish trade representative in Berlin (1921-22); Irish representative Berlin (October 1922-February 1923); called to the Inner Bar of the Irish Free State (1926); Irish Minister to the Vatican (1929-33); Irish Minister to Germany (1933-39).

Blythe, Ernest (1889-1975) TD; Dáil Éireann Minister for Trade and Commerce (1919-22); Provisional Government Minister for Local Government (1922); Minister for Health and Local Government (1922-23); Minister for Finance (1923-32); Vice-President of the Executive Council (1927-32).

Bonar Law, Andrew (1858-1923) British Prime Minister (Conservative 1922-23).

Bourdillon, Francis Bernard (1883-1970) British Naval Intelligence (1916-19); British delegation to the Paris Peace Conference (1919); Upper Silesian Commission (1920-22); Secretary to the Irish Boundary Commission (1924-25); Secretary of the Royal Institute for International Affairs (1926-29); Foreign Office Research Department (1943-45).

Brennan, Joseph (1887-1976) Educated at Clongowes Wood College, University College Dublin and Cambridge University; Principal Officer, Department of Finance (February 1922-21 February 1923); Secretary, Department of Finance (22 February 1923-1927); Chairman of the Currency Commission (1927-43); first Governor of the Irish Central Bank (1948-53).

Byrne, Edward J. (1872-1940) Roman Catholic Archbishop of Dublin (1921-40).

Campbell, Gordon (later **2nd Lord Glenavy**) (1885-1963) Secretary, Department of Industry and Commerce (1922-32).

Chamberlain, Austen (1863-1937) Leader of the British Conservative Party (May 1921-October 1922); member of the British delegation at the 1921 Treaty negotiations; Foreign Secretary (1924-29).

Churchill, Winston (1874-1965) Secretary of State for the Colonies (1921-22); Chairman of Cabinet Committee on Ireland; member of the British delegation at the 1921 Treaty negotiations; responsible for the transfer of services to the Irish Provisional Government (1922); Chancellor of the Exchequer (1924-29).

Cohalan, Daniel F. (1865-1946) Irish American politician; Judge of the Supreme Court of New York State; chairman of the Irish Convention held in Philadelphia (February 1919); active in the Friends of Irish Freedom, broke with Eamon de Valera and Joe McGarrity in 1919.

Connolly, Joseph (1885-1960) Senator (1928-36); Consul General of Ireland in the United States of America (October 1921-November 1922); Minister for Posts and Telegraphs (1932-33); Delegate to the League of Nations (1932).

Cope, Sir Alfred 'Andy' (1880-1954) Assistant Under-Secretary for Ireland and Clerk of the Irish Privy Council (1920-22); Secretary of the National Liberal Association (1922-24).

Cosgrave, William Thomas (1880-1965) TD; Minister for Local Government, Dáil Éireann (April 1919-September 1922); Minister for Local Government, Provisional Government (January-August 1922); Chairman of the Provisional Government (August-December 1922); President of the Executive Council of the Irish Free State (1922-32); Acting Minister for Finance (September 1922-September 1923); Acting Minister for External Affairs (July-October 1927).

Craig, Sir James (1871-1940) Prime Minister of Northern Ireland and leader of the Ulster Unionist Party (1921-40).

Craig Martin, William Irish Free State Honorary Consul in Shanghai.

Crawford, Lindsay (1865-1945) Sometime Grand Master of the Independent Orange Order, expelled after advocating Home Rule; Sinn Féin representative in Canada, Irish Free State Trade Representative in New York (1922-29).

Cremins, Francis T. (1885-1975) Clerical Officer, General Post Office (1900-22); Higher Executive Officer, Publicity Department, External Affairs, (1922-25); Higher Executive Officer, Department of Lands and Fisheries (1925-29); head of League of Nations Section, External Affairs (1929-34); Permanent Representative at Geneva (1934-40); Chargé d'Affaires at Berne (1940-49).

Curran, Michael Vice Rector, Irish College, Rome (1920-30); Rector (1930-38).

Curtis, Lionel (1872-1955) Colonial Office Adviser on Irish Affairs (1921-24).

Dawson Bates, Sir Richard (1877-1949) Northern Ireland Minister of Home Affairs (1921-43).

Dempsey, Vaughan Bebe Assistant, Irish Free State Office in Paris (January-December 1923); Trade Representative in Paris (1923-29); transferred to Dublin as Higher Executive Officer, Department of Industry and Commerce in 1929.

Devlin, Joseph, (1871-1934) Nationalist MP for Belfast (1902-18), leader of the Nationalist Party in Northern Ireland (1920-34); MP in Westminster and Belfast parliaments.

Drummond, Sir (James) Eric (1876-1951) Secretary General of the League of Nations (1919-33).

Duane, Cornelius Assistant, Irish Free State office in Berlin (1923); Irish Free State Representative in Berlin (1923-24).

Devonshire, Victor Christian William Cavendish, 9th Duke of (1868-1938) British Secretary of State for Colonial Affairs (1922-24).

Egan, Frank Irish Representative in Chile (1919-23).

Eliassoff, M.H. Higher Executive Officer/Second Secretary, High Commissioners Office, London (1923 -37).

Fahy, John Vincent Accountant and head of the General Section, Department of External Affairs, Dublin.

Feetham, Richard (1874-1965) Judge of the South African Supreme Court; Chairman of the Boundary Commission (1924-25).

Figgis, Darrell (1892-1925) TD for Dublin County (1919-25). Acting Chairman of the Irish Free State constitution committee (1922). Author of various books on Irish history and politics.

Fisher, J.R. (1855-1939) Journalist (Editor of the *Northern Whig* (1891-1913)) and barrister; British government nominee as Northern Irish representative on the Boundary Commission (1924-25).

FitzGerald, Desmond (1889-1947) TD; Dáil Éireann Substitute Director of Propaganda (17 June 1919-11 February 1921, 15 July 1921-8 September 1922) (subsequently styled Secretary for Publicity, August 1921, then Minister for Publicity, January 1922); Minister for External Affairs (1922-27); Minister for Defence (1927-32); member of Seanad Éireann (1938-47).

Flynn, Charles J. (1884-1938) Irish Free State Revenue Commissioner (1923-25).

Gasparri, Cardinal Pietro, Cardinal Secretary of State, Vatican City.

Gavan Duffy, George (1882-1951) TD; Educated in France and at Stonyhurst College, Lancashire, England; Sinn Féin representative in Paris (1919-20); roving envoy in Europe (1920-21); representative in Rome (1921); Member of the Irish Treaty delegation (October-December 1921); supported the Treaty; Minister for Foreign Affairs (10 January-25 July 1922).

Grattan Esmonde, Osmond (1896-1936) Educated at Downside and Balliol College, Oxford. Dáil Éireann representative in USA, Canada, Australia, France,

Madrid and Rome (1920-22). Department of External Affairs, Dublin (1922-23); TD for Wexford (1923-36).

Hankey, Sir Maurice (1877-1963) British Cabinet Secretary (1916-38).

Harding, Edward J. Assistant Secretary Colonial Office (1921-25); Assistant Under-Secretary, Dominions Office (1925-30); Permanent Under-Secretary Dominions Office (1930-39).

Healy, Cahir (1877-1970) Nationalist MP, House of Commons, Westminster (1922-24, 1931-35, 1950-55); Northern Ireland House of Commons (1925-65); interned (1921-24, 1941-42).

Healy, Timothy M. (1855-1931) Nationalist MP for Wexford (1880-83), Monaghan (1883), South Londonderry (1885-86), North Longford (1887-92); leading anti-Parnellite after the 1890-91 split in the Irish Parliamentary Party; MP for North Louth (1892-1910), North Cork (1910-18); Governor General of the Irish Free State (6 December 1922-31 January 1928).

Howard, Sir Esme British Ambassador to the United States (1924-30).

Kennedy, Hugh (1879-1936) Educated at University College, Dublin; called to the Bar in 1902 and to the Inner Bar in 1920; Legal Adviser to the Provisional Government (1922); member of the committee appointed to draft the Irish Free State Constitution (1922); Attorney General (1922-24), though Kennedy only took up the post on 1 March 1923; TD for Dublin South (25 October 1923-June 1924); Chief Justice of the Irish Free State (1924-36).

Kerney, Leopold Harding (1881-1962) Irish Consul at Paris (1919-22); opposed the Treaty; Republican Envoy in Paris (1923-25); Commercial Secretary, Paris Legation (1932-34); Minister to Spain (1935-46).

Kiernan, Thomas J. (1897-1967) Educated at University College Dublin and London University; Inland Revenue (1919-24); Secretary High Commission, London (1924-35); Director of Radio Éireann (1935-41); Minister to the Vatican (1941-46); Representative to Australia (1946-50); Ambassador to Australia (1950-55); Minister to Germany (1955-56); Ambassador to Canada (1956-60); Ambassador to Washington (1960-64); Author of several books on financial and historical subjects.

Larkin, James (1876-1947) TD and Trade Unionist, resident in the USA from 1914 to 1923, jailed 1920-23 for labour agitation; returned to Ireland and founded the Workers' Union of Ireland; secured recognition from the Communist International in 1924 and visited Russia as a representative of the Irish Section of Comintern; TD for Dublin North (1927-32, 1937-38, 1943-44).

Lester, Sean (1888-1959) Former news editor of the *Freeman's Journal*; Publicity Office and League of Nations Section, Department of External Affairs (1923-29); Irish Free State Permanent Representative to the League of Nations (1929-34); League of Nations High Commissioner in Danzig (1934-37); Deputy Secretary General of the League of Nations (1937-40); Secretary General of the League of Nations (1940-46).

Loughnane, Norman G. (1883-1954) Chief Secretary's Office (1920-22); Colonial Office representative in the Irish Free State (1922-24).

Luzio, Monsignor Salvatore Papal emissary to Ireland (1923).

Macaulay, William J. Babbington (1892-1964) Royal Navy (1914-18); Inland Revenue (1918-25); Secretary, Irish Legation, Washington (1925-30); Consul General, New York (1930-34); Irish Minister to the Vatican (1934-40).

MacDonald, J. Ramsay (1866-1947) British Prime Minister (Labour 1924, 1929-31) (National Government 1931-35).

McDunphy, Michael Assistant Secretary to the Provisional Government (1922) and to the Executive Council (1922-37).

McGann, Gearoid Senior Private Secretary, Department of the President of the Executive Council.

McGilligan, Patrick (1889-1979) TD; educated at Clongowes Wood College and University College, Dublin; Private Secretary, Minister of Home Affairs (1922); Secretary to the High Commissioner's Office London (1923); elected as Cumann na nGaedheal TD for the National University of Ireland in November 1923; later represented Dublin North-West and Dublin-Central; Minister for Industry and Commerce (1924-32); Minister for External Affairs (1927-32); Minister for Finance (1948-51); Attorney General (1954-57); called to the Bar (1921), called to the Inner Bar (1946); Professor of International Law at University College, Dublin.

MacNeill, Eoin (John) (1867-1945) TD; Educated at St Malachy's College, Belfast; Dáil Eireann Minister for Finance (January-April 1919); Minister for Industries (April-August 1921); Ceann Comhairle during the Treaty debates; supported the Treaty; Minister without portfolio in the Provisional Government (January-August 1922); Minister for Education (August 1922-December 1925); Irish Free State representative on Boundary Commission (1923-25); brother of James McNeill; Professor of Early and Medieval Irish History at University College, Dublin (1909-41).

McNeill, James (1869-1938) Educated at Blackrock College and Emmanuel College, Cambridge; sometime member of the Indian Civil Service; member of the Irish Free State Constitution Committee (1922); Irish Free State High Commissioner in London (1922-28); Governor General of the Irish Free State (1928-32); brother of Eoin MacNeill.

MacWhite, Michael (1882-1958) Served in the French foreign legion (1914-18); secretary to Irish delegation to Paris peace conference (1920); Irish representative to Switzerland (1921-23); Permanent Representative to League of Nations (1923-28); Irish Minister to the United States of America (1928-38); Irish Minister to Italy (1938-50).

Marquis MacSwiney of Mashonaglas Unofficial Irish representative to the Vatican (1922-23); Irish delegate to the League of Nations Assembly (1923, 1924).

Mulcahy, General Richard (1886-1971) TD; educated at Christian Brothers

School, Thurles; Acting Minister for Defence (January-April 1919); Chief of Staff of the IRA in the War of Independence; pro-Treaty; Minister for Defence in the Second Dáil (January-August 1922) and for National Defence (Provisional Government, August-December 1922); Minister for Defence (1922-24); Chief of Staff of the National Army (1922-23); Minister for Local Government (1927-32); founder member of Fine Gael (1934); leader of Fine Gael (1943-59); Minister for Education (1948-51, 1954-57); Minister for the Gaeltacht (1956).

Murphy, Sean (1896-1964) Educated at Clongowes Wood College and University College, Dublin; former Solicitor; Secretary, Irish mission to Paris (1920); Representative of the Irish Free State in Paris (1923); Administrative Officer, Department of External Affairs (1925-27); Assistant Secretary (1927-38); Minister to France (1938-50); Ambassador to Canada (1950-55); Secretary of the Department of External Affairs (1955-57).

O'Byrne, John (Born 1884) Member of the Irish Free State Constitutional Committee (1922); Irish Free State Attorney General (1924-26); High Court Judge (1926-40).

O'Hegarty, Diarmuid (1892-1967) Secretary to the Dáil Ministry (1919-22); Secretary to the Irish Treaty Delegation (1921); Secretary to the Provisional Government (1922) and to the Executive Council (1922-32).

O'Higgins, Kevin (1892-1927) TD; educated at Clongowes Wood College and Maynooth College; Minister for Home Affairs (1922-24); called to the Bar in 1923; Vice-President and Minister for Justice (1924-27); Minister for External Affairs (1927); assassinated 10 July 1927.

O'Kelly de Gallagh, Count Gerald (1890-1968) Educated at Clongowes Wood College; Sinn Féin envoy to Switzerland (1919-21); Irish representative to Belgium (1921-29); Minister Plenipotentiary to France (1929-35); Special Counsellor at Paris and Brussels Legations (1935 -48); Chargé d'Affaires at Lisbon (1948-68).

O'Shiel, Kevin (1891-1970) Adviser to Michael Collins on Northern Ireland affairs (1922); Assistant Legal Adviser to the Provisional Government and the Irish Free State Government (1922-23); Director of the North-Eastern Boundary Bureau (1922-25).

O'Sullivan, John Marcus (1881-1948) TD; educated at Clongowes Wood College, University College Dublin and the Universities of Bonn and Heidelberg; Parliamentary Secretary to the Minister for Finance (1924-26); Minister for Education (1925-32); Professor of Modern History at University College, Dublin (1908-48).

Phelan, Edward J. (1888-1967) Educated at St Francis Xavier College, Liverpool and the University of Liverpool; British civil servant (1911-19); Chief of the Diplomatic Division, International Labour Organisation (ILO) (1920-38); Deputy Director General, ILO (1938-41); Director, ILO (1941-46); Director General, ILO (1946-48).

Pollock, Hugh M. Northern Ireland Minister of Finance (1921-37).

Smiddy, Timothy Anthony (1875-1962) Educated at St Finbar's College, Cork, University College, Cork, and later at Paris and Cologne; Professor of Economics at University College, Cork (1909-23); Irish Representative in Washington (1922-October 1924); Irish Free State Minister in Washington (1924-29); High Commissioner in London (1929-30); member of the Tariff Commission (1930-33); head of Combined Purchasing Section, Department of Local Government and Public Health (1933-45).

Stephens, E.M. (1888-1955) Barrister-at-law; Joint Secretary of the Irish Free State Constitution Committee (1922); Secretary to the North-Eastern Boundary Bureau, Dublin (1922-26).

Thomas, James H. (1874-1949) Trade Union Leader and Labour Politician; Colonial Secretary (1924); Dominions Secretary (1930-35).

Waller, Bolton C. Researcher at the North-Eastern Boundary Bureau (1922-26).

Walshe, Joseph Patrick (1886-1956) Educated at Mungret College and University College, Dublin; former Jesuit seminarian and teacher at Clongowes Wood College, and solicitor; Irish delegation in Paris (November 1920-January 1922); Secretary to Dáil Ministry of Foreign Affairs (February 1922-August 1922); Acting Secretary, Department of External Affairs (September 1922-7 August 1927); Secretary, Department of External Affairs (8 August 1927-May 1946); Ambassador to the Holy See (May 1946-September 1954).

Whiskard, Sir Geoffrey Granville (1886-1957) Assistant Secretary, Chief Secretary's Office, Dublin and Irish Office London (1920-24); Assistant Secretary, Colonial and Dominion Offices, London (1924-29).

List of Documents Reproduced

1922

No.	Title	Main Subject	Date	Page
1	Memorandum, O'Shiel to Cosgrave	Development of Northern Ireland policy	25 Sept.	1
2	Memorandum by O'Shiel	Establishment of North-Eastern Boundary Bureau	14 Oct.	7
3	Memorandum, O'Shiel to Cosgrave	Establishment of North-Eastern Boundary Bureau	21 Oct.	12
4	Memorandum, O'Shiel to all members of the Provisional Government	Boundary Commission	Sept./ Oct.	15
5	Letter, Connolly to Cosgrave	Revival of anti-Treaty position in United States	7 Dec.	18
6	Letter, Smiddy to FitzGerald	Support for Irish Free State in United States	8 Dec.	21
7	Letter, Murphy to FitzGerald	French public opinion and support for the Irish Free State	11 Dec.	23

1923

No.	Title	Main Subject	Date	Page
8	Telegram, Smiddy to External Affairs	Attack on New York Consulate	1 Jan.	24
9	Memorandum, McDunphy to Executive Council	Anti-Treaty activity in Britain	1 Jan.	24
10	Telegram, Smiddy to External Affairs	Attack on New York Consulate	3 Jan.	25
11	Memorandum, Flynn to Cosgrave	Irish Free State customs frontier	3 Jan.	25
12	Letter, Walshe to Murphy	Closure of Irish Office in Rome	3 Jan.	26
13	Letter, Smiddy to FitzGerald	Intelligence operation in the United States	6 Jan.	27
14	Letter, Smiddy to FitzGerald	Attack on New York Consulate	6 Jan.	28
15	Letter, Stephens to O'Shiel	Establishment of the Boundary Commission	10 Jan.	29
16	Despatch, Healy to the Duke of Devonshire	Anti-Treatyite activity in United States	12 Jan.	30
17	Executive Council minutes	Anti-Treatyite activity in Britain	13 Jan.	31

No.	Title	Main Subject	Date	Page
104	Letter, Crawford to Smiddy	League of Nations	27 July	144
105	Letter, MacWhite to FitzGerald	Boundary Commission	4 Aug.	145
106	Letter, Kennedy to FitzGerald	Application to the League of Nations	4 Aug.	146
107	Letter, McNeill to FitzGerald	Irish-American politics	9 Aug.	147
108	Letter, FitzGerald to Drummond	Application to the League of Nations	11 Aug.	147
109	Letter, MacWhite to FitzGerald	Admission to the League of Nations	14 Aug.	148
110	Despatch, Healy to the Duke of Devonshire	1923 Imperial Conference	15 Aug.	149
111	Letter, MacWhite to FitzGerald	Admission to the League of Nations	16 Aug.	149
112	Memorandum by Walshe	League of Nations Assembly	28 Aug.	150
113	Memorandum by O'Shiel	1923 Imperial Conference	undated	151
114	Letter, Walshe to FitzGerald	Admission to the League of Nations	4 Sept.	151
115	Letter, MacNeill to Agnes MacNeill	Journey to Geneva	6 Sept.	152
116	Letter, FitzGerald to Mabel FitzGerald	Journey to Geneva	undated	154
117	Letter, FitzGerald to Mabel FitzGerald	League of Nations Assembly	undated	155
118	Speech by Cosgrave	Admission speech to League of Nations	10 Sept.	156
119	Letter, Stephens to O'Shiel	Admission to the League of Nations	11 Sept.	157
120	Letter, MacNeill to Agnes MacNeill	League of Nations Assembly	14 Sept.	157
121	Letter, MacNeill to Agnes MacNeill	League of Nations Assembly	15 Sept.	158
122	Letter, MacWhite to Walshe	Registration of the Anglo-Irish Treaty with the League of Nations	17 Sept.	160
123	Letter, Stephens to O'Shiel	League of Nations	17 Sept.	160
124	Letter, MacNeill to Agnes MacNeill	League of Nations Assembly	17 Sept.	161

1924

1925

1926

1922[1]

No. 1 NAI DT S1801

Memorandum by Kevin O'Shiel to William T. Cosgrave (Dublin)
(Confidential)

DUBLIN, 25 September 1922

To
The President.
NORTH EASTERN POSITION.

1. In order that you may be fully informed on this important matter I have done a rough Memo. of what I know about the work of the late Chairman[2] in this connection.

Much of it will probably be familiar to you, but there may be parts here and there which will be helpful to you.

2. I had a good deal to do with North Eastern Affairs during the late administration. My work in this connection fell mainly under the following headings:-

(1) Acting as M.O.C's[3] proxy on the Sinn Féin Advisory Committee for Ulster, and acting as a member, but mainly as his agent on his own Provisional Government Advisory Committee in Ulster.

(2) The drafting for him of letters, documents, statements, newspaper articles, etc.

(3) Furnishing him with Memoranda on the subject from time to time.

3. *The Advisory Committees.*

These were, and still are (although they have become nearly obsolete of late) two distinct Advisory Committees on Ulster Affairs, viz., the Sinn Féin Advisory Committee and the Provisional Government Advisory Committee.

(1) *The Sinn Féin Advisory Committee.*

This body was created after the Meeting of the Ard Fheis about February last by certain disgruntled Northern Sinn Féiners (chief of whom was Eamonn Donnelly[4]) for the supposed purpose of guarding against Partition, but in reality

---

[1] See introduction for the provenance of documents number 1 to 7.

[2] Michael Collins.

[3] Miceál O Coileáin (Michael Collins).

[4] Former Director of Elections for Sinn Féin (1918 and 1921), anti-Treaty during civil war, Republican MP for Armagh (1925-29), Fianna Fáil TD for Laois-Offaly (1933-37), Republican MP for Belfast Falls, died 1944.

to molest and obstruct us in every conceivable way. The Meeting that formed this Body took place on the night of the day that the Ard Fheis was postponed. It was held in the Mansion House and none were admitted save the Northern delegates to the Ard Fheis, and the members of the Standing Committee. De Valera was present but neither A.G.[1] nor M.O'C. In the absence of these latter de Valera had the field to himself and succeeded in turning in his favour a considerable section of those who were hostile to him. De Valera appealed to this Assembly in the most barefaced and dishonest manner imaginable. He denounced Partition in every mood and tense and of course gained enormously with such an audience. He talked ad nauseam about fighting Partition and the Belfast Government to the death and drew rousing applause from the throats of many enthusiasts who, since the trouble in the North, have trekked as far South as they possibly could.

Before concluding[,] this Assembly established what it called a Sinn Féin Committee on Northern Affairs. This Committee was to consist of a couple of delegates from every Comhairle Ceanntair area in the Six Counties together with two members from the Standing Committee selected so as to represent the Treaty and the Anti-Treaty sides.

The inaugural Meeting of this Advisory Committee was fixed for a date a few weeks subsequent in Belfast.

At the next Meeting of the Officer Board (which, as you will recollect, took the place of the Standing Committee after the Collins – de Valera Ard Fheis[2] Agreement) the matter of this Committee came up for discussion. I was present representing M.O'C, and de Valera was in the chair.

The question of the status and authority of this Committee arose and after a great deal of argument and considerable difficulty I got a Resolution passed decreeing that the Committee would be a purely subordinate Body to the Officer Board and directed and controlled in every way by that Board. It was to be nothing more than a mere Advisory Committee on North Eastern Affairs, with no power whatever to carry into effect any Resolution it may pass without first submitting same to the Officer Board and receiving its express sanction.

I was present at its first Meeting in Belfast, and at subsequent Meetings in Belfast and Derry. My work was mainly that of defending the policy of the Government which was frequently attacked by the incorruptibles, and obstructing the malicious proposals of de Valera and the hare-brained proposals of Eamonn Donnelly.

Time and time again these two, along with that warlike old veteran, Mr. Archibald Savage, did their very best to get proposals passed committing the whole Six Counties to a hopeless guerrilla warfare with Craig's Government.

By pointing out to the ladies and gentlemen of the Committee that it was primarily a matter for themselves as to whether they adopted warfare or peace, and that in the event of warfare *they* and *not* people like myself, Mr. de Valera and Mr. Savage, who enjoyed existence in the comparative security of Dublin, would suffer, I succeeded in weakening their ardour for war, and at length

[1] Arthur Griffith.

[2] The 'Collins-de Valera Pact' of 20 May 1922 under which pro- and anti-Treaty candidates contested the June 1922 election in agreed proportions.

they compromised on a Resolution adopting passive resistance proposed by a lady member at a Meeting held shortly after the murder of some women in Belfast by the Orangemen.

This Committee had a sufficiently large Die-hard majority and influence to elect Mr. Micheal Carolan – a well known Die-hard, now in our keeping – as its Secretary. He was to be salaried at the rate of £500 a year, and this figure was accepted and endorsed by the Officer Board.

The headquarters of this Advisory Committee was to be Dundalk, although I strongly opposed this and suggested Belfast.

By making it a purely subordinate Body to the Officer Board we completely destroyed the effectiveness of this Committee and within three months of its establishment it had practically died of inertia, although no definite action was taken to wind it up or rescind the Resolution ordering the payment of the £500 per year to Mr. Carolan.[1]

(2) *The Provisional Government Advisory Committee on the North East.*
This Committee was established by M.O'C. for the purpose of enabling him to obtain advice on North Eastern affairs from those who were friendly disposed to the Free State in the North.

It was formed by simply writing to some 30 or 40 prominent Northerners who had been identified with, or at least sympathetic to the National Movement, asking them to attend a general Meeting in Dublin.

This Meeting took place in the Council Hall here under the Chairmanship of M.O'C., A.G. and yourself (I think) also being present. I think two or three of the five Bishops invited were also there.

Before we departed a Committee was elected from this general Body with representatives from every County in the North Eastern Area and it was decided that the first Meeting of this Committee would take place in Belfast.

The first Meeting was held in Belfast on the 15th May last.

Sub-Committees.
Having considered such matters as the Collins-Craig Pact No. II,[2] Craig's Advisory Committees in connection with the said Pact, the Boundary Commission, etc. etc., it was agreed that two Secretaries should be appointed to act as Joint Secretaries of the Committee.

On this matter I quote from my report of the proceedings to M.O'C. as it may enable you to understand more clearly why it was considered necessary to appoint two Secretaries:

> 'There was considerable discussion about these Secretaries and the whereabouts of the G.H.Q. of the Committee. In order to understand this better it is well that I should remind you that there is a big "Home" question in Ulster as well as an "external" one. This is the eternal pull between the Country and the City, between the nine Counties (as it once was) the Six Counties (as it now is) and Belfast. This jealousy, this ruralism

[1] Handwritten note: 'which still remains in the books of the Standing Committee of Sinn Féin'.
[2] See DIFP vol I document No. 259.

v urbanism is very old; not exactly as old as Ulster, but certainly as old as the City of Belfast. It applies not only to Nationalist Organization, but also to Unionist where, if possible, an even stronger antagonism prevails.

The Ulster countryman, on any point that is neither political nor religious, will unite willingly against the alleged dominance of Belfast. I do not know, but you may probably have a similar condition of affairs in the South, e.g. Cork City v The Munster Counties. But to return.

The Belfast men wanted a single office to be situated in Belfast and all subordinated to one General Secretary in Belfast. The 'Ruralista' did not object to Belfast having an Office and a Secretary, but they also wanted an Office in the country. When your idea of Joint Secretaries was mooted the 'Ruralista' immediately jumped at it. After one of those long urban-rural Ulster wrangles to which I am accustomed it was finally agreed that:

(1) Two Joint Secretaries should be appointed at £300 per annum each.

(2) Two Offices, one in Belfast and the other in Clones.

One Secretary to look after *Belfast* in *Belfast*, and to be purely concerned with Belfast affairs. The other Secretary to be stationed in Clones, and to be purely concerned with *rural Ulster* affairs.

(Frank Crummey[1] will do the Belfast Secretariat, and the privilege of obtaining the Rural Secretary was imposed on me.)

They were very keen for O'Driscoll to take the second Secretariat, but he did not want to do so. I am at a loss to know who to appoint. A number of them were keen on a Six-County man. However, O'Driscoll has promised to help me in the matter.

Although the Ruralists were against it [,] it was insisted upon by Belfast that the Belfast Office should be the principal Office, and should get a copy of the records of the other Office.

The Belfast Secretary would be the man to summon the whole Committee.

The Ruralists succeeded in getting a very wide measure of autonomy on this matter for themselves. For instance, it was agreed that their Secretary would send *direct* to Dublin all reports for propaganda purposes that might reach their office, furnishing, later on, a record for the Belfast Office, which was to be considered always the Head Office.

(I am personally of opinion that this is a very satisfactory arrangement for both sides. To begin with, it recognises the existence of *Facts*. There are two points of view on the 'Ulster Question', viz., the rural view-point and the Belfast City view-point. The Ruralists say that *they* have the key of solution for, without them[,] Belfast could not exist and therefore the Belfast Parliament could not exist. The Belfast fellows say that they have suffered most, and that the question, being really a Belfast question, will be solved by Belfast.

According to this arrangement provision is made whereby two machines are erected for getting the best from the two different angles of view.

[1] Former Intelligence Officer, 3rd Northern Division, IRA.

It is also a wise provision to have Belfast recognised as the Headquarters for it is bound to happen that a time will come when some Headquarters will have to act for the whole.)

(10) *Local Committee.*
It was agreed that the Rural Section on its part, and the Belfast Section of the Committee on its part should make provision to collect all the information possible and send it down to Dublin.

The Rural Section propose to establish small local Committees throughout their sphere of operations for this purpose and also for the purpose of carrying out all the injunctions of the Committee.

The Rural Section's Committee would also set about collecting information for the Boundary Commission.

Another of its activities would be to endeavour to ascertain the Protestant Anti-Partitionists in the various districts.'

Finance of the Committee.
The Committee passed a Resolution requesting the Government for a Grant of £1,000 to cover their expenses for three months, the idea being that they would return whatever monies they did not want.
This is a rough detail of their estimate:

(1)	Belfast Office	£250.
(2)	Clones Office	75.
(3)	Members' travelling expenses	100.
(4)	Organization, setting up of Local Committees ...	500.

Present Position of this Committee.
Owing to the intensive campaign carried on by the Northern Government this Committee never got very far with its work.

Shortly after this Meeting hundreds of Northern Sinn Féiners[,] whether of the Free State or Irregular variety, were arrested wholesale by the Specials and interned in the Northern Prisons and on board the 'Argenta' Prison Ship (now moored off Larne Harbour). This Committee was greatly reduced and broken up by these arrests. Mr. Frank Crummey, the Belfast Secretary was arrested and is, I understand, at present on the 'Argenta'. The fact that he was a member of two or three Committees under the North Eastern Government by virtue of the Craig-Collins Pact No. II did not save him.

Mr. Cahir Healy of Enniskillen, a prominent member of the Committee and an enthusiastic Free Stater was also arrested, as well as many others.

Hence the work of the Committee has practically ceased, and it is moribund at the moment.

The Rural Secretary.
After much searching I discovered a suitable person for the position of Rural Secretary, viz., Mr. Sean Carty of Belleek. He was formerly Secretary to the North Fermanagh Comhairle Ceanntair of Sinn Féin and is one of the very best and most conscientious workers in the movement I have come across. He alone, and with practically no assistance from either Dublin or Fermanagh,

organized that most difficult constituency for Sinn Féin. He established 17 Clubs in that small half Orange, half Hibernian constituency, which was indeed an achievement. He was thereupon appointed Sinn Féin Organizer for the whole County Fermanagh. He was Battalion Commandant of the Belleek Volunteers and was one of the principal persons concerned in the capture of Belleek Barracks in the Autumn of 1921. It was solely owing to his strenuous efforts that almost the entire West Fermanagh establishment of the I.R.A. threw in their lot with the Free State, although they were cajoled and threatened and finally harassed by Pilkington and Bradshaw and Seamus Devins of Sligo to make them turn with them.

I suggested Carty's name to the late Commander-in-Chief and one of his last directions to me was to go ahead and get Carty to establish the Clones Office. I was also to go to the Treasury and endeavour to get from them a portion at least of the monies asked for by the Committee.

Matters however, became so upset by the recent great tragedy of the late Chairman's death that I had not time to do any of this work.

Roughly that is how the position now stands with respect to these Committees.

At the time I told Carty that the late Chairman had endorsed his appointment as Secretary to the Clones Office, and he is now in Dublin waiting to see how things develop.

I do not know whether you will decide to continue this Committee or not, but in any event I would strongly recommend Carty to you for some position of trust in either the Committee or any North Eastern Department that you may decide to establish. He is thoroughly conscientious, efficient and conversant with all the facts in the extremely complicated Northern situation, and above everything else takes a tolerant view on the Partition standpoint and even on the Orangemen.

The Acting Belfast Secretary.

There is just one other matter I should mention to you before I depart from the subject.

On the arrest of Frank Crummey, the Belfast Secretary, his place was immediately taken by Mr. McLarnon. McLarnon, like Crummey, is a National Teacher, and, like Crummey, is subsisting on the salary paid him as a Teacher by our Education Ministry (I daresay he will now be paid by the Northern Ministry).

McLarnon's work hitherto was that of collecting information and sending it up to us. He and Crummey are both prominent Belfast Volunteers and engaged, I think, largely on the intelligence side.

McLarnon is working, I understand, under great risks. He wants no remuneration himself, but wants access to some small fund out of which to pay actual working expenses. His typist, a very sound girl, I believe, has been receiving up to this a mere pittance of a salary. The late Chairman was aware of these facts, and had undertaken to supplement her salary.

I just mention these matters to inform you fully as to how matters stand now in connection with the late Chairman's activities in the North. It may be that you may make other arrangements in this connection, but it is well, at any rate, that you should have all the facts fully before you.

Articles on the North Eastern Situation.
I frequently drafted Memoranda, statements and letters to the Press on Northern matters for M.O'C., and also I frequently advised as to policy on this subject, but I must admit that he did not always take my advice!

About two months before his death he asked me to do for him a series of 12 Articles on the North Eastern situation for the American Press. It so chanced that I had collected a large quantity of material on the Ulster question with a view to preparing a book on the matter. I may say that two years ago I arranged to furnish the Talbot Press with such a work. I started the book a good time ago, but never had time to complete it. However, when M.O'C. asked me to do him the 12 Articles I decided to use the data I had collected for the book in the Articles. I was only able to supply him with the two first Articles (which are probably now amongst his papers) and a plan or scheme of the lines along which I was proceeding. Now, that he is gone I intend to continue with my Talbot Press commitment, and bring the matter out in book form as originally arranged.

Conclusion.
This then is roughly how the late Commander-in-Chief's activities in connection with Northern matters stood at the time of his death, in so far as I am personally aware.

In a rough and ready Memo. of this nature it is obviously impossible to take up your time by going more into detail. What I have given you is the merest outline. There are many important items in connection with the late Commander-in-Chief's Northern administration on which I have not touched at all, as for example the two Collins-Craig Pacts, particularly the last one, with its whole series of contingent commitments; the Boundary Commission; the Belleek-Pettigo and general frontier situation; the extraordinary alleged rumour at the end of April last that there was an agreement between the two sections (Regular and Irregular) of the Army to invade the Six Counties in force, about which I personally had no definite information beyond what I received from outside sources in the Six Counties, etc. etc.

I am sending you further a supplemental Memo. on some important aspects of the Northern situation, which I hope may be useful.

[signed] Caoímhghín Ó Síadail
Assistant Legal Adviser

No. 2 NAI DT S4743

Memorandum by Kevin O'Shiel on the organisation of the North Eastern Boundary Bureau

Dublin, 14 October 1922

THE BOUNDARY COMMISSION ORGANIZATION, ETC.

By a Minute of the Cabinet dated the 2nd day of October last[1] I was made responsible for the entire preparation of our case for the forthcoming Boundary

[1] Not printed.

Commission, and given authority to make all the necessary arrangements for carrying out the task expeditiously and efficiently.

In order to make for the necessary despatch and thoroughness I considered that it was essential to condense the entire scheme of work into one central bureau which would be divided into a number of Departments or divisions, with special work appropriated to them and in charge of competent and well-qualified individuals – All these divisions, of course, to be responsible to me for their conduct of that part of the work entrusted to them, and I, on my part, to be responsible to the Cabinet for the completion and delivery of the whole task in good time for the Boundary Commission.

In starting off on the work of organising the necessary machine I received a number of disappointments from persons who had practically promised to assist me in the work and on whose assistance I was relying. This occasioned an initial delay in my plans, but it worked out for the best as it so happened for, in the meantime, I was enabled to meet and discuss matters with prominent representatives from the North East and to adjust my arrangements in view of their suggestions.

I found it extraordinarily difficult to procure the services of fully qualified persons to undertake the most important task of research and investigation. This was largely accounted for by the necessarily temporary nature of the undertaking and the quite reasonable reluctance of good men to leave, at this time of much change, their permanent positions with whatever possibilities they might carry with them.

Eventually I succeeded in establishing the framework of the organization and am now able to report to you the following achievement in this connection:

Taking into consideration every aspect of my work and in order to secure the maximum results in the minimum time I have proceeded to organise along the following lines:

NORTH EASTERN BOUNDARY BUREAU

(A) *Research Division and Central Office, (16, Kildare Street)*
In charge of a Secretary and staff.
Attached to this will be a number of experts who will be remunerated by us and called in occasionally for consultation. Scale and further details later.

(B) *Publicity Division*
In charge of a competent person with a small staff.
Details later.

(C) *North-Eastern Local Division*
In charge of a supervisor and a number of legal agents who will be responsible for their own areas.
Details later.

I will now explain the proposed working of the above scheme.

(1) The Research and Investigation Division has been set up and has now actually commenced work in the Offices recently occupied by the Constitution Committee at 16, Kildare Street. I have put this section in charge of Mr. E.M.

Stephens, B/L who, in my opinion, is amply qualified for the work. In addition to his legal and other qualifications I may mention that he has just completed a period of eight months service as Secretary of the Constitution Committee, and his experience in that connection will be most valuable in his present position.

I suggest that Mr. Stephens should be remunerated at the rate of £700 per year. This, I think, is a very reasonable figure when the special circumstances of the case are taken into account.

To begin with it is a *purely temporary post*. There is no guarantee of any permanence in connection with it, or even that it shall last longer than four months at the outside. Then he has left aside for the present all his usual work, and he will of course have to do work overtime both on Sundays and week days. He is aware of the obligations which the position entails and is quite prepared to perform them.

With Mr. Stephens in Kildare Street is the remains of the staff of the Constitution Committee. As far as I remember[,] this consists at present of Mr. Meara, an expert indexer (whose services will be most valuable)[,] one clerk and two lady typists.

As I have said there is in existence now at least the framework of a staff, and they are actually engaged at present on the preparatory work of their inquiry according to a complete scheme of work with which they have been provided. From this on though it will be essential to augment this staff very considerably, and I may have to make occasional requests for additional help as time goes on. Already we are trying to procure the services of an expert statistician, as well as a couple of competent men to look up certain special matters in Libraries, etc.

We will require frequently to consult with and seek the advice of well known authorities and experts who for many reasons we could not take over as fully-paid officials. I am at present consulting with a number of these people with a view to arranging a satisfactory *via media* which will enable us to call upon their advice at any time, and get them to furnish us with Memoranda and reports that we may request from time to time.

We may also have to obtain wholly individual and special work. For instance, I have a few men already on the task of exploring every possible aspect of the Silesian, the Schleswig-Holstein and the Hungarian Plebiscites, and also the special position of Alsace-Lorraine (the attempt made to Germanise it, etc. etc.).

(2) *The Publicity Division*

I consider this an extremely important division to be run in close co-operation with the Research Division. This Division will be under some competent person with both literary and Northern experience.

The functions of this Section will be:

(1) To provide either through the Government Publicity Department or direct, whichever is most convenient, the daily Press of Ireland, Great Britain, America, and the World generally, with suitable and effective articles and circulars bearing on the situation. (This could be conveniently done by sending out a weekly bulletin to all the principal papers).

(2) To get in touch with all the friendly British and foreign Journals with a

view to getting them to assist in publishing the weekly circulars and special articles that may be issued from time to time, and also in guiding their own policy along lines somewhat similar to ours in this matter.

(3) To publish occasionally pamphlets, leaflets, etc. etc. bearing on the various aspects of the case and get them distributed, especially in those parts where there is a hostile propaganda.

(4) To anticipate Sir James Craig's forthcoming Press Campaign and to answer Sir James Craig's arguments when they are brought forth.

(5) To run, if it becomes necessary, a small propaganda sheet *chiefly* for the consumption of those Anti-Partition Unionists who live in areas like Derry City, Newry, etc. etc.

I consider this Division of immense importance in connection with our whole Boundary campaign. We cannot underestimate the vast influence of the Press in all modern politics. We have seen great wars created, Governments overturned and many other things of equal importance done purely through a vigorous Press propaganda.

No one knows better than Sir James Craig the might and power of the Press, and even whilst we are discussing he is making his arrangements to launch forth a vast Press campaign when the proper moment arrives.

It cannot be forgotten [that] the whole 'Ulster question' as we know it in modern times, with its plea for the special treatment of an arbitrarily chosen group of people, has been created solely and absolutely by a gigantic and carefully arranged Press campaign.

The 'No Home Rule' and the 'No surrender' campaign of the early part of the century, and later the Partition Campaign have been purely manufactured by the great Press organization of the late Lord Northcliffe.

Therefore, we cannot underestimate the advantages of a judiciously arranged and timely Press campaign.

It will be recalled that in the two recent European examples of Partition – viz., Silesia and Schleswig-Holstein an enormous literary propaganda was carried on throughout Europe by the various partisans. Prior to the taking of these two Plebiscites one could not enter into a hotel or public lounge on the Continent without finding scattered about the tables and desks enormous quantities of literature from the various viewpoints in many languages.

I do not propose that we should organise this Division on so extensive or ambitious a scale, but I do think much can be done in this direction to influence world opinion, and through world opinion, *not* the North-Eastern Government, *not* the Northern Unionist, *but* the British Government and the Chairman of the Boundary Commission. The importance of this will readily be seen when it is realised that *it will be the organised force of public opinion and that alone which will eventually decide whether the Boundary Commission will lean towards our side of the case or the Pro-Partition side.*

Hence, the use of a capable and competent editor in this connection will be extremely valuable, and by no means a waste of time.

I have elsewhere outlined a scheme along which I think this Division should work.

(3) *North Eastern Local Division*
This is an important and necessary Division of the work. We want some machinery for keeping us in touch with the various people concerned in the entire North East, but particularly in those parts where the 'wishes of the inhabitants' will certainly be with us.

This will be a big Division and will require considerable expenditure, but it is, nevertheless, essential to the proper working of the whole scheme.

What I propose to do is to put certain districts in charge of a competent person, preferably a legal man, as he would have most experience for the purposes required. I would throw on that man the onus of making up the case for remaining with the Free State for that particular area over which he has charge. He would furnish me in Dublin with frequent and ample reports, and would also be required to answer any query that may be sent up to him by the Research Division. I propose, therefore, that such a person should be appointed over the following districts:

(1) Fermanagh County
(2) Tyrone County
(3) Derry City
(4) South Derry County
(5) Newry District (including South Armagh and South and East Down).

Later on we may have to appoint some person to look after the special internal areas of Nationalism, such as the Glens of Antrim, the Shores of Lough Neagh, West Belfast and Rathlin Island; but for the present these are the most important areas.

All these men will be under a Supervisor, who, for the present at any rate, will pay special attention to these little islands of Nationalism in addition to his general work of going round and keeping the various Committees, that these agents will start in their own districts, at work.

I propose to appoint Sean O'Hanrahan, Solicitor, Omagh as Supervisor of the entire Northern area.[1] The question of his remuneration does not yet arise. For the present, at any rate, he is agreeable to accept only out-of-pocket expenses.

All the agents mentioned above will, of course, have to be remunerated. I will furnish later, when I have had time to consult with Mr. O'Hanrahan and others, what I would consider reasonable remuneration.

This is a very important section of the work as it will provide most of the practical work in connection with the Commission. All reports coming in from this quarter will be carefully examined by us with a view to seeing that the cases of the districts do not conflict in any way with our general scheme for the whole case of the North East stated.

I am able to state now definitely that the following gentlemen have been appointed as our agents to the following districts. They have all been chosen because of their experience in registration work and their personal capacity, and I will propose later that they be paid weekly in order to enable us to dispense speedily with their services should they prove to be unsatisfactory.

[1] O'Hanrahan was a former Sinn Féin Director of Elections in Tyrone.

Derry City – Mayor O'Doherty. I was personally against this appointment but the general consensus of all whom I consulted was that it would be very inadvisable to ignore him, as he 'possesses the Bishop's conscience'. I was assured that his son[,] young Hugh C. O'Doherty, who is a fairly[1] capable Solicitor, and quite steady, would do most of the work.

Derry County (South) – Mr. P.J. Agnew, Solicitor, Magherafelt. (This man did a lot of work for Sinn Féin in connection with the Revision Sessions, etc.)

Tyrone County (North and Mid) – Mr. Alec Donnelly, Solicitor, Omagh.

Tyrone County (South and East) – Mr. T.J.S. Harbison, M.P., Solicitor, Cookstown.

Fermanagh County – Not yet filled.

Newry District (including Down County South and East)
(Armagh " South)
Mr. John H. Collins, Solicitor, Newry.

[signed] Caoímhghín Ó Síadail
Assistant Legal Adviser

No. 3 NAI DT S4743

Kevin O'Shiel to William T. Cosgrave (Dublin)
Dublin, 21 October 1922

To/
The President and Minister of Finance.[2]
A Chara,
Re: *NORTH EASTERN BOUNDARY ORGANIZATION*
I have much pleasure in reporting to you now that organization in connection with the above matter has been largely completed and that work in the Research and North Eastern (Local Organization) Divisions is now well under way.

In my report to you of the 14th instant[3] I outlined the plan of work and the personnel, in so far as that could be ascertained at the time. I am now able to supply much, though not all, of the details that I was unable to do then.

This is the position of affairs in connection with the North Eastern Boundary Bureau at the moment.

1. *RESEARCH DIVISION AND CENTRAL OFFICE*
This Division is now established in the offices formerly occupied by the Constitution Committee. It is in charge of Mr. E. M. Stephens, B.L. and the staff etc. is as follows:

Research Division and Central Offices
Secretary – E.M. Stephens, B.L. (To be remunerated *at the rate of* £700 per annum as from Wednesday the 11th instant).

[1] The word 'very' in the original has been crossed out and replaced with 'fairly'.
[2] Cosgrave held both posts from 22 August to 6 December 1922.
[3] Above No. 2.

Staff – Messrs. Meara and Seamus Redmond (on loan from the Department of Agriculture).
Miss Saunders and Miss Kane (on loan from the Insurance Commission).
Mr. Ruth – expert on vital statistics (on loan from the office of the Registrar General).

With the exception of Mr. Ruth these are all former members of the staff of the Constitution Committee, which we have merely taken over.

Running in connection with this Research Division will be a small Board or Committee of experts to advise and collect material about the various subjects on which they are authorities. By the time this Committee is fully organised it will consist of about 6 or 7 persons. So far, only two have definitely promised to assist in this capacity. These are, Mr. Joseph Johnston, F.T.C.D.,[1] a Northerner himself from Tyrone, who has undertaken to furnish a report on transport and regional economics, and to collect and arrange all material bearing on this important subject; and Mr. Smith-Gordon, Manager, National Land Bank, who has undertaken to do likewise with regard to finance, banking, rate of exchange, currency, etc., showing how all these matters will be very greatly affected by a) Partition of any kind and b) an uneconomic Partition.

No rate of remuneration for this work was suggested as yet. It was thought best that as Mr. Johnston was in a position to devote most time to the work, he should undertake his branch first, and that the financial questions arising from the treatment of the economic situation should be passed on to Mr. Smith Gordon. I may say that Mr. Johnston commenced work on his subject some time ago.

I also communicated with Dr. George O'Brien and Professor Mitchell Henry of the Queen's University, Belfast.

I heard from Dr. George O'Brien who said that he would be willing to give us any voluntary assistance in his power, but that he was not in a position to make himself responsible for any particular branch of the work.

I have not yet heard from Professor Mitchell Henry (whom you may recall as the well known writer on Sinn Féin from an Ulster angle), but I expect he will be agreeable to do work for us, as this is his pet subject. I have yet to get a few good historians to trace the work of Plantation and Partition from A.D. 1500 upwards.

A number of experts are already engaged on work in connection with the Silesian and the Schleswig-Holstein Plebiscites.

You may take it now that with regard to this Division work is in full swing on the following aspects: economic, statistical, Silesian and Schleswig-Holstein Plebiscites, and that within the next week work will have commenced on both the historical and financial sides.

NORTH EASTERN LOCAL DIVISION

I have made great headway with this Division and have definitely appointed the following Legal Agents to the following districts:

---

[1] Fellow of Trinity College Dublin.

(1) *Tyrone County* -		
North and Mid District	–	Mr. Alec Donnelly, Solr., Omagh.
East and South District	–	Mr. T.J.S. Harbison, M.P., Solicitor, Cookstown.
(2) *Newry District* (Embracing South and East Down and South Armagh.)	–	Mr. John H. Collins, Solr., Newry.
(3) *South County Derry*	–	Mr. P.J. Agnew, Solicitor, Magherafelt.

There yet remains to be filled corresponding positions for Fermanagh County, Derry City and Belfast District (including all Antrim County, Rathlin Island and parts of Down and Armagh).

TERMS OF APPOINTMENT AND SUGGESTED REMUNERATION FOR LEGAL AGENTS
Every one of these Legal Agents have been (and will be) appointed on the following definite and unmistakable terms:

(1) That they furnish the Bureau, before the 6th December next, with at least one clear copy of their brief containing the whole case stated for their district.

(2) That they send to the Central Office short but frequent reports as to how the work for the Commission is progressing in their district.

(3) That they supply any information bearing on the matter which the Central Office may from time to time request, and in general, work in close co-operation with the Central Office.

These Agents appointed have already been supplied with full and definite instructions elaborating these terms. If you desire it, I will send you on a copy of the instructions sent. It is rather a lengthy document, containing five pages of foolscap, and I forbear to trouble you with it.

There is no doubt that these Legal Agents have their work 'cut out' for them in real earnest. It will take them all their time to provide us with their respective 'cases stated' for their respective districts between this and the 6th December, next. They have represented to me that they will have to give up all other work until this work is completed. Now October and November are the harvest months of the country Solicitor. The Autumn Quarter Sessions, which are the largest Quarter Sessions in the year, take place during these months, and they generally reap the major part of their incomes at this period.

Those of them who have agreed to accept the position of Legal Agent will, of course, have largely to forego their legal Court work in order to accomplish our work. For this reason they will have to receive adequate remuneration, and after consultation with them and other less interested parties it was suggested that they should be paid each a fee of Sixty Guineas, when the work which they have severally contracted to deliver up completed to us on the 6th December has been so furnished to us. This is by no means an exorbitant fee under the circumstances. It works out at about £10.10. per week, which is certainly not high professional pay for temporary and most arduous work.

Beyond this fee they will have to be paid reasonable expenses, where such expenses are incurred in the prosecution of our work. There are a sufficient number of us who are conversant with those parts of the North to be able to check and keep a strict account of such expenses.

Mr. O'Hanrahan, the Supervisor, is at the moment engaged on a tour round the various districts, instructing the Agents and giving them their bearings. Unfortunately the Minister of Home Affairs, whom I have to thank for the loan of this gentleman, will be requiring his services at the end of a week. However, by that time the Agents will all be hard at their several tasks, and the Government will not be put to further expense in this connection as in future I will undertake the direct supervising myself.

THE PUBLICITY DIVISION

I have not yet got this Division into working order, but it will certainly be functioning before this day week. I have asked Mr. Milroy to undertake this *most important* end of the work, but he has not yet replied definitely.

Propaganda in this direction has become even more important than ever in view of the political crisis and the likelihood of a General Election and the return of a 'Die-hard' Government in Great Britain. If a 'Die-hard' Government comes into power in Great Britain we will have to organise and exert every ounce of world opinion that we have in order to influence the Boundary Commission Chairman against Craig's conception of Article 12 of the Treaty.

In conclusion I would like respectfully to suggest to you that should you see your way to sanction the above mentioned amounts – as Minister of Finance[1] – you will do so as soon as possibly convenient, as the matter is most urgent.

The work is taking shape rapidly, and is, I think, as far advanced as possible in the time. I trust that by the end of November we will be in a position to provide the principal information on all branches and to have the greater part of the General Case Stated drafted and ready for the printers.

[signed] Caoímhghín Ó Síadail
Assistant Legal Adviser

No. 4 NAI DT S8892

Memorandum by Kevin O'Shiel to each minister in the Provisional Government (Very Urgent)
Dublin, undated but September/October 1922

To/
Each Minister.

THE NORTH EAST and THE COMING BRITISH ELECTIONS

The dramatic collapse of the Lloyd-George Government resulting in the forthcoming General Election in Great Britain has raised a number of urgent and vital issues in connection with the North East, which require to be dealt with immediately.

I. *The Question of our contesting certain North-Eastern Seats*

The most immediately critical of these issues and one upon which a decision

[1] Cosgrave was holding the Finance portfolio as well as that of President of the Executive Council.

will have to be made at once, is the question as to whether or not we should advise our people in the Six-County area to contest those Constituencies in which there is an excellent chance of their being victorious.

It should be explained that the British General Election will apply to the Six-County Area for the purpose of electing 13 members to the British House. Whilst the voting will be according to the old direct method, the Constituencies will remain as at present arranged under the Proportional Representation Act.

This matter is only *particularly pertinent to the Constituency of Tyrone-Fermanagh*. This great Constituency will presently be called upon to return 2 members to the Imperial Parliament by the direct method of voting. Should a contest take place *it is an absolute certainty that two Nationalist or Anti-Partition members will be returned by a clear majority of from 8,000 to 9,000 over the nearest Unionist candidate*. About this result there is not the slightest shadow of doubt whatever.

Personally, I think that this great opportunity of proving once more that Tyrone-Fermanagh, the great territorial centre piece of the Six Counties, does not want to remain under a Belfast Parliament, should be availed of. This is particularly important in view of the forthcoming *Boundary Commission*. For the Boundary Commission will want every available argument in order to maintain even half our case, and, in my opinion, we certainly should not turn down that golden opportunity that is now offered to us through such a contest.

It does not much matter whether the individuals concerned will, or will not go to the Imperial Parliament. The great thing is that they stand on one plank and on one plank only, viz., Anti-Partition against the inclusion of the two Counties of Tyrone and Fermanagh in the Northern Parliament and for their remaining part of the Saorstát.

I am firmly convinced that should this policy be sanctioned it will enormously strengthen our hands at the Boundary Commission. In the face of such a result what arguments can Sir James Craig put up against these Counties remaining with us?

At any rate, it is a matter on which a decision will have to be made at once, as time presses. The nominations will take place within a week, and if our people are to be advised to engage upon the contest, they will have to make their preparation at once. I may say that the locals all favour a contest. I have been speaking to a number of them, and they [all] are unanimous.

Another reason why we should advise our people to contest this particular seat is that if we do not[,] Mr. Harbison, M.P., the sitting member, and another Devlinite[,] *certainly will*. The Nationalists will undoubtedly vote for them as against the Orange candidates and we will, in consequence, lose a good deal of prestige.

II. *Electioneering at British Elections*

1. The Ulster Unionist Council have made extraordinarily elaborate arrangements to take a prominent part in this General Election in Great Britain. They have actually sent over hundreds of Speakers and intend to address at least 600 Meetings at which the 'Cause of Ulster' will be put before the British Electorate.

2. Now, what are we to do about this? Are we to ignore it or to take measures

to anticipate and counteract it? We may say that Ireland has nothing further to do with Great Britain. But this is not the case. Until the Constitution and the Boundary Commission have been safely steered through to success we must keep a very attentive eye on Great Britain and British politics.

Now it is quite obvious that this British Election is a most important one from our particular standpoint. If a powerful Die-Hard Unionist majority is returned it will be very bad for us, especially for our interpretation of the Boundary Commission. What would suit our development at this stage best would be a weak British Government, that is to say, one which has *only just a working majority*. If we ignore the North Eastern incursion into Great Britain, it is bound to have an enormous effect on the British Electorate and in so light[1] a contest it may play a decisive part in the Elections.

3. The question then arises that if we decide to counteract this prejudicial propaganda, what precise measures should we take?

It would obviously be both unwise and undignified for us either to hitch ourselves on to any particular British Party, or to take a part in the campaign *as an Irish Government*. But I think between these extremes a number of middle ways offer themselves. For instance, what is to prevent a number of individuals from Ireland going across and counteracting any hostile propaganda where it may be presented. Or even a particular Irish Party could take an active part, *as a Party*. For example, the Irish Labour Party could do a lot of good in this way.

4. But apart from this our main propaganda in Great Britain should be undertaken by the Irish Societies and Organizations there. For example, the Irish Self-Determination League and the U.[nited] I.[rish] L.[eague] of Great Britain under T.P. O'Connor (who is now altogether with us) could do much in counteracting Craig's propaganda.

5. *Main Point in Craig's Propaganda*

There is no doubt at all that Craig's propaganda will centre around the Boundary Commission. His tone of argument will be mainly

a) That 'Ulster' is a self-contained, economic and homogenous entity within its Six Counties.

b) That he never asked for Home Rule. All he asked for was to be allowed to remain part of the United Kingdom, and now that a Parliament has been thrust on him all that he asks is to be let alone to govern it without interference from 'Southern Ireland'.

c) That 'Ulster's' Present territory was guaranteed to 'her' by the 1920 Home Rule Act – an Act of the British Parliament, just as sacred and as binding as the Treaty Act.

d) That all the Six Counties are peopled overwhelmingly by Loyalists.

e) That surely the fair-minded British people would not have any part in flinging him and his Loyalists to the Barbarism of Southern Ireland.

f) Then much attention will, no doubt, be paid to the 'appalling conditions' in 'Southern Ireland', especially the awful happenings to 'Southern Loyalists'.

---

[1] The author may have meant to use the word 'tight'.

Now, these are arguments which, if left to themselves, are bound to have an effect on the British Electorate, but which are quite simple to confute. Therefore, I think it will be essential to have some of our people there to counteract such arguments.

6. *Publicity Campaign in England*
Craig and his supporters have always believed in propaganda. Their case for the special treatment of the Pro-British thinking people of the North of Ireland has been almost entirely created by a vast Press campaign. I hear that they have already made their preparations for a vast Press campaign in Great Britain during this Election. It is essential to counteract this, and I am endeavouring to get in touch with prominent British Journals that will probably support us and will be glad to publish our stuff and make use of our statistics. Leaflets will also have to be printed and distributed through the various Organizations in England favourable to us. In the Boundary Bureau we are at present preparing suitable stuff for publicity purposes in England. We can supply stuff for leaflets etc.

7. It has just occurred to me that some of our prominent Election experts, like Dan McCarthy, should be placed in control of a distributing and organising centre for getting in touch with and using English parties favourable to us.

8. The whole matter, at any rate, is extremely important, and I would be very glad of your comments on it *immediately*.

Mise,
[copy letter unsigned]
Assistant Legal Adviser

No. 5 NAI DFA ES Box 30 File 197

Handwritten letter from Joseph Connolly to William T. Cosgrave (Dublin)
DUBLIN, 7 December 1922

A Chara[1]

At Dr MacNeill's suggestion I am putting before you the position in America leading up to my return from New York so that you may, at first hand, know the circumstances that prompted my action & decided me to withdraw from the responsibility as Consul General there. It is desirable that I should do so, more particularly as Mr FitzGerald T.D. Minister for External Affairs in the interview which I had with him, did not seem to appreciate the position. Moreover Mr Blythe with whom I had most contact in my American work & to whom I addressed a request for an interview, did not reply.

Before returning in September to resume my work I expressed the belief that the political activities of the Irish Americans were, in so far as Ireland was

[1] The Irish-American community had divided over supporting the 1921 Treaty during early 1922. By late 1922 the worst of the physical and rhetorical clashes over the divide seemed to be over. Mary MacSwiney's hunger-strike in late 1922 reinvigorated the anti-Treaty groups in the United States and this, combined with a feeling of ministerial inaction in Dublin regarding his post, led Connolly to write this letter to William T. Cosgrave. (See also No. 6 below.)

concerned, dying quickly and that in my judgment it was desirable that this should happen. It was my hope that after a period of quiescence we could launch such activities as would most fittingly represent the racial activities in its material & cultural pursuits & in a manner which would reflect the most creditable side of our 'Home' life to our own people there & to the Americans generally. It is unnecessary to outline in detail the constructive programme intended. Much of the preliminary work was underway & the records will give full information on the matters pertaining thereto.

A short time ago it was quite evident to me that the activities of the American Assoc. were being carried on with increasing difficulty & that the spasmodic efforts to galvanize it into life were not likely to be successful to any appreciable extent. It must be remembered however that in so far as articulate expression of views in America was concerned no other organization of any account was operating. The Friends of Irish Freedom organization is a spent force & the result of the recent election when Surrogate Cohalan was utterly routed was ample confirmation of the opinion & advice expressed by me & shows how futile & unwise was the effort made by the Government in sending out an ambassador to secure the support of that body. Support from it would have been a source of weakness to the Government in its American work. I stated so last spring & I repeat it now & I claim that events have proven that my estimate was a correct one.

Several weeks ago events in Ireland were causing grave uneasiness in the States but it was not until Miss MacSwiney[1] was arrested & on hunger strike that anything like an old time revival of interest in the A.A.R.O.I.R.[2] took place. From that time there was a new interest infused into the Association's activities & many who had dropped out of action began to drift back to their groups. Many of the supporters of the F.S. openly denounced us. An agitated atmosphere was growing & growing quickly & even people who were apathetic a week before were becoming tense & 'worked up' about the position.

At all times I have kept aloof from the various political & factional elements amongst the Irish Americans & I claim that the Consulate was in the unique & enviable position of being clean & above all their differences & enjoyed the goodwill & co-operation of all those with whom we had to work. It was quite evident that we were not going to be allowed to continue so. On all sides there was continued pressure & agitation on the grounds that to allow Miss MacSwiney to die was to alienate all sympathy & support & would leave Ireland an object of reproach to all our friends in the States. It is well to remember that this was mainly due to the extraordinary reverence that is attached to Terence MacSwiney's memory & that nothing in modern times so completely stirred the whole American imagination as his hunger strike & death. If I may express a personal opinion without wishing to claim any attention for it save in so far as one may claim the conscientious right of a citizen, I felt that to allow Miss MacSwiney to indulge her idea of heroic self-sacrifice was going to destroy

[1] Mary MacSwiney, sister of the Lord Mayor of Cork who died on hunger strike in 1920, Terence MacSwiney.

[2] The American Association for the Recognition of an Irish Republic.

our work in the States & what was infinitely more important to me – was likely to produce a very bad aftermath in Irish life at home.

The cumulative effect of the inquiries, reproaches etc. decided me to communicate with you, but at this time I had a visit from Mr Peter McSwiney & Miss Sheehy-Skeffington.[1] The interview was short. I refused to be dictated to or bullied into action & stated that I had my own views & was already dealing with my opinions to the only authority with which I was concerned. I allowed a good deal for Peter's natural agitation & state of mind but told him quietly & firmly that he could threaten pickets or anything else but I refused to give him or anyone else any guarantees of my action nor would I discuss it with them. My cable to you on the 9th was the expression of what I saw & felt & I realized that apart from my feelings, if the Consulate was to escape a serious set back & if our work there was not to be very much discredited the only sane course was to leave things in such a way that the staff could carry on without *direct official* representation available as the stalking horse for attack. Moreover I may say frankly that in the prevailing position at the time my influence & power of achievement in National work there were sure to be rendered futile. My subsequent cable to you explains the rest. I went into all matters on hand with the vice-Consul Mr D.J. MacGrath & furthermore got a guarantee from him that he would endeavour to carry on the work & reply to the critics that he was simply carrying on his clerical duties pending developments.

I had to book my passage home & the Shipping Co., in direct violation of a promise given to me, published my name on their departure list before sailing time. On the day of departure I was inundated with pressman but refused to give any information or particulars. The press statements are the usual stories which American journalists serve up when they get no authoritative statement. I had already seen some of these & Mr McGrath very kindly promised to take up with some of the worse offenders.

These are the circumstances of my decision to return & whilst regretting that the work into which I had put all my mind & energy has had to be terminated under such regrettable circumstances, I feel satisfied that my action was conducive to the real interests of our National activities in the States & the preservation of the work of the Consulate.

Mr FitzGerald's approach on the matter suggested that of a minister [and] a very minor civil servant but *I regret* to say that my position in America was never such. The Consulate despite all my efforts to the contrary had inevitably its political reflections & was unquestionably, to the Americans interested, the accepted representation of the Home Government. Without any reflection on other representation that exists it was the real & only recognized representation that was there & as such had to take cognisance of the feelings & expressions of our people who made our work possible in our *officially* unrecognized position.

I went to America at the request of An Dáil in Sept. 1921 without any Civil Service rating or guarantee. I abandoned a profitable business & exiled myself from the pleasantest possible domestic & social life. I have no regrets for having done so. I have suffered very serious material loss but when I reluctantly

[1] Hanna Sheehy-Skeffington.

consented to go I did so with the idea of National Service & I worked day & night in America with the same stimulus.

I feel satisfied that at least some of my work was worthwhile & at all events am content that despite all temptations & offers my work was honestly & conscientiously carried out.

If there is any amplification of this statement desired or if there are any points in connection with our American or other interests in which my experience can help the information will at your command.

I am
Faithfully Yours
JOSEPH CONNOLLY

No. 6 DFA ES Box 28 File 175

Timothy A. Smiddy to Desmond FitzGerald (Dublin)
CHICAGO, 8 December 1922

A Chara:
I beg to report to you the following interviews which I had during the last few days:-
Dr Constantine E McGuire: He stated that, as the result of conversations which he had with people with different points of view on the present Irish situation, he was of opinion that the Irish Free State would act wisely as regards American opinion if it were to execute no more rebels. (1) He said that the opinion of the average type of Irish American who is a supporter of the Free State does not approve of these executions, and that some among them, if this policy is persisted in, may give their support to the Irregulars: that the idea of execution for political offences is not popular in the U.S.A. and that it is hardly ever resorted to.

(2) There is the American who has never interested himself sympathetically in Irish affairs – one might speak of him as the average American – and who either believes that the Irish Free State is adopting the only policy which is effectual for the maintance of its existence or who are indifferent in the matter.

(3) Finally, there is the active supporter of the Irregulars whom the present policy of the Irish Free State will incite to further activity to influence many Irish Americans to rally to the Irregulars. It will lead to reprisals in Ireland and, possibly here.

He is also of opinion that the association of the setting up of the Free State with executions may have a future historical significance that may perpetuate obstacles for its functioning and may act in the minds of the young as an incitement to future rebellions.

Mr Hugh O'Neill of Chicago – a leading citizen of this city, a Clans man and one who played a very prominent part in organising the Americans against the Black and Tan regime, had intimate connections with de Valera when here, also Sir Roger Casement, etc.

Mr J.A. McGarry of Chicago who has had associations similar to those of O'Neill and who was the backbone of the Irish here since his early manhood.

Mr O'Mahony, a very prominent supporter of the Irish cause here.

The opinion of these three men is that the Irish Free State is pursuing the only policy consonant with the maintenance of its very existence: their regret is that it was not pursued at an earlier date. If it had, probably Mr Collins would be alive to-day. They are particularly wrathful with de Valera whom they regard as the prime cause of the present situation. They state that he divided and broke the influence of the Irish in this country; he returned to Ireland and accomplished the same there. According to them the Irregulars have no supporters worthy of the name in this town (Chicago). Their present supporters are a few discontents of no status whatever in Chicago, and they are unable to raise any funds. There was a meeting here last week of the various Councils to consider their attitude towards the present situation in Ireland with the result that by a majority they declared in favour of the Free State. The Napper Tandy Council met also last week with a similar result.

I asked these gentlemen their opinion about a propaganda to counter the activities of the Irregulars in the U.S.A. They strongly disapproved of it. They say in the first place there is no need of it as the supporters of the Irregulars will not gain adherents to their cause; they will get no money, and any kind of active propaganda would create an impression that their power is greater than it is. It is better to ignore them. The most effective propaganda is frequent dignified statements from the Government of the Irish Free State showing that it is functioning successfully and is determined to do so, and that it is going to pursue a policy to achieve that end. The recent statements that have appeared in the papers here dealing with Ireland are effective for this end. With the successful functioning of the Government hostility on the part of the Irregulars will become innocuous or disappear.

A public statement to the effect that the Cabinet of the Irish Free State has decided to pay off its obligations to the American people would have most desirable results. It will establish the Free State Government highly in the esteem of the American people, and raise the financial credit of the country, especially, at a time when other countries are trying to have their debts to this country cancelled. It will be very effectual publicity.

I had the pleasure of meeting Mr Patrick J. Collins, brother of the late General Michael Collins. In many respects he is very like him and seems a very intelligent and alert man. His views are similar to those I have recited above.

Rev.Wm.F.Cahill, who is responsible for the paper published here weekly, called the 'Irish Republic', copies of which I have sent you; he was also the president of the Central Council for the A.A.R.I.R. in Illinois.

In company with Mr McGrath I interviewed him to-day in connection with the lists of subscribers to the Second Loan issued here. We received very bad accounts of him; perhaps, to some extent prejudiced. He received us genially and told us he would help us in our inquiries. Before going to him we had already ascertained that every thing was in order as regards the Second Loan. He discussed politics a little and expressed a desire to have some one mediate and bring both parties to some common understanding. He mentioned the name of the Most Revd Dr Mannix[1] as a probably effective arbitrator. This is the third indication I have experienced recently of anxiety on the part of the supporters of the Irregulars to effect a settlement.

He mentioned that the Irish Americans are at present quite apathetic as regards Ireland, and that they would prefer to discuss Armenia and the Turk to discussing Ireland; also, *one could not obtain a nickle* at present for the Irish Cause.

One hears many conflicting views on the present situation from those who were interested in the Irish cause. Personally, I am of opinion that those who wish well to the Free State and who disapprove of the execution of rebels will not give any active support to the Irregulars, and that the ultimate success of the Free State will make them forget their resentment. One thing is certain; the supporters of the Friends of Irish Freedom are either strong supporters of the actions of the Free State or are indifferent. The average American gives his notional assent to the policy of the Free State Government, as also all the important Newspapers with few exceptions.

Mise, le meas,
[signed] T.A. SMIDDY

P.S. The announcement made by Harvey, American Ambassador in London, a cutting of which was sent to you, will be productive of much good here for the Free State.

No. 7 NAI DFA ES Paris 1922-23

Extract from a letter from Sean Murphy to Desmond FitzGerald (Dublin)
(118-1922)

PARIS, 11 December 1922

[Matter omitted]
I am enclosing some cuttings from the French press. The proclamation announcing that the execution of Rory O'Connor and Liam Mellows was an official reprisal for the assassination of Sean Hales, had a very bad effect here. Journalists and others whom I met including Monsieur Goblet considered it a very serious tactical mistake as far as opinion outside Ireland is concerned. The French in particular have a horror of reprisals. They all agreed that the executions were perfectly justifiable on the ground that these men were in rebellion against the lawful government, but they compared the reprisals to the recent executions in Greece. They also commented on the execution of Childers on the charge of having a revolver in his possession, when the government had various other charges to try him on. These remarks were made by people who are friendly to the Government, and not critically.

Is mise, le meas mór,
[signed] SEÁN Ó MURCHADHA

[1] Catholic Archbishop of Melbourne, Australia.

1923

No. 8 NAI DFA ES Box 30 File 200

Timothy A. Smiddy to Department of External Affairs, Dublin
NEW YORK, 1 January 1923

Ginnell Adherents led by Mrs. MacSwiney forcibly ejected from Consulate.

SINBAD[1]

No. 9 NAI DT S1753

Memorandum by Michael McDunphy for the Executive Council
DUBLIN, 1 January 1923

IRREGULAR ACTIVITY IN GREAT BRITAIN
POSITION OF BRITISH GOVERNMENT.

(a) In a letter dated the 15th December[2] addressed to the Governor General, the Duke of Devonshire furnishes particulars of a Meeting held in London on the 6th December under the auspices of the I.[rish] S.[elf] D.[etermination] L.[eague] as typical of the propagandist activities of irregular sympathisers in Great Britain.

While anxious apparently to assist the Irish Government in coping with this phase of the irregular movement, he states that as at present advised, so long as these activities are not directed against order and good Government of Great Britain and do not involve any actual breach of the peace, his Majesty's Government do not propose to take any action *except on the initiative of the Irish Government*.

Should the Irish Government so desire however, they are prepared to consider action on the lines indicated in a memorandum submitted by the Home Office (copy of which is attached).[3] Briefly this memorandum advises that persons who by their overt acts or speeches in England show that they are acting in furtherance of seditious or rebellious objects in Ireland, could on warrants issued on proper information in Ireland be arrested in England and conveyed to Ireland for trial on charges of seditious conspiracy &c.

The matter is submitted for consideration by the Irish Government.

(b) The continued production in Great Britain of Irregular publications, such as 'The Republic of Ireland' and the 'Workers Republic' is a similar problem on which his Grace would like to have the views of the Irish Minister.

[initialled] M. MACD

---

1 Telegraphic designation of Timothy A. Smiddy.
2 Not printed.
3 Not printed.

No. 10 NAI DFA ES Box 30 File 200

Telegram from Timothy A. Smiddy to Department of External Affairs, Dublin[1]
(Copy)
NEW YORK, 3 January 1923

Police clear Irish consulate of fifty Irregular invaders. De Valera force including many women and Muriel MacSwiney go to Mayor Hylan to get him to recognise their claim. Mayor replied that from their own statement the Free State is the legal occupant of the premises. The law must be observed in this country and we must stop being ridiculous.

No. 11 NAI DT S1955A

C.J. Flynn to William T. Cosgrave
(Copy)
DUBLIN, 3 January 1923

The President,

CUSTOMS FRONTIER.

1. Article 74 of the Constitution provides that during the present financial year all taxes and duties shall continue to be assessed, levied and collected in like manner as immediately before the Constitution.
2. The effect of this provision is that all Customs and Excise duties in Great Britain and Ireland are at present collected on a common basis leaving the Free State Revenues from these sources to be worked out on an agreed basis of attribution. The whole of Great Britain and Ireland remains the fiscal unit and dutiable goods may be moved between places in the two Countries without any Revenue restraint or formality.
3. At the end of the financial year (i.e. on 31st March) the above arrangements cease and the Irish Free State becomes an independent fiscal unit (unless any legislative provisions in the contrary sense are made in the meantime). All goods coming from Great Britain and Northern Ireland will become subject to the same Customs formalities as goods from Foreign Countries and Customs duty will be payable on all dutiable goods entering the Free State from whatever destination.
4. For this purpose it will be necessary to surround the Free State with a complete Customs ring. So far as the sea-frontier is concerned this does not present any great difficulties as Customs Staffs are at present located at all the main ports, and it will only be a question of strengthening these staffs and perhaps stationing staff at points where staff is not employed now. The land frontier (i.e. the boundary between Northern Ireland and the Free State) is at present quite open and the object of the present note is to point out the necessity of taking immediate steps to prepare the necessary machinery to constitute the Customs barrier between the Free State and the North on the 1st April next, if necessary.

[1] Copies also sent to William T. Cosgrave and Hugh Kennedy.

5. *Article 13* of the Adaptation of Enactments Act 1922 empowers the Minister of Finance to make regulations to adapt the Customs Acts to a land frontier, but before such regulations can be definitely drafted it will be necessary to make extensive enquiries as to the character of goods traffic and the main arteries of such traffic across the border, to consult traders and carriers, and possibly to discuss certain phases of the question with British Customs representatives. It will also be necessary to give a fair notice of the impending changes to Merchants and others in the Free State with full instructions as to the Customs procedure that will have to be followed.

6. Assuming that it is the intention that the Free State should stand on its own fiscal legs from 1st April next it is of the utmost importance that a tentative scheme for the provision of a Customs frontier organisation should be completed at the earliest possible date and I suggest that I be authorised to take the necessary steps for the preparation of a scheme to be submitted for approval in due course.

(signed) C.J. FLYNN

No. 12 NAI DFA Letter Books (Paris 1923-24)

Joseph P. Walshe to Sean Murphy (Paris)
(195/23) (Copy)

DUBLIN, 3 January 1923

A Chara,

I am instructed by the Minister to ask you to be ready to proceed to Rome for the purpose of clearing up affairs there within a few days. Count O'Byrne[1] should reach Paris on the 7th or 8th from Saint Jean de Luz. He will explain to you the whole position as far as possible and will give you any introductions, authorisations etc. which may be necessary.

The object of your mission will be:

a) To close up the house and get rid of the staff.

b) To find out if there is any possibility of keeping the house until the expiration of the lease without a tenant being in occupation.

If the landlord still insists on not accepting any successor to Count O'Byrne there is not much use in holding on to the lease for the remaining few months as presumably the option to renew only held good for the immediate successor of Gavan Duffy.[2]

In that event you can only try to persuade him to return portion of the rent paid and surrender the lease immediately.

Gavan Duffy apparently left at least one loophole in the agreement and the landlord has availed himself of it to nullify the lease after Count O'Byrne's departure.

In the circumstances when a representative is finally sent to Rome he will have to look for another residence.

To maintain the house without an occupant might lead to serious compli-

[1] Count P.J. O'Byrne, Irish representative in Rome (1922-23).

[2] George Gavan Duffy, Irish representative in Rome (1921), Minister for Foreign Affairs (January-July 1922).

cations as presumably we should be held responsible for thefts or injury to furniture, and all things considered the Minister advises surrender now in order to avoid complications and annoyance.

You will of course be careful while in Rome not to give the impression that we are either abandoning the post or intend to make an immediate appointment.

Le meas,
[copy letter unsigned]
Rúnaidhe

No. 13 NAI DFA ES Box 28 File 185

Timothy A. Smiddy to Desmond FitzGerald
WASHINGTON, 6 January 1923

INTELLIGENCE

A Chara:

For some time I have had operating secret service agents, especially during recent weeks. I also secured the services of six competent men in connection with the recent trouble in the Consulate Office.[1] The secret service that I have had operating up to now is not organised, and I am of the opinion that for some months to come there is need of a thoroughly well organised intelligence service in New York especially. For this purpose it is essential to appoint an Organiser of Intelligence on this side who would direct and report on the activities of his subordinates. Naturally, such an organisation will be expensive, but I am of the opinion that it is necessary and may produce satisfactory results. I can procure an organiser on this side who, I am of the opinion, would be more efficient on account of local knowledge than one sent from Ireland, unless you wish to have an agent from Ireland cooperate with him.

I have had the movements of Mr. Briscoe[2] watched and reported to me for the last six weeks and I was prepared for his activities with regard to the Consulate. He is a great intriguer and I am endeavoring, if possible, to find out if there is any connection between his activities and Bolschivist propaganda. Mr. George McGrath will give you an account of his Dublin social relations. He officially calls himself here an 'Irish Republican Soldier'.

I sent you cables with reference to information I got about the shipment of guns which I trust was of some use: unfortunately, I could get no details.

I have learned from inside sources that an attempt was contemplated, after the execution of Mellowes,[3] on the lives of Geddis (sic),[4] the Representative of the Irish Free State in Washington, and Judge Colohan, and that attempts will be made to carry out their intention should de Valera be shot. They will not succeed in getting away with action of this kind in America as easily as they are, unfortunately, doing in Ireland.

I have got the names of some of those who are active in the shipping of guns, and also of the Liverpool gun men whom I am having carefully watched.

[1] See No. 8 and No. 10 above and No. 14 below.
[2] Robert Briscoe.
[3] Liam Mellows.
[4] Sir Auckland Geddes, British Ambassador in Washington (1920-24).

Lawrence Ginnell[1] came to the states by Halifax and through the Canadian border. By this method they avoid the difficulty of getting a pass-port to the United States. Perhaps, you could take up this matter at your end. I shall also endeavour to see what can be done on this side. I am about to take up the subject with the Bureau of Immigration and Labor, and the activities of some of the Irregulars with the Department of Justice.

Mise, le meas,
[signed] T.A. SMIDDY

No. 14 NAI DFA ES Box 30 File 200

Timothy A. Smiddy to Desmond FitzGerald (Dublin)
WASHINGTON, 6 January 1923

A Chara:
I enclose some clippings of the New York papers which give substantially accurate accounts of the trouble we had at the Consulate Office. On Tuesday last a large number of the followers of de Valera endeavored to get access to the Consulate Office: Mrs. Muriel MacSwiney[2] was particularly active. Lieut. Gegan blocked her entry. They were then informed by Lieut. Gegan that unless they left the building they would be arrested. All left except two pickets. The women formed themselves into a deputation to put their grievances before Mayor Hylan, who told them to seek redress through the ordinary procedure of the courts. This advice was so displeasing to them that they picketed, with eight large placards, the Town Hall. On the following day, Wednesday, the manager of the building, 119 Nassau Street, decided, and made known to some of the Irregulars, that any individuals who would attempt picketing inside the building would be arrested. Since then all is calm and quiet in the Consulate Office.

Subject to your approval I appointed Mr. Lindsay Crawford a few days before, installing him in the office of the Consulate as Acting Consul. On the day he took over his duties the trouble began – Wednesday, December 27th. I cannot speak too highly of the manner in which Mr. Crawford acquitted himself in the performance of his duties during the trying ordeal to which we were subjected. He is a man in whom absolute reliance can be placed, and I was fortunate in having secured his services at such a critical moment.

Mr. McGrath was evidently terrified by the threats of the Irregulars, as he did not come near the office after Friday, December 20th. I had counted on his remaining at the office for a week extra in order to initiate Mr. Crawford into the details of the work. As I have also dispensed with the services of an assistant mail clerk who did not report himself during the above proceedings the work of this office will be much retarded until Mr. Crawford and new staff will adjust themselves gradually to the routine and special work of the office.

---

[1] Former Dáil Éireann Director of Propaganda (1919-21), Special Representative to Argentina (September 1920 to March 1922), opposed the Treaty.

[2] The wife of Terence MacSwiney, the former Lord Mayor of Cork who died on hunger strike in 1920.

I have sent Mr. J.P. Kerr, who was attached to the Finance Office in Washington, to the Consulate Office to help Mr. Crawford in routine work.

The Irregulars attempted to scare Mr. Crawford by their usual methods of intimidation. I was unable to take any action until Saturday, December 30th when I paid rent to the manager of the building personally, and got from him receipt for same. This obtained for me recognition as the occupant of the rooms of the Consulate. The attorneys for the estate in which the rooms are located, the Messrs. Gillespie, did not feel disposed to cancel and surrender to me the lease, though they verbally recognized the Free State as the tenants. Mr. Gillespie was to have seen me to discuss further details about his recognizing me as tenant but he failed, as also my lawyers failed, to get in touch with him. I have a suspicion he avoided designedly the issue at stake. In the first and only interview I had with him he emphasized the fact that I ought to get the intruders removed from the Consulate through the procedure of the courts. But from this method I was very adverse; the case might have been submitted to a magistrate or a law court and there was a possibility of a 'snap' decision being given against us, especially as the lease was not in my name, or the name of the Free State: and this would be prejudicial to the more important case of the funds. Hence, our policy was to throw on the intruders the onus of making good their pretentions in the courts.

Throughout these proceedings I cannot praise too highly the interest, attention, and valuable advice given by our lawyers, especially Ex-ambassador Davis, Mr. Cannan, and Judge Colohan. Lieut. Gegan was impartial and determined in seeing that the law was adhered to.

I am enclosing copies of the pretentions that Ginnell presented at the Consulate and sent me here at Washington. I believe he is due to arrive at my offices in Washington and leave after him his 'larva' as he did in New York, but he shall meet with much more drastic treatment here than he experienced in New York.

Mise, le meas,
[signed] T.A. Smiddy

P.S. I have enclosed newspaper cuttings dealing with the above in another letter.

No. 15 NAI NEBB Box 25

Extract from a letter from E.M. Stephens to Kevin O'Shiel (Dublin)
Dublin, 10 January 1923

A chara,
[Matter omitted]
The Boundary Commission derives its authority from the Treaty and should be treated in all respects as an international Commission.

The first step of our Government towards the setting up of the Commission would be to communicate with the British Government stating that they were proceeding to select their member on the Boundary Commission and asking the British Government to call upon the Government of Northern Ireland to appoint its representative and to appoint the Chairman.

The general arrangements as to the place of meeting, staff, procedure and other preliminary matters should then be made by the Chairman, in consultation with the Governments interested.

As to the appointment of a representative there is varying practice. The best course appears to be to appoint a person of recognised judicial capacity, who, although the representative of the Government interested, is distinct from an advocate. The case can then be supported by an advocate according to the ordinary practices of judicial tribunals.

The procedure usually followed by Boundary Commissions is substantially that laid down for the Hague Arbitration Court for International Arbitrations; that is to say, the case should be put forward in writing on behalf of each Government which appears as a claimant before the Commission. The investigation of these cases forms the subject of the enquiry and they should be supported by the documents on which they rely annexed to the cases when furnished.

A verbal statement of the case on behalf of each party may be made by their representatives, but this is sometimes considered unnecessary.

The procedure to be followed by the Commission in investigating the cases put forward is to be determined by the Commission itself. It may visit the locality, take plebiscites, call experts on economic and geographic conditions or hear any other parties who in the opinion of the Commission could assist them in coming to their decision.

Their decision when arrived at is, of course, binding on the parties who submitted their cases for adjudication.

Mise, le meas,
[copy letter unsigned]
Secretary

No. 16 NAI DFA D1976

T.M. Healy to the Duke of Devonshire (London)
(Secret)

DUBLIN, 12 January 1923

My Lord Duke:
With reference to Your Grace's Secret Despatch of the 13th ultimo[1] transmitting a copy of a Despatch from His Majesty's Consul General at New York with regard to activities of Irregulars in the United States of America and the rumoured shipments of arms, etc., to Ireland, I have the honour to thank Your Grace for the information therein contained and to state that my Government will be greatly obliged if they can be kept supplied with any similar information which reaches the Colonial Office regarding Irregular activities in the United

[1] Not printed.

States of America, particularly as to the shipment of arms and the movements of suspected persons between Ireland and America.

I have the honour to be,
My Lord Duke,
Your Grace's most obedient humble Servant,
(Sgd) T.M. Healy

No. 17 NAI DT S1753

Extract from minutes of a meeting of the Executive Council
(C.1/29)
Dublin, 13 January 1923

IRREGULAR ACTIVITIES IN GREAT BRITAIN
A message from Mr. Sturgis[1] of the Colonial Office was read in which he stated there was a marked increase in Irregular activities in Great Britain and suggesting that a senior officer of the Intelligence Organisation be sent over at once to confer with the British Authorities on the matter.

It was the opinion of the Executive Council that a senior Intelligence Officer should cross to London not later than Monday night the 15th instant.

The Secretary was instructed to advise the Commander-in-Chief[2] accordingly.

At a later stage of the Meeting a reply from the Commander-in-Chief was read in which it was stated that Comdt. General O'Hegarty, Director of Intelligence would cross to London on Monday night.

This was approved.

No. 18 NAI DFA ES Box 28 File 185

Extracts from a letter from Timothy A. Smiddy to Desmond FitzGerald (Dublin)
(Private and Confidential)
Washington, 15 January 1923

I mentioned in my letter of the 6th Jan.[3] the necessity of organising an efficient *Secret Service in the U.S.A.* The necessity has become so urgent that I have engaged the activities of some of the most efficient Secret Service agents in New York. For tracing the connection of the Reds with the Irregulars – especially Larkin's[4] affiliations – I have secured the agents who have worked on this organisation and who are still pursuing their investigations for the U.S.A. Department of Justice. I cabled you to-day for authorisation for the expenditure necessary for this work as also for discovering by whom guns and ammunition are being exported from this country to Ireland.

Naturally it is impossible to give an estimate of the cost of work of this character

---

[1] Mark Sturgis.
[2] General Richard Mulcahy.
[3] Above No. 13.
[4] James Larkin.

but in my opinion it is absolutely vital. However it can be discontinued at short notice: and it is better to utilise some of the large Secret Service organisations on this side than organise one ourselves afresh.

I shall give you the following details which I have already obtained:-

Larkin: He is an Hon. Member of the Soviet Council of Moscow. When a Captain Kirkpatrick was imprisoned in Russia and the American Government sought his release from the Soviet Government the latter agreed to do so on the condition that the American Government would release Larkin.
The American Government did not agree to this arrangement.
A Mr. Kollowski, agent of the Soviet Government was deported from here and when he returned to Russia he had charge of the prison in which Captain Kirkpatrick was: he treated Kirkpatrick inhumanly. He returned recently to the United States and was arrested and is now serving a sentence of a few years in a Federal prison. When on trial here Captain Kirkpatrick who had meanwhile been released gave evidence against him for the maltreatment to which he subjected Kirkpatrick.
It is believed by Secret Service agents in this country that Larkin was an agent of the British Government who sought his release from prison here some time ago with the object of having him go to South Africa.
This happened at the time of the strong Separatist movement led by Hertzog.

This connection was affected by the agents I have employed.

Cullen: This man is, I am informed, of Irish descent born in Liverpool. He is here many years and is a violent Communist. I was told by another Secret agent that he was the most violent of the Irish Reds in New York and that the followers of Mrs Muriel MacSwiney were in close association with him. That he was a Gunman ready to act. This information was mentioned to me in connection with the intention to shoot if opportunity presented itself Geddes, Judge Coholan, and your representative after the execution of Mellows. On the same occasion it was mentioned that this attempt would be carried out if De Valera were executed.

When discussing with the Secret agents to whom I have referred above they stated that Larkin had in their opinion some connection with the Bomb explosion in Wall Street with the intention of demolishing Morgan's Bank. They also mentioned that an Irishman by the name of Cullen was the driver of the cart that took the Bomb. They have not sufficient evidence to indict him. When I mentioned that I was informed from another source that Cullen was a very dangerous individual and a most violent Irish Communist in New York they saw therein a confirmation of their opinion of that man. He is an intimate associate of Larkin and Larkin's brother, Peter Larkin. He frequents the house in which Peter Larkin resides.

Peter Larkin is another Irish Communist and was recently active in Montreal where Mrs Skeffington organised a meeting with the co-operation of the Communist Council of Montreal. Naturally this meeting was not held ostensibly under the auspices of this Council.

A man named *O'Brien* is another Irish Communist of the type of Cullen with whom he is intimately associated though not quite so violent.

Patrick McClellain, Irish Communist and great friend of Jim Larkin. He headed the Amnesty meeting on last May day for the Release of Political prisoners.

Tallantyre: This man is of Irish descent, born in England, spent nine years in Canada, and is now an active member of the United Communist party.

O'Flaherty: Born in Ireland, an active Communist.

Gallagher: Communist who endeavoured to organise a Bank in the West with the object of collecting money from Irish Americans. The project did not succeed.

Some of these latter have been indicted with Russian Anarchists.
At present they are on bail – in all about twenty – having given Bonds to the value of $225,000. The fact that the Anarchists have been able to find readily this money shows they have large financial resources.

The United Communist party spent in propaganda work in U.S.A. for the eleven months ending November last $1,880,000: they have 67 Communist publications with a total circulation of eight million a month.

It is quite obvious that the Russian Communists will utilise the Irregulars to endeavour to establish in Ireland a Soviet form of Government, while the Irregulars will willingly accept their aid to destroy the Free State.

The head of the Detective Service in New York is greatly concerned over the Larkin incident and is strongly of opinion that he will be made the rallying ground for a fresh assault in Ireland. He is prepared if necessary to sign an affidavit as to his affiliations on this side, in case your Government desires to take steps on his arrival there.

The publicity and propaganda incidental to his release will add considerably to his prestige and make his entry into Ireland a grave problem for the Government. Whatever action is taken by your Government with regard to Larkin should be carefully considered and based upon grounds that will clearly and definitely align public opinion on the side of the authorities. No trivial technical charges should be put forward in this case. In my judgement it is time to awaken the Irish people everywhere to the dangers that lie in the present open alliance between de Valera and those who are seeking to impose the Soviet form of Government.

No more important issue could be raised in the coming elections than this.

I shall inform you of any further details I shall obtain about the connections between the Communists and Irregulars on this side.

As regards guns and ammunition: A man named McGee seems to be mainly instrumental in shipping guns from Hoboken; there is associated with him a Mr Reynolds. I am having these men carefully watched at present.

No. 19 UCDA P80/384

Desmond FitzGerald to the Director of Intelligence, Lieutenant General Diarmuid O'Hegarty

DUBLIN, 17 January 1923

A chara,

The despatch from Geneva[1] was read at to-day's meeting of the Executive Council. It was decided to send a messenger across to our Representative in Geneva,[2] to see if steps can be taken to have the woman representative of the Irregulars watched and arrested on her return to England or Ireland.

It was considered likely that she might have with her papers of importance. Our messenger was instructed to endeavour to see the D.I. in London, and to see if it could be arranged would also assist.

Mise, le meas,
[copy letter unsigned]
Minster for External Affairs

[enclosed despatch][3]

During the Christmas Holidays a female messenger from the Irish Republicans arrived at Lausanne with despatches from de Valera to the Bolshevik Commissary, Chicherin.

The contents of those despatches were most edifying as they showed without a shadow of doubt that whilst not openly espousing the Bolshevik cause in Ireland the 'Irregulars' were working hard with the Irish Communist Party as witnessed by the destruction of property which their co-operation had brought about during the past six months. This destruction could be intensified during the Winter season were it not for the fact that their financial resources were almost exhausted and the channels through which they had been able to obtain arms in the past were now cut off owing to the vigilance of the Free State's secret police.

'Without material,' said one of the despatches, 'it would be impossible to continue the struggle and failure at the present moment would mean the perpetuation of the Capitalistic Free State Government in Ireland for another generation.' Under those circumstances the 'irregular' leader felt that he could depend on the Moscow Government for a loan of ten thousand pounds in English money as well as for a supply of arms and ammunition which could easily be landed from a schooner of 200 tons burden in a western Irish port. The loan as well as any other debts due to the Soviets would be paid off as soon as the American money which was now the subject of litigation in the States was forthcoming.

Chicherin has transmitted the despatches to Moscow and whilst awaiting a reply the female messenger of de Valera and Co. can be seen disporting herself in the palatial hotel where the Soviet Delegation has its headquarters.

---

[1] Printed below.
[2] Michael MacWhite.
[3] Received from Michael MacWhite, Geneva, no date given.

No. 20 NAI DFA ES Box 29 File 189(4)

Timothy A. Smiddy to Desmond FitzGerald (Dublin)
WASHINGTON, 23 January 1923

A Chara:
A report given last week to the American papers by Mrs Despard from Paris, (a cutting of which has already been sent to you) stated that, hence forth, women who were found in possession of arms were liable to the death penalty. I enclose another cutting on the same subject.

The women Irregulars here are excited over the announcement and have started activities to incite public opinion against it. Mrs Corliss – a most active Irregular – told Judge Cohalan last Friday over the 'phone that he would be held as one of those responsible for any execution of women unless he issued at once a statement denouncing such a policy. Naturally, he would do no such thing.

As far as I can gather from conversations with many of our *real* friends here executions of women – if such be contemplated – would not be good policy from the point of view of sympathy for the Free State in U.S.A.: they would very much deplore it.

In the event of such executions being rendered necessary state as explicitly as possible to the press the real reasons for them. The bare statement 'in possession of arms' will give to the Americans a very inadequate impression of the enormity of their deeds.

Mise, le meas mór,
[signed] T.A. SMIDDY

No. 21 NAI DFA ES Paris 1922-23

Vaughan Dempsey to Desmond FitzGerald (Dublin)
PARIS, 25 January 1923

A Chara,
[Matter omitted]

IRREGULAR PROPAGANDA

I have certain reasons for knowing that there will be in the near future an intense effort made by the Irregular party to obtain a position in France as distinct from the Free State. You already have knowledge in your hands of this contemplated move. In view of this I would respectfully and urgently suggest that the position of this office be regularised by means of letters accrediting us, for otherwise there is no possibility of our being taken seriously by the French Government. If we are to counter-act this move of the Irregulars, then we must be officially recognised at the earliest possible moment.

If the Government decides to take action against the representatives of the Irregulars in Paris it will be irksome if not futile owing to the absence of recognised status of the Free State in France, without which recognition and accredition the French Government cannot take official cognisance of any action brought by our Government.

Otherwise, since we don't exist officially in France, the whole atmosphere and condition of Irish affairs in France will take upon themselves the appearance of political bickering which will be irritating to the French Government and will seem undignified if not ludicrous to the French people – thus we lose in prestige.

Is mise, le meas mór,
[signed] VAUGHAN Ó DÍOMASAIGH

No. 22 NAI DFA ES Paris 1922-23

Joseph P. Walshe to Vaughan Dempsey (Paris)
DUBLIN, 26 January 1923

A Chara,
Mr. KERNEY has written the following letter dated the 22nd January to this Department:

> 'I have to inform you that my appointment as Irish Consul in Paris has been confirmed by the Government of the Irish Republic and that consequently all further communications which you may wish to send to this Consulate should reach me through the medium of my Government.'

The Minister wishes you to ask Kerney to hand you over the finances he has on hands as well as the office furniture. A list of the furniture[1] is enclosed. His money on hands at the end of December was: 22,558 francs.

The best attitude to adopt is that you take the handing over as a matter of course.

The property and money belong to the Irish Government and to refuse your request would be patent dishonesty.

I attach, a formal letter giving you power to take over from him.

If he refuses to hand over perhaps you could convey to him that a notice will of course be issued to the Irish press warning all traders etc. to have nothing to do with him. Naturally the Irish Government can only treat him as a common thief and must arrest him as such when he arrives here.

Le meas,
[signed] S.P. BREATHNACH[2]
Rúnaidhe

No. 23 NAI DFA ES Paris 1922-23

Joseph P. Walshe to Leopold Kerney (Paris)
DUBLIN, 29 Janaury 1923

A Chara,
I am instructed and authorized by the Minister for Foreign Affairs of the Irish Free State Government to take over from you all office effects, including furniture, papers and files of every description, and all correspondence to date.

---

[1] Not printed.
[2] Joseph Patrick Walshe, Secretary, Department of External Affairs.

I am also instructed and authorized to demand and receive from you moneys declared as balance on hands on the 31st December 1922.

I should be obliged if you will expedite the transfer to me of this balance and property.

le meas,
[copy letter unsigned]

No. 24 NAI DFA ES Paris 1922-23

Extract from a letter from Vaughan Dempsey to Desmond FitzGerald (Dublin) (Copy) (Unnumbered)

PARIS, 29 January 1923

MR. KERNEY

A Chara,

As you probably anticipated the matter would not reduce itself to a simple question of presentation of authorization and consequent immediate handing over. Kerney refused to make any definite statement on the spur of the moment, but informed me that he must first communicate with what he calls his Government and act according to the instructions which they will give him. He regards the matter as similar to the case at present being conducted in America in connection with the Republican Funds, and considers that the Free State Government will probably have to institute proceedings against him in the French Courts.

As regards the balance in hands on the 31st December, Kerney is doubtful as to the validity of the Government's right to claim it, seeing that, as he informed me, the Consulate had not then come under the Ministry of Finance of the Free State, but was nominally still under the old Dáil at that date. In instituting proceedings therefore it will be necessary to remember this argument of the Irregulars, and to prove that the Free State has taken over the property as well as the responsibility of the old Dáil.

All these remarks are merely information as to Kerney's way of looking at this affair, gleaned in the course of conversation with him. The chief fact is that Kerney refuses to give any definite reply as to his line of action, and declines to hand over property, and balance until advised by his 'Government'.

Under the circumstances, there was nothing left for me to do on my own initiative, I await instructions as to the next steps to be taken. Either a prosecution can be commenced in the French Courts, or a bailiff can be placed in possession of his apartment acting under a judge de paix but in these two instances it would, it seems to me[,] be advisable to await a definite refusal on the part of Kerney to surrender the property of the Government. I would suggest as the best, least expensive, and more dignified method, that the Free State seek official recognition as a State by the French Government, and when this is accorded, official action can be taken supported by the Government of this country.

Is mise, le meas mór,
[copy letter unsigned]

No. 25 NAI DFA ES Paris 1922-23

Vaughan Dempsey to Desmond FitzGerald (Dublin)
(137/1923)

PARIS, 31 January 1923

A Chara,
To-day I have issued the following notice to the Press through Radio: 'The Irish Minister for Foreign Affairs informs the Press that Mr. Sean Murphy of the Bureau Irlandais, 28, rue Pauquet, Paris, has been appointed Acting Trade Agent for the Irish Free State. All communications should be addressed to him until further notice'.

In view of the transfer to this office of the duties of Trade Agency it is necessary that the whole system be organised on a thorough basis with a comparatively intense publicity in order to ensure that the cleavage between Free State and Republic be made as definite as possible and that there should not be left an interval of stagnancy and indecisiveness during which the Republican representative can make headway. Also it will be essential, until we are accredited[,] to work with discretion and tact, seeing that, as I informed you in one of my recent communications, we are not recognised by France. Under these circumstances if we give opportunity to Kerney to enter into controversy with us, there is the possibility of his turning the whole affair into something like a political dogfight, and if there are any public incidents I am informed by people in administerial circles that the French Government would probably expel the whole circus bag and baggage, Free State and Irregulars and let us fight out our differences elsewhere. Whereas if we are accredited this cannot happen, and we can apply at once for the expulsion of the Irregulars with all the right and dignity of an accredited Government. But in all this I would respectfully suggest that we must act quickly and not leave things to chance, for apart from public incidents it is to be taken for granted that the Irregulars will commence widespread propaganda here, and on account of the intensely anti-English mood of the French at this moment, it is not unlikely that they would be prepared to support the Republic as being anti-English and not the Free State which they have not been able to regard as anything else but a part of the British Empire. (I have certain reason for knowing that 'Anti-English' will be the chief component of Kerney's propaganda).

In reference to propaganda I would like to mention that this office has never paid anything to journalists for articles. Now a number of journalists began to cultivate this office with protestations of sympathy with Ireland, etc., and wrote articles in support of the Free State. Of course no one with a knowledge of French journalists could be deceived into a belief in the disinterestedness of their protestations. They soon found that they were not being offered remuneration for their work and so they quit. There are still two left who are better stayers than the rest, but even they are beginning to insinuate that their services are worth money. In view of this it may be essential to take into consideration the necessity for judicious payment for propaganda and journalistic influence on questions which are vital to a proper understanding of our position as against that adopted by the Irregulars.

In this connection I would suggest that the appointments paid to M. Bourgoeois (sic) be discontinued as his services are to my mind, of no practical utility to the working of this office.

I have written at some length in this and recent communications because I consider it my duty to give you as clear an impression as possible of the situation here, in view of recent events, and offer my opinion of the course of action entailed by the conditions in Paris.

I would be glad to receive detailed instructions from you for my guidance during the absence of Mr. Murphy.

Is mise, le meas mór,
[signed] VAUGHAN DÍOMSAIGH

No. 26 NAI DFA ES Box 31 File 200

Joseph P. Walshe to Timothy A. Smiddy (Washington)
DUBLIN, 1 February 1923

A Chara,
I am instructed by the Minister to forward new books per H.S. For ordinary purposes you may find the Unicode useful. For secret wires use the other. Instead of adding the actual date as heretofore, add the total number of days in the month minus the number of the actual date. Thus wiring on the 15th February, you add 13 (i.e. 28 – 15) on the 21st add 7 (i.e. 28 – 21) etc.

The Minister is most grateful for all the information and suggestions supplied for this and other Departments.

The Postmaster-General and the Minister for Agriculture wish their special thanks to be conveyed to you.

Since your Offices have been purified, there is no reason to fear henceforth that our letters might fall into the wrong hands. The present irregular system of answering your letters in cryptic general terms or not at all will cease forthwith.

The Minister wishes me to reaffirm on his behalf his entire confidence in your discretion and his complete approval of all the steps you have taken in the difficult matters you had to deal with.

There was no question at any time of dispensing with Mr. Crawford's services.

The question was whether somebody with more experience of Trade matters should not be appointed Trade Agent leaving Mr. Crawford free to assist you. When a final decision has been taken you will be advised.

We are asking the British Government to notify their Ambassador and the American State Department that you are duly appointed Agent of this Ministry 'for the purpose of studying the methods of public Administration in the United States and looking after financial interests of the Irish Free State'.[1]

Le meas,
[copy letter unsigned]
Rúnaidhe

[1] See No. 27 below.

No. 27 NAI DFA D1976

Desmond FitzGerald to T.M. Healy (Dublin)

DUBLIN, 1 February 1923

Sir,
I am to ask your Excellency to inform the British Government that Professor Timothy SMIDDY, 1045 Munsey Building, Washington, is the duly appointed Agent of this Ministry for the purpose of studying the methods of public administration in the United States and looking after financial interests of the Government of the Irish Free State in that country.

I am further to ask your Excellency to request the British Government to make known Professor SMIDDY's position to the State Department and to the British Ambassador in Washington.

I have the honour to be,
Sir
Your most obedient Servant,
DESMOND FITZGERALD
Minister for External Affairs

No. 28 NAI DE 5/96

Joseph Brennan[1] to Timothy A. Smiddy (Washington)
(Copy)

DUBLIN, 1 February 1923

Dear Professor Smiddy,
As you have already been advised, Mr. Slattery is leaving today to take up duty with you, and I avail of the opportunity to send you this note by him.

With reference to the Funds issue, the course which you have adopted and the way in which you have handled this whole matter has my very best approval and the Government wish me to convey to you their great satisfaction at the successful way you have guided the whole case.

The Government are also deeply grateful to you for the tactful way in which you have met and defeated the attack made on the Consulate Office in New York by Ginnell and his followers, and they appreciate the great help given you by Mr. Lindsay Crawford.

I understand that Mr. George McGrath and Mr. FitzGerald are in communication with you as to the matter of staff and funds. The Government will be only too pleased to approve of any requirements that you may think necessary for the Washington and New York Offices.

Secret Service: We would like to keep the amount ($6,000.00) advanced to you yesterday within this Financial Year, but we realise you are the best judge of what should be done. $6,000.00 is all we have authority for at the moment.

Currency: The Finance Department here are in agreement with your views that no change in currency can be made just at present. We have now secured

[1] It is unclear who sent this document.

for this Department the services of Mr. J. McElligott, late Editor of 'The Statist'. He remarks on Currency that 'The rise in sterling is due to the depreciation in gold, and even if English currency attains parity with the United States dollar, this will not be the same as the restoration of the gold standard in England. The latter will probably yet involve a further period of deflation, with attendant ill-effects, unless gold prices take a turn different to that which they are at present assuming. An appreciation in gold will, of course, mean a fall in gold prices.'

With very best wishes for your continued success in the hard duty before you,

Mise, le meas,
[copy letter unsigned]

No. 29 NAI DFA ES Paris 1924-26

Joseph P. Walshe to Vaughan Dempsey (Paris)
(213/23)

DUBLIN, 2 February 1923

A Chara,
In reply to your letters to the Minister and to myself, I am to say that the difficulty of the Paris position is fully recognised. We are taking the first steps to regularise it by informing the British Government that SEAN MURPHY has been appointed Acting Trade and General Agent. The letter has been sent through the Governor General to-day. The British Government has been asked to make known Sean Murphy's position to the British Ambassador in Paris and to the French Foreign Office. I enclose a patent for him, and one for you to be used in his absence, both in duplicate.

Mr. Kerney's last draft £300 was sent by us on the 8th December. The Minister agrees that it is essential to maintain official dignity at all costs and to avoid any unseemly 'bickering'. It might be well to write Kerney about the Office effects and Finance. Merchants here will of course have nothing more to do with him and I can't believe that he will wish to keep the files of their correspondence.

As to getting the French Authorities to move, great prudence must be exercised and the antics, if any, of the irregulars in Paris must be regarded in their proper perspective.

The Minister thinks it wiser to have somebody of Bourgeois' type at hand in case of need even if the need arises rarely. He would like to know if Sean Murphy's view agrees with yours on this point.

For the moment you cannot do more than watch events, replying to communications as far as possible.

We shall advise you when we hear that your position is known to the British and French Authorities.

Le meas,
[signed] S.P. BREATHNACH
Rúnaidhe

Patents will be forwarded in Irish & French within a few days. Thanks 'Carte Politique'

No. 30 NAI DFA ES Box 28 File 181

Telegram from Timothy A. Smiddy to Department of External Affairs (Dublin)[1]
(Copy)

WASHINGTON, 2 February 1923

Estero,[2]
Keeping intimate contact Larkin movement. He expressed himself to an individual last Friday as bitterly hostile to President and members of Free State Government. He said wants to clear English out of Ireland and the Countess belonged to his organisation. That he was going home soon. Also states there is a law that prevents me (?) (him)[3] landing at any British port. If Larkin returns Ireland of his free will can come USA when he wishes. If deported cannot return here for further activity. If you consider expedient can have him deported at once. Larkin and Frank P. Lawyer making more effective co-operation of Soviets with Irregulars here. Larkin's intention to intensify Soviet methods in Ireland. Reply prompt.[4]

SINBAD

No. 31 NAI DFA ES Paris 1922-23

Vaughan Dempsey to Desmond FitzGerald (Dublin)
(142/1923)

PARIS, 3 February 1923

Publicity

I send enclosed two cuttings which I have taken from to-day's papers.

Once the letters of credit which it has been decided to send to this Office are presented, the French Government will act of its own volition to defend our interests, and if we consider it expedient, a word would suffice for the expulsion from France of the ex-Trade Agent.[5]

In reference to the de Valera interview I would be glad if you would ask President Cosgrave to consent to send to this Office the substance of an interview which would tend to remove the impression created by this communication of de Valera. I could arrange to have this interview spread through the Press here.

It is my opinion that these words of de Valera fall at an unfortunate moment for us[,] seeing that the French mentality at the moment as regards Irish Affairs is confused and sceptical and inclined to give acceptance to the ideas expressed in this interview as the only explanation of the continued state of war in Ireland.

The mere fact of de Valera being still at liberty to give such an interview will incline the French to give substance to his assertions.

---

[1] Copies also to William T. Cosgrave and Hugh Kennedy.
[2] Telegraphic designation of Department of External Affairs, Dublin.
[3] As typed in original.
[4] Handwritten note: 'Reply sent: "take no action".'
[5] Leopold Kerney.

Hence I would earnestly request that a counter-communication be supplied this office as soon as possible.

De Valera's representatives are also trying to pass other interviews in French papers as I am informed by the 'Victoire'.

le meas,
[signed] VAUGHAN Ó DÍOMSAIGH

No. 32 NAI DFA ES Box 32 File 218

Joseph P. Walshe to Frank Egan (Chile)
(41/23)

DUBLIN, 7 February 1923

A Chara,

I am directed to acknowledge your letters Nos: 71, 72, 73, enclosing communication from Mr. SIMPSON, which has been transmitted to the Trade Department, Ministry of Industry and Commerce.

With regard to the matter of the British Legation, the Minister is of opinion that this also is a question for local decision.

In the present anomalous position, while on the one hand every thing that can be done should be done to emphasize Ireland's distinct Nationality and Statehood, at the same time there is no reason why Irish Citizens, since the Treaty with England, should put themselves to any inconvenience or at any disadvantage, through not making use of the British Consular machinery etc. Until Irish Representatives are officially accredited to foreign countries it is the only legal machinery available.

Le meas,
[copy letter unsigned]
Rúnaidhe

No. 33 NAI DFA ES Rome 1921-23

Sean Murphy to Desmond FitzGerald (Dublin)

8 February 1923

A Chara,

I am in receipt of your letter *N° 216.*

As your instructions in reference to giving up the house were very definite I did not think it necessary to report to you as to the opinion of the Irish Colony in this connection. I merely shut up the house and left it vague as to whether the Government would form an office later on or not. With regard to a report on the general situation in Rome I thought it better to reserve that until I was in a position to know the opinion of the prominent people there.

I am enclosing herewith a short report.

Is mise, le meas mór,
[signed] SEÁN Ó MURCHADHA

[enclosure]
REPORT

The general opinion in Rome amongst the Irish Clergy with regard to the present situation in Ireland is in favour of the Free State. There are however some exceptions. In some cases though supporters of the Free State the opinions were critical of the actions of the Government.

For example amongst the Irish Dominicans, who are almost entirely in favour of the Free State, they consider the action of the Government in regard to the measures taken against the Irregulars (executions etc) unwise and unduly severe. They say that facts prove that these measures have failed, and that their continuance will only exasperate the country. They criticize the Government for not making a more determined effort to solve the problem by other means.

The Irish Christian Brothers are I think entirely in favour of the Free State and agree that the Government have done all they can to settle the question without resorting to extreme measures, but that now there is nothing left for them to do. They consider that the Government is only doing its duty to the country in using every means to restore order.

The Rector[1] of the Irish College, on whom I called and with whom I had a short conversation, pretended that he was in favour of neither one side or the other, and that his only thought was, how an arrangement could be brought about to end the present strife. I saw from the trend of his arguments that he blamed the Government for the present state of things. He suggested that the only way peace could be restored was the acceptance by the Government of Document No 2. I am reliably informed by other clerics that he is very definitely pro-Irregular. I was not able to gather the opinion of the students but was told that they were careful not to voice an opinion one way or the other at least in public. I also met the Vice-Rector,[2] but he was very careful in all his remarks. I would be inclined to think that his feelings were with the Irregulars, but that his common sense leads him to the Free State. To get out of the difficulty he avoids giving any opinion.

Dr MacGuinness, the General of the Carmelites who is as you know at present in America, is definitely and actively pro-irregular.

Dr O'Gorman the Augustinian, who has I believe considerable influence[,] being a consultor to the Holy Office, is strongly Free State and a supporter of the Government. Though there were some things which he did not personally approve of, he refrained from criticism on the ground that the Government knew the situation better than anyone outside the country, and that their actions were guided by that knowledge.

As far as I could gather the Vatican is favourable to the Free State. Dr O'Gorman told me that even during the war the Vatican[,] as such, was not hostile, though there were certain personages there who were distinctly anti-Irish.

With regard to the petition presented by the Irregulars asking for the condemnation of the Irish Bishops, all the Irish priests in Rome looked upon it as an act of madness which will have no result. With regard to the report given

[1] Monsignor John Hagan.
[2] Michael Curran.

to Irish press by the presentors of the petition, I hope to have some definite information in a few days which I will send you.

The Irish Jesuits in Rome were all in favour of the Free State and supporters of the Government.

The only layman I met was the Marquis MacSwiney. He was very useful to me and gave me a great deal of assistance. He is a strong Free Stater and a supporter of the Government. He is engaged in forming an Irish Section in the Vatican Library. The section is now almost complete, and is very representative. He seems to have influence at the Vatican, and as far as I could find out is well thought of there.

The opinion with regard to the Delegation was practically all in favour of closing. During the war its only possible function was to counteract English Propaganda, now there was nothing to do. The continuance was considered as an expensive luxury. Until such time as the nominee of the Irish Government was recognised by the Vatican there would be absolutely no use having anyone in Rome. The opinion was that the Vatican would not take any step towards recognition until some other country had led the way. The Vatican Court is very conservative, and in such matters is very slow to move.

These views coincide exactly with the superficial opinion that I was able to form during my short stay.

SEÁN Ó MURCHADHA

No. 34 NAI DFA ES Box 34 File 241

Charles Bewley to Joseph P. Walshe (Dublin)
(26B/K)

BERLIN, 10 February 1923

A chara,

You will remember that I mentioned to you in Dublin in October that I wished to retire in the course of the New Year. I also mentioned the matter to Mr. Gearoid O'Lochlainn[1] when he was recently in Berlin.

I now beg formally to tender my resignation, and will be glad if you will let me know the earliest date on which it would suit you that it should take effect.

I will also be glad [for you] to let me know at your earliest convenience what arrangements you wish made with regard to transferring the funds of this office, the office itself etc.

My resignation is, as you are aware, dictated purely by personal reasons, and, as I would be reluctant that it should in any way be used for propaganda against the Government, I would be glad if you would see that a correct version is published in the Press.

Mise le meas mór
[signed] C[HARLES] BEWLEY

[1] Gearoid O'Lochlainn, Department of External Affairs.

No. 35 NAI DT S2027

Secret and Confidential memorandum on the Boundary Question to every member of the Executive Council, with covering letter by Kevin O'Shiel
DUBLIN, 10 February 1923

A Chara,
Herewith further Memo. on Boundary Question.

As many more are to follow, and as all will be of the *utmost importance*, please put into special File for swift and convenient reference.

Mise, le meas,
[stamped] CAOÍMHGHÍN Ó SÍADAIL
Assistant Legal Advisor

SECRET & CONFIDENTIAL
THE BOUNDARY COMMISSION – WHEN?

Having given a good deal of attention and study lately to the question as to *when* the Boundary Commission should proceed to function I have come to the conclusion that it would be nothing short of folly on our part to raise the issue *now* or at any time until there is a decided change in general conditions.

There is a foolish notion abroad that delay will tend to defeat, or at least to weaken our case in the Boundary Commission. In another Memo. I have analysed the reasons behind this notion and found, as I suspected, that there was not the slightest foundation to support it.

Far from defeating or weakening our Boundaries case, delay will have just the opposite effect. It will tend to strengthen and consolidate it.

The following are the reasons upon which this opinion is based:

I. *(1)* The prevailing bad condition of the country bears directly and insistently on the whole civil and constructive fabric of the Government. At the moment we can only prepare and perfect plans to put into force as soon as the reign of terror is overthrown and the reign of law re-established.

This is particularly true of our greatest internal problem – the matter of our future boundaries.

Our case on the Boundaries is overwhelmingly strong and has been rendered even more so by our recent researches on European Precedents.

(2) Whether therefore as a weapon to force Craig to come to suitable terms with us, or, in the last resource, to push to the ultimate our advantage at the Boundary Commission our case, politically, economically, geographically, historically and according to the Treaty Article itself (as further emphasised by Versailles Precedents) would appear to be absolutely unanswerable.

(3) Our case stated and the Commission itself provide us with extremely valuable diplomatic weapons which we can, and, in my opinion, should use for all we are worth in order to effect an enduring and lasting settlement on a basis not in conflict with the ideal of National Union. (This point I am developing more fully in another Memo.)

To use these valuable weapons to their fullest advantage peace all over the jurisdiction of the Free State is an *essential condition precedent.*

(4) Before we embark on the settlement of this great problem it is imperative

that we should be in the strongest possible condition, backed up by the united strength of a peaceful and law-abiding Nation.

We must be in a position to maintain public order and to *guarantee the protection of the lives and property of possibly future citizens.*

Clearly then, it would be folly for us to join issue on this grave matter *before we are robust enough to face the strain.*

What a ridiculous figure we would cut – both nationally and universally – were we to argue our claim at the Commission for population and territory when at our backs, in our own jurisdiction is the perpetual racket of war, the flames of our burning railway stations, and the never failing daily lists of our murdered citizens!

We would have then to meet the retort, 'What do you want with more territory and more population when you cannot maintain order in the territory you have or protect the lives and property of the population who declare their allegiance to you.'

(5) Suppose the Boundary Commission proceeded to function now and an arrangement was suggested in *lieu of it* which would meet our views and the ideas of Northern Nationalists, how would we undertake to guarantee anything to possible contracting parties?

No matter what we might say, no matter what documents we might sign to this effect, it would be all negatived by the daily and nightly turmoil going on behind us. The Irregulars would see to it that our undertakings would soon be broken.

(6) Here is another aspect. The Boundary Commission is bound to awaken great international attention. Once proceedings are opened many journalists, publicists, experts, etc. will be attracted to our shores, and a searchlight of most unenviable publicity would thus be thrown on the state of affairs in Saorstát.

We can depend upon it that the supporters of a separate 'Northern Ireland', having a very bad case on the merits, would work up this end of it for all they were worth. It is quite possible, too, that under existing circumstances they would get the support of many of those gentlemen, even those who would, under more favourable conditions, be prepared to stand up for us.

It is significant in this respect that the '*Daily News*' has lately taken up such an attitude in commenting on the Glenavy episode.[1]

II. *(1)* Another reason why delay is essential is the present condition of opinion in Great Britain. And in this connection we must remember first of all that a strong Tory Government is at present in power in Great Britain. The traditional policy of the Tory Party has always been one of hostility to Irish aspirations and of friendship to the Orange Cause. This Government is now carrying out the Treaty because *it has to*, because the Treaty is more than a mere statute, because it is in fact an international contract. The

[1] A private letter from Lord Glenavy, a former southern Unionist leader and the newly elected Chairman of the Senate, to Sir James Craig urging Northern Ireland to join the Free State with its regional autonomy and territory intact, had been leaked at the end of January and provoked fierce criticism in the *Irish News*.

declared opinion of the strong Die-Hard element and the secret opinion of the remainder of the Party is that the Treaty was really an act of betrayal; that the loyal population was betrayed in order to conciliate irreconcilable 'Celts', who could never be reconciled.

The actions of the Irregulars in the Free State have made it possible for Tories to say 'We told you so. Once Home Rule is granted to the Irish they will fight amongst themselves. They do not belong to that type of population which is ripe for self-government, etc. etc.'

They are able too to point to the peaceful conditions of 'Loyal Ulster' and contrast that with conditions in the Free State.

(2) I have it on excellent authority – from good friends of ours in Great Britain – that it would be most unwise for the Irish Government to raise this issue at the present juncture. It is the opinion of these people that if it were brought up at present the Northern Ireland Members and their supporters in the House of Commons would immediately protest against any handing over of territory from 'the peaceful North to the disorderly Free State', and that under present conditions such a protest would carry great weight in the House and in the Country.

If we forced the Boundary Commission now on the ground that it was an essential part of the Treaty we may be pretty certain that, driven to such a strait, the British Government would insist on the Craig interpretation.

The opinion of these British friends of ours is that Ireland has lost and is losing much valuable support in Great Britain. The English public and newspapers take a very gloomy view of conditions in the Free State.

The unsettled conditions here have badly hit big English enterprises which formerly dealt largely with us. London too is full of émigrés who have no reason to love us and who take every opportunity to speak bitterly of us.

I am informed further that in the Clubs intervention at an early period is freely spoken of. This being the case feeling against a Boundary Commission, and certainly our interpretation of Article XII., would be very easily stirred up.

I may mention here that I have found that the special propaganda I arranged for Great Britain has fallen flat owing to the many sensational and tragic news items which come from Ireland every day, and which completely overshadows my stuff. I have called off the publication of some of our best points until more favourable conditions. At the present time they would fall deadly flat and thus lose much, if not all, of their far reaching effects. The British people are at the moment not at all in a mood to listen to what they would call the ventilation of more 'Irish Grievances'.

III. A further and very important reason for delay arises if we have made up our minds to join the League of Nations.

In view of our international status not only *under* the Treaty but *by the very fact of the Treaty itself*, it is most important for us to pay the greatest attention to all our initial actions as they may probably result in the establishment of fundamental precedents with far reaching effects on our future development.

Most important of these is the international significance of the Boundary Commission under Article XII. That Commission by international law (which the Treaty of London, 6th December, 1921, entitled us to receive the benefit of) is a Commission composed of two representatives of the Government of Great Britain and one representative of the Government of the Irish Free State to decide the future Land Frontier between these two States. The fact that the two States are members of the same Commonwealth or alliance does not alter the international aspect of the matter. Neither does the fact that one of the States has an autonomous province called 'Northern Ireland' within its sovereignty alter this aspect or reduce it to the dimensions of a mere domestic arbitration.

It is clear then that we should neglect no means of strengthening our international position before we embark on any such delicate affair as the Boundaries issue. For this reason we should certainly take steps to join the League of Nations.

I hope in another Memo., which will follow soon, to elaborate in considerable detail the case for and against our joining the League of Nations. Here I will content myself with merely indicating roughly some of the very great advantages:

(1) The League is naturally more ready to intervene on the behalf of a member than of a non-member.

(2) If we are a member of the League of Nations at the time the Boundary Commission becomes rife we will be able to press the international significance of the Commission with greater and more telling force.

(3) The League has interfered on behalf of a number of countries in connection with Boundary disputes.

(4) Whatever the League's decision may be on the matter of our possible appeal *the Assembly of the League cannot refuse to hear the case of a member-State, and this will at least secure a measure of world-wide publicity which we could not get otherwise.*

(5) Membership of the League gives an additional recognition of the new relationship towards England attained by Ireland under the Treaty and thereby strengthens and enhances the Treaty itself *as a solemn contract between two countries which are both recognised internationally.*
It is obvious that this increased recognition strengthens the whole Treaty position and makes our case for interpreting our relationship with Great Britain, by the international code of law, practice and procedure, all the firmer in every direction.

(6) Membership of the League marks very definitely before the world the immeasurable distance in status between Saorstát and Northern Ireland. The latter cannot, under any present circumstance be a member of the League and the admission of Saorstát would make all the more evident that it is a Boundary dispute between a State internationally recognised and a province subordinate to another State.

CONCLUSION

In conclusion let me sum up very briefly the whole case against forcing on this issue at present.

If we join issue now on this grave matter we shall do so under the worst possible circumstances, and with only a few of our big cards in hands when we want them all.

The issue, if decided now, will only have the effect of an arbitration. To begin with, in our present weak and exhausted state the British Government, at the clamourings of the Die-Hards, on whom it mainly relies, *may insist on the Commission acting on special terms of reference which may in effect only direct a mere alignment of the Boundary line.*

The 'Morning Post' which at the moment, owing to the Conservative Party being in power, enjoys an enhanced influence and some official inspiration, declares that whether Craig appoints a Commissioner to the Boundary Commission or not *will depend largely on the terms of reference.*

Our case is, of course, that the terms of reference are contained in Article XII. according to international precedents. It is obvious then that against such dangerous possibilities as these we should consolidate all our international advantages, and, in so far as we enjoy freedom of action, refrain at least from raising this matter until such consolidation has been effected.

It is impossible at the moment to give a date when the Boundaries Question should be raised by us, but I am convinced that we should not at any rate go out of our way to seek it until

1) The time is opportune
2) Our case is fully completed
3) We have made full use of all the privileges and advantages given us by our new position, particularly those of membership of
   a) the League of Nations
   b) the Imperial Conference
4) The unnatural folly of Partition has been demonstrated by the operations of a Customs chain along the present utterly untenable frontier

and finally until

5) Every effort towards accomplishing an agreement with the North-Eastern Government along lines in conformity with the ideal of National Union has been fully and patiently exhausted.

[stamped] Caoímhghín Ó Síadail
Assistant Legal Adviser

No. 36 NAI DFA P646

Text of financial agreements between the Irish Free State government and the British government

London, 12 February 1923

I.

(A.)–*Completed and Pending Purchase Agreements.*

It is agreed that:-

1. The Free State Government undertake to pay at agreed intervals to the appropriate fund the full amount of the annuities accruing due from time to time, making themselves responsible for the actual collection from the tenant-purchaser.

2. The security for such payments shall be primarily a Free State guarantee fund similar to that under existing legislation, and, secondarily, the central fund of the Irish Free State.
3. The British Government shall continue as at present to provide the stock and cash necessary to finance purchase agreements pending at this date. Should any question arise as to whether any case is a pending agreement, the same shall be referred to Mr. Justice Wylie,[1] whose decision shall be final.
4. The British Government shall provide out of monies voted by Parliament, the cost of interest and sinking fund on bonus and excess stock as already issued or required for pending purchase agreements, together with the remuneration of the Banks of England and Ireland for management, subject to a contribution by the Irish Free State at the rate of £160,000 per annum.

Provided that such payments on both sides shall be without prejudice to the ultimate financial settlement.
5. The cost of administration of land purchase in the Free State area, except as provided under paragraph 4 above, shall be borne by the Irish Free State.

(B.)–*Completion of Land Purchase (new scheme).*
1. The terms of any new scheme which the Free State Government may propose to enact after such consultation with landlords and tenants as they may think necessary shall be subject to the concurrence of the British Government in consideration of the guarantee mentioned below.
2. The Free State Government shall finance any such new scheme by the issue of an Irish stock at 4 ½ per cent., the capital and interest of which, subject to agreed provision for redemption, shall be guaranteed by the British Government in the same way as it might guarantee a Colonial or Dominion Government loan.
3. The Free State shall provide security for payment of interest and sinking fund under the new scheme as under (A) 2 above.

(C.) The Free State agrees to continue the Office of Public Trustee without prejudice to the right of any beneficiary to apply to a competent court for the transfer of his trust.

II.—*Compensation.*

It is agreed that–
1. The division of cost shall be on the basis of existing arrangements (i.e., heads of working arrangements, paragraph 5, and the supplementary instructions to the Compensation (Ireland) Commission).
2. The general principle shall be that of a quarterly refund by the British Government on the following basis:-
(*a*) The Commission shall report, in respect of the awards made by them in any quarter, in what shares the aggregate amount of these awards is apportionable between the two Governments. On payment being made by the Free State Government on foot of any award made in the said quarter, the Free State Government shall be entitled, by quarterly demands, to recover from the British Government an amount equal to such a percentage of the payment (including

[1] William Evelyn Wylie (1881-1964), later a High Court judge of the Irish Free State.

any advance adjusted therein) as the aforesaid share of the British Government forms of the combined shares of the two Governments, after deducting from the product of the above percentage a fixed sum of £83,333 6s. 8d.

The said sum of £83,333 6s. 8d. shall be taken into account for this purpose for not more than twelve quarters.

(*b*) Such demands shall be discharged by the British Government in the course of the settlement from time to time of mutual cash liabilities between the two Governments.

(*c*) For the purpose of (*a*) all awards made up to the 31st March, 1923, shall be deemed to have been made in the quarter ending on that date, and the first demand of the Free State shall be in respect of payments made up to that date.

(*d*) The payments made under this arrangement shall be deemed to be provisional, and subject to final adjustment at the conclusion of the Commission's enquiry.

(*e*) The British Government waives in favour of the Free State Government any claim to benefit under the Agreements between the two Governments and Lloyd's Underwriters and certain other Insurance Companies.

III.—*Payment under the Irish Railways Settlement Act.*

The British Government agree not to press for a refund by the Irish Free State of any portion of the above, but reserve the right to claim in the ultimate financial settlement that the whole of the payments made under Section II of the Railways Act, 1921, and under the Irish Railways (Settlement of Claims) Act, 1921, both in Great Britain and Ireland should be treated as public debt for the purpose of Article 5 of the Treaty. The Free State Government take note of this reservation without prejudice to its position in the ultimate financial settlement.

IV.—*Refund of Cost of Munitions.*

The British Government agree that the cost of munitions of war supplied to the Irish Government up to the present date shall constitute a debt to be funded for the purpose of adjustment at the ultimate financial settlement (the exact amount due to be settled by agreement) on the understanding that the Irish Free State agree to pay cash for future supplies.

V.—*Royal Irish Constabulary.*

The Free State Government, without prejudice to their position at the ultimate financial settlement, agree to repay to the British Government 75 per cent. of the pensions and compensation allowances payable to ex-members of the Royal Irish Constabulary under the Constabulary Acts, subject to the exception mentioned in Article 10 of the Treaty.

The British Government agree to waive their claim for any contribution in respect of extra statutory non-recurrent payments made in connection with the disbandment of the Force.

VI.—*Haulbowline Dockyard.*

1. It is agreed that lands and buildings shall be transferred to the I.F.S. subject to the understanding that such lands and buildings shall be treated generally in the same way as military establishments under the 'Heads of Working Arrangements.'

2. (*a*) As regards fixtures, unerected plant and floating craft, the I.F.S. claim under the Treaty and Constitution, and on the analogy of military establishments, whatever is needed for carrying on the yard in working order.
(*b*) The British Government, while holding that there is a broad distinction in principle under the Treaty between naval and military services, and that the claims of the I.F.S. under paragraph 2 (*c*) above are therefore inadmissible on legal grounds, are nevertheless prepared without prejudice to agree in the procedure proposed in paragraph 3 below as a practical working arrangement.
3. If the Admiralty desires to remove for its own purposes any of the fixtures, unerected plant or floating craft, the I.F.S. will agree to the removal of so much as will not prejudice the working of the yard subject to the I.F.S. being given credit in the ultimate financial settlement for such part of the property removed, as is not surplus to normal requirements (on the analogy of military movables under the 'Heads of Working Arrangements').
4. (*a*) The I.F.S. contends that 'normal requirements' mean the requirements of the yard when carried on as a dockyard, whatever be the use to which it is put hereafter by the I.F.S.
(*b*) The British Government contends that normal requirements mean actual requirements.

Decision on this point to be reserved for the ultimate financial settlement.

5. It is agreed that a cash payment shall be made on account of the British claim for a refund of the cost of maintenance of the yard on the principle agreed under Head IX of this Agreement.

VII.—*Local Loans.*

1. It is agreed that the Free State Government shall make payments to the Local Loans Fund on account of outstanding arrears at the fixed rate of £25,000 a quarter as from the 1st April, 1923, until such time as the amount of irrecoverable debt on this account can be ascertained and agreed between the two Governments.
2. As regards future collection, the principle laid down in Article 4 (iii) of the Order in Council of the 1st April, 1922, shall continue to be applied between the British Government and the Free State Government pending further consideration.

VIII.—*Annuities under the Irish Railways Acts, &c.*

The Free State Government agree, without prejudice to the ultimate financial settlement, to pay to the Treasury the amounts due for payments of annuities arising from expenditure in the Free State under the Railways (Ireland) Act, 1896, the Public Offices Site (Dublin) Act, 1903, the Telegraph Acts and the Military Works Acts.

IX.—*Recoverable Charges.*

It is agreed that in future not less than 80 per cent. of these charges shall be paid by the Free State on account immediately on presentation of the claim, a reasonable period being allowed for discussion of any question which may be raised as regards the balance.

X.—*Property Losses in Irish Rebellion*, 1916.

The British Government agree to meet payments remaining to be made in respect of property awards already made, and the Free State Government to accept liability as from the 1st April, 1923, in respect of awards for personal injuries outstanding.

XI.—*Claims against Local Authorities for Extra Police.*

The British Government agree to withdraw this claim.

XII.—*Arrears of Taxes as on April* 1, 1922.

The British Government agree that all such arrears are collectable by the Irish Government for the benefit of their Exchequer.

JOHN W. HILLS　　　　L. T. MACCOSGAIR

No. 37 NAI DT S1955A

Memorandum on Customs Frontier with Northern Ireland

DUBLIN, 13 February 1923

To: Each Minister, Mr Flynn and Mr Brennan[1]

A Chara,

CUSTOMS & EXCISE DUTY.

Determination of Respective Revenues of Saorstát Éireann and Six County area.

Herewith for your information is a copy of a memorandum on the above subject which is to be considered at a Special Meeting of the Executive Council to be held at 10 a.m. tomorrow morning the 14th instant. The Meeting will commence punctually at the hour stated and it is the wish of the President that every Minister shall be in prompt attendance.

Mise, le meas,
[copy letter unsigned]
Gníomh Rúnaí

Customs and Excise.
Alternatives to Customs Frontier.

The President,[2]

1. In accordance with your directions I have prepared the following memorandum on the alternative arrangements that might be made for the determination of Free State Customs and Excise Revenue if it were decided to suspend temporarily the setting up of a Customs Frontier between the Free State and Northern Ireland. It is assumed that the object would be to postpone the Frontier temporarily and to make temporary arrangements to tide over the

[1] C.J. Flynn (Revenue Commissioners), Joseph Brennan (Department of Finance).

[2] Handwritten note by William T. Cosgrave: 'Establishment of Customs Frontiers not to be postponed. L[iam] T. MacC[osgair] 14/2/23'.

interval from 1st April. In those circumstances there are, I think, but three feasible alternatives, viz:-

(a) To collect all Ireland Revenue and attribute between Northern Ireland and the Free State on a presumptive basis (e.g. population).

(b) To collect the Revenue for Great Britain and Ireland on a uniform basis but attribute to Free State on a statistical basis.

(c) To continue present arrangement under which all Ireland Revenue is in the main determined on a statistical basis and attributed between Free State and Northern Ireland on a presumptive basis.

(a) *All-Ireland Collection of Revenue.*

2. *System described.* Under this arrangement all-Ireland would be treated as a fiscal unit. A complete Customs ring would be set up round Ireland: Customs duties would be payable on all dutiable goods imported into Ireland from all countries (including Great Britain) and Customs and Excise drawbacks would be payable on exported drawback goods to all destinations (including Great Britain). The official machinery for such a system exists in skeleton and for its completion would only require the strengthening of the Staffs at the Customs ports. The Revenue as collected in Ireland would be the true all-Ireland Revenue and its distribution between the Free State and Northern Ireland would fall to be made on some presumptive basis (e.g. population), to be agreed upon between the Governments concerned.

3. *Free State position.* The objections to this system from the Free State point of view are that it connotes a uniform tariff and a uniform basis of collection and assessment of Customs and Excise duties for the whole of Great Britain and Ireland – (this could only be avoided by the grant of fiscal autonomy to Northern Ireland and the acceptance by them of an agreed tariff – a contingency which need not be considered). This implies the adoption by the Free State Parliament of the British Tariff in its entirety and of any modifications that may be made in it as a consequence of the new British budget. The system has the advantage that it does not violate the principle of Irish unity and that it is free from the criticism, to which the Frontier system is open, that it recognises and tends to stereotype the present boundary between the Free State and Northern Ireland.

4. *British position.* Looked at from the British point of view the primary objection to this system would probably be that[,] despite uniformity of tariff, it involves the treatment of Northern Ireland by Great Britain as a foreign country for Customs purposes, and vice versa. This might well prove an insuperable difficulty in itself as it would evoke intense opposition in the North of Ireland and would also be unpopular amongst the British trading community doing business with Northern Ireland. There would, however, be the further difficulty that the arrangement would require legislation in the British Parliament and it is extremely unlikely that the present British Government would, even if it could, ask Parliament for the necessary powers. Apart from the possibility that the scheme might yield a little more Revenue to the North (and this is entirely problematical) it has no compensating advantages either to Northern Ireland or Great Britain.

(b) *Collect Revenue for Great Britain and Ireland as a unit but attribute to Free State on a Statistical basis.*

5. *System explained.* This is really an extension of the existing arrangement described at paragraph 8 below. In addition to the collection of statistics of the movements of dutiable goods between the Free State and Great Britain as at present, statistics of the movements of dutiable goods between the Free State and Northern Ireland would also be collected. The complete statistics thus collected would give the total quantities of dutiable goods retained for consumption in the Free State. The quantities so ascertained would form the basis for the determination of Free State Revenue. This arrangement would necessitate the employment of a small number of Customs officers along the frontier to collect the statistical returns but it would not involve any machinery for the bringing to account of or the collection of duties on dutiable goods passing to and fro. The transit of free goods would be perfectly unrestricted as now and the arrangement would not involve any appreciable interference with the trade and traffic between the Free State and the North.

6. *Free State position.* This system has, from the Free State point of view, all the disadvantages of system (a) above, with very few of its compensating advantages. It would involve the temporary surrender of fiscal autonomy without achieving even the semblance of fiscal unity. Whilst it could not be described as stereotyping the present boundary between the Free State and the North, the presence of Customs officers along the boundary to collect statistics might be construed as an official recognition of its existence. It has the advantage over the existing arrangement that it would provide a firmer basis for the determination of Free State Revenue and would eliminate the speculative division of Revenue between the Free State and Northern Ireland which is inherent in the present system.

7. *British position.* The only objection that I can see from the British point of view is that this arrangement would probably require legislation and that the time available is very short, but the British legal advisers are really the only competent people to judge. It would probably involve a small additional cost for increased staff as compared with the present system but, on the other hand, it would mean a very great saving in staff as compared with a 'Customs frontier' regime.

(c) *Continue present arrangement.*

8. *Present arrangement.* The arrangement in force at present is to collect statistics of trade in dutiable goods between Great Britain and Ireland. These statistics coupled with the particulars of Customs and Excise Revenue actually collected in Ireland (as a whole) furnish a basis for the determination of true all Ireland Customs and Excise Revenue. The all-Ireland Revenue thus determined is divided between the Free State and Northern Ireland on a presumptive basis.

9. *Free State position.* This system is equally open with systems (a) and (b) to the objection that it involves a temporary surrender of fiscal autonomy. In theory it is open to the further objection that *all* the statistical returns now go to London and that the accounts are prepared there. On the other hand these accounts are available for any detailed scrutiny or examination that the Ministry of Finance may wish to impose and it has the merit that it saves duplication of work and

staff and the expense which this involves. If it were desired to continue the system there would moreover be no physical difficulty in arranging that duplicate returns should be supplied to the Free State and a duplicate account prepared here.

10. *British position.* I cannot see any objection, from the British point of view, to a continuance of the system. On the contrary it would save them considerable expense in the way of staff and considerable trouble in the way of administration. It has also, from their point of view, the merit that it would not require further legislation as it is already provided for in their 'Irish Free State Constitution Act' of last year.

General

11. *Schemes compared.* Of the three schemes there is no question but that scheme (a) would be the most desirable from our point of view. For the reasons stated in paragraph 4 it seems probable that neither the British Government (nor the Northern Government whom they would no doubt consult) would be prepared to accept this scheme, and for that reason I am afraid that it must be regarded as outside the sphere of practical politics. As between schemes (b) and (c) there is not, from our point of view, a great deal to choose, but the balance of favour undoubtedly rests with scheme (b). On the other hand scheme (b) would probably require legislation in the British Parliament whereas scheme (c) would not, and it may therefore be assumed that as between the two schemes they would press for (c). Either (sic) of the three schemes would require legislation in the Oireachtas.

12. *Questions for decision.* The fundamental objection to the Customs Frontier, from our point of view, is that it may be regarded as stereotyping the present boundary line between the Free State and Northern Ireland and might, to that extent, prejudice our position before the Boundary Commission. The fundamental objection to the alternatives discussed above is that they all imply acceptance by the Free State not only of the existing British tariff and its administrative system, but also of any modifications that may be made by the British Parliament so long as the arrangement continues. If there were any probability that the Boundary Commission were likely to sit and complete its deliberations in the early future there would be a very strong case for postponing the frontier. If there is not, it may be difficult to justify postponement, with its consequences, to the Oireachtas. We are now in the middle of February with only six weeks left in which to prepare the necessary machinery for the arrangements to operate from 1st April. Whatever these arrangements are to be they will involve considerable negotiation and discussion and it is therefore essential that the position should be cleared up without delay. The points for decision are:-

I. Is the establishment of a Customs Frontier as from 1st April to be postponed or not?

II. If the decision is in the affirmative, which of the schemes discussed above is to be introduced as a temporary substitute for the frontier?

No. 38 NAI DT S1955A

Extract from minutes of a meeting of the Executive Council (C.1/46)
DUBLIN, 14 February 1923

CUSTOMS FRONTIER BETWEEN SAORSTÁT ÉIREANN AND THE SIX COUNTY AREA
A memorandum from the Finance Department setting out alternative arrangements to the setting up of a Customs barrier between SAORSTÁT ÉIREANN and the Six Counties was considered.

It was decided that arrangements for the establishment of a Customs frontier should be proceeded with at once, so as to be in operation as from the 1st April next.

No. 39 NAI DFA ES Box 29 File 189

Timothy A. Smiddy to Desmond FitzGerald (Dublin)
WASHINGTON, 19 February 1923

A Chara:

PUBLICITY

I enclose a description of the meeting Sir Horace Plunkett[1] addressed in New York on February 8th, 1923, as also a cutting from the Montreal Standard, January 29th, and a letter I had inserted by a Mr Donleavy in the Evening World.

Having been acquainted before hand that an attempt was to be made to break up Sir Horace's meeting by local Irish radicals and Irish Communists, which a number of the waterfront 'tough element' was ready at hand to carry out, the New York Police were duly informed. Mr - - -[2] and his men were there in force and prevented what might have been a serious interruption.

Sympathetic prominence and a very full report is given to the President's ultimatum to the Irregulars in the Sunday New York Times and other papers. I would again urge regular statements by President and Ministers to Foreign Press Correspondents.

Mise, le meas,
[signed] T.A. SMIDDY

No. 40 NAI DFA ES Box 34 File 241

Gordon Campbell[3] to Joseph P. Walshe (Dublin)
(C.263)
DUBLIN, 19 February 1923

I am directed by the Minister of Industry and Commerce to refer to your minute (T/21/23) of 15th instant attaching copy of a letter of resignation received from

[1] Sir Horace Plunkett (1854-1932), agriculturalist and politician, founder of the Irish Co-operative Movement, Member of the first Irish Free State Senate (1922).
[2] Blank in original document.
[3] Secretary, Department of Industry and Commerce.

Mr. Bewley.[1] I am to say that the question whether an Office is for the time being to be retained in Berlin appears to be a matter rather for the Minister of External Affairs than for the Minister of Industry and Commerce. It is felt that at the moment there would be no justification for maintaining an Office in Berlin merely for trade purposes in view of the present conditions in Germany but if on general political grounds an Office is retained in Berlin this Ministry would like to make use of it so far as possible for trade matters.

[signed] GORDON CAMPBELL

No. 41 NAI DT S2027

Secret and Personal memorandum by Kevin O'Shiel to each member of the Executive Council with attached memorandum by Joseph Johnston
DUBLIN, 19 February 1923

A Chara,

CUSTOMS ON THE IRISH-BRITISH LAND FRONTIER

1. I send you herewith for your *special attention* a Memo. prepared at my request by our Economic Adviser, Mr. Joseph Johnston, F.T.C.D. with regard to the forthcoming exercise of our fiscal sovereignty. This Memo. contains suggestions which will, if adopted, have effects of a very far-reaching nature on the North-Eastern Position.

2. Now, that there is no doubt that the fiscal frontier is going up in April next and that our fiscal independence will be exercised, it is well that the new position thereby created should be carefully reviewed with the object of deriving for ourselves the very best results.

From the political standpoint of the North-Eastern Position with which we are dealing, this is the experimental year. Aiming, in the ultimate, for full National Union, political and economic, we look upon all matters at hand arising out of the Treaty of London as cards towards the achievement of this object.

And we are convinced that the Customs Frontier if well used is one of the greatest cards in this policy.

3. It is anticipated and understood that owing to conditions in Ireland caused largely by the criminal action of the Irregulars, we will not be able to use to the fullest advantage the Customs weapon. By this I mean nothing in the nature of an economic boycott of the Belfast Government, but merely the creation and carrying out in the Free State of a fiscal policy in accordance with particular and special wants of all Ireland.

It will take Belfast some time to appreciate that the fiscal policy of the Free State is the policy most natural for them, and one which best suits them in every respect; and that the British fiscal system is based on purely British conditions, which are essentially different from Irish conditions.

When the North-East see across their Border, actually abutting them, a fiscal policy in operation based on natural causes which they share in common with the rest of the Island, it will not take very long for a feeling to develop towards a Customs Union, and thence Political Union.

[1] See No. 34 above.

4. We should not, however, make the big blunder of handing over this concession for nothing. We should do nothing towards a rapprochement on this question (and, of course, nothing against it). It is now for the Belfast Government to make overtures and suggestions to us. We can afford to wait, and, in spite of all that has been said, pro and con, I am of the opinion that a position will presently develop in which they will be most anxious to meet us, and discuss, with a view towards settlement, this and other big outstanding questions.

It is time enough for us when the discussion arises to formulate our terms. (Johnston deals with this well in his Memo.)[1] At any rate, let it be a good bargain on our part as well as theirs, and in accordance with the principle so well understood by Northern psychology, 'nothing for nothing'.

5. It is said that our taxes are likely to be higher than Northern taxes. This state of affairs can only arise over one out of two alternatives occurring[:]

(1) On our increasing our taxes above their present standard in our next budget.

(2) On our maintaining present taxation (which is identical with British taxation); and on Britain[,] in her next budget, lowering considerably her taxation.

On this I have got the views of our experts, and whilst I do not know anything about our fiscal policy, or what it is likely to be the experts reply[:]

(1) As to increasing our taxation, a great mistake and only increase internal trouble like unemployment, etc. without gathering in anything like a correspondingly large amount of money. Such a decision would play directly into the hands of the Six Counties, and probably oblige us ultimately to seek a Customs adjustment with them.

(2) It is possible that Britain may, for political purposes, reduce taxation slightly on certain commodities, but I am advised that it is not likely that she will pursue this policy to any appreciable extent. Her international debts and liabilities (e.g. with America) are huge, and she is doing all she can to gather in all the money she can, even to the extent of calling upon such little places as the Channel Islands and the Isle of Man to come to her assistance with comparatively insignificant sums.

6. Even in the event of the taxation in the two parts of Ireland remaining the same[,] the North-East will be inconvenienced and will suffer to a greater extent than we will. It is quite clear then that if we can alter our taxation in the manner suggested by Mr. Johnston the effect on the North-East will be even more uncomfortable, to put it lightly.

I am strongly of opinion that during this most important experimental year every effort should be made to take the fullest advantages out of this important fiscal weapon along the lines suggested by Mr. Johnston.

[stamped] Caoímhghín Ó Síadail
Assistant Legal Adviser

[1] See enclosure with this document.

[enclosure]

Secret

Suggested modifications of schedules of Customs and Excise Duties.

A writer in the Morning Post of 6th February, 1923, deals with the Boundary Question from the point of view of the fiscal policy of the Free State.

He points out that the present boundary is exceedingly awkward from the customs point of view and urges the necessity of 'a reasonable rectification which would get rid of the more inconvenient salients and make it conform more conveniently to the railway and other great traffic routes.' This means that the North wishes to take the whole of North Monaghan into their territory at least so far south as to include the whole of the railway from Portadown to Clones in their area. They also wish to include Pettigo District Electoral Division and perhaps one or two neighbouring Districts in that part of County Donegal. In East Donegal they quite clearly wish to include at least enough territory to give them the whole of the Great Northern Railway from Strabane to Derry and they would probably take the whole of the Inishowen Peninsula if they got it. As against that they would probably surrender a large part of West Fermanagh and possibly some part of the Clones No. 2 Rural District in South East Fermanagh. They might possibly be willing to let South Armagh go, but less willing to forego any part of South Down.

The effect of such a transference would be to round off the Northern Railway system at the expense of ours. By gaining possession of Clones and East Donegal they would have complete control of the railway system connecting Portadown with Clones, Enniskillen and Derry. But our railway communications from Dundalk via Clones to Cavan, via Clones, Cavan and Inny Junction to Sligo, via Clones, Cavan and Mullingar to Ballina, Achill and Clifden will be interrupted. In fact to get by rail from Dundalk to Connaught or Donegal, without passing through Northern territory[,] would involve a journey to Dublin.

Even if the North obtained such a 'reasonable rectification' of the boundary, although they would have simplified their railway problem, they would still be in most serious difficulties as soon as the new Boundary became a Customs frontier. For the new Boundary would still cut the market regions of Derry, Strabane and Enniskillen to the quick, and would almost certainly be fatal to the latter town in particular. (For the effect of a Customs barrier on market towns see memorandum on that subject.)

The chief interest of the article in the Morning Post is that it betrays a sensitiveness to the possible effects of Free State fiscal policy on the excluded area, an effect which it is dishonestly or ignorantly suggested that a 'rectification of the boundary' will minimise or remove.

It is stated in the article that 'a reasonable Southern Ireland would recognise the necessity of conforming to the United Kingdom Customs and Excise for business reasons.'

In this connection it may be pointed out

(1) That even if the Free State took over the whole of the existing British schedule of Customs and Excise Duties without a single modification, once the Free State begins collecting these duties within its own area the Customs barrier will automatically go up and the effect on the market regions of Derry,

Enniskillen and Strabane will be nearly as unpleasant as if there was a considerable difference in the respective schedules of duties and dutiable articles.

(2) As regards the effect of a Customs barrier on the existing market regions of Six County Towns a 'rectified' Boundary is very little better for the Belfast Parliament than the present boundary.

The fact is that if the North succeeds in holding Derry City, Tyrone and Fermanagh, Derry City, Strabane and Enniskillen will be practically ruined by the mere fact of the existence of a Customs barrier.

Free State fiscal policy and *North East Ulster.*

Fiscal separation, even if we retain the same rates of duty on the same articles as the British, will make the commercial position of these important Six County Towns absolutely untenable. But there are a few changes and modifications which, if introduced by the Free State into the fiscal system, would exercise a powerful leavening influence on the commercial outlook of Northern business men and cause the land frontier to be a much greater nuisance to them and to the British tax-gatherer than to us.

The vast bulk of British and Irish indirect taxation is derived from the Customs and Excise duties on tea and tea substitutes (e.g. cocoa), alcoholic beverages, tobacco, sugar, and 'sugar composite' articles. For example the tax on confectionery, condensed milk, and table waters is really a tax on the sugar contents of these articles. It would be safe to assert that 99 per cent of the revenue derived from indirect taxation is derived from the Customs and Excise taxes on these commodities, their substitutes, and on the composite articles into which one or other of them enters as a raw material.

In present financial conditions it may be laid down that the Free State must consider the fiscal system primarily from the point of view of revenue productions. And, therefore, the taxes on the articles mentioned above must be continued though not necessarily at the same rate as that imposed by the British. It will be undesirable for many reasons to increase any of the rates and if the rate on any one of them is to be reduced the effect on revenue must be kept carefully in view.

The present tax on spirits and possibly also on wine and beer (stout) is probably higher than the point at which a maximum revenue would be obtained. Poteen drinking etc., is notoriously rampant. The effect of a[,] say[,] 25 per cent reduction on the duty on spirits would probably be to cause such a shifting of public demand from 'poteen' to whiskey, as actually to increase the revenue obtained from whiskey without any increase in the *total* consumption of intoxicating spirit. The social and fiscal evil of illicit distillation would consequently be more easily dealt with. Much whiskey that had paid duty to the Free State would be smuggled across the Border thus increasing the revenue of the Free State and 'making the foreigner pay.' Free State border towns and seaside places would become a popular resort for thirsty 'bona fides' from the North-east and from Great Britain. And all this would help to swell Free State revenue.

The writer in the Morning Post contemplates such action on the part of the Free State and he is good enough to admit that in that event the 'North would be seriously handicapped and would have a huge task in holding its frontier against smugglers.'

Taxes which should be swept away altogether.

During and since the war customs duties have been imposed on certain articles imported into these islands with a view to protecting the corresponding British industries. Such, for example, are the $33^1/3$ per cent ad valorem duty on clocks, watches, motor cars and cycles and musical instruments imported from abroad. Under the Safeguarding of Industries Act of 1921 there us also a similar $33^1/3$ per cent customs duty imposed on an enormous range of 'key industry' goods, e.g., optical glass, theodolites, thermometers, and other scientific glass ware, galvanometers, and other scientific instruments, gauges and measuring instruments of precision, 'of the types used in engineering machine shops,' etc., etc.

In addition there is the 'British Dye-stuffs Acts' under which German or other foreign dyes can only be imported from abroad under a licence.

The object of all these duties and restrictions is frankly protectionist but the industries they seek to protect are confined exclusively to Great Britain.

The effect of these duties in Ireland is:

1. To increase the cost of certain instruments and machines used in engineering and shipbuilding works.
2. To increase the cost of the dyes used in the textile industry. This, so far as it goes is injurious to the linen industry, but much more so to the cotton industry on account of the great relative importance of dyes in the latter industry.
3. To add to the difficulty and expense of properly equipping the scientific departments of Irish Universities, North and South. In effect this is a tax on education and we have evidence that its effect in this respect is appreciated by the authorities in the Queen's University, Belfast.
4. To add greatly to the labour involved in the collection of customs revenue at the ports.
5. To hamper and impede business men interested in the import of any of these 'protected' articles in view of the troublesome formalities that have to be complied with.

N.B. It may be stated confidently that the revenues derived even by Great Britain from the taxes on these articles is utterly insignificant and the revenue accruing to the Free State from a continuation of these taxes would probably not exceed the direct and indirect cost of collection.

As the industries 'protected' by the tariffs are not represented in the Free State or in Northern Ireland either[,] there is no earthly reason why these tariffs, devised exclusively in the supposed interests of certain cross channel industries, should be retained by the Free State. 'Northern' Irish industries derive no protection from these taxes either, and in fact suffer from them to an even greater extent than Free State industries do, but no doubt they will regard this loss as part of the price they gladly pay for the privileges of British citizenship!

There is evidence in the Morning Post article referred to that this aspect of the matter is beginning to be appreciated in the North. The writer attributes to the Free State the intention of abolishing the restrictions on the import of German dye-stuffs. He then goes on to say that if the Free State is able to give effect to this 'the effect on Northern Ireland will be inconvenient in two respects. The textile manufacturers of the North will be working under an extra burden as compared with the South in regard to their expenditure on dye-stuffs; and the guarding of the frontier against smuggling from the South into the North of German dye-stuffs will be a heavy task.'

The writer is unable to suggest any direction in which a compensation might be obtained by the North from this incidental disadvantage of British citizenship.

The moral (sic) of the Free State is obvious. Let us abolish not only the import restrictions on dye-stuffs but the whole congeries of taxes on foreign motor-cars, clocks, galvanometers, thermometers, optical instruments 'et hoc genus omne' and multiply the problem of guarding the Northern frontier against the vigorous smuggling industry in all these articles which will at once spring up.

In this matter the interests and sympathy of the Northern business man will be with the southern smuggler and against the whole pro-British policy underlying the key industries['] duties. And it will soon dawn on his rapidly developing political intelligence that so far as fiscal policy is concerned the Free State system is more in his interests than the British system.

One of the incidental effects of the successful smuggling of key industry goods into Northern Ireland will be to compel the British customs authorities to keep almost as close a watch on the trade from Northern ports to Great Britain as they would keep on the trade from Free State ports. For otherwise key industry goods will be smuggled not only into Northern Ireland but from Northern Irish ports to Lancashire and elsewhere, where the demand for them is very urgent. The British custom authorities will have to abandon the attempt effectively to guard the land frontier and while conniving at the use of smuggled goods in Northern Ireland concentrate their attention on preventing such goods finding their way into Great Britain from Northern Ireland.

And so, Northern Ireland will have the worst of both worlds for her trade with Great Britain will be watched just as closely as the trade of the Free State while she will not enjoy the legitimate advantages of Free State fiscal independence.

American tariff on imported linen.

At present the linen industry in Ireland as a whole is hampered in its export trade by the American tariff on imported linen. Most of the linen mills and factories are in the Six Counties but there are a few in the Free State, e.g. in Dublin, Drogheda, Dundalk and Castleblayney. I am not aware whether any of these Free State linen concerns export direct to America, but if they do a vigorous effort should be made by our representative in America to induce the American Government to take off the tariff on linen exported to America from *Free State* linen factories. If Irish-American sympathy could be enlisted it ought to be possible to achieve this.

Political reactions of suggested Free State fiscal policy.

A fiscal system of the kind outlined would lead very soon to a movement among Northern business men for a Customs union with the Free State. The political price in terms of Irish unity which they would offer in the first instance would probably not be very high. If any offer at all is made I think it would be advisable to arrange a Customs Union for one year at the best political price the Free State can obtain *for the first year*. As a condition of renewal for a second year *the political price should be raised*, and so on from year to year until we all wake up suddenly to realise that by slow degrees the Free State has in fact reabsorbed the Northern Territory.

This procedure is in accordance with Northern psychology. The Northerner has made the 'splendid gesture' of marching out of the Free State with a flourish of trumpets. His back is now turned to the Free State, but he is quite noticeably taking one or two backward steps in the direction of that Institution. There is a story told of a man who walked backward into a circus and when passing the pay desk tried to avoid payment by pretending that he was going out. This is evidently the Northern attitude and policy. And it is safe to prophesy that he will gradually back into the Free State, that he will pay the political price of re-entry, and that the fiscal policy pursued by the Free State, if it is of the right kind, will be *the* deciding factor in inducing him to return.

But we can have no fiscal policy at all until we decide to exercise our fiscal independence.

(signed) JOSEPH JOHNSTON

No. 42 NAI DFA Letter Books (Paris 1923-24)

Joseph P. Walshe to Sean Murphy (Paris)

DUBLIN, 1 March 1923

A Chara,
I am instructed by the Minister of External Affairs to forward the attached amended patent in French and English.[1]

The French Government was informed by the British Ambassador in Paris on the 13th inst. that you had been appointed as 'Acting Trade and General Agent of the Irish Free State in Paris.'

The Minister wishes that you should forthwith act accordingly and make yourself known officially to the chief officers of the Ministries which may now or at any future time be useful for the purposes of our Paris Office.

It is also desirable that you should leave your cards on the British Ambassador and Consul without delay.

The Canadian High Commissioner would be able to give you valuable information as to his own position vis a vis the French Government and the British Ambassador.

You will naturally proceed with great caution in all things concerning the extent of your powers, and whenever any question is put by the British regarding them you will have to confine yourself to the words 'TRADE AND GENERAL AGENT' without committing yourself to define the implications of the word 'GENERAL'. On the other hand you should seize on every opportunity given by the British to create precedents in our favour. Thus if you are asked by them to look after the interests of Irish Citizens or do anything whatsoever concerning Irish interests which formerly came within the sphere of the British Missions, you should seize the opportunity offered no matter what the difficulties involved.

The Minister fully appreciates the difficulties of your position and the delicate

[1] Not printed.

and responsible nature of the task committed to you as the first recognised Irish Agent in Paris, and he feels confident that you will carry it out with all due zeal and discretion.

It is essential that you should realise how vague the position of the Nations forming the British Commonwealth still remains with regard to Foreign Affairs, and how much depends on the individual discretion of those who are in a position to influence that side of our political evolution.

The implications of your new responsibility will be given our attention immediately.

A list of your requirements as to Staff, etc. should be sent as soon as possible.

I attach a list of personalities, whom in the opinion of M. Blanche, you should visit at the earliest opportunity.[1] The British should be visited first.

M. Blanche suggests that the Office of the Protocole would give you every information as to procedure. Advice or documents on this would be most valuable to us.

Le meas,
[copy letter unsigned]
Rúnaidhe

No. 43 NAI DFA Letter Books (Department of the President 1923-28)

James McNeill to Desmond FitzGerald (Dublin)
(V.4.) (Copy)

LONDON, 2 March 1923

My dear Minister,
I am anxious to have a clearer understanding about my duties and responsibilities. I thought of writing to you earlier but did not wish unnecessarily to trouble you and the Ministry with matters which would adjust themselves with the help of time and patience.

As advised by Mr Walshe's telegram Sir Philip Hanson[2] came here this morning. I was ill and unable to see him at 10.30 when he arrived, but told Mr McGilligan beforehand that I would see him in the afternoon. He came at 2.30 p.m. and told me that he had instructions from the Finance Department to inquire as to premises. He had no written instructions and no communications from the Finance Department addressed to me to state what his duties were. He had heard already from Mr McGilligan and Mr MacDonnell[3] that an offer had been made on my behalf for other premises, the offer being made on such terms as would prevent its being binding if a better bargain could be secured. He had been to see Norway House and was told of other premises by the Board of Works people here. Some of these at least were those which were suggested to us and regarded as unsuitable. We discussed the possibility of sub-letting a part of the premises (2nd floor, Kinnaird House, Cockspur St.) for which an offer of £2750 had been made. I explained why I thought that subletting of a part of these somewhat large premises would have to be

[1] Not printed.
[2] Hanson was Chairman of the Commissioners of Public Works in Ireland.
[3] Solicitor for the Irish High Commission.

considered as a possibility but not as a necessity. He asked me as to details of the accommodation I should need with reference to Norway House. I told him that while I wished to be in no way discourteous to him I was not prepared to explain my proposals to him. I added that I was personally dissatisfied with the attitude of the Finance Department and that I did not think it right that anyone should be sent over here to deal with the arrangement about premises without any written instructions and without giving me formal information. He thought that financial control was necessary. I agreed with him but told him that I did not care for the way it was exercised in this and in other cases which were at the moment irrelevant.

I now wish to state that I am not prepared now or at any time to explain my proposals to officials of the Finance or any other Department who come over here with instructions about my work which are not communicated to me. I do not doubt that Sir Philip Hanson was carrying out instructions and I am sorry that he should experience anything unpleasant as a consequence of my strong dissent from the methods of the Finance Department. I tried to make that clear to him.

As regards the control of the Finance Department, I have no wish to evade proper control, but do not care to have my arrangements upset nor to have officials sent here by the Financial Department to anticipate my proposals or relieve me of my duties, whether their intentions are communicated to me or not.

The anxiety for transferring responsibility from my shoulders has lost us a suitable set of premises and caused the numerous enemies of the Free State some satisfaction. It has not helped us in the matter of terms.

The withholding from me of all information regarding the agreements[1] come to at the recent conference has caused some official difficulty. I have asked orally and more than once in writing for a copy of the agreement which is supplied to Government Departments here.

The Ministry of Finance in its letter, No. 657 of 19/2/23,[2] states that that Department has arranged *directly* with the British Government that equipment for my office shall be requisitioned from the Office of Works here. I think that that is a politically objectionable arrangement, and I also think that it is desirable that I should ask British Government Departments for any facilities. If I am in difficulties I shall inform you as Minister of External Affairs. It is unnecessary to adopt a procedure which suggests that neither the Minister of External Affairs nor the High Commissioner knows his business, even if it is assumed that the Board of Works can always supply my needs most economically.

When there was urgent need for munitions the Colonial Office was informed a day before I received any intimation. The officials in the Colonial Office are courteous and helpful, but if they only are informed I can do nothing, while if I am treated by my Government as other High Commissioners are treated by theirs the public business will benefit. Neither the Colonial Office nor any other office will take the High Commissioner very serious if he is kept in the dark or side-tracked.

Both Mr Crowley and I have been informed orally that the former is to

---

[1] See above, No. 36.
[2] Not printed.

work under my general control. There has been, so far as I know, no formal communication to either of us. The Colonial Secretary inquired of the Governor General what Mr Crowley's duties were. Had I been duly informed I should have told him before inquiry was made. He does not ask other Governments about the duties of their officers working under the control of High Commissioners.

A stream of precedents is swelling which will render the status of the High Commissioner of the Irish Free State something very different from that of his Canadian colleague. There is an anxiety in some quarters here to minimise his status. I am not concerned with my own importance, but you will readily understand that I do not want my tenure of this office, however short, to have been marked mainly by having it treated as unimportant as some people here would wish. Obviously the High Commissioner cannot be an Ambassador but he need not be an office boy. I am writing to you separately about the proposed definition of my duties which Sir Mark Sturgis wrote about.

Meantime, as Sir Philip Hanson will doubtless let you know that I declined to go fully into my proposals with him, I thought it right to place frankly before you the facts and opinions which are contained herein. I am sorry to cause you personally any trouble and I have no wish to raise official controversies, but I think that neither I nor anyone else can reputably serve as High Commissioner if needful information is withheld and needless interference is practised in the guise of financial control. Economy is a very good thing when not extended into the region of official courtesy. If my view, based on some experience of financial control and administrative responsibility and possibly strengthened by a belief that the Free State will suffer from an undue effect to work in close conjunction with British departments, is held to be mistaken I have no wish to claim any personal consideration. I cannot carry out a system which is, to me, unintelligible, wastes time and money which might be spent more usefully, and is calculated to lower the repute of the Irish Free State. If you think that on the grounds of either ill-health or incompetence I should cease to impede financial efficiency as authoritatively recognised I shall quietly make way for a healthy or competent successor, who enjoys having some of his work undone, some done by somebody else, and most of the remainder rendered difficult or impossible.

[signed] James McNeill

No. 44 UCDA P4/503

Memorandum by Patrick McGilligan

London, 4 March 1923

Mr. Curtis came on Tuesday, 20th February, to discuss several matters with the High Commissioner. Two important matters were mentioned. Mr. Curtis wished to know if the recital of the duties of the High Commissioner contained in the demi-official letter dated 25th February (copy herewith)[1] might be regarded as an official definition, and asked if any Press announcement would

[1] Not located.

be opportune. Mr. McNeill said that until he was installed in the new offices Press notices had better be postponed. He also stated that the recital was a draft of his own, to which the Minister of External Affairs took no exception, but that his Government had had no time to consider and define the scope of the High Commissioner's duties. Mr. McNeill thought that in any case an exact definition could not easily be given as no one knew exactly what duties might be entrusted to the High Commissioner. There appeared to be some anxiety to have the duties defined. Mr. Curtis thought that the words underlined in the enclosed draft of the d.o. letter might be deleted. Mr. McNeill agrees. They may seem to imply criticism of either or both Governments and add nothing essential. Mr. Curtis wished that the Irish Free State Government should formally approve of the definition.

Mr. Curtis also referred to the question of Irish Free State representatives abroad and the passport system. He stated that the Foreign Office understood that the Irish Free State had succeeded to a system established in pre-treaty times. Till the Irish Free State Constitution was adopted it was thought undesirable to move in the matter. But, he said, the Governments of countries where Irish Free State representatives were maintained from time to time asked as to the status of the Irish Free State representatives and, especially in connection with passports, it was desirable to clarify the position. Mr. McNeill stated that he knew that the passport question was under consideration. Mr. Curtis pointed out that a good deal of confusion would arise if passports were issued in Ireland and travellers found no-one competent to deal with the return passport, and that consular work necessitated the issue of an authoritative 'Exequatur' to the consul in each country. He said that he thought it would be best if the Secretary for the Colonies raised the question now in a formal despatch and Mr. McNeill assented. Mr. Curtis had discussed the passport question with President Cosgrave.

[signed] P. McGilligan

No. 45 UCDA P80/415

Handwritten memorandum from William T. Cosgrave to Desmond FitzGerald (Dublin)

Dublin, undated, but probably 1923[1]

M[inister for] External Affairs.
Re Appointment of Irish Rep[resentatives] abroad.
I don't know whether the High Com[missioner] is aware of the position of these Rep[resentative]s abroad. If not you will have to consider going over & personally seeing [the] Duke & giving [the] High Com[missioner] all the information at your disposal.

This is a business which requires careful handling. These[2] Reps are generally poor stuff & while our national position must be safeguarded we can't have them making a mess of things.

L.T. MacCosgair

[1] As there is no indication as to the date of this memo, it is inserted here because the text deals with topics similar to those addressed by Cosgrave here.
[2] Could be 'Those'.

No. 46 NAI DFA ES Paris 1922-23

Sean Murphy to Desmond FitzGerald (Dublin)
(72/1923)

PARIS, 14 March 1923

OFFICE

A Chara,

I have to-day discovered my exact position with regard to the French Government.

Monsieur Goblet made inquiries for me at the Foreign Office. At first they did not seem to be aware of any intention on the part of the Government to recognise an Irish Agent in any shape or form. Finally they discovered correspondence on the subject and the position according to the Chef du Protocole is as follows.

The French Government consider me as being introduced to them by the British Embassy as Commercial Agent of the Irish Free State. I have no consular or other status. I am in exactly the same position as the Canadian Commissioner with this difference that the French Government recognise me to be the Commercial Agent and in the case of the Canadian Commissioner they do not officially know of his existence. They mentioned that they regarded the recognition rather as a personal thing, that is to say that their action does not mean that they recognise an Irish Commercial Agent. They recognise me in that capacity, owing to the request of the British Embassy. The Foreign Office has informed the various ministries of my presence here and has issued instructions to them to facilitate me in every way.

I intend visiting the various personalities mentioned in the list at once. I did not do so before, because I was told it would be very foolish to take any step until I knew exactly what the position was in regard to the French Government.

Is mise, le meas mór,
[signed] SEÁN Ó MURCHADHA

No. 47 NAI DT S1932

Extract from the Report of the Committee on the Allocation of Functions among Government Departments (The 'Blythe Committee')

DUBLIN, 14 March 1923

[Matter omitted]

3. Proceeding on this basis the Committee is of opinion that the general administrative work of the country could effectively be done by nine Ministries (including Departments which it is hereafter recommended should be under the President's control) and the Attorney-General's Department. These nine Ministries, with a general indication of their functions, are as follows:-

PRESIDENT:	Executive Council, General Policy, External Affairs, Publicity.
MINISTRY OF FINANCE:	Finance, Taxation, Civil Service, Public Works, Stationery Office.

MINISTRY OF DEFENCE:	Defence matters.
MINISTRY OF LOCAL GOVERNMENT:	Local Government, Public Health.
MINISTRY OF EDUCATION:	Education.
MINISTRY OF LANDS & AGRICULTURE:	Agriculture, Forestry, Land Settlement, Land Purchase.
MINISTRY OF HOME AFFAIRS:	Judicial machinery, Police, Prisons.
MINISTRY OF INDUSTRY & COMMERCE:	Industry, Commerce, Fisheries.
MINISTRY OF POSTS & TELEGRAPHS:	Postal, Telegraph and Telephone services.

Also the:

ATTORNEY GENERAL:	Law Officer of the State.

If the Attorney-General is not a member of the Executive Council (and if a Minister he must be a member of the Council as with his functions he could not be one of the Ministers responsible to the Dáil) it is recommended that the President should answer for him and his Department in the Dáil.

4. It is considered that the above general division of functions, while relating allied services and establishing Departments in which Ministers would have an approximately equal division of work, would also provide the country with Governmental machinery sufficient for its needs. It contemplates two less Ministers than there are at present, the work of the Ministry of External Affairs being allocated to the President and the Ministry of Fisheries to the Ministry of Industry and Commerce. In the political circumstances of the present time it is considered that the Ministries of External Affairs and Fisheries should be retained but that sooner or later the work of the Ministry of External Affairs would by comparison with the work falling on other Ministries not justify the expense of a separate Minister and that in the case of Fisheries, while desirable for the time being to have a separate Minister responsible for putting the fishing industry on its feet again, the development of the fishing industry will before long not involve questions either of policy or of administration essentially different from those with which the Ministry of Industry and Commerce will be dealing.

5. The Committee has considered the proper allocation of existing functions and Departments among the several Ministers recommended above, with the addition for the time being of a Ministry of External Affairs and a Ministry of Fisheries. Existing Departments are so numerous and in a number of cases so complex in their organisation that final conclusions as to their proper redistribution cannot at present be arrived at. It is contemplated that the Ministries Bill should only indicate broadly the functions of each Ministry and that it should include a power to the Executive Council to decide as to the allocation of particular machinery necessary to perform these functions. The Executive Council could then by order attach existing Departments to particular Ministries, or split existing Departments up and allocate portions to different Ministries.

[Matter omitted]

No. 48 NAI DT S3332

Kevin O'Shiel to each member of the Executive Council (Dublin)
(Secret)

DUBLIN, 14 March 1923

IRELAND AND THE LEAGUE OF NATIONS

A Chara,

1. I send you herewith a further Memo. from our Mr. Waller on certain aspects of the routine and procedure necessary should we decide to join the League of Nations, which was prepared in reply to queries put to him by me.[1]

2. In so far as our investigations in the Bureau have guided us we are unanimous as to the desirability of Saorstát Éireann joining the League of Nations at the earliest possible moment. I need not here put forward our reasons for this conviction, as that has already been done amply in previous Memoranda, which are on your files.

Suffice it is to say that in so far as our particular work on the Boundary Question is concerned it is absolutely essential for us to make use of every position opened to us by the Treaty of London, 1921 in consolidating and solidifying our international status and thereby giving beforehand a strong international complexion to our Boundary dispute which, quite conceivably, will be vigorously challenged on this head before the Boundary Commission.

3. Apart from the League of Nations it is also our opinion, towards the further advancement of this objective, that we should avail ourselves of our right to join the Imperial Conference.

Our idea is, that in the event of a contention over the judgment of the Boundary Commission we should first take the matter before the Imperial Conference – given that provision is made either in its constitution or its precedents for the consideration of such disputes – and in the event of receiving no satisfaction there, go thence to the League of Nations.

4. At any rate we should lose no time in consolidating every inch of our position. You will see from the Memo. attached that Mr. Waller favours an early application for membership to the League in order to cope in time with the great volume of procedure necessary.

He suggests also that we should register the Treaty first of all as a mere 'non-conforming' outsider.

Whether or not we should do so is a matter for Governmental policy. An objection occurs to me that by doing so we gain no immediate good, and perhaps only 'blow the gaff' on our future policy of joining the League. However, as against this, it can be urged that, once we make formal application to the League Secretariat for admittance, it will be the public property of the world within a few hours afterwards.

5. In order to provide against any little disagreeableness or sourness that may arise from an imperial quarter – although of course it should not – we might perhaps send in our applications for both the League and the Imperial Conference together.

[1] Not printed.

6. I would be glad to have your views on the important points raised by this and previous Memoranda on the question of our joining the League.

The above are my own views and the views of those working with me in the North-Eastern Bureau.

Mise,
[signed] Caoímhghín Ó Síadail
Assistant Legal Adviser

No. 49 NAI DT S1955A

Extract from minutes of a meeting of the Executive Council
(C.1/65)
Dublin, 16 March 1923

CUSTOMS FRONTIER.
The Meeting had under consideration representations made by various business interests with a view to inducing the Government to postpone the coming into operation of the new Customs barrier between Saorstát Éireann on the one hand and Gt. Britain and Northern Ireland on the other.

After prolonged discussion it was decided to adhere to the decision already made in the matter, viz, that the new Customs regulations should come into force as from 1st April next.

No. 50 NAI DFA ES Box 34 File 241

Desmond FitzGerald to Charles Bewley (Berlin)
Dublin, 20 March 1923

My dear Bewley,
I am very sorry to hear that you have decided to leave us. Of course I know well that you prefer to be in Ireland, and I appreciate all the steps you have taken to ensure that your leaving should cause us as little inconvenience as possible.

I hope to see you as soon as you return to Dublin.

With best wishes for the future, and with full recognition of your loyal service.

Yours very sincerely,
[copy letter unsigned]
Minister of External Affairs

No. 51 NAI DFA 26/102

Michael MacWhite to Desmond FitzGerald (Dublin)
(N.S. 30/23)
Geneva, 24 March 1923

A Chara,
With reference to your letter No 180,[1] I had a conversation with Sir Eric

[1] Not located.

Drummond's Private Secretary and, as a result, I am in a position to enclose a form of application for membership of the League, which has been drafted by its legal advisers and which has evidently been approved of by the Secretary General himself.[1] The simplest lines possible were considered to be the most suitable.

I also enclose you a copy of covering letter I had from the forementioned Private Secretary, as well as copies of requests for admission made by Hungary, Finland and Albania, which may be of service to you.[2]

I may mention that, in order to figure on the Agenda of the next League Assembly, it is necessary that the application for Membership should be received here not later than the 1st of May. The Sub Committee appointed to deal with the admission of new members will meet as soon as possible, perhaps the second day after the opening of the Assembly, when our delegates should be present in order to give any explanations required. It will be necessary to have about two dozen copies of the Constitution and Treaty and the same number of Mr. Lloyd George's letter to the late President Griffith.[3] A short memorandum on Military, Naval and Air Forces should also be disponable though, in my opinion, all explanations should as far as possible be verbal.

When forwarding your application for Membership it is not necessary to send any documents in support of it as those would only be held up until such time as the Sub Committee on Admissions meet, which cannot be before the opening of the Assembly.

Is mise, le meas,
[signed] M. MacWhite

No. 52 NAI DT S3332

Extract from a memorandum by Bolton Waller on admission to the League of Nations

Dublin, 24 March 1923

[Matter omitted]

IV. *REASONS FOR IRELAND'S JOINING THE LEAGUE.*

That the Irish Free State is eligible for membership of the League and would immediately be admitted is scarcely open to question. As established under the Treaty of 1921 it comes under the category of a 'fully self-governing State, Dominion or Colony['] (Covenant Article 1) and in particular has the same constitutional position of Canada – an original member of the League. A refusal to admit would strike at the position of the Dominion, whose support of the application is assured. Not less certain is the support of the British Government, not merely because admission to the League was held out to Ireland as one of the advantages of accepting the Treaty, but also because otherwise Great Britain would have to admit before all the world that the Treaty was a sham. Scarcely less certain is the support of the other smaller States which are members of the

[1] Not printed.
[2] Not printed.
[3] Not printed.

League. They will be glad of any addition to their numbers such as will increase their strength relative to the Great Powers. The necessary two-thirds majority seems to be assured, and indeed it is difficult to mention any State which might be expected to raise opposition.

Of the advantages both for Ireland and the world arising from membership of the League the following are the chief:-

(a) *Recognition of Status.*
Membership will secure a new and world-wide recognition of the status attained by the Irish Free State, membership being in fact at the present day one of the tests of the attainment of full self-government and of complete nationhood, as is witnessed by the eagerness to join the League displayed by all the small states constituted since the War. The appearance at the Assembly at Geneva each year of three representatives of the Government and people of Ireland will bring Ireland in a tangible shape before the world. To delegates from Eastern Europe or South America Ireland will cease to be a name, and will become a reality and a force in world affairs. The result cannot under present conditions be attained in any other way. On the other hand abstention from the League would certainly be misinterpreted, however wrongfully. It would almost certainly be supposed that there was some flaw in Ireland's title to membership, as being too small or still too much under English control. It would be regarded as in the position of Newfoundland, which was considered too small, or the Crown Colonies which are not self-governing. This impression, however mistaken, it might be very difficult to eradicate.

In particular, the position in relation to Great Britain will be made plain, namely that the Treaty of 1921 is an international Treaty between two countries internationally recognised.

Again, the difference of status between the Irish Free State and Northern Ireland will be made more explicit. The latter as was pointed out by Mr. Lloyd-George in his letter to Sir James Craig of November 14th, 1921, (See Cmd. 1561) could not be admitted to the League, both on account of its size and as not being 'fully self-governing.'

(b) *Security.*
One reason for the eagerness of small States to enter the League has been that it provides, if not a complete, yet at least a considerable security against aggression on the part of any other State. While the League at present leaves much to be desired as regards its power of preventing aggression, it at any rate provides a means of publicity and of protest against any aggressive act, publicity which has several times proved of great value, as in the case of Albania above. If aggression is feared, membership of the League is at any rate one means of protection against it.

(c) *Influence in world affairs.*
Membership of the League gives to small nations a voice in world affairs which they did not possess and could not have secured previously. At the meetings of the Assembly or Council it is not merely the size or military strength of nations which gives them influence, but the character and abilities of the men they send to represent them, this marking a great change from earlier diplomacy.

It is remarkable to how great an extent the leadership in the Assembly has been taken by men representing small countries, Nansen of Norway, Hymans of Belgium, Lord Robert Cecil representing South Africa, Motta of Switzerland are notable examples. If Ireland sends men who can carry similar weight, and who can help in improving relations between other countries (sitting on arbitrations etc.) it will not only be to the advantage of the world but to the honour of Ireland herself.

(d) *Share in the co-operative activities of the League.*
Membership involves the right to share in the various schemes of international co-operation enumerated in Part 11 (a). The advisability of taking part in these, and the advantages to be gained thereby, need no emphasis. In particular a share in those bodies which deal with international communications and transport seems almost a necessity for a country which desires to promote her international trade.

There will also be a desire to help forward the various humanitarian activities of the League.

(e) *Work for world-peace.*
Lastly, the League, notwithstanding its faults and weaknesses, is in aim and intention an organisation working for world-peace and better international relations. Ireland, or any other country which has those objects in view, can by its membership and support of the League do much to bring about their attainment.

A word may be said on some of the objections which can be brought against joining the League.

First, it will be said that the United States has refused to join, and that the best policy for Ireland is to follow that example. Such a policy might be sound if Ireland was situated on the other side of the Atlantic. But Ireland is and must be part of the European system, and for European States membership of the League and its subsidiary organisations is becoming almost a necessity of prosperous life. No real analogy can be drawn between an isolated country like the United States and a country like Ireland, small and necessarily linked with the European system. Moreover, the United States is at present the most powerful country in the world, and as such is certain to exert a great influence in international affairs, whether a member of the League or not (though many consider that her influence has been greatly weakened by abstention). For Ireland the case is entirely different. Refusal to enter the League does not in her case mean a position of influence, but a position of isolation in which she can be completely ignored.

Secondly, it may be urged that the League is a sham, that it is entirely under the control of the victors in the Great War, or is dominated by the Great Powers, or again that it is in fact powerless to carry out its avowed aims. For all these objections there is a considerable basis. The League is by no means as free or as powerful as might be desired. But the important fact is that with regard to all these three objections the League shows signs of steady improvement. It is by no means only a League of victors since three of their former enemies have now been admitted, and since many former neutrals are playing a prominent part. It is less and less dominated by the Great Powers as is shown not merely by the position of leadership in the Assembly held by representatives on the Council of the less powerful States (see Part 1 (b)). As regards the powerlessness of the League, it must be admitted that up to the present it has not had opportunity to deal with any international dispute of the first magnitude (though Upper Silesia might be so regarded). But the dissolution of the Supreme Council of the Allies which formerly arrogated the main power to itself, and with the virtual breakdown of the Entente, the League is almost certain to gather strength as the one real international organisation still existing. There are increasing indications of its ability to deal with large questions. It must also be remembered that the League has only been three years in existence, and much of its attention has necessarily been given to setting up and developing its own organisation, methods, procedure, etc. It could not be expected to reach full effectiveness rapidly, considering that it is a unique and unprecedented development in world affairs.

But even if all the objections on the ground of the powerlessness of the League were sound, they would not constitute a conclusive argument against Ireland's entry. The advantages of securing recognition and of sharing in its co-operative activities would still hold good. This also is an additional reason. Whatever be thought of the present League, it is admitted on all hands, even in the United States, that some sort of association of nations is a necessity. The League may possibly have to be altered radically and changed into some better association. But it is certain that if that should happen the countries which are members of the present League will have a considerable voice in determining what changes are necessary and what form the new association should take, while small nations which have stood aloof would again be very probably ignored.

More probably, however, if the catastrophe of another world war can be averted, the present League will gradually reform itself and evolve into a more genuine and effective organ of international co-operation and of peace. That it should do so is to the supreme interest of Ireland as of any other small country to which peace and freedom are the first necessities. Whether it will succeed in doing so depends entirely on the members of the League themselves. In bringing about this evolution Ireland as a member would be able to play a part not inferior to that of any of the smaller European countries, and in fact superior to many of them. If Irish influence, not merely at home but exercised as it can be in many parts of the world, should be thrown definitely on the side of the League it might easily be one of the decisive influences making for world peace.

No. 53 NAI DT S1967

Extract from minutes of a meeting of the Executive Council (C.1/75)
DUBLIN, 27 March 1923

BRITISH EMPIRE EXHIBITION.
Reference was made to the fact that it had already been provisionally decided (Ref.C.1/41 of 2/2/23)[1] to participate in the British Empire Exhibition to be

[1] Not printed.

held in London this year, but in view of the pressing necessity for reducing expenditure to the lowest possible level, it was now decided not to take part in the Exhibition in question.

No. 54 UCDA P4/856

Kevin O'Shiel to each member of the Executive Council
DUBLIN, 29 March 1923

IRELAND and THE LEAGUE OF NATIONS

A Chara,

1. I send you a further Memo.[1] on the League of Nations prepared at my request by our Mr. Waller, and I would ask you to attach it to your File and study it *most carefully* in conjunction with the preceding Memoranda.

2. The Memo speaks eloquently for itself and I do not intend to do more than draw your particular attention to certain very interesting and important points raised in it.

3. The Question of Expense
Mr. Waller is at present investigating more closely the important matter of expense in connection with joining the League. On page 4 he shows the present method of dividing the annual expenditure incurred by the League into numbers of payable units and then assessing groups of those units to the various Member-Nations. This would go to show that the question of expense is largely arbitrary and dependent wholly on the League's annual expenditure.

It is probable that we will be assessed in the degree of the Nations shown in the table on page 4, which correspond to our size, viz., the group, Netherlands and South Africa at 15 units, and the group, Denmark, New Zealand, Norway, Peru and Switzerland at 10 units; or Finland at 5 units. On this table a unit would appear to represent £878.10.

There is no reason why we should be called upon to contribute more than the Republic of Finland, a Nation resembling us very nearly in many ways. It is almost exactly our size in population, and is in a similar category to us in as much as it has, after a long servitude, only enjoyed freedom within recent years. Also, it has had a trying time of civil warfare with its native Bolshevik 'Irregulars' before it settled down to ordered and regular government.

Doubtless, these were the reasons why it was let off so lightly. Our case is just as strong and it is not likely that we will be called upon to pay at the same rate as countries which have enjoyed years of settled and ordered government. If these arguments hold good our subscription to the League annually should not exceed £4,392.10 at the current rate.

4. Minorities
It will be noted (on page 8) that certain minorities in European countries have been put under the special protection of the League. This is valuable, as it is possible under this heading, should the worst come to the worst, to make such a case for the minorities within Northern Ireland that we could at least threaten

[1] Further to No. 52. The memo referred to is not printed.

to ventilate their grievances at the League.

We have a very strong case in this direction should we ever consider it politic to employ it, e.g., gerrymanderings, abolition of Proportional Representation, &c. &c.

Another strong point that we could raise in this connection is the parallel of the Lausanne Conference between Turkey and Greece, Great Britain and certain countries, which sat some time ago. At that Conference the question of the several large Christian minorities under Turkish rule came under review. Lord Curzon put forward as his solution that these homogeneous entities within the Turkish jurisdiction should be given autonomy. Kemal Pasha vigorously resisted this proposal, on the grounds that minorities in a State had no right of special audience or special treatment at an International Conference; that if they wanted such special treatment the proper authority for them to treat with was their own central and sovereign Government. Eventually, I think these minorities had to be content with Kemal's promises.

Now, the point is, if the official British solution for Christian minorities under heathen Turkish rule is that they are entitled to some small degree of autonomy and *not* to either (1) incorporation with a neighbouring Christian power or (2) independence on their own account – why should Northern Ireland be allowed by Britain to break completely away from Irish jurisdiction and incorporate itself with Great Britain?

In this case there is no question of throwing 'Ulster' under a non-Christian community; it is a case of two Christian communities[,] yet 'autonomy' is never suggested. The only remedy is secession for the minority.

This is a point I think we could raise with effect should the opportunity arise. I am having a Memo. prepared on the discussions and agreements in the Lausanne Treaty, which may throw more light on this interesting aspect of the question.

5. Northern Ireland

With regard to our special province of North-Eastern affairs, I am strongly of opinion that we should join the League next September.

Such action must greatly strengthen our case at the Boundary Commission. It has been pointed out that in view of Article 10 of the Covenant we may be compelled to recognise the 'status quo' at the time of our joining, which would mean the present jurisdiction of An Saorstát.

However, as against this it is pointed out

(1) That Article 10 of the Covenant is most indefinite and, although discussed, has never yet been authoritatively defined, and

(2) That the terms of the Treaty of London, 1921, recognising in effect our de jure right to the whole territory of Ireland and providing for a Boundary Commission, would completely over-rule Article 10. For this reason it might be advisable to register the Treaty under the Secretariat of the League.

Another aspect of this North-Eastern position is that by our joining the subordinate and petty status of Northern Ireland will be even more marked than at present. It is interesting to note in this connection that Sir James Craig has always been most anxious to send representatives from the Six Counties to the League of Nations.

On page 20 Mr. Waller recalls Mr. Lloyd George's letter to Sir James Craig stating that his area could not be admitted to the League because of its diminutive size, and of the fact of its not being 'fully self-governing'.

6. Our Status

Mr. Waller puts our case for joining the League very clearly. It is well known that the admission of the Dominions to the League of Nations as separate Member-States was achieved only after a very hard tussle indeed.

When the League was opened to the Dominions as separate Nations it was regarded as their greatest constitutional victory. By this fact they were admitted to be 'Nations' in the international sense, having impliedly, at all events, the several distinctive rights and privileges of Nations.

It is noteworthy too that they signed the Treaty of Versailles in their new distinctive capacity as 'Nations'; and their separate signature of that Treaty undoubtedly prepared the way, 'by Constitutional practice and procedure' for the novel and far-reaching action of Canada recently in signing a Treaty with the U.S.A. without the hitherto all-essential sign manual of the British Ambassador.

For all these and other reasons it appears to me that we should avail ourselves of our *undoubted right as a Nation* to join the League, especially as this right was only conceded to our sister Nations in the Commonwealth after a tough struggle.

The cost is nothing like as great as many people suppose. The greatest figure we could be charged on last year's estimates would be that chargeable to Denmark, New Zealand, Norway, Peru and Switzerland, viz., £8,784 (i.e. 10 units). And it is quite reasonable to suppose, as I have pointed out, that we should get Finland's measure of £4,392.10.

This is surely an insignificant figure to pay to enable the Voice of Ireland to be raised and heard with effect once more in the Councils of the Nations of the World.

[stamped] CAOÍMHGHÍN Ó SÍADHAIL
Assistant Legal Adviser

No. 55 NAI DFA ES Box 28 File 181

Timothy A. Smiddy to Desmond FitzGerald (Dublin)
WASHINGTON, 30 March 1923

A Chara:

INTELLIGENCE

James Larkin has recently obtained a subscription of $15,000 from his supporters in Chicago for the purpose of purchasing a vessel from the U.S.A. Shipping Board to be loaded with food and clothing for the distressed people of Ireland.

He arrived in Washington a few days ago with introductions to two influential people here from Mr James K. McQuire of New York who is supposed to be friendly to the Irish Free State – an indication of the complex people one has to deal with here. He interviewed Dr Constantine McQuire to whom he got an introduction. He was informed by him that the Shipping Board would want to know a lot about it, and, perhaps, would impose a number of restrictions, and insist on inspection. He left Dr. McQuire discouraged but quite determined in his object. He then went to Mr Philpin the Manager of Sales of the Board. I am taking the necessary action. Dr McQuire informed me he was frank and direct in all his statements and disclaimed any intention to meddle one way or another in politics, avowing, none the less, his Republican aspirations. He said a Labor Committee for relief had been organized here, to combat the results of destruction and unemployment.

My recent correspondence on the subject of Jim Larkin shows clearly that he is active on the side of the Irregulars; there need be no doubt of this.[1]

Mise, le meas,
[signed] T.A. SMIDDY

No. 56 NAI DFA ES Box 34 File 241

Cornelius Duane to Desmond FitzGerald (Dublin)
BERLIN, 6 April 1923

A chara,
You are, I am sure, aware by this time that I have taken over the office and the office funds from Mr. Bewley. In his letter dated April 6[2] he has pointed out to you the enormous increase in the cost of living in Berlin as well as the increased work which, owing to his retirement falls to me. He has also informed you that the last instalment of my salary should have been paid on the 15th of last month. I believe moreover that he explained to you fully the exact position of a foreigner living at present in Berlin. I am sure you will appreciate the case and consequently that you will have hardly any objections to increase considerably my present rate of remuneration here. As a matter of fact I can scarcely manage to float myself on £200. I would suggest to you that under the new circumstances my salary should be on the basis of £500 a year. Otherwise I would have to consider seriously the advisability of retiring if I am still allowed what I consider to be an insufficient yearly salary.

Of course I can assure you that, come what may, I do not intend to treat you in the manner you have experienced quite recently from another of the European capitals.[3]

I should be glad to hear from you on this matter as soon as possible as at present I may frankly say that I am at the end of my financial resources.

I should also like to make suggestions to you as to how the proposed new salary might be paid to me.

Le meas mór,
[signed] C. Ó DUBHÁIN

[1] See No. 30.
[2] Not printed.
[3] Possibly a reference to Leopold Kerney in Paris.

No. 57 NAI DFA ES Box 28 File 181

Timothy A. Smiddy to Desmond FitzGerald (Dublin)
(Absolutely Confidential)

WASHINGTON, 11 April 1923

James Larkin:- There is a break of a definite nature between Larkin and the Irish Radicals who are of the Irish Communist party but who subordinate their Communism to Republicanism and who are anxious to support de Valera in his efforts to destroy the Free State. Miss MacFadden of 53, Jane Street New York, meeting place of the Irish Republican Communists, is the leading spirit of this group; her two associates and intimate confederates are Albert Hickland, No 323, West Twenty Third Street, New York, and Tim Sullivan also of 53, Jane Street. In this latter address James and Peter Larkin reside when in New York.

These people complain that Jim goes out of his way to declare personal war on both the Free State and de Valera. In a letter to de Valera[,] Larkin stated that even if the Free State were defeated and driven out of office to-morrow the Republicans would at once be confronted with the Labour question, and that he could see no difference between Ireland governed by English, Free State, or Republican bourgeois so far as the working classes were concerned; and that, finally, it would be easier, more advisable and better politics for de Valera to revise his programme in harmony with Labor's demands before getting rid of the Free State than after such an event. It was stated that this was very painful to de Valera who wrote to Larkin pleading against anything that might cause any further dissension on this side of the Atlantic; but Larkin would not give way an inch and insists on his rule or ruin policy.

Larkin was told by above that any remarks about bourgeois or middle class people came with very poor grace from him, as it was the bourgeois, that got him out of Sing Sing when his own bunch could not do anything for him: also, there was a good deal of money being sent to Larkin personally for the cause and Larkin and his friends persisted in holding on to it, refused to account for it, and devoted it to the Labor cause instead of Ireland's cause.

One of the above said that they had to move very carefully so as not to let the other side know that they had another split within their ranks. De Valera sent, on advice from this side, instructions, under seal of the Irish Republic to the effect that all of the existing credentials for organizers, collectors, representatives, propagandists, etc., in the U.S.A. are cancelled and new ones are issued. Headquarters at 8, Forty First Street New York, are to be the only authorized place to which remittances are to be sent, or whence orders are to be received: all other places are declared non-official.

It is stated that this means a lot of trouble and will create ill feeling; but it cannot be helped: that Larkin and his friends cannot be allowed to wreck us just as we are getting our summer programme ready. 'We could not openly disavow Larkin, and he cannot afford to antagonise us openly, so we took the best way out of it. Now we can get down to business and knock the ground from under Larkin's friends. Larkin will not take orders from any one so we had to make the order a general one.'

Miss MacFadden stated after the round up in England and Scotland that it did not matter what the other side did, that they would just keep on until there was no one left; also that the Irregulars had good friends in Belgium and Germany and even England who were willing to supply them with guns, and who actually are supplying them in small quantities.

Miss MacFadden stated on the 26th March 'If we could only get enough equipment over there we would put an end to it in short order. But we cannot get any of the larger stuff there, and it is hard to win a war with small arms. We must find a way; we have plenty money.' 'The loss of the stuff (amunition captured by our special secret service) was nothing, but we are being watched very closely' and she knew that it was the British Government who are working hand and hand with the Free State; the British were watching every thing like a hawk. [']We know for a fact that it was no accident on [the] part of the policeman, and that other plans were interfered with and had to be abandoned'.

Note. It is of the utmost importance that the above information be kept absolutely secret as any leak would identify a very special agent and thereby close one of our channels of information as also seriously imperil him.

No. 58 NAI DFA 26/102

Extract from a letter from Michael MacWhite to Desmond FitzGerald (Dublin) (NS 39/23) (Copy)

GENEVA, 11 April 1923

A Chara,

I should like to remind you again that if your application for Membership to the League does not arrive here before May 1st, it cannot figure on the Agenda of the next annual Conference, which is to meet in September. The advantage of having the application figure on the Agenda is that the matter can be dealt with as soon as the Assembly meets and will consequently permit the Irish Delegates to take an effective part in the proceedings. On the other hand, if it arrives later, it may be dealt with only when the rest of the Agenda has been disposed of.

I should also like to bring to your notice the subject of a conversation I had with Sir Eric Drummond a few days ago, with reference to the demand of admission by the Irish Free State. According to him this demand should not be presented through the British Foreign Office as, in that case, it would be likely to cause you a certain amount of prejudice in the eyes of foreign Delegates. There is nothing in the League Covenant to prevent the Government from applying direct through its own representative which is, I presume, what it intends doing.

[Matter omitted]

Is mise, le meas,
[signed] M MACWHITE

No. 59 NAI DFA D2075

T.M. Healy to the Duke of Devonshire (London)
(No. 89) (Copy)

DUBLIN, 12 April 1923

My Lord Duke,
I have the honour to advert to Your Grace's Despatch No. 80 of the 15th February,[1] with reference to the question of Communications from His Majesty's Government to the Government of the Irish Free State on International Affairs, and to inform you that my Ministers are of opinion that it would be advisable to continue provisionally the understanding arrived at between the late President Griffith and Mr. Winston Churchill, mentioned in paragraph 3[2] of your Despatch, whereby such communications and consultations were deferred until such time as the Irish Government should be in a position to deal adequately with matters of this nature.

I have the honour to be,
My Lord Duke,
Your Grace's most obedient,
humble servant,
(Sgd.) T.M. HEALY

No. 60 NAI DFA Secretaries' Files S2

Sean Lester to Desmond FitzGerald (Dublin)

DUBLIN, 16 April 1923

MEMO TO MINISTER FOR EXTERNAL AFFAIRS.[3]
I am informed that Father Conry, Secretary to Monsignor Luzio, spoke to several Pressmen this afternoon in the course of which he said that Monsignor Luzio would intervene in Irish affairs when sufficient number of the Public Bodies had requested him to act. Father Conry further said that when Monsignor Luzio would go in he 'would go in as Pius 11th.' He further stated that it was a pity the Irish Government insisted on treating Monsignor L. as a private individual simply because he had not credentials, and that when Monsignor Luzio was leaving the Pope[,] His Holiness told him that when he had settled the Ecclesiastical matter he was to 'hold himself free for peace.' He praised the 'Irish Times' Leading Article of this Monday morning and said it was a pity the other newspapers had not similar articles. He mentioned that Monsignor

---

[1] Not printed.
[2] The despatch referred to consultation between Britain and the dominions on questions of Imperial Foreign Policy. Paragraph 3 of the despatch refers to this process, the relevant section reading: 'Mr Griffith and members of the Provisional Government intimated that they did not wish to begin the consideration of matters of this nature until such time as their Departmental arrangements for dealing with communications on the subject were more fully advanced.'
[3] Copy also sent to W.T. Cosgrave for information.

L. had an interview for two hours with President Cosgrave but that as the Government did not publish anything about it he did not feel free to do so. None of this matter was for publication over Monsignor Luzio's name but was intended apparently as 'inspiration'.

On Saturday Fr. Conry had an interview with the Press on his invitation. I have not the full particulars of what he said then but it also was designed not for publication over his name but to 'feed the Press'.

Regarding the paragraph on Saturday morning in the 'Irish Times' inviting the Councils in Ireland to ask Monsig. Luzio to intervene[,] I have reason to believe that this was published on the suggestion of Fr. Conry. In this connection it should be noted that a similar paragraph appeared in other Irish papers several days before and the 'Irish Times' does not look up the back files of its rival organs for news.

[signed] SEAN LESTER
PUBLICITY DEPARTMENT

No. 61 NAI DFA 26/102

Desmond FitzGerald to Sir Eric Drummond (Geneva)
(Copy)

DUBLIN, 17 April 1923

Sir,
In accordance with the terms of Article 1 of the Covenant of the League of Nations, I have the honour to request that the Free State of Ireland may be admitted as a Member of the League of Nations, and that this request may be placed on the agenda of the next Meeting of the Assembly of the League.

The Government of the Irish Free State is prepared to accept the conditions laid down in Article 1 of the Covenant, and to carry out all obligations involved in Membership of the League.

The Government will send representatives, empowered to give all necessary explanations, to the Assembly, and it will be glad in the meantime to give any information relevant to this application which may be required.

It is requested that this application may be brought without delay to the knowledge of all the Members of the League.

I have the honour to be,
Sir,
Your obedient Servant,
[copy letter unsigned]
Minister of External Affairs

No. 62 NAI DT S2198

Extract from minutes of a meeting of the Executive Council (C. 1/85)
DUBLIN, 12 noon, 17 April 1923

MONSIGNOR LUZIO.
Reference was made to a statement appearing in the morning's issue of the Irish Independent that Mgr. Luzio was,

> 'now free to devote his entire services to the interests of peace, and that in this capacity he will be directly representing the Holy Father, and that Mgr. Luzio's time and services will be at the disposal of all those, no matter what their political convictions may be who desire the fulfilment of that end',

and quoting a message given by Mgr. Luzio through his Secretary, to the representative of that paper.

It was decided that a letter should be sent to His Holiness the Pope drawing attention to the fact that Mgr. Luzio, having come to the Free State under the cloak of an ecclesiastical mission, was now endeavouring to interfere in the domestic affairs of the country without having sought or received permission from the Government, and pointing out that his action was an encouragement to the Forces of disorder and anarchy operating against the Government and the people.

It was arranged that the Minister of Education[1] should prepare Headings for a letter, to be drafted by the Minister of External Affairs in consultation with the Attorney General[2] and that the draft should be submitted to the Executive Council at tomorrow's meeting.

It was further decided that His Grace the Archbishop of Dublin[3] should be advised of the action taken by the Government in regard to the matter.

No. 63 NAI DFA Secretaries' Files S2

Sean Lester to Desmond FitzGerald (Dublin)
DUBLIN, 17 April 1923

MEMO TO MINISTER FOR EXTERNAL AFFAIRS.[4]

MONSIGNOR LUZIO.
I have had a talk with Mr. Hooper, Editor of the 'Freeman'[,] regarding Monsignor Luzio. He is quite convinced that the Monsignor's action in inviting the local authorities to appeal to him to intervene between the Irish Government and the rebels is likely to prolong the trouble. He confirmed my information of yesterday evening regarding the attempts by Father Conry to 'inspire' the Press and get Press support for his intrigue (if I may use that term). How successful this has been may be noticed from the news columns of both the 'Irish Times'

[1] Eoin MacNeill.
[2] Hugh Kennedy.
[3] Edward Byrne.
[4] Copy to W.T. Cosgrave for information.

and 'Independent' this morning which contained about half a column relating to Monsignor Luzio's activities, and portion of which was directly dictated by the Monsignor's Secretary. The general feeling seems to be that if the Government is not to find itself in a predicament with the Irish people apparently appealing outside the authority of that Government, some action should be taken. One suggestion is that a representative should be sent at once to Rome to ask for Monsignor Luzio's recall, and another is that a statement should be made authoritatively announcing that Monsignor Luzio is apparently sent to Ireland to settle some ecclesiastical matter, and that he was received as an act of courtesy by the President but that Monsignor Luzio has no political mission to Ireland, otherwise he would have come armed with the proper credentials; or something to this effect. Regarding the first suggestion a courier could reach Rome in two days and see the Cardinal Secretary of State on the third day. If it were thought desirable that the mission should not be undertaken by an official of the Government but by a Cleric, the name of a very able Clergyman occurs to me. This is the Rev. Dr. Walsh, who is, I think, Assistant Vicar General of the Augustinians. Dr. Walsh knows Rome very well, and at one time acted as Secretary to Cardinal Sortolli during his time as Legate in the United States.

The 'Freeman' refused to publish the matter which reached them in much the same form as it appeared in the other two papers and it is possible that they may take some more definite action in the matter – but this cannot be counted on.

I do not know what information you have about Father Conry, but he was ordained in Rome and remained there living on his private means until 10 years ago or so when the Pope issued an order that no Priest was to remain in Rome unless he had some appointment. I am told that Fr. Conry then endowed a Canonry in Rome and himself became the first Canon. He was out there for some years and has lately been living in Bray looking after some property left to him by his father. Monsignor Luzio brought over with him an Italian Secretary but on his arrival Father Conry took up the position and the Italian Clergyman returned to Rome.

No. 64 NAI DFA Secretararies' Files S2

Extract from a memorandum by Kevin O'Shiel
to each member of the Executive Council
(Strictly Confidential)

Dublin, 19 April 1923

MGR. LUZIO and THE NORTHERN QUESTION
[Matter omitted]
6. It is said that designing and imprudent advisers are endeavouring to use the Monsignor's position to stampede the Government into calling a Truce with irregularism and opening up parleys with de Valera.

Some of these advisers are said to be foolish, but well-meaning people; others are said to be in sympathy with de Valera and are probably endeavouring, on his directions (now that their conspiracy is on the verge of collapse) to improve as far as possible 'the maximum terms of settlement for his Party under the circumstances'.

The plan of campaign appears to be to send representatives on the q.t. to the various County Councils and Local Bodies who suggest to these Bodies to call special Meetings and request the Monsignor to work for peace.

Should the Monsignor lend himself to this very obvious manoeuvre at this late stage in the day it will be tantamount to an act of gross discourtesy to the Irish Government, in so much as he had refused to recognise the lawful Government of the Land to which he had come as Envoy from perhaps the greatest world power, and had endeavoured to engage whilst in that country, on a line of policy in direct conflict with the policy of the de jure and de facto Government.

In this connection it is also well to recall that the present Government has the emphatic endorsement and support of the highest moral authority in the Land, viz., the Irish Hierarchy.

On the 11th October last the Hierarchy met at Maynooth and addressed a most important pastoral letter to the Priests and people of Ireland. In this now famous pastoral the Bishops declared that the killing of National Soldiers was murder, and that the seizing of public and private property was robbery, and that persons guilty of these crimes could not be admitted to the sacraments, should they persist in such evil courses.

Priests who approved of this 'saddest of all revolts' were declared to be false to their sacred office and guilty of grievous scandal, and they were forbidden, under pain of suspension, to advance such doctrine publicly or privately.

This being the solemn, deliberate and unanimous ruling of the highest Christian Authority in Ireland, the alleged activities of Mgr. Luzio appear all the more extraordinary, and, considering them in conjunction with the reported grant of the Benediction of the Holy Father to one who comes under the Bishops' interdict, one would have to draw the conclusion that the Roman Authorities were in direct conflict with the grave and considered opinion of the Irish Church.

Apart from this, as I have said in the beginning, an unofficial Vatican-made settlement with the Irregulars would have the most calamitous results on our Northern policy.

[stamped] Caoímhghín Ó Síadail
Assistant Legal Adviser

No. 65 NAI DFA Secretaries' Files S2

William T. Cosgrave to Cardinal Gasparri (Rome)
(Copy)

Dublin, 19 April 1923

Excellency,[1]
The Ministers who constitute the Executive Council, the lawfully established Government of the Irish Free State, (Saorstát Éireann,) realising the Holy

[1] See No. 62 above.

Father's abiding and most paternal interest in the well-being of our dear country, desire through me as President of the Council, to submit for His Holiness's consideration the position which has arisen with reference to the visit to this country of the Right Rev. Monsignor Luzio.

Your Eminence will be aware that for some months past certain persons in Ireland have sought by force of arms to overthrow the lawful government of this State, elected by the people, and to destroy the Treaty between Great Britain and Ireland which has been solemnly approved and ratified by the elected representatives of the people of both countries, and which guarantees to us the abstention of Great Britain from all interference in the government of our country. The persons so in revolt against the lawful government by the people have attracted in their train all the lawless and criminal elements which exist in varying degree in every community, as well as those who have the most noxious moral, social and political theories to forward by any means whatever wherever opportunity offers. Hence it is that this minority in revolt have to their account a campaign darkened by murder, rapine and arson, and the note struck on the far side of Europe has found an echoing cord (sic) among these unhappy destroyers of social order.

It is gratifying to be able to assure Your Excellency that this young government and its devoted and much-enduring Army have been able to cope with the situation so full of danger that met it at the outset of its career. The forces of disorder have been gradually but surely overcome, and the revolt has now almost burnt itself out, leaving but dying embers soon to be quenched, if not encouraged to flame again by hopes foolishly aroused of achieving some even partial success.

We understand that the Right Reverend Monsignor Luzio was despatched to this country by His Holiness to transact business of an ecclesiastical character. He had no political or diplomatic mission, and therefore was not accredited to this Government which was not officially cognisant of his visit and had no official intercourse with him.

We have learned, however, that the Right Reverend Monsignor, having disposed of his ecclesiastical business, has got into close touch with some of the persons in armed revolt against this Government and indeed against the social and moral order. His Secretary has sought the support of the Press and of public bodies for a call to him to act as intermediary between the Government and the revolters against the authority of the Government. His Lordship has given audience to a number of those in revolt (including persons who have constituted themselves a pretended government).

Though the Right Reverend Monsignor has in fact produced no credentials from His Holiness for intervention in political affairs in this country, and has not presented himself officially to the Government as in any way authorised by the Holy See to intervene, his clerical position, and his previous ecclesiastical mission give to his actions a special character. The consequence is that the embers of revolt are not allowed to die. The unskilled hand of a man who has no real knowledge or understanding of the affairs of this country is fanning into continued life the destructive fires with which he should not meddle.

I can assure Your Excellency that this Government is far from wishing to show the slightest disrespect to any religious dignitary, even though it might complain of scant respect shown by him to its dignity or authority. It is, however, obvious that the circumstances of Monsignor Luzio's extended visit are in the highest degree embarrassing to the Government in its onerous work of restoring peace and order, and that serious mischief may flow from his actions.

I have, therefore, respectfully to ask Your Excellency to arrange that Monsignor Luzio's visit may not be prolonged beyond what is absolutely necessary for the completion of his ecclesiastical business (if not yet complete). In the meantime his intervention in the domain of politics or rebellion cannot be countenanced by my Government.

On my own part I take this occasion of offering my dutiful homage to His Holiness, and my humble respects to Your Excellency.

I am, with respect,
Your Excellency's
Most humble and most obedient servant,
[copy letter unsigned]
President of the Executive Council of the Irish Free State

No. 66 NAI DFA 26/102

Michael MacWhite to Desmond FitzGerald (Dublin)
(N.S. 44/23) (Copy)

GENEVA, 20 April 1923

A Chara,
On receipt of your communication No. 196,[1] I made an appointment with Sir Eric Drummond and handed him your letter of application for Membership[2] this afternoon.

It created immediate excitement in the Secretariat and amongst the members of the Council which is sitting at present. To say it was welcomed would scarcely describe its reception for it was considered as the most important application that has been made since the formation of the League and more so even, than if it came from Germany or Russia.

The application was forthwith made public and as there are about fifty foreign journalists here at present, in connection with the Council Meeting, there is no doubt its publicity will be widespread.

Is mise, le meas,
[signed] M. MACWHITE

[1] Not printed.
[2] No. 61 above.

No. 67 NAI DFA ES Box 28 File 185

Extracts from a letter from Timothy A. Smiddy to Desmond FitzGerald (Dublin)
(144/23)

WASHINGTON, 20 April 1923

A chara:

POLICY

[Matter omitted]
All the active Irish-Americans – supporters of Irish Free State, as well as Irregulars – are against Ireland's entry into League of Nations.
[Matter omitted]
Personally I am of opinion that in the 'long run' in the U.S.A., the advantages of marking in every way possible – and the League of Nations does it in a high degree – Ireland as an independent State will outweigh any present hostility. In fact, the Administration at Washington is only seeking a Diplomatic way of entering the League.
[Matter omitted]

Mise, le meas,
[signed] T.A. SMIDDY

No. 68 NAI DFA ES Box 28 File 184

Timothy A. Smiddy to Desmond FitzGerald (Dublin)
(140/23)

WASHINGTON, 20 April 1923

A Chara:

INTELLIGENCE

In a conversation I had recently with the Assistant Director of the Department of Justice, Washington D.C.[,] he informed me that there is no law in the U.S.A. against export of arms to a friendly country even though they are known to be used against that country. Such export of arms if accompanied by men organized to use them is an indictable offence as it comes under the heading of an expeditionary force.

Some few years ago a temporary embargo was put on the export of guns to Mexico. But this was chiefly in the interest of the U.S.A.

With reference to the Ammunition captured on February 24th, the Authorities here took action and the Federal Government indicted the individuals who were arrested because *it is illegal to move Ammunition or guns from one State to another without license.* And this ammunition had been moved from New Jersey to New York.

The absence of a law here against the export of arms renders our work difficult. As far as I can ascertain there is no ammunition or guns being exported at present from the Eastern States of U.S.A. But there is always the possibility of a few guns, and even Thompson machine guns, being smuggled by sailors on the Liners; and during transit placed for safety, sometimes, in Engineers stores. This has happened, I am informed, on many occasions on Liners going to Liverpool and, especially, Glasgow. Hence, the necessity of examining the baggage of all sailors at these ports – if possible.

The Irregulars at New York and Philadelphia[,] especially Joe McGarrity, are feeling highly nervous at present and have, as far as I can ascertain, ceased gun-running activities. They know they are being watched carefully. If definite discoveries of munitions are not being made at present (and I believe there are few, if any), the activities of our agents are having the effect of, at least, seriously impeding the efforts of the Irregulars to ship them.

Mise, le meas,
[signed] SINBAD

No. 69 NAI DFA ES Box 28 File 186

Timothy A. Smiddy to Desmond FitzGerald (Dublin)
(142/23)

WASHINGTON, 20 April 1923

A Chara:

INTELLIGENCE.

I have been informed by the 188-4-1 of 328-7-2[1] that the Emmigration[2] Authorities are proceeding with the deportation of Martin Lavan. Much influence is being brought to bear by Finnerty and influential Irregulars to have him retained here, as they state that he will probably be executed if he returns to Ireland.

The 188-4-1 of 328-7-2 will strongly press his deportation. Lavan's passage to U.S.A. was facilitated by a stewardess on board ship and was looked after while in New York by Mrs Sheehy Skeffington. I am to obtain the name of ship he came by. I shall be glad to know if you are interested in this man's deportation from the U.S.A.

It is announced here that Mrs Sheehy Skeffington is about to return to Ireland soon. She has been the most active of publicists in the U.S.A. for the Irregulars and has circulated everywhere the most atrocious lies about the Free State.

She says when she returns to Ireland she will probably be put in Mountjoy where she will hunger strike and as she will not be allowed to die she will be released.

Is it possible or feasible to prevent her entering the Free State.

Mise, le meas,
[signed] SINBAD

[1] Code sequencing cipher unknown.
[2] Immigration?

No. 70 NAI DT S3332

Extract from minutes of a meeting of the Executive Council (C. 1/89)

DUBLIN, 3.45 pm, 21 April 1923

LEAGUE OF NATIONS.

The President reported that he had received a message from Mr. Curtis[1] of the Colonial Office stating that the British Government wished to be informed as to what attitude on their part would be most helpful to the Free State in connection with its application for membership to the League of Nations, and suggesting that a note intimating the wishes of the Irish Government be addressed to each of the Colonial Governments and to the Imperial Government.

The matter was referred to the Minister of External Affairs for a report.

No. 71 NAI DT S2027

Strictly confidential memorandum to each member of the Executive Council by Kevin O'Shiel

DUBLIN, 21 April 1923

THE BOUNDARY ISSUE AND NORTH-EASTERN POLICY

1. These questions of the first magnitude have been wisely held back until all our preparations have been completed and until an opportunity most favourable for us has turned up.

Fortunately, circumstances governing our commitments on these great issues have favoured us and enabled us to play for time and such a suitable opportunity in which to raise these matters.

It so chanced that Article 12 of the Treaty, which prescribes the method for adjusting the present admittedly imperfect Land Frontier laid down no time limit, and we are thus well within our rights in awaiting an opportune moment – so important a factor for the success of our negotiations.

2. Apart from the excellent, and, in itself, conclusive reason that we are not ready, there were other excellent reasons why the Boundary Commission, in so far as we are concerned, has not yet been created. Chief amongst these was the state of turmoil and anarchy prevailing in Saorstát, which monopolised, and rightly monopolised all the Government's time and energy. To have raised the Boundary issue any time within the past six months would have been utter folly and would have played directly into the hands of Craig and his British Tory allies.

3. Happily the forces of the Government have prevailed against the forces of disorder, and the chaotic revolt against the people may now safely be said to be in its death agony. With the near advent of Peace and the prospect of the restoration and solid entrenchment of the Reign of Law, the opportune moment for dealing with this issue will have arrived.

[1] Lionel Curtis.

4. I set down here very roughly a few notes on the present aspects of the situation for the information of the Ministry.

The period covering the negotiations seems to me to fall naturally into four distinct stages, viz.,

a) *A Preliminary Stage*, in which the opening announcement of policy which will set the ball rolling will be made, the British Government formally acquainted of our purpose and the Boundary Commissioners all duly appointed.
b) *A Functioning Stage*, in which the Boundary Commission will be engaged at its actual work as prescribed by Article 12.
c) *A Stage terminating* with the promulgation of the Commission's findings, and
d) *A Final Stage* (possibly) in which the findings of the Commission may be challenged, under certain circumstances, before a Higher Tribunal.

Now, as I have pointed out in earlier Memoranda, we should manoeuvre for a position during all these stages in which we will be able to effect friendly contact with the North-East and over a round table conference hammer out a better and more lasting type of agreement than that provided by the very imperfect Boundary Commission. The Boundary Commission should only be regarded as merely an excellent weapon for furthering our great objective, viz., National Union.

It is clear that Stages a) & b) and, in a lesser degree, Stage c) are capable of presenting many opportunities for the establishment of such contact. For example, in Stage a) after the official announcements have been made and the British are duly acquainted of our purpose and the Boundary Commission appears very imminent it is by no means unlikely that Britain may make some move to both Craig and ourselves to meet in London and endeavour to fix up the thing. Failing that, other opportunities equally valuable will present themselves during Stage b). We have a far stronger case than is generally imagined. The British Government, undoubtedly, won't like to 'let down Ulster', but, on the other hand, it certainly won't like to offend us. We will be Members of the League presently and our voice there, should we will it, will count as something if used against her, and in alliance with France, Belgium and other countries that are not friendly to her at the moment. Besides, she fully realises by this time what it is to upset the international Irish 'Hornet's Nest' on her shoulders. Without doing anything childish like tearing up the whole Treaty because of the Commission's going against us, we can yet use our really powerful position as a Dominion in many ways against her, which will certainly not be pleasant.

All this England well knows and just such an impasse is created which will force her to cry out 'Can't you both come together and settle the confounded thing!'.

Our propaganda, etc. during these Stages will help towards this possibility.

If we go as far as Stage c) without any conference or suggestion of a conference I am afraid prospects of an amicable settlement will be hopeless indeed, and we will have to rely on the findings of the Commission and trust to the chance of bringing them up for review before the League of Nations or the Imperial Conference.

5. A curious crux will arise during Stage a) if Craig carries out his oft repeated threat and refuses to nominate a Commissioner. Craig will be thus acting once again along the traditional North-Eastern lines of ignoring any British Statutes that may be hostile to his policy. This action of his will add greatly to our moral prestige in the matter. We will, no doubt, notify Great Britain of this act with a view to getting her to take disciplinary action against her subordinate Parliament.

Should Craig continue and should Britain take no action we will be given a valid reason for bringing the whole matter up before the League of Nations or the Imperial Conference.

But that is not likely to happen, as British diplomatists are too shrewd to let it go to that extent. It is more likely that Craig will swallow his brave 'never, nevers' and appoint his man. But the most likely solution is that Britain will come to Craig's relief at this stage and suggest a conference. This would suit us down to the ground and is just what we are manoeuvring for.

I have it on fairly good authority that Britain will never let the matter get as far as a functioning Commission.

This being so it is all the more reason why we should, openly at any rate, keep a stiff upper lip, and make a show of being very resolute and determined as to pressing forward our claims. A little bit of the Ulster dourness and thick headedness at this stage will produce excellent results. Legally and morally we will be in the right and Craig will be in the wrong, and we should use this card for all we are worth. Depend upon it[,] Craig will not be sorry of a way out of the impasse created by his oft repeated determination to have nothing to do with the Commission.

6. *Deputations from the North-East* – There are signs that these deputations are becoming active again. At present a Hibernian deputation has been formed and awaits the word to see the President. I have already submitted my views on this. In my opinion it would be unwise for the President to receive a Hibernian deputation at this stage before a Sinn Féin deputation. This would be tantamount to admitting that Devlin had the Government's ear, and would have a very bad effect on our supporters, and create great jealousy.

My opinion is that either the President should call together our own Advisory Committee, which contains Sinn Féin as well as A.O.H.[1] representatives, and address them first; or better still, ignore all Northern Ireland groups and make his first statement on future Northern policy from the Dáil, which is, after all, the Parliament of the Nation, and as such, representative of the entire Nation. This, to my mind, would be the best and safest course, particularly as we have decided to deal with this problem as a great *National* problem, and not as a petty parochial problem, and one purely in the interests of the people of Tyrone, Fermanagh and Down, etc. etc.

This statement should not be made until peace is definitely here, as it would be highly unwise for us to open up this affair until that event. In the meantime deputations should be informed that the President intends shortly to make an official statement on Northern policy in the Dáil, and that therefore he cannot receive any deputations, etc. etc.

[1] Ancient Order of Hibernians.

7. *'Festina Lente'* – My view is that this should be our motto during all the Boundary negotiations. Haste at any time would be very bad. I feel that time is on our side and that we have all to gain by going slowly and cautiously.

We should allow a good measure of time to elapse between every interval, as after the first outburst of indignation from the North-East a much more tolerant spirit will mature according as the thing becomes more and more inevitable. With perfect Peace behind us and the Reign of Law solidly re-established in Saorstát we will puncture ab initio much of Craig's strongest argumentations.

I suggest that the steps in the negotiations should take the following form and order:

(a) *The ball opens by a Governmental statement to the Press* (and through the President's Secretary to Deputations) that as soon as Peace has been completely restored – a consummation which is shortly expected – it is the President's intention to make an official statement on future Northern policy in the Dáil.

(b) *The President makes statement in the Dáil* – This statement should take the form of a strong but unimpassioned pronouncement on our Treaty Rights under Clause 12 and on our adherence to those rights, and our intention of pressing our case on for the Boundary Commission.

It should display also a strong feeling of friendship for the North-East and a hope that now that the Reign of Law has been restored in Saorstát they may, at the eleventh hour, unite with us, etc. etc.

This statement should also explain that the Boundary Commission is an International Commission and therefore a matter solely for the Government as representing all the People of Ireland, and that in this the Government is carrying out procedure along International precedents. (This to out any interference as *by right* which certain groups may put forward.)

(c) *Our Boundary Commissioner is nominated* – (In this connection I hope presently to submit some names to the Executive Council for its consideration. Let me say here that we will require in this connection a man of great weight and sagacity, and one of irreproachable name. It matters not from what part of the country he hails, or even if he should come from outside our shores, as long as he has the requisite qualities. He should be a man without prejudice on the Northern Question, yet one who has a thorough mastery of the situation and with sufficient backbone to fight his corner hard and well, if necessary. Above all, he should be a person who is prepared to act on the Government's slightest suggestion – to go hard when the Government tells him to go hard, and to soften when the Government tells him to soften. This is particularly important in view of the possibility of negotiations for settlement proceeding *outside* the Commission, whilst the Commission is actually functioning.

An ideal person, in my opinion, would be Mr. James McNeill, our High Commissioner in London.

It may in the ultimate be necessary to ask him to take up this temporary work as I cannot, at the moment, imagine a more suitable person in every way).

(d) *Notification to Great Britain of our Purpose and the Name of our Commissioner.* (This is merely formal and will probably be answered formally by Britain, notifying us of her Commissioner and that of Northern Ireland.)

These then are the immediate steps in connection with the Boundary Commission.

8. *Work in the Bureau.*

Mr. Stephens, secretary of the Bureau, is preparing a Report on the present stage of the work there. As this Report will be very shortly in the hands of Ministers, I will say nothing further here save that the work will be found to be very forward in every way. All our research and investigation work is practically concluded, and at the present we are engaged on two things, viz., the preparation of a 'Handbook on Ulster', and in drafting the introductory statement of claim of our case, which will accompany the several historical, economic, statistical and geographical annexes.

We have made our claim for two lots of territory – a maximum demand which we can argue well from the wishes of the inhabitants point of view, but not so well from the economic and geographic point of view, and a minimum demand which will give us all Fermanagh and the greater part of Tyrone, East and South Derry, South Armagh and South and East Down, and which is supported with unanswerable statistical, economic and geographic arguments.

[stamped] Caoímhghín Ó Síadail
Assistant Legal Adviser

No. 72 NAI DFA ES Box 30 File 202(3)

Extracts from a report from Irish Consulate Offices, New York, to Department of Trade and Shipping on Irish trade possibilities in the United States, by Lindsay Crawford
(Copy)

New York, 25 April 1923

IRELAND'S OPPORTUNITY

With an increasing volume of imports into the United States, enterprise and sound judgment should enable Irish firms to find an expanding market for their surplus produce. No one can forecast the future. Whatever the outcome of the present forward movement, and despite the tariff, there is a market for those who cater to a select trade. Ireland cannot hope to compete with the mass production of American factories working on cheap lines, but the demand for better quality that now prevails provides an opening for superior Irish-made products.

That Irish products rank high in the estimation of American buyers is evidenced by the dishonest attempts to pass off inferior American-made commodities as 'Irish' or 'Irish-made'. Irish exporters must realize that competition today is keener than ever, and that countries hitherto little known are now exporting to America goods for which Ireland hitherto had a world-wide reputation. Inferior Chinese handmade lace – Irish style – is fast supplanting the Irish make and frequently advertised and sold as 'Real Irish'. Cotton imitations of Irish poplin are sold as 'Irish Poplin'. Motor rugs of inferior quality are sold as 'Donegal motor rugs'. Unscrupulous trading has wrought serious injury in money and reputation to Irish producers. The fault partly lies with the Irish producer, in his failure to adopt more intelligent and aggressive methods in the merchandising of his goods. The present generation cannot afford to rest upon the reputation of the past. The public memory is short-lived and a country is known industrially not so much by its achievements in the past as by its present samples and pushfullness in advertising its wares.

An export trade calls for more, not less, effort and intelligent handling than are necessary in a home trade. Too often the surplus produce is shipped overseas as a pious hope rather than a business certainty, and without any intelligent appreciation of the condition of the American or other market to which the goods are sent. When shipments turn out badly, the exporter decides that it is a losing business and not worth while. Business in the United States is a science in which efficiency and aggressiveness are the last words. Only by a close study of American tastes, wants and business methods is it possible to carry on a satisfactory export trade. Last year a Donegal manufacturer of homespuns and hose visited the United States. He returned with new ideas, having found out what the American people wanted, and is now finding a market for all he produces. How many Irish manufacturers think it worth while to investigate American conditions on the spot and see for themselves the openings for new lines of goods which the manufacturers of other countries annually explore? The old method of sending to the United States the surplus of commodities that are manufactured to suit Irish and European needs is an exploded commercial heresy. An export trade carried on chiefly as an outlet for surplus trade, and as a mere temporary measure for the deflation of stock, cannot be strictly classified as a sound export business.

That the U.S. tariff is not an insurmountable obstacle may be inferred from the increasing imports of foreign goods into this country. That there are methods by which the prohibitive effects of the new tariff may be minimised is seen by the large store combine that has been formed by several American houses, to be known as the Associated Dry Goods Corporation. Its annual purchasing power in the principal markets of Europe amounts to several millions of dollars. These importing firms have joined forces in the creation of this huge central purchasing agency to be represented in London, Paris and Berlin, and hope in a short time to enrol other firms, eventually having a purchasing power in Europe of many millions annually. Boston, New York, Buffalo, Baltimore, Newark, N.J., Louisville and Minneapolis are cities at present represented in this combination. It is hoped to offset the tariff by cutting down the purchasing expenses abroad. These department stores, it may be added, conducted a vigorous campaign against the Fordney-McCumber Tariff law. Having lost in the fight they have turned their business experience to the formation of an agency by means of which the worst effects of the new Customs duties may be mitigated. Such a combination may in time monopolize the textile and sundry output of Europe and fix the prices at both ends. Its ostensible aim is to meet American-made competition by the lowering of import values to American competing levels. It may be that the experiment will have to face the hazards of combine laws which at present are being rigorously applied.

[Matter omitted]

GENERAL CONCLUSIONS

That Irish producers should regard with intensive interest the present and future trade possibilities of the United States as a market for Irish goods, and that opportunities are presented for the sale of superior Irish-made products, are the conclusions intended to be drawn from this report. Ireland stands to gain commercially by the publicity in recent times, as it has directed attention anew to the undeveloped resources of the country and her remarkable showing in trade activity in abnormal and depressing times. That the American trade in imported commodities for which Ireland is famous should, through any lack of Irish enterprise or adaptability, be diverted to other countries less known is not to be considered.

SOME SUGGESTIONS

The question of the merchandising of Irish commodities is one of pressing importance, in view of the high state of efficiency in other countries. The tendency in the United States is towards collective activity. In textiles consideration should be given to the feasibility of establishing central show-rooms in London and New York for the purpose of encouraging more direct contact between the Irish manufacturer and the foreign buyer. A capable salesman, with an exhibit of all the latest Irish products, would aid considerably in the expansion of the export Trade. The same principle might apply to other surplus commodities. Much of the pessimism which experience of the export trade has engendered in Ireland is due to avoidable mistakes in merchandising. The confidence of the buyer, and greater satisfaction in trading, would follow some concerted plan for the establishment of permanent relations between producer and buyer through central show-rooms in the large buying centres. In Canada, where the U.S. tariff has led to intensive cultivation of other foreign markets, University Extension courses for Export Managers are provided by Canadian universities in co-operation with the Department of Trade and Commerce. A thorough training in export business is there regarded as a condition precedent to success. In the new era upon which Industrial Ireland now enters, efficiency in export trade must not lag behind that of other countries now entering into keen competition for foreign trade, much of which Ireland is capable of supplying.

No. 73 NAI DFA Secretaries' Files S2

Report on mission to Rome by Sean Murphy
(Copy)

ROME, 26 April 1923

REPORT ON MISSION
by
Sean Ó Murchadha

On arriving here on Sunday evening I called immediately to see Marquis MacSwiney. He was unfortunately not at home, but I saw him at 11 o'clock on Monday morning. I explained to him the object of my mission, and the situation generally in connection with Monsignor LUZIO's visit to Ireland. He thought the best thing to do was to go at once and present my credentials to the Under Secretary of State and ask for an audience with the Secretary of State. We went together to the Vatican and he introduced me to Monsignor Pizzardo, Under Secretary of State. I gave him my credentials and explained shortly the reason of my visit. I let him see that Monsignor LUZIO was making the position very difficult for the Government. He was very gracious and said he would see the Secretary of State, and would let the Marquis know by letter the day and the hour of my audience with the Secretary of State.

About four o'clock on Monday afternoon the Marquis received a note from the Under Secretary stating that the Cardinal would be pleased to receive me at any time after 9.30 on the following morning. That evening I discussed the case with the Marquis and asked his advice as to what points should be most stressed. He considered that the best attitude to take was that the Government were afraid lest through the indiscreet actions of Monsignor LUZIO the Holy See might be placed in an awkward position. The strong points in our case according to the Marquis were the following:-

(1) That Monsignor LUZIO took as a Secretary a subject of the country to which he had been sent. This is altogether against the customs of the Vatican in such matters.

(2) The fact that the Monsignor did not get into touch with the Government until he had first seen the Irregulars. That he remained a month in the country without in any way informing the Government of his presence.

(3) The intended meeting at COUNT PLUNKETT's house.

The third point the Marquis was of opinion would carry great weight because it showed that it was the Monsignor's intention to take part in an irregular meeting.

In the course of our conversation the Marquis told me that Cardinal GASPARRI did not read English. He volunteered to translate the President's letter into Italian if the Cardinal so wished.

At 11 o'clock on Tuesday morning the Marquis and myself were received by the Secretary of State. The Marquis introduced me, and I presented the President's letter to his Eminence saying that I regretted that the object of the first mission of the Irish Free State to the Holy See was not as pleasant as the Government would wish. The Cardinal took the letter and said: 'Unfortunately I do not read English'. Whereupon the Marquis said: 'If your Eminence wishes I will translate it'. The Cardinal replied that he would be very pleased if he would. He listened very carefully while the Marquis translated and once or twice showed that he was worried and annoyed. When the Marquis had finished he said in French: 'Undoubtedly the situation is very serious.'

I said that if his Eminence wished I would give him a short resumé of the case. In this exposé the Marquis gave me extraordinary assistance, because he was able to remark to the Cardinal that most of Monsignor LUZIO's actions were against the Customs of the Holy See. We told his Eminence that Monsignor LUZIO arrived in Ireland on the 19th March, and that it was only on the 9th of April that he intimated his desire to see any member of the Government. We pointed out that he had taken CANON CONRY as his Secretary; that the Canon had given several interviews to the Press stating that the Monsignor had been sent by the Holy Father in the interests of peace. Finally when an interview with the President was asked for, it was expressly stated by the Monsignor's Secretary to be unofficial. In this interview the situation was fully and carefully explained to Monsignor LUZIO by the President. When asked for credentials the Monsignor simply said he had been sent by the Holy See, but gave no document of any kind. After the interview a campaign was carried on in the Press by the Monsignor's Secretary to the effect that if a sufficient number of public bodies expressed the desire the Monsignor would be glad to intervene. We explained to the Cardinal that this placed the Government in a very difficult position, as it was known that Monsignor LUZIO had had an interview with the President. Owing to this, and to the petition previously presented to the Vatican on behalf of the Irregulars, and the communiqué subsequently issued to the Irish Press in reference, which contained grave statements that the Holy See unfortunately omitted to contradict, the impression might easily be created that the Vatican was inclined to give undue consideration to the Irregulars' claims. This seeming benevolence on the part of the Holy See at a time when the Irregulars were definitely beaten caused the Government great anxiety. We then informed his Eminence of the proposed meeting between Monsignor LUZIO and prominent Irregulars at Count PLUNKETT's house. We pointed out how in giving up the opportunity of making important captures by occupying the house and preventing the meeting, the Government had rendered a signal service to the Holy See. The Government's action had saved the Vatican from being compromised, not only in the eyes of the Irish people, but before the world at large. The Cardinal said the question was very serious and very urgent, and that he would go immediately and see the Holy Father. He asked us to wait for him in his ante-chamber.

When we were in audience about twenty minutes the Cardinal Dean of the Sacred College was announced, and the Cardinal sent word to him to wait. He remained with us for fully half an hour longer. He then saw the Dean for a few moments. After the Dean, the Minister for Hungary was announced and he informed him that he could not see him as he had to see His Holiness at once, and asked him to come and see him the following day.

He returned to us about forty minutes later and told us with apparent satisfaction that: 'Monsignor LUZIO's ecclesiastical business had come to an end and that he would be recalled immediately by wire.' I thanked His Eminence and said that though I would not presume to ask for an audience knowing how occupied His Holiness was, nevertheless I would be very glad to kiss the Holy Father's hand. The Cardinal replied that he quite understood my desire to see the Pope, but that in order that I might see the Holy Father he would send me an invitation to the Beatification ceremony on Sunday next. We then thanked His Eminence and withdrew.

All during the audience the Cardinal was very gracious. He seemed very impressed by the action of the Government in connection with the proposed meeting at Count Plunkett's house.

After the interview, I sent you the following wire: 'Audience to-day with Secretary of State. Papal Delegate will be recalled immediately by wire. Writing'. In all this matter the Marquis MacSwiney has given me invaluable assistance, in fact but for his help, knowledge of the Vatican, and influence I could never have succeeded in getting the audience so quickly. Before and at the interview he helped me in every way. His presence was very valuable, as owing to his friendship with the Cardinal he was able to press points that I would not have been in a position to do. He advised me to say that it would be appreciated if after the departure of Monsignor LUZIO the President were to send the thanks of the Government to the Holy See, for acceding to their request in this matter.[1]

The Marquis has just let me know that this morning the Under-Secretary of State has informed the Agency Stefani that Monsignor LUZIO's mission has come to an end, and that the Prelate was returning to Rome. The Marquis asks that this communication be considered as STRICTLY CONFIDENTIAL.

(Signed) SEAN Ó MURCHADHA

No. 74 NAI DFA D2185

T.M. Healy to the Duke of Devonshire (London)
(Copy) (Confidential)

DUBLIN, 2 May 1923

My Lord Duke,
I have the honour to acknowledge the receipt of Your Grace's Confidential Despatch of the 6th ultimo[2] on the subject of the proposed Imperial Conference and Imperial Economic Conference to be held in October next, and in reply to convey to you, on behalf of my Ministers, an expression of thanks for the cordial invitation of His Majesty's Government to representatives of the Irish Free State to attend the Imperial Economic Conference, and to the President of the Executive Council to attend the Imperial Conference.

2. My Ministers will be glad to arrange in due course for suitable representatives to attend the Imperial Economic Conference.

3. The President of the Executive Council is not at present in a position to say whether it will be possible for him to attend the Imperial Conference but he will be glad to do so if the circumstances of the time permit.

I have the honour to be,
My Lord Duke,
Your Grace's most obedient,
humble Servant,
(Sgd.) T.M. HEALY

No. 75 UCDA P4/878

Handwritten note by Hugh Kennedy on the registration of the Anglo-Irish Treaty at the League of Nations

DUBLIN, 2 May 1923

So far as we know the Treaty has not been registered with the League of Nations. The question of an application by us to have it registered is closely involved in the question of our membership of the League.

The question of its being incumbent upon the British Gov[t] to present the

[1] No. 78 below.
[2] Not printed.

Treaty for registration is one between the British Gov[t] & the League & we do not propose to invite a justified rebuff by making representations to the British Gov[t] on the matter.

No. 76 NAI DFA ES Box 28 File 186

Cable from Timothy A. Smiddy to the Department of External Affairs (Dublin)
WASHINGTON, 3 May 1923

Major Kelly one of chief heads Irregulars in USA sailed twenty first April with Ginnell's body. Chief motive consult with Dev and important Irregs. Watch him closely. Irregulars will attempt arrange meeting between Dev and Larkin for agreement on common policy.

SINBAD

No. 77 NAI DT S2198

Extract from minutes of a meeting of the Executive Council
(C. 1/99)
DUBLIN, 12.30 p.m., 5 May 1923

Sent to President and Att. General.

MONS. LUZIO.
The Secretary read a report furnished by Mr. Sean Murphy[1] in connection with his mission to Rome regarding Mons. Luzio.

The result of his mission had been most satisfactory, and Mons. Luzio had been recalled.

It was decided that a letter of thanks[2] should be sent by the President to His Holiness the Pope for the gracious manner in which His Holiness had acceded to the representations of the Irish Government and that a letter of appreciation should also be sent to the Marquis MacSwiney for the valuable assistance rendered by him in connection with this matter.[3]

It was arranged that the Attorney General should draft both letters.

No. 78 NAI DT S2109

William T. Cosgrave to Cardinal Gasparri (Rome)
DUBLIN, 8 May 1923

May it please Your Excellency,
Permit me on my own behalf and on behalf of the Government of the Irish Free State to invoke Your Excellency's kind offices to express to the Holy Father our sentiments of grateful appreciation of the gracious consideration of His Holiness, evidence of the undiminished affection ever shown by the Holy See towards Ireland, whereby the embarrassment caused by the manner of the Right Rev. Monsignor Luzio's intervention in our affairs has been brought to

---

[1] See No. 73 above.
[2] See No. 78 below.
[3] Not printed.

an end and Monsignor Luzio has been able to take his departure without further difficulties ensuing.

I beg also to assure Your Excellency of our gratitude for the kindness shown by Your Excellency personally to the bearer of my letter, of which he has informed us.

With renewed expression of gratitude and humble devotion to the Holy See,

I am, my Lord Cardinal,
Your obedient servant,
[signed] LIAM C. MACCOSGAIR
President

No. 79 NAI DFA Secretaries' Files S2

Report on mission to Rome by Joseph P. Walshe

9 May 1923

VISIT OF THE MINISTER OF EXTERNAL AFFAIRS (MR. DESMOND FITZGERALD) TO ROME
29th April - 9th May, 1923

OFFICIAL DIARY

29th April ...	The Minister arrived in Rome. Interview with the Marquis MacSwiney, arranged beforehand by Mr. Sean Murphy who had already conveyed to Cardinal Gasparri the President's message about Monsignor LUZIO.
PRELIMINARIES	It was decided that the Marquis should go with Mr. Murphy the following morning to see Monsignor Pizzardo, Secretary to the Cardinal Secretary of State to inform him of the purport of the Minister's visit and to secure an appointment.
30th April, morning VISIT TO MGR. PIZZARDO	The Marquis pointed out to Mgr. PIZZARDO that the Minister had come to express the gratitude of the President and the Cabinet for the prompt action taken by the Holy See in recalling Mgr. Luzio and to put the relations of the Holy See with Ireland on such a friendly basis that no hitch could in future occur between them. Mgr. Pizzardo was particularly cordial and showed much anxiety to repair the harm that had been done by Mgr. Luzio's visit and seemed impressed by the fact that the Government considered it advisable to send a Member of the Cabinet to explain the whole situation to the Holy See. The interview with Cardinal Gasparri was arranged for 7 o'clock the same evening.
Evening	The Minister accompanied by Marquis MacSwiney, Messrs. J. Walshe and S. Murphy went to the Vatican.

INTERVIEW WITH CARDINAL SECRETARY OF STATE

After a few minutes wait in the Council Chamber, the Minister and the Marquis were conducted to the study of the Secretary of State. The Minister having been introduced was greeted very affably by the Cardinal. The Minister explained the situation at great length, referred particularly to the Con Murphy incident and assured the Cardinal that the Government had ample reason for arresting him (Documents produced showing that Con Murphy's house was distributing centre for Irregular despatches). The Cardinal urged that the telegram sent to the Archbishop of Dublin was in no sense an order. The question of intervening to secure Murphy's release from prison was left entirely to the discretion of the Archbishop. The telegram was occasioned by the great number of wires sent from Ireland and America, all stating that Murphy's imprisonment was due to his visit to Rome.

The Minister went on to explain that the release had taken place before the Government had any knowledge of the telegram to the Archbishop, that in any case the Government, had they desired, could have prevented the departure of Con Murphy for Rome, that it was not the wish of the Irish Government to prevent peaceful action of any sort by the Irregulars least of all to prevent them putting their case before the Holy Father.

VISIT OF MESSRS. CLERY & MURPHY TO HOLY SEE

Both the Minister and the Marquis emphasised the bad impression created by the attitude of the Vatican towards the visit of Messrs. Clery and Con Murphy to Rome. A notice appeared in the Irish and Foreign Press about January of this year saying that these gentlemen had come to Rome to protest against the interference of the Irish Bishops; that they had seen the Cardinal Secretary of State who promised to communicate their memo. to Cardinal Logue to obtain further information; that they had received an assurance that the Sacred Congregation would study the matter. This Press notice remained uncontradicted by the Holy See with the result that Irish Catholics of whom the vast majority support the Government were gravely alarmed. Their political convictions remained unshaken but the apparent consideration shown by the Vatican to the enemies of the established Government and its apparent indifference to the express public declaration of the Bishops had been a source of grave scandal and disedification to them. These feelings and doubts were accentuated when the report

BAD IMPRESSION IN IRELAND

of Mgr. Luzio's intended visit was published and the people could only conclude that the Holy See believed all the reports received from Ireland and the U.S.A. against the Bishops and the established Government. The report, still uncontradicted[,] that the Papal Benediction had been sent to Con Murphy gave still further ground for anxiety.

The Cardinal was evidently much perturbed at this exposé of the situation created by the interference of the Holy See, and he hastened to explain to the Minister that the action of the Holy See had been misinterpreted. The Papal Benediction was *not* sent to Con Murphy. It was understood in Rome that the elections were to be held in May and Mgr. Luzio's presence in Ireland was regarded by the Holy See as a means of aiding the Government to convince the people that the result of the elections should finally decide the controversy.

EXCUSE FOR MGR. LUZIO'S VISIT

To complete his explanations the Minister informed the Cardinal of the visit of the Red Cross Delegates to Ireland; their inspection of the prisons: their excellent impression of the prisoners' treatment. With 10,000 prisoners on their hands the Irish Government could not allow the hunger-strike to be used as a means of obtaining release even if death supervened in some instances.

The Marquis here interrupted to impress on the Cardinal how pained and surprised the Irish people would be if the Holy See intervened on behalf of rebel strikers when no steps whatever had been taken on behalf of Terence MacSwiney, whose sufferings had lasted for seventy days or on behalf of Thomas Ashe who had been killed by inexpert physicians while being forcefully fed.

ATTITUDE OF HOLY SEE TO TERENCE MacSWINEY

Cardinal Gasparri did not admit that the Holy See had been indifferent to the case of the two Irishmen mentioned. Mr. Lloyd George at that time had made strong representations to the Vatican in order to get hunger-striking condemned, but the Pope refused to take action.

Before leaving the Minister impressed on the Cardinal how happy he was to find the Holy See so favorably disposed to the Government of the Irish Free State. He felt quite confident that henceforth similar painful incidents would not occur; that doubts would be solved by open and amicable communication. The President and the Ministers were now as always in the past devoted to the Holy See. The Irish Government would do all in its power to make the relations now begun ever closer and more cordial.

1st May: Morning

Officials of the Vatican Library. The Minister was introduced by the Marquis to Mgr. Mercati, Prefect of the Library, whom he thanked in the name of the Irish Government for the facilities given to the Marquis in the founding of an Irish section of the library. Mgr. Mercati's present post was held immediately before him by Pius XI.

VATICAN LIBRARY

VATICAN SECRET RECORDS

In the Records section, the Minister was received by Mgr. Ugolini, Cardinal Gasquet's First Assistant Keeper of the Records.

Amongst other interesting MMS. Mgr. Ugolini showed to the Minister a series of Minutes of Papal Bulls addressed to Irish Bishops during the period immediately preceding the Anglo-Norman invasion.

Evening: 6 o'c.

Visit to Mr. Theo Russell, British Minister Plenipotentiary to the Holy See.

Visit to British Minister Plenipotentiary.

The Minister informed Mr. Russell of the purport of his visit. Mr. Russell was extremely courteous and expressed his desire to help and facilitate the Minister in every way during his stay in Rome. He seemed amazed that it had been possible to arrange the interview with Cardinal Gasparri so soon after the Minister's arrival.

During a short general discussion on Roman Affairs, he remarked that he had never come in contact with the Irish College Authorities but he hoped that with the new order of things amicable relations might be established. Mr. Russell regretted that the fact of his being still without a house prevented him entertaining the Minister as he should have wished. He agreed that the Minister should leave his card on the head of the Italian Government.

Mr. Russell's relations with the Irish College

7 o'clock

Visit to Cardinal Vanutelli, Dean of the Sacred College.

VISIT TO CARDINAL VANUTELLI

The Minister having been introduced by the Marquis told the Cardinal that though his visit was very short and only semi-official he could not leave Rome without presenting his respects to the Cardinal and through him to the Sacred College. It was well known that the sympathies of the Cardinal were always strongly pro-Irish.

Cardinal Vanutelli replied that it gave him very very great satisfaction to meet a member of the Irish Government. He had indeed a great affection for Ireland and he almost considered himself an Irishman since he had been honoured with the freedom of her chief cities (Cork, Dublin, Drogheda). He would be delighted to inform his colleagues of the Minister's act of courtesy. He asked the Minister to convey his best wishes to the President and the Government.

2nd May, Wednesday

CARDINAL RANUZZI

Visit to Cardinal Ranuzzi di Bianchi, Protector of the Constantinian order of Saint George.

After having inquired about the situation in Ireland, he told the Minister how desirous he was that a distinct branch of the Order should be founded in Ireland. Branches had already been established in France and England.

The Order is somewhat similar to that of St. John, but is exclusively Catholic.

3rd May, THURSDAY

In view of the impending change in the method of selecting Bishops in Ireland, the Marquis, at the Minister's request interviewed the Brazilian and Portuguese Representatives for the purpose of finding out what system was in operation in their respective countries, neither of which has at present a concordat with the Holy See.

The Bishops are selected by the Nuncio resident in Rio and Lisbon without direct reference to either the local clergy or the Government.

Before recommending his choice to Rome, the Nuncio finds out unofficially whether the individual is a persona grata with the Government, but the wishes of the local clergy are completely ignored.

4th May, FRIDAY 11 o'clock

Audience with the Pope The Minister accompanied by the Marquis and followed by Messrs. Murphy and Walshe arrived at the Vatican. The party was ushered to the Throne Room, Military honours being given by the officers of the Guards in all the halls leading to the Pope's private study. Mgr. Confalonieri, the Maestro di Camera, conducted the Minister and the Marquis to the antecamera segreta (to which only Cardinals and personnages of high rank are admitted) to await the Audience.

After a few minutes they were led into the Pope's private study in which the Pope very rarely receives visitors.

When the Minister had kissed his ring the Pope invited him to sit in a chair placed immediately in front of his writing table.

THE MINISTER

The Minister spoke briefly to the Pope about the attachment of the Irish Government and people to his person and office; about the strong Catholic spirit in Ireland which had lasted for centuries and was still as strong as ever. The legally constituted Government of Ireland not only represented the views of the overwhelming majority of the people in every political matter but also in their attitude towards the Holy See.

THE POPE

The Pope who spoke for almost half an hour assured the Minister that every time he offered the Holy Sacrifice, Ireland was present in his thoughts. During his stay in Poland as Nuncio he often thought of the similarity between the history of the two peoples. He referred to the work of the Irish Missionaries in Northern Italy. BOBBIO had been the centre of an intense intellectual and religious movement. (Messrs. Murphy and Walshe were introduced at this point.) In a short time – probably about September – a Papal rescript would be issued restoring the ancient abbatial title of Bobbio.[1]

[1] A handwritten textual note reads '13th Centenary of foundation of the Abbey'.

The Holy Father spoke at length about the Irish MMS. in the Ambrosian Library of Milan (of which he had been Curator before coming to Rome) especially about the Antiphonarium of Bangor with its scoliae in old Irish. His study had made him familiar with the Irish characters in which these MMS. were written.

The Pope gave his Benediction to the four present and through them to their relatives and friends 'according to their intention'.

He had previously asked the Minister to convey his special blessing to the President and Ministers of the Government.

The Pope accompanied his visitors to the ante-camera segreta to examine a set of books which the Marquis had received for the new Irish section. He was particularly pleased to see the bound volumes of 'Hermathenae' presented by the Provost of Trinity College.

The Holy Father, with further good wishes to the Minister and his friends, bade Good-Bye.

SATURDAY, 5th May 6 o'clock

Interview arranged by the Marquis with Signor Contarini, permanent Director of Foreign Affairs.

Interview. The Minister was very cordially greeted by Sig. Contarini. The latter conveyed Sig. Mussolini's regrets to the Minister that his departure for Milan prevented him receiving the Minister personally. If the Minister remained a few days longer, Sig. Mussolini would be very gratified to have an opportunity of meeting him.

Signor Contarini inquired about the exact relations between the Irish and British Governments and expressed great pleasure on hearing from the Minister that the relations were amicable.

Signor Contarini hoped that it would soon be possible to have a trade convention with Ireland and that the most cordial relations would be established between Italy and Ireland.

The Minister left his card on the British Ambassador.

MONDAY, 7th May 6 o'clock

The Minister visited Cardinal Von Rossum, head of the Propaganda. The Cardinal displayed an intimate knowledge of Irish affairs and declared himself greatly pleased at the strong position of the new Government, owing to its wise and just administration.

TUESDAY, 8th May.

The Minister left Rome.

[signed] S.P. BREATHNACH
Rúnaí

No. 80 NAI DFA P83

Sean Lester to William T. Cosgrave (Dublin)

DUBLIN, 10 May 1923

MEMO: TO THE PRESIDENT.

Mr. Mark Sullivan of the 'New York Tribune' and a well-known political writer in the American Reviews arrived in Dublin to-day. Professor Smiddy had advised us of his arrival. He came to see me and we had half an hour's conversation. Although warned by Professor Smiddy that he would probably want to talk about the League of Nations and had no strong Irish sympathies, I found him to take a very sympathetic view of the situation and appeared to have a good understanding of it. He is an Irish man and has relatives in Cork whom he visited. He was rather surprised at the normal conditions prevailing in Cork County, and mentioned that he had talked to some farmers who are sympathisers with the Irregulars, declaring the latter to consist of the 'best of the old I.R.A.' As supporting the view that the trouble is nearly over[,] these men told him that they hoped there would be no more fighting for another twenty years.

He intended staying in Dublin only until tomorrow as his principal business is in London, Paris and the Ruhr. He may however change his mind if he finds the situation very interesting and remain until Sunday. He will attend the Dáil this evening for the discussion on the Finance Bill and the debate on the de Valera document.

I asked him some questions about the situation in America and propaganda there. He says that the number of de Valera supporters in America is quite inappreciable. Americans are puzzled by de Valera's attitude. They generally understand that the Free State has the same position as Canada and they see across their borders that Canada is contented and prosperous and mentioned the Treaty signed separately by Canada a few months ago as showing how her position is still advancing. (In this connection he remarked that it was only a matter of waiting until it would not embarrass the British Government for the Canadian Government to appoint a resident Minister at Washington.)

I asked him what effect the Irregular Missionaries were having on American public opinion, and he said that as far as he could judge, and he was a working journalist in touch with all the affairs of the day, they had no influence. He pointed out that the American papers had not reported the meetings held by these people not because of any hostility but simply because they were uninteresting and had no news value. He said that the touring lecturers would go into a town and hold a meeting in some small suburban church where their audience would consist of a small group of Irregular supporters. I asked him to compare these activities with those of the old Sinn Féin delegates. He described the scenes he himself had frequently witnessed a couple of years ago and very emphatically said that a comparison was ridiculous. As to the funds they were gathering he said an American might part with a few dollars on the purely charitable plea while not supporting the political aims of the Irregulars, but that there will be no more of the old subscriptions of 50 and 100 dollars until the time came for capital investments in the Free State. In his opinion the American public which formerly helped and supported the Sinn Féin movement was now behind the Free State. He was interested in the question of whether Ireland would in the future adopt a free trade or protectionist policy, and the amount of the British war debt that would be apportioned to the Free State. I told him in this connection that neither of the subjects had been yet decided and explained to him the present fiscal system.

He did not ask any questions about the League of Nations, and mentioned once or twice that he did not think of dealing with the Irish situation but had passed through Ireland for the purpose of showing his wife and family the country. He said that once things settled down here Irish Americans, he was certain, would be only too anxious to invest capital in this country, and that he thought the tourist traffic in Ireland could easily be made a tremendous business in the future.

[copy letter unsigned]
Director of Publicity.

No. 81 NAI DFA ES Box 29 File 178

Timothy A. Smiddy to Desmond FitzGerald (Dublin)
(152/23P) (Strictly Private and Confidential)
WASHINGTON, 10 May 1923

A Chara:
I received to-day copy of letter 28th April sent by Director of Publicity[1] to Trade Agent – Mr L. Crawford. On receipt thereof I sent you a cable[,] copy of which I enclose.

Mr. L. Crawford, as I have already stated, is, in my opinion, competent to act as Trade Agent. But I am convinced that on account of his political connections here the Government would act unwisely in giving him any *responsibility or control of Publicity*. He is most intimately associated, socially and politically, with a group here who are now leading a strong attack on the Irish Free State Government for their application to enter the League of Nations. They will also most probably institute in the near future strong propaganda against anything *suggestive* of complacency on the part of the Irish Free State with its inclusion in the British Commonwealth of Nations.

My most difficult position here has been to try and keep this group well disposed to the Irish Free State: and until your Government decided on entering the League of Nations, I was to some extent successful; and I still hope to be able to moderate their hostility or at least take the sting out of it.

When I appointed Mr Lindsay Crawford to take temporary charge (under my control) of the then 'Consulate Office' I had mainly in view his reliability for the situation that then arose, as also for his qualifications as provisional Trade Agent. I have also utilized his office occasionally as a medium for the distribution of publicity directly under my control. But at no time did I

[1] Sean Lester.

contemplate that he should have any responsibility or control of publicity which has sometimes important implications of policy. Hence, it is absolutely essential that any directions from the Government re. publicity or its distribution should come only through this office.

Again, as in all cases when responsibility is divided efficiency will be impaired and responsibility itself will vanish.

Mise, le meas,
[signed] T.A. SMIDDY

No. 82 NAI DFA ES Box 28 File 185

Timothy A. Smiddy to Desmond FitzGerald (Dublin)
with two enclosures on intelligence matters
(184/23)

WASHINGTON, 11 May 1923

A Chara:

INTELLIGENCE.

I enclose two memoranda which contain almost verbally some conversations which took place last week between some of the chief organizers of the Irregulars in New York.

I respectfully request that on no account shall it be made public as its origin would be thus easily traced. Hence, I have marked it absolutely private and confidential.

Mise, le meas,
[signed] T.A. SMIDDY

[enclosure one]
ABSOLUTELY PRIVATE AND CONFIDENTIAL.

Speaking about the death of Laurence Ginnell, the 'Ambassador' of the Irish Republic. Miss - - - said, [']that was a very hard blow in more than one way. Of course, we all knew that Ginnell was a very sick man, but, dying as he did, has caused a lot of complications we didn't foresee, but should have. We could not very well supervise Ginnell's accounts as we could do with one of our own people, and, in consequence, there's a lot of trouble before us, getting Ginnell's financial affairs straightened out – if we ever do.

I don't mean to say that there was anything wrong on Ginnell's part, but there must be fifteen or twenty thousand Dollars that we don't know how to go about looking for. Mrs Ginnell is on the way back to the old country and we couldn't very well demand any accounting from her.

Miss - - - said, there is always something good about most things, no matter how bad they may look and taking Ginnell's body back to Ireland has given Major Kelly an opportunity to make a flying visit back to Ireland. You can bet that Kelly will make good use of his time while he's in Ireland. It will be a good thing too, for Major Kelly will get right in touch with the President (de Valera). The best of it is they (Free Staters) won't dare to interfere with Kelly, whereas any one else would be watched like a hawk.[']

The following conversation took place a few days later:

[']As was said before[,] Ginnell had a lot of Money in his possession, and a lot of incomplete transactions in the air, when he died. Some of these transactions and funds were in the name of the Republic, but most of them were in Ginnell's personal account. Now we're up in the air, and don't know where to start in at to straighten things out and our people in Philadelphia and Washington are quarrelling like dogs, so the first thing we know it will be in the newspapers and that will destroy or cripple our movement for funds.

Mrs Skeffington and Peter McSwiney decided that it would be best to let the matter drop, but unfortunately Joe McGarrity and Joe O'Doherty don't pull together on the subject.

O'Doherty wants to have all Ginnell's affairs straightened out, regardless of any scandal it might cause, while McGarrity believes that silence and diplomacy is the best policy at this time. So it means that we have another split in our ranks, right at the very top this time. Major Kelly we hope, will be able to get the President (de Valera) to advise O'Doherty the proper thing to do. One thing is certain[,] we cannot afford to have any more trouble in our ranks, or we might as well throw up the sponge. There are quite a number of Irish-Americans who resent the attitude of some of the emissaries that are coming over here.'

[enclosure two]

ABSOLUTELY PRIVATE AND CONFIDENTIAL.

At a private meeting of some of the chief organizers of the Irregulars the following conversations took place:-

'Our organization was getting unwieldy, splitting up into factions, and fighting like cats and dogs, until, finally we lost so much ground over here, that it was hurting the people on the other side (Ireland) who are depending on us for their supplies. And, then in order to make our organization effective, we had to get rid of a lot of 'dead timber' without antagonizing them, if possible, and practically organize all over again, with a very small and effective central body, and we are going to take in some new material.'

[']We are going to operate along Fenian lines.[']

The conversation then turns to the reported cessation of hostilities in Ireland, and the published accounts of peace overtures by de Valera. Continuing Miss - - - said [']the fight is only starting. There have been some very bad losses to our side, but in a very short while there will be a new kind of war-fare, and some of the Free State politicians will not find their jobs so attractive, and possibly their lives so secure, as they think they are. Something is in the wind just now and if certain elements get together there will be a great surprise.'

On being asked what the surprise would be Miss - - - made the following reply: 'We have got the situation lined up nicely here. What I mean in fact, is the Irish Labor element. If we can get Jim Larkin to line up and "take programme" from the President (de Valera) well, things will pick up once more; if not, the trouble will get to be more personal. A terrible vow had been made by the prisoners in Irish Jails, forfeiting the lives of Mulcahy and Cosgrave and all their assistants in the Free State. Well, it may be decided that the friends of those poor prisoners will take up the vow for them.'

Speaking of the Strike on the Ships Miss - - - said 'It's been a Godsend to us in one way, because we have been able to send a couple of good men over to England, and if the strike keeps on, or spreads, we will be able to do still better. Before when we had a friend aboard one of the regular ships, he soon became known, now we can drop one or two men on any ship that's having trouble, simply as strike breakers or "scabs" as they are called, and nobody is any the wiser. Men secured at the last minute before sailing are not scrutinized as closely as if they were secured in regular times, and we can use different men occasionally, instead of using the same ones continually.'

Asked about Larkin Mrs Skeffington said 'that allowances would have to [be] made for Larkin in any future plans. As between what J.L. calls a "bourgeois government" and what de Valera calls Jim's "communism" there is a middle ground that I'd like to see both of them standing on. It is my idea that Ireland will best work its destiny out as a co-operative commonwealth, and I have so stated many times. I would not be a bit surprised to see the President (de Valera) and Larkin get together on the subject and when I get back to Ireland, if I am left out of jail long enough, I'll do all I can to get Jim and the President to adopt common ground, for the fight is going on just the same.'

Mrs Skeffington is going to Ireland in a couple of weeks, simply to confer with de Valera, and to give him a complete report from our central Executive Committee.

No. 83 NAI DFA ES Box 29 File 189/2

Timothy A. Smiddy to Desmond FitzGerald (Dublin)
(161/23)

WASHINGTON, 12 May 1923

A Chara:

DIPLOMATIC RECOGNITION AT WASHINGTON

During the last four or five months many events have made me realize the imperative necessity of obtaining Diplomatic Recognition for the Irish Free State at Washington. The following three reasons in themselves justify action being taken at the earliest possible date. Any move in this direction has been delayed, I presume, in consequence of a desire to await the decision of the Canadian Government to appoint a Representative at Washington. As I shall point out later our action in the matter should no longer be contingent on that of Canada. The three reasons above referred to are.

(1) The evidence such recognition would give of the International Sovereignty of the Irish Free State which will go a long way to render ineffective the activities of the Irregulars and their supporters in this country.

(2) It will have a very satisfactory effect on the settlement of the suit that is pending the Court.

(3) It will aid us considerably in coping with the activities of the Irregulars by giving us direct access to the State Department and helping us to obtain an embargo on the exportation of arms to the Irish Free State.

A further reason worthy of consideration is that if such recognition were authorized by the British Government at an early date, and before the Imperial Conference is held in September next, it would prevent the possibility of

Ireland's Diplomatic Representation being made contingent on decisions that may be arrived at in that conference.

Finally, it will remove from the opponents of the Irish Free State all grounds for asserting that Ireland is not a Sovereign Power – as far as most Nations can be such at present.

For the above reasons during the last month I have endeavoured to ascertain the attitude of the Government at Washington towards the recognition of the Irish Free State, and also the present attitude of the Canadian Government towards the appointment of a Diplomatic representative at Washington. I am enclosing two reports dealing with these investigations.[1]

Mise, le meas,
[signed] T.A. SMIDDY

No. 84 NAI DT S2027

Memorandum to each member of the Executive Council by Kevin O'Shiel (Dublin)
(Strictly Confidential)

DUBLIN, 17 May 1923

OUR TERRITORIAL DEMAND AT THE BOUNDARY COMISSION

1. The Memoranda sent you herewith comprise

a) Report on possible Boundary Lines

b) Report on Economic and Geographic Conditions governing the suggested Minimum Line

c) Report on Economic and Geographic Conditions governing the suggested Boundary Commission or Middle Line.

(N.B. These Reports are referred to hereinafter as Reports 'A' 'B' and 'C' respectively.)

2. Our standpoint has been that the Boundary Commission must be an international Boundary Commission between the two distinct and co-equal Governments of Saorstát Éireann and Great Britain, and not in any sense a mere Royal Commission under the aegis of the British Parliament.

Hence our case must take the form of a demand for a definite and specific piece of territory.

3. The Memoranda attached herewith have been prepared at my request by our experts for the information and assistance of Members of the Executive Council in order that they may be facilitated in coming to a conclusion as to what would be the best possible Line of the three suggested to base our Case on for presentation to the Boundary Commission.

When Members of the Executive Council have had time to consider these data carefully I would suggest that the whole matter be discussed and finally decided at a Meeting, whereat I can display maps and charts illustrating the various positions.

4. *The Maximum Line* – The effect of the Maximum Line will be seen to be to put a total of 781,488 Ulster people under our flag and 800,208 Ulster people

[1] Not located.

under the British flag. Free Staters would form 66% of the population of the proposed Free State Ulster and 22% of the population of the proposed Belfast Parliament area. The net result of a decision on this Line would be to give us all Ireland save the County Antrim, the extreme North-East corner of the County Derry, portion of North and Middle County Armagh (exclusive of Armagh City) and all the County Down save the North and Middle portions.

The Maximum Line represents the greatest possible amount of territory we could get under the Boundary Commission, and can only be supported on one argument, viz., the wishes of the inhabitants.

It is approximately 148 miles in extent and offends against every conceivable geographic and economic principle. Yet there is a precedent for its successful argumentation, viz., the Silesian Boundary dispute precedent where, it will be recalled, Lord Balfour decided on the division of the industrial and economically self-contained Silesian triangle on the ground that by the terms of reference the 'wishes of the inhabitants' were paramount and above every other consideration.

5. *Minimum Line* – This Line represents not only the minimum territory that we should get but the best possible line, taking into account the three considerations in the terms of reference, viz., wishes of the inhabitants, geographic and economic considerations. It will be seen that it restores to us a considerable slice of County Derry, including Derry City, nearly all County Tyrone, save a small quadrangle bordering on the Lough shore, the Southern portion of the County Armagh and the Southern portion of the County Down, including the Borough of Newry and all the County Fermanagh.

From the population standpoint we would get 604,102 and the Belfast Parliamentary area 977,594 inhabitants of All Ulster's 1,581,696 inhabitants. Of our population only 179,421 people and of the Belfast Parliamentary area population only 266,135 people would be living under a Government not of their own choice.

The length of this Line is approximately 124 miles, and is thereby the shortest possible under the circumstances.

6. *Middle Line (or Boundary Commission Line)*

Fearing that the urging of the Maximum Line would enable the Chairman of the Commission to take a high and mighty attitude and refuse to consider our propositions on the ground of 'utter unreasonableness', and that the putting forward of the excellent and, in my opinion, almost uncontrovertible Minimum Line in the first instance would be a huge tacticable blunder inasmuch as it would leave no margin for the Chairman to concede something to 'Ulster', I requested our experts to furnish me with an alternative course. The result is the 'Middle Line' or 'Boundary Commission Line', as described in Report 'C'.

It will be seen that this Line concurs mainly with the maintainable 'Minimum Line' but bulges out in three places into a number of salients all of which may be, if necessary, surrendered to enable the Chairman of the Commission to yield something from our absolute demand – a very difficult thing for him to do if we put up at once the strong Minimum Line.

This Line, the 'Middle Line', is most arguable as it stands, on the ground that it alone of all the Lines practically balances the number of unwilling citizens in each area. They are:

208,191 pro-Belfast Government people in the Free State
227,760 " Free State " " " " Belfast area.

[stamped] Caoímhghín Ó Síádhail
Assistant Legal Adviser

No. 85 NAI DT S2027

Memorandum to each member of the Executive Council
by Kevin O'Shiel (Dublin)
(Strictly Confidential)

Dublin, 22 May 1923

CHANGES IN BRITISH GOVERNMENT and BOUNDARY COMMISSION

1. The resignation of Mr. Bonar Law from the Premiership has created a position which the Government would be well advised to watch closely, in particular with regard to its North-Eastern policy.
2. I am of opinion that the best course for the Government to adopt is to stay its hands in making any move towards acquainting the British of our intentions with regard to Article 12 of the Treaty until the present indefinite position of the British Government is cleared up and until we see exactly what its new personnel is likely to be.
3. The success of the Boundary Commission depends so much on there being good men in power in England at this stage – men, not necessarily favourable to us, but prepared to deal straightly and honourably with us.

It is invidious to prophesy but judging from his antecedents and his close touch and frequently avowed friendship with 'Ulster' Lord Curzon would not be a suitable person in power for our purposes. He would appear to be too much committed to Craig to make it easy for him, even if he so desired, to deal impartially in this matter.

Lord Balfour would be better as he is less rigid and narrow than Curzon and can always be relied upon to throw any side over board once he is convinced that there is danger to the Empire in adhering thereto.

(N.B. I think we will succeed in convincing him of this according as the Boundary Question develops.)

4. The best alterations for us under the circumstances would be the taking into the British Government of the Conservative signatories to the Treaty, viz., Mr. Austen Chamberlain, Lord Birkenhead and Sir Robert Horne. It appears highly probable that some, if not all, of these persons will be brought in to strengthen the British Government, as it is very much in need of new blood.
5. No harm can be done to our cause by holding our hands until things take definite shape across the water.

Were we to reveal our hands at this critical moment by despatching the preliminary letter to the British Government we might influence against us the future personnel and complexion of the British Government, whereas if we remain quiet for the moment persons well-disposed towards us may be given positions of prominence that would make them helpful to us in the reformed Administration.

[stamped] Caoímhghín Ó Síádhail
Assistant Legal Adviser

No. 86 NAI DT S2027

Memorandum to each member of the Executive Council by Kevin O'Shiel, with covering letter by O'Shiel
(Strictly Confidential)

DUBLIN, 30 May 1923

A Chara,
I send you herewith a rather lengthy Memorandum on North-Eastern policy and the Boundary Commission.
2. Although it is unusually long it is important and contains carefully considered views and most carefully thought out plans in connection with the Boundary Question.
3. I trust you will have time to read it carefully as I intend to apply shortly for a special Meeting of the Executive Council to consider the Alpha and Omega of the whole North-Eastern position, and the information in this Memo. will assist you at such a Meeting.

Mise, le meas,
[stamped] CAOÍMHGHÍN Ó SÍÁDHAIL
Assistant Legal Adviser

[enclosure]
Strictly Confidential

29th May, 1923

THE BOUNDARY ISSUE
(N.B. Ministers are requested to read this Memo. in close conjunction with my Memo. on *'The Boundary Issue and North-Eastern Policy'* circulated on the 22nd April.)[1]
1. With the complete collapse of the Irregulars the time seems opportune for starting the ball rolling in this tremendously important issue of the North-Eastern Boundaries.
2. Since I have been entrusted with this very important matter I have endeavoured to steer a course as near to the policy of the late General Michael Collins as was humanly possible under the circumstances.

The late General never made any secret of his distrust in the Boundary Commission as a means of settlement per se. He used frequently to remark that 'the Boundary Commission will settle nothing'. He realised that even after the Boundary Commission had sat and made its decisions, and even if those decisions conceded to us our ultimate claim there would still be an 'Hibernia Irredenta' to disturb the peace of future generations. Not only that but there would be an increased feeling of intense hatred amongst the Northern secessionist populations against the rest of Ireland. Though the territory of Saorstát might be broadened, the gulf between Saorstát and these populations would also be broadened. So fully aware of all this was the late General that on a number of occasions he went out of his way to establish contact with the Belfast

[1] Above No. 71.

Authorities in the hope that such contact would lead to a better and more enduring settlement between Irishmen.

3. Being convinced of the truth of General Collins' policy and at the same time bearing in mind that the Government is under solemn pledges to carry out the entire Treaty – Article XII no less than the other Articles – I have endeavoured to plan out a line of policy in the matter which seeks to reconcile these two somewhat disparate positions, which whilst enabling the Government to hold strongly to its pledges, yet allows ample room for the operations of statesmanship.

4. I have outlined the plan in many previous Memoranda. It is roughly to look upon our ultimate objective as not the securing of more territory, but as the securing of *National Union*. Everything else should be subordinate to this great object, and should be used or left according as circumstances show whether it would further or retard *National Union*. Hence the Boundary Commission must be regarded as a weapon, probably *the* most important weapon in this diplomatic war for National Union; and our aim should be to extract from it and its 'bye-products' every ounce of value, and only in the last resource, when all else fails and in the event of the North-East determining to continue obdurate to the bitter end, let it take its course to the ultimate.

5. It is, of course, clear to Ministers that once the ball has commenced to roll in this game we shall be to a greater or lesser extent victims of circumstances. I mean by this that the position will be that of a ball rolling down a hill which may be frequently side tracked and frequently compelled to slow, but which, once started, can never be absolutely stopped until it reaches the foot of the hill, unless it is side tracked into a hollow.

(The hollow in this case would represent National Union! It is a poor metaphor, but, I think, helps to make the position clear.)

6. The recent preliminary letter[1] which it was intended to despatch some weeks ago to Mr. Bonar Law will require some alterations in view of the accession of Mr. Baldwin to the Premiership of Great Britain. It should be despatched as soon as these alterations have been made.

7. *THE NEW BRITISH PREMIER*

Mr. Stanley Baldwin, the new British Premier, is, as far as I can learn, a person having strong Die-Hard sympathies. It will be recalled that he was the mover of the motion in the Tory Revolt at the Meeting of the Conservative Party, which was the direct cause of clearing out the Lloyd George Government and discrediting Chamberlain and Birkenhead.

I have no doubt that he has strong pro-North-East sympathies and may have committed himself to those people by pledges in former days. But the great outstanding fact remains that as Bonar Law's successor in title he is committed as steadfastly to the Treaty as the two former Premiers.

Many people are under the impression that we could get most from the Boundary Clause by delaying until a Liberal or a Labour Government comes into power in Great Britain. But I take the view that our best chance is to deal with this question whilst a Conservative Government is in power. Apart from

[1] Not printed.

the fact that Conservatism is traditionally much straighter and honester in its dealings than the other parties, there remains the most important point that by forcing a Conservative Government to deal with Article XII, *we eliminate from the British Parliament the largest possible measure of opposition.* By this I mean that it would be utterly impossible for the Conservatives to adopt a strong 'pro-Ulster' and anti-Irish attitude, as their party is in power and has pledged itself to carry out the Treaty in good faith.

The Liberal and Labour Parties in the Commons will be strongly in our favour (if for no other reason than that they largely depend upon the huge Irish vote), and thus the situation will be considered in a Parliament in which the one potentially hostile Party to us will be largely gagged because of the fact that it is the Government in power responsible for carrying out the Treaty.

Now, with a former Die-Hard in complete control I have no doubt that the vehement 'pro-Ulster' enthusiasm of the Die-Hard Tories will be largely held in check. The position is a delightful one for our purposes – almost Gilbertian.

8. *A PROPAGANDA CAMPAIGN*

The success of the entire Boundary negotiations – whether on the one hand they result in *National Union*, or on the other hand they result in a transfer of extensive territories under our flag – will depend enormously on the quality and persistence of our Propaganda. To my mind the Propaganda that will accompany the various stages of the proceedings is almost as important an element as the Boundary Commission itself.

This Propaganda will fall naturally under two main headings, viz., (a) Home and (b) Foreign.

(A) Home – With regard to Home Propaganda the work will be more *negative* than *positive*, and will be directed more towards controlling and checking as diplomatically as possible any foolish and unreasonable eruptions in our own Press which at a critical moment might conceivably deal us a nasty blow. Our Weekly Bulletin will, of course, keep going in its present quasi-official capacity. It may be necessary too to get our Press to work up certain aspects now and again. In this connection I have got into friendly alliance with the 'Freeman' people who are, as usual, willing and anxious to assist us in every way; and also the North-Western Publishing Company. This Company has its Headquarters in Omagh, and produces weekly the following papers, circulating in the following districts:

(1) 'The Ulster Herald' – Mid, South and East Tyrone.
(2) 'The Strabane Chronicle' – North Tyrone & East Tirconnaill.
(3) 'The Derry People' – Derry City, part of Co. Derry and Innishowen Peninsular, Co. Tirconnaill.
(4) 'The Fermanagh Herald' – Co. Fermanagh, South Tirconnaill, North Leitrim and parts of Co. Sligo and West Cavan.
(5) 'The Frontier Sentinel' – Newry Borough, South & East Down, South Armagh and North Louth.

It will be seen that this combine affords a perfect chain of opinion round the entire debatable area. These papers are naturally inclined to be a bit 'Irredentist', but we can rely always on their help so long as we are determined on the Boundary Commission.

We can also rely on the 'Derry Journal' in this connection, I think.
(B) *Foreign* – Once the Boundary Commission negotiations get well under sail this will be far and away the most important field for our active propaganda.

This section falls naturally into three heads, viz., (a) British (b) Commonwealth & U.S.A. (c) Continental.

At the present moment the major part of the material for our *'Handbook on the Ulster Question'* is at Press and we hope in a short time to have the book launched. It will be a concise synopsis of all that it is prudent to release of our Case Stated. It will be divided into the following sections, viz.,

Historical – Dr. MacNeill and Mr. J.W. Good
Statistical – Mr. Stephens and Mr. G.A. Ruth
Economic – Mr. Joseph Johnston
European Boundary Commissions – Mr. Waller
How Union was effected in Other Countries – Mr. Waller
The Question of Minorities and Analogous Continental Cases thereon – Mr. Murphy

It will be provided with 9 or 10 maps and diagrams (many of them the original work of the Bureau) and an excellent index, so that information can be readily obtained.

It is intended to distribute this work *free* to all Statesmen, Public Representatives, Political Bodies and Newspapers, etc. in Great Britain, U.S.A. and the Dominions, as well as to Foreign Embassies, Consulates, etc., the League of Nations, etc.

Apart from this the Handbook will also be on sale in all these countries.

British – When I was in London before Xmas I obtained a good deal of information with regard to the best methods of placing propaganda in Great Britain. My investigations led me to the conclusion that in that country articles to be generally read must be first signed by prominent and influential publicists, and secondly, printed in prominent, popular and influential papers. Whilst there I met several leading Journalists who expressed themselves willing to be of any assistance. Many of them were, however, not very well informed (It was the extraordinary ignorance on the situation displayed by our friends there that made me think of preparing the 'Handbook'). For these our Publicity Department are preparing a series of skeleton articles with copious references from the strong British standpoint. When the series is complete and when the time is ripe I will go to London again and 'place' them.

These skeleton articles will deal with such topics as

(a) *Danger to the Commonwealth of Failure to carry out Clause XII of the Treaty* – Dealing with the terrible power the Irish Race are all over the World and especially in the Nations of the Commonwealth; their numbers and instances of their influence overseas (e.g. number of Dominion Statesmen of Irish blood, etc.); how fiercely they resent Partition and how ardently they are depending on Article XII to reduce the Partitioned area to a minimum.

Then there is the other point that failure to carry out this Clause would simply play into the hands of the Irregulars and give them a renewed lease of life, etc. etc.

(b) *Sir James Craig should assist the supporters of the Commonwealth in Ireland* – Sir James Craig and Carson by their unwise and foolish pronouncements and illegal actions in 1912-14 were the main causes of modern physical force movement in Ireland and contributed more than any other persons to the destruction of the Union in Ireland (under 'Home Rule' the United Kingdom would be preserved; now it is gone). Here copious quotations from past utterances of Ulster Unionists.

The men who have done most to maintain the integrity of the Commonwealth [are the] present Irish Government, which carried out to a successful conclusion a war against Irregulars, Craig cannot now say these men [are] not in earnest about [the] Treaty. Debt of £20,000,000 put on Ireland by these necessities and many of the best men in Ireland [are] dead, e.g. Pres. Griffith, General Collins.

(N.B. it is to be remembered that these articles will be written by Englishmen *purely from the British point of view.* The point about this particular article is to counteract Craig and the Die-Hards should they attempt to repeat their 1912-14 tactics – a most probable contingency – by reminding the British public of the pickle these tactics led them into at the time of the European War.)

In general these articles are planned a) to impress British Commonwealth and American opinion with the excellence of our case b) with the manifold dangers in the Boundary Situation and the general danger of turning the Irish Race against them – especially now when they can appeal to World opinion with a case at least as excellent as that which compelled the Treaty.

The Dominions – Our particular wooing of the Dominions is of course due to the fact that it must have a big effect at the *Imperial Conference*. It should not be too difficult to get Dominion opinion overwhelmingly behind us on this matter, as they will be directly concerned both because of analogous problems of a similar nature (e.g. Rhodesia, Newfoundland) and because of the power of the Irish in these countries. We should also 'give the tip' to Irish papers in the Dominions to begin to wax enthusiastic about the Boundary Commission, so that pressure can be brought to bear in time on the Dominion statesmen who will go to the Imperial Conference.

Continental – We must also try to enlighten Continental opinion in view of the League of Nations – a possible Court of Appeal in the last result. For this purpose we could not do better than print some thousands of copies of Mr. Y.M. Goblet's 'La Frontiere de l'Ulster', also sundry articles on the topic from 'La Revue des Deux Mondes'.

Other Propaganda Methods – We should also make use of other methods which were very much in vogue at the time of the Home Rule agitation in 1912, viz., invite distinguished Foreign and British Journalists to visit the disputed regions, and write up their experiences.

9. *IMMEDIATE STAGES IN THE ISSUE*

These will be, first of all, the despatch to Mr. Baldwin of the informal preliminary letter, notifying him of our intention to acquaint him formally of our purpose with regard to the Boundary Commission.

When a reply has been received from Mr. Baldwin the President should thereupon make his statement on Northern policy somewhat along the lines outlined in my Memo. of the 22nd April.[1] It is essential to wait for Mr. Baldwin's

[1] Above No. 71. This memo is dated 21 April.

reply to see what exact line he takes before the President makes his Dáil statement. I agree that whilst this statement should not contain as many direct and friendly references to the North-Easterners as the statement of the 6th December, it would not be polite not to make some reference to the Government's friendly intentions towards the Belfast Government. It would at least maintain the continuity of the consistently friendly policy of the Government to the Belfast Government.

'FESTINA LENTE' – With these two steps the issue will be very definitely and very decidedly joined. We may expect ominous rumblings from Belfast and much solemn pledging of what they will or will not do in the event of certain circumstances. We must, at this period, keep resolutely the level and calm attitude that we have adopted since the advent of this Administration. Nothing is more baffling, nothing more cooling for the excitable Belfast temperament than this calm, objective, temperate and somewhat aloof attitude. As I have said before our motto must be 'festina lente!', giving plenty of time for the significance of every step in the game to sink deeply in. Time is now on our side. Three months ago it was on the side of Sir James Craig. It is for us now to use this valuable weapon of time to our best advantage.

After the President's statement the next important step – unless before that time a London Conference is suggested – will be the nomination of our Boundary Commissioner.

About this I have already said something in my last Memo. and will say nothing further here. The game we are playing, or will be playing, in connection with this matter of the Boundaries, is very definitely, decidedly and undisguisedly *a political game*, and as such we should not hesitate to use politics to help us. The most ideal way to go about the task would be to work steadily along, step by step, and then, after giving latitude for much discussion on possible Commissioners, appoint, on the eve of the Election, our Commissioner, and after this dynamic stroke go to the country. There is no doubt that such a stroke at such a time would enormously benefit the Government at the hustings; and, as I have said before, it is essential to have this Government returned if this North-East Question is to be dealt with in a sane and statesmanlike fashion.

However, it is problematical at this moment whether we will be able to hold back the functioning of the Commission until after the Elections, if the Elections will not take place until September or October.

Personally, I would not like to see the Commission actually sitting when the Government was making its appeal to the country. Much valuable negotiation time would thereby be lost, as it is not likely that the British Government would make proposals of a considerable nature to a Government which was not in existence and which, as far as it knew, may not be in existence. Then again, were the Commission operating whilst the Government was at the country it is impossible to say what trick or decision might be played or made.

If possible, our Commissioner should be appointed, but the Commission *should not sit until the return of the Government*, and in the meantime one of the strong planks at the Election should be the Boundary Commission, or the complete implementing of the Treaty.

Returned on this issue (amongst others) our position would be enormously strengthened, and we could confidently look forward to seeing something definite and enduring accomplished.

10. *POINTS OF VIEW ON THE BOUNDARY COMMISSION*
Ministers may not be aware that there are no less than four definite and distinct opinions in Ireland on the Boundary Commission, its usages and disadvantages, etc.

(a) There is the view-point – which is the Government's view-point – that the next great milestone to be reached in the progress of this Nation is the achievement of complete *National Union*. The advocates of this viewpoint consider everything in connection with Northern policy subordinate to this achievement.

Whether they are psychological Republicans or not – hoping to see Ireland termed *'Poblacht'* at some future time – they consider the chief advantage of the Treaty position is to enable them to halt a little on the way in order to get their separated countrymen united to them before they march forward to the ultimate goal.

(b) There is the point of view of people who consider that the next milestone must be, *not* National Union, but the ejection from the Constitution of that nefarious conglomeration of words called the 'Oath of Allegiance', and also sundry other demoniacal but utterly powerless phrases referring to a person called the King and expressing the right of Citizens of the Saorstát to appeal to the British Council – all precedental deadletters.

These people who are in mental affinity with Irregular philosophy are hoping against hope that there will be a crash of the first magnitude with regard to the Boundary Commission, e.g., that Craig will refuse to nominate his Commissioner or that the Commission will not deal fairly with us. In these events their view is that it should go forth to the World that we have been let down and betrayed on the Treaty, and that we should thereupon repudiate the entire Treaty and set to work ourselves to eject[1] the objectionable features from the Constitution. Persons of this school with whom I have had conversations are avowedly more anxious for this consummation out of the Boundary Commission than for the consummation of National Union. The idea behind their reasoning is, 'far better to get us all united in Saorstát first before we consider the North-Eastern position'.

This opinion has many adherents amongst the official opposition. Ministers can see that there are possibilities in this course should the dice be weighted against us in the ultimate.

(c) There is the point of view of the North-Eastern Irredentists, who cannot see farther than the sheer carrying out of the Boundary Commission as soon as possible, and who are mainly concerned with the inclusion within the Free State of their own Parish.

Their reasoning is that Partition is odious, and a crime and that if it is to exist they have a *right* to get out of the partitioned area as soon as possible. When confronted with the argument 'What of those who will be left behind?',

[1] The word originally was 'reject', but the 'r' has been crossed out.

they reply, 'It is to their advantage that "Northern Ireland" should be cut down to a minimum, as it cannot hold out without a hinterland and is bound to come in'. They regard themselves as the real advocates of National Unity.

(d) There is the point of view of the East Ulster Nationalists who are avowedly in favour of scrapping the Boundary Commission and accepting a compromise co-operation settlement with Craig. Their reasons for this are chiefly the opposite reasons to the people in (c). In other words, they realise that no possible Boundary Commission could possibly get them out, and that therefore their best interests are served by having as big a hinterland of people of their own way of thinking as possible.

These people have also a less altruistic but none the less potent reason for this point of view. It is this. They know full well that it is only within a North-Eastern area that their discredited politico-sectarian A.O.H. will get a chance to recuperate and support 'leaders' of the type of Mr. John D. Nugent in place and in power.

In their heart of hearts many of these people, in spite of their utterances, are really not anxious for the advent of National Union at all.

These are the four schools of thought on this Boundary issue amongst the people for whom the Government can speak.

11. *A POSSIBLE CONFERENCE AND OUR PROPOSAL*

As I have said we are angling for and hoping for the maturing of a position when the British Government, either because it realises the dangers itself, or because it will have become aware of them owing to pressure exerted through our propaganda, will invite both Free State and Belfast to London to a Conference to see what better plan than the Boundary Commission can be arranged. Should this Conference come off it will be second only in importance to the Treaty of London. It will in itself partake of something in the nature of a second Peace Conference and may probably sit for weeks and even months before it hammers out an enduring settlement.

But given the Fact of the Conference and the existence of the present Government, I have no doubt whatever that if we manoeuvre the 'Problem of Ulster' at this stage to a Round Table Conference in London the representatives of the various interests and countries will not rise from that table without having worked out a new Treaty of Settlement – this time amongst Irishmen with England possibly as a Guaranteeing Power in order to soothe North-Eastern susceptibilities, and I cannot see any reason why that settlement should not be based on *National Union*.

We should be prepared to meet that time – prepared to have a number of well-drafted proposals ready to set before that Conference, our minimum terms to be exposed first and then so on to our maximum – unless (which is not likely) they accept some one or other of the intermediaries.

(N.B. At the present moment we are drafting a number of proposals in the Bureau to meet this contingency.)

FEDERAL UNION
It is my belief that unless something very wonderful occurs National Union must first take a Federal form. We cannot expect Belfast to relinquish altogether its Government (of which it is so proud) and become merged in us. Besides, there are sufficient differences to justify an autonomous Parliament in that corner of Ireland. There will have to be mutual concessions on the Minorities point, and probably, if it is urged, on [the] Educational point. And it is quite possible that such a change in our present order will compel us to alter our Constitution somewhat.

THE OBJECTIVE
National Union, and not the Boundary Commission, nor the removal of objectionable portions of the Free State Constitution is, therefore, our next great objective. The Government that reaches this goal will live in history as the Government that performed the greatest piece of initial statesmanship in Ireland and laid the most solid and enduring foundations of peace.

It is my belief that this immortal achievement is within the grasp of the present Government. This indeed would be a splendid Crown to its successes.

[stamped] CAOÍMHGHÍN Ó SÍÁDHAIL
Assistant Legal Adviser

No. 87 UCDA P80/520

Hugh Kennedy to Joseph P. Walshe (Dublin)
(298/23)

DUBLIN, 4 June 1923

A Chara,[1]
1. I have your minute of the 31st ultimo,[2] with reference to the legislation complementary to our application for admission to the League of Nations.
2. In my opinion, a very simple Act will fulfil the requirements of Article 1 of the Covenant of the League of Nations, which provides that an applicant for admission must give effective guarantees of its sincere intention to observe its national obligations and must accept such regulations as may be prescribed by the League in regard to its military, naval and air forces and armaments.
3.[3] I suggest that the first requisite before settling the draft Bill is to procure from our representative at Geneva information as to the nature of the guarantees which are usually required and of the regulations which are usually imposed as a condition of admission. The Bill might then take the form of an authority to the Minister for External Affairs or to the President to give the necessary guarantees and undertakings, but it is obvious that these should be specified as far as possible before the Parliament can be asked to pass the measure.

---

[1] Handwritten note by Walshe: 'Phelan writing in ref[eren]ce to the nature of the guarantees and obligations.' S.P.B.
[2] Not located.
[3] This paragraph has been highlighted by a pencil line down the right margin.

4. Having obtained the information, the Minister should present his proposals as fully as possible to the Ministry of Finance for sanction and, having obtained sanction of that Ministry, should submit the proposals or, if possible, the Bill in draft for approval. If approved, the Bill can then be sent to the Parliamentary Draftsman, and it will probably be found convenient to introduce the Bill in the first instance in the Senate.
5. As soon as the Minister has the proposals in a tangible form, I am sure that the Parliamentary Draftsman will be happy to make an appointment with him to discuss the form of the Bill in detail.

Mise, le meas mór,
[signed] AODH UA CINNÉIDIGH
(HUGH KENNEDY)
Ard-Aturnae

No. 88 NAI DT S1801C

Extract from minutes of a meeting of the Executive Council
(C.1/116)

DUBLIN, 5 June 1923

NORTH EAST ULSTER.
1. Mr. Kevin O'Shiel submitted a statement[1] with reference to the case to be made by the Free State before the Boundary Commission and illustrated his points by reference to maps, diagrams etc. prepared by the North East Boundary Bureau.

He indicated a suggested Boundary line, the effect of which, if established, would be to give to the Free State, all Ireland except Co. Antrim, the extreme north east corner of Co. Derry, portion of north and mid Armagh (excluding Armagh city) and north and mid Co. Down. This might be regarded as the *maximum* claim of the Free State.

He indicated also a second Boundary line, the establishment of which would give to the Free State, all Ireland except Co. Antrim, the extreme east portion of Co. Tyrone bordering on Lough Neagh, the eastern half of Co. Derry, the northern portion of Co. Armagh and the northern portion of Co. Down. This should be regarded as the minimum claim of the Free State beyond which they could not recede.

These suggested lines were approved for the purpose of aiding the Boundary Bureau in preparing a case for the Boundary Commission, but not necessarily as the actual basis for the ultimate presentation of the case.

2. It was decided further that a letter[2] should be addressed by the President to the Prime Minister of Great Britain informing him that the Irish Government were now ready to present their case to the Boundary Commission and that it was their intention to send a formal communication on the subject to the British Government at an early date.

[1] See above No. 84.
[2] See below No. 89.

The Attorney General was instructed to prepare a draft letter for the President's signature and to submit it to the Executive Council at its next meeting.

3. Mr. O'Shiel mentioned also that the Boundary Bureau had in course of preparation a Hand-book on the Ulster question with special reference to the Boundary question.

He was authorised to include in the book, a map of Ulster and the surrounding areas indicating the population – ratios in the Six Counties for and against the inclusion of the Free State. It was emphasised that any reference to Ulster should clearly indicate that this title refers to the whole province of Nine Counties, and that 'Northern Ireland' consists of only six of these counties and has no title whatever to the name of Ulster.

No. 89 NAI DT S1801C

William T. Cosgrave to Stanley Baldwin (London)
(Copy)

DUBLIN, 9 June 1923

Dear Prime Minister,

Immediately upon the Houses of the Parliament of Northern Ireland presenting an address pursuant to Article 12 of the Anglo-Irish Treaty which had the effect of suspending the powers of the Government and Parliament of the Free State in the Six North-Eastern Counties of Ulster, the Government of the Free State took in hands the preparation of the case to be submitted on our behalf to the Boundary Commission constituted under the same Article. Our preparations are nearing completion and we shall be very soon in a position to announce to you the name of the Commissioner we are nominating and to ask that the Commission proceed with its task.

I am aware that many within the Six Counties, whose interests before the Commission are common with ours, have also been steadily working at their cases for inclusion in the area under the authority of the Government and Parliament of the Free State and I believe that they are ready, or practically ready, to meet the Commission.

I assume that any interests adverse to ours have similarly got to work since the presentation of the addresses made the Commission inevitable, but my colleagues and I think it fair to you that I should let you know a little in advance that a formal request that the Commission proceed will be made shortly on our part. There will thus be a greater opportunity of considering the personnel of the Commission so far as its nomination rests with the British Government and the Government of Northern Ireland and any hitch or delay upon the receipt of our formal note may be avoided.

Yours sincerely,
[signed] L.T. MACCOSGAIR

No. 90 UCDA P80/385

S. Ó hOgáin to Desmond FitzGerald (Dublin)

DUBLIN, 11 June 1923

A Chara,

I regret my inability to return Professor Smiddy's papers earlier, but to-day was the first opportunity I got of reading them at my leisure.

I have attached a list of reports of which I would be obliged to have copies or extracts for permanent reference.

These reports are undoubtedly valuable in so far as they reveal the revival of Fenianism amongst a section in New York who are apparently thinking in terms of a personal vendetta against the chief opponents of Irregularism. It is not easy to appraise the exact value of the reports from this point of view. For instance the agent's admission to work an extremely exclusive circle was too easy, and obviously many of the statements made in his presence from time to time are exaggerations. At the same time this does not affect the importance of his reports. Making all allowances it looks as if a secret organisation was being set up, and as if members were thinking along the lines of continued physical action.

So long as we hold the irregular leaders as prisoners I believe we have hostages against anything in the nature of assassination, but in proportion to the completeness of their defeat the irregulars will have recourse to secret organisation. Necessity will compel them to this course, and apart from your reports I have reason to think that they are remodelling their broken organisation on a secret basis.

One assertion which lends credence to the genuineness of the reports is the intention to restrict the numbers of the organisation. The Irregulars have probably learned enough by experience to know that secrets cannot be confided to a great number, and if they organise on a small secret scale I can see very serious difficulty in penetrating their organisation at home.

Now your agent seems to offer a possible means of penetration at least in America, and it would be to my mind a vital mistake not to work him for all he is worth. If we have an agent within the secret irregular organisation in America we will have made a great stride.

It will be possible through him not only to keep in touch with their programme but also to work up connections in Ireland. An agent in important irregular circles in America is at a point d'appui because the irregulars are bound to use America extensively for finance and owing to the freedom with which they may organise there. Besides at home our people are much more reticent and guarded in their statements, while in America our people are talkative. For instance the British S.[ecret] S.[ervice] made much greater headway against our organisation in America than in Ireland only a few years ago.

I am strongly of opinion that the connection established by Professor Smiddy should be tried out fully, and that further Professor Smiddy should have powers to extend his activities where prospects are good.

This raises the question of control. I am not authorised to make any official proposals, but I would suggest that the regularising of all this work in America and elsewhere might with advantage be along the lines of Police Attachés to our Consulates. At the recent International Police Congress in New York such a proposal received general approval. In our case besides dealing with questions of extradition passports etc., such Police Attachés would be in a position to control Intelligence activities and could keep in direct communication with Intelligence Headquarters at home.

Such suggestions are needless to say purely informal. My authority does not extend to such matters, but Intelligence work has convinced me of the necessity of some definition on such points.

Mise, le meas,
[signed] S. Ó hOGÁIN MAJOR GENERAL
DIRECTOR OF INTELLIGENCE

No. 91 NAI DT S5685

Extracts from a letter from Edward Phelan to William T. Cosgrave (Dublin)
(Personal)

GENEVA, 22 June 1923

Dear President Cosgrave,
[Matter omitted]
During the conversation with Sir Eric Drummond the question of the method of communication between the Irish Free State and the League was touched on. I told Sir Eric that I had suggested that the best course would be for you to communicate with the League through your representative in Geneva and that the League should send its communications to you in the same way. Sir Eric saw no objection to this course being followed. As a matter of fact, the League communicates directly with Canada and Australia. So far as the International Labour Office is concerned which, as you know, is autonomous, communications pass directly from the Office to all of the British Dominions at the request of the Dominions themselves. I think it might be useful if a letter were addressed to the League indicating that the method of communication through your representative in Geneva is the one which you would prefer to be followed.
[Matter omitted]

I have already sent to Mr. Kennedy a certain amount of information regarding the detailed organisation of the work of the Assembly and I am preparing certain further information for him on points of procedure which he raised during my conversations with him. Needless to say I shall be glad to afford him or any of the members of the Irish administration any information or assistance in my power which may be of use in connection with the preparations for the arrival of the Irish Delegation in Geneva.
[Matter omitted]

Yours very sincerely,
[signed] E.J. PHELAN

No. 92 UCDA P4/859

Hugh Kennedy to Arthur Matheson[1] *(Dublin)*

DUBLIN, 23 June 1923

1. In confirmation of our discussion on the subject of the Bill relating to the League of Nations, I have to say that the Minister of External Affairs sent forward his proposal for a Bill at my request. Under the Covenant of the League of Nations, of which I have lent you a print, you will observe that it is provided that applicants for admission must give effective guarantees of their intention to carry out their international obligations, and also must give undertakings to comply with international regulations for the restriction of armaments.
2. It occurred to me that if Parliament had not sanctioned the giving, by the Executive Council, of such guarantees and undertakings, any nation which was not well disposed to our admission to the League might raise it as an objection and cause the postponement of our admission for another year. I think, therefore, such a Bill is required.
3. There is a further reason why such a Bill should be presented at an early date and it is this that it will enable each House of the Oireachtas by its vote on the Bill to give its approval to the action of the Executive in applying for admission. The Senate has already shown some jealousy in the matter.
4. My view of the Bill is that it should be a very short enabling Bill and that it need not go into the details under the several headings set out in the letter from the Ministry.
5. I think it should commence with a recital of the fact that application for admission was made by the Executive Council. I think it should recite the clause of the Covenant of the League of Nations which requires the guarantees and undertakings, and it should then enact in the first section a provision that it be lawful for the Executive Council to give the guarantees, and in the second section that it be lawful for the Executive Council to enter into the necessary undertakings. It does not seem to me that anything more than this is required.

[copy letter unsigned]
(HUGH KENNEDY)
Attorney General

No. 93 NAI DFA Letter Books (Department of the President 1923-28)

Joseph P. Walshe to Diarmuid O'Hegarty (Dublin)
(P/54/23)

DUBLIN, 30 June 1923

A Chara,

KERNEY'S POSITION

With reference to the President's note to the Minister of External Affairs, I am instructed to state that our Representative in Paris is known to and recognised by the French Government and the British Embassy in Paris.

Consular powers have not yet been acquired by any of our Representatives

[1] Parliamentary Draftsman.

but the question has been raised with Mr. Curtis and an early favourable solution is expected.

Mr. Murphy approached the French Government three months ago with a view to putting an end to Kerney's activities. While expressing readiness to assist the Free State Government in every possible way, the Quai d'Orsay officials told Mr. Murphy that it was unusual to take cognisance of foreign political agitators so long as their activities did not endanger the good relations between the French Government and the foreign Government concerned.

Kerney's consular and diplomatic powers are purely subjective. They interest nobody except the readers of the Parisian weekly funny Press. He is not received by the French Authorities.

The 'Irish and Foreign Trading Corporation' has only itself to blame for such accidents, if it addresses letters in English without indicating street or number to a City of over three million inhabitants.

The Minister will be very glad to give the President any further explanation should he require it.

Le meas,
[copy letter unsigned]
Rúnaí

No. 94 NAI DT S5685

W.T. Cosgrave to Edward Phelan (Geneva)

DUBLIN, 4 July 1923

Dear Mr. Phelan,

I was very pleased to hear from you and to learn that your interest in Ireland and in our approaching membership of the League had remained as lively as during your visit to us.

While I should like very much to be quite certain of going to Geneva for the Assembly, I can not yet foresee events with sufficient clearness to be able to say that I am definitely going.

I appreciate very much Sir Eric Drummond's kindly anticipation of my visit and I am looking forward to meeting him as well as our good friends General Smuts[1] and Mr. Mackenzie King.[2] We shall doubtless have many things to discuss together about the relations of the Nations of the Commonwealth to each other and to the League.

With regard to the method of communication between the Irish Government and the League, I must confess to feeling surprised that any other method than the direct should have been contemplated.

New Zealand alone of the Commonwealth Nations made a formal request to the League that the channel should be the Colonial Office.

We have made no such request and by making our original application for admission through Mr. MacWhite we indicated clearly the channel through which we desired communications to be sent.

Mr. FitzGerald is considering the question of sending one or two officials to

[1] Jan Christian Smuts, Prime Minister of South Africa (1919-24).
[2] William Lyon Mackenzie King, Prime Minister of Canada (1921-26, 1926-30).

Geneva some time before the Assembly meets. They will be very glad to avail of your kind offer of assistance.

Yours very sincerely,
[copy letter unsigned]

No. 95 NAI DFA ES Box 28 File 185

Unknown[1] *to Timothy A. Smiddy (Dublin)*
(Private and Confidential)
WASHINGTON, 10 July 1923

Dear Professor Smiddy:
I had a visit last evening from Lieut. Gegan: he has been making some special investigations for me about the C—C—. He had a long interview with Archbishop Hayes who was very much interested and also very sympathetic. The Archbishop said he would find out all he could do to help us and greatly appreciated the fact that we did not want any publicity; he said that he had already forbidden any secret meetings to be held in any church; also that no Priest's name was to appear on any programme or pamphlet. In a few days after this interview the Archbishop sent for the Lieut. and told him that he had summoned the Priests whom he knew to be Irregulars and bound them by a solemn oath not to divulge anything he would say to them; he then asked them if they had any ammunition stored in Church, gymnasium, or school, or anything that they had no legal right to store. They said that there was nothing there *now* and promised that there never would be anything from now on. The Archbishop said that he was doing his best to keep the Irregular Priests down. He went on to say that the Irish Free State had his whole hearted support and he was pleased to see they had made so much headway already. He stated that he was willing at any time to do what he could to help us.

He also told the Lieut. that Mrs H. Skeffington had called on him, and had asked him to issue an appeal to all congregations for money to help the widows and orphans of the Irish Republicans. This the Archbishop refused to do and said that he had no sympathy with the Irregulars and he would not be a party to raising funds to buy ammunition and guns. He was next worried by a delegation of men (Irregulars); and to use his own words he said 'he never saw such a tough looking lot in his life'.

The Archbishop said that the Irregulars would be a hard lot to get rid of, and was sure they would do their best to rise again 'so long as they had so many well paid loafers among them'.

The Lieut. spoke about the 318-11-6[2] and said that he had now no following worth talking about, and that he would not trust him very far; he is a power loving man who wants to be everything. I was interested to hear the Lieut. thus express himself. On the other hand I was not surprised as I have had the same opinion myself. The Lieut. has not seen 'Plaster' for some considerable time and does not talk of him as he used to. Perhaps, he, too, has got tired of his stupidity.

---

[1] Possibly one of Smiddy's agents.
[2] Code, no cipher known.

I enclose a letter sent to Judge Cohalan by some of the Irregulars. Mr Crawford wants to have it photographed but I did not think it was worth the trouble; it may be that the name is familiar to the Intelligence Department.

Yours sincerely,
[copy letter unsigned]

No. 96 NAI DT S1801C

Memorandum on the Boundary Commission
circulated to each member of the Executive Council, with covering letter
by Diarmuid O'Hegarty

DUBLIN, 6.00pm, 11 July 1923

A Chara,
In accordance with the suggestion made at the Cabinet Meeting held yesterday, a memorandum regarding the arguments advanced in connection with the proposed issue of a formal letter on the Boundary Commission to the British Government is transmitted herewith for your information.

Mise, le meas,
[copy letter unsigned]
Rúnaí

[enclosure]
SECRET AND CONFIDENTIAL.
BOUNDARY COMMISSION – Memorandum.

1. The following memorandum is intended merely as an outline of the arguments for and against immediately forwarding an official request to the British Government to have the terms of Clause 12 of the Treaty put into operation.
2. Representations have been made to the President from various sources that the present time (within the next 12 months) is not opportune for pressing for the carrying out of this Clause. These sources have been The Governor General, certain Railway Directors, and others. The Railway people feel that advantage could be taken of the Railway situation in Ireland to secure the unity of the country. They have not made any clear case as to how this could be effected beyond the suggestion that it might be done through Railway Grouping and through pressure on Railways partly within the Six Counties. The Governor General is concerned by the fact that in the opinion of a leading personage in political and journalistic circles in England, the late Prime Minister[1] of that country is not favourably disposed towards the Boundary question, and that as long as he wields his present influence, quarters that might otherwise be friendly will not be inclined to assist us openly.
3. There is general agreement that certain progress must have been made in the matter of the Boundary Commission before the coming General Election. It is anticipated that this election will take place early in September (about six

[1] Andrew Bonar Law.

or seven weeks from now). There is no difference of opinion amongst Ministers as to the necessity for having matters at a pretty advanced stage as regards the setting up of the Commission by that time, and a semi-official communication on the subject is already on the British Cabinet Agenda. The possibility of protracted delay before taking the preliminary steps cannot therefore be entertained.

4. The matter in immediate question is whether the formal official request should be issued at once or whether it should be delayed until about the first of August. The whole matter depends upon the rapidity or otherwise with which events will move once the official request has been formulated.

5. On this there exists divergent views, some being of opinion that events will progress rapidly, and that if the official letter were delayed until August 1st the situation at the time of the election would be somewhat as follows:- The British Government would have noted the request and agreed to do its part to fulfil the contract and possibly would have elected the Chairman. It would in all probability have notified the Northern Government of the intention to proceed with the Commission, but the Northern Government would probably not have replied. The possibility of the opponents of the Government being furnished with ammunition by Craig's refusal to nominate a representative would thus be obviated, and the Government would not be faced either immediately before or during the election with the necessity of formulating and disclosing its future policy in the event of Craig's refusal. On the other hand the Government should go to the country with the statement that they had taken the necessary originating steps and with their representative appointed.

6. Other members feel that there is no likelihood of rapid progress being made in the setting up of the Commission. They fear that there will be extended delays at every stage. The British Government will take no action until the formal letter has been received by them; when it has been received they will not rush a decision; the consideration at the Cabinet will be prolonged; and it may easily happen that no satisfactory progress will have been made by Election time. This, they urge, would be disastrous as their opponents would make great capital out of the assertion that the Government were taking no action in the matter.

7. Government supporters are becoming anxious at our delay. Hitherto it was understood that we could not be expected to move until we had restored normal conditions in the 26 Counties, but now that things are almost normal all over our area, this excuse no longer holds.

8. Even if things move so rapidly that the Irish and British Governments have appointed their representatives and that Craig's reply has been received they urge that this will be all to the good. Any reply from Craig will strengthen the Government's hands – if he consents to appoint his Commissioner, it will be of advantage – if he refuses, the Government will be in a position to call upon the electorate to rally to their support in their efforts to compel the terms of the Treaty to be carried out.

9. The Ministers who hold these latter views urge strongly that the official letter in the matter should issue without delay.

10.The President has placed Mr. Ormsby Gore[1] in possession of his views that the Government could not go to an election until the Irish representatives and the Chairman had both been appointed. This is a further argument for immediately taking up the question formally with the British Government.

No. 97 NAI DFA ES Box 37

Extracts from a letter from Michael MacWhite to Desmond FitzGerald (Dublin)
(N.S. 77/23)

GENEVA, 12 July 1923

A Chara,
I enclose you a number of Legal and Diplomatic Documents which it is necessary to submit to the Fourth Assembly of the League of Nations in connection with the application of the Free State for admission.[2] I have gone thoroughly into the matter with the Legal Advisers of the League and discussed the contents of these documents with them. They suggested that as the Treaty, from the English point of view, is one between Great Britain and Ireland so, from the Irish point of view, it is between Ireland and Great Britain and should figure accordingly on our documents.

Now, it will be necessary to have those documents printed in pamphlet form, about the same size as that of the 'Parliamentary Debates'. It must be in Irish, English and French as the latter two are the official languages of the League. The Irish part should be in Gaelic type as, otherwise, it has no significance for foreigners.

[Matter omitted]

The Booklet should be well turned out as from a propaganda standpoint, outside altogether of its legal and diplomatic aspect, it will be invaluable. Each language should form a separate part, but the title could appear in the three on the cover.

[Matter omitted]

Is mise, le meas,
[signed] M. MACWHITE

No. 98 NAI DFA Letter Books (Paris 1923-24)

Osmonde Grattan Esmonde to Sean Murphy (Paris)

DUBLIN, 27 July 1923

A Chara,
As you are already aware, most of the prominent Powers have recently appointed, or are about to appoint, Consuls-General in Dublin to look after their relations with the Irish Free State. Within the last two months the Belgian and Argentine representatives have arrived, and the Italian Consul has been promoted to the higher status.

[1] Parliamentary Under Secretary of State for the Colonies.
[2] Not printed.

We understand that Germany has appointed her Consul-General who is expected in the near future.

With the suppression of the Rebellion and the happy return to normal conditions, the social life of the Capital is reviving, and it would be a source of much regret to the Irish Government if in the usual official functions and ceremonies the Representative of France should be precluded because of his rank from taking the privileged place of honour which is his due and which the Government is so anxious to give him.

The Minister would be very glad if you could bring this matter to the notice of the Ministry of Foreign Affairs, and at the same time acquaint them of the very high regard – and indeed affection – in which M. Alfred Blanche is held, not only in official circles but among all sections of the Community.

Taking into consideration the friendly relations of the Free State with the British Government, and our admitted right to intervene in the conduct of British Foreign Policy, there are probably many other aspects of the case which might strike you and to which you might refer when bringing the matter to the notice of the French Authorities.

Le meas,
[copy letter unsigned]
O.G. Esmonde

No. 99 NAI DT S3332

Seán McEoin to William T. Cosgrave (Dublin)
Athlone, 19 July 1923

Sir,
As promised in our conversation on Friday night last I send you hereunder what is necessary for us to do for our Consuls.
(1) To send a letter to him authorising him to act on behalf of An Saorstát at the League of Nations.
(2) To instruct him that all letters for the League of Nations would be sent through him from you, and that he was to receive all letters for you from the League of Nations same as Canada and South Africa.

These at the moment are the most important things requiring immediate attention. The next is for us to suppress the Visas same as England has done to England for Swiss people or subject. At the moment the condition of affairs are for a Swiss to come to England he requires no Pass Port or Visa. For Swiss to come to Ireland he had to apply to the British Consul in Switzerland and pay £1 (one pound) or in other words England is acting as the toll or gatekeeper of the road to Ireland. This can be stopped at once by our Minister suppressing the Visa.

The next important item is for at least a Delegation of six to be appointed for the League of Nations with six substitutes. One of the advantages that is to [be] gained is that we can always send one of these men to the Government of any Nation and that they must be received as an Ambassador should be received, being a Delegate of the League of Nations. These Delegates will take with them copies of the Treaty, Constitution, Acts by both Parliaments ratifying the Treaty. These should be brought first for registry in the League of Nations, and secondly copy to be given to each Delegate from each Country. There are 52 Countries represented at the League of Nations, so for this purpose 100 copies would at least be necessary. This is part propaganda and to inform the Nations of the World as to what actually our Status amongst the Nations of the World really is.

The next thing that is mentioned is that you make special arrangements for this Delegation with reference to travelling to the League of Nations viz. that each Delegate is served with a copy as to his appointment as Delegate to the League of Nations, so that he travels under a sort of what is known as Diplomatic Pass Port and surely not what I travelled under.

The next thing to be done is to immediately instruct MacWhite to retain Hotel accommodation for the Delegates in Geneva, as if we let it go any longer it will be very difficult to get place, and you must have a decent place. When admission is gained to the League of Nations our first speech must be in Irish, of which you will have two translations, one in English and one in French. It would be wise that the second speech be in French and the third in English, so as to show the world, that we are Statesmen equal to any Nation of the World.

This is nearly all the information I got about the matter, with the exception that all the different groups of the small Nations are very friendly to us, and I think Mr. MacWhite has written a Memo on this matter to the Minister of Foreign Affairs. Sir Eric Drummond, President of the League of Nations was very pleased with MacWhite's statement to the Press after application to the League of Nations. I know for a fact that it has caused France to become doubly friendly to Ireland, and made all the rest of the small Nations start to ask about Ireland, because up to the issue of that statement, they were all of the opinion that Ireland coming into the League of Nations simply meant another vote to England. MacWhite's statement opened their eyes to the fact that this was not so.

It is also suggested that we immediately start to ratify separately some of the Treaties between the different groups of Nations for instance Opium Treaty for the prevention of Drug traffic, the White Slave Traffic, and all these various Treaties that are registered between the different groups of Nations, of which each Nation must subscribe independently. It seems at the moment that we are taking no steps in the matter simply because England is a party to the Treaties that I mention, and that some of our Solicitors maintain that England having ratified, it is not necessary for us to do so.

I wish to point out that it is the United Kingdom that has ratified them, which at the moment thank God only refers to Great Britain and a little spot on the North East corner of Ireland, and therefore is another step forward in our International Status, as the National ratification by us independently of each of these Treaties would have a widespread effect and would place us high in the limelight as an Independent Nation. I attach a memo by the International Law Adviser to the League of Nations.[1] I do not think it is necessary to make any explanation of it as it thoroughly explains itself, with the exception of the

[1] Not located.

five points raised in para 3. and under one and two headings.

Having more or less described this to you verbally I wish to point out that Canada has broken practically with England on the 1st. and 2nd. point mentioned and that for to raise our own status as Canada raised hers we must support Canada in this action at the Imperial Conference. I also attach translation of an article from a French Paper 'L'OEUVRE' on the 27th. June.

I wish to impress very strongly on you all the points raised in this letter as I feel the matter very keenly and as I have pointed out to you in our conversation for good or evil a certain amount of responsibility of the Treaty to Ireland rests upon my shoulders. I therefore believe that it is incumbent for me to see that Ireland gets every inch and ounce of freedom out of the Treaty that can be got out of it, and that as pointed out in memo attached we must under no circumstance let England or the Northern Government round off any of the corners, but that instead that we push them out and take the full benefit of it including the Boundary Commission of which England is a party to and must uphold and interpret in the spirit in which the Treaty was written.

I know well that it is only necessary to draw your attention to these matters to have them made right.

Yours to Command
[signed] Seán McEoin
Major Genl
G.O.C. Troops Athlone Command

P.S.
I forgot to mention the fact that it would be well if you appointed some good lawyer to watch the development of all the other Dominions and to keep you posted and informed upon the different precedents as they are created. You will kindly note that attention to this matter is drawn in the memo.

[initialled] SM

No. 100 NAI DFA ES Box 16 File 106(4)

Memorandum on the Boundary Question to each member of the Executive Council by Kevin O'Shiel

Dublin, 19 July 1923

OMINOUS ACTIVITIES ON PARTS OF THE NORTH-EASTERN BORDER

1. *Belfast Government Police Circulars* – Some time ago we received information from an authentic source that two confidential circulars from the Office of the Inspector General of the Ulster Constabulary had been despatched on the 31st May and the 1st June respectively to the various Border-County headquarters of that Force.

The earlier of these circulars declared that the 'Northern Government was determined to resist the Boundary Commission, if supported properly by the Imperial Government', and requested its officials to have the opinions of prominent local Nationalists forwarded to P.R. Gilfinnane, a D.[istrict] I.[nspector] of the 'C' Specials on the G.H.Q. Staff of the Force in Belfast 'in the event of a plebiscite being decided on by the Commission'.

It is necessary to explain that 'Nationalist' in the vernacular of the Orangeman has now come to mean exclusively one who holds the view of the A.O.H. section. It was generally hoped a few months ago that the retainers of this Order might be prevailed upon to cast in their lot with the Northern Secessionists, as relationship was rather strained between them and the Sinn Féin element. That phase has now happily passed, and these people can be now relied upon to stand by us for the Treaty.

The second circular requested the County Inspector of the Police to furnish the Head Office 'without delay' with a list of the stations situated on the Border that he considered it necessary 'to have Vickers Guns planted, also the names of men in the County suitable to man same'.

2. *Provocative Actions by Specials* – Shortly after this move a recrudescence of extremely provocative conduct, reminiscent of the Border disturbances of a year ago, manifested itself amongst particular groups of Specials along the Southern Fermanagh Border.

I have already submitted some instances of this conduct for the consideration of the Executive Council, notably the instance of the wanton, wilful and most unnecessary destruction of the bridge on the Swanlinbar-Enniskillen road, and the treatment meted out to the local people who endeavoured to mend it. This has been all very clearly set out in the Memo. of Mr. Johnston of the Bureau, circulated about a week ago, who paid a special visit to the locality for investigation purposes.

The Defence Department quite lately provided further evidence of this growing 'war atmosphere' on the part of the Specials in a statement circulated recently setting forth the extraordinary treatment of a number of Co. Waterford pilgrims (men and women) on their way to Lough Derg. This occurrence took place at Garrison and Belleek, if I remember right.

3. *Treatment of Our Chief Customs Officer at Clones* – I am able to supply a still further and very bad instance in the copy attached letter of Mr. P. McCartan, our Chief Customs Officer at Clones, to his brother Mr. Hugh A. McCartan, our publicity agent in the Bureau.[1]

Ministers may remember that recently at my request Mr. H.A. McCartan paid a visit to Clones in order to enable me to supply Ministers with an accurate account of the Twelfth celebrations in the Free State. The man Robinson complained of, Mr. McCartan tells me, watched both his and his brother's movements all that day. Mr. McCartan in a covering note to me comments aptly as follows:-

'You will see that the letter more than confirms all that I have said in my reports regarding the offensive and provocative conduct of the Specials on the Border. It seems to me that these people are deliberately trying to stir up trouble. If one of our people in the Six Counties had acted as Mr. Robinson did he would be promptly arrested and placed on the "Argenta". The press has been silent on this episode so far, but it might be considered whether the facts should

[1] Not printed.

be conveyed to it. The contrast between the Free State attitude towards the Orange procession and the "Specials" treatment of a Free State official and clergyman is very marked. Sir James Craig may not be aware that the conduct of the Border "Specials" is the only real danger to peace'.

4. *Object of all this* – I think we can no longer shut our eyes to the fact that the Specials, acting very obviously on instructions from some superior quarter, are now deliberately endeavouring once again to stir up trouble along the delicate and dangerous Border regions. With commendable 'restraint' they have remained quiet and inoffensive for months past, and now for no apparent reason (for the Border was never freer from trouble than it is to-day) their whole attitude undergoes an immediate and sudden change.

The object of all this is obviously to create a position of actual warfare along the Border so that they will be able to assert, as they did last year under similar circumstances with considerable success (see the 'Times' 'Daily Mail' of the period) that they are being attacked from the South, who are trying to indulge in Korfanty[1] tactics, and so prejudice the Commission's findings in their favour.

Instances have recently re-occurred of continued firings at night into the Free State by gangs of armed Specials.

All this is very sinister and I am strongly of the view that representation should be made to the Duke.[2] For, if this dangerous humour continues there is bound to be a conflagration on the Border in a short time, and then Craig may get the entire ear of the Duke. It would be well, therefore, for us to make some representation now, so that we could get, as it were, our say in first. And we could not choose a better moment for this, with such excellent evidence now quite fresh.

5. *Troops Along the Border* – May I suggest that it would be a very good thing if, from this on, our side of the Border was guarded by our best, most reliable and most seasoned troops, as it is more than likely that our men there will be submitted to a great test of patience and endurance before the Boundary negotiations are over.

It would be well that no troops (or as few as possible) who are natives of the Province of Ulster should be stationed along Frontier Posts, as human nature being as it is their naturally strong Irredentist sentiments may at an awkward moment get the better of them with disastrous consequences.

[stamped] CAOÍMHGHÍN Ó SÍADAIL
Assistant Legal Adviser

---

[1] Wojciech Korfanty (1873-1939) Polish politician. Originator of the Korfanty Line, a Polish-German boundary in Upper Silesia. The line was never accepted as the official border, but provided a basis for a compromise border, which was less favourable to the Poles. Forces led by Korfanty occupied the German section of Silesia in May 1921, until they were forced out by British troops.

[2] The Duke of Devonshire, the Secretary of State for the Colonies.

No. 101 NAI DT S1801C

T.M. Healy to the Duke of Devonshire (London)
DUBLIN, 19 July 1923

My Lord Duke:
I have the honour to refer to the terms of Article 12 of the Treaty between Great Britain and Ireland signed on 6th December, 1921,[1] and to acquaint Your Grace that, pursuant thereto, my Ministers have nominated Dr. Eoin MacNeill, T.D. Minister for Education and a member of the Executive Council, to be the representative of the Government of the Irish Free State upon the Commission which is to determine the boundaries between Northern Ireland and the rest of Ireland as provided therein.
2. My Ministers desire me to request Your Grace to be good enough to move His Majesty's Government to take the necessary steps on their part for constituting the said Commission.

I have the honour to be,
My Lord Duke,
Your Grace's most obedient,
humble Servant,
(Sd.) T.M. HEALY

No. 102 NAI DFA ES Box 29 File 189(5)

Lindsay Crawford to Timothy A. Smiddy (Dublin)
NEW YORK, 23 July 1923

Dear Mr. Smiddy:
Mrs. Skeffington sailed from Montreal last week by the 'Empress', that calls at Liverpool.

Our friend Jerome called here on Saturday. He had one of his usual fairy tales about your withdrawal from the Washington Office. He is strongly of the opinion that the war will be resumed after the elections. Jerome intends visiting Ireland this summer for a more or less permanent stay in connection with some commissions he has undertaken. He will probably take his family with him.

I just learned today from Mrs. MacFeat that she has been very unwell. Apparently she is all right again.

I am glad to report that both the Clan [na Gael] and A.O.H. Conventions show a determination to stand by the Free State. The resolutions of the Clan were unanimous, as forwarded to you last mail. Joseph Mac- rallied all his forces at Montreal for the A.O.H. Convention, but he was defeated by a three to one vote. He was not there himself but was ably represented from Philadelphia and Boston. Ex-Congressman Michael Donoghue was elected President of the A.O.H. in succession to Judge Deery. Mr Donoghue is a splendid type and a great friend of the Judge. He is an out and out supporter of the Free State, and with his control of the A.O.H. monthly magazine and propaganda funds, will be a powerful influence on our side during the coming year. I saw

[1] See Appendix No. 3 for the text of the Treaty.

him on his way through here yesterday, and he told me that the enemy had left Montreal very much crestfallen.

The Irregulars are keeping up their meetings here, but they are badly divided amongst themselves, and the attendance at their meetings is very small.

Yours very truly,
[signed] LINDSAY CRAWFORD

No. 103 NAI DT S5685

Edward J. Phelan to William T. Cosgrave (Dublin)
(Personal)

GENEVA, 24 July 1923

Dear President Cosgrave,

I was very glad to get your letter of 5th July[1] and to learn that although you cannot yet be absolutely certain of being able to come to Geneva, nevertheless you hope to be able to do so on the occasion of the Assembly. I sincerely hope that circumstances will make your visit possible as the forthcoming Assembly promises to be of special interest and importance, and the presence of other Dominion Prime Ministers will render it desirable that the head of the Irish Delegation should be yourself.

I have heard from the League that they have now been officially informed that the channel of communication between them and your Government should be through your representative at Geneva and the obscurity which existed in this connection would now seem to have been cleared away. No similar communication has yet been received by the International Labour Office, but I have no doubt it will follow. As I pointed out to you during our conversation in Dublin, the International Labour Organisation is an entirely autonomous international body and the precedents created with it are of equal legal importance with those created in connection with the League.

Interest continues to be manifested in various quarters on the continent on the participation of the Free State in the Assembly. There appeared recently a very important leading article in 'L'Oeuvre', one of the most important of the Paris newspapers, of which a translation appeared in 'The Freeman' about ten days ago. I am enclosing a copy of 'The Freeman' translation in case it should have escaped your notice, as it is typical of the interest which is being displayed and of the general attitude of continental political observers.

I presume preparations are now in hand in Dublin for the organisation of the Delegation to the Assembly. Needless to say, if I can be of any assistance by furnishing you with information or in any other way, I shall only be too glad to do so. May I perhaps in this connection remind you of the importance of having ready the Free State passports for the Delegation to the Assembly? I had been hoping to see the announcement that they had been prepared but I gather from the account of a recent discussion in the Dáil that certain technical difficulties have been encountered which I hope, however, it will be possible to surmount before the departure of the Delegation.

[1] No. 94 above, actually dated 4 July.

I was specially interested in the concluding paragraph of your letter indicating that the question of sending one or two officials to Geneva before the meeting of the Assembly was under consideration by the Minister for External Affairs. I sincerely hope that it will be possible for them to come at an early date, as the interval between now and the opening of the Assembly is very short if they are to examine the working of the League machinery and return to Dublin in order to assist in the final preparations.

I have noted in the Press the formidable legislative task with which the Government and the Dáil are faced during these coming weeks, and also the vigour and efficiency of the campaign which you and other Ministers are managing nevertheless to conduct throughout the country in order that it may be better informed of the achievements under the Treaty and the work which still lies ahead. It would seem impossible for you to find time for international preoccupations, but you have already so often achieved the impossible that I am looking forward with confidence to the arrival of a Delegation which will be equipped to profit by the really extraordinary opportunity which the meeting of the Assembly will provide. I need only add how much I personally hope that you yourself will be able to head the Delegation, and I can assure you that you will meet on all sides in Geneva with the very warmest welcome.

Yours very sincerely,
[signed] E.J. PHELAN

No. 104 NAI DFA ES Box 37

Extract from a letter from Lindsay Crawford to Timothy A. Smiddy (Washington)[1]

NEW YORK, 27 July 1923

Dear Mr. Smiddy,
[Matter omitted]
While our friends remain supporters of the Free State, there is evident uneasiness at the announcement that the President will attend the League Assembly. Apart from the local arguments in favor of such a course, it is significant that on this question all factions on this side are united against the entry of Ireland. If a step has been taken which cannot be retraced, the next best thing in my judgment is for the Irish representatives to implement, by some decisive pronouncement, the statements sent out by MacWhite regarding Ireland's independence of Great Britain in the League. This can only be done in the Assembly. Much stress was laid last night by several speakers on the point, that whereas United States would enter the League with one representative, the British Empire would be represented by six votes. Including Ireland, it would mean seven votes. I can see where the League might be utilized on behalf of Irish independence – as a spectacular appeal to the world – but cannot conceive of any action that would improve her international status, seeing that India is on the same footing as the other dominions in the League, and that the jurisdiction of the League is definitely restricted in respect of

[1] See No. 81 above.

matters affecting the territorial integrity of the British Empire. All the influences at present arrayed in the United States on the side of the League are concerned in denying the charge that the British Empire has seven votes in the League, against the one that would be allowed the United States, and will do all that is possible to prevent the realization of the extra votes of the Dominions as separate and independent votes. Thus, in respect of international status, Ireland, should she enter the League, may possibly find arrayed against her the combined forces of Leaguers and anti-Leaguers in United States, in any effort to secure a separate and independent status in the League as a leverage for more extended recognition in international relations. The effect on relations at Washington cannot be underestimated. My growing conviction is that Ireland will stand better at Washington by keeping out of the League. The next President will have as definite a mandate as Harding,[1] to keep the United States out of European entanglements, and sympathy for Ireland will be considerably weakened by taking action that may be interpreted as part of the British propaganda for inducing America to break with the Washington tradition.

Yours very truly,
[signed] LINDSAY CRAWFORD

No. 105 NAI DFA ES Box 37

Michael MacWhite to Desmond FitzGerald (Dublin)
(N.S. 90/23)

GENEVA, 4 August 1923

A Chara,
I was invited yesterday to lunch with Major Abrams who is Secretary to the Sixth Commission which is to deal with the admission of Ireland. Much to my surprise there was a third party – Mr Ormsby Gore, Under Secretary for the Colonies. From what I learned afterwards the latter was responsible for the arrangement as he wished to meet me.

Needless to say the conversation turned principally on Ireland. The Under Secretary expressed himself as being greatly impressed by his visit to Dublin last month and was loud in his praise of the members of the Government who, taking the circumstances into consideration, had performed a task which was bordering on the impossible.

Referring[2] to the Boundary Commission he stated that it was a most disagreeable subject for all the three parties concerned but that President Cosgrave was quite right in raising the issue at present. He did not, however, think that the Free State was yet strong enough to absorb any great portion of Northern Ireland. He added that Carson's action in 1912 created a new situation in Ulster and that the Belfast leaders were growing more and more jealous of the more extensive liberties of the Free State. The forcing of the Boundary question might have the effect of pushing Craig and his followers to demand Dominion status which if granted would mean that the barrier between North

[1] Warren G. Harding, President of the United States of America (November 1920-2 August 1923).
[2] This paragraph has been highlighted with thick pencil lines down each margin.

and South would become permanent.

During the conversation I only made the vaguest references to the issues raised as I fully realised their importance and my own incompetence to discuss them. It seemed to me however that the English Government are very much embarrassed by the Boundary question and that he wished me to inform you of the points he raised. They did not impress me very much. On the other hand I am convinced that the more we make our weight felt abroad while this subject is under discussion the more amenable will the English Cabinet be in giving a more reasonable interpretation from our point of view, to the Boundary Commission clause of the Treaty.

Is mise, le meas,
[signed] M. MacWhite

No. 106 NAI DFA ES Box 37

Hugh Kennedy to Desmond FitzGerald (Dublin)[1]
(417/23)

Dublin, 4 August 1923

MINISTER OF EXTERNAL AFFAIRS,
Your reference 33/23:[2] I think the proper line of reply to the enquiry contained in the letter of 25th ultimo from the Secretary-General of the League of Nations would be, having expended a certain necessary quota of politeness in acknowledging the document, to mention that this country has just emerged from a state of armed rebellion directed to the overthrow of the Government; that the rebellion has failed, but that certain military measures are still requisite for the complete establishment of permanent tranquillity. Whence, as could be pointed out, it would be obvious that the present military, naval and air establishments of the Irish Free State are such as were requisite for handling the situation actually existing and are not indicative of the establishments which would be maintained by this State on a peace basis. You could then go on to say that the establishments to be maintained on a peace basis would be governed by Article 8 of the Treaty made between Great Britain and Ireland, and signed at London on the 6th day of December, 1921. You could then add that while the maximum limit has thus been made the subject of a Treaty Agreement, the actual establishments within that limit, which it is proposed to maintain in the future, have not yet been decided and will presumably come under early review by the Irish Government on the complete restoration of peaceful conditions in this country. You might contribute further to the information contained in this suggested letter by sending him a copy of the temporary Army Act, which the Parliament of the Free State has just passed.

[signed] Aodh ua Cinnéidigh
(HUGH KENNEDY)
Ard Aturnae

---

[1] See below No. 108.
[2] Not printed.

No. 107 NAI DFA Minister's Office Files (1924-25)

Handwritten letter from James McNeill to Desmond FitzGerald (Dublin)
LONDON, 9 August 1923

Dear D.[esmond] F.[itzGerald]
I had a talk to-day with Mr. Justice Cohalan. We talked rather generally, & he told me some facts connected with de V.[alera]'s visit to the States. I am sure that he will appreciate having monies[1] taken for him, & I felt that Tom[2] would not mind being troubled with an appeal for aid.

He seemed to be anxious to impress me with the need for understanding that our friends in America must be regarded primarily as American citizens though of Irish race or even of Irish birth, & that the Irish in America who remained 'the Irish in America' could effect nothing[3] of value. He also stated that much financial aid would be forthcoming if our actions indicated that we were not tied up to England economically, that we would actively set about developing outside markets.

I told him of Sunday's political meeting & gathered that he would like much to see for himself the public attitude. I suggested nothing.[4] You now know what he would like.

Yours sincerely,
JAMES MCNEILL

No. 108 NAI DFA ES Box 37

Desmond FitzGerald to Sir Eric Drummond (Geneva)[5]
DUBLIN, 11 August 1923

Monsieur,
J'ai l'honneur d'accuser réception de votre lettre du 25 juillet.

Voici les renseignements que vous voulez bien me demander:-

L'Article 8 du Traité entre l'Irlande et l'Angleterre détermine l'importance de nos forces militaires.

Texte de l'Article 8:

'8. With a view to securing the observance of the principle of international limitation of armaments, if the Government of the Irish Free State establishes and maintains a military defence force, the establishments thereof shall not exceed in size such proportion of the military establishments maintained in Great Britain as that which the population of Ireland bears to the population of Great Britain.'

Les honourables membres de la Commission Permanente se rendront compte que le Gouvernement de l'Etat Libre a été obligé de lever une armée volontaire

---

[1] Not discernible.
[2] 'Jim'? – not discernible.
[3] Not discernible.
[4] Not discernible.
[5] See above No. 106 and below No. 111.

de quelque quarante mille hommes pour défendre l'Etat pendant une courte période de troubles intérieurs. Ces troubles étant maintenant heureusement terminés les soldats reviennent à la vie civile aussi rapidement que le marché du travail peut les absorber. Le Gouvernement a la ferme intention de réduire l'armée au stricte minimum de ses besoins dès que tout danger à l'Etat aura été définitivement écarté.

Nous n'avons que les premiers éléments d'une Marine Marchande. L'organisation de nos flottes navales et aériennes n'a été guère entamée.

Notre attitude à l'égard des armements est simple. Nous n'avons pas un seul ennemi parmi les pays du monde et nous entrons dans la Société pour aider dans son admirable projet de convaincre toutes les nations que c'est par la paix seule que les hommes pourront atteindre le bonheur.

Veuillez agréer, Monsieur le Secrétaire Général, l'assurance de ma plus haute considération.

(signed) D. FITZGERALD
MINISTRE DES AFFAIRES ETRANGÈRES

No. 109 NAI DFA ES Box 37

Extract from a letter from Michael MacWhite to Desmond FitzGerald (Dublin)
(N.S. 94/23)

GENEVA, 14 August 1923

A Chara,

[Matter omitted]

It is also of utmost importance that our Delegates should have Irish Diplomatic passports as the effect that would be produced did they travel on English ones would be deplorable. As a last resort type-written passports would suffice, as there is no law to the effect that they should be printed.

There are several other matters in connection with the League Assembly the details of which would require to be arranged in advance. For example, if our Delegation intends to do any entertaining the dates should be fixed during the first few days so that they would not clash with other engagements. As I have already informed you, the Members of the League form several groups and our attitude to all those should be defined.

In case the President comes, he should have his speech prepared beforehand. It would produce an excellent effect if this were delivered in Irish. French and English translations should be ready for distribution to the Delegates and the press at the same time. It would not do to speak partly in English and partly in Irish as it would make a bad impression on the Assembly.

As the President's stay in Geneva must necessarily be very short, he should be in a position to meet with as many European Statesmen as is possible in the time but to go into every detail by correspondence is not only unsatisfactory but impossible. This can only be done by a general discussion. Under the circumstances I could, if you think it necessary, go to Dublin towards the end of the month and talk over the whole situation.

Is mise, le meas,
[signed] M. MACWHITE

No. 110 NAI DFA D2185

T.M. Healy to the Duke of Devonshire (London)
(Confidential)

DUBLIN, 15 August 1923

My Lord Duke,
I have the honour to acknowledge the receipt of Your Grace's Confidential Despatch of the 28th May last,[1] enclosing the Agenda for the Imperial Economic Conference to be held in October next, and to express, on behalf of my Ministers, agreement in general with the proposed subjects for discussion.
2. My Ministers would be glad to be informed of the latest date for receiving further subjects for inclusion in the Agenda of the Imperial Economic Conference. They also wish me to urge the desirability of discussing at the Conference the establishment of reciprocal measures by which Government Loans of all the Dominions might become trustee investments throughout the Empire.
3. The President desires me to express his general agreement with the proposed Agenda for the Imperial Conference.

I have the honour to be,
My Lord Duke,
Your Grace's most obedient,
humble Servant,
(Sgd) T.M. HEALY

No. 111 NAI DFA ES Box 37

Michael MacWhite to Desmond FitzGerald (Dublin)

GENEVA, 16 August 1923

A Chara,
I have received your letter relating to our military, naval and air forces for transmission to the Secretary General of the League of Nations.[2]

In glancing through Article 8 of the Treaty as set out in your translation I notice that the importance of our military establishments with relation to the military establishments of Great Britain shall be in the same proportion que la population irlandaise par rapport à la population britannique.

In International law the words underlined have a significance which differs considerably from the original version of the Treaty. The latter says: 'which the population of Ireland bears to the population of Great Britain'.

'Population britannique' may be taken as meaning the whole population of the British Empire and not exclusively of Great Britain. Such an interpretation would, of course mean that our army should be considerably smaller than that allowed under the Treaty and would be likely to create complications of a serious nature for us in the future.

[1] Not printed.
[2] Above No. 108.

Under the circumstances, I think it advisable to use the translation of Art. 8, as it appears in 'Diplomatic and Legal Documentation' because it is more concise and less likely to be misinterpreted.

You will, therefore, excuse me for taking the liberty of returning the letter for those corrections, the importance of which cannot be overestimated, but which must have inadvertently escaped your notice.

Is mise le meas,
[signed] M. MacWhite

No. 112 NAI DFA ES Box 37

Memorandum by Joseph P. Walshe for members of the Irish delegation to the League of Nations Assembly

Dublin, 28 August 1923

ADVICE TO DELEGATES
– Position of Delegates –

It is customary in every country for the Ministry of External Affairs to give advice to political missions before they leave for Foreign countries.

In this instance the need scarcely exists as our international relations are still too vague to afford a basis for defining our attitude. The Delegates are however respectfully urged to adapt themselves to cosmopolitan usages in all matters of dress, tenure and general decorum. French writers on the manners of diplomatists insist on the necessity above all things of avoiding singularities and idiosyncrasies and of conforming in apparently trivial things (e.g. usage in doffing one's hat) to accepted customs and conventions.

The Delegates will hold council among themselves about their attitude towards the other nations of the Commonwealth. It is the opinion of this Ministry that while relations with these latter should be most cordial, we should endeavour to associate for the most part with Delegates of other nations of Europe, especially the smaller nations.

This will emphasize our real position as one of the old nations of Europe and will obviate any impression which might be created in the United States by too frequent association with the British Group.

The Delegates, i.e. The President, the Minister of Foreign Affairs and the Minister of Education have primary right of séance at the Sittings of the Assembly, the substitute Delegates (The Attorney General, Marquis MacSwiney and Mr. Esmonde) have equal rights of séance with the Delegates at Commissions and can at all times replace the Delegates at the Assembly. It is quite in order, e.g. for Delegates to sit at the back of the Hall while substitute Delegates sit at the Assembly table. There is no real distinction except that no more than three members of the Delegation can sit at the "table" at the same time. The Deputy Delegate, Mr. Kevin O'Shiel, can take the place of any of the delegates in case of absence.

No. 113 UCDA P4/909

Handwritten memorandum by Kevin O'Shiel on the 1923 Imperial Conference
GENEVA, undated

From what I have gathered in conversation with C.[1] & from information received from home there is every likelihood that a big drive will be made at the forthcoming Imperial Conference by interested parties[:]

a) to make radical and far reaching alterations in the prevailing plans of Imperial Preference and,
b) to achieve at least the thin end of the wedge in a future comprehensive scheme of federation.

It is almost certain that suggestions will be made to carry the present plan of imperial preference very much further than at present and it is quite likely that such proposals may receive the support of influential dominions who may be materially affected in an advantageous way by the new proposals. Now the danger is that Ireland may have to take a certain attitude towards such proposals [and this] may create new difficulties between her fiscal policy and that of the Northern area.

My information is too hazy as yet to say very definitely what these proposals are likely to be but it is almost certain that they will be put forward with a view to prejudicing us in connection with the Boundary Commission.

No. 114 NAI DFA ES Box 37

Extract from a letter from Joseph Walshe to Desmond FitzGerald (Geneva)
DUBLIN, 4 September 1923

A Chara,

1. There has been no development in matters concerning this Department requiring your personal attention.
2. The reports of the receptions accorded everywhere to the President and Ministers have produced an excellent effect on public opinion here. Well affected people rejoice that the position of the President, as head of the State, has been definitely asserted abroad. (The 'Excelsior' refers to him 'tout naturellement' as President de la Republique Irlandaise). The disaffected are dismayed as they feel that they are losing one of the best weapons in their armoury.
3. The results of the elections would have been overwhelmingly in favour of the Cumann na nGaedheal were it not for extremely bad organisation in a large number of districts. Mr Bewley, lately employed as our representative in Berlin, informs me that the mass of the electors in his constituency did not know even the names of the candidates.

The prevailing view here is that the majorities secured by the Ministers have more than compensated for the unexpected number of deputies elected in the irregular interest. There is complete confidence in the Government's power to carry through whatever programme it wishes to propose for legislation.

[1] Identity unknown.

A commonly held opinion gives the Irregulars six months playacting before coming into the Dáil and becoming a constitutional party.
4. With the sanction of the Vice-President, the following telegram has been despatched to the Minister of Foreign Affairs, Japan:

> 'Gouvernement et peuple Etat Libre d'Irlande envoient message profonde sympathie avec Gouvernement et peuple Japon à cette houre de terrible épreuve.'[1]

It was thought better to send the telegram in your name, the supposition being that you had wired instructions from Geneva.
[Matter omitted]

Le meas mór,
[copy letter unsigned]
Rúnaí

No. 115 UCDA LAI/G/215

Handwritten letter from Eoin MacNeill to Agnes MacNeill
GENEVA, 6 September 1923

My Dearest Taddie –
It is just a week, almost at this hour, since I left you. It seems like a year. Now don't take that for philandering. It is the variety of experiences that has expanded the time. We began with a very stormy passage to Holyhead. Only the Attorney-General and myself, of all our party, succeeded in keeping our heads up. The Marquis, who stayed with me on deck, had to bow to Boreas and pay a small tribute. I got only a few hours sleep in the train. James[2] met us in London. In Paris, we had a civil & military welcome at the Gare du Nord. You will have seen the photo in the Freeman, which does not include me. We had a long journey from Paris to Genoa, though it was a splendid train, the Paris-Rome express. In Genoa we arrived in the dark of the morning between 4 and 5. We were again officially received. During our stay, two automobiles were placed at our disposal by the Prefetto, and we had an escort of two generals of Fascisti, who were very pleasant companions. The journey in the Prefetto's cars from Genoa to Bobbio was splendid beyond description. Almost the whole way, the road winds along the sides of deep mountain gorges. There are river beds – at this season mostly dry – hundreds of feet below us, and crags and forests above us. Only the Aran Islands can match the industry of these northern Italians. In the wildest and deepest slopes, every perch of ground that can be cultivated is cultivated. Little terraces of earth are artificially built up, often supported by stone walls, and in them are grown vines, potatoes, vegetables, maize etc. The people are very industrious, & they are handsome, with broad square shoulders and good carriage. Many of them have fair or red hair and a light complexion. Others are very dark and, as the Irish proverb says, má 's

[1] There had recently been a catastrophic earthquake in Japan.
[2] James McNeill, Irish High Commissioner in London, brother of Eoin MacNeill.

peacadh bheith beidhe, tá daoine damanta. In places that from a distant view seem fit only to support goats, there is a thick population. They have to climb to get to their houses. When we passed the highest part of the range we came on Italian troops going through manoeuvres. We then reached the valley of the Trebbia, also a zigzag gorge between high mountains, with water in the rivers below. Bobbio is in this valley. When we reached it, the whole population of the town & district were out to meet us. There was a great scene of excitement and repeated cries of Viva l'Irlanda. We were received by the Sotto-prefetto and the local Fascisti, and presented to Cardinal Ehrle and the Bishop of Bobbio. There were between 150 & 200 visitors from Ireland, many of them old acquaintances. I am keeping a copy of an Italian paper with a two column account of the celebrations. Besides the religious ceremonies which were extraordinarily impressive, there was a banquet at which the Cardinal presided, with our President on his right and myself on his left. Before we left, the Cardinal gave each of us a relic of St. Columbanus. Our journey by road back to Genoa (three hours – 80 or 90 miles of zigzag) was partly by night, and the lighted towns in the valleys below us looked like bits of the starry sky turned upside down.

Now I have to dress for dinner, and I shall tell you about Genoa afterwards.

Dinner being over, I resume about Genoa. Genoa was a great city in the Middle Ages & is a great city now. It is one of the chief trading ports on the Mediterranean. It is a great manufacturing town. With all that, it is full of both ancient & modern beauty, but seems modern rather than ancient. It is built on hills overlooking the port. It consists mainly of high buildings of many stories, most of the people live in flats. The buildings however are not run together in blocks of great length, but stand out from each other like castles. They are of a light coloured stone, & look bright & cheerful, rising one above another & facing in all directions, some of them on very high ground, with their backs to steep hills, so that you can walk in at the top story. The mountain slopes all around are covered with villas, some small, some great mansions. What catches you is the amount of solid but bright & ornate stonework – almost as if the whole city & surroundings consisted of the best class of buildings in the best parts of Dublin. The people are of the fine north Italian type that I have spoken of, & seem very industrious. Genoa is more busy at 7 a.m. than Dublin is at midday, & its activity goes on till after midnight. I have got a great respect for northern Italy after what I have seen.

From Genoa we took the train to Milan on our way to Geneva. Our Fascisti officers came with us & stayed with us till we left Milan. The first part of the railway journey was through the mountains, with scenery almost as grand as on the road to Bobbio. The railway winds through deep gorges, with many tunnels. Then it runs out into the plain of Lombardy, full of rich cultivation. We had a couple of hours in Milan, & spent much of the time in the Cathedral. I never liked the extraordinary ornate architecture of this Cathedral, il Duomo, when I saw it in pictures, that is the exterior, & I like it no better having seen it in the reality, but inside it is by far the most impressive building that I have ever been in – vast & massive & majestic, a complete contrast to the exterior which is crowded over with all the art & ornament possible in cut stone.

From Milan we took the train northward, first through the same rich plain, full of luxuriant crops of every kind. In Ireland we don't know the meaning of agriculture. There is a slow gradual rise till we reach the foot of the Alps. The train runs for miles along the side of Lake Maggiore, a beautiful sheet of blue water, with its banks & islands decorated with beautiful homes & gardens, & plenty of woodland. Then we run up into the Simplon Pass, miles & miles & miles through a wild valley between grand mountains, every bend of the line showing us a fresh piece of the most magnificent landscape. All this disappears when we run into the Simplon Tunnel, & spend about 25 minutes getting through it. When we got out of the tunnel, night had fallen, & we came on in darkness to Geneva, arriving about midnight.

Here our quarters were not yet ready, and Desmond & I were stowed away in a high up pension, which I shall ask you to ask him to describe. In the morning we came over to our hotel, the Hotel Bellevue, which is the H.Q. of our delegation, with our flag flying from its windows. I am sending a postcard with a photo of the hotel. The lake, Leman, is to the left of the trees. Geneva is a very beautiful city.

We have met many representatives of nations & personages of their entourage, & have been received with friendship & interest on all hands. Today, the President, Desmond, & myself went to lunch with Lord Robert Cecil. I afterwards attended one of the sittings at the Palais des Nations, & found it dull enough, except to watch the people from all parts of the world. This evg. I dined at the League of Nations Club (I am not sure of the name) with M. Edouard Phelan, whom I met last year in Paris, the secretary of the International Labour Bureau. It is late now, so good night. More again:

With love,
EOIN

No. 116 UCDA P80/1404

Extract from a handwritten letter from Desmond FitzGerald to Mabel FitzGerald[1] (Dublin)

GENEVA, September 1923

My dear Mabel
Sorry not to have written before. Usual trouble when I get a chance no paper. People coming every minute &c. I started off four times yesterday to send a wire and stopped each time.

History of last few days this. I was to come straight to Geneva but Italian Consul and [three words not legible] at D. Laoghaire both besought me to go to Genoa as Fascisti there know me. Frightful crossing to England, everyone sick, short time in London. [Matter omitted]
Rough crossing to France, reception at Calais, at Paris. No time for anything in Paris. So many of us, always someone lost. Had dinner at Grand Hotel, not finished till nearly 11 o'c. Usual trouble nearly missing train in morning. Arrived Geneva 5 a.m. Saturday. Fascist reception. Slept morning. Drove with Fascisti

[1] Mabel McConnell, FitzGerald's wife (married 1911).

to see all town afternoon, nothing in the evening. Sunday all except Kennedy & I went to Bobbio. Fascist took us [three words not legible] to Sta. Margherita, Porto Fino, Rapallo. More beautiful than any place ever seen. Came back first thing Monday, arrived 1.30 a.m. Tuesday, fiddled all yesterday. This morning just summoned to meeting. All details when I return. Hope all is well. Children returned? Hope Gladys[1] well.

Sincerely,
D.

No. 117 UCDA P80/1404

Handwritten letter from Desmond FitzGerald to Mabel FitzGerald (Dublin)
GENEVA, September 1923

M[y] D[ear] M[abel]
I had meant to write often but things are impossible. Everything has gone splendidly in one way but our interior economy is a continual muddle. You will have seen news in the papers. We have a continual series of meals – meals that last anything from two to four hours. You can imagine how I enjoy it. Everyone is very charming. But the strain of politeness, good behaviour and over eating tell on one. Arrangements at present mean that I get back to Dublin on Friday night. It is always possible that I may be delayed. We change (or rather our plans are changed) several times a day. I have not seen much of Geneva. On Saturday we went for lunch to a Mrs MacCormack of Chicago – she has a chateau at Nyon. Of course I was furious at being let in for another meal. But it was actually very pleasant. The lady was versed in Dawson and knew a certain amount about glandular secretions. That made conversation easy. Asked her if she knew Miss Cramer and it appeared that she did. Mr Cramer (now married) was at Nyon a few days before. She asked me if I had heard of Vincent O'Sullivan. I of course was able to give his full literary history. There were a great many people at the lunch, but it was arranged so sensibly that it didn't pall. Several tables instead of one long one.

Our dinners at night go on till somewhere about midnight. If possible after that I slip off with Diarmuid to what I might call the Geneva Reaton's, it is quite pleasant as there are always people to talk to and an occasional life history.

That is about all here. I should like to know how things are at home. How children got on in North. Is Gladys still there. Any news from my people?[2] I hope to see them on way back. Arrangement now is that we are due to arrive in London about 7:15pm and leave by morning train. So I might be able to run down in the evening if there is not some confusion amongst us. I am writing this in the League. Every speech is translated into the other language. Very wearisome.

D

[1] Gladys Hynes, a close friend of the family.
[2] Desmond FitzGerald's mother, brother and sister who lived near West Ham in London.

No. 118 NAI DT S3332

Speech by William T. Cosgrave to the Assembly of the League of Nations on Ireland's admission to the League of Nations[1]

GENEVA, 10 September 1923

On behalf of Ireland, one of the oldest and yet one of the youngest nations, and speaking for the Irish Government and the Irish Delegation, I thank this Assembly of the League of Nations for the unanimous courtesy and readiness with which our application to be admitted to membership of the League has been received and approved.

Ireland, in ancient times linked by bonds of culture and of friendly intercourse with every nation to which the ambit of travel could carry her far-venturing missionaries and men of learning has to-day formally, yet none the less practically, entered into a new bond of union with her sister nations, great and small, who are represented in this magnificent world-concourse.

With all the nations whose spokesmen form this Assembly, Ireland joins to-day in a solemn covenant to exercise the powers of her sovereign status in promoting the peace, security and happiness, the economic, cultural, and moral well-being of the human race.

Lofty ideals have inspired the best minds who have faith in the power of good will and of joint international endeavour to operate for good through this Council of the Nations. It is our earnest desire to co-operate with our fellow-members in every effort calculated to give effect to those ideals – to mitigate, and whenever possible, to avert the ancient evils of warfare and oppression; to encourage wholesome and to discourage unwholesome relations between nation and nation; to enable even the weakest of nations to live their own lives and make their own proper contribution to the good of all, free even from the shadow and the fear of external violence, vicious penetration, or injurious pressure of any kind.

In the actual proceedings which we have witnessed, we have seen a keen appreciation of the fact that nations are interdependent in matters of economic and intellectual development. We hope that the means of closer intercourse provided or initiated through the League of Nations will be helpful to the economic and educational progress for which Ireland is looking forward and always striving.

We willingly testify that the advocacy of these ideals has strongly attracted us towards the League of Nations, and if as yet the means provided have not always proved fully effective to secure their worthy ends, we are mindful of our national proverb, 'Bíonn gach tosnú lag' ('every beginning is weak'), and we trust that in time to come, adequate means and faithful use of them will justify our common hopes. Our history and the instinct of our hearts forbid us to think that temporary or even recurrent failures can deprive a just and steadfast purpose of the assurance of success.

[1] Cosgrave began this speech with a brief introduction in Irish; it is reproduced in English in No. 134 below.

Ireland counts on having no enemy and on harbouring no enmity in the time to come. She counts also on bringing forth fruits worthy of liberty. *Si tollis libertatem, tollis dignitatem.* These are the words of a famous Irishman of the sixth and seventh century. Inscribed on his tomb at Bobbio in Italy, they met our eyes when, a few days ago, a happy conjuncture enabled the members of this Irish Delegation to assist at the celebration of the thirteenth centenary of Saint Columbanus, pioneer of Ireland's moral and intellectual mission among the nations of Western Europe.

We shall return to our own country to take part with our own patriotic people in the enormous work of national construction and consolidation. The kind welcome, the cordial words of understanding, that have greeted us here on the part of every nation whose representatives we have met, will not be forgotten. They will cheer and sustain us in that work, and they will remind us, too, that as the life of a man is bettered and fructified beyond measure in the harmonious society of men, so must the life of nations reach a much fuller liberty and a much fuller dignity in the harmonious society of nations.

No. 119 NAI NEBB Papers Box 25

Extract from a letter from E.M. Stephens to Kevin O'Shiel (Geneva)
DUBLIN, 11 September 1923

A chara,
[Matter omitted]
Everyone here was delighted at the reception which Ireland got at the League of Nations. It was very well reported in the Press, and I think will make a tremendous impression in the country. It just came at a time when everyone's attention was focussed on the League.
[Matter omitted]

Mise le meas,
[copy letter unsigned]

No. 120 UCDA LAI/G/217

Handwritten letter from Eoin MacNeill to Agnes MacNeill
GENEVA, 14 September 1923

Dearest Taddie,
Beyond making fresh acquaintances daily, there is not much here to write home about. We meet them at the League Assembly, at Committees, at lunches, teas, dinners. The Marquis is in Heaven on these occasions and I am in a mild Purgatory. Kevin O'Shiel is at home, that is to say, he is so deaf that it makes no big difference. On that topic, I may say that my own hearing, which used to be of the best, is much duller recently, and this is a great disadvantage when the conversation is in French. MacWhite also is quite at home, he revels in talking to people of all tribes and tongues. The four of us now constitute the Irish Delegation, and I am Chef de Délégation, which causes me to get an extra dose of invitations. MacWhite is fluent in French and also in Danish. The Marquis is

perhaps the best linguist in Geneva. He speaks Irish, English, French, Italian, Spanish, Portuguese, German, and some Russian.

A strange thing befell MacWhite, I think it was on Saturday, the day when our demand passed the Commission. That morning, early, he got the news that his wife had given birth to a son.[1] Naturally we all congratulated him. In the afternoon, when he was away somewhere on our business, word came that the baby was very ill. I was the first to hear it, and from the wording of the message I guessed that the child was dead. I was right and wrong. The same day that the little son was born, their only other child, a girl of a year and a half, died suddenly. Mrs MacWhite was in a nursing home for her delivery, and they had sent the other little one to be tended in the meantime. It took ill internally that day about 3 p.m. and was dead before 4. Mrs Mac does not know yet about the death. Next day, I went with Mac to see her at the home, and she was looking well and happy. Of course I stayed only a minute. They are naming the son Eoin. All our delegation attended the funeral of the little girl. MacWhite is an old and faithful backer of Griffith's policy, and it was a strange thing that two great joys & one great sorrow should come to him in one day. He has worked hard for Ireland in Geneva and the friendship of so many nations for us is largely due to his work. I would like you to understand that every representative here regards our entrance into the League as an international recognition that Ireland is a sovereign independent state. Quite a number of them speak of the Irish Republic and write to us as its delegates.

We dine this evening with the Jam Saheb. Kennedy and Esmonde left here for Ireland last evening. Kennedy has made a great impression here. I am eagerly awaiting a letter from you especially to know if you will face the journey. Let me know too if you want any cheques.

EOIN

No. 121 UCDA LAI/G/218

Handwritten letter from Eoin MacNeill to Agnes MacNeill
GENEVA, 15 September 1923

Dearest Taddie –
Someone told me that James had gone to Dublin for a holiday. If so, he will be interested in this little story. Yesterday evening our delegation, with some others, were the guests of His Highness the Jam Saheb of Jamnagar, once better known as Ranjitsinji, the famous cricketer. I had the place of honour on the right of the host, the guest on his left being a Persian prince, Mirzakhan. On my right was another Persian delegate and opposite to me a Siamese delegate. Beside him and opposite to the Jam was a dignitary named Hosein Imam, who wore a skullcap and a long black robe like a soutane. The attendants wore brilliant oriental uniforms. The party was almost wholly Irish, English, and Asiatic. During the chat, Hosein Imam gave the Jam a list of the exports of Persia. I

[1] Eoin MacWhite (1923-1975), joined the Department of External Affairs, later serving in Spain and the Netherlands.

said he had forgotten one. They both turned to me with surprise and interest and asked what one. I said 'cats'. They laughed, and Hosein said that was indeed so. Do you know, he said, what was the merchandise of the first caravan that came through the Khyber Pass when it was opened at the end of the Tirah campaign? There was a caravan of 23 camels, and they were all loaded with cats. I thought, but did not say, that it would be a good export trade for Ireland to develop. That is not the point of my story, but merely an example of the diplomatic conversations of Geneva. The Jam spoke to me about the unequalled quality of Irish woollens. He said they were almost everlasting but not quite. The gay uniform of a lackey in front of us, emerald green, was of Irish manufacture. It was bought ten years ago. The Jam had been trying some time ago to get more of the same stuff in Ireland but had not succeeded, and he wondered if I could help him. I said I would have a try, and I explained that during the Big War the Irish manufacturers had been full up with orders for army uniform material and recently with orders for the Irish Government. Later, when we were taking leave, the Jam again said he hoped I would try to help him about it, and I said I would.

I am writing by this post to Desmond FitzGerald on the subject. Only that I am ignorant of the rearrangements in the Ministry of Trade & Commerce, I could write there also. What I want you to do is to call round on Mr. O'Riordan[1] in Merrion Avenue and tell him what I have told you about the request of this Indian Prince. It might lead to a good order, as the Jam has a little army and no end of uniformed followers. I would suggest that Mr O'R would first call at Desmond's office and tell him that he had heard through you, and then that Mr O'R himself would write to His Highness the Jam Saheb, Hôtel de la Paix, Geneva, saying that he had been informed at the Ministry of External Affairs and asking for particulars of the goods required. Mr O'R will understand that he would be doing a service to the Irish Delegation and, let us hope, to Irish business. Who knows how much might develop? There are plenty of Indian princes who might follow suit.

I have just been discussing with MacWhite the idea of hiring a shop front in Geneva during next year's Session of the League, for a display of some of the best Irish manufactures. You might mention the idea to Mr O'Riordan. We have people here from the whole world, even from countries like the United States & Russia, which have not joined the League.

I am wondering when a letter from you will reach me. Do think seriously about coming out here before I leave. All my own expenses here are paid, and by the end of my stay I hope to have actually saved as much as I had to spend on outfit, and most of the outfit will last me a long time. I have only had to buy a black soft hat, 25 francs, to go with morning dress. Occasionally I treat myself to a row (mind the pronunciation) on the lake at 1 franc per hour.

This day I lunched with the Polish Delegation and sat next to the celebrated Nansen[2] whose enterprise for the discovery of the Pole is so well known. The sledded Polack was very friendly and the ice was good.

[1] E.J. Riordan of the Department of Industry and Commerce.

[2] Fridjof Nansen, Norwegian explorer whose work repatriating prisoners of war and refugees set the basis for later international refugee work.

I have not managed to get a kippered herring since I came here. The other day at some banquet, I found a rasher of bacon on my plate. Glory be, I said, this reminds me of home. The waiter laughed. I said to him in my best French that he was very intelligent. 'Oh yes,' he said, 'I have been at Dublin and Cork and Killarney and Belfast and Portrush.' On the other hand, I have also been eating caviare, which is said to [be] more expensive now than ever. Will you ever write?

EOIN

No. 122 NAI DFA 417/105

Michael MacWhite to Joseph P. Walshe (Dublin)
(N.S. 103/23)
GENEVA, 17 September 1923

A Chara,
I have been requested by the Delegation here to ask you to be good enough to send
(1) instructions empowering them to take the necessary steps to have the Anglo-Irish Treaty registered;
(2) That the date of registration be left to our discretion as to whether it should be done immediately or left over until the Assembly adjourns;
(3) That a certified copy of the Treaty be sent us. We can supply the French translation.

This matter should be seen to immediately so that we may be prepared for any eventuality.

Most likely you have seen the article in the 'Times' stating that we are definitely submitting the dispute about the Boundary to the League. This is interesting and shows a certain amount of nervousness in view of the fact that no dispute or conflict has so far arisen on the matter between the two governments concerned. It may be advisable for some member of the government to have an interview published on the subject to the effect that it is hoped that the Boundary question would be settled amicably by the parties concerned without reference to any third party.

Is mise, le meas,
[signed] M. MACWHITE

No. 123 NAI NEBB Papers Box 25

Extract from a letter from E.M. Stephens to Kevin O'Shiel (Geneva)
DUBLIN, 17 September 1923

A chara,
The moral effect which joining the League of Nations has produced in this country far exceeds anything that was anticipated. It seems to have convinced the people that the Treaty really did secure international recognition as a separate State. It has also had a tremendous effect on the northern question. The 'Times' and even the 'Morning Post' suggest settlements of the Boundary

question and discuss the whole matter from a much more reasonable point of view.

Rumours have appeared in the Press that steps were being taken to register the Treaty. Curiously enough this has produced almost as great an impression as joining the League itself. Even Mary MacSwiney has said that if the Irish representatives succeed in having the Treaty registered they would have done a good thing for the country. How she reconciles this with the idea that the Treaty imposes permanent slavery on the country I do not know. You can however see from this statement that the irregulars feel the whole Geneva transactions the greatest blow they have yet received.

A statement appeared in today's Press from the Attorney General that the registration of the Treaty had not been considered. There is a feeling here that if the Treaty is not registered after what has been said that it will be because England has succeeded in preventing it. Could you let me know what is being done. Judging from opinion here I think its registration has become absolutely essential to our case with the north. Waller has been out sick for the last few days. I will get him to write you his views as soon as he returns.
[Matter omitted]

Mise le meas,
[copy letter unsigned]
Rúnaidhe

No. 124 UCDA LAI/G/219

Handwritten letter from Eoin MacNeill to Agnes MacNeill
GENEVA, 17 September 1923

Dearest Taddie
Still no news from you. We have seen the Dublin papers giving the accounts of the President's return, and they show us that the Dublin people have grasped the significance of what has been happening in Geneva. I see that the Diehards in the London press have also risen to a comprehension, and are making foolish and futile attempts to recover a foothold. Events have justified to the letter the interpretation of the Treaty that I have given from the first. It is sad that so much sorrow has been caused by the political ignorance and silly vanity of those who took the contrary view. Imagine the madness of these people sending two women[1] to Geneva to prevent the representatives of other nations from recognising Ireland as their equal. Now I see that some Diehard fool of an official in the entourage of the British Delegation here or perhaps in the League secretariat, which has many English employed & must include some Carsonites, has betrayed a guilty conscience towards Ireland by starting a racket in the London 'Times' about the registration of the Treaty & the Boundary question. In the gossip of this place, he got hold of a fact, namely that a night had been spent here in preparing a French translation of some of our principal documents. He supposed that this happened after Pres. Cosgrave's departure & that the

[1] Hanna Sheehy-Skeffington and Mary MacSwiney.

Treaty was the only document, & he inferred that the purpose was to have the Treaty registered by the League of Nations. He further inferred that the object of doing this was to appeal to the League in the 'Dispute' about the Boundary clause. What are the facts – At the earliest possible moment after our arrival, and while the President was still here, we found it necessary to have French translations of all the principal documents on the subject of our status, as the majority of the delegates, even of those who know more or less English, understand documents of the kind much better in French. The translating had nothing at all to do with registration of the Treaty, for a translated version of the Treaty would not be authentic. But the strangest part of his assumption was that a 'dispute' already existed between us & the British Gov^{t}. about the Boundary clause. Of course there has been no such dispute. The two Gov^{ts} have not even yet begun to discuss the effect of the clause beyond the appointment of Commissioners. One English journal after another has followed the 'Times' lead, assuming a dispute. This proves only one thing, that these journals do not mean fair play for the clause. Nous verrons.

I have formed a very strong opinion that James[1] ought to come to Geneva. He would get a good deal of insight here into the international situation in general and into its aspects for us in particular. Why should not you plan with him to come along, and bring Máire with you, for a trip on the Continent is more educative than half a year of stewing.

Your letter has just arrived. As you have managed to get through the lines in a fortnight, I hope you will keep the road open. If you see Sommerfeld, give him my best regards. Tell him I have met Nansen. I suppose Seumas[2] thinks there are compensations for a bad knee. Love to all.

EOIN

No. 125 UCDA P80/535

Extract from a handwritten letter from Eoin MacNeill to William T. Cosgrave (Dublin)

GENEVA, 19 September 1923

My dear President,

The Times 'canard' about registration has obviously arisen from some Diehard in the entourage of the British Delegation here or of the Secretariat of the League. It was telegraphed from here. We see that it has been taken up seriously by the London Press. We have had no occasion to refer to the matter in any public way here. When it is mentioned to us in conversation we quote the facts, namely [1] that it is true that we have gone to extra trouble to provide everyone who needs them with French versions not only of the Treaty but of all the principal documents that go to define or illustrate our position, seeing that the great majority understand such documents much better in French than in English; (2) that we for our part do not consider the similar work done by practically every Delegation a matter for press telegrams, nor do we go about to collect information as to what other delegates may do in the late hours in their hotels,

[1] James McNeill, Irish High Commissioner in London, brother of Eoin MacNeill.
[2] Seamas?

and we should not desire that any reputable Irish journal would encourage this kind of thing; (3) that the question of registering the Treaty is still one to be decided for us; even though the British press seem anxious to make a decision inevitable; (4) that the League Covenant enables any Treaty or agreement between *members of the League* to be registered; (5) that press opinions do not affect the facts of our status; (6) that British journals themselves must explain their assumption that a dispute exists between us and the British Govt. on the Boundary clause, seeing that no such dispute has arisen, and that we have always expected that this clause, like every other clause in the Treaty, will be fulfilled honestly and amicably on both sides. In fact, the relations between our governments are not reflected in the sinister attitude of certain British journals. It may also be noted that the Times telegram indicates that our work of translation was undertaken after your departure, whereas you are aware that it was completed before your departure from Geneva.

[Matter omitted]

We are still extending the circle of our friends here, and our digestions have so far proved equal to all occasions. We were glad to see how Dublin has appreciated the significance of events. Our own Diehards seem to be as much rattled as our neighbour's.

EOIN MACNEILL

No. 126 NAI DFA Unregistered Papers

Memorandum on the wireless and cable facilities of the Irish Free State prepared for 1923 Imperial Conference

DUBLIN, 19 September 1923

SUMMARY

The existing means of cable communication with Great Britain are sufficient for the present traffic and leave ample reserve for growth so far as telegraph traffic is concerned. It is anticipated that in the next few years additional telephone outlets will be needed, but the time is not yet ripe for making definite recommendations. No need is felt for wireless communication with Great Britain.

Direct communication between the Irish Free State and the British Dominions either by wireless or cable would be extremely costly to provide and the traffic from the Free State would be insufficient to render such services remunerative; it is thought that it would not be possible to attract traffic from other countries for such Irish Free State services.

There are good prospects of wireless development so far as the ship and shore stations are concerned.

The memorandum deals with the various questions solely in their technical aspects; the limitations which may be imposed by, for example, political considerations, have not been considered.

WIRELESS

(a) *TO GREAT BRITAIN*

Excluding stations which may be controlled by Government Departments other than the Post Office, for example the Ministry of Defence, there are no Wireless Stations owned by the Irish Free State capable of transmitting to points outside the Free State.

Except for emergency purposes there is little scope for wireless telegraphy between the Irish Free State and Great Britain; the existing cables provide sufficient channels for the traffic between the two countries. It is hoped to formulate shortly a scheme for small portable wireless stations to be used in emergencies in the Free State, for example, between the mainland and outlying islands when the cables are broken down, and these emergency wireless stations could serve in time of need for communicating with Great Britain.

Commercial wireless telephony to Great Britain is not yet practicable.

(b) *TO BRITISH DOMINIONS*

A Free State owned wireless station to work to the Dominions would not be remunerative. Since about 1906 there has been a growing demand from the public for a chain of wireless stations linking the Dominions to Great Britain and after many vicissitudes the scheme is now being put into execution. The first stations of the Imperial Chain, Leafield (Oxford), and Cairo, have been found to lack power for reliable communication with the Dominions and a much larger and more powerful type of station is now proposed. The scheme in its latest form is that the Dominions shall arrange for their own stations, the Imperial Government shall own one station in Great Britain, leaving any other stations required in Great Britain to private enterprise. It is believed that the Marconi Company propose to erect in England two stations at the outset. At the moment negotiations are in progress between the British Government and the Marconi Company as to traffic pooling arrangements, in order that the available traffic may be distributed equitably. The capital cost of these modern long range stations is in the neighbourhood of £400,000; there is not likely to be sufficient traffic from the Irish Free State, even aggregating the traffic for all the Dominions, to keep such a station fully loaded, and it would be almost impossible to come to satisfactory working arrangements with the various Dominion Governments about the working programmes to enable the traffic available to be handled expeditiously.

(c) *SUGGESTED NEWS TRANSMITTING STATION FOR NORTH AMERICA*

There is some scope for a wireless station, large, but not so powerful as the Imperial Chain stations, to work to North America with news traffic, but since its success hinges upon the arrangements for collection of news, principally from England, it is a matter for private rather than Government enterprise. It would be well to bring this matter under the notice of the people likely to be interested. Commercial firms are not likely to spend money on schemes such as this until they are reasonably sure that conditions are stable. Land lines from England would be needed for the station.[1] The Marconi Company might be induced to consider the possibilities of using Clifden for such a news

[1] Handwritten marginal note reads as follows: 'At the moment we are discussing re-opening of the Station with the Marconi Co[mpan]y. It will work to Canada and U.S.A.'

transmitting station; their organisation would allow them to arrange to receive acknowledgments and requests for repetitions at their larger stations in England. The Western Union or Commercial Cable Co[mpan]y might consider such a station as a supplement to their cables.[1]

(d) *COAST STATIONS AND THEIR DEVELOPMENT*
The Irish Free State operates on behalf of the British Government two coast or 'ship and shore' wireless stations, Valencia, Co. Kerry and Malin Head, Co. Donegal, which are used for sending messages to and receiving messages from ships. Valencia is the more powerful station; the average working ranges over open sea are approximately:-

	DAY	*NIGHT*
VALENCIA	450 miles	1,000 miles
MALIN HEAD	300 miles	500 miles

Both stations use the spark system which, however, is being rapidly displaced by the more modern continuous wave system. The present position is that the larger ships are equipped with both spark and continuous wave plant, the smaller ships having spark plant only.

Valencia and Malin Head are profitable stations in normal times; it would be of considerable financial advantage if the Saorstát owned these stations. There are opportunities for profitable development; it would be practicable to provide at the stations additional equipment for continuous wave working and to operate both this and the spark system simultaneously with less overhead charges for each system than separate stations would require. Though outgoing messages for ships would no doubt be dealt with largely by British Stations, for most of the messages originate in Great Britain, with well organised stations incoming traffic, which is more profitable than outgoing, could readily be obtained, for the shipboard operators are interested in getting their traffic cleared to a shore station as quickly as possible. Though wireless has developed considerably in the past few years the geographical positions of Valencia and Malin Head are still of advantage, and the stations have the further advantage that reception there is less liable to interference from other wireless stations, a trouble which multiplication of wireless services is making quite serious in Great Britain.

A proposal has been submitted to the Secretary suggesting that the services be obtained of an Irishman now in the British Post Office, who has had long experience in the actual running and control of Coast Wireless Stations. He would be on the staff of the Engineering Department, and could train the wireless station staffs to a state of high efficiency. The operating staffs are at present employees of the Irish Free State but there is reason to believe that the British Post Office Authorities are considering the question of sending over English staffs to the stations. If the stations be handed over to the Irish Free State the most efficient way of controlling them would be for the staffs as well as the plant to be primarily under the Engineering Department.

[1] This sentence is a handwritten addition to the text.

(e) *DIRECTION FINDING APPARATUS*
It is anticipated that in the near future a demand from ship owners will arise for facilities from the Irish Coast Stations for ships' direction and position finding by wireless. The bearing or direction of a ship can be obtained from a single wireless station, but to find the actual position of a ship[,] readings from two, preferably three stations are needed. Valencia and Malin Head are so situated that readings from them both are not likely to be of much use to ships and actually readings will be needed from Irish and British or French Stations. It is possible too that a need will arise for a position finding station on the South East Coast of Ireland. Additional equipment would be needed to enable Valencia and Malin Head to give these direction readings, and at the outset the service would not be remunerative. It would however work in well with the other duties of the Stations and, if efficiently performed, would reflect credit on the Saorstát.

CABLES
(a) *GOVERNMENT OWNED*
(1) *To Great Britain*
All the existing Government owned submarine cables landing in the Irish Free State connect it to Great Britain. The cables are in the joint ownership of Great Britain and the Irish Free State, provide sufficient channels for the present telegraph traffic and give an ample margin for growth in traffic. No improvement in the cable facilities to Great Britain is needed, so far as telegraphs are concerned but it is hoped that increased telephone traffic will, within the next few years, necessitate additional trunk channels. Developments in wireless telephony and in 'wired wireless' may be such that when the time comes for providing these additional channels means other than cable will be the most economical.

Details of the present cables are as follows:-
Howth to Abergeirch, Wales.
One telephone cable, two circuits.
Howth to Trescastell, Wales.
Two telegraph cables, one seven wire, one four wire, in all eleven telegraph circuits.
Newcastle, Co. Wicklow, to Abergeirch, Wales.
Three telegraph cables, four wires each cable, in all twelve telegraph circuits.
Blackwater, Co. Wexford, to Fishguard, Wales.
One telegraph cable, four wires, four telegraph circuits.
Blackwater, Co. Wexford, to Abermawr, Wales.
One telegraph cable, four wires, four telegraph circuits.

(2) *TO BRITISH DOMINIONS*
The cost of providing direct cables from the Irish Free State to any of the British Dominions would be considerable and the traffic from the Free State is not sufficient to justify any such cable. It would be difficult, if not impossible, to obtain from other countries traffic for the Dominions to go over a cable, if such there were, owned by the Irish Free State.

(b) *PRIVATELY OWNED*
The following privately owned submarine cables land in the Irish Free State. Except one cable from Waterville to Weston-Super-Mare, they are single wire telegraph cables.
At Valencia, Co. Kerry.
Three cables from Hearts Content, Newfoundland.
Two cables from Penzance, England.
At Waterville, Co. Kerry.
Two cables from St. Johns, Nova Scotia.
Two cables from Canso, Nova Scotia.
One cable from Fayal, Azores.
One cable from Havre, France.
Three cables from Weston-Super-Mare, one being a two conductor cable.

The cable stations at Valencia and Waterville are now used principally as cable repeater stations, only one land line being rented by the Companies, and it is anticipated that the Cable Companies will be reluctant again to rent the long Irish land lines they have recently surrendered, though prolonged freedom from interruption to land lines may make it advantageous for the Companies to use land lines with the short Ireland-England cable link rather than the long submarine cables from England direct to Kerry. Settled conditions may also induce the Companies to terminate in Ireland rather than in England any future long submarine cables they may find necessary. The Cable Companies might be induced to erect in Ireland wireless stations to supplement their cables. The Eastern Telegraph Co[mpan]y is considering such a scheme for their Indian traffic. The point has been raised above under Wireless (C).[1]

[signed] J McCandless,
Assistant Engineer in Chief

No. 127 UCDA P4/910

Extracts from a handwritten letter from Kevin O'Shiel to Hugh Kennedy (Dublin)

Geneva, 20 September 1923

A Chara Dhíl
I send you herewith under separate cover copy of document No. 20/41/13 which is a memo. approved by the Council of the League of Nations on 19th May 1920, dealing with the question of the registration of Treaties.

It would seem quite clear from this document that the intention of the Council was to get all 'treaties and international engagements' in the widest sense of those terms, entered as the Records of the League.

On p. 5 I have underlined part of art. 3 which seems to bear out this as it refers to any international engagement or act by which nations or their Governments intend to establish legal obligations etc. The expression is 'nations or their Governments' and seems to cover all cases of members of the League. Elsewhere too the document will be found interesting as for example par. 4

[1] This sentence is a handwritten addition to the text.

which lays it down in a rather peremptory manner that 'registration is necessary for *all* Treaties' which become or have become finally binding.

Paragraph 6 makes suggestions as to how Treaties should be registered, dealing with the routine of procedure; and par. 8 makes it clear that 'Treaties or international engagements' may be presented for registration by one party only. Altogether I think you will find the document highly interesting. We had some difficulty in securing a copy.

Some days ago the Jurists' Committee rang me up and suggested that I should take your place thereon in your absence. I mentioned the matter to the Doctor[1] who was of the opinion that I should go and hold a watching brief. I have attended a number of sittings since, but owing to the fact that I have a great deal of work in connection with the Sixth and other Commissions I have not been able to attend regularly. However I am watching the proceedings as well as I can and hope to give you an accurate account of what was done. As a matter of fact they are not progressing very quickly and I scarcely see how they will be in time for this Assembly.

I have heard it from a number of reliable sources that this Treaty[2] will never pass through the Assembly as the opposition both to it generally and to particular clauses is very strong. I cannot of course say how accurate this information will prove to be but undoubtedly there will be quite vigorous opposition at the Assembly.

At the Jurists' Committee a point turned up the other day which serves to give an idea of the partisan feeling that still unfortunately prevails. The point I may mention was later happily adjusted to everybody's satisfaction at the Fourth Commission. The point was this: the Jurists' Committee wrote a letter to the 4th Committee suggesting some changes in the draft Treaty. One of those changes was in effect that as ex-enemy countries like Austria, Hungary & Bulgaria, now members of the League were bound in the first instance by the terms of the Treaty of Trianon and Versailles before they could be bound by the Covenant, and that as it was laid down in those Treaties that the very limited armies of those countries could not be used outside the frontiers *ergo* it was only right & fair, 'meet & just' that the special extra peace guarantees of the Mutual Guarantee Treaty should *not* be put into effect with regard to them!

In other words, as (for example) Hungary had been strictly forbidden by the Peace Treaties (a) to raise more than a certain number of soldiers & b) to employ those soldiers outside her frontiers, *therefore* she could not assist the League in any combined punitive expedition against an erring member and that *therefore* she was not entitled to receive the added security contained in the provisions of the Mutual Guarantee Treaty!

I have a busy time of it sitting on the Sixth Commission and substituting on one or other of the others. The Sixth Commission dealt with the Finnish recommendations in the case of Eastern Carelia (a kind of Finnish Six Counties) and practically accepted in toto the entire Finnish recommendations. This afforded me an opportunity to say a few words in support of the Finns of a non-committal and friendly nature which I did, being followed in almost

[1] Eoin MacNeill.
[2] The Draft Treaty of Mutual Guarantee.

identical terms by the Latvians, the Esthonians and the Poles. The matter was unanimously adopted by the Sixth Commission & today by the Assembly. The Finns have been profuse in their gratitude for my few words.

By the way the Marquis scored quite a big success on the Intellectual Cooperation Commission. He secured the representation of Ireland and of the Finns and Hungarians on the Permanent Special Committee of this Commission. Quite a thing this as there was opposition from an ambitious Frenchman who had other plans. Nevertheless in the 'final round' the Frenchman came round & the Marquis carried the day by 33 votes to 1 (Portugal) against, with 9 abstentions (including Norway, Sweden & Denmark). Norway played him a dirty trick as she (Norway being a lady in this particular Commission) promised to support his motion in the sub-committee but turned round afterwards and abstained. I will tell you about this in detail when I see you.
[Matter omitted]

By the way a nice young man called *Antrobus*[1] has taken a kindly interest in us lately and shows it by doing us the honour of sitting on our bench at the Assembly beside us. He is there every morning before we arrive and always greets us with a winning smile. We rather fancy the intention is to let people see how *near* the connection actually is and how fraternal the interest is in the newest of dominions. There are other reasons also which are obvious.

Please excuse this hasty & very rough scrawl, but I am writing it at the Assembly where it is hard to give one's whole mind to it on account of the buzz. It is likely we shall be returning on Sunday week.

Kindest regards to Mrs. Kennedy
Mise do chara,
[initialled] C. O'S

No. 128 UCDA LAI/G/220

Extract from a handwritten letter from Eoin MacNeill to Agnes MacNeill
GENEVA, 21 September 1923

Dearest Taddie,
I had your telegram yesterday. I think at this stage we must postpone the project. I am now anxious myself to get back home at the earliest moment when we can leave this place. I have not much to tell you. Everyone seems to hope & wish that the business here will end by Saturday evening and we are discussing arrangements to start for home on Sunday morning, this day week.
[Matter omitted]

We have the same daily round of meetings, most of them very tiresome & stuffy. The weather for the past week has been atrocious, except yesterday. Today has been constant heavy rain with some thunder & lightning, & I have now to start out for tea at the Château de Coudrée, nearly an hour's journey from here on the French shore of the lake between Geneva & Girains les Bains, being invited by the owner M. Bartholoni, Deputy for Haute Savoie. This

[1] M.E. Antrobus of the Colonial Office.

coming week we shall have to entertain some of those who have been our hosts at dinners, lunches or teas.

I wish it was over & that I was back at home.

EOIN

No. 129 NAI DFA 417/105

Joseph P. Walshe to Michael MacWhite (Geneva)
(No. 234/23)

DUBLIN, 22 September 1923

A Chara,

The Minister having examined the matter of your letter[1] with his Colleagues requires answers to the following questions urgently:

1. If the Treaty were presented in the ordinary way for registration, would it be accepted by the usual registering authorities, or would it be referred to the General Secretary for his decision?

The Ministers desire the most exact and authoritative statement as to various possible lines of action on the part of the League Authorities following an attempt to register.

2. What are the implications attached to the date of registering with special reference to (1) above?

3. What form meets the League view of a 'certified copy' of the Treaty?

Le meas,
[copy letter unsigned]
Rúnaí

No. 130 UCDA LAI/G/221

Handwritten letter from Eoin MacNeill to Agnes MacNeill

GENEVA, 23 September 1923

Dearest Taddie,

I sent off a letter to you this morning dated the 21st by mistake.[2] This is Sunday, and this day week I hope to be on my way home. I told you I was going to tea at the Château de Coudrée, I have been there & back. There was a crowd of guests, nearly all French – I only noticed one Japanese in addition to myself who were not French. The Château is the most richly furnished mansion I have ever seen. MacWhite, who is a repository of information, tells me that the Bartholoni family are descended from a native of Florence who had to become a refugee in France some three centuries ago. They kept up the family tradition of banking & became very rich. The Château is a very old one, but not medieval. It is built in a square with a courtyard inside, a square donjon towards the courtyard, & round turrets from the ground up at the outside corners. It is a moderate size, but contains magnificent apartments & exquisite furniture and is quite a museum of ornamental work of the last three centuries.

[1] Above No. 122.
[2] Above No. 128.

Monday
Today our delegation entertained nearly a score of journalists at lunch. We have had to give some entertainments in revenge for those to which we have been invited, & so far our arrangements have been successful. This evening I am to be a guest of the Cuban delegation. But I *am* tired. Nearly all the social functions and every one of the League functions, which are every day, morning or evening or both, are wearisome to me, though evidently pleasant to others. That is one of the disadvantages of being happy at home. I have gone off several times to enjoy myself rowing on the lake in a boat all to myself. Today is fine, and I have just been admiring a wonderful sunset. While it was raining a deluge in Geneva, the Alps to the east were getting covered with snow. As the sun went down, the high mountains turned from white to a delicate rose colour & the lower mountains near us became purple. A little later, the rose colour was in the sky and the snow took the faintest shade of green – perhaps it was only the contrast. Still my favourite air is 'Go day, come day, God send Sunday'.

EOIN

No. 131 NAI DT S3439

Gordon Campbell to Diarmuid O'Hegarty (Dublin) enclosing a Memorandum on the Imperial Conference by E.J. Riordan (19 September 1923)

DUBLIN, 24 September 1923

Secretary, Executive Council.
I am directed by the Minister of Industry and Commerce[1] to forward for distribution to the members of the Executive Council copies of a Memorandum on the Agenda for the Imperial Economic Conference so far as particulars are available in this Ministry.

Some technical points arise on the items[2] – 'carriage of goods by sea' and 'workmen's compensation' and memoranda can be prepared on these if necessary. These items, however, appear to be of no importance.

[signed] Gordon Campbell

MEMORANDUM.
IMPERIAL ECONOMIC CONFERENCE.
1. The following items, extracted from the Preliminary Agenda of the above Conference, are those which mainly concern this Ministry, viz:-

(2) Co-operation in assistance to Imperial Development.
(3) Trade Development.
(6) Unification of Law and Practice in the Empire on matters bearing on Trade Development.
(7) Commercial Intelligence and Statistics.
(9) External Commercial Relations of Empire.
(14) Carriage of Goods by Sea.
(15) Economic co-operation.
(16) Workmen's Compensation.

[1] Joseph McGrath.
[2] The word 'enquiries' has been crossed out and 'items' written in its place.

2. Several of these items are of secondary importance, so far as An Saorstát is concerned, but others are likely to be discussed very fully, and, no doubt, efforts will be made to influence the Saorstát Representatives in favour of one or other of the policies to be advocated.
3. For example. The South African delegates propose pressing for an arrangement whereby the British and Dominion Governments would give a much more favourable preference to British and Dominion products, thereby making it almost impossible for countries outside the Commonwealth to place goods, similar to those produced within the Empire, on the British and Dominion markets. New Zealand is reported as favouring this proposal, and Australia is inclining in the same direction. Canada, on the other hand, appears to look less favourably on such a proposition. India, too, is unlikely to acquiesce in it, and, to a large extent, British interests do not view it favourably, for the reason that, it must, if adopted, result in compelling Great Britain to adopt an extensive Tariff Policy, not alone in respect of many manufactured goods, but of food products as well.
4. Adherence to such an arrangement would, of course, commit An Saorstát to a corresponding Tariff Policy. How this would work out in practice can only be conjectured – we have no reliable data on which to base an opinion.

It is conceivable that under such conditions the British market for Irish agriculture and dairy produce might prove more lucrative and extensive than heretofore. That is a possibility, but, what is practically certain is, that the cost of the vast quantities of manufactured goods, raw materials, etc., imported into An Saorstát would rise in price; that our trade with countries other than the British Commonwealth would nearly, if not altogether, cease – both in respect to imports and exports; and it is highly probable that, on balance, An Saorstát would lose rather than gain by adopting such a course. Further, Britain, Ireland's chief competitor so far as manufactures are concerned, would find herself equipped with increased facilities for placing her products on the Irish market, and for preventing existing Irish industries from expanding or potential ones from coming into being.
5. The weight of domestic opposition in Great Britain to the adoption of the policy advocated by South Africa, seems to preclude the probability of the British Government adhering to that policy. Consequently, one may presume that there is little, if any, risk of its passing beyond the debating stage. Nevertheless, South Africa may succeed in persuading the British Government to concede a portion of the claim advocated by its delegates.
6. The following factors should be taken into account, namely, that insufficient statistical data are available to enable the Government to estimate the true volume of Saorstát trade with Great Britain and the British Dominions; that such data will not be forthcoming, in reliable form sooner than the middle of next year; that only now evidence is being procured which should assist them in determining the form which the Saorstát trade policy should take in the immediate future; that this question of trade policy has yet to receive consideration by the Ministry before it can be decided; that it is inevitable, that whatever form it may take at the outset must be subjected to variation from time to time, as fuller knowledge is acquired of the resources and needs of the State.

7. Canada's attitude is summed up in the undermentioned excerpt from a speech delivered by her Minister for Marine, viz:-

Mr. Lapointe[1] said (according to the 'Montreal Gazette'), with reference to the Imperial Conference:-

'Every proposal made there shall have to be considered on its merits, but the Canadian policies must be discussed and decided on in Canada, and by Canadians, and the Parliament of Canada must be the supreme authority in the matter. Under the present circumstances I do not see that we should subscribe to any new scheme involving military or naval expenditure, and this will undoubtedly be the opinion of Canada's Parliament.'

8. Owing to the present unpreparedness of the Saorstát to frame a definite trade policy, based on reliable knowledge of the very many intricate factors which must enter into the making of such a policy, the obvious course for the Saorstát delegates to adopt at the Imperial Economic Conference seems to be to attend as observers; to acquire as much information as possible, directly and indirectly, from the proceedings and from intercourse with the other delegates, but to refrain from entering into the discussions on this occasion, except in so far as their spokesman might make a general statement outlining the reasons why the Saorstát delegates are unable, off-hand, to express definite views on the subjects under discussion or commit their Government in any way, at that stage, in respect to same. The procedure to be adopted by Canada, as set out in par. 7 above, might be considered as being applicable to the Saorstát Government on this occasion.

(Sd.) E. J. Riordan
19.9.23.

No. 132 NAI DFA 417/105

Michael MacWhite to Joseph P. Walshe (Dublin)
(N.S. 107/23)

Geneva, 25 September 1923

A Chara,

I beg to enclose you herewith a copy of a Memorandum dealing with the Registration of Treaties which was approved by the League Council three years ago.[2] Articles 3 and 4 of this Memorandum are of special interest in so far as our position is concerned.

With reference to the questions put in your letter No.234/23[3] I wish to state (1) That any Treaty presented to the League for registration should, in the first instance, pass through the hands of the Secretary General.

We are not in a position to make any authoritative statement as to the possible lines of action on the part of the League authorities following an attempt to register.

[1] The Canadian Minister of Marine and Fisheries.
[2] Not printed.
[3] Above No. 129.

(2) It would be advisable to make no attempt at registration whilst the Assembly is sitting. And
(3) The meaning of the term 'certified copy' is explained in Article 6 of the accompanying Memo.

Is mise, le meas,
[signed] M. MACWHITE

No. 133 UCDA P4/887

Extract from a letter from Michael MacWhite to Hugh Kennedy (Dublin)
GENEVA, 28 September 1923

Dear Mr. Kennedy,
[Matter omitted]
We have followed the work of the Commissions pretty closely and were able to intervene effectually in some of the debates. We were canvassed by all parties but we succeeded in sailing on an even keel. Canvassing for the election of Members of the Council is now in full swing but as there are many undercurrents it is as yet impossible to say who will be the winners outside of Czecho-Slovakia and Spain. The results will, however, be known before this letter reaches you.

Our independent attitude in all matters here has produced a good effect. Even our friends across the water have nothing to criticise unless it be the lack of enthusiasm we have shown towards them.

With best wishes
Yours very sincerely
[signed] M. MACWHITE

No. 134 NAI DFA 26/102

Extracts from the report of the Irish delegation to the Fourth Assembly of the League of Nations (September 1923)
DUBLIN, September 1923

1. *COMPOSITION OF THE DELEGATION OF IRELAND*

The Delegation of Ireland to the Fourth Assembly of the League of Nations was composed of the following:-

(1) *First Delegate and Chief of the Delegation:-*
President W.T. Cosgrave, T.D., President of the Executive Council of the Irish Free State;

(2) *Delegates*:- Dr. Eoin MacNeill, T.D., Minister for Education, Mr. Desmond FitzGerald, T.D., Minister for External Affairs, Mr. Hugh Kennedy, Attorney General, the Marquis MacSwiney of Mashonaglas and Mr. O. Grattan Esmonde, T.D.

(3) *Substitute Delegate*:- Mr. Kevin R. O'Shiel, Assistant Legal Adviser to the Executive Council;

(4) *Secretary-General*:- Mr. Michael MacWhite, Representative of the Irish Free State in Geneva;

(5) *Experts and Attachés*:- Mr. Diarmuid O'Hegarty, Secretary to the Executive Council of the Irish Free State, Mr. Gearoid McGann, Principal Secretary to the President, and Col. Joseph O'Reilly, Assistant Secretary to the President.

The Delegation left for Geneva on the evening of the 29th day of August, 1923 by the Mail Boat from Dun Laoghaire.

2. *OFFICIAL RECEPTION OF THE PRESIDENT BY THE GOVERNMENT OF THE FRENCH REPUBLIC*

The most notable incident on the journey to Geneva was the official reception accorded to the President by the Government of the French Republic.

When the boat arrived at Calais Pier she was boarded by the Sous-Prefect of the Department of the Pas de Calais, by the Mayor of Calais and by the local Deputy, who in the name of the Government of France extended a very cordial welcome to the President on the occasion of his first official visit to that country. These gentlemen accompanied the President and the Delegation to the train, where they saw them off. That evening they were met on the arrival of the train in Paris by a high Military Officer from the Maison Militaire, representing the President of the Republic, as well as by representatives of the French Foreign Office.

On his homeward journey from Geneva the President was received at Paris in a similar manner by the French Government.

3. *THE DELEGATION AT GENEVA*

A section of the Delegation arrived at Geneva on the 1st September, and were joined a few days later by the President and the main body from Bobbio, whither they had gone to attend the celebrations in honour of Saint Columbanus.

During the Session of the Fourth Assembly the Delegation fell naturally into two periods – the first period from the 3rd September till the 12th September, when the entire Delegation was present under the direction of the President; and the second period from the 12th September to the end of the Session, during which the Delegation comprised the Marquis MacSwiney of Mashonaglass, Mr. O'Shiel and Mr. MacWhite, under the Chairmanship of Dr. MacNeill.

The chief event during the first period was the admission of Ireland into the League of Nations. This occurred at the Fourth Plenary Meeting of the Assembly on Monday the 10th September.

4. *THE COMMITTEES OF THE ASSEMBLY*

For the better despatch of business the Assembly of the League appoints six Committees for the duration of the Session, and delegates to each of these Committees certain specific classes of work appearing on the agenda or arising during the deliberations. These Committees are composed of one representative from each Member State, and it is their duty to deal in the first instance with all matters and to submit reports and recommendations thereon to the Assembly for discussion and final decision.

The importance of these Committees is very great for in nearly every instance since the establishment of the League (and certainly in every instance at the recent Assembly) their recommendations and resolutions are passed by the

Plenary Meeting of the Assembly without alteration.
[Matter omitted]

Apart from these Six Main Committees, which can now be said to be practically permanent adjuncts of the Assembly, there are other Special Committees appointed by the Council or by the Assembly, and many Sub-Committees appointed by the main Committees for the consideration of particularly urgent matters.

An important Special Committee of Jurists was set up by the Council to co-operate with the Third Committee in drawing up the final draft of the Treaty of Mutual Assistance.
[Matter omitted]

Professor Barthelemy was elected Chairman and M. Rolin Secretary of this Committee. On Mr. Kennedy's departure to Ireland Mr. O'Shiel was appointed by the Council to take his place.

Perhaps the most important of the Sub-Committees was the Sub-Committee of the Sixth Committee charged with the special duty of examining into the request for admission into the League of any new State. It consisted of seven Members elected from the Delegations of Great Britain, Finland, France, Italy, Latvia, Persia and Roumania.

Other important Sub-Committees were:-

A Sub-Committee appointed by the Third Committee to draft for its consideration an interpretation of the provisions of Article 10 of the Covenant affected by the Canadian Amendment;

A Sub-Committee appointed by the Fifth Committee to consider a Resolution effecting a change in the Constitution of the Committee on Intellectual Co-Operation, on which the Marquis MacSwiney of Mashonaglas was co-opted; and a Sub-Committee appointed by the Sixth Committee to deal with the matter of Eastern Carelia put forward by Finland.

PART II

1. ADMISSION OF IRELAND INTO THE LEAGUE OF NATIONS

[Matter omitted]

Amid scenes of remarkable enthusiasm the Delegates of Ireland proceeded to their appointed seats in the Hall. All the representatives in the Assembly, as well as the occupants of the diplomatic, press and public galleries stood up and for several minutes applauded the new delegates. The President then called upon President Cosgrave, the First delegate of Ireland to address the Meeting. The President spoke as follows:- Opening in Irish he said:-

'In the name of God, to this Assembly of the League of Nations, life and health. We are Delegates from Saorstát Éireann, from its Parliament and Government, who have come to you to signify that Saorstát Éireann desires to acquire Membership of the League of Nations and to participate in the great work of this League. You have unanimously agreed to this request. We have found welcome and generosity from you all. We thank you, and we pray that our peace and friendship may be lasting.[1]

[Matter omitted]

[1] No Irish original has been found, the remainder of the speech is reproduced as No. 118 above.

2. STATUS AND INFLUENCE OF IRELAND

The remarkable reception accorded to Ireland on her admission into the League was certainly one of the outstanding features of the recent Assembly. There is no doubt that the large group of little Nations who form a clear majority in the League welcomed the coming of Ireland as an important and useful addition to their class and as a country that was likely to take an impartial and courageous stand on all essential matters affecting those principles of liberty and harmony upon which the foundations of the League are said to have been laid, and which are the only certain safeguard of their own existences.

A large number of Delegates was found to have a pretty accurate knowledge of the main incidents of the history of Ireland – her manifold sufferings, her age-long struggle for liberty, her triumph, her freedom from international entanglements of any kind – and this knowledge led them to the opinion in the words of one great European Statesman, that 'Ireland although in the category of the little Nations geographically was in the category of the Great Nations morally'.

Thus very much was and will be expected of the Delegation of Ireland at Geneva.

The Irish Delegation maintained throughout the proceedings the position of representatives of a free and independent State linked by the terms of the Treaty of London to Great Britain and the other States in the British Commonwealth, and cultivating a spirit of friendship and friendly consultation with these States.

In accordance with the custom in Geneva the national tricolour was flown from the apartments of the delegates, and from the official motor car of the Delegation, and its novelty created a good deal of interest amongst the general public.

On one occasion a statement was made by M. Adatci, the Japanese Delegate on the Second Committee, involving not directly the status of the Free State but the constitutional position of all the Dominions. The incident occurred during a debate in the Committee on the problem of the status of foreigners when M. Adatci used words implying that in his view the countries of the British Commonwealth were subordinate in status to Great Britain. The Marquis MacSwiney, the Irish Delegate, immediately corrected the implication and was strongly corroborated by the British Delegate, Sir Hubert Llewellyn Smith. The Canadian Delegate, Col. Graham, Canadian Federal Minister of Railways, subsequently saw Dr. MacNeill, Chairman of the Irish Delegation, and spoke to him in warm approval of the Marquis's action.

The presence of the Delegation in Geneva during the whole of the proceedings of the Fourth Assembly gave it the opportunity of testing the accuracy of some of the charges levelled against the League. One of the commonest allegations is that the League is entirely controlled by the great Powers, of which Great Britain is the dominant influence. Whatever may have been the case in the early days of the League the great Powers certainly cannot now be said to control the League, although they naturally possess a considerable degree of influence in its Councils, and Great Britain is most decidedly not the dominating factor that ill-informed people imagine her to be.

The recent Assembly was remarkable for the activity of the little Nations and the strong tendency amongst them to assert themselves on the big important issues. This was a notable departure from their attitude at the past Assemblies when, with few exceptions, they remained largely quiescent on all important matters, allowing the big Powers to have it mostly their own way.

It will be interesting to watch the development of this tendency amongst the little Nations – for, at the moment, it is not much more than a tendency. Fortunately, the atmosphere in the League is favourable for its development, and there would appear to be a genuine desire amongst the little States themselves to act purely on principle when they can, as they have realised that in the ultimate their best and surest safeguard is the just and impartial operation of the League Covenant.

It will take time for this tendency to develop and grow into a strong movement, but it must come if the League is to endure as a real peace tribunal.

3. THE DISPUTE BETWEEN ITALY AND GREECE

This tendency of the little Nations to assert themselves manifested itself very strongly during the debates on the Italo-Greek episode.

In the course of the existence of the League the little States have seen only too much evidence of the avoidance of inquiry into actions which deliberately defied the Covenant, when these actions had been committed by one of the great Powers. On the other hand, when the smaller Powers initiated this bad example there was an immediate inquiry resulting sometimes even in the putting into operation of the punitive clauses of the Covenant against the offending country.

The Italo-Greek affair raised anew the whole question of the competence of the League to interfere in the event of a dispute between two Member-States. Undoubtedly, Greece had weakened to some degree the claim of the League's rights in such matters by her appeal in the first instance to the Council of Ambassadors, a Body created by the Peace Treaties, and which has become an anachronism since the operation of the League.

Nevertheless, the little Nations taking alarm at the disposition of the Council of the League to overlook the violation of the fundamental principles involved in the dispute, instinctively came together and expressed very openly their profound disappointment at the Council's attitude. Their displeasure had effect for, at a Meeting of the Council on the 29th September Lord Robert Cecil raised the question again, and it was unanimously resolved by all Members including Italy that they were 'in agreement that any dispute between the Members of the League likely to lead to a rupture is within the sphere of the action of the League, and that if any such dispute cannot be settled by diplomacy, arbitration or judicial settlement it is the duty of the Council to deal with it in accordance with the terms of Article 15 of the Covenant'.

Furthermore, they decided to refer to a Committee of Jurists four questions on the matter of competence. The Jurists are to have their answers to these questions ready for the Meeting of the Council in December.

At the debate in the Assembly on this resolution a good number of the small independent Nations expressed their relief at the favourable ending of the unhappy incident in this very definite and unanimous recognition of the important principle of the right and competence of the League to interfere in such disputes.

This was the particular occasion on which Dr. MacNeill spoke with such good effect on behalf of the Delegation of Ireland.

In the course of his remarks Dr. McNeill said that the chief anxiety that beset the minds of the participants in that Assembly had been, not lest a particular set of events should result in a particular rupture of peace, not that a solution might not be found for a particular difficulty, but lest the work to which they had all put their hands might be undone, and the hopes which so many Nations had reposed in that great effort of good will to establish the foundations of peace might be brought to nothing. He hoped he was speaking the minds of all present when he said that there was assurance, real assurance, in the words of the statement presented by the President of the Council. He concluded with these words:

'There is only one other thing I desire to say. The test of our desire for peace, the test of our sincerity, the test of our fidelity to the principles and the solemn engagements to which we have subscribed, must be held to be our willingness, our readiness when a rupture arises, to have recourse in the first instance to the means of settlement which the League of Nations can afford.'

This was the first interference of Ireland in the Assembly since the day of her admission, and the speech of Dr. MacNeill was commented on with approval and satisfaction in many quarters.

[Matter omitted]

7. FINLAND AND EASTERN CARELIA

A matter which was of special and peculiar interest to the Irish Delegation was the dispute between Finland and Russia over the district now known as Eastern Carelia, which was brought before the Sixth Committee and subsequently before the Assembly by the Finnish Delegation.

Carelia is a large district embracing all South-Eastern Finland, that portion of the Government of Petrograd which is adjacent to Lake Ladoga, and part of the Governments of Olonetz and Archangel, extending on the East as far as the White Sea.

Carelia was a Duchy invaded and conquered several times by both Swedes and Russians. By the Treaty of Noteburg in 1323 it was partitioned between the Duchy of Novgerod and Sweden. The Eastern and Southern portions of Carelia were annexed to Russia by virtue of the Treaty of Nystadt in 1721; the remainder formed part of the Duchy of Finland and shared its fate during the following centuries.

The population of Carelia probably does not exceed 300,000 persons who are overwhelmingly of the Finnish race, speaking a dialect of the Finnish language. Indeed Carelia is not only in population Finnish, but it is source of some of the finest and most beautiful of the ancient Finnish sagas and folk-lore including the great Finnish epic of 'Kalevala', which comes from the Eastern part of the district.

The only distinction which exists amongst the people of Carelia is a religious distinction, the people of Western Carelia being of the Lutheran confession, which is the faith of the great mass of the Finnish race, whilst those living in Eastern Carelia are almost all members of the Orthodox Greek Catholic Church. Amongst these two communions of the same race there would appear to have been some contentions in the past, though never of a very violent or prolonged nature as their common language, customs and culture did much to assuage the sharpness of their religious divisions.

Western Carelia is entirely within the ambit of the present Republic of Finland, whilst Eastern Carelia, since the Russo-Finnish Treaty of Dorpat (October 14th, 1920) is now entirely included in the territories of the Russian Federal Soviet Republic.

Eastern Carelia is bounded on the West by the present frontier of Finland, on the South by Lake Ladoga, on the East by Lake Onega and the shore of the White Sea, whilst on the North it adjoins the Kola Peninsula. It has an area of about 150 square kilometres and a population of about 250,000.

The Treaty of Dorpat which was signed on October 14th, 1920 concluded the war between the Republic of Finland and the Russian Soviet State and defined the present boundaries between the two countries. Eastern Carelia went entirely to Russia, but Russia guaranteed in the Treaty itself, and more definitely by a special solemn declaration which is an Annex to the Treaty, that Eastern Carelia would be an 'autonomous territory' enjoying the 'full rights of national self-determination belonging on federative principles to the Russian State'.

Finland was also promised by the same declaration that the Eastern Carelian dialect of the Finnish language would be the language of the local administrative jurisdiction and popular education, and furthermore, that a local militia corps would be formed which would supersede the garrisons of the Russian standing Army in the district.

In November 1921 the Minister of Foreign Affairs for Finland called the attention of the Council of the League to the situation created in Eastern Carelia by the non-application of the provisions of the Treaty of Dorpat which had been registered at the Secretariat of the League the previous March. The Latvian, Esthonian and Polish Governments supported the action taken by Finland, and the Lithuanian Government requested the Council of the League to use 'its prestige to find a peaceful settlement which would safeguard the legal rights of the interested parties'.

The Council declared its readiness to consider the question with a view to arriving at a satisfactory settlement if the two parties concerned would agree, and requested one of the interested State Members of the League which was in diplomatic relations with the Government of Moscow, to ascertain that Government's intentions in that respect. The Soviet Government declared that the question of Eastern Carelia was one of domestic policy, and refused to support further efforts for mediation. Subsequently, the Finnish Government requested the Council of the League to obtain from the Permanent Court of International Justice in accordance with Article 14 of the Covenant an advisory opinion on the question of Eastern Carelia, and on the 21st April, 1923 the Council adopted the following Resolution:-

'The Council of the League of Nations requests the Permanent Court of International Justice to give an advisory opinion on the following question, taking into consideration the information which the countries concerned may equally present to the Court.

Do Articles 10 and 11 of the Treaty of Peace between Finland and Russia signed at Dorpat, October 14th, 1920, and the annexed declaration of the Russian Delegation regarding the autonomy of Eastern Carelia constitute engagements of an international character which place Russia under an obligation to Finland as to the carrying out of the provisions contained therein?'

The Permanent Court of International Justice after having considered the question at its Meeting on July 23rd, 1923 laid down that the Powers Members of the League of Nations in signing the Covenant had accepted the obligation resulting from the provisions of the Covenant concerning the peaceful settlement of international disputes, but that for those countries which were not Members of the League, and consequently not affected by the Covenant, the case was different and the League could not deal with any such dispute without their consent. Therefore, the Court decided by a majority that it was not competent even to give an advisory opinion in this particular dispute.

But the question was too important for Finland, and consequently the Finnish Delegation at the recent Fourth Assembly of the League of Nations raised the matter again. It came before the Sixth Committee in the ordinary course, who in turn sent it for special consideration to a Sub-Committee. The Sub-Committee drafted the following Resolution:-

'The Assembly of the League of Nations

Recognising the importance of the question of Eastern Carelia

Notes the declaration of the Finnish Delegation that the Finnish Government in the absence of any decision or any contrary opinion pronounced by international jurisdiction maintains its right to consider the Clauses of the Treaty of Dorpat and the Supplementary Declarations relating to the Statute of Eastern Carelia as agreements of an international order:

And requests the Council to continue to collect all useful information relating to this question with a view to reaching as satisfactory a solution as ulterior circumstances may permit'.

This Resolution came before the Sixth Committee at its Meeting on September 20th, and was strongly supported by Mr. Kevin O'Shiel, the Irish Delegate on the Committee, and by M. Meierovics, the Latvian Delegate, and by Poland, Lithuania and Esthonia. Mr. O'Shiel expressed the interest which the Delegation of Ireland took in this important matter, and declared that no harm could be done to any country interested by throwing more light on this dispute. The League of Nations was primarily established for the purpose of smoothing away the causes of contention and healing the discord between Nations, and not for dealing with the peace that might exist between Nations.

This motion was ultimately unanimously adopted by the Fourth Assembly, and thus Finland has been able to keep public interest alive in a question of such great importance to her.

No. 135 NAI DT S3332

Memorandum by Kevin O'Shiel on the Boundary Issue and League of Nations Policy

GENEVA, September 1923

SOME POSSIBLE DANGERS IN THE N.E. SITUATION:

1. *The Welcome of Ireland:* Perhaps the most unexpected and remarkable feature of Ireland's admission to the League of Nations was the astonishing and universal welcome she received from all the Nations. That this welcome was spontaneous and sincere there can be no manner of doubt, and it displayed, on the parts of the assembled peoples a far more intimate, acute and sympathetic knowledge with our history than any of us had given them credit for. It also spoke well for the efficacy of the old Dáil propaganda, which, carried on against seemingly overwhelming odds, sowed seeds which have now fructified in a very fortunate manner and at a very opportune moment for us.

2. Great Britain said 'Yes' to our admission and applauded our entry and the President's speech,[1] but in spite of those overt manifestations of goodwill it would be unwise for us to ignore the underlying fact that Great Britain was by no means too pleased by the extent, enthusiasm and unanimity of the welcome or by the nature of the speech, with its strong implications.
Great Britain finds now the country that for so many centuries she has been trying to suppress and coalesce with her own population not only free and amongst the free nations of the world, but also enthusiastically accepted by each and all of those nations as a friend, and, most disconcerting of all, *showing all the signs of being accepted by them as a nation of great influence and great importance, and likely to play a big and independent part in future world policy.*

3. It is well perhaps to mention here that the enthusiasm of our welcome by the little nations in particular was not wholly altruistic. There was a design in it. They welcomed us as yet a further useful addition to *their class*, the class of the little nations, and saw in our entry the prospects of one more vote against the designs and potency of the big powers which have always frightened them and against which they have always been struggling since the formation of the League.

4. To return to Great Britain. All these developments are, quite naturally, embarrassing and considerably upsetting to that country, particularly the prospects of our becoming a great moral influence in the League especially amongst the little Nations. In the League, as England knows so very well, there are several precedents for the rise to great influence and weight of quite small, numerically weak and economically poor countries. There is the well known case of Finland, a recently liberated country with a population not greater than that of Saorstát which, in a few years membership of the League has attained

[1] See No. 118.

to a degree of great importance and influence amongst the Northern Countries.[1] Similarly with Czecho Slovakia, another poor and rather small country, and Cuba which has attained to the position of Presidency of the entire Assembly. Perhaps the most disconcerting reflection for Britain is the thought that we may act far more independently than she would naturally wish. Efforts have been made by the Imperial Government to get all States in the Commonwealth to act and vote as much as possible together. And so far (at least on the great crucial questions), she has largely succeeded. Hence the fear that we may develop along another line in the League than that of the other Dominions is causing her a good deal of anxiety. It is not however the fashion for English statesmen to remain long idle when a line of policy is being carried out by another country (especially one by the Dominions) which they deem to be not in accord with the best interests of their country. And herein lies the main source of danger to us.

4a. All signs and omens that I have been able to read appear to me to point in the same direction, viz., that England, thoroughly alarmed at the success of our League venture will at once, indeed has actually set about the task of endeavouring to bring us to boot. This she will do in many and various ways with her usual persistence and patience, and with all the resources of her extraordinarily clever and successful diplomacy.
In this constitutional pull between England and ourselves most of the odds will be on England's side. It is true that we have now got into the Council of Nations once again, but once the Assembly is over and the great concourse of Nations at Geneva disperses[,] England will have most of the field to herself. She will be able to work through her great world chain of Ministries, Ambassadors and Consuls, and if she puts herself to it, it is quite conceivable that ere the meeting of the next Assembly she may have succeeded in clipping our wings considerably.

5. It is, I think, plain that Britain will make a huge effort to keep down our status to the dimensions of say New Zealand. There are many signs that in this task she has commenced work. Her papers lately, the 'TIMES' and the 'DAILY MAIL' have devoted considerable space to this aspect of the Irish question. Figgis' article to the 'Daily Mail' shows all the signs of having been prompted from London in order to clear the way for the 'Daily Mail' to reply. Probably F. was approached by a 'Daily Mail' Agent and asked to write on those lines. Then recently in the 'Times' there appeared a rather instructive leader on Ireland. There was praise in it but it ended up with just the suspicion of a threat. 'Ireland is at the cross-roads. She can elect to remain a loyal dominion or she can endeavour to use her new status as a stepping stone towards separation. *Mr.* Cosgrave has not yet said which of these roads he is going to travel. All we are certain of is that Britain cannot and will not concede another inch.' etc., etc. These are not the exact words but they are the meaning.

[1] 'Northern Counties' in the original.

It is therefore clear that this whittling down of our status campaign has already commenced. In obedience to some instructions the press has got active and there is no doubt activity in many other channels as well. Now, whilst the Press is dangerous and will have to be watched, the most dangerous events for us in the near future are –

(1) the Imperial Conference,
(2) any negotiations in connection with the Boundary Commission,
(3) the Boundary Commission itself.

Whatever may have happened had we not gone to Geneva there is I think no doubt but that we will now find all manner of little tilts at our status on these occasions.

IMPERIAL CONFERENCE: This conference should be carefully watched as it is most likely that a big effort will be made to create an entirely new preferential tariff which in effect may almost nullify the importance of the present Customs frontier. I know that Britain is extraordinarily anxious to get our Customs barrier removed, and to my mind its existence is one of our strongest weapons.

NORTH EASTERN NEGOTIATIONS, BOUNDARY COMMISSION, ETC.: The time will soon arrive for the maturing of this matter when again the greatest vigilance will be needed. It is probable that the British themselves may call some sort of a conference ere the B.C. sits in order to see if something may not come out of it other than the actual B.C.

Owing to the way things went in Geneva[,] Britain may now be depended upon to play more vigorously the game of the North-East irreconcilables. She will not do it openly of course, but will be very strong on the point of their "difficulties" etc., etc.

Proposals for the abolition of the Customs frontier are almost certain to be made at this juncture. We will, of course, turn down the suggestion of the U.K. frontier and then an attempt will be made to arrange commercial understandings with us so as to achieve the same thing, in that guise.

Finally (bearing in mind that the real objective in these conversations will be the whittling down of our status) a proposal as follows may be made should we prove to be sufficiently difficult:-

(1) Irish political union in some shape or form to be effected: provided that
  (a) All the Six Counties remain under the local Belfast Parliament.
  (b) Ireland to enter into an arrangement with Great Britain to remove for ever the Customs barrier.

(N.B. under this heading it will be represented to us that 'Ulster' turns naturally for trade purposes to Great Britain. Now more so than ever since the Boycott limits Belfast trade with the South and West. Therefore, this is an absolutely imperative condition precedent to Ulster coming in.)

  (c) The Union Jack to be incorporated on the Irish tricolour flag (as in the other dominions) and the King's Head to be replaced on the stamps.

(N.B. It will be represented that this is essential to solace Ulster sentiment.)

  (d) Special terms for 'Ulster' with regard to the control of patronage, finance, the Army and the Police.

(e) A solemn written guarantee by the Saorstát Government that it will remain for ever loyal to the King and the Commonwealth.

And as a quid pro quo for all this

(f) 'Ulster' to guarantee certain safeguards for her minorities in the matters of education and the exercise of the franchise, etc.

Now, it is quite probable that in the ultimate such a proposal may be put up to us and we will be called upon to decide whether we will accept or refuse it. The dangers in either event are big and very obvious. Supposing we refuse it, it will be then represented to the entire world that NOT Ulster but ourselves are the intolerant and unreasonable people. Ulster will be represented as having made superhuman sacrifices for the sake of Irish union and Irish peace. Sir James Craig will become the hero of the hour, and we will go to the B.C. in the position of the most unreasonable of unreasoning beings.

On the other hand, should we accept it we shall undoubtedly have gained the political semblance of national union (a very big thing indeed) but we shall have come down at least 50 degrees in our world status.

So as can be seen the situation has its pit-falls of which we must be careful.

Personally I think the arguments on our side were never stronger. The President's Government has restored peace and achieved a stable Govt, out of chaos. Irishmen have died and much Irish blood has been shed for the Treaty position.

We cannot din in this argument too often and also the argument that Irregularism though broken is by no means dead. It is with us always present. The 44[1] Irregulars are in this sense a blessing in disguise and we can use the fact of their existence repeatedly in our conversations with the British.

Please excuse these very rough and disconnected notes. They are not intended to be anything more than merely the roughest notes written down during odd intervals which I send in this rough form in the hope that they may be of some assistance.

C. O'S.

No. 136 NAI DFA Unregistered Papers

Statement by William T. Cosgrave to the 1923 Imperial Conference

LONDON, 1 October 1923

Mr. Prime Minister,[2] I wish to express my very real appreciation of the welcome you have extended to us and of the pleasing references you have made to our inclusion in this conference. I also appreciate very highly the cordial welcome extended to us by Mr. King, Mr. Massey and General Smuts,[3] and the great interest in Ireland shown by General Smuts in his speech. He is perhaps the best able to appreciate the difficulties through which we have passed as he also gave ready and most valuable assistance to bring about the position which leads to our presence here to-day. In your statement, Sir, you have referred to

[1] A reference to the 44 anti-Treaty Sinn Féin TDs elected at the 1923 General Election.
[2] Stanley Baldwin.
[3] General Jan Christian Smuts, Prime Minister of South Africa (1919-24).

problems which, both in size and number, over-shadow our own immediate difficulties and it gives us hope that besides settling our own affairs we may give some assistance in the solution of problems affecting the whole world. We come to this Conference in good faith, with an earnest desire to render what assistance we can in the solution of the problems to be faced, and to carry out with good faith and good will our part of that undertaking which you on your side have faithfully honoured in the past, realising that it is only in the exercise of these great attributes that it is possible for us to reach the desired end. This business is new to us and it is not possible for us to express opinions upon the many great and important matters which have been mentioned in your speech. The troubles and difficulties of our present situation and the circumstances surrounding it make my immediate association with the Conference less than I would wish. You, Mr. Prime Minister, will appreciate that and I am sure His Grace the Duke of Devonshire will do so also. I would say it is a very real pleasure for me to be here and to have witnessed such a cordial and whole-hearted reception. We realise our responsibilities and we are prepared to take over and shoulder the burdens, which are common burdens. I was very much gratified with the concluding paragraphs of the Prime Minister's speech and with the statement made by General Smuts that the real objective of this conference is to further the cause of peace.

No. 137 Reprinted from *Correspondence between the Government of the Irish Free State and His Majesty's Government relating to Article 12 of the Treaty* (Dublin, 1924)

T.M. Healy to the Duke of Devonshire (London)
DUBLIN, 2 October 1923

My Lord Duke,
I have the honour to acknowledge the receipt of Your Grace's despatch of the 22nd ultimo,[1] in which is conveyed an invitation on behalf of His Majesty's Government to the President of the Executive Council, together with such of his colleagues as he may see fit to appoint, to attend a joint Conference with representatives of His Majesty's Government, and of the Government of Northern Ireland, to discuss matters arising out of Article 12 of the Treaty of December, 1921.
2. As Your Grace is probably aware, the Constitution of the Executive Council will not be complete until Mr. MacNeill, who has been nominated Minister of Education, and who is at present absent at Geneva, has complied with the terms of Article 17 of the Constitution.[2] Immediately on his return within the next few days a reply to the despatch will be forwarded.
3. My Ministers have thought it due to Your Grace that this explanation of the delay in replying should be communicated.

I have, etc.,
T.M. HEALY

[1] Not printed.
[2] The Oath of Allegiance.

No. 138 NAI DT S3332

Extract from a report on the Fourth Assembly of the League of Nations (September 1923) by Eoin MacNeill

DUBLIN, 4 October 1923

[Matter omitted]

Almost throughout the month, the Italo-Greek crises dominated the minds of the Assembly, though it was little discussed in the formal proceedings. At the outset, the Council came to the conclusion that it would not be practicable to deal with this affair through the instrumentality of the League. Their reason undoubtedly was a fear that Italy, rather than submit the issues to the League, would withdraw from the League. In that case the League would suffer a severe shock from the withdrawal or would be forced to attempt to impose its will on one of the principal powers. If it failed in this attempt, it would be still more fatally discredited. My opinion is that the attempt would not have been made. I could find no evidence of any disposition on the part of the other three powers of the Big Four – Great Britain, France, and Japan – to compel Italy to conform to the letter and spirit of the League Covenant. The Council adopted a very ingenious way out of the difficulty, which agitated many of the small Nations, especially those of the Baltic group, who felt that the resort to force by Italy, if not dealt with by the League, might involve the practical annulment of the Covenant and render the League useless for the protection of small States and the preservation of Peace. The murdered Italian Officers had been engaged on a special task to which they had been appointed by the Council of Ambassadors.[1] The result is known. Greece agreed (having no help for it) to pay Italy 50 million *lire* and Italy agreed to evacuate Corfu. On the second last day of the session of the Assembly (Sept. 28th) the Council of the League presented a report to the Assembly on the subject of this settlement – in which the League had no part – and embodied in the report a declaration of the competence of the League to require its members to observe the Covenant. This was obvious *façade* – windowdressing. Nevertheless it was probably the wisest and most effective course that could have been taken in the circumstances.

In the discussion on the Council's report, Nansen voiced the feelings of the Baltic group and of many other small States in a speech which showed deep dissatisfaction with the whole affairs and the handling of it. He was proceeding to impugn the conduct of Italy when the President stopped him. Later in the discussion, I made a short speech, in which I excused the Report on the ground that the League was still too immature to make full use of its formal powers. I said that the affirmation of competence – which I quoted – would give some reassurance. I ended by saying that it was the plain duty of all members of the League – a duty to which they were solemnly engaged – to have recourse to the League *in the first instance*, before taking any hostile step, when a dispute should arise that threatened a rupture of peace. We were afterwards assured

[1] The following is handwritten in the margin: 'The Council of the League referred the examination of the affair, and also the settlement of it, to the Council of Ambassadors'.

by many that my speech gave wide satisfaction and gained very general approval.

The fact is that the non-representation of the United States and Germany tends to leave the League ineffective for its main purpose, the maintenance of international peace. Germany originally refused to join, and is now believed to be willing, but France opposes.

The smaller nations in the League do not act in concert. There are three chief groups. There is an American group, including all the American States south of Mexico as well as the Republic of Haiti. Mexico is not a member. The S. American member states number 19, more than a third of the total. They are already protected by the Monroe Doctrine and are consequently not heavily concerned in the efficiency of the League to prevent aggression. A group in close touch with France comprises Poland, Czechoslovakia, Yugoslavia, and Roumania. To these may be added Abyssinia, the last admitted Nation. The Baltic group, Denmark, Norway, Sweden, Finland, Esthonia, Latvia and Lithuania, act more or less together, with a leaning toward Great Britain. Hungary is isolated, and so apparently is Greece. China exercises little influence in proportion to its enormous population and territory, hardly if at all more than Siam and Persia.

The Irish Delegation maintained throughout the position of representatives of a foreign independent state linked by the terms of the Treaty to Great Britain and the Dominion States, and cultivating a spirit of friendship and friendly consultation with these. This is also the attitude of Canada, South Africa and Australia. New Zealand claims this status less pronouncedly, though I do not know if anything inconsistent with it could be specified.

The position of India is sufficiently seen in the fact that the head of the Indian Delegation is Lord Hardinge, who may represent Indian economic and cultural interests to some extent, but is politically a representative of Great Britain. India is the only member of the League that has not autonomy or any constitution properly so called, and is a member by virtue of specific inclusion under the original Covenant, not having the qualifications for admission otherwise.

The full Status of Ireland was universally admitted. Once at a meeting of a Commission, the Japanese Delegate present used words implying that in his view the countries of the British Commonwealth were subordinate in Status to Great Britain. The Marquis MacSwiney immediately corrected the implication, and was corroborated by the British Delegate, Sir Hubert Llewellyn Smith. The Canadian Delegate, Mr. Graham, Canadian Minister of Defence, afterwards spoke to me in warm approval of Marquis MacSwiney's action. Many delegates spoke of the Saorstát as *la Republique Irlandaise*, as also did various press organs. At the same time, I wish to observe (1) that we always avoided making unnecessary protestations, and (2) that we adopted a wholly friendly attitude towards Great Britain, and gave expression to this attitude whenever any particular occasion arose. I should also add that nothing was done or suggested on the part of the British Delegation to limit our freedom of action.

One incident arose, which, I think expressed the desire of the British Delegation or of some members of it to honour Lord Robert Cecil and perhaps to advance his prestige. Almost at the end of the session, when the Italo-Greek composition became known, Sir Willoughby Dickinson circulated for signature by the 'Commonwealth' group a letter in which the first part congratulated the League on the success of the settlement and the second part attributed the success 'largely' to the work of Lord Robert. When Sir W. D. placed this letter before me, during the sitting of the Assembly, I saw that it already bore the signatures of the chief delegates of the Dominions. He indicated that the letter was to be published. I said that I would gladly testify to the good work of Lord R. Cecil but that I could not sign without consulting my colleagues. In my own mind, I objected to the procedure of asking me to sign a joint statement when I had not been consulted in the preparation of it, and I thought that part of the intention of the document was to advertise the signatories as representing a distinct unit – which, however proper elsewhere, was not desirable in connection with the League of Nations. Sir W. D. then left me an unsigned copy to show to my colleagues. On reading it, I came to the conclusion that the first paragraph, claiming success for the League in settling the Italo-Greek crises would stultify both the League and the signatories and be nowise helpful to Lord R. Cecil. My colleagues all agreed with this view. I called that evening on Sir Lormer Gouin, chief of the Canadian Delegation, who had signed the letter, and explained to him my objection to signing. I did this, lest I should be made out to have slighted the other signatories. Sir Lorner became uneasy and asked me if I had a copy of the document. I showed him the copy. He then said that he had signed it without much examination, regarding it merely as a compliment to Lord Robert Cecil. I said I would gladly bear witness to Lord Robert's excellent work, but that this document began with a statement which I did not believe to be at all true. Sir Lorner said that he thought he could make a good defence for the statement. I replied that I did not doubt his ability, it was my own ability to defend the statement that I could not sustain, and so we parted. I then wrote to Sir W. Dickinson, explaining that our delegation could not agree to sign and why. Mr. MacWhite has copies of the correspondence. He sent me a rather lame reply and I have heard no more of the document. Next day, the last day of the Assembly, our delegation called on Lord Robert Cecil to take leave, and, without mention of the proposed round robin, we congratulated him on his personal work and in particular on the peaceful ending of the Corfu affair.

The second matter of importance was Canada's proposed Amendment of Article 10 of the Covenant. This was long and warmly debated in the First Commission, in which I was a Member. There was strong opposition to the amendment, which proposed to allow each State to decide whether it would participate in warlike measures adopted by the Council of the League. Since unanimity is necessary for amendments to the Covenant, this amendment, being opposed by many States, was withdrawn, and a resolution was substituted interpreting Article 10 in a mitigated sense. My belief, which I could explain if required, is that the whole discussion was about nothing. In any case, it did not affect Ireland particularly, since our Constitution, which was put in along with our claim to admission, expressly requires the assent of the Oireachtas to any participation in war. The interpretative resolution was adopted by the Commission and afterwards by the Assembly, but will have no binding force, as it was not adopted unanimously.

The question of the admission of Abyssinia brought some interesting facts to our knowledge. Abyssinia retains the tradition of a very ancient civilisation, with a distinct language, literature, and customs and institutions, but has been almost wholly out of the current of modern development. For some time past, an organisation of the State has been going on under the direction of Frenchmen serving the Abyssinian Government. The British in Egypt and Somaliland, the Italians in Eritrea, would prefer Abyssinia to remain weak and disorganised, with a view to establishing 'spheres of influence' and ultimately to annexation, and there is evidence of an understanding to that effect. Neither Britain nor Italy directly opposed the claim of Abyssinia for admission to the League, but some objection cropped up on the ground of slave trade said to be tolerated by Abyssinia. In the end, Abyssinia has obtained admission, and since this means a guarantee of territorial integrity on the part of all Members of the League, it is to be expected that the aims of Britain and Italy to the contrary will be found to be abandoned. The existence of such joint aims on the part of two of the 'Big Four', if it were generally known to the smaller States, would help to explain the impotence of the League in certain directions.

There was, in fact, only one notable success in the work of the League to be reported to the Fourth Assembly, namely, the reconstruction of the State finance of Austria. The details deserve to be studied by us. Similar work under League auspices has been undertaken for Hungary.

An American organisation in favour of the entry of the United States into the League was represented early in the Session, and came into touch with our Delegation. The opinion was expressed by some of the Americans that Ireland's adhesion to the League would have great effect in the United States. Some said it would mean a turn over of a million votes. It was suggested that we should send a mission to the States to advocate America's entrance, but we did not believe that we were entitled to undertake such a step or that it would have the desired effect if we undertook it.

It would be well, however, if all our spokesmen were clear on this point. The American objection is partly a party affair and partly based on argument. The Republicans are anti-League and scored heavily by Wilson's inability to make good. The main argument is that joining the League would impair American sovereignty. This argument was mainly based on Article 10 which can be interpreted to read that America could be compelled against her will to take part in Old World quarrels – she is already bound by the Monroe Doctrine in the New World. Again, the idea is put forward that the League will evolve into a 'super-state'[,] a kind of world empire which would be operated through alliances and combinations within the League. This idea finds support in the exceptional position of the Big Four and in the grouping of the small nations. On the other hand, it is a crude and mistaken notion to think that the liberty of any country is diminished by entering the League. One might as well imagine that the citizen of a free state has less liberty than a man who is a citizen of no state. The members of the League are themselves vigilant opponents of the 'super-state' idea, and nothing would do more to reduce the Big Four to a level of equality with other States in the League than the entry of America. It goes without saying that America's adhesion would immensely strengthen Ireland's position. It would be well if friends of Ireland who have the ear of the American public would take the matter up over there.

There are side-shows to the League's work which do not seem to be in the way of accomplishing much, though they enable some fine things to be said and also some inanities. Marquis MacSwiney took a useful part in criticising certain proposals and in procuring amendments. In particular, he spoke successfully in favour of a wholly amended form of a Spanish proposal to set up a sort of super-university; he secured the inclusion of Ireland, in a League commission for international cultural purposes; and he effectively converted a proposal for the encouragement of boy scouts and girl guides on their travels into a proposal for the encouragement of travelling students. The Marquis helped our position by speaking in French on most occasions, though he did not ostentatiously avoid speaking English at times. He showed great discretion, and held his own tenaciously but with courtesy, so that he evoked no hostile feeling. He was probably the best linguist in the Assembly, being able to speak English, French, German, Italian, Spanish, and Portuguese with complete fluency, and to some extent several other languages, including Irish.

Mr. O'Shiel was diligent and efficient as usual and secured to make his mark and create good feeling towards Ireland in every quarter where he found an opportunity.

I cannot speak too highly of the work of Mr. MacWhite. His wife's illness and the death of his child did not prevent him from being of constant and valuable service. He has good tact and judgment and a remarkable knowledge of political personages and the press. Besides being an active member of the Delegation, he did all its secretarial work, including the laborious work of exchanging cards, arranging for invitations, and taking charge of our agenda and Timetable.

I must also put on record the invaluable assistance that our Delegation received throughout the Session from Mr. Edward Phelan. Mr. Phelan has a remarkable knowledge of European politics and Politicians and of technical matters connected with the League. He was always watchful for the advantage of Ireland, and his advice never failed us and never misled us. Mr. Kennedy is aware of the trouble he took in the early days of our work at Geneva and he continued to place himself equally at our service until our departure. He and Mr. MacWhite more than made up for the inexperience of the rest of us and it is due to them that our Delegation[,] without any straining for effect, kept abreast of the other Delegations generally.

Our quota of contribution to the League was fixed at £10,000. In view of the assessment on other States, we are satisfied that this is a moderate charge. I cannot say without inquiry when this contribution falls due, Mr. MacWhite will ascertain that, if he does not know it already. I presume it will be the subject of a special Vote in the DÁIL.

It might be well if the Marquis, MacWhite and O'Shiel sent in special reports without delay to External Affairs. Presumably some statement of the work of the Delegation and the effect of its participation will have to be presented to the DÁIL at an early date. I think such a statement should come in the first instance from External Affairs, and if there is any criticism I could reply.

We had to make some return for the social invitations which we so abundantly received. The accounts will show that we acted prudently in this respect. The social Meetings give good opportunities of getting on friendly terms with the representatives of various countries.

I would urgently represent that a special official in the Department of External Affairs should in future have charge of League of Nations affairs. I do not know whether it would be found possible to assign this duty to Mr. O'Shiel. His work on the Boundary Commission must now be nearly complete. It may be found possible to maintain a current of international relations through this medium, whereas it is impossible to keep up relations with many countries in the old-fashioned diplomatic way. There will be questions of the Labour Conference, Customs Conference, the permanent Committees of the League, etc., which will need special attention, and the proceedings of the Council of the League, of which Ireland is not a Member, will require to be kept in view.

The election of the non-permanent members of the Council resulted satisfactorily from our standpoint. The permanent members are the Big Four. The others are chosen by election. Each Delegation votes for six, and the six who get most votes are elected. Five of the six who received our vote were elected, and we calculated beforehand that this would be the result, though we were not certain which one of our six would fail to get in. There was much canvassing for the votes, and it may be remarked that those who were actively engaged in canvassing recognised our freedom to vote as we pleased without being bound to act with any State or group. Our object was to have as many as possible of the more outstanding and independent among the small nations put on the Council.

Our policy with regard to the League should be to strengthen the position of the small nations, by which I mean all the nation states of small or moderate size which are not looking for bits of Africa or Asia. As I have said above, most of these are formed into groups and the support of those groups is sought after by France and England, while there are possible combinations within the Big Four, involving their supporters and friends among the small nations. This state of things tends towards the old European policy of balance and power, which has always led to unrest and wars. It tends to nullify the principles and aims adopted by the League, and to make it possible for the stronger members, or for the weaker with the backing of the stronger, to act as if they were not members of the League and as if the League did not exist. The League will not realise its aims and principles until the small nations break away from the group system and act in harmony.

Not a few of the Delegates of other countries expressed the intention of visiting Ireland soon. It must be pointed out that we have no arrangements in view for the suitable reception of visitors of international importance. Our estimates provide £150 for the purpose! Our Ministry consists entirely of men of small means – in fact it is a Ministry of the Proletariat. I do not think that any official plan of entertaining representatives of other nations is at present possible. I therefore think that we should look for a non-official plan. We have placed a number of fairly wealthy men on the Seanad, and these might form the nucleus of a citizen's union of hospitality which, at the Government's request, would undertake the function of entertaining the Nation's guests. I am quite sure that this method would, if adopted, be far superior to any governmental plan, however magnificent, and that it would be characteristic and distinctive of Dublin and of Ireland.

Before we left Geneva I had a long and friendly conversation with M. Hanotaux, Mr. Phelan acting as interpreter. Hanotaux was chief of the French Delegation, though the nominal chief was Leon Bourgeois, who was present only for a few days. Hanotaux was formerly Foreign Minister for France and ranks as one of the statesmen of France. It was at his request that I went to see him at his Hotel. He conversed for about an hour. He opened the conversation by expressing gratification at the new status acquired by Ireland, and assured me of the desire of France to establish the most friendly relations with Ireland. I said that Ireland was no less desirous of cordial relations with France and that the people of Ireland had always been attracted towards France. I took care also to make it clear that in the new state of things it was our intention to cultivate amicable relations with Great Britain, a position which he said he fully appreciated. He then said that there were two relationships, economic and intellectual, which he desired to see fostered between us. I outlined to him the economic position of Ireland, her large export and import trade, probably nine-tenths of it at present confined to Great Britain. I said that even in our trade with France, Great Britain was middleman probably for nine tenths, and the conversion of this into direct trade would be a gain to both France and Ireland. He showed the keenest interest in this view, and went on to suggest that a plan of trade agencies for Ireland in France would be more productive of result than the operation of consulships, though he did not state it just so plainly. (I may remark here that Mr. Dempsey[1] in Paris, on our way back, without having heard of my conversation with Hanotaux, expressed the same view very emphatically. He said that the Consulate, by the rules of consular action, was actually tied up from opening lines of trade which a trade agency could open up). M. Hanotaux added that, if agents on behalf of Irish trade went to work in ports like Havre or Bordeaux, he hoped they would have recourse to the French Government for special facilities and we could rely on such facilities being accorded. In the matter of intellectual relations, he said the French Government would welcome the establishment of a hostel in Paris for students from Ireland, and he recommended such a hostel, because Paris might not be conducive to studious habits for youths at large in the city. I thanked him for the suggestion – (if it is acted on, it may mean that the French Government will help, perhaps in providing the building) and I said that we might also hope for a plan of interchange of University professors for occasional terms of lectures, a suggestion which drew his approval.

There is no doubt that this interview was of a very special and significant character and ought to be followed up.

I made close enquiry about the Spahlinger Institute at Geneva for the cure and prevention of tuberculosis. Dr. Spahlinger made proposals of such importance that I propose to deal with them in a special memorandum, as they have no particular relation to the business of the League of Nations.[2]

EOIN MACNEILL

[1] Vaughan Dempsey of the Irish office in Paris.
[2] Not printed.

No. 139 NAI DFA D3601

Extracts from a memorandum prepared by Joseph Walshe for the Imperial Conference on the Irish Free State's position regarding the signature of treaties by Dominions

DUBLIN, undated, but autumn 1923

Though Canada has been making Treaties since 1874 the Halibut Treaty with the U.S. of 2nd March, 1923 was the first which was not signed by the British Ambassador.

The usual procedure prior to the Halibut Treaty was to enter into negotiations with the foreign country and to keep the British Ambassador informed of the progress being made. He was then invited to sign with the Dominion Plenipotentiaries.

The following is a resumé of the events leading up to the exclusion of the British Ambassador at the signing of the Halibut Treaty.

It should be remembered that the United States not being a signatory to the Versailles Treaty and not being a Member of the League of Nations was not a party to the international recognition of the Dominions implied (according to the Dominion view) in the position given to the Dominions as signatories of the Treaty and as Members of the League. It was therefore particularly necessary for Canada to make use of the first opportunity to get her international position recognised by the U.S.A.

On June 27th, Lapointe,[1] Minister of Marine and Fisheries, definitely claimed to have obtained that recognition. 'I claim that by signing and accepting the signature of Canada on that Treaty the United States have recognised the international status of Canada, and it should not be the part of Canadians to criticise that status'.

There has been no contradiction of this statement from English or American authorities.

[Matter omitted]

What the Halibut Treaty has effected.

1. It has broken down the theory of Lloyd George, Hughes, Massey, Curzon,[2] and the other reactionaries that the diplomatic unity of the Empire was to be maintained by making the British Foreign Office the sole executive agent of all the Commonwealth Nations in all matters of external policy.
2. It has broken down what was in effect the practice of the British Cabinet to occupy towards Dominion Cabinets the position which it rightfully occupies towards the British people, i.e. of the King's substitute.
3. It has made impossible the continuance of the present system whereby the Governor General is a subordinate of the Colonial Office instead of being a personal Representative of the King.

[1] Ernest Lapointe, Minister for Marine and Fisheries (1921-24).

[2] David Lloyd George, British Prime Minister (1916-22); Charles Evans Hughes, United States Secretary of State (1921-25); W.F. Massey, Prime Minister of New Zealand (1912-25); Marquis Curzon of Kedleston, British Foreign Secretary (1919-24).

4. It has opened the way for the independent appointment by each Dominion of Consuls and Ministers Plenipotentiaries with full appropriate powers.

It is therefore of the utmost importance to give the strongest support to MacKenzie King[1] when the question of signing Treaties is being discussed. It is the only item on the Agenda of the Political Conference which really matters. New Zealand and Australia will take the reactionary side.

(Signed) S.[EOSAMH] P. B.[REATHNACH]
Rúnaí.

No. 140 NAI DT S3439

Memorandum by the Department of External Affairs on the 1923 Imperial Conference

DUBLIN, autumn 1923

IMPERIAL ECONOMIC CONFERENCE.
MEMORANDA BY THE MINISTRY OF EXTERNAL AFFAIRS
on the following subjects:-

1. Historical Outline.
2. Attitude of the Dominions.
3. 'Consultation' in Foreign Affairs. Opinion of Chief Canadian Liberal Paper.
4. Imperial Preference. Adverse Canadian Opinion.
5. Signature of Treaties by the Dominions.

[Matter omitted]

IMPERIAL CONFERENCES.

UNIFORM TENDENCY Steady refusal on part of Dominions to consider any form of Federal or Constitutional Union and an ever increasing insistence on their status as independent Nations within the Empire.

Steady increase in the insistence by the British Government on the importance of the problem of defence, and in the sentiment on the part of the colonies in favour of inter-Imperial Commercial preference.

CONFERENCE BEGAN: No particular importance.
1) 1887 (Colonial)
2) 1897 "
3) 1902 "

HISTORICAL SUMMARY
1907 CONFERENCE
FIRST STEP TOWARDS COMMONWEALTH.

EVERY FOUR YEARS
1) An 'Imperial Conference' was to be held every four years or oftener if need be.
2) It was to have no executive or legislative authority.

[1] W.L. MacKenzie King, Canadian Prime Minister and Foreign Secretary (1921-26).

POWERS
3) It was to be a Conference between governments represented normally by Prime Ministers for the discussion of questions of 'common interest' whose decisions were only to be effective if *endorsed by the respective parliaments.*

The question of defence was shelved owing to British discussion with Germany for limitation of armaments.

The British Government of the day had come into power on Free Trade policy and could not accede to desire of Dominions for Imperial preference policy.

1909 CONFERENCE – DEFENCE.
Called to consider situation created by new German naval programme.

Australia agreed to maintain in Australian waters under her own control a fleet unit of one dreadnought, three armoured cruisers, and destroyers.

Canada agreed to keep two smaller units, one in the Pacific, the other in the Atlantic.

New Zealand and South Africa promised to contribute in ships or money directly to British Navy.

All undertook to increase their national forces and to train them on uniform lines for the purpose of co-operation in the event of war.

1911 CONFERENCE.
The Dominions having accepted a share in defence were allowed to discuss foreign policy.

1917 IMPERIAL WAR CABINET
The Prime Ministers of the Dominions came to London to attend special meetings of the British Cabinet to discuss the problems of the war and possible conditions of peace.

1918 IMPERIAL WAR CABINET
This Cabinet again convened remained in session as the supreme directing body until the Armistice and went to Paris in 1919 as the British Empire Delegation to the Peace Conference.

The Dominions insisted on separate representation at the Peace Conference on the ground that they had done more to win the war than several of the participating nations.

1921 CONFERENCE.
CONTROL OF FOREIGN POLICY.
The Conference was recognised as the body which formulates the policy of the Empire especially in foreign matters. The British Government becomes charged with the duty of carrying out that policy in the intervals between the conferences, subject to such consultation as is possible through resident or visiting ministers or the cables and the mails.

The British have made a pretence of consulting the Dominions by sending innocuous 'confidential' despatches to the Dominion Governments long after any possible advantage could be gained or disadvantage avoided by the Dominions.

The question of 'consultation' on foreign affairs is regarded as the most important item on the Agenda for the coming Conference.
[Matter omitted]

No. 141 NAI DFIN 826/5

Extract from a memorandum by Joseph Brennan on Irish Free State financial policy

DUBLIN, 5 October 1923

[Matter omitted]
The suggested creation of a Department of Law should not hastily be accepted. The question of incorporating External Affairs with the staff of the Executive Council and the President's Office and attaching the whole to the President might be considered. The abolition of a Publicity Branch seems called for.
[Matter omitted]

No. 142 NAI DT S1801C

Kevin O'Shiel to William T. Cosgrave (Dublin)
(Strictly Confidential)

DUBLIN, 5 October 1923

A Chara,
Re: Reply to British Government's Boundary Letter
On a more careful examination of the British Government's letter to us suggesting a Conference on the Boundary Question a number of points have occurred to me which require care in dealing with as I think they are of very great importance.

2. In the first place I am of the opinion that our reply should be drafted in preparation for publication, for it is almost certain that sooner or later this correspondence will have to be published. Therefore, it is necessary to choose very carefully the words and phrases employed in the answer, as some or all of them may eventually attain an importance and significance out of all proportion to their meaning at the present moment.

3. A mere acceptance without qualification of the British invitation to a Conference in the form in which it appears in the Duke's letter would commit us to a Conference purely and mainly on the unexecuted provisions of Article 12 dealing with the Boundary Commission. This acceptance of a Conference to deal with the Boundary matter instead of holding fast to our Treaty rights in the matter, must tend to weaken very much a final resort to the method prescribed in the Treaty for dealing with the Boundary matter. Such an acceptance by us would undoubtedly be construed by our Irradentists and the large body of Southern opinion that supports them, as being a virtual waiver

of our Treaty rights under Article 12. The cry of their being 'betrayed again', after many assurances of standing by the Treaty, would rise up with greater vehemence than ever. On the other hand, such an unqualified acceptance would give immense gratification to Craig, who all along has said that there will be no Boundary Commission. The Northern Press would come out with long articles to this effect showing once again the wonderful leading powers of Craig.

From the words of the British despatch it is quite clear that the phrase 'the matters in question' in the second paragraph refers back to 'the provisions of Article 12 of the Treaty' in the final line of the first paragraph. From the British standpoint it is apparently to be a Conference solely and only on Article 12 and the Boundary Commission, and in my opinion should not be accepted as it stands.

4. In preparing our reply we should prepare it with a view to its utility in keeping us right in the event of the proposed negotiations breaking down. Therefore, I think we should courteously, but firmly[1] and in guarded sentences, hold to the point of view that ample provision has already been made in the Treaty for dealing with the question of the Boundaries, but that we never had, and have not now, or at any future time, any objection to meet our fellow countrymen of the North and discuss with them matters of interest to our common country, with a view to adjusting in an amicable manner the entire relationship that at present exists between the Six Counties and the rest of Ireland, which in our opinion has proved detrimental to Ireland as a whole, and which will be an ever present obstacle to the goodwill and concord between Great Britain and Ireland until it is finally settled in a manner satisfactory to all concerned.

We should mention that it is in this spirit that we enter the Conference, and we should lay stress on the fact that we have always been ready to discuss matters with these Northern people, but whilst doing so we should give ourselves any amount of scope to retreat back *on to an unshaken Article 12 position*.

We should make it perfectly clear now whilst there is time, and before anything happens that may militate against us, that we enter this discussion *without prejudice to our rights under Article 12 of the Treaty*.

I feel that this is very important and most necessary even for the position and prestige of the Government in this country in the event of anything going wrong.

Even if we are a trifle strong in the letter Britain will understand as we can, if necessary, cause her to know that the reason is largely due to the great body of opinion in the country represented by the 44 Irregular T.D's. These 44 Irregular T.D's are, at the present juncture, almost a blessing in disguise, as they will enable us to fight a much harder fight in this great matter of the future North-South relationship, and (possibly) drive a harder bargain than we could have done, say before the last Election.

We can blame everything on to them and the British cannot say anything in reply. I am particularly anxious about our keeping the way clear for an easy

[1] This word is unclear, it may also read 'grimly'.

retreat back on to Article 12, as recently I read a very illuminating article in the 'Morning Post' which admitted that Craig's interpretation (viz., a mere revision of the Boundary) of the meaning of Article 12 was wrong and that our interpretation (viz., the transfer of large tracts of territory and population) was right. The 'Morning Post' went on to say that the only decent solution was for Britain to give us large pecuniary compensation.

Please excuse this rough note, but I thought you should know the position as we in the Bureau have been able to see it.

Mise, do chara,
[signed] K. O'SHIEL
Assistant Legal Adviser

No. 143 UCDA P4/897

Edward J. Phelan to Hugh Kennedy (Dublin)
GENEVA, 6 October 1923

Dear Attorney General
I have just seen in the Freeman that you are likely to become a member of the Dáil. My best wishes and congratulations.

I have also seen Darrell Figgis' question about the registration of the Treaty and the President's answer. In connection therewith:- I have recently been having the League records examined in order to prepare a statement for our forthcoming conference concerning the signature and ratification of the amendment to Art. 393 of the Treaty[1] and I have incidentally had my attention drawn to two interesting facts. First of all you remember that during the Assembly Cecil[2] signed the said amendment for the 'British Empire'. It seems that all the Dominions have since signed separately. 'British Empire' must therefore be taken to mean Great Britain and those parts of the Empire not separately represented in the League. The Dominions were apparently more watchful than I thought. I think it may be taken as certain that they signed in virtue of their proper powers and that no 'powers' were issued to them by the F.O. Secondly the member of my staff who was examining the protocol of amendment, which is of course the original, was able to inspect a number of registered Treaties. The form is almost uniformly as follows. Each certified copy is accompanied by a letter to the Secretary General more or less in these terms:- 'In accordance with Article 18 of the Covenant of the League of Nations, I have the honour to forward herewith a certified copy of the Treaty between — and — signed at — the — day of etc. and to request you to register it in conformity with the stipulations of the abovementioned Article'. The letter is signed by a Minister and the copy of the Treaty is certified in a very simple formula which states that it is an exact copy. This declaration typed on the last page of the Treaty is also signed by a Minister.

It is also interesting that the Treaty Registration Official mentioned the Irish Treaty and said that if it were presented, in his opinion it would have to be

[1] Treaty of Versailles.
[2] Lord Robert Cecil, British delegate to the League of Nations.

registered. This of course was only an opinion expressed in conversation between two non-British officials dealing at the moment with another function of the registration department. But it was expressed spontaneously and is therefore interesting.

By the way[,] there are six precedents for the registration of a Treaty between two parts of the British Empire, or perhaps it would be better to say a sixfold precedent. India and Great Britain have each ratified six of our Labour conventions, Unemployment, Night Work of Women, Minimum Age, Rights of Association, Minimum Age for Stokers, Medical Examination for Young persons at Sea. These conventions are all registered with the League under Article 18. The ratifications are all given in accordance with Article 405 of the Treaty which states that they shall be 'formal ratifications'. If you find the point interesting I can send you fuller details and references to texts in the Official Bulletin. I don't imagine however that there will be any legal argument on the question if it should be decided to register. As a matter of fact Article 18 would seem to make it a clear obligation.

I was a little disturbed by a paragraph in the 'Freeman' of 3rd Oct. stating that the Free State had approved & thus become a party to an Anglo-French Convention on Oyster Fishing. No indication of the procedure was given and the report is perhaps inaccurate. It seems to me a case where an awkward precedent might be created if we are not careful.

I read with great interest the G.[overnor] G[eneral]'s speech. I imagine I can see your hand in one or two touches of constitutional interest.

With kindest regards
Yours very sincerely
[signed] E.J. PHELAN

No. 144 NAI DFA D1801

T.M. Healy to the Duke of Devonshire (London)
(No. 286)

DUBLIN, 8 October 1923

My Lord Duke,

I have the honour to advert to Your Grace's Despatch No. 573 of the 22nd ultimo,[1] in which is conveyed an invitation on behalf of His Majesty's Government to the President of the Executive Council, together with such of his colleagues as he may see fit to appoint, to attend a joint conference with representatives of His Majesty's Government and the Government of Northern Ireland, to discuss matters arising out of the provisions of Article 12 of the Treaty of December, 1921.

2. My ministers are bound equally to His Majesty's Government and to their own people to observe and abide by the terms of that instrument, and they have faithfully and scrupulously fulfilled their obligations in that respect

[1] Not printed.

and maintained the position created by the Treaty with the steady support of the Irish people and at the cost to them of much suffering and heavy material loss.

3. The procedure for determining the boundary between Northern Ireland and the rest of Ireland has been fixed by the Treaty and by Statute both of the United Kingdom and of the Irish Free State. It would be indeed a source of gratification to my Ministers if, at the same time, a discussion such as that suggested, would open up a prospect of remedying the present unsatisfactory position of Northern Ireland in relation to the rest of the country in a manner compatible with the fulfilment of their trust to their people, and fair and reasonable to the parties concerned, the more so as such a result would remove a cause of contention tending to impair the future amicable relations between Great Britain and Ireland.

4. In this spirit, and with this desire, my Ministers are prepared to confer as suggested, and they accept the invitation of His Majesty's Government in the hope that a basis may be found for the harmonious co-operation of the whole Irish people for their common weal.

5. They will accordingly be glad to learn at Your Grace's early convenience the date suggested for the meeting.

I have the honour to be,
My Lord Duke,
Your Grace's most obedient,
humble Servant,
[signed] T.M. Healy

No. 145 NAI DFA Unregistered Papers

Statement by Eoin MacNeill to the Imperial Conference on Ireland's position in the League of Nations

London, October 1923

I may say that the Irish Free State has arrived at nothing nearer to a definition of foreign policy than is expressed in its adhesion to the League of Nations and I was very much gratified to hear on all sides today, from Lord Robert Cecil[1] and from the representatives of other States who have spoken, the view expressed that the foreign policy in which we, as a group of nations ought to be interested – I shall not say to which we ought to be committed but in which we ought to be interested [–] should be in harmony with the principles underlying the League of Nations. I sincerely trust that will always be so. If it is so there will never be any difficulty in our following a common course together and following it effectively. Speaking as the junior among you and representing a junior State among you, I have no hesitation in saying that if a test of those principles arose and if the League of Nations through its properly accredited organs required a certain duty to be done, a certain amount of pressure, in whatever form desired, to be applied, I am perfectly certain that

[1] British delegate to the League of Nations Assembly.

the nation for which I sit here would not be behindhand in doing that duty. I should like to emphasise the point of view that I have expressed because, as an observer in Geneva, I did my best to estimate the feeling that was abroad, especially among the smaller nations, and I should say undoubtedly it was a feeling of dissatisfaction rather than a feeling of want of confidence, a feeling of desire that the objects of the League should be made effective[,] which is I think the next thing to the operative will that they should be made effective. On this question in general I did my best to express the view of the Irish Delegation in a statement that I made at the meeting of the Assembly on the 28th September and I shall not take up the time of this Conference in repeating that view now. I should like to join with those who have spoken already in offering a testimony, a stronger testimony than my own personal testimony, when I say that, so far as I know, and I have heard of nothing to the contrary, it was the unanimous feeling of the representatives of the nations at Geneva that Lord Robert Cecil had done as much as could be done to maintain the prestige and the effectiveness of the League of Nations.

No. 146 NAI DFA 417/105

Michael MacWhite to Desmond FitzGerald (Dublin)
(N.S. 120/23)

GENEVA, 12 October 1923

A Chara,

During the past week I have had inquiries made through reliable sources that could not very well be associated with us as to the attitude likely to be adopted by the League Secretariat in case we present the *Anglo-Irish Treaty for registration.*[1]

The information I received is to the effect that, though it may be disagreeable to certain people, there is no other course open to them than to proceed with the registration in the ordinary way.

The relations between Iceland and Denmark are, in many instances, similar to those between an Saorstát and Britain only, on the whole, our constitutional position is much stronger and, besides, we are members of the League. Nevertheless, an agreement signed between those two countries has recently been registered and published by the League in volume XIV of the Treaty series. I may add that it was the Danish Government that made application for the registration of the Article in question.

Is mise[,] le meas
[signed] M. MACWHITE

[1] The words italicised have been underlined in pen in the original.

No. 147 NAI DT S1983

Diarmuid O'Hegarty to Eoin MacNeill (London)
DUBLIN, 17 October 1923

A Chara,
The President would be glad if you would keep a lookout for a suitable opportunity of sounding the British and the others on the possibility of our having an ambassador at Washington.

From various points of view it would be of immense advantage not only to us but also to some of the other members of the Commonwealth.

We will write you about this in the course of a day or two.[1]

Mise, le meas,
[copy letter unsigned]

No. 148 NAI DT S1983A

Diarmuid O'Hegarty to Eoin MacNeill (London)
DUBLIN, 19 October 1923

A Chara,
Further to my letter of 17th instant,[2] the President has asked me to elaborate somewhat his views regarding an Ambassador at Washington.

On May 10, 1920, Mr. Bonar Law announced in the British House of Commons that it had been agreed 'that His Majesty, on the advice of His Canadian Ministers, shall appoint a Minister Plenipotentiary who will have charge of Canadian affairs and will be at all times the ordinary channel of communication with the United States Government in matters of purely Canadian concern, acting upon instructions from and reporting direct to the Canadian Government. In the absence of the Ambassador the Canadian Minister will take charge of the whole Embassy and of the representation of Imperial as well as Canadian interests. He will be accredited by His Majesty to the President with the necessary powers for the purpose. This new arrangement will not denote any departure either on the part of the British Government or of the Canadian Government from the principle of the diplomatic unity of the British Empire'.

This declaration appears to establish the constitutional right of Canada to appoint Ministers-Plenipotentiary empowered to deal with purely Canadian matters, and hence an effort on our part to establish a similar right would not have the appearance of breaking new ground. The fact that a Canadian Minister has not yet been appointed is attributed in some quarters to an objection on the part of Canada to the proposition that he would be charged with the

[1] See No. 148 below.
[2] No. 147 above.

representation of Imperial interests in the absence of the Ambassador[,] with the implication of subordinate status.

A Minister-Plenipotentiary at Washington would be of great value to us in many directions. In the first place it would add to the national dignity and be a manifestation to our people here that our status is what we claim it to be and not what the Irregulars pretend. This fact would in addition be made clear to our people in the United States and would tend to dispel the misapprehensions which have been created by Irregular propaganda and thus close down a source of revenue and moral support to the Irregulars.

Such an appointment would also, by reason of the diplomatic privileges which the holder would possess, enable us to deal more efficiently with a number of important matters of commercial interest to us and to the United States, e.g., tariffs on our products, as for example lace, cured fish, etc., financial accommodation in the event of our endeavouring to float external loans, and sundry other similar questions. In addition it would put us in a position to keep leaders of Irish opinion in the United States in close touch with our views and our policy here and thus to prevent the exploitation of the national spirit of the Irish race there by political adventurers.

This latter point is of general importance to all the partner States in the Commonwealth, as the hostile attitude to the Commonwealth which pre-Treaty events in Ireland have induced could thus be assuaged and the growth of a friendly feeling would have beneficial reactions all round.

I need hardly say that the considerations set out above are merely intended as general suggestions which would doubtless occur to you if you get any suitable opportunities for discussing the matter.

Mise, le meas,
[copy letter initialled] D O'hÉ
Rúnaí dón Ard Chomhairle

No. 149 NAI DFA ES Box 241 File 240

Cornelius Duane to Joseph P. Walshe (Dublin)
with enclosure on Irish-German relations
(86 C/D)

BERLIN, 19 October 1923

A Chara,

I am forwarding you two copies of a report on suggested improvements that might be carried out at the Berlin office. On Sept. 20th I put forward the view to the Ministry of Industry & Commerce that alterations were necessary and on being requested by that Ministry to give an outline of the proposed alterations I reported as in the enclosure.

Mise, le meas,
[signed] CONCHUBHAR Ó DUBHÁIN

[enclosure]

Position.

The office is situated in a residential quarter in West Berlin and is far removed from the business, political and financial centre as well as from the majority of the great railway stations. The manufacturing part of this city lies in the North and the business section runs roughly from Potsdamerplatz to Alexanderplatz. An office located between the former square and Friedrichstr. would be most convenient for Irish people to find (should they require any assistance) as well as for a Trade Representative because he would have only a little travelling to do to get into the business part of the city at once.

The political centre of Berlin is the Wilhelmstr. – the seat of the German Government. Now and again it happens that I must travel thither for information on one thing or another as raised by one or other of the Irish Ministries. The amount of time thus lost is by no means negligible and while I am absent from the office the only person in the place is the typist.

Again the banking centre is in the Behrenstr. which is not very far from the Wilhelmstr. From the point of view of monetary transactions the speed with which these are carried out by the big banks is an advantage not to be enjoyed at any of the branch offices in this neighbourhood.

Finally it would be far easier for German business-men to visit an office in the vicinity of Potsdamerplatz than in the Kaiser Allee. I am sure I would have seen more of them if I were in a more central position.

These are the main reasons why I disapprove of the location of the present office.

Office Staff

May I refer to your letter of May 12th[1] and in particular to the instructions appended for the guidance of Trade Representatives abroad. I think it is quite impossible to carry out efficiently these instructions single-handed as work has considerably increased here during the last few months. At the moment it falls roughly under the following heads:

(a) general correspondence,
(b) the compilation of a list of German importers of Irish products,
(c) reports on German economic conditions,
(d) a further section might with advantage be introduced viz: propaganda.

General correspondence is nothing more than routine work, varies in size and quality from day to day but is of no great importance.

The second heading is really important and demands a good deal of time and honest endeavour before a development of trade sets in. It is always easy to find exporters here only too anxious to flood Ireland with all sorts of goods: it is not so easy to find importers anxious to buy either raw or finished products from Ireland. It is only too obvious that concentration on the German import trade must, for a long time, be a matter of supreme importance in the relations between this office and the German trading community. It may not be generally known that Germany is, even still, one of America's best customers. Let it be hoped that Ireland will take up the running soon.

[1] Not printed.

As regards economic reports (monthly, annual and special) I have only to repeat what I said in my letter of May 28th[1] – that really first class up-to-date reports on special topics belong to the domain of specialists and can best be treated by them. Less pretentious reports could be prepared here.

You may think it strange that I attach importance to propaganda but I am convinced that far more attention should be paid to it than heretofore. Irish people are usually classed as 'English' here just as if they were natives of Yorkshire or Cornwall. The reasons are not too difficult to find. Our former relations with England have given the impression to the German people that Ireland was to all intents and purposes nothing more than a province of Great Britain. We have had the same legal system, the same currency and for all practical purposes the same language. It is not so easy to explain away to even an intelligent German the significant story on the passport 'British subject by birth'. If we had a language barrier we would have a great asset in our favour. It is painful to see that some well-known Irishmen of the past such as Swift, Steele, Goldsmith etc. are at once classed as English writers. Perhaps of 50 000 Germans not one knows that G.B. Shaw has any Irish connections whatever. Some German works on Finance that I have seen always refer to Prof. Bastable as 'der englische Schriftsteller' (the English writer). Now and again one finds references to Ireland – chiefly to her martial spirit. Recently she was quoted by the 'Lokal-Anzeiger' against Stresemann when he proposed to compromise with France. I venture to suggest that French pressure in the Ruhr forces the German press to select the one outstanding example where active resistance, after passing through the passive stage, was successful. It will take some time before Germany comes to realise that Ireland has really come out of the corner. It is our duty to make our status clear to the German people and not the duty of the German people to go and look for the facts.

The above outline is intended to convey that very much good can be derived from this country to the immediate advantage of Ireland but the means necessary to achieve that fuller development must be taken. For quite a long time there has been enough work for two in this office and I suggest that the Ministry might well consider the appointment of a second person to Berlin. With a division of labour and with earnest co-operation much useful work can be effected. An Irishman may be appointed, but unless he is acquainted somewhat with the country and with the language he cannot do very much progressive work until after the lapse of six months or a year. Supposing that the matter is postponed until later then it may be advisable to secure the assistance of a trained German economist who would be content to work for a very moderate salary. The salaries paid to many German officials of high rank with years experience behind them would, when converted into Pounds, astonish even those acquainted with circumstances on this side. A suitable German assistant would have the advantage of being able to readily locate sources of material and to condense very much of it in a short space of time. Most of the officials here have been trained in one or other of the various Universities of the country and in general one notices that practically the whole

[1] Not printed.

German Civil Service is recruited from these seats of learning. As a temporary solution I would commend this to your attention. I am not out to over-rate German ability as I hold that ability is just as high in Ireland. Of course there is in this country the narrow group of very great men (shining lights in the world) but they have sacrificed their lives to their work. I should regret that an intelligent human being should ever show the German symptoms of insatiable interest in any department of the sphere of Knowledge.

Again in order to preserve the continuity of work in this office the presence of a second person is desirable. Cases arise when I must come to the assistance of people out here on business of one sort or another. That means I have to vacate the office and consequently the sequence of work is snapped. That is readily understood as I cannot be in two places at the one time. It would indeed be desirable if some foreign visitors from Ireland learned to distinguish between a Trade Representative in the service of the Irish Free State and a commercial traveller privately employed. Not all individuals believe that the State has got its rights too.

If a good connection is to be built up then I think the sooner a second Irishman is sent out here the better. It would afford opportunities of getting into personal contact with the leading political, business, educational and artistic circles in the country and would serve, if properly used, to bring the name of Ireland most vividly before the best and most influential elements in this country. On the political side we would have very little to gain at present in Germany as the country is politically sick at heart. At the same time the British Embassy did not lose sight of the necessity for trying to have a voice, as far as possible, in moulding German foreign policy. For a long time the Berlin Foreign Office was heavily under the influence of the British Ambassador – Lord D'Abernon, whose genial smile was a greater puzzle to the wiseacres of Wilhelmstr. than the apparently inconceivable action of France when she occupied the Ruhr. However the scales have fallen from the eyes of the German politicians and they now see that 'a man may smile and smile again and still he'd be a villain'.

Ireland's interests would be along the lines of business and I can assure you that if one went about among the bigger concerns in this city one would get some very concrete business proposals that would be of interest to Ireland. My view is that German capital and technical skill should be enticed to Ireland to make up for our deficiencies in that line. In that way we may aspire to catch up rapidly on the world which is advancing at such a bewildering rate in all departments. I submit that something can be said in favour of the view.

Legal Adviser

Now and again it happens that Irish firms come to have differences, chiefly in matters of contract, with German firms of the smaller type and write here for what really amounts to legal advice. As I am unacquainted with the German legal system I cannot very well advise in such matters unless I consult a lawyer. As cases are bound to turn up periodically I would suggest that the Delegation should pay for the advice outlining the procedure to be adopted by the Irish firm but that the interested firm should meet all other expenses. Experience shows that writing begets only writing and time goes for nought. Much better to know at once what might be done than to go on an assumption that the affair will right itself somehow and sometime.

These are the main points I am asking the Ministry to consider. There are other minor items but as they are not pressing I do not refer to them in the above outline. I am submitting to your consideration a necessary minimum which sooner or later must be allowed for if this office is to be as efficient as it might well be. The fact remains that single-handed I cannot attend to everything though I have striven to do so as far as possible.

No. 150 UCDA P4/898

Edward J. Phelan to Hugh Kennedy (Dublin)
(Personal and Urgent)

GENEVA, 26 October 1923

Dear Attorney General

I am sending you herewith a copy of a document which was received by the I.L.O. this morning.[1]

It is a ratification of an amendment to the Treaty of Versailles which was adopted by the International Labour Conference and which is effected in virtue of Article 422 of that Treaty to which you can refer.

The text of the amendment and of the protocol which embodies it for the convenience of those Members of the League who prefer a process of signature as a preliminary to ratification may be found in the Official Bulletin of the I.L.O.

I asked the British Delegation if it was meant to be a ratification binding the whole Empire including the Free State. They said they thought it was. I pointed out that an en bloc ratification raised certain difficulties as regards the I.L.O. Were we to count it as one ratification or as seven, in order to calculate the total of ratifications necessary to bring the amendment into effect? They asked me to suspend publication until they could consult London.

You will remember I told you when you were in Geneva that Cecil had signed this Protocol for the 'British Empire' but that I thought it could be argued that his signature only covered the Empire in so far as it was in the League, and at the date of his signature An Saorstát was not a member. The Dominions have since also signed. Thus the same game has been played as at Versailles. The Dominions have insisted on separate signature and the Foreign Office has countered them by a unique ratification.

But as regards the Free State the position is infinitely more grave. The Free State has not even been given any opportunity of deciding whether it is in favour of the amendment or not. It might be opposed to it.

If London replies that this ratification covers the Free State the whole of our international status disappears and the value of the Treaty with England is seriously compromised unless such action is immediately challenged.

I will inform you immediately we receive the London reply and I would suggest that if it is to the effect that the Free State is covered we should

[1] Not printed.

immediately create a precedent on the other side by an individual ratification of say the Court Convention by the procedure of an Act of the Oireachtas authorising the President to ratify or by some other similar procedure.

In any case I would hope that we should decide to proceed to an individual ratification of the Court Convention or of some other convention as soon as possible as the longer we wait the greater is the danger of a precedent being made against us, as I greatly fear may now prove to be the case.

Forgive this hurried note. We are in the throes of the last days of the Conference[1] and working all night. The Irish delegation have made a good impression though of course they were very upset at the tragic end of Senator McPartlin.[2]

I hope your election goes well. I am expecting that as soon as you are free from its preoccupations you will let me know if you agree with the proofs I sent you about the beginning of the month for the second edition of the Treaty pamphlet. I hope you got them all right.

With best wishes
Yours very sincerely,
[signed] E.J. PHELAN

No. 151 NAI DFA Unregistered Papers

Statement by Desmond FitzGerald to the 1923 Imperial Conference
LONDON, 29 October 1923

Prime Minister, on our country I do not need to say we have no racial distinctions at all. Indians in Ireland have the same position as Englishmen or South Africans. It seems to me that this matter falls more or less into two classes. There are the Indians in the Dominions and the Indians in the Colonies and mandated territories etc. Now we recognise the Dominions as independent Sovereign countries, having a perfect right to look after their own affairs and we really have no right to interfere there, and in the mandated territories and protectorates they are controlled by the British Government and we have no responsibility. So all that I can do really is to give an opinion. We have no responsibility in the matter; but, if we had responsibility, we should have to protest very strongly against any racial distinctions being made. We, who are not Anglo-Saxons, have suffered a good deal in the past from being treated as an inferior race. Putting myself in the position of an Indian, I do not think that the Indian representatives here are of an equality with us, because they are not really here in a representative capacity; they are not really sent by an independent Indian Government, and they cannot really be regarded as equal with the rest of us. If I were an Indian, putting myself in their position, I would recognise that this hypersensitiveness that they have about their treatment outside of India arises really from the fact that they have not, so far, reached the degree of self-government that the rest of us have reached. With regard to Indians in the

[1] The International Labour Conference.
[2] Senator McPartlin died while attending the International Labour Conference in Geneva on 20 October 1923. He was the first member of the Irish Free State Senate to die in office.

Protectorates and so on, the Government which is primarily responsible for those places being the Government which is also responsible for India – it seems to us unjust that there should be any distinction drawn between Indians and other British subjects in those places. At the same time it seems to me that the only solution of this trouble, which comes from racial sensitiveness, is for Indians to be in a position to make real reciprocal arrangements and to make bargain for bargain. The only way that this Indian trouble is really going to be solved is for that progress towards self-government – whatever form of self-government they consider suitable for themselves – for that progress to be hastened with all speed so as to avoid what Sir Tej and the Maharajah indicated – revolutionary methods taking the place of evolutionary methods. We in our country must necessarily sympathise whole-heartedly with the Indians both in their protests against their inferior race treatment and in their feelings as to the freedom of their country. We also recognise quite plainly here that we have no right to dictate to the other Dominions as to what they do in their own areas. That is all I have to say, Prime Minister.

No. 152 NAI DT S3439

Eoin MacNeill to William T. Cosgrave (Dublin)
LONDON, 30 October 1923

My dear President,

From the published statements of prominent men in Great Britain, it is quite evident that a great British political conflict, with Protection as the main issue, is now imminent. Under the circumstances, in my opinion the Imperial Conference is now only a side-show, except in so far as the Protectionist policy in Britain may benefit by any act of the Conference. General Smuts adheres to his intention to leave for South Africa on November 9th. I think I ought to return to Ireland this week. I have accepted no engagements beyond Thursday.

Further, we have formed a strong view that this Conference should not continue a practice which has crept into former Conferences (at which we were not represented) of *passing resolutions*. We are prepared to act on our own responsibility in refusing to adopt *any* resolution, but we should be in a still stronger position if we were instructed to that effect also. Though it is understood that such resolutions cannot bind Governments it is clear that they may embarrass them, and in any case they are not consonant with the principle that each minister is constitutionally responsible to his own legislature only. We have made our view on this point clear to several of the representatives of the other States, and will use the earliest suitable opportunity of making it clear to all.

There will probably be a dissolution of Parliament here late this year or early next year.

Mr. Curtis[1] called on me to-day about the date of the preliminary conference on the N.E. question. He suggested that I should put forward January for the

[1] Lionel Curtis, Colonial Office.

further conference. I however said that I thought the preliminary conference should meet without delay and should fix the date for the further conference.

Yours sincerely,
[signed] EOIN MACNEILL

No. 153 NAI DFA Unregistered Papers

Memorandum prepared for the Imperial Conference by J.J. Walsh on the attitude of the Irish Free State to civil and commercial aviation
DUBLIN, 31 October 1923

In so far as the general question of civil aviation is concerned, the Irish Administration is prepared to co-operate in any proposals which may be made in order to facilitate Air Services, commercial or postal, and it is believed that the Irish Government would be prepared to bear its share of any expenditure necessitated by a common scheme.

Ireland, however, is very particularly interested in the development of air traffic between America and Europe, and as its ports are the nearest in Europe to America, it is thought that it is in a position to facilitate air communications generally, and in particular the transit of mails.

We are yet only at the beginning of aerial transport, but it is evident that even at the present stage of aerial development transport by aeroplane, where this is practicable is a great deal quicker than transport by sea or land, and that, in the case of mails from and to America there would be an immense gain in time if all the outgoing mails were sent by aeroplane to the farthest out land port in Europe and the incoming mails taken off by aeroplane at that port.

That port is either Galway or Queenstown.

At present American Mails incoming to Great Britain and a considerable proportion of those for Ireland, are landed at Liverpool, Plymouth or Southampton. In point of time Galway and Queenstown offer appreciable advantages over these ports. The respective distances are as follows:-

	To New York	*To St. John's*
	Miles	*Miles*
Galway	2800	1705
Queenstown	2815	1730
Liverpool	3050	1930
Plymouth	2980	1870
Southampton	3100	2002

If the average speed of the mail boats be taken as 20 miles an hour – which is probably on the high side as only the very fast boats will maintain that average – we find that:

Queenstown is	13	Hours nearer	N.Y. than	Liverpool	&	10	hrs. nearer	St John's
"	9	do	do	Plymouth	"	7	do	do
"	15	do	do	Southampton	"	14	do	do

while Galway is an hour nearer. If then, the principle of taking off mails at the nearest land port is a good one, that port should be Galway or Queenstown, and the Irish Administration favour Queenstown as being the more convenient of the two ports. The time occupied in aerial transport from Queenstown to

London would be slightly more than that occupied from Liverpool, Plymouth or Southampton, but not appreciably, and it is evident that the adoption of the principle of sending mails to and from the nearest land port by aeroplane would result in a general acceleration of approximately one day to correspondence for Great Britain and the Continent and more than that in the case of Irish correspondence generally. It has been agreed that first steamers picking-up mails off St Johns could land them at Queenstown within three and half days and by the use of Air transit between New York and the former point the distance from New York to London should be covered in four days. If seaplanes were used the mails could be taken directly from the ship, which could be met when in sight of port, and a material further acceleration would thereby be effected.

In putting this suggestion forward, the Irish Administration desires again to emphasize the fact that it is prepared to facilitate in any way in its power the general object in view.

It should be stated that a big aerodrome is situated within a dozen miles from Queenstown. This would be ready for use within a brief period.

sd. J.J. Walsh
Postmaster General,
Irish Free State

No. 154 NAI DT S3439

Diarmuid O'Hegarty to Eoin MacNeill (London)

Dublin, 31 October 1923

A Chara,

I am desired by the President to acknowledge and thank you for your letter of 30th instant[1] and to say that he has shown it to the other members of the Executive Council and they all agree you should return as soon as possible.

I would like to add that the President is not at all too well since his brother's[2] death and that he has been induced to agree to go away for a short holiday. This, in the opinion of the other members, would make your presence here all the more desirable.

Mise, le meas,
[copy letter unsigned]

No. 155 NAI DT S3439

James McNeill to Edward J. Harding (Colonial Office, London)
(Copy)

London, 1 November 1923

Dear Mr. Harding,

I am desired by Mr. Desmond FitzGerald to write you as follows with reference to the Committee to deal with the status of High Commissioners.

[1] No. 152 above.

[2] Philip Cosgrave, Governor of Mountjoy Jail.

High Commissioners are the representatives of one Government to another Government. It therefore seems that, as outside countries largely look to the representatives accredited in London for guidance as to the status, etc. of Dominions, the fact that the representatives of the Dominions in London have no definite diplomatic standing tends to create in foreign countries a wrong impression of the true status of the Dominions. For this reason alone it seems highly desirable that High Commissioners should be given definite diplomatic status.

The question of 'Extra Territoriality' in this connection seems also worthy of consideration and it would tend to clear the air if the precedence of High Commissioners were defined.

Yours sincerely,
[copy letter unsigned]

No. 156 NAI DT S1801C

Handwritten letter from Eoin MacNeill to Kevin O'Higgins (Dublin)
LONDON, 2 November 1923[1]

Dear Kevin
I called on the Duke of Devonshire this morning as a sort of leavetaking. When I made the appointment I thought I might be returning today or tomorrow, but I have to stay now over Tuesday. He asked me what about the Boundary question. I said that since I had been appointed commissioner I thought it proper to leave the other aspects of the matter in other hands, & I repeated what I said to Curtis who called on me a few days ago, that I thought the premiers & Cosgrave ought to meet without delay and settle the further proceedings. The Duke seemed to think that some delay might be needed, but I pointed out that this preliminary meeting might not last more than an hour and could be fitted into time among other engagements. He said that the conference itself could hardly meet before January, but I said that the preliminary conference would be best able to settle that.

The fact is that a big political fight is coming on in Gt Britain over the Protection issue and they are unable to think of anything else. The Impl Conference has nearly done its business, and from our point of view it has done it fairly well.

I think I wrote to the President[2] saying that FitzGerald and I were agreed that no resolutions ought to be adopted by the Conference. As I hear the President is taking a holiday perhaps you would take the matter up and have us put in a position to say that this is also the view of our government. To my mind it is quite unconstitutional and may cause inconvenience and even friction if the Conference follows the precedent of 1921 in adopting resolutions. In fact, one of the 1921 resolutions regarding the status of Indian (Hindustan) residents in the Dominions was raised by question in the Canadian parliament, and the then premier, Meighan, had to say that the resolution had no binding force,

[1] MacNeill was in London attending the 1923 Imperial Conference.
[2] See No. 152 above.

though he was a member of the Conference that adopted it. Nevertheless, the same resolution was referred to by the Indian delegation at the present Conference as having the force of a binding pledge. At the '21 Conference Smuts refused to vote for this resolution. Now it is evident that to pass resolutions that have no binding force is futile, & that resolutions give occasion for variance and friction. Moreover, each minister at the Conference is responsible solely to his own gov^t^ and legislature, and cannot take on any other responsibility, and no minister has plenipotentiary powers on any matter great or small. The only effect of these resolutions is to create difficulties, and they tend to lessen, in appearance if not in fact, the independent status of the members.

The same applies in some degree to the adoption of reports sent up from committees of the Conference, unless it is made clear that adoption means no more than placing the reports on record for the information and advice of the respective governments. We, FitzG. and I, intend to make this clear, but on this point also it would be well if we could say (if necessary) that this is our gov^t's^ view.

If there is any correspondence about the prelim. conference, I think we shd ask to have it at the earliest possible date. It will probably be necessary for you to take the President's place.

Lloyd George is due back this day week, and there are bound to be developments. The situation will be worth watching.

Yours sincerely,
EOIN MACNEILL

No. 157 NAI DT S3439

Extract from minutes of a meeting of the Executive Council (C.2/16)
DUBLIN, 3 November 1923

IMPERIAL CONFERENCE
(a) *Address to the King.*
The following suggested alterations in the text of the Address which it was proposed to present to the King at the close of the Imperial Conference were agreed on:-

References to the 'Throne' to be replaced by references to the 'Crown'.
References to the 'British Empire' to be replaced by 'British Empire and Commonwealth'.

In addition it was suggested that Dr. MacNeill should inform Mr. McKenzie King, Prime Minister for Canada, of these alterations and to enlist his assistance with a view to getting the words 'British Empire' altered for all future purposes to the 'British Empire and Commonwealth'.

(b) *Adoption of Resolutions.*
A letter was read from Dr. MacNeill in which he stated that he and the Minister of External Affairs were opposed to the adoption of any Resolutions by the Imperial Conference.[1]
The Executive Council agreed with this view.

[1] See above No. 152 above.

No. 158 NAI DT S3439

Diarmuid O'Hegarty to Eoin MacNeill (London)
(Confidential)

DUBLIN, 3 November 1923

A Chara,

Your letter of the 26th ultimo to Mr. O'Higgins[1] was read at to-day's meeting of the Executive Council, and I was instructed to send you a reply.

(1) IMPERIAL CONFERENCE

(a) Your view on the question of the adoption of resolutions by the Imperial Conference was agreed to by the Ministry.

(b) We received confidentially from Mr. Loughnane a copy of a draft address to the King, which they propose to adopt at the termination of the Conference. This document is of course very confidential, and I gather that it was not the intention to consult the Members of the Conference individually in its regard. We have suggested the following alterations to Mr. Loughnane:-

(1) That the opening sentence, which reads 'We the Prime Ministers and other representatives of the British Empire etc.' should be altered to read 'We the Prime Ministers and other representatives of the British Empire and Commonwealth of Nations, etc.'

(2) That all references to the Throne should be replaced by references to the Crown, and

(3) That the phrase 'Many and serious problems which confront the Empire' should be altered to read 'many and serious problems which confront the British Commonwealth'.

While we have indicated these changes to Mr. Loughnane we have also suggested to him that in view of Parliament reopening on the 14th instant, it is possible that none of our delegates will be present when the address is moved. The President asked me to mention this matter to you so that, if you consider it desirable, you could indicate to Mr. King that we had made the suggestion of introducing the phrase 'British Empire and Commonwealth of Nations' in future reference to what is now generally known as the 'British Empire'.

(c) The Cabinet noted that you had intended to return on Tuesday, but I have subsequently been given to understand that your return may be delayed for another day or two. In connection with this matter we will be glad to know what are Mr. FitzGerald's intentions with regard to his stay. We presume that unless there is something of importance to be dealt with at the remaining meetings of the Conference – which would necessitate his remaining – he would desire to return with you.

(2) BOUNDARY QUESTION

You will have seen in the Press that certain information regarding the proposed Conference was allowed to leak out either in Belfast or in London, that the question of the Boundary Commission was raised yesterday on the adjourn-

[1] Not printed.

ment by Mr. Milroy,[1] and that the President replied. On yesterday evening, following Sir James Craig's statement that he had accepted the invitation to the Conference without conditions, we asked the British Government to agree to the publication of the documents in this morning's papers. The Duke of Devonshire replied to the effect that in consultation with the Home Secretary he had authorised the issue of the official communique, the text of which appears in this morning's papers, and that he hoped in view of this publication that we would not insist on the publication of the full text of the correspondence for a few days. We represented that this action had rendered matters difficult here and asked whether there was any grave reason, in view of Sir James Craig's statement, for further withholding publication. We also regretted that we had not been consulted before the communique was issued by Downing Street. A reply was received at a late hour last night, in which they said there was no intention of breaking faith in the matter, that they had drafted the communique hurriedly, with a view to stopping press misrepresentations, and that they thought it would be desirable to defer publication of the full correspondence for a few days.

In view of this and of your early return, and in view also of the fact that our position was made pretty clear in the President's reply to Mr. Milroy, we thought it as well not to press for publication until you return. The British have been informed accordingly, and I send you this information so that you may be abreast of recent developments.

The Cabinet have considered very carefully the question of urging the holding of a preliminary meeting at an early date, but in view of the new 'Protection' issue and of the probable developments within the British political arena, which may be expected to manifest themselves within the next week or two, they feel that the preliminary Conference would be somewhat in the nature of a 'Marking Time' business, and might be turned to political use by either of the opposing parties in Great Britain. For this reason they think it better that we should not make any definite move in the matter until the situation clarifies itself somewhat. If there is a probability of a General Election in January, it is unlikely that the main Conference could usefully be held before then.

REGISTRATION OF THE TREATY AT GENEVA

When Mr. FitzGerald left last week he was to consult you as to whether the present was a suitable time to move in the matter of the Registration of the Treaty with the League of Nations. We have not heard whether he has taken any action in the matter, and perhaps you will ask him to send me a note for the information of the Ministers here.

Mise, le meas,
[initialled] D O hÉ

[1] Seán Milroy, TD for Cavan (1921-25).

No. 159 NAI DT S3439

Desmond FitzGerald and Eoin MacNeill to Diarmuid O Hegarty (Dublin)
LONDON, 5 November 1923

A Chara,
Your letter of 3rd instant[1] received.
1. *IMPERIAL CONFERENCE*
(a) We note that you agree with us as to the undesirability of adopting resolutions at the Imperial Conference.
(b) We note the amendments you suggest to the draft Address to the King. We have not seen this draft Address. We shall see Mr. Mackenzie King.
(c) With reference to our return, on Thursday next, 8th instant, a general report on the whole Conference will be produced. We are advised that it is important that we should be present on this occasion. This will be the last point in the Imperial Conference of any importance. We shall probably therefore return at the week end.

2. *BOUNDARY COMMISSION*
(a) *Publication of Correspondence.* Noted.
(b) *Date of Preliminary Meeting.* We think consideration of the date of this meeting should be left till our return.
(c) *Registration of Treaty at Geneva.* In our opinion registration of the Treaty at Geneva has no bearing whatever upon the Boundary Commission. We think that there is no great urgency in this matter and as we believe that a satisfactory precedent exists we think details of this precedent should first be obtained. Mr. Kevin O'Shiel may have such details.

Mise, le meas,
[signed] D. FITZGERALD & E. MACNEILL

No. 160 NAI DFA EA 1-26

Memorandum by the Irish Delegation regarding the Resolutions and Conclusions of the Imperial Conference and the Imperial Economic Conference
LONDON, 5 November 1923

The Imperial Conference is a consultative body, and has no legislative or executive status. The participant ministers are responsible solely to the Governments and Legislatures of their respective states. The acts and recorded proceedings of the Conference must accordingly be understood to be purely of the character of advice and information and to have no binding force on the governments or on the participant ministers.

It must follow from this that the acts and proceedings of the Conference should not in future take the form of resolutions. Though a resolution of the Conference does not bind the governments of the states it may appear to commit a minister to a responsibility other than his constitutional responsibility.

[1] See No. 158 above.

Moreover, a difference in opinion may arise between the participant members on the subject of a resolution, and it is not desirable that such differences should be forced without necessity to become a matter of decision and record and eventual publicity.

It should also be understood that, in adopting the Reports of its Committees, the Conference does no more than place such Reports on record for the advice and information of the respective governments and legislatures.

No. 161 NAI DFA 26/102

Letter from Michael MacWhite to Desmond FitzGerald (Dublin), enclosing a report on the admission of Ireland to the League of Nations
(N.S. 143/23)

GENEVA, 7 November 1923

A Chara,
I enclose you herewith some notes on the Admission of Ireland to Membership of the League of Nations and on the work of the Delegates on the different Commissions.

I regret that owing to pressure of work at the time I received your letter on this subject it was overlooked until now.

Is mise, le meas,
[signed] M. MACWHITE

[enclosure]

THE ADMISSION OF SAORSTÁT ÉIREANN TO MEMBERSHIP OF THE LEAGUE OF NATIONS.[1]

The unanimous admission of the Irish Free State to membership of the League of Nations has been considered by many keen observers to be the most important, as it certainly was the most popular, event of the Fourth Assembly. By this act, Ireland entered into a Treaty with the 53 other Members of the League, by virtue of which her independence is guaranteed against any possible interference from outside her own shores. In addition she has entered into the domain of international affairs and definitely broken down the isolation wall which caused her to be known on the Continent as an 'island beyond an island'. Henceforward, she is a part of the European Comity, to whose civilisation she contributed so unstintingly during the Middle Ages.

The Sixth Committee which dealt with the admission of new Members unanimously recommended that of the Irish Free State. Its independence de jure and de facto was recognised in accordance with the terms of the Constitution. The stability of the Irish Government was unquestioned and it was taken into consideration by the Committee that 'provision for the final delimination of a part of the boundary has been made in the Treaty, dated Dec. 6th,1921, embodied in the fundamental law constituting the Irish Free State'. Article 12 of the Treaty had, therefore, to come to the official cognisance of the League before the case for the admission of An Saorstát was complete and it

[1] Handwritten note on top right hand corner: 'Original handed to Minister 13/11/23'.

seems, ipso facto, that if a dispute arises over the implementing of the clauses of this Article, an appeal may be made to the League under Article 13 of the Covenant.

In proposing the admission of Ireland, the Chairman of the Sixth Committee, Mr. Meierovics, Prime Minister of Latvia, said that he felt bound to express in the name of his Government and of the Lettish people, the sentiments of strong sympathy which they felt for the noble Irish people to whose aspirations the Lettish people, rendered sensible by their own painful past, always showed the strongest sympathy. As the admission of a new State requires a two-third majority, a vote was taken by roll call to which the forty-six Members present responded in the affirmative. On the announcement of the decision, there was an extraordinary outburst of applause from all parts of the Hall which did not subside until the Irish Delegates had taken their seats.

In his address to the Assembly immediately afterwards President Cosgrave drew attention to the fact that from that day 'Ireland joined in a solemn covenant to exercise the powers of her sovereign status in promoting the peace, security and happiness[,] the economical, cultural and moral wellbeing of the human race'. He also emphasized the international character of the Anglo-Irish Treaty. This did not pass unnoticed. Writing in the 'Revue Politique et Parlementaire' a few days later, Professor Barthelemy, of the Faculté de droit, one of the French Delegates to the Fourth Assembly, remarked that the admission of Ireland was a remarkable international event and that, if ever England would be tempted to go back on the concessions to which she has consented in the document which President Cosgrave, in his thanks, intentionally qualified as an 'International Treaty', Ireland will have the right to appeal immediately to the League of Nations. Professor Barthelemy's words carry all the more weight as he was Chairman of the Jurists' Committee during the sitting of the Assembly. This is also the opinion of all the Delegates with whom I have come in contact and it proves, if proof were wanting, that by getting into the League Ireland has consolidated her international status, and considerably strengthened her constitutional position.

The part played by the Irish Delegates has also proved to the other nations, in a most convincing way, that the Irish people are not, as an insidious propaganda endeavours to make out, unfitted to take an intelligent part in international affairs. On some of the Committees it was thought sufficient to have Irish backing to get an amendment through. The votes of the Irish Delegates were amongst the first to be canvassed and, because of the weight attached to their influence, they were frequently asked to support motions made by the big as well as the small powers. The support given by the Irish Delegation to Finland on the Eastern Carelian question and to Dr. Nansen on the question of refugees made a very good impression and considerably increased Irish prestige amongst the powers which form the Baltic Group. When the decision of the League Council regarding the Graeco-Italian dispute came up before the Assembly for discussion, Lord Robert Cecil suggested that Professor MacNeill should speak on the question, as his words would carry considerable weight. His remarks, which were in wide and general terms irrespective of the case under consideration, went further than those of any other Delegate as he emphasized the fact that, in cases of dispute, the League should be appealed to in the first instance. Even the Italians were relieved by his speech as, unlike the other Delegates, he did not single them out as the only culprits.

In conclusion, it may be remarked that through the League Assembly the Irish Delegates were brought, for the first time into direct diplomatic contact with the Ministers and Ambassadors of other States. As Delegates to the League they were all on the same level and questions of prime importance which, under any other circumstances, would have been impossible could have been, and were, freely discussed. The relations thus established will be of exceptional value to the Free State and will, in many instances permit of direct communications with other Powers without the aid of any outside intermediary. For Ireland has now an interest for the League Members which, heretofore, she did not possess. She is popular in the Assembly and influential in the Committees. By employing those qualities to the best advantage she can command universal respect and obtain for herself a position in the international arena which few States, whether they be great or small, can possibly ignore.

WORK OF IRISH DELEGATES ON THE COMMITTEES

Immediately after the admission of Ireland the President and the Minister of Foreign Affairs were obliged to leave Geneva, to be followed a day later by Mr. Kennedy and Mr. Grattan Esmonde. The Delegation, until the end of the Assembly, was then constituted as follows: Dr. Eoin MacNeill, the Marquis MacSwiney, Mr. Kevin O'Shiel and Mr. Michael MacWhite, the three first as Delegates and the last as Substitute Delegate. The following appointments were then made to the different Committees:

1st Committee	Dr. MacNeill
2nd "	Marquis MacSwiney
3rd "	Mr. MacWhite
4th "	Mr. MacWhite
5th "	Marquis MacSwiney
6th "	Mr. Kevin O'Shiel

The work of the first Committee was confined to Constitutional questions, which included the proposed Amendments to Articles 10 and 16 of the Covenant. Its work was practically over before the Free State Representative was entitled to sit on it. The Second Committee dealt with Technical organisation, such as Health, Communications, Transit, etc. The Third Committee occupied itself almost solely with the Report of the Temporary Mixed Commission for the Reduction of Armaments. From the point of view of the great powers, this was considered to be the most important question dealt with. From our own point of view, however, it had but a secondary interest. In connection with this Committee, a Jurists' Drafting Committee was appointed, consisting of eight of the most competent lawyers, amongst the Delegates. Mr. Kennedy was specially invited to sit on the Jurists' Committee and, after his departure, he was replaced by Mr. Kevin O'Shiel.

The Fourth Committee dealt with the Budget of the League and all financial matters appertaining thereto. Outside of the technical and economic aspect of the question considered there was little room for the intervention of our representative except in the question of Near East Refugees and in support of a scheme for the establishment of an International University Information Office, in connection with the League. The question of Intellectual Co-operation was dealt with by the Fifth Committee and, owing to the intervention of our representative there, Irish culture was recognised and it is possible that it will, at a later date, be represented on the Committee of Intellectual Co-operation. The Sixth Committee treated political questions, minorities, boundaries, etc. Outside of the Finnish demand concerning Eastern Carelia, which had our support, there was nothing of any particular interest before it.

With regard to the whole Irish Delegation, its work at the Assembly and on the Commissions, it was remarked that everything was businesslike and went off as it should. There was no hitch or faux pas that could be attributed to it by its severest critics.

No. 162 NAI DFA ES Box 34 File 241

Cornelius Duane to Joseph P. Walshe (Dublin)
BERLIN, 13 November 1923

A Chara,
If my present letter contains the element of surprise the explanation is due to the extraordinary pressure of present circumstances which force me to request you to be good enough to transfer me from Berlin to some other part of the foreign service or to recall me to Dublin.

During the last six weeks the cost-of-living went so high that I was barely able to make ends meet with my present salary but the last fortnight ushered in such an upward price-wave that financial embarrassment and, to a minor extent, hunger loom in the immediate future. I do not propose to ask you, by way of solution, for a further increase of salary because money is no reward for the physical strain to which one is at present subject in this city. I should infinitely prefer an immediate recall to Dublin where the whole situation could be reviewed – eliminating from the discussion the possibility of my return to Berlin. Unfortunately as I am forced to live virtually in restaurants and as all price increases in food-stuffs are immediately reflected in these places I find that life is now on the verge of being unbearable. Just imagine 5 goldmarks for a cutlet or 4 goldmarks for 'ham and eggs', both of which cost about one goldmark six months ago. I am selecting two very ordinary examples but other prices stand well up to this standard. It may seem that, with billions of paper-marks, one could find a temporary solution but such is not the case. The money swindle in Berlin has long ago gone beyond the bounds of an art: it may be classed as a perfect Science. Take the last week as an example. On Saturday the official rate of the Pound, as fixed by the Reichsbank, was 2 900 000 000 000 marks but in spite of all the regulations I succeeded in getting 6 billions for a Pound or in other words more than twice the official rate. Yesterday the Pound stood at the same official level yet I got exactly twice the amount. Were it not for such strokes of luck I would have written this letter a week earlier. Of course shop-keepers and restaurant-proprietors see the swindle and fix prices in gold marks well above the level in many other foreign cities. Speculation has therefore been stimulated and is now wilder than ever. The active speculator buys dollars in Berlin at the official rate and sells next day in Prague, Danzig or Amsterdam at four times the official rate, returns to Berlin, buys again, repeats the journey and so on. As my position is not that of an exchange speculator I have got to face the higher cost-of-living without any special reserves at my disposal capable of meeting it.

The political unrest does not worry me in the least because, as far as my knowledge goes, the various revolutions described in the English and auxiliary Irish press have not in reality taken place. The English press is looking merely for sensational headlines and at the moment Germany is the best hunting ground for such. The Irish ambush has given way to the German 'revolution' with this important difference – the ambush was a reality but the German revolutions are unrealities. Generally speaking such universal unrest does not contribute to anything in the nature of economic or industrial progress but it cannot last indefinitely and a distracted Europe must ultimately make up its mind to secure order as a preliminary to progress. How long Germany remains in the melting-pot is a problem not readily answered even by experts.

The political structure of Germany has been shattered and the economic has been in agony since 1918. The very obvious signs of hunger and want moving side by side with luxury cannot but create a despondent feeling on any unprejudiced observer. Added to this I find that the feeling of solitude and the losing of touch with Dublin intensify the gloom and force me to take refuge in flight from an impossible position. I had hopes of being able to continue this veritable rear-guard action some time longer but I find the moment has now come when an immediate capitulation is the only hope. On no account can I see my way to stay on any longer than December 15th. Physical endurance does not permit me to prolong the period.

I need hardly say that my cash resources are low at the moment and estimated expenses in connection with my retiral would be as follows:

Salary for November	£ 25.-.-
" up to December 15th	" 12.10.-
Travelling expenses	" 20.-.-
total	£ 57.10.-

I must ask the Ministry to notice this matter and in particular that my salary does not allow me to make any outlay for travelling expenses.

At the moment the Government Account stands at about £ 8.- but this sum would hardly be enough to cover all expenses up to December 15th. An extra sum of about 5 or 6 £ may suffice but that is a matter which can be settled during the next few weeks.

In conclusion I have to thank the Ministry for the confidence it placed in me in appointing me to take charge of this office and hope that I may be deemed worthy to enjoy that same confidence in some other part of the service. At the same time I have to express my regret for any inconvenience that I may cause the Ministry when I ask to be removed at such short notice from Berlin.

As the contents of this letter are of interest to the Ministry of Industry and Commerce I am forwarding that Ministry a copy.

Le meas mór,
[initialled] C Ó D

No. 163 NAI DT S1667A

Joseph P. Walshe to Diarmuid O'Hegarty (Dublin)
(D11/3/38)

DUBLIN, 22 November 1923

With reference to your Minute of the 6th[1] instant regarding accommodation in Government Buildings, I am directed by the Minister to make the following observations:-

As this Ministry is being constantly visited by Consuls and foreigners interested in the Saorstát, it should be housed in some part of the Government Buildings more easily accessible from the street. Incidentally, our present apartments have the negative advantage of being so constructed as to allow of a constant current of air between the doors and windows to banish the odours of decaying chemicals exuding from the waste pipes.[2]

The Publicity Department, which need not necessarily be in the same floor as the Ministry of External Affairs requires one small room and two large rooms allocated as follows:

The small room to Mr. Lester, Director of Publicity
One large room for Typists and general work
The other to be used as Press Room.

The Ministry of External Affairs requires six rooms allocated thus:

1 Small room for MINISTER
2 Ante-room for Private Secretary
3 Small room for Secretary
4 Larger room for two Administrative Officers
5 Small room for Accountant and Assistant
6 Large room for files, register, records, clerical officer, typists, librarian.

These suggestions do not provide for the possible transfer of other services to this Ministry nor for the Passport Department which presumably will continue to be housed in Hume Street.

[signed] S.P. BREATHNACH
Rúnaí

No. 164 NAI DFA ES Box 17 File 16

Joseph P. Walshe to Gordon Campbell (Dublin)
(08/1/181)

DUBLIN, 22 November 1923

The Secretary
Ministry of Industry and Commerce.

Further to our 'phone conversation this morning we have wired to Mr. Duane of the Berlin Office that his resignation has been accepted. He has been instructed to close the office and dispose of the furniture.

[1] Not printed.
[2] The Department of External Affairs was located in the same complex as the College of Science on Merrion Street in Dublin.

As conditions of living in Berlin have become impossible and as there is no need, in the view of both our Ministries, for retaining an Office there in the present circumstances, the Minister of External Affairs considers that the consideration of a new appointment can be postponed indefinitely.

[copy letter unsigned]
Rúnaí

No. 165 NAI DT S1967

Extracts from a letter from M.H. Eliassoff to Joseph P. Walshe
(V. 177/504)

DUBLIN, 7 December 1923

I am to suggest that the question of taking part in the British Empire Exhibition may now be reconsidered in the light of the following facts.

When originally participation was decided on[,] the proposal was to erect, in a prominent site, a pavilion of from 15,000 to 20,000 sq.ft. in area, and to incur an expenditure of about £30,000. The financial and political outlook in March rendered it improbable that this outlay would be profitably incurred.

[Matter omitted]

All the countries, dominions and colonies of the British Commonwealth of Nations, except the Irish Free State, Gambia and North Borneo, are exhibiting. The absence of two small colonies with a total population less than that of Dublin and suburbs will not be noticed. The absence of the Irish Free State is noticeable, especially as the total value of our trade with Great Britain is so great, and as many of our products are saleable in the markets of the Dominions and Colonies, as well as in other countries, from which potential purchasing agents will attend the exhibition. Non-participation may, in the near future, affect the attitude of the administration and of British traders and consumers.

[Matter omitted]

The High Commissioner was informed, and believes it to be a fact, that the offered site can be sold to a private firm for £1,000. It will be assigned free to the Irish Free State, all Dominions being allowed free sites. He believes that the outlay of about £7,000 would be well repaid by the stimulus given to Irish trade, and asks that the question of participation be again considered as early as possible. There would still be time to construct a pavilion, arrange for the allocation of space, and transport the exhibits to be displayed. It may be thought desirable that the Department of Industry and Commerce should consult industrial and commercial associations immediately as a preliminary to a decision.

The Managing Director is most anxious, for many intelligible reasons, that the Irish Free State should be represented, and his anxiety on this point will ensure that difficulties with the administration of the exhibition regarding details will be minimised. He asked that a decision be reached within a week.

[signed] M.H. ELIASSOFF
p.p. Secretary

No. 166 NAI DT S5685

Edward J. Phelan to William T. Cosgrave
(Personal)

GENEVA, 8 December 1923

My Dear President
When you were in Geneva I had several talks with you on the question of the Status of the Free State particularly as regards ratification of treaties or conventions.

A very grave situation has now arisen to which I think your personal attention should be drawn.

An amendment to Article 393 of the Treaty of Versailles is at present under ratification. (Art. 393 concerns the composition of the Governing Body of the International Labour Office.)

A ratification was communicated to the League about a month ago by the British Government. The question was raised as to what the ratification covered, and, in particular, whether it covered the Irish Free State. The British Delegation communicated with London and the following communication has just been received from the British Ministry of Labour by the International Labour Office:-
'I have made enquiries as to the scope of H.M's ratification of the amendment to Article 393 and find that as I anticipated the ratification applies to the whole Empire and extends to the Irish Free State as well as to Canada, the Commonwealth of Australia, New Zealand, the Union of South Africa, and India. We would suggest therefore that in describing the ratification in official publications the most suitable formula would be to say that it is on behalf of the British Empire, Canada, the Commonwealth of Australia, New Zealand, the Union of South Africa, the Irish Free State, and India.'

Publication of the ratification was held up pending the receipt of information concerning its exact application. Publication will now have to be made and it seems to me that the effect will be disastrous. It will amount to an official intimation to all the Members of the League that our independence and sovereignty are non-existent and it will entirely stultify your speech at the Assembly.

I was very much distressed and discouraged by the resolution adopted by the Imperial Conference concerning ratifications, but this goes very much further. The Free State has never had this amendment communicated to it, has not signed it, and has had no opportunity to consider it.

I am communicating the above information to you and to the A.G. confidentially and therefore it cannot be used officially. I was very much afraid that something would be done to diminish our Treaty rights in this way and that was why I urged that we should forestall any such attempt. It is now too late to prevent this precedent being created against us although something may be done after it becomes an official fact. I think however that we should immediately proceed to ratify independently say the Court of International Justice Treaty so as to protect ourselves by a precedent on the other side. I wrote to the A.G.[1] and to O'Shiel when first this ratification was put in[,] drawing attention to the circumstances which would arise and I have no doubt

[1] See above No. 150.

but that the A.G. has considered the matter. I also fully explained the matter to Professor Whelehan[1] before he left Geneva.

You will I hope forgive me for adding to your many preoccupations but I think you will agree that the matter is of the first importance and that unless action is taken at once our whole position will be gravely compromised.

I have been delighted to see the success of the loan and I hope you will accept my congratulations.

With kindest regards
Yours very sincerely
[signed] E.J. PHELAN

No. 167 NAI DT S5685

Edward J. Phelan to Gearoid McGann (Dublin)
(Copy)

GENEVA, 8 December 1923

Dear McGann,
I have written a personal letter to the President,[2] concerning a ratification which has been put in by London to an amendment to Art. 393 of the Treaty of Versailles, which you will doubtless see. I have also written to the Attorney General[3] and to O'Shiel.[4]

Would you draw the President's attention to the extreme gravity of the question which I have no doubt you will readily realise. I foresaw that something of this kind would arise and that is why during the Assembly and since, in a series of letters to A.G. and to O'Shiel, I have been urging that we should take the first step and affirm our rights under the Treaty by ratifying a convention on our own before a precedent of joint ratification from London had been created.

But this is much worse. The Free State has not been consulted on this amendment. She is to be internationally bound by London without having had the opportunity to express an opinion. The text of the amendment has never even been officially communicated to her from Geneva. If London can bind us internationally in this way, all sovereignty resides in London. If London can bind us in this way legally, still more so can she alter by the exercise of this sovereign power any arrangement between us and her such as the Treaty. Our whole position goes by the board and the Treaty becomes Home Rule and no more. I cannot believe that we will accept such a position which makes the President's speech to the Assembly just so much vain bombast and reduces the Collins-Griffith Treaty to a fraud.

I have been studying the legal side of the question and have written suggesting to the A.G. a method by which we can ratify independently. O'Shiel knows the procedure I propose. It consists simply in the Oireachtas empowering

[1] J.B. Whelehan, Department of Industry and Commerce, Government of Ireland delegate to the International Labour Conference (1923).
[2] See above No. 166.
[3] See below No. 168.
[4] Not located.

the President by an Act. Since the Oireachtas includes the King, and an Act gets the G.[overnor] G[eneral]'s. assent, it would not be against British Constitutional procedure which requires the King for ratification. The British could not object because to the British constitutional lawyer the King would have made the President his Agent. (There is also a South African precedent.) It is to me incredible that we should accept any other procedure. In view of Articles 1 and 12 of our own Constitution I do not think any other procedure is constitutional.

That is why I am very disturbed by the resolution of the Imperial Conference on the negotiation and ratification of Treaties. I wish I knew what you think of it in Dublin so as to know what line to take here.

I have thought out my system very fully. I know there are difficulties and objections which may be urged but I think they will all be met. I am leaving Geneva on the 11th. and will be in London the 15th., 16th., 17th., 18th., and 19th. for a meeting of one of our Commissions. I have suggested to O'Shiel that if there are any questions that are obscure it might be possible for him to come to London on one of these days. The points are difficult to explain by letter and I can't use my office secretary. By the way will you apologise to the President for my amateur efforts with the typewriter but I wanted to spare him a struggle with my handwriting. If O'Shiel should not be in London, I believe Dermot[1] is over fairly often. Would it be possible for him to make a visit coincide with the days while I am there.

Anyway do ask the President to give the matter his most careful consideration. It seems to me that the Foreign Office is betting on our ignorance and general desire to be pleasant, hoping that the precedent will be created and that we shall be trapped. It is a tragedy that we should have let precious months go by and not have established our own legitimate precedent as we so easily might have done any time since our admission to the League.

Now all we can do is to get a precedent to put up against theirs but we must do it at once or when the British ratification with the description of it given in my letter to the President goes out to the Governments our whole international status will seem to them to have been a bluff.

So I trust you to do what you can. Any assistance I can give or any help in any way is of course at any time at the President's disposal.

Yours,
E.J. PHELAN

No. 168 UCDA P4/900

Edward J. Phelan to Hugh Kennedy (Dublin)
(Personal)

GENEVA, 8 December 1923

My Dear Attorney General
The question of the power of the Free State to ratify Treaties has now come to a head.

[1] Diarmuid O'Hegarty.

You will remember the history of the signature and ratification of the amendment to Art. 393 of the Treaty of Versailles. I wrote you that the British had sent to the League a ratification entirely general in form and that the question had been raised with the British Delegation as to its application. The British Delegation (to the Labour Conference) asked us to suspend publication and to ask the League to do likewise until they could enquire from London.

The Ministry of Labour has now written to us as follows:-

'I have made enquiries as to the scope of His Majesty's ratification and find that, as I anticipated, the ratification applies to the whole Empire and extends to the Irish Free State as well as to Canada, the Commonwealth of Australia, New Zealand, the Union of South Africa, and India. We would suggest, therefore, that in describing the ratification in official publications the most suitable formula would be to say that it is on behalf of the British Empire, Canada, the Commonwealth of Australia, New Zealand, the Union of South Africa, the Irish Free State, and India.'

As soon as we communicate this statement to the League they will publish and we will be obliged to do the same as it concerns an amendment to the Labour part of the Treaty and therefore will be reproduced in the Official Bulletin of the I.L.O.

I had already been very distressed and discouraged by the resolution of the Imperial Conference which to my mind is contrary to the Treaty. Its drafting however is not rigid and in any case it is only a 'voeu' submitted to the various Governments. I had hoped therefore that under it our position could still be maintained. But this last goes much beyond even the most rigid application of the I.[mperial] C.[onference] resolution. The Free State has never been consulted on the amendment in question. She has not received the text and has not signed the protocol. Her position in fact becomes that of a colony and the President's declarations in his speech at the Assembly are stultified before all international opinion.

However, you will realise better than anyone how grave are the results and implications. I can see no means of stopping publication. Ten days perhaps remain which will be consumed in the communication of the above reply to the League, in printing etc. But the above information is conveyed to you confidentially and cannot be used officially. The only thing I can see is that the Free State should at once create a precedent of independent ratification, say of the Court Treaty, and contest the above ratification after she is officially informed of it.

I have already suggested for your consideration a method of ratification which I think squares with the Constitution and which can also be defended by Empire practice. There is a South African precedent, an instrument of ratification signed by Smuts and the Governor General (see Official Bulletin of the I.L.O. Vol. 4 page 400).

I should very much like to be able to have a chat with you about the situation and about the I.C. resolution. I am at a loss to understand it and I should very much like to have your views so as to know the line to take here. I shall be in London on 16th.17th.18th. and 19th. I suppose there is no chance that yourself or O'Shiel or anyone familiar with the legal view might be in London at that time. If you should wish to write to me in London, International Labour Office

26 Buckingham Gate will find me, on the abovementioned dates. I shall be leaving Geneva on the 11th.

I enclose a copy of what may be called the 'enacting' clause of the Court Treaty in case you should want to consider it.

I have been following with interest the Courts of Justice Bill in the Dáil. I imagine it must be giving you an immense amount of work but you should draw considerable satisfaction from its progress.

I see that an interpretation bill has also been presented. I should be very glad if you could have a copy sent to me.

If I can give you any information with regard to ratification precedents I shall of course be only too glad and if I can do anything to help in any other way I hope you will not hesitate to ask me.

With kindest regards and best wishes

Yours very sincerely,
[signed] E.J. PHELAN

P.S. I should be glad if you would let me have a line to inform me if you get this letter. I am aware how busy you must be and I dont want to press you to answer when you have so many more important things on hand. But I should like to know that you get these confidential letters and the occasional texts I have sent you. I have had no acknowledgement of my four or five previous letters and I should like to be sure that they have not been 'lost in the post' or otherwise failed to reach their destination.

No. 169 NAI DFA ES Box 37

Michael MacWhite to Desmond FitzGerald (Dublin)
(N.S. 169/23)

GENEVA, 10 December 1923

A Chara,

I enclosed you with my letter No.144[1] a copy of an Instrument of Ratification by the British Government and, at the same time, called your attention to the fact that the said Instrument was meant to cover not only the British Empire, but also the Dominions. A question was raised from Geneva as to the validity of this assumption but the latest information is that the British Government insists on adhering to it.

A letter from a British Parliamentary Secretary to a League official dealing with this matter has come to my knowledge. The following is an extract:-
'I have made inquiries as to the scope of H.M. ratification of the Amendment to Art.393 and find that, as I anticipated, the ratification applies to the whole Empire and extends to the Irish Free State as well as to Canada, the Commonwealth of Australia, New Zealand, the Union of South Africa and India. We would suggest, therefore, that in describing the ratification in official publications the most suitable formula would be to say that it is on behalf of

[1] Not printed.

the British Empire, Canada, the Commonwealth of Australia, New Zealand, the Union of South Africa, the Irish Free State and India.'

Now, if this interpretation is accepted by the Government it means that Saorstát Éireann would be bound by decisions of the British Government although such decisions may not have the sanction of the Oireachtas. As a result, the Executive Council and the Dáil would be placed in a very invidious position and the prestige of the Saorstát would be considerably diminished both at home and abroad. If Treaties and Conventions can be ratified on our behalf, without even asking by your leave, it would be a matter of indifference for all practical purposes whether we agree to those Conventions or not.

If this Instrument of Ratification is registered, it will be published immediately afterwards. It will then be too late for us to take any steps in the matter. In order to delay the registration, I am writing to the International Labour Office asking for a certified copy of the Amendment to Article 393, on the pretence that the Irish Government wants to consider it, along with other Amendments to the Covenant with a view to future ratification. This demand commits us to nothing but it will oblige the League to consider the situation that would be created and will make them doubt if the British Instrument, already submitted, holds good for Ireland.

The Government should profit by the delay thus created and take steps to ratify the Statute of the Permanent Court of International Justice. This will commit them to nothing more than Membership of the League has already committed them. It will, however, prove to the League authorities that the British Imperial Ratification is not binding on the Irish Free State and that the Irish Free State cannot be committed to anything without the approval of the Executive Council or of the Oireachtas.

I shall be obliged if you let me know as soon as possible the decision of the Government on this matter for, whatever steps they take must be taken immediately if they are to be effective.

Is mise, le meas,
[copy letter unsigned]

No. 170 NAI DT S1801C

Extract from minutes of a meeting of the Executive Council (C.2/30)
DUBLIN, 10 December 1923

BOUNDARY QUESTION

Reference was made to the arrangement verbally communicated through Mr. Loughnane that a preliminary conference between the representatives of the three Governments concerned on the subject of the Boundary question should take place on the 15th inst. It was pointed out that no written confirmation of this arrangement had been received and in view of this and of the uncertain position in Great Britain following the recent General Election it was felt that it would not be desirable to initiate formal steps in regard to the Conference at the moment.

It was arranged that the Minister for External Affairs should acquaint the

High Commissioner in London with the general circumstances and with the Government's views thereon in order that he might ascertain and report upon the position as it exists at the moment.

No. 171 NAI DT S1967

Gordon Campbell to Diarmuid O'Hegarty (Dublin)
(C. 1331)

DUBLIN, 12 December 1923

I am directed by the Minister of Industry and Commerce[1] to refer to your minute of 10th December enclosing a memorandum from the High Commissioner on the subject of participation in the British Empire Exhibition and to say that this Ministry has seen little sign of any public interest in the Exhibition on the part of industrial or commercial concerns in the Saorstát. Some time ago certain of the Shipping and Railway Companies enquired whether the Saorstát intended to participate but they have not since pursued the matter. Practically no other enquiries have been received from industrial or commercial concerns.

Since traders and manufacturers themselves are not taking any present interest in the matter it is unlikely that any great commercial advantages would result from such an Exhibition as it would be possible for this Ministry and the Ministry of Agriculture to organise in the time available. Some good results could undoubtedly be expected if energetic manufacturers or traders in the Saorstát could be got to utilise the opportunities presented by the Exhibition and some such persons could be found.

The question, however, appears to this Ministry largely a political one, a decision depending upon whether non-appearance at the Exhibition may tend to prejudice Irish trade. It is considered that it would for various reasons and that for the sake of the outlay mentioned by the High Commissioner, viz., £7,000, it would be a mistake to risk this prejudice. The fact that the Saorstát do not intend to participate was adversely commented on in several directions at the recent Imperial Economic Conference and much the same reasons apply to participation in the Exhibition as applied to participating in the Economic Conference. If it were possible to organise a proper Exhibition in the Saorstát itself within the next 12 or 18 months it would be better business to do so but enquiries have been made as to the possibility of this and the conclusion has been reached that such an Exhibition cannot be organised in the Saorstát before the Summer of 1925 at the earliest.

I am to add that the Minister is doubtful as to whether the general advantages to be expected from participation would not be largely neutralised if it was necessary to occupy a small Pavilion in line with the Newfoundland and Fiji sites. In such a Pavilion the importance of Saorstát trade in relation to Great Britain and the Dominions would be unduly depreciated. It is difficult to decide how far this effect might be created without actually seeing the proposed

[1] Joseph McGrath.

location and its relation to other buildings. The plan referred to in the fourth paragraph of the High Commissioner's letter was not available to this Ministry.

GORDON CAMPBELL

No. 172 NAI DFA 417/105

Michael MacWhite to Joseph P. Walshe (Dublin)
(N.S. 174/23)

GENEVA, 13 December 1923

A Chara,

It is scarcely possible, at the present moment, to throw further light on the question raised in your letter No.293.[1] All the higher officials of the League are absent in Paris, assisting at the quarterly meeting of the League Council. They are not expected back for another week. Mr. P.[helan] is also absent in London.

Strictly speaking, no real precedent exists for the *Registration of the Treaty of December 6th, 1921*. There has been a case where India has separately ratified a Labour Convention which is very likely what Mr. P. referred to, but that can scarcely be taken as an example. The situation of Ireland, at the time of the negotiation of the Treaty, was unique and no analogy can be found for it. Since Ireland joined the League, matters have, however, considerably changed. The Covenant imposes on her the obligation of registering the Treaty and, however obnoxious it may be to certain League officials to do so, I do not see how they can avoid it. There is no doubt but the British dislike registration of the Treaty. Their anxiety on the subject has frequently made itself felt in League circles. I am now perfectly satisfied that the inquiry made some time ago by a League official on this subject was on behalf of the British and not on behalf of the United States Minister as it pretended to be.

I am also of the opinion that the British attitude is largely one of bluff. In my preliminary discussion on the *inter se* Article with the British Delegate here, a few weeks ago, he stated that he would agree to no alteration. When on the following day, after my amendment had been handed in, he found that I was not intimidated in the least and that there was likely to be a big debate on the matter in public, he accepted the final article by which all the other Articles in the Statute were subordinated to the Covenant.

It seems highly improbable that the British Government would intervene after a demand had been formally made to have the Treaty registered, as they desire at all costs to be able to show a united front in so far as the Commonwealth of Nations is concerned. Besides, if the League stretched a point or two in favour of Great Britain, it would create a very bad impression, particularly in the United States, but that is exactly what neither Great Britain nor the League can afford under the present circumstances.

I will endeavour to have further inquiries made regarding registration as soon as the League Officials return but, in the meantime, I think it advisable that a certified copy of the Treaty and the acts of ratification of same be sent

[1] Not printed.

here to be held in readiness for presentation when the Government should so desire.

In view of my letter of December 10,[1] referring to the British instrument of ratification it is all the more necessary that an immediate decision be taken on the matter.

Is mise, le meas,
[signed] M. MacWhite

No. 173 NAI DT S1983A

Extract from minutes of a meeting of the Executive Council (C.2/33)
Dublin, 11.30 am, 17 December 1923

POWERS AND DUTIES OF THE DEPARTMENT OF EXTERNAL AFFAIRS.
Consideration was given to a reply drafted by the Minister of External Affairs to Colonial Office Despatch No. 689 of the 29th November relative to the powers[,] duties and functions of his Department as provided for in the Ministers and Secretaries Bill at present before the Oireachtas.[2]

The draft was approved subject to the omission of all references to the proposed appointment of a Minister at Washington.[3]

No. 174 NAI DT S1983A

Draft despatch to be sent by T.M. Healy to the Duke of Devonshire (London)
Dublin, 18 December 1923

My Lord Duke,[4]
I have the honour to refer to Your Grace's Despatch No. 689, of the 29th ultimo, with regard to Clause I (11) of the 'Ministers and Secretaries Bill 1923' at present before the Oireachtas, and to inform Your Grace that My Ministers thoroughly concur with the opinion expressed in paragraph 2 thereof to the effect that there will be need for consultation with His Majesty's Government should any question arise in the future as to special Diplomatic representation of the interests of Saorstát Éireann abroad in any particular instance.

It is on this understanding that they desire me to inform Your Grace that they have been convinced of the urgent necessity of appointing an Irish Minister in the United States of America.

They have decided that Mr. Timothy A. Smiddy would be a suitable person to assume that position, and would be glad if His Majesty's Government could cause enquiries to be made as to whether such an appointment would be acceptable to the President and Department of State at Washington.

---

[1] Not located.
[2] The detailed draft reply is reproduced below as No. 174. The actual reply was much shorter and is reproduced as No. 177.
[3] See below No. 177.
[4] This draft despatch, though not sent, has been included because of the scope of information it contains, especially when compared with the final text of the despatch as sent (No. 177 below).

In the event of a favourable reply, they would be glad to receive credentials for Mr. Smiddy from His Majesty the King, in the form already employed in the case of Plenipotentiaries sent for specific purposes to represent, and negotiate on behalf of the other Dominions.

My Ministers are confident that Your Grace will appreciate the considerations which have prompted them to arrive at this decision. The financial and commercial interests of Saorstát Éireann in the United States are very considerable and the pressing problem of Irish emigration to America has for a long time engaged the earnest attention of My Government. They have found, in dealing with these matters, that they are severely handicapped through lack of an official mouthpiece at Washington: – but they have been influenced also by a consideration of still graver import. Your Grace is aware that the vast majority of the Irish Race is settled in America, of which a misguided section is keeping alive, by propaganda and financial support a revolutionary movement which, for the time being, the Government of Saorstát Éireann has succeeded at the cost of much blood and treasure, in suppressing at home. My Ministers cannot but view with dismay the prospect of an indefinite continuance of this activity, and they are confident that nothing could more effectively eliminate it, or more effectively consolidate the relations between our people and the rest of the Commonwealth, than the presence of an Irish Diplomatic Representative in the United States.

My Ministers are fully aware that although the Dominion of Canada decided some years ago to appoint a Minister at Washington, the appointment, and the necessary understandings consequent upon such an appointment have not yet been made. They are convinced that by a frank exchange of views such an arrangement can easily be arrived at, whereby the Irish Representative, while transacting the business which only affects Saorstát Éireann, will act in the closest and friendliest cooperation with the British Ambassador (and the representatives of other Dominions should such be appointed) in all matters which might affect the interests of other members of the Commonwealth, or of the Commonwealth as a whole.

No. 175 UCDA P4/901

Extract from a letter from Hugh Kennedy to Edward Phelan (London)

DUBLIN, 18 December 1923

My dear Mr. Phelan,

This is a preliminary note by way of reconciliation. I humbly admit that I have received your series of most important and informing letters and documents and that I have from day to day meant to write you a long letter discussing various points upon the matters of your communications; but unfortunately on my return from Geneva, I was plunged into my own contested election and immediately after that, was plunged into very important Bills in the Dáil, which were special concerns of mine. I have had my first breathing space since I saw you last during the last two days, and I am breathing rapidly as I look round upon the accumulation of office work that waits to be tackled.

I hope to write you a long letter soon, but in the meantime I write you this line upon the subject of yours of the 8th, written at Geneva.

The matter which you raise with reference to the amendment of Article 393 of the Treaty of Versailles is of course a serious matter calling for definite action on our part. Fortunately, we are in a position to take the matter up, as we have been informed officially of it since the receipt of your letter. Suffice it to say now that we have the matter in hand with a view to definitely asserting our position.

I was not present myself at the Imperial Conference in London, but I understand that our representatives were not dissatisfied with the course matters took in relation to treaties. Clear, separate, national ratification by the government and parliament of each Dominion is recognised as essential before any Dominion is committed to any particular treaty.

[Matter omitted]

With kindest regards,
Very sincerely yours,
[copy letter unsigned]
(Hugh Kennedy)
ATTORNEY GENERAL

No. 176 UCDA P4/902

Extract from a handwritten letter from Edward Phelan to Hugh Kennedy (Dublin)
PARIS, 19 December 1923

My Dear Attorney General
I was delighted to get your letter of 18th Dec[1] (850/23) in London this morning. I realise how busy you must have been. My anxiety was that any of my letters should have gone astray, & in the particular case of Art 393 I was anxious to be sure you had been made aware of the critical situation.

After writing you I reflected on the matter from the point of view of the I.L.O. & suggested to Thomas[2] that we could not take the responsibility of transmitting the reply which I quoted in my last letter to the League. He agreed & I wrote an official minute in that sense to Butler who was in London. Butler accordingly wrote to the Ministry of Labour who were thus led to throw the responsibility of instructing the League to publish back on the Foreign Office. I hoped that this would have given you longer time. In fact as you have now been seized officially it has been even more effective.

I am glad to hear that you have now the matter in hand & I have no doubt you will find a way out of the tangle which will fully safeguard our position.

There was apparently a deliberate attempt to commit us to a fatal precedent. Only the accident that the I.L.O. has to tread carefully when a question affecting two Members of the Organisation arises allowed you to be officially seized & thus given the chance to maintain our rights.

I personally think therefore that we should protest very strongly against

[1] Probably No. 175 above.
[2] Albert Thomas, Director General of the ILO.

this attempt to 'jump our claim' & should ask for sanctions against the British Office responsible. I think it would be a mistake on our part to let the matter pass or accept any casual excuse that it was a clerical error.

It is not clear from your letter as to *what* you have been informed of officially. Have you been informed that the ratification was actually communicated over your heads without consultation, or have you been asked whether you agree to a ratification being made as if the document now in Geneva had never been sent?

We have all the rights of the case on our side & I would like to see us take a very definite attitude that we are not amused & that we will decide whether or not to ratify in our own good time.

As for the Imperial Conference resolutions I shall only be satisfied when I have your own opinion. I am as I told [you] very unhappy about them. I cannot trace any contribution of ours in them. On purely internal evidence I would imagine that we just took them because we were told that they summarised existing procedure & we didn't know any better. I think we should weigh them & interpret them very carefully before we decide to follow them. The preference resolutions of the I. Conference have now been torn to shreds by the British election & we may treat the ratification resolution the same way. I should be very happy if we did, as it seems to me in contradiction both with the Treaty & Constitution.

[Matter omitted]

With best wishes,
Yours very sincerely,
[signed] E.J. PHELAN

[Matter omitted]

No. 177 NAI DT S3444

T.M. Healy to the Duke of Devonshire (London)[1]
(Despatch No. 361)
DUBLIN, 21 December 1923

My Lord Duke,

I have the honour to refer to Your Grace's Despatch No. 689 of the 29th ultimo,[2] with regard to Clause I (11) of the 'Ministers and Secretaries Bill, 1923', at present before the Oireachtas; and to inform Your Grace that my Ministers concur in the opinion expressed in Clause 2 thereof, to the effect that there will be need for consultation with His Majesty's Government when the question arises of diplomatic representation of the interests of Saorstát Éireann abroad in any particular instance.

I have the honour to be,
My Lord Duke,
Your Grace's most obedient humble servant,
[stamped] T.M. HEALY

[1] A much more detailed draft version of the despatch is reproduced directly as No. 174 above.
[2] Not printed.

No. 178 NAI DT S3452

T.M. Healy to the Duke of Devonshire (London)
(No. 362)

DUBLIN, 22 December 1923

My Lord Duke,
I have the honour to refer to Your Grace's Despatch No. 695 of the 6th instant,[1] transmitting a copy of the text of an Amendment to Article 393 of the Treaty of Versailles and the corresponding Articles of the other Treaties of Peace which was adopted by the General Conference of the International Labour Organisation of the League of Nations during its Fourth Session on the 12th October, 1922.
2. My Ministers realise that it is unnecessary to remind Your Grace that they are responsible for acts done in the name of, and on behalf of the Irish Free State, and that a ratification of which they had no previous knowledge as in the present case could not include the Free State. This particular matter was not submitted to my Ministers for approval and has not been examined by them, and they trust that in the circumstances His Majesty's Government will, in order to avoid any misapprehension arising, cause it to be made clear that the ratification which has been signified has not been so signified on behalf of the Irish Free State.

I have the honour to be,
My Lord Duke,
Your Grace's most obedient humble Servant,
[stamped] T.M. HEALY

No. 179 NAI DT S1971

Joseph P Walshe to Diarmuid O'Hegarty (Dublin) enclosing a memorandum (copy) from Desmond FitzGerald to Walshe and with explanatory notes by Walshe
(D3/12/91)

DUBLIN, 28 December 1923

A Chara,
The attached report of his interview with the British Authorities on the use of the description 'British Subject' in Irish Passports has been received from the Minister.

I have sent a copy to Mr. Kennedy.

Please be good enough to ask the President whether the report should be circulated to the Members of the Executive Council.[2]

[signed] S.P. BREATHNACH
Rúnaí

I enclose a few explanatory notes on the British contentions.

[initialled] S.P.B.

[1] Not printed.
[2] Handwritten note by Cosgrave: 'circulate to all members of the Exec[utive] Council and ask for ob[servation]s by Monday'.

[enclosure 1]

21 December 1923

J. P. Walshe, Esq.,
Secretary,
Ministry of External Affairs,
DUBLIN.

Yesterday I saw Curtis, Martin, Passport Officer, and Adams of the Foreign Office. Adams is a most objectionable person. Curtis's line was that the description 'Citizen of the Irish Free State' and the omission 'British Subject' was a breach of the Treaty (1)[1]. Adams said the British Government had entered into an agreement (I think he referred to the League of Nations 1922) that all British passports would state clearly that the bearer was a British subject (2). It was impossible for Consular agents to know whether a man was or was not a British subject and the omission would cause endless trouble and confusion (3). At one stage he said that they were not going to have Irishmen in America going about saying that they are not British subjects (4). I told him his arguments did not interest me, but that if Curtis demonstrated to me that the failure to state clearly that the bearer is a British subject is a breach of the Treaty that that would influence me. Adams said that his instructions were not to yield on the point. In the earlier stages they suggested that we should agree to their despatch, but they were prepared, if I insisted, to put the matter before the Cabinet, and they could assure me that no British Government could agree. I said that there was no question as to whether or not it would come before the Cabinet because our reply must necessarily take up the argument and not agree.

These are the chief points of the discussion. Of course they urged hundreds of considerations and quoted numerous examples. To my mind if they can make a good case for its being a breach of the Treaty or causing international complications we shall have to fall back on the proposal to print in 'Whether bearer has the status of a British Subject – Yes or No' (5).

I strongly objected to the attitude of the Foreign Office man. I shall be glad if you will get Kennedy on to the question of the Treaty. I suggested at one time that the term 'British Subject' included everyone from Mr. Baldwin to an undiscovered savage in British Guiana, that there was no uniformity of position for the holders of passports with such a description, instancing the difference between say Mr. Baldwin going to South Africa and an Indian coolie who would not be allowed to vote or to have his shop in certain parts of Natal, and in other places would not be allowed to own lands in uplands. They said that all holders of passports in the King's name, described as British subjects would have equal consideration and protection of His Majesty's Consular representatives. They could not, of course, interfere with South African legislation, but if the undiscovered savage, say, went a little further into Lorenzo Marques (Portuguese) all the power of the British Empire would be behind him for his protection.

[1] These numbers in parentheses refer to the numbered explanatory notes in Walshe's enclosure 2 below.

They instanced some celebrated case of a man who was either a Portuguese Jew or Spanish Jew who had been naturalised British, and for the protection of whom they nearly went to war.

A point that I did not make was the point arising out of the Lausanne Treaty, viz: that if we agreed only to the ratification on our behalf of the general Treaty and not of the two additional Conventions – the Trade Convention and the Rights of Foreigners – then, in Turkey a Turkish Government would have to distinguish between citizens of the Irish Free State and Englishmen or people from any Dominion which ratified the reciprocal Rights of Foreigners agreement. I think in view of the fight I put up with them that we must be prepared for a little more delay in the issue of the passports and send another despatch something on the lines of the one I prepared holding in reserve the proposal to print an additional line on the front page. I am seeing Curtis this afternoon and may have more to add to this.

Later:
I saw Curtis this afternoon. He was much less emphatic alone. In talking to him he seemed rather to justify their action on the ground that we asked the British Government to take action. This rather suggests a new trend of thought; for instance, that we might in a later despatch say that if they objected to notifying Governments under these circumstances we ourselves would notify them, or we might say, in the event of our having to agree, that we reserved to ourselves the right to make a separate arrangement with any other Government – say with the American Government – that they would accept passports or similar documents from us in which the bearer was described as a citizen of the Irish Free State. This brings to one's mind the existing arrangement between Canada and America. Obviously the Canadian Government must have made an arrangement with the American Government about the Identification Cards (6). It seems to me doubtful that the Canadian Government describes holders of Identification Cards as other than Canadian citizens. With regard to Smiddy it seems better to wait before taking action in this matter until there is a new Government here.

Think about the Canadian Identification Cards and their analogy to the passport arrangement and you will see that it may give us an entirely new ground to combat the 'difficulty with Foreign nations' plea.

I expect to be here until Monday, probably in Monte Carlo on Wednesday. Keep me informed of what Kennedy says and what you yourself think about this.

D. FitzGerald

[enclosure 2]

EXPLANATORY NOTES[1]

1. There can be no question of a breach of the Treaty except by interpreting Article 2 as binding us to follow Canadian precedent so closely as to include forms of every description.

[1] The numbers 1 to 6 refer to the numbers in parentheses in the above document.

We have already departed from Canadian usage in some important respects, e.g. in the preamble to Acts of Parliament.

All the Dominions without exception use the description 'British Subject' on their passports.

2. There is no such agreement. There was a *resolution* of a Passport Conference in 1920 referring to the material make-up of the Passport. None of the parties have acted on the resolution. There was no question as to the nature of the description of the bearer.

3. This is mere bluff. The Consular Agents can be instructed to treat all the holders of Irish passports as having the status of local or Imperial British subjects. When the holders are local British subjects only (foreigners having seven years residence in Ireland on the 6th December, 1922) there will be a definite clause inserted on the passport to that effect. Where no qualifying clause is added to the description 'Citizen of the Irish Free State' (the vast majority of cases) the bearer is to be regarded as having the status of an Imperial British subject. The British Consular Officers have very much more complicated instructions than this to carry out.

4. This is the real motive of the British objection. From our point of view to describe a citizen of the Saorstát as a British subject or as having the status of British subject would be detrimental to our interests at home and in the States.

British sentiment and Irish sentiment are definitely opposed on this point. But the issue is more vital for us. The British can afford to dispense with the form for the reality since our international status is definitely that of British subjects.

5. Mr. Kennedy suggests as the limit of compromise that the question 'Whether bearer has the *status* of British subject? (Yes – No)' should be added on the description page of the Passport. It is felt however that the difficulty of explaining the distinction to ordinary people would be considerable.

6. There is no reliable information to hand yet about the Canadian system of Identification cards. In any case it is a local arrangement and the description of status employed would have no significance of a general international application.

[signed] S.P. BREATHNACH
Rúnaí

No. 180 NAI DFA LN16

Michael MacWhite to Joseph P. Walshe (Dublin)
(N.S. 185/23)

GENEVA, 31 December 1923

A Chara,

After the admission of the Saorstát to Membership of the League of Nations reference was usually made in League documents to 'Ireland' and not to the 'Irish Free State'. Recently, however, this order of things has been changed, most probably, at the request of the British Foreign Office.

The International Labour Office has, I understand, also had a communication from the British Ministry of Labour protesting against the employment of the word 'Ireland' instead of 'Irish Free State' by the Chairman of the Governing Body of the Labour Office in his speech on the opening of the Fifth International Conference.

I have, also, reason to believe that the legal lights of the British Home Office are anxiously looking for a formula by means of which the ratification of Conventions by Great Britain will not be binding on 'Northern Ireland'. Their argument is that as the Imperial Parliament does not legislate for 'Northern Ireland' in matters relating to Labour, Commerce, Education, Health, etc. they must avoid implicating the Belfast Parliament without the consent of the latter. The object of this line of argument would be to make a case in favour of the admission of 'Northern Ireland' to separate Membership of the League of Nations.

On the other hand, the British Government did not hesitate to include the Saorstát in the instrument of ratification of the Amendment to Article 393 of the Treaty of Versailles without even consulting the Irish Government beforehand on the matter. From this, it is evident that there are some high officials in the British Foreign and Home Offices as well as in the Ministry of Labour whose anti Irish activities cannot be ignored.

Is mise, le meas,
[signed] M. MACWHITE

No. 181 UCDA P80/396

Rough notes by Joseph Walshe on the role of the Department of External Affairs
DUBLIN, undated, late 1923 or early 1924[1]

I) The Ministry of External Affairs will be a source of profit to the country:

a)	Passport visas	50,000 people expected from the U.S.A. in 1924 i.e. over £100,000 (visa £2-5)
	Issuing of passports	£10,000 per annum

II) Objects of the Ministry

(A) To establish and maintain with the chief countries of Europe and America such friendly relations as will lead to the Universal political recognition of Ireland as a distinct, sovereign state of the Commonwealth.

~~And to~~ B) ~~To coop~~[?] To encourage and coordinate ~~To coordinate the work of the Irish people To invite the cooperation people of Irish race/ people who have become~~ the work of people of Irish race in every country on behalf of the Motherland.

III) Work

Consuls	Under jurisdiction For. Affs in every country. Work has two sides

[1] There is no indication on this document of a specific date, other than a reference to 1924.

	A) political	Passports, protection, contact with local government[1]
	B) commercial	
	B) dealt with by I & Com	
	A) by Foreign Affs.	
Diplomatic Agents	For Affs alone Diplomacy intimate connection with Country's trade. If the right agents can influence government personages trade can be created etc.	

[1] Words would appear to be 'local government'.

1924

No. 182 NAI DFA D1971/1/01

Michael MacWhite to Joseph P. Walshe (Dublin)
(N.S. 01/7)

GENEVA, 9 January 1924

A Chara,
I have been asked by several persons here as to how and when they may be able to get *Irish passports*. There are a number of persons employed by the League of Nations who are classified as citizens of the Irish Free State. I happen to know that one at least of those could not justify such a claim but, in order to demonstrate that the English Members of the staff are not too numerous, some of the latter are marked down as Irish or Indians, etc. Another reason also for this is that, in case we should ask for some Free State citizens to be appointed to the staff of the League Secretariat, we would be informed that the number of our nationals is already more than could proportionately be justified. It is only when they apply for Irish passports and justify their claims to citizenship that we can rightly say how many of our people are on the League staff. In the meantime, four or five members of the Secretariat and three from the Labour Office have repeatedly asked me when they can have an Irish passport issued to them.

As for myself, my passport expired last September and, even if I wished to, I could not get it renewed here as I have not been registered at the British Consulate. Until such time as I get a new one it is impossible for me to go outside of Switzerland.

Is mise, le meas,
[signed] M. MACWHITE

No. 183 NAI DT S1971

Joseph P. Walshe to Diarmuid O'Hegarty (Dublin)
enclosing a memorandum to each member of the Executive Council
on Irish Free State Passports
(No. 5/8)

DUBLIN, 11 January 1924

PASSPORTS
I am instructed by the Minister to ask you to kindly have the outstanding question about Passports brought before the Cabinet at the first opportunity.

I enclose a copy of Passport[1] and a Memo. for each Member of the Executive Council.

[signed] S.P. BREATHNACH
Rúnaí

[enclosure]

11th January, 1924.
To: *EACH MEMBER OF THE EXECUTIVE COUNCIL.*

PASSPORTS
Issue Outstanding: Use of the description: 'BRITISH SUBJECT'

TO BE DECIDED WHETHER:
1) The Citizens of the Saorstát shall be described as British Subjects. (The British demand)
or
2) As having the status of British Subjects, i.e. All Irish Free State Citizens not included in the class of non-British Subjects referred to in 3 below shall write 'Yes' after the question 'whether bearer has status of British Subject'. (The Attorney General's suggested compromise)
or
3) As citizens of the Irish Free State without qualification. (A qualifying clause is added in the case of non-British subjects who acquired Saorstát citizenship under Article 3 of the Constitution. The Clause sets forth that the holder not being a British Subject is entitled to the good offices of British Consular Representatives only as a matter of courtesy, no protection being afforded in the country of origin unless the bearer has ceased to be a subject thereof.)

NOTANDA re (1)
The British contend that there should be a 'clear indication on the face of the Passport whether the holder is or is not a British Subject.' This description, they claim, is necessary both from the point of view of the relations with Foreign Governments and of the convenience both to the holder of the passport and to British Consular Officers abroad. They do not object to the description 'Citizen of the Irish Free State' provided it follows that of 'British Subject'.

NOTANDA re (2)
The Minister of External Affairs refrained from putting forward the compromise in (2) above at the recent Conference in London.[2] The description 'British Subject' whether used as an individual description or as an indication of the category by virtue of inclusion in which certain privileges are obtained is odious to the ordinary Irishman, and its introduction in any form into the Passport would be followed by serious political difficulties here and in the U.S.A.

---

[1] Not located.
[2] See above No. 179.

NOTANDA re (3)
The British had no serious reasons to oppose the case put up by the Minister of External Affairs namely, that the Request in the name of His Britannic Majesty was a sufficient indication to foreign Governments and to British Consular Officers of the privileges and protection to which the holder was entitled. The British Consular Officers are bound to extend protection to every Subject of the King and an explicit declaration that bearer is a British Subject would neither decrease nor increase the degree of protection to which he has a right.

The qualifying clause in 3 above obviates all possibility of confusion.

The basis of the British contention is that Irish Citizenship is purely local and that outside the area of the Irish Free State, Irish Free State Citizens are British Subjects in nowise distinct from other British Subjects whatever their place of origin might be.

The Minister of External Affairs holds that this theory is false. The right which we are about to exercise of not adhering to the Convention fixing the regime for foreigners in Turkey will oblige the latter country to make a distinction between Irish Free State Citizens and British Subjects from England and from such of the Dominions as adhere to the Convention. This distinction will become increasingly necessary.

In deference to a British request we have already yielded on an important point by omitting the words 'on behalf of the Irish Free State' before the words 'in the name of His Britannic Majesty'.

The Minister of External Affairs recommends that in our reply to the British we should refuse to agree to the use of the description 'British Subject' reiterating that the wording of the Request excludes any possibility of difficulties arising with Foreign Governments or British Officers abroad.

If the British establish to our satisfaction that insuperable difficulties would be created with Foreign Governments by the omission of the description 'British Subject', the Minister recommends that the Attorney General's compromise should then and then only be proposed.

No. 184 NAI DT S1971

Extract from minutes of a meeting of the Executive Council (C.2/41)
DUBLIN, 3 pm, 14 January 1924

Minister for External Affairs
PASSPORTS.
The memorandum from the Minister for External Affairs on the subject of the description of Irish citizens as British subjects in the Passports of Saorstát Eireann was considered.[1]

It was agreed that the Minister for External Affairs should instruct the High Commissioner to seek an interview with the new British Secretary of State for Foreign Affairs[2] on this matter and urge upon him the considerations which affect the council.

---

[1] See above No. 183.
[2] Ramsay MacDonald who was also Prime Minister.

No. 185 NAI DT S3452

Edward J. Phelan to Eoin MacNeill (Dublin)
(Confidential) (Copy)

GENEVA, 17 January 1924

Dear Professor MacNeill,
Things have again become very critical as regards the question of our international status.

You will remember my last letter of 8th December,[1] concerning the ratification of the amendment to Article 393 of the Treaty of Versailles.

I was delighted to hear from you on 17th December that the matter had been brought before the Cabinet and that appropriate action would be taken.

I gather that a protest has been made but what has been the result?

The objectionable instrument of ratification is still with the League and no communication has been received by the League from London in connection therewith.

If, as I understand is the case, the Free State Government protested to London, the protest has just been conveniently shelved.

The League are now in the process of informing the Members of the ratification in question. They are obliged to take this course and cannot delay any longer. They have waited, or rather been persuaded to wait, for over two months and in the absence of anything official they have been obliged to go ahead.

You will remember I suggested that as a countermove we should ratify the Court Treaty.

The League have now been privately informed on high authority that the Free State is to be considered as covered by all the British ratifications of League Treaties communicated before the Free State became a member of the League.

I warned the Delegation to the Assembly that step by step we would be hemmed in and our status whittled down. It has now happened and our inertia is allowing our status to be undermined if not destroyed.

As regards the Labour Conventions, in application of the above doctrine the League have written officially to the Labour Office refusing to communicate to the Free State those conventions which were the subject of British ratification before Ireland joined the League – and this despite the fact that they have been the subject of separate ratification or non-ratification by Canada, S. Africa, etc.

The I.L.O. will raise certain objections on purely international grounds, so there will be a little time before it is announced that the Irish Free State is a party to a certain number of conventions on which it was never consulted, but as regards the League conventions it is more serious. Instructions were given to Flynn[2] and to MacWhite to object to a certain article in the Customs and Transit conventions which was judged to diminish our independence and which had been reproduced from the Barcelona Conventions. It now appears that we

[1] Not printed.
[2] C.J. Flynn, Revenue Commissioners.

were a party to the Barcelona Convention all the time! I can imagine nothing which could harm our prestige more. The authority of our representatives at such conferences is completely destroyed and their instructions will become a laughing stock in diplomatic circles.

Can we not pursue actively an immediate policy of staking out the status which we won with the Treaty with England before it is whittled down and diminished to something much less than the Irish people ever understood they accepted?

I have already drawn attention to how this is happening but only to the most urgent cases. There are others. There is a correspondence regarding the status of the Six Counties – the question of their separate representation in the international institutions will be the next to be raised and the way is being prepared now. The thing is yet in its initial stage but the whole thing is one manoeuvre. While we are absorbed in internal affairs we are losing inch by inch what we won with the Treaty. Day by day it gets more serious and it becomes more difficult for us to act. But act sooner or later we must. For instance the Labour Government in England is sure to result in enhanced importance and great publicity being given to our Labour Conventions. If questions are raised in the Dáil as a consequence, our situation is that the League considers us bound by the British ratifications. I cannot pretend to judge opinion in Ireland but surely the necessity for such an admission would be dangerous.

I see these questions of status very clearly here and I am very perturbed at our inaction. It may be justified by reasons of which I know nothing, but not knowing them I cannot but feel a certain responsibility for pointing out the dangers we are running and the way in which we are losing ground.

That must be my excuse for worrying you again.

With kindest regards and best wishes,
Yours very sincerely,
Signed – E.J. PHELAN.

No. 186 NAI DT S5685

Edward J. Phelan to William T. Cosgrave (Dublin)
(Personal)

GENEVA, 17 January 1924

My Dear President
I venture to write to you once again on the critical situation concerning the international status of the Free State.

The developments during the last few days are so important that I think they merit your personal attention.

I understood from letters received from Dr. MacNeill and the Attorney General[1] in December that the question of the British ratification of the amendment to Article 393 of the Treaty of Versailles had been taken up. You will remember that that ratification covered the Free State although the Free State had never been consulted.

[1] Probably No. 175 above.

That ratification is still in the possession of the League and the League has received no communication from London in connection therewith.

Hence if any representations have been made to London on the subject they have been conveniently shelved.

The League is obliged to notify the ratification to its Members, and after having been persuaded to wait nearly three months it has now decided to go ahead. Notification is now being made.

But there is another development. The League has been informed on high authority, but unofficially, that the Free State is bound by the ratification of League Treaties given by the British before Ireland became a Member of the League.

The Labour Office has been in correspondence with the League concerning the Free State and the Labour Conventions. The following is an extract from an official letter from the League to the Labour Office:-

> 'It appears, therefore, that as regards the abovementioned conventions, there is no occasion for any action to be taken by the Government of the Irish Free State with a view to examining and ratifying the Conventions, since they are already in force as regards the Free State, in virtue of instruments of ratification already deposited.'

The League have in preparation a list of ratifications of League Treaties. In accordance with the above doctrine the Free State will appear in it as party to a number of Treaties on which she has never been consulted. From some of them other Dominions have dissented and are not parties.

I do not need to insist how grave is the menace to our status.

You gave instructions to our delegates at the Customs and Transit Conferences to object to a certain Article which was reproduced from the Barcelona Conventions. It now seems that we were parties to the Barcelona Conventions all along. What will be the respect with which our delegates and their instructions will be treated at future Conferences if this position is admitted?

I ventured to warn you at the Assembly that attempts would be made to whittle down our status in this way and that advantage would be taken of our concentration on internal problems. It is very difficult for me to write in full detail but it is going on in many directions. For instance the relation of the Six Counties to the International Organisations is being discussed. It is yet in its initial stage but no doubt a claim for the separate representation of the Six Counties will be the next step.

I know how many and how great are the problems with which you are faced at home but I feel sure you will forgive my anxiety concerning these external problems which are of such vital importance. Day by day the affirmation of our status is being made more difficult and if these things are allowed to go unchallenged *internationally* it will become impossible.

I have already suggested to the Attorney General the steps I think we could take.[1] There may be other and better methods but in any case it does seem to me that we should act without delay.

Once more I hope you will understand and forgive my insistence and that

[1] Above Nos 168 and 176.

you will not hesitate to ask me at any time for any assistance that I may be able to render.

With kindest regards and best wishes

Yours very sincerely
[signed] E.J. PHELAN

No. 187 NAI DT S3452

Memorandum on Edward J. Phelan's letter of 17 January 1924
DUBLIN, undated

With regard to the ratification by the British Government of Article 393 of the Treaty of Versailles, the first intimation the Irish Government received was by the despatch from the Colonial Office No: 695 of the 6th December 1923.[1] A reply was sent to that despatch on the 22nd December[2] asking the British Government to make it known that this ratification did not extend to the Irish Free State. On the 22nd January a reply was received from the British[3] stating that as the amendment was to affect the Treaty of Versailles it was necessary that the ratification should extend to the whole Empire. A draft despatch has now been prepared asking the British Government to get the King to issue a separate ratification in respect of the Free State.

Mr Phelan is incorrect in stating that the Irish Free State is to be considered as covered by all the British ratifications of League Treaties communicated before the Free State became a member of the League. In two instances at least Ireland is not included in the ratification namely:-

The Convention concerning the rights of Association and combination of Agricultural workers adopted at Geneva in 1921.

The Convention concerning Workmen's Compensation in Agriculture adopted at Geneva, November 1921.

Conventions adopted in 1919 & 1920 have been ratified in respect of Great Britain and Ireland. This is of course true of all Treaties and Conventions made before the establishment of the Irish Free State.

With regard to the Labour Conventions which Mr Phelan says the League have refused to communicate to the Free State. We have received most of these Conventions from the British. I do not think that the attitude of the League can be objected to, as only members are entitled to be supplied with copies of the Conventions, and I presume that as we were not members at the time these Conventions were made we can hardly claim copies of these Conventions as of right.

Mr Phelan states that in a little time an announcement will be made that the Irish Free State is a party to a certain number of Conventions on which it was never consulted. This will probably happen, but there is no means of changing the position, as we are undoubtedly bound by certain Conventions which were made before the establishment of the Irish Free State. The Barcelona Convention is one of these. It is unfortunate that it is the first Convention into which the

[1] Not printed.
[2] See No. 178 above.
[3] Not printed.

'Inter Se' clause was introduced. The British have been asked for an interpretation of this clause, but as at the moment we are not in possession of an exact interpretation, it is difficult to say whether it is more harmful to our prestige than the Washington Treaty by which we are likewise bound. Recently Conventions have been signed at Geneva to which the Irish Free State was a party, into which a clause was introduced modifying the 'Inter Se' clause to the effect that:

> 'Nothing in the preceding articles is to be construed as affecting in any way the rights or duties of a contracting State as member of the League of Nations.'

This clause at least safeguards our rights as a member of the League.

Mr Phelan suggests that we should pursue actively an immediate policy of staking out the Status which we won by the Treaty before it is whittled down. Since the establishment of the Free State the status acquired under the Treaty has been in no way diminished. Mr Phelan has a wrong impression of our position under the Treaty. He seems to think that we are quite free to act as we please with regard to Treaties and Conventions made before the establishment of the Free State, this of course is not the case. The Treaties which he considers diminish our status were made before we had any status. We can withdraw from certain of these Conventions and Treaties on giving the prescribed notice, but in the majority of cases such withdrawal at the moment would not be beneficial. The reference to the Status of the Six Counties is very vague and it is difficult to gather from Mr Phelan's letter in what capacity the Six Counties would be represented in the International Institutions.

If questions are raised in the Dáil with regard to Labour Conventions by which we are bound owing to British Ratification before our entry into the League of Nations, they would seem to be answerable by the statement that we are in the same position with regard to these Conventions as to outside Treaties which we have inherited owing to our position prior to the Treaty.

No. 188 UCDA P4/427

Gearoid McGann (President's Office) to each member of the Executive Council, Hugh Kennedy and Diarmuid O'Hegarty, enclosing a memorandum (Copy) by William T. Cosgrave on the proposed Boundary Conference

DUBLIN, 17 January 1924

I attach hereto suggestions by the President on the line to be adopted at the proposed Boundary Conference. The President would be glad if you would read them over and favour him with your comments and any other suggestions which you might wish to make bearing on the matter.

[signed] G. MAG GCANAINN

N O T E S by *THE PRESIDENT*
IN CONNECTION WITH THE PROPOSED BOUNDARY CONFERENCE

The Conference will probably suggest an economic unit – ALL IRELAND, and it is conceivable that it would be accompanied by some financial accommodation on the Treaty clause referring to Army Pensions and our liability in respect of the National Debt, that a sum would be fixed for the former and that the British would waive the latter or consideration postponed for 10 or 20 years.

In considering what propositions we would give favourable hearing to, I recommend first of all the consideration of the ultimate goal as the best method of arriving at some practical solution.

The ultimate goal is Dáil and Seanad for all Ireland. This is not a likely probability, and appears so far off as to be out of the arena of practical politics for the present.

The next and more likely probability is a Parliament for the two parts of Ireland, as at present, apart from the number of counties in each; that is, 26 and 6, or 27 and 5, or 28 and 4, etc., etc., with a link of the two Cabinets.

I am of opinion that Sir James Craig will propose the following:-

The two Parliaments to remain as they are and the two Cabinets to function as the Council of Ireland, Northern Parliament constituencies to return members to English Parliament.

It may be that I take a too sentimental view of the representatives of North-East in the British Parliament, but it is a loss of prestige to us, and I think the British would like to get rid of them. I don't know what we could give in return for this, and I don't see any grave reason why we should not withdraw opposition to the handing over of reserved Services.

If, then, the situation develops on these lines, viz., a PARLIAMENT OF 26 AND OF 6 COUNTIES WITH AN OVER INSTITUTION OF TWO CABINETS, there are many weaknesses in this latter proposal – such as 7 for and 7 against, 8 for and 6 against (the 6 not accepting the decision), and so on. Any such complexity will have Craig suggesting the British Chairman, who would enter on level terms between us and not on the basis now existing, that is, Saorstát Éireann and a subordinate legislative in North-East.

If there be a Joint Cabinet, it must be laid down that –

1. WE PRESIDE.
2. THAT MAJORITY RULE PREVAILS.
3. THAT THE CHAIRMAN HAS A CASTING VOTE.

If this proposition, viz. two Cabinets, prevails – the next question that will arise is the economic unit.

An economic unit presupposes that the North-East will demand the same fiscal policy as Great Britain. Any such proposition, however, is a derogation of status and, of course, cannot be entertained if the North-East insists.

I am of opinion that these proposals without corresponding accommodation towards the minority in the North-East are more than we could stand for and that we would not have any justification in agreeing to them.

The next point to consider is what possible arrangement can be made which will make for ultimate union in the circumstances?

The North will not forego the Ulster Constabulary! How can they be made to forego it? Only by cutting them off from Great Britain and giving them also a Local Militia. What do we gain and lose by this? I think a Local Militia and liability for their own Constabulary is the only basis, and this implies loss of representation in the British Parliament.

If this be agreed our first line is:-

1. Withdrawal of all penal acts against minority, we undertaking to recommend minority to go into Parliament; Reconstruct Constituencies in North-East on a par basis, that is, a fair allocation to both Unionists and Nationalists in the Franchise and consequently representative – Craig and so many, Nationalist and so many – equal number of both sides, with a British Chairman to give a casting vote; retention of P.R. for ten years; disqualify any persons not taking their seats.
2. Retention of Customs Barrier.
3. Rectification of Boundary so as to make it a more suitable line.
4. Two Cabinets to meet, as outlined above on page 2.
5. Withdrawal of claim of British to any War Debt; Liability of Ireland to War Pensions of say £1,350,000 a year –
   (Northern Ireland £600,000.)
   (Irish Free State £750,000.)
6. Representation in Senate of Northern Ireland either by extending its numbers or some way to get in the proportion to which minority is entitled.

The designation of All-Ireland as 'IRISH FREE STATE – SAORSTÁT ÉIREANN' with the Northern Parliament having all its rights guaranteed.

This may mark the division more strikingly, but as that is likely in any case, we get a fairer deal for our people in the North. We cut away entirely from England. We have full control in the major part of the country and North-East is left without its reserves and may possibly look more to us than across.

No. 189 NAI DT S1801D

Memorandum by E.M. Stephens (Dublin)
on the memorandum of 17 January by William T. Cosgrave[1]

DUBLIN, 18 January 1924

A chara,

I have gone carefully through the President's notes on the Northern situation, a copy of which you gave me. I think, from what you said, that the notes were made before I furnished the President with our Memorandum on the 'Possible Basis of Union',[2] which contains material which I hope may be of use on the subjects he refers to.

The President reviews the situation with ultimate political union as the goal in view, while, at the same time, he says that this is, for the moment, out of the region of practical politics. In other words, his view is that while the goal of national union may be still a long way off, everything which is done now should be done with the idea of assisting the evolution of National union.

From reading the notes in the light of this idea, certain questions occurred to me which I would like to suggest for consideration.

The President suggests that Sir James Craig will urge that union might be made by retaining the two Parliaments and having a Council of Ireland formed

[1] No. 188 above. Circulated to all members of the Executive Council, Diarmuid O'Hegarty, Hugh Kennedy and Kevin O'Shiel on 21 January 1924.
[2] Not printed.

from the two Cabinets. Could this be done without taking away from the power of the Dáil, or would it be possible to form a Council of Ireland from the Cabinets? There seems to be a constitutional difficulty in this, as the Council of Ireland has legislative powers, and would probably tend to develop under such a scheme into something in the nature of a Federal Parliament. If such a scheme was put into operation would not certain important powers have to be handed over to the Council by the Dáil?

There seem to me to be four possible arrangements, some of which would be very undesirable.

(1) The Northern Parliament could remain, as it is at present, subordinate to Westminster.

(2) It could become subordinate to the Oireachtas instead of to Westminster.

(3) It could become, jointly with the Dáil, subordinate to a third body for all Ireland.

(4) It could acquire control of Reserved Services and so become a Dominion Parliament.

Is not this last alternative very dangerous? Would it not enable the North to join the League of Nations and act in every way with the same independence as the Free State? Is it not moreover contrary to the Treaty?

The President raises the question of the representation of the North in Westminster. Is not this inseparably connected with the arrangement for the North to make an Imperial Contribution? Under any but a Tory Government will this not become a very serious financial embarrassment? If this is so does not the reason already exist for the abandonment of representation in Westminster by the North? While fiscal union is, of course, possible without political union, is any political union possible so long as representation at Westminster continues? It would seem to be dangerous to our status.

The President refers to the Customs barrier as something which we must retain. I am not quite certain whether his note referred to the whole Customs barrier of the Free State or the land portion of the barrier between us and the North. Could not this be moved to the sea if the North agreed to accept our fiscal system? Could not such an arrangement be made without prejudice to the Boundary Commission or to our political position generally, with universal popular support all over Ireland? I always think this side of the question requires first attention, because if the fiscal systems, in force in the North and in the Free State, once diverge, and new vested interests spring up, political union will become daily more difficult. I am certain that the wisdom of the Government in their attitude towards fiscal matters has impressed the North, even more perhaps than the success of the Loan, which must itself be partly attributed to the feeling of security created by their attitude towards these matters.

All the questions raised by the President's notes are very complicated and very interdependent. I am passing you on these which occur to me off-hand, as I think you said the President was circulating his notes with a view to getting general suggestions.

Mise, le meas,
[signed] E.M. STEPHENS
Rúnaidhe

No. 190 NAI DT S1801D

Memorandum relating to the situation in Northern Ireland by Kevin O'Shiel
DUBLIN, 28 January 1924

RE. NORTH-EASTERN POSITION

With regard to the President's notes of 17th January in this matter and Mr. Stephens letter of the 18th January in reply,[1] the following points occur to me.

1. *GENERAL SITUATION:* There is no doubt that the atmosphere has greatly altered in our favour during the past few weeks. A considerable obstacle to our chances of success either at a Conference or a Boundary Commission was the presence in power of a Government which had by tradition and natural affinity strong bonds with the ruling caste in the Six Counties. And since the accomplishment of the Treaty the three Governments which held sway in Great Britain – Mr. Lloyd George's, Mr. Bonar Law's and Mr. Baldwin's – apart altogether from the more enlightened outlook of individual leaders[,] depended mainly for their existence on the strong Tory Die-hard influence. This influence was a continual menace to the full satisfaction of our rights under the Treaty for the Tory Die-hards were not only in complete sympathy with the aims and objects of Northern ascendancy but were in many instances directly connected by blood with the great aristocratic, commercial and landlord families in the Six Counties. The Duke of Abercorn, Lord Londonderry, the Marquis of Dufferin and Ava etc. could pull enormous influence in British Tory circles. All of these noblemen have residences in England and most of them entertain widely so that their social influence is immense. It is noteworthy that the recent Baldwin Government did everything it could to strengthen the Northern Government. It got very large grants of money for all sorts of things from Police to the building of Parliament Houses and Governor's residence and even such things as 'compensation' for their share in the College of Science!

2. *NORTHERN GOVERNMENT AND THE GENERAL ELECTION:* The Northern Government committed a big blunder during the recent British general election in putting all its cards on the Conservative Party and in particular identifying itself with the extreme Die-hard element in that Party. Large numbers of well paid but not very discreet Orange enthusiasts were despatched to British constituencies during the election with the benediction of the Northern Government to propagand in the Die-hard cause. These persons mainly devoted themselves to vitriolic onslaughts on Labour and Socialism. The General Election resulted in what was virtually the downfall of the Unionist Party and a victory for the Radical and Socialist elements that Sir James Craig and his friends were so overanxious to keep out.

On the other hand, we were careful to regard the contest as a purely British affair and no persons spoke during the election in our name.

---

[1] See above Nos 188 and 189.

3. *SURVEY OF THE POSITION:* It has and is being continually urged by its critics that the Government has been extremely negligent and tardy in connection with enforcing the Nation's rights under Article 12 of the Treaty. The Government has been accused of an almost criminal delay in putting the Boundary clauses into operation. A little retrospection will show the value of the delay and the satisfactory nature of its results.

The Government has no cause to regret that it deliberately delayed the discussion of the Boundary clause until the chaotic conditions that existed in the country were removed. A year ago an appalling condition of affairs obtained in the Saorstát. The country was in a chronic state of commotion and disorder. Murders, assassinations, ambushes and the wholesale ruthless destruction of property were the order of the day. Pessimism was in the ascendant and in London most of our friends had made up their minds that what they termed 'the experiment of the Free State' was a calamitous failure. The 'prophecies' that had been so lavishly made by our enemies – that we were a 'bankrupt State' and 'an unstable people' ruled by 'inculpable and unprincipled' rulers were being gradually accepted by the bulk of British people as accurate, and in even friendly quarters we were being admonished to 'take a leaf out of "Ulster's" book' and to make ourselves worthy of 'Ulster', etc., etc.

It is enough here to say that everything that was thought and said about us and our Government has been completely falsified, and, mainly due to the enormous efforts of the Government, our national position – political and financial – was never so strong as it is today. Tory Diehardism, a very vital and powerful influence, has been largely swept out of British politics and with it the significance and domination of Northern Orange ascendancy. The old order can be said to have vanished and we have now got to face a new order of things.

4. *THE NEW BRITISH GOVERNMENT:* It is too early yet to form a comprehensive and just opinion of the attitude of the new Labour Government in Great Britain towards us, especially as for a long time their Party have been more or less inarticulate about Irish affairs (save for occasional outspoken references made by their more extreme adherents).

Taking the worst view first, it is possible to conclude from the responsible statements of their leaders during the past four or five important years that they are not likely to turn out very much better than the other British Parties. It must be remembered that during the pre-Truce days British Labour defined its attitude towards us and declared its policy to be a grant of Dominion Home Rule which is identical with the policy of the Liberals and the progressive Conservatives. They were never called upon to elaborate the details of such a policy and hence we have no official record of how the Party intended to deal with the North-Eastern Question. The new Colonial Secretary (the Cabinet Minister who will have most to do with us) Mr. J.H. Thomas, has never shown himself conspicuously friendly to us. If my memory is correct, he came across to Ireland at the time of the Railway strike, organised against the transport of British military and munitions of war, and did his best to wreck it. At any rate no funds during that episode were forthcoming from his Union (the N.U.R.) for Railwaymen in Ireland who had suffered because of their action. During the debates in the House of Commons on the Treaty, he supported the Treaty but I have a recollection that he expressed himself particularly pleased with regard to the special treatment of 'Ulster'.

Thomas has always been regarded in England as a moderate Labour man. He is a 'trades-unionist' as distinct from a 'socialist' and his actions and his speeches have frequently brought forth praise from his ultra Die-hard organs. He is not an idol of the rank and file of British labour and they have frequently accused him of pandering too much to the 'bosses'.

He has the reputation of being very clever and shrewd with a good deal of the wiliness of his distinguished countryman Lloyd George.

The new Premier, Ramsay MacDonald has the reputation of being an honest politician but as far as we are concerned he is a dark horse. He should be well acquainted with Orangeism as it is by no means insignificant in his part of Scotland. If we are to judge from his statement issued since he has become Prime Minister, on India, he cannot be considered very advanced as in that statement he deprecated the activities of Indian nationalists and told them pretty plainly in words that might have been used by a member of the late Government that if Indian Nationalists did not renounce unconstitutional methods, whether active or passive, they would find they would be met.

On the whole, however, I think we can assume that the new British Government as a body will be inclined to deal fairly with us in this matter of the Boundaries if for no other reason than that its main support in many parts of Britain are Irish people, as are many of its best and ablest organisers.

As against this the one thing we may expect to be up against from this on is a strong and united Tory opposition to any scheme that would seem to 'let Ulster down'. Whether this will have the same effect on the Labour Government as the Tory opposition had on the Liberal Government in 1912 remains to be seen.

5. *THE POINT OF TIME:* During the forthcoming Conference and any further conference or meeting that may take place we should bear in mind two things which should govern the question of duration:

(a) that the present British Government has not a very secure footing and is liable to be thrown out of office at any moment, and

(b) that we should see to it that the Local Government Board elections in the Six Counties that are due to take place in May, should not take place before this question is definitely decided. Owing to the gerrymandering that has been going on we can take it that great changes in favour of the Partitionists will result from these elections which will be fought on the new register.

Another thing to remember is that whatever happens to British Governments the civil servants remain intact and will certainly endeavour to carry on the old tradition.

6. *THE CONFERENCE:* I come now more directly to the points raised by the President in his Notes.[1] I agree largely with his first point that the Conference

[1] Above No. 188.

will probably suggest the absorption of all-Ireland into one economic unit in consideration for which we may probably be offered considerable financial accommodation on the Treaty clauses.

The danger lies in what precise form this economic union will take. Few things have caused greater uneasiness to the British than our determination to exercise our fiscal independence and the resultant necessity of a Customs barrier. It has frequently been suggested that we should, in view of the North's acceptance of some form of union, agree to 'bring all Ireland within the United Kingdom fiscal unit'. I think the cause of this uneasiness is more at the prospect of possible developments of independent fiscal policy rather than at any immediate fears. We are, however, almost certain to be faced with this suggestion at some stage or another, which of course would be utterly impossible from our standpoint.

7. *THE TWO CABINETS:* I take it that this point in the President's notes means that such a body will deal first mainly with the 'reserved services' as the 'Council of Ireland' in the 1920 Act. Legislation would be necessary to give such a body definite Parliamentary shape – as its functions in this respect would be mainly legislative – and also to provide for the number of representatives from North and South. The danger I see in this is its tendency to treat the Six or Four Counties, or whatever it may be, as the equal of the Free State, thereby providing precedents that it may be difficult for us to confute at a later date.

8. *NORTHERN M.Ps. IN WESTMINSTER:* I agree with the President that the presence of Northern M.Ps. at Westminster is a big loss of prestige to us and that it is highly important for us to cut them out of Westminster. If we achieved nothing else but the cutting of all financial and political bonds that bound the North-East to London and thereby caused them to look *in* to Ireland rather than *out* of Ireland, it would be a very big step on the road to National union. Should the North-East agree to accept something of this nature we might consent to withdraw opposition to the handing over to them of some at least of the reserved services on condition, say, that they accepted the general principle of an Irish Federation; otherwise they might progress towards full Dominion status, which would be dangerous. Also, if they decide to come closer to us in this respect I see no objection to the suggestion to meet them with regard to Constabulary and a Local Militia, accompanied, of course, by satisfactory guarantees from them as to the position of minority members in those forces.

9. *A POSSIBLE BASIS OF AGREEMENT:* The six or seven points outlined in the last page of the President's notes provide, I think, a possible basis of agreement. At any rate they represent the minimum that we could accept without much danger to our own position and provide a ground for possible future development towards a closer union.

To such a plan I would make one addition, namely, the acceptance of all-Ireland as a distinct economic unit, power being given to the 'Council of Ireland' or whatever central body is set up to regulate the details involved. Of course I do not mean by this suggestion that we should do anything to limit our own sovereign fiscal powers, which are amongst the most valuable powers we possess and which we should be very careful to preserve intact.

10. *OUR ATTITUDE AT THE CONFERENCE:*
In conclusion, I would like to submit a few points on our attitude at the forthcoming London Conference.
(1) We should bear in mind that we are not responsible for this Conference; that it has been called by the British Government, and that all we have agreed to do is to accept their invitation without prejudice to our rights.
(2) The onus is on the British Government to explain in greater detail why they have called this Conference and to submit for our consideration any plans for settlement.
(3) We should not let the Conference develop into a discussion on the Boundary question. No good could come of such a discussion. I have reason to believe that the North-East is very anxious for this.
(4) We should not commit ourselves to anything until we see what the British Government have to say. When we are in possession of their scheme we can ask for a little time in which to consider it. Of course should it be a plan that we could not possibly accept we can say so at once.
(5) If pressed to put some plan before the Conference we can excuse ourselves on the ground that we have no plans for the solution of the difficulty other than the Treaty which we readily admit is not perfect but under the circumstances and in view of the rigid attitude of the North-Eastern Government we cannot conceive a better.

We can point out that we have endeavoured to meet the North-East but it has quite plainly on several occasions ruled out all prospect of affiliation with us. The plan in the Treaty, had they not opted out, met them, we thought very generously.

It is no harm at all if we appear at first a little 'difficult' as there is a danger of our being taken for granted across the water as being 'very accommodating', creating thereby the preconception in the minds of British arbitrators that whatever compromise is made for settlement purposes must be made by us, the North-East on the other hand being taken for granted as being constitutionally static and unbending.

We can blame public opinion in the Saorstát for our attitude. We can point out that the Government and people of the Saorstát fought a trying civil war in which hundreds of excellent lives (including General Collins) were lost, and put a debt of many millions on the country in order to maintain the Treaty.

The result is that the people of the Saorstát, having suffered for the Treaty position, are now keener than ever on seeing that the Treaty is honoured to the letter. What they would consider as a 'letting down' on the part of the Government over Article 12 would certainly not consolidate the existing state of peace in the country and might lead to further commotion with the Irregulars coming out on top and proceeding to 'purge' the Constitution.

The Government has to satisfy the Oireachtas on any scheme that may be forthcoming from the Conference and it will take a very good scheme to satisfy the legislature that the Boundary Commission could be waived, etc.

THE MINORITY IN NORTHERN IRELAND:
The forthcoming Conference will probably only be a preliminary affair to lead up to a more serious meeting. That being so it would be a fitting occasion for us to urge the matter of the treatment of the minority in the Six Counties, e.g., the 'Argenta'[1] and the incarceration of Cahir Healy which Sir John Simon has declared to be an affront to the House of Commons. We should ask for the release of the 'Argenta' prisoners as a way of creating a more favourable conference attitude (incidentally the release of those men on our initiative would have an excellent home effect).

GERRYMANDERING OF CONSTITUENCIES, THE ABOLITION OF P.R. AND THE RESTITUTION OF 'PROPERTY QUALIFICATIONS' FOR LOCAL GOVERNMENT ELECTORS IN THE SIX COUNTIES:
We should protest very strongly against these interferences with minority rights. The restitution of 'property qualifications' should have a telling effect on Labour mentality. There is the notorious fact too of the establishment of a Special policeman's Orange Lodge to be called the 'Peel Loyal Orange Lodge'.

The Bureau, I understand has prepared a dossier on the treatment of Minorities by the Belfast Government.

In conclusion, it is my belief that we should be able to hold out, under the prevailing conditions, for a good hard bargain.

No. 191 NAI DT S1801D

Rough notes by Diarmuid O'Hegarty on the conference held to discuss the forthcoming meeting in London on the Boundary Question (Strictly Confidential)

DUBLIN, 28 January 1924

There were present:-
1. The President, Professor MacNeill, Messrs. O'Higgins, Kennedy, Blythe, O'Shiel, Stephens, McElligott[2] and O'Hegarty.
2. Mr. Stephens undertook to provide each of the Delegates with a dossier containing pronouncements on the Boundary Question by British and Northern politicians, a copy of the Craig-Collins Pact and a number of schemes for settlement which had been propounded from time to time.
3. Mr. McElligott undertook to examine the possibility of any proposal for Fiscal Union and generally the financial position of Northern Ireland as disclosed in its Balance Sheets.
4. Mr. Stephens was of opinion that if a discussion on Fiscal Unity took place, it might be possible to get agreement as to the desirability of the same Fiscal system, so far as Customs and Excise were concerned, being adopted for all Ireland. This would involve some settlement of the Authority which would impose other taxation (e.g. Income Tax) on Northern Ireland, and both Mr.

[1] The *Argenta* was a prison ship moored in Belfast Lough.
[2] J.J. McElligott (Department of Finance).

Stephens and Mr. McElligott expressed themselves of the opinion that this could be met by giving this competence to the Northern Parliament, thus obviating the Northern representation at Westminster. Professor MacNeill and Mr. O'Shiel were both in agreement that this aspect should not be allowed to side-track the main issue.

5. Mr. O'Higgins raised the question as to the effect of the inclusion of Tyrone and Fermanagh in Saorstát Éireann on Northern finances and strength. The general opinion was that though they could hold out from the Financial point of view, they would nevertheless be very much weakened, notwithstanding that in such case they would be dealing with a more homogenous and industrially centralised population, and their Police requirements would be considerably reduced. It was pointed out that they would be faced with exorbitant over-head charges, and that we would obtain a complete Railway system to their disadvantage. The possibility of their merging in the British system was mentioned, but was considered unlikely.

6. Professor MacNeill thought a hard and fast stand should be made on the plebiscite system with the smallest possible area as unit. The Northern reading of Article 12 as providing merely for a rectification of the boundary gave away any case which might be put up regarding the sanctity of County boundaries, and hence would prevent them from using this as an argument for a plebiscite on a County basis.

7. The likely procedure at the forthcoming Conference was considered. The President was of opinion that Mr. MacDonald would open with an expression of his desire for a solution and his hope for a United Ireland, and that after hearing replies from both parties would adumbrate his proposals.

Our contribution in the first instance would be to the effect that the only real solution was a Parliament of all Ireland. Craig would probably reply on a 'what we have we hold' basis. He would use the 1920 Act as his argument.

The Attorney General and others pointed out that the 1920 Act was an arbitrary division of Ireland without the consent of either population, that a United Parliament with a Northern Parliament subordinate thereto would not affect what the North held, as it would cover 'reserved matters'. The boundary provided by that Act disposed of large areas against the will of the population. Tyrone and Fermanagh had in two elections rejected the division. The Treaty provided machinery for revision of this injustice, and it was the duty of the British Government who had created the injustice to see that this machinery was availed of. Professor MacNeill was anxious that very sympathetic treatment should be accorded to the Labour Ministry unless they showed that they were unfair.

8. Mr. O'Higgins said that no Irish Government could face the people having given away the Boundary Commission unless the North agreed to return to the position which existed before they opted out. It would be politically impossible for them to do that. Mr. Stephens urged that if there was a proposal to return to this position two questions should be attended to (a) the boundary as agreed should be sealed by the Treaty machinery of a Boundary Commissioner and (b) the protection of minorities in the Northern area.

9. Delegates will be briefed by Mr. Stephens on the expulsion of Catholics from Belfast, the Peel Orange Lodge, the gerrymandering of constituencies

and local electoral districts, and the re-introduction of the property qualification for Local Government franchise.
10. A further Conference will be held before the departure of the Delegation.

No. 192 Reprinted from *Correspondence between the Government of the Irish Free State and His Majesty's Government relating to Article 12 of the Treaty* (Dublin, 1924)

T.M. Healy to J.H. Thomas (London)
DUBLIN, 29 January 1924

Sir,
I have the honour to acknowledge receipt of your despatch of the 24th instant,[1] relative to the Conference with representatives of His Majesty's Government and of the Government of Northern Ireland proposed in the Duke of Devonshire's communication of the 22nd September last, acceptance of which by my Ministers was signified in my Despatch of the 8th October.[2]
2. The date suggested for the first meeting of the Conference, viz., Friday, 1st February, will be convenient to my Ministers, and President Cosgrave, accompanied by the Minister for Home Affairs and the Attorney-General,[3] will attend at No. 10 Downing Street on that date.[4]

I have, etc.,
T.M. HEALY

No. 193 UCDA P4/911

Marquis MacSwiney of Mashonaglass to Desmond FitzGerald (Dublin)
(Copy)
DUBLIN, 29 January 1924

A Chara,
I see in this morning's papers that the Secretary-General of the League of Nations, at the request of the Council, has sent a letter to the governments of Nations, Members of the League, suggesting that certain measures be taken with a view to enforcing the League's decisions in connection with the illegal traffic in harmful drugs.

Referring to a private conversation on the subject which I had the honour of having with you, and the Honourable Ministers for Education and Finance,[5] a short time ago, I beg to come and ask you, in my capacity of Delegate of the Free State of Ireland at the Fourth Assembly of the League of Nations, to take into consideration the following points which have come to my mind as a result of my personal active participation in the work of the Fifth Committee of the League which, amongst other various matters, dealt precisely with the question of the *Traffic in Opium and other Dangerous Drugs*.

[1] Not printed.
[2] No. 144 above.
[3] Kevin O'Higgins, John O'Byrne.
[4] The Conference met as arranged on 1 February, and adjourned on 2 February for a period not exceeding 28 days.
[5] Eoin MacNeill, Ernest Blythe.

I consider it is not only expedient, but urgent that the Government of the Free State of Ireland, following the example of governments of various other foreign States which have come into existence in the course of the past few years, should ratify at an early date, and have its signature put to the Convention of the Hague of January 23, 1912, which was intended to suppress the illicit traffic in habit forming narcotic drugs.

Although, through the mercy of God, the People of Ireland have not so far been affected to any considerable extent by an evil which, in many other countries of Europe, as well as of America, and the East, has steadily been growing for some time past, reaching in certain cases the proportion of a national calamity – yet I am of opinion that the Government of the Free State of Ireland cannot afford to look on with apparent indifference to what is going on elsewhere, without exposing itself to the risk of being severely criticised and blamed by Governments of Nations, where the use of dangerous drugs is prevalent, and even, on account of the peculiar geographical position of this Island, of being actually accused of secretly favouring a traffic which is as highly remunerative as it is immoral. The manner in which such a charge was brought up in full Committee last September by the Delegate of Great Britain against the Government of the Helvetic Confederation, makes me feel that the Government of the Free State would be well advised to take without delay such steps as may be necessary with a view to making an attack such as this absolutely impossible.

Another consideration which, to my mind, would make it eminently desirable for the Government of the Free State of Ireland, to ratify and sign as soon as possible the Hague Convention, consists in the fact that the Government and People of the United States of America take the keenest interest in the campaign for the repression of the traffic in noxious drugs. Of this interest we had, last year, a very striking instance when, notwithstanding the attitude of aloofness assumed, and constantly observed from the very start by that Government towards the League of Nations, the late President Harding commissioned the Hon. Stephen G. Porter, of Pennsylvania, Chairman of the Committee on Foreign Affairs of the House of Representatives to go to Geneva, at the head of a special Delegation including Bishop Brent, and other distinguished personalities, with the object of attending the sittings of the Fifth Committee, in which the question of opium and harmful drugs was to be discussed, and of informing that Committee, and consequently the Assembly of the League, of his Government's views on the matter. On the advice of the Hon. Minister for Education, first Irish Delegate at the Fourth Assembly, I put myself immediately in touch with the Hon. S.G. Porter, and the Members of his Delegation, and by the support I was able to give to their policy, in the course of the discussions, and votings which subsequently took place, was fortunate enough to secure their confidence and approval. I think there can be no doubt as to the satisfaction which an early ratification of the Hague Convention on the part of the Government of the Free State of Ireland would produce both on the Government of the United States and on the Irish community out there.

Furthermore, I would still like to call your attention to a point which, I believe, deserves to be borne in mind by the Government of the Free State of

Ireland, particularly as it does not only apply to the Hague Convention, but to many other international treaties of the kind which, from time to time, have been negotiated, ratified, and signed by the Government of the *then* United Kingdom of Great Britain and Ireland. So long as the Government of the Free State of Ireland does not denounce, in the usual official form any of these Treaties, the Irish Nation remains bound by them just as if the status of the country, from an international point of view, continued to be the same as it was prior to the Anglo-Irish Treaty of December 6, 1921, and to the admission of the Free State of Ireland in the League of Nations on September 10, 1923. However, it is up to the Government of the Free State, when an occasion arises, either to denounce such Treaties or Conventions, or to ratify them in its new capacity of a Government of a Sovereign State. Now, it seems to me, that in many cases, but most particularly in that of the Convention of the Hague, it would be of the utmost importance, especially from a moral point of view, that the Government of the Free State of Ireland should ratify and sign it as the Governments of so many other sovereign States which have come into being as a result of the European War, have lately been doing, thus showing at a time that it is quite awake to the powers it derives from the new Status of the Nation, and its position as a State Member of the League, and that it is anxious to use these powers for the purpose of contributing its share to the material and moral progress of the World at large.

Is mise, le meas mór,
[copy letter unsigned]
MAC SUIBHNE MAGH SEANA-GHLASS

No. 194 NAI DT S1801D

Rough notes by Kevin O'Shiel of a conference held in the President's Room with the Governor General (Confidential)

DUBLIN, 30 January 1924

1. Present:
   THE GOVERNOR GENERAL,
   THE PRESIDENT,
   THE MINISTER FOR HOME AFFAIRS,
   ATTORNEY GENERAL and
   MR. KEVIN O'SHIEL.

The Governor-General commenced by giving a brief summary of what, from his experience of them, he considered would be the likely attitude of the new British Government. On the whole he considered that RAMSAY MacDONALD and his Ministers would be inclined to deal fairly and justly with us. He mentioned in particular MR. HENDERSON[1] whom he thought likely to be exceptionally favourably disposed towards us as during the Black and Tan

[1] Arthur Henderson, British Labour MP (1923-24, 1929-31, 1935-51), Home Secretary (1924), Foreign Secretary (1929-31).

regime he came across to Dublin as part of a Labour mission of investigation and told Sir Hamar Greenwood[1] in strong language what he thought of him.

2. The Governor-General impressed on his listeners the necessity of remembering in their dealings with the Labour Government that in spite of its undoubted friendliness toward Ireland, it was absolutely ignorant about Irish affairs. It did not know, he declared, the A.B.C. of the general situation and in particular the North-Eastern situation. The delegates, he said, should not hesitate to explain the whole situation from A. to Z. to these men as their minds have been in the main occupied with such matters as wages, trades' union affairs and continental internationals, etc., etc. and they have never had time to get a good grasp of the Irish situation.

In particular they should be told all about the passing of the 1920 Act – that it was passed through the British Parliament at a time when the greater part of Ireland was subject to a tyranny and could not express its opinion and that in that Parliament not one member for any Irish constituency, Nationalist or Unionist, recorded their vote for the measure.

3. The treatment of the Catholic minority in the Six Counties is another matter we should stress, laying particular emphasis on the pogroms, the imprisonment of large numbers of Catholics without trial, the absolute immunity extended to criminals who were not Catholics, the driving out of their homes of Catholic men for no conceivable reason, many of whom could not be accused of belonging to any political party, the special consideration meted out to Irregulars and those who were opposing the Government of the Saorstát (e.g. Frank Aiken permitted to wander about County Armagh unmolested and to consolidate his plans against us; he attended Mass and funerals openly all during the trouble of last year and at present cycles openly along the open country in County Armagh). The vexatious arrest and imprisonment, without trial, of our people who go to their homes in the Six Counties, including Military Officers of high rank.

On the other hand in the Free State there is perfect religious and civil freedom. We hold none of their people prisoners without trial. Protestant citizens throughout the Saorstát are as free to take part in their legitimate avocations as Catholics, and as a matter of fact none of the Protestant communities have uttered a word of complaint against the Saorstát Government. Many Protestants are members of the Oireachtas but in no sectarian sense, having joined one or other of the several national parties.

If they complain about the size of our Army and Police Force, we can say that this necessity is occasioned by the inimical attitude of the Belfast Government which is working so strongly against us, and that we will have to continue this for our own protection.

HISTORICAL ARGUMENT: We should not neglect, the Governor-General declared, to urge strongly the historical argument which he considered very strong. We should point out that Ireland was always one compact unit, economically, geographically and historically. At no time in history was it ever

[1] Chief Secretary for Ireland (1920-22).

divided or partitioned, certainly never in the present disgraceful manner. The Six Counties are especially Irish. County Down, for instance, contains St. Patrick's grave and St. Brighid's; Shane O'Neill's grave is in County Antrim, and in Tyrone and Fermanagh are the memorials of many battles and culture sacred to Irish memory.

A STIFF ATTITUDE: The delegates, he declared, should preserve a very stiff and unbending attitude, being careful never to yield an inch. It must not with us be a case of *addition* but of *subtraction*. We will gain nothing by yielding, and may gain – if we are to gain at all – by adopting and maintaining all through a good firm attitude. Look at Craig. He is like a piece of iron. He never yields, for he knows that should he yield he would be torn to pieces in Belfast within twenty-four hours afterwards.

Craig and his Government are exceptionally intimate with very influential British political and social circles and they are informed through these quarters of exactly what they are to expect.

Delegates should, of course, be as sweet as honey with MacDonald and the other Ministers. They can say whatever they like in private or speaking separately with British Ministers to show their reasonableness and moderation, but at the meetings of the Conference let them be as hard as granite.

[initialled] C.Ó S.[1]

No. 195 NAI DFA Letter Books (Department of the President 1923-28)

Desmond FitzGerald to William T. Cosgrave (Dublin)
(54/14) (Copy)

DUBLIN, 1 February 1924

My dear President,

The American Legislature is now considering a Bill to revise their immigration arrangements. At present immigrants are allowed in to the extent of 3% of nationals resident in U.S. in 1910. The new proposal is that it should be 2% of nationals resident in U.S. in 1890 plus 2% extra of blood relatives of those already there. So far there has only been a general quota for the late United Kingdom, but the American census has details of Irish in America as distinct from English, Scotch, etc., so that it would be possible for the Americans to define a separate Irish quota. This would be a gain for Irish would-be emigrants, as I calculate that it should amount to about one-half of the whole quota for the late United Kingdom, and with 'blood relatives' possibly even more, as nearly all our people going to America have relatives there already.

Professor Smiddy has been instructed to ascertain:

1) If it would be possible to have separate quota for Free State.
2) Failing that, if it could be arranged that there would be separate quota for whole of Ireland.

I think No. 1 is impossible, as though the American Government have figures

[1] Caoímhghín Ó Síadhail.

for Ireland they have no return showing their residents from the separate counties of Ireland.

Professor Smiddy cannot approach effectively the State Department (or even the Labour Department which is specially concerned with this matter) in his present unaccredited position.

It would be well therefore if he had special powers to deal with this. This does not mean that he should necessarily become Minister Plenipotentiary. He could have special powers to deal with this specific matter without prejudice to the question of his being accredited with full powers as Diplomatic Representative of the Free State.

In the event of our getting quota for all Ireland, it would be necessary for us to enter into an arrangement with the Northern Government to allot proportion of quota to Free State and proportion to Northern Six Counties.

What do you think of the feasibility of:-

1) Approaching British Prime Minister on the matter of special powers for Smiddy,
2) and Craig on the matter of quota for Ireland and division of that quota between his people and ours?

Yours sincerely,
[copy letter unsigned]

No. 196 NAI DT S1801D

Memorandum of notes made by William T. Cosgrave at the London Conference on the Boundary Question (Secret)
LONDON, 2 February 1924

We have given long and careful consideration to the proposals which have been put before us – not because of any value in themselves or of any contributory advantage towards ultimate benefit to our country – but for the sole purpose of assuring our North-Eastern friends that it is our desire and our hope and our wish to bridge differences not of our making, and difficulties for which we have no direct or indirect responsibility.

The proposals as outlined did not justify us in submitting them to any one outside of the Executive Council, and no useful purpose is served in considering them.

They are relatively and substantially inferior to the proposals of a kindred character in the Act of 1920 – which was definitely repudiated by our people. Nor do they constitute any apology for non-fulfilment or delay in carrying out the provisions of the Treaty.

We think it desirable to say that partition in the Act of 1920 must be regarded in the light of the maximum demand of the Northern Government. This proposal had never been accepted by any person on behalf of the majority of the Irish people and was responsible for breaks in former conferences.

In essence, therefore, the majority of the Irish people had on all occasions on which the 26 county and 6 county distribution had been tabled definitely and finally rejected that form of solution.

We will not consider nor put before anybody of our people any proposal less workable in substance and reality than that which has been confirmed by the two Nations.

The proposals would vitiate the Constitution we have adopted and which has been sworn to by 108 elected representatives of our Parliament – and which the 109th would also swear to maintain but that he is detained in gaol in Great Britain. It has been sworn to by every member of our Senate.

We are not asked in these proposals to share our independence with the Parliament of Northern Ireland, but to limit our independence and to give the Northern Parliament a veto on our legislation and a share in our administration of services withheld from it.

In any proposals for accommodation we are satisfied no useful purpose can be served in experimenting on unknown paths. Negotiations on the basis of ultimate union, however attractively they may be staged, are of no avail if we know definitely that one of the three parties to this Conference is in advance committed to a policy against such an end.

Negotiations on the basis of a trial period of a given number of months or years are of no avail if there be no goodwill and earnest purpose on both sides to such an instrument to safeguard minorities and to placate objections on the part of minorities.

No. 197 NAI DT S1801D

Extract from minutes of a meeting of the Executive Council (C.2/48)
DUBLIN, 4 February 1924

BOUNDARY CONFERENCE.
The President reported on the visit of the delegation to London during the week ended the 2nd inst. in connection with the Boundary question and presented to the meeting a copy of proposals made by the British Government.[1]

It was arranged that the Minister for Finance[2] should draft, for consideration by the Council, a note addressed to the British Government, intimating, with reasons stated, that the proposals are unacceptable to the Government of the Irish Free State. In addition each member of the Council is to prepare a memorandum embodying his views on the proposals, for consideration in conjunction with the draft reply.

No. 198 NAI DT S1801E

Secret memorandum and covering note from E.M. Stephens to William T. Cosgrave relating to the London Boundary Conference
DUBLIN, 9 February 1924

A Dhuine Uasail,
From the notes which you gave me, I have made draft criticisms of the proposals for submission to the next meeting of the Conference, and now enclose draft for consideration.

[1] Not printed.
[2] Ernest Blythe.

I also enclose for consideration draft counter-proposal, based on the Treaty, outline of possible further concessions, which I think should be very reluctantly made, and outline of powers with which it would be impossible to interfere without injuring our status.

I return herewith your notes, the notes of the Minister for Home Affairs and Conference Proposals.[1]

Mise, le meas,
[signed] E.M. STEPHENS
Rúnaidhe

[enclosure]

SECRET. February 8 1924

DRAFT CRITICISM OF PROPOSALS.

The policy of the Government of the Irish Free State has always been directed towards the creation of a united Ireland. It could only consider a suggestion for postponing the Boundary Commission if it was clearly shown that by doing so an opportunity would be afforded for a definite step being taken towards union.

From our examination of the present proposals we cannot see that any such step is suggested, nor do we think that even coupled with such a suggestion the proposals could be accepted by the Dáil.

Their general effect would be to give the Northern Parliament an absolute veto on legislation over services in the Free State, now under the control of the Oireachtas, which it is proposed to put under the control of a body which would only legislate by double majority. The machinery proposed seems unworkable and no suggestion is put forward as to what is to take place at the expiration of the suggested period.

Taking the proposals in order, our comments are as follows:-

1. There is no indication of any purpose for fixing a period of one year for the duration of any working arrangement which may be come to between the two Governments, and such an arrangement would only lead to further feeling of uncertainty.
2. It is not clear to whom these services would revert at the end of the year.
3. Joint responsibility is necessarily only temporary and is a doubtful method even for a short period.
4. The proposal for creating a joint legislative body is in itself practicable, but the powers now proposed are too few to justify the creation of a legislature.
5. The 'double majority' plan is wholly unacceptable.
6. Alternative sittings in Dublin and Belfast would not be possible.
7. The postponement of the Boundary Commission on the basis of these proposals would be impossible, as it would not be accepted by the country.

[1] Not printed.

No. 199 NAI DT S1801E

Memorandum by Kevin O'Shiel on the Boundary Question and London Conference
DUBLIN, 11 February 1924

THE BOUNDARY QUESTION AND THE CONFERENCE.
I. THE BRITISH PROPOSALS.
The British Government, as I thought, made proposals to us on this matter on the conclusion of the recent London Conference. Their proposals are not very detailed, but general as they are it is quite clear that their acceptance by us as they stand is out of the question. In substance they are practically identical with the Council of Ireland provided for in the discarded 1920 Act. Indeed the powers of the body described in the proposals are exactly those of the Council of Ireland[,] the differences between the two bodies being entirely with respect to their compositions. The proposals set forth in effect that the British Government and the Saorstát Government will mutually relinquish control of what may be called Council of Ireland Services, viz:

(1) Certain Private Bill legislation (1920 Act sub-section 7).
(2) Any powers which the two Irish Parliaments may mutually delegate to the Central Body, (sub-section 10).
(3) Powers in connection with railways and fisheries and the administration of the Diseases of Animals Acts (excepting powers in connection with railways that are wholly situated in one or other of the two areas) (sub-section 10).
(4) Capacity of the Central Body to pass resolutions suggesting legislation to either or both Parliaments on matters of general importance to the entire country, but in respect of which the Central Body has no powers, (sub-section 10).

The Saorstát and British Governments having relinquished control the intention is that these meagre services will be made responsible to a legislative body composed of the Senate and Dáil of the Saorstát and the Senate and House of Commons of 'Northern' Ireland, sitting jointly in Dublin and Belfast alternately. Were it intended that legislation in this large body was to be put into effect by a clear majority vote of the entire body something might be gained, but this is not so. There must be majorities in both Parliaments even though sitting together jointly before any bill passed by them could become law within their respective areas; and, after that contingency, the administrators of such legislation are to be 'the proper Ministers in Northern Ireland and the Free State *jointly*'.

Apart from the 'unworkableness' of this arrangement it does not bring us nearer a feasible union scheme than we were a year ago. Indeed the ideas underlying the Collins-Craig Pacts would have been wider in their application had they matured. A further point in the proposals is the suggestion of granting certain protection to minorities within the 'Northern' Ireland area. This suggestion is too vague to be of any value at the moment. Much more specific undertakings in this respect in the second Collins-Craig Pact came to nothing.

Taking the British Proposals generally I fail to see in what respect they mark an advance on the 1920 Act plan. The meeting of the two Pacts has a certain sentimental value but no actual value. Even the Council of Ireland was much nearer to an all Ireland Pact than this body for it had, as a body, definite legislative powers which the proposed conjoint Parliaments, *as a body*, will not have. Supposing that we accept these terms what will be the result?

For the sake of unity we shall have consented to the delegation of certain powers to this central body. Great Britain will do likewise for the Northern area. The conjoint Parliaments meet together in either Dublin or Belfast, but, as a united body they have no power. Legislation must be passed by the two Parliaments separately to be effective. As we enjoy the greater status this involves a loss of prestige to us and (if anything) a gain to the North East. The North East is called upon to sacrifice nothing. Its members will still attend Westminster; it will still (presumably) receive all manner of doles from Westminster and its education, legislation, specials, police etc., remain intact. By this scheme none of the 'painters' binding it to England will be severed.

Is there not a great danger of such a plan tending in time to pull the whole of Ireland, through the North, more and more towards London? I know it is one of the main points that this scheme is to be given a trial, 'without prejudice to the Boundary Commission', for twelve months. But in spite of this statement[,] supposing that it were possible for us to accept the scheme[,] such a delay would, in fact, be very prejudicial to the Boundary Commission, and, to our case generally. It would take from our position a good deal of its present strong morale, for this arrangement, cumbersome as it is, is quite likely to work out alright for a year, at the expiration of which *the onus of upsetting it, will be thrown upon us*. Before the expiration of that year we will be gravely and repeatedly admonished by a unanimous British press not to do anything to disturb a plan which had brought Irish Peace over the whole land, and this press will demand a further period of trial for the plan. It will thus be much more difficult for us to retreat back on to the strong Treaty position and take our stand on the Boundary Commission. The delay will have given away a considerable degree of the strength of our position.

Again, whilst delay during the past eighteen months, owing to the circumstances that prevailed[,] was essential and necessary[,] we have I think arrived at a time when much further delay, without the definite prospect of a good union settlement that we could confidently recommend for acceptance to the Dáil[,] would be very dangerous to our position in every way. As long as the Boundary Question is unsolved one way or another it will be an element of instability and insecurity in the State from this on and the lesser of many evils will be some kind of a settlement of this question, either by the Boundary Commission operating or by some definite plan which all sides will mutually agree to accept. Certainty, even if it is unpleasant is better and healthier than living in continual uncertainty.

II. OUR REPLY:

For the reasons already stated I am of opinion that the British Proposals should be definitely turned down, in a short time, say a week or ten days, as any longer delay would only create amongst the public of all the places concerned a false optimism by creating the impression that we considered the terms sufficiently good to warrant a fair period for their consideration.

We should reply to this effect sending also something in the nature of counter-proposals. There is no reason for our Counter-Proposals to be a degree more explicit than their proposals. In my opinion they should take the form of a general offer to the North-East through the British Government to accept Irish Union as the Saorstát has accepted the Commonwealth Union. Whilst I believe that this is the moment for stating our maximum claim for Union, we should so draft it that it should not appear that we were out for our whole 'Pound of Flesh'. That would be bad tactics as it would provide Craig with a slogan and the British Press a theme. It would be said that we were not dealing fairly with Craig, and that we were not genuinely anxious for Union, etc., etc.

In the most diplomatic language possible we could strike a claim now for complete Irish Union pointing out its *GEOGRAPHICAL* and *ECONOMIC EXISTENCE* and its *absolute and admitted need in the best interests of all the People in Ireland.*

We could then proceed that we are quite prepared to give the North-East all the reasonable guarantees with regard to any matters which they are timid about, e.g., *education, administration, economics, religion, fiscal policy,* etc.

These proposals would be more in the nature of a *'feeler'* to see [to] what extent the North-East is prepared to go for an amicable adjustment of the difficulties.

POSTPONEMENT OF L. G. B.[1] *ELECTIONS IN NORTHERN IRELAND.*
We should express our willingness to sit in conference with the North-East to hammer out the details of any scheme of Union as long as it may be necessary, but we should also take care to mention that before we could do so it will be necessary for the Belfast Government to postpone the forthcoming Local Government elections for a twelve months. *This is very important.* County Council and Rural District Council elections are due to take place in the Six Counties in May next on the *new register* and for *gerrymandered areas.* The new register has operated disastrously against Nationalist electors. The old property qualifications have been restored, P.R. has been abolished, the electoral areas have been terribly gerrymandered and hundreds of Special Police from outside places have been put on the Tyrone and Fermanagh registers.

The result of these forthcoming elections will most certainly be that the County Councils of Tyrone and Fermanagh, now Nationalist, will go Unionist, as well as *ALL* the Poor Law Unions and Rural District Councils in both Counties. As showing the sweeping nature of these 'reforms', here are the results of the last P.R. elections for comparison:-

TYRONE:

(1) COUNTY COUNCIL.	NATIONALIST.
(2) 6 POOR LAW UNIONS.	5 NATIONALIST, 1 UNIONIST.
(3) 6 RURAL DISTRICT COUNCILS.	4 NATIONALIST, 2 UNIONIST.

FERMANAGH:

(1) COUNTY COUNCIL.	NATIONALIST.
(2) 3 POOR LAW UNIONS.	1 NATIONALIST. 2 UNIONIST.
(3) 3 RURAL DISTRICT COUNCILS.	2 NATIONALIST. 1 UNIONIST.

[1] Local Government Board.

It must be remembered with regard to this country that since the establishment of Partition, 2 Nationalist R.[ural] D.[istrict] C.[ouncil]s. have been abolished and Amalgamated with strong Unionist ones.

It is also more than probable that Magherafelt R.D.C. and P.[oor] L.[aw] U.[nion] in County Derry will go Unionist, as well as the R.D.Cs. and P.L.Us. of Newry No.1, Downpatrick and Kilkeel (Co. Down) and Armagh and Newry No.2 (Co. Armagh).

It will be seen from above how disastrous it would be for us to permit these elections to take place either whilst the Conference is sitting or before any definite setting-up of the Boundary Commission takes place.

It is clear that no matter what we may say about gerrymandering and packing registers, *AFTER* these elections no argument of ours will prevail against the *GREAT FACT* that those districts, once in favour of a Dublin Parliament, have all gone in favour of a Belfast Parliament. It will give the Belfast Government's tenure of those lands infinitely greater security and will most gravely prejudice our case in the event of a Boundary Commission being set up. We will be in the position of persons who have handed away the most telling part of their case and guilty of breaking the equity maxim that *'Delay defeats Equity'*.

In these circumstances the Government's strong home position would be much weakened and it would be accused of having been weak and having been 'fooled and tricked; kept talking until Craig was able to get this election through', etc.

We cannot, therefore, afford to postpone settlement one way or another of the Boundary matter beyond 1st March unless Craig agrees to a postponement of these elections.

Another reason that makes this still more imperative is that we are dealing with a British Government whose position is extremely insecure. It might be bowled out at any moment and our position would be once more one of uncertainty and doubt. Should a general election take place tomorrow, a not unlikely contingency, the Boundary matter would be once more 'put by' and Craig could go on with his election plans for converting formerly solid Nationalist areas into part of the new 'homogeneous Ulster'.

III. OUR POSITION:

i. Whilst the achievement of *IRISH UNION* is an objective greatly to be desired and whilst big sacrifices should certainly be made for it, we cannot dare to make sacrifices that would undermine the Government's authority and position in the country. Sacrifices, too, must be mutual, and if we give in any point we must see to it that we get something in return, that the North-East also gives.

ii. At the moment it is more important for the present Government to have the confidence of the people of the Saorstát and to continue in control at least until the Nation is 'out of the wood' than for any form of Union to be agreed to which would have the effect of jeopardising their position in the country.

iii. The Government should therefore neither accept nor agree to any terms which would imperil its position in the Saorstát and thereby engender once again a period of chaos and disorder. The Government should not be called upon from any external source, nor for any reason, to meet and deal with violent opposition and disturbance once more. It has kept faith well and truly with Great Britain in connection with its Treaty obligations. No person can deny this fact. The observance 'in the spirit as well as in the letter' of the signed bond of our responsible statesmen as endorsed by our legislature has cost Saorstát Éireann blood, money and treasure. It is therefore extremely reasonable for the Government to stipulate that *it should not be called upon to accept any adjustment of the Treaty which would have the effect of endangering in any way the present peace and security of the Saorstát.*

iv. If we find the 'Non-Possumus' attitude prevailing, and both the British Government and Craig expecting us to do all the compromising we should cut the matter short and fall back on the Boundary Commission before it becomes too late. There is no doubt at all that the easiest course for us now and all along would have been to have stood out rigidly for a Boundary Commission. By not doing so we have shown ourselves to be reasonable and anxious to secure Irish Union if at all possible. We have delayed long for this consummation, but we cannot at this stage afford further delays. So therefore, if Craig continues obdurate and obstinate we will have to slip back quickly into the rock of the Boundary Commission which after all has solemn Treaty sanction.

v. Should we be compelled to adopt a rigid attitude there is no doubt that it will be extremely popular in the Saorstát. It may weld the people of the Saorstát firmly together and will certainly give the Government added prestige. Such an attitude will, as I have said, be most popular at home; nevertheless I do not think it should be adopted save as a last resource when it has become pretty clear that Craig will not budge an inch and that the British Government will do nothing definite to make him. At any rate we will have to make up our minds quickly as *TIME from this on will be running against us and in favour of Sir James Craig.*

Should Craig be able to manoeuvre us past the elections he will then be able to snap his fingers at us and as he will have an excellent case to go before the Boundary Commission in which there is no definite method prescribed for ascertaining the wishes of the inhabitants he may agree to appoint his Commissioner.

IV. POSSIBLE TREND OF EVENTS SHOULD WE STAND BY THE BOUNDARY ARTICLE:
The Labour Government, I hear, is most anxious that this matter should not come to a Boundary Commission during their term of office. They are frankly frightened at its complications and feel that their own difficulties will only begin then.

Craig has repeatedly declared that he will not recognise the Commission on the ground that the 1920 Statute secured him his present territory. What will happen then?

We must make it clear that we cannot afford to fight any more Civil Wars. One was quite enough for any Government to be called upon to undertake in defence of the Nation's plighted word. Any new settlement that may involve further trouble will therefore be out of the question.

As a 'last resource argument' we can urge that the Boundary Commission is part of the Treaty which we fought for. It must therefore operate. Let it be diplomatically made known that if there is to be no Boundary Commission by reason of the North-East's malfeasance and Great Britain's acquiescence in that malfeasance, there will be no further need for our maintaining the Treaty in its entirety. We can then let it be known that if all-Ireland Union is out of the question we can at least have complete union amongst all sections in the Saorstát. A general election would then take place on the question of revising the Constitution and repudiating the Clauses dealing with Finance, etc. in the Treaty that have not yet been executed. Let it be made known also that there will be no intention of any 'War against Ulster' at any time. Constitutionally the above can be achieved without any war.

Our case and our position could hardly be stronger for this 'last resource' attitude. And if Labour sees that, after having exhausted every 'avenue' to Irish Union as far as we could possibly do so and displayed our undoubted anxiety for settlement, we are determined in letting events take their course according to the Treaty (we might also, at this stage, register the Treaty at the League of Nations) which after all is the easiest and popular course for us, it is not by any means impossible that at the last moment it might effect a big and sensational change of front.

C. Ó S

No. 200 NAI DFA ES Box 29 File 191

Timothy A. Smiddy to Desmond FitzGerald (Dublin)
(6/24)

WASHINGTON, 11 February 1924

A Chara:

POLICY

The need of recognition has been recently made manifest in dealings I had with some of the government departments in Washington. While they have always been willing and ready to supply me with any information I sought, yet, they will not take action in important (and sometimes in small) matters without a direction from the State Department; and the latter will not act without a formal request from the British Embassy.

For instance in the recent case of the registration of Dr Russell by the Department of Agriculture for the export of meat and meat products from Dublin to the U.S.A. the chief officials put many difficulties in the way of such recognition. One of the difficulties put forward by them either displayed gross ignorance of their own regulations, or else it was only a pretext. This difficulty was promptly removed by the intervention of the British Embassy who requested the State Department to give a direction to the State Department to register Dr Russell.

In this connexion Mr Broderick, Commercial Counsellor to the Embassy, a Dublin man and one of the ablest (if not also imperialistic) in the Embassy raised with me the following question: 'Have any arrangements been made with the British Foreign Office by the Free State Government by which the Embassy could take action with the State Department here in matters similar to the above, and in still more important matters, such as extradition?' He stated they were only agents of the Foreign Office; and, hence, that they should get a direction from the l[at]t[er] advising them to act on my instructions as Representative of the Irish Free State.

Sir Auckland Geddes[1] when I approached him last year on somewhat similar subjects made no such comment but directed the Secretary of the Embassy to facilitate my work, which he did most cordially whenever I made any request. Now, I do not mean to imply that Mr Broderick did not, and is not, anxious to help: he is; but he said the relations between me and the Embassy ought to be put on a formal basis.

It is then obvious that my relations both with the U.S.A. Government and the British Embassy are informal: both have acted – the former in many cases the latter in all cases – when I asked them to get things done. But in the case of both[,] anything they did for me was purely by act of grace.

It will be undignified, without official credentials, to attempt any longer to induce the government departments of the U.S. *to take action* in important matters that concern the Irish Free State. Last year, and recently, I attempted it with a measure of success through personal and social influences because it was tentative and there was the expectation at an early date of my recognition as an accredited representative. But you will agree it would be undignified for the Free State to pursue these attempts any further; and an invidious situation would be provoked if I were to call in the aid of the British Embassy in the event of the failure of my own efforts.

Hence, my relations to the Government Departments of the U.S.A. and to the British Embassy is anomalous and somewhat invidious whenever *action* on behalf of the Irish Free State is to be initiated by me here. However, there are no difficulties to be encountered where information only is sought in my capacity of a political or economic observer.

The Canadian Representative is theoretically in the same position. Officially, he acts through the British Embassy, but his offices, being in the Embassy he can ring up a government department directly – even the Department of State – and indicate his request *as from the British Embassy*. Some three [years][2] hence Mr Mahoney[3] – the Representative – consented to have his office (at the request of its officials) in the Embassy; he did so as a purely tentative and *vocational* arrangement to suit his own purpose. As soon as a Minister will be appointed at Washington (which he thinks to be imminent) the offices of the Canadian Embassy will be independent of the British Embassy.

Hence, immediate action is necessary to remedy this anomalous position either by arranging with the British Foreign Office that the Embassy here take action on my direction in matters that affect only the Free State, or by the Foreign Office directing the British Embassy to have me recognized as the accredited representative of the Irish Free State by the President of the U.S.A. and by the State Department. Naturally, this latter plan is the better. It will facilitate all the relations of the Free State with the U.S.A. Government, and it will indicate in a striking manner to the Irish Americans that the Irish Free State is a self-

[1] British Ambassador to Washington (1920-24).
[2] Word missing.
[3] M.M. Mahoney, Canadian Representative in the United States (1921-27).

governing, independent nation, and will tend in an effectual manner to counteract the Irregular campaign here and illustrate the futility of the American people to subscribe moneys for the establishment of an ideal which is practically achieved.

The suggestion of Secretary of State Hughes that provision be made in the Johnson Immigration Act, 1924, so as to warrant a separate immigration quota for the Irish Free State is a good omen. The ground is prepared and I believe ready in Washington for an application for recognition. Is the British Foreign Office ready to present it?

At your convenience I shall be favoured by your remarks on this subject,

Mise, le meas,
[copy letter unsigned]

No. 201 NAI DT S1801E

Extract from minutes of a meeting of the Executive Council (C.2/50)
DUBLIN, 12 February 1924

BOUNDARY QUESTION.
Consideration was given to a number of memoranda prepared by members of the Exec: Council outlining their views with regard to certain proposals made by the British Government in connection with the recent London Conference on the Boundary question.[1]

The memoranda were referred to the Minister for Education[2] who is to prepare in conjunction with the Secretary to the Council a draft reply to the British Government intimating that the proposals could not be accepted by the Government of Saorstát Eireann.

The draft is to be circulated to the members of the Executive Council and their observations thereon communicated to the Minister of Education at the earliest possible moment.

The Minister for External Affairs[3] is to inform the Colonial Secretary that the Government of Saorstát Eireann desire that the Conference should be resumed without delay.

No. 202 NAI DFA D1976

T.M. Healy to J.H. Thomas (London)
(No. 66) (Copy)
DUBLIN, 19 February 1924

Sir,
In reply to the Duke of Devonshire's Despatch No. 604 of the 15th October, 1923, I have the honour to inform you that my Ministers concur in the action taken by Mr. Chilton[4] in ignoring letters and telegrams addressed to him by

[1] Not printed.
[2] Eoin MacNeill.
[3] Desmond FitzGerald.
[4] Counsellor, British Embassy, Washington (1921-28).

Branches of the American Association for the Recognition of the Irish Republic in the United States, on the subject of the detention and possible trial of prisoners in Ireland. My Ministers would, however, be glad to receive for information copies of any such communications which might emanate from sources of political or social importance in the United States.

2. They would also suggest that in any cases where Mr. Chilton was of opinion that an acknowledgment should issue, the writer might be invited to address himself direct to the Secretary of the Executive Council, Government Buildings, Dublin.

3. It is presumed that His Majesty's Government would not desire that the receipt of such copies of communications by my Ministers should be regarded as confidential.

I have the honour to be,
Sir,
Your most obedient, humble Servant,
[stamped] T.M. HEALY

No. 203 NAI DT S1983

T.M. Healy to J.H. Thomas (London)
(No. 79) (Copy)

DUBLIN, 3 March 1924

Sir,

My Ministers desire me to inform you that they are convinced of the urgent necessity of appointing an Irish Minister Plenipotentiary and Envoy Extraordinary to the United States of America.

2. They have decided that Mr. Timothy A. Smiddy would be a suitable person to assume that position, and they would be glad if His Majesty's Government would cause immediate enquiries to be made as to whether he would be persona grata to the President and to the Department of State at Washington.

3. In the event of a favourable reply, they would be glad to receive letters of credence from His Majesty the King for transmission to Mr. Smiddy.

4. They are confident that you will appreciate the considerations which have prompted them to arrive at this decision. The financial and commercial interests of the Free State in the United States are very considerable, and the pressing problem of Irish emigration to America has for a long time engaged the earnest attention of my Government. They have found, in dealing with these matters, that they are severely handicapped by reason of the fact that their representative at Washington has not been accredited to the Government of the United States. They feel sure, moreover, that nothing could be more effective in promoting amongst Irish people in America cordial relations with the Nations of the Commonwealth than the presence of an Irish Minister Plenipotentiary in the United States.

5. In view of the extreme urgency of finding a solution for the financial and immigration questions directly affecting them, my Ministers request that the British Ambassador at Washington be immediately instructed by telegraph to

communicate with the United States Government in reference to Professor Smiddy's appointment.

I have the honour to be,
Sir,
Your most obedient, humble Servant,
[stampted] T.M. HEALY

No. 204 NAI DT S1971

T.M. Healy to J.H. Thomas (London)
(No. 80) (Copy)

DUBLIN, 4 March 1924

Sir,
With reference to the Duke of Devonshire's Despatch No. 722 of the 14th December 1923,[1] regarding the issue of Passports by the Government of the Irish Free State, I have the honour to state that my Ministers have given the matter further careful consideration and in order to meet the difficulties raised by His Majesty's Government, they would be prepared to agree to describe holders of Passports, other than those described in paragraph 3 below, as 'Citizen of the Irish Free State and of the British Commonwealth of Nations'.
2. This description would, in the view of my Ministers, remove all possibility of confusion by His Majesty's Consular Officers abroad or by Foreign Governments.
3. In the case of persons who acquired Irish Citizenship on December 6th, 1922 by virtue of Article 3 of the Constitution, the words 'and of the British Commonwealth of Nations' would be omitted from the description on the Passport and the qualifying Clause set out in Paragraph 3 of my Despatch No. 339 of the 27th November, 1923,[2] would be inscribed in each case.

I have the honour to be,
Sir,
Your most obedient, humble Servant,
[stamped] T.M. HEALY

No. 205 NAI DT S1801E

T.M. Healy to J.H. Thomas (London)
(No. 95)

DUBLIN, 15 March 1924

Sir,
I have the honour to acknowledge the receipt of your telegram of the 11th instant[3] transmitting extracts from a despatch received by you from the Governor of Northern Ireland, containing a proposal that the next Meeting of

[1] Not printed.
[2] Not printed.
[3] Not printed.

the Conference on the Boundary Question should be postponed until the 24th April next, in view of the illness of the Premier of Northern Ireland.
2. My Ministers regret to learn that the condition of Sir James Craig's health continues to be a cause of uneasiness, and that he is obliged on medical advice to abstain for the present from all work and anxiety, but they trust that the measures prescribed by his medical advisers will speedily restore him to health.
3. It is now suggested that the Conference be further postponed, and in this connection the statement is made in the letter from the Secretary to the Cabinet of Northern Ireland[1] 'that the questions being dealt with at the Conference have been awaiting a decision for over two years and that it is not unreasonable in the circumstances to ask for a further delay of a few weeks'. My Ministers, however, desire me to point out that the provisions of Article 12 of the Treaty did not become operative until after the 6th December, 1922. My Government had its energies engaged from that date in setting up the machinery of Government and creating the various Departments of State, as well as in suppressing disorder and armed violence which showed themselves during the transition period.
4. As soon as my Ministers felt that they had set the machinery of Government on a secure and ordered basis they appointed their representative on the Boundary Commission, viz: Dr. Eoin MacNeill, T.D., Minister for Education, and the appointment was notified to your predecessor in my despatch No. 206 of the 19th July[2] last. At the same time a request was made that the necessary steps should be taken by His Majesty's Government to complete the constitution of the Commission.
5. The delay which has since intervened has been agreed to by my Ministers at the request of His Majesty's Government in the hope that a settlement would be arrived at which would bring about not merely a formal unity but a cordial and harmonious reunion of the people of Ireland. With this object in view they agreed to participate in the Conference in London on the 2nd ultimo, which was summoned to consider the problems arising out of Article 12 of the Treaty.
6. These problems have been rendered more acute by events which have occurred in Northern Ireland during the period which has elapsed since Article 12 of the Treaty became operative. Administrative changes have taken place, the result of which will be, after the Northern Local Government Elections of May next, practically to disfranchise the Nationalist population in large areas adjacent to the Boundary, and further similar measures are foreshadowed in the Speech from the Throne at the opening of the Northern Parliament on the 11th instant.
7. In the circumstances my Ministers feel that the effect of further postponement would be to deprive of the benefits of the Treaty those persons whose interests Clause 12, without which the Treaty would never have been accepted, was specially designed to protect, and they ask, therefore, that His Majesty's Government will take the necessary steps to complete the constitution of the Boundary Commission without further delay.

[1] Wilfred Spender.
[2] No. 101 above.

8. My Ministers wish me to make it clear that this request is not to be regarded as closing the door to further amicable discussion between the Governments concerned. They have at all times shown themselves, and will continue to show themselves, even during the sittings of the Boundary Commission, willing to give the most careful consideration to any representation from His Majesty's Government or the Government of Northern Ireland which would appear to offer any hope of a genuine settlement on the basis of the re-union of Ireland.
9. In this spirit they considered the proposals made by the Secretary of State for the Colonies at the Conference held in London on the 2nd ultimo, and they desire me to enclose, for the information of His Majesty's Government, a copy of a statement which they had prepared for presentation to the Conference on its reassembly.[1]

I have the honour to be,
Sir,
Your most obedient humble Servant,
[stamped] T.M. HEALY

No. 206 NAI DT S1367

T.M. Healy to J.H. Thomas (London)
(Confidential)

DUBLIN, 27 March 1924

Sir,
I have the honour to inform you that the Duke of Devonshire's Despatches of the 20th August and 3rd December 1923 and your Despatch of the 5th February, 1924, relative to the proposed amendments to Article 16 of the Covenant of the League of Nations, have received the careful attention of my Ministers.[2]
2. Wide divergence of opinion still exists amongst Member States of the League as to the exact nature of the obligations contracted under Article 16. My Ministers feel that the proposed amendment raises difficult and very important questions which require, and as they anticipate, will be subjected to, serious examination at the next meeting of the Assembly of the League. They wish to be free to weigh the various considerations which will be offered, and are therefore reluctant to prejudice such action as they may decide upon after full debate of the matter.

I have the honour to be,
Sir,
Your most obedient, humble Servant,
[stamped] T.M. HEALY

[1] Not printed.
[2] Despatches not printed.

No. 207 NAI DT S1801F

T.M. Healy to J.H. Thomas (London)
(No. 120)

DUBLIN, 7 April 1924

Sir,

I have the honour to refer to your despatch No. 203 of the 1st instant[1] and to state that my Ministers have given careful consideration to your earnest request that they should not 'ask His Majesty's Government to call upon the Government of Northern Ireland to appoint their Commissioner until the representatives of the two Governments have had time to resume their conversations'.

2. With regard to the suggestion in paragraph 3 of your despatch, my Ministers desire me to say that this important matter has in their opinion now become so pressingly urgent that they could not take the responsibility of permitting the indisposition of any of their representatives to cause any further delay. Had the President or any other member been unable to attend the Conference in person, his place would have been taken by a representative appointed for that purpose.

3. While my Ministers are anxious to consult the convenience both of His Majesty's Government and of the Government of Northern Ireland, they cannot, for the reasons stated in my despatch No. 95 of the 15th ultimo,[2] agree to the continued postponement of the settlement of this problem, and they consider that the personnel of the Boundary Commission should be completed not later than the 1st May next.

4. In the meantime, however, since Sir James Craig is due to return from his voyage on the 24th instant, they would be prepared, in the spirit referred to in paragraph 8 of my despatch mentioned above, to send representatives to confer with representatives of His Majesty's Government and of the Government of Northern Ireland on the following day, provided that they are assured on behalf of His Majesty's Government, that if the resumed Conference does not result in, or give promise of, a more satisfactory solution of the Boundary question than that provided for in Article 12 of the Treaty, steps will be taken by His Majesty's Government to complete the constitution of the Boundary Commission not later than the 1st proximo.

I have the honour to be
Sir,
Your most obedient humble Servant,
[stamped] T.M. HEALY

[1] Not printed.
[2] See above No. 205.

No. 208 NAI DFA Minister's Office (1924-25)

Extracts from a letter by James McNeill to Desmond FitzGerald (Dublin)
LONDON, 8 April 1924

My dear Minister,
I have just heard for the first time that the Committee of the British Empire Exhibition were going to issue invitations to about 1,200 people to attend the ceremony of opening the Exhibition by the King on 23rd April, and that High Commissioners were being asked to propose the names of persons to be invited.
[Matter omitted]

I must, as I conceive, attend. Absence would be regarded as wilful discourtesy. I think I must also propose at least ten other names. If, as seems likely, President Cosgrave is in London I think he must attend. In any case I think I should ask for an invitation for him, even if eventually he is unable to attend. If you, or the Ministers of Agriculture and of Industry and Commerce could attend[,] the names should be sent in. If the Ministers could not come the Secretaries of the Departments might be invited, or any of the three who could come. The Governor General would of course be invited, but I must include his name in any list sent in by me. The Chairman of the Senate[1] should be suggested in my opinion.
[Matter omitted]

As the matter is very urgent please have a reply sent to this as soon as possible.

Yours sincerely,
[signed] JAMES MCNEILL

No. 209 NAI DFA Minister's Office Files (1924-25)

Handwritten minute from William T. Cosgrave to Desmond FitzGerald
DUBLIN, undated, but mid-April 1924

I don't approve issuing invitation unless people can come. Personally I have no time for such matters. If people have any doubts regarding our leisure time the sooner they are disabused the better & it is the business of the High Comm[issioner] to let it be known that our offices are whole time demanding very long hours of attendance.

I have no patience with their semi social events. If in the future when an opportunity for Ministers of this State to devote time to such affairs our proximity to England must not presuppose our absorption in these festivities & events. We have our own.

L T MACC[2]

[1] Lord Glenavy.
[2] L[iam] T. MacC[osgair].

No. 210 NAI DFA ES Box 29 File 191

Timothy A. Smiddy to Joseph P. Walshe (Dublin)
(4/24) (Copy) (Confidential)
WASHINGTON, 18 April 1924

A Chara:

INTELLIGENCE.

You will see by newspaper cuttings, posted to you under separate cover yesterday, that further attempts are being made on part of the Irregulars to prevail upon Congress to use its influence to obtain de Valera's release.

One of the reasons alleged for doing so is that he is an American Citizen who does not owe allegiance to the Irish Free State because an actual Republic does not exist.

These appeals to Congress will be ineffective as you will see from the statement of Secretary Hughes.[1] They will tend to keep the name of de Valera in the limelight, but, except [for] a small, well organized and articulate group of Irish-Americans in New York and Boston, the American people and press have long since ceased to be interested in de Valera and his propaganda.

The Advent of 'recognition' will confirm the people of America in their belief that the Irish Free State contains the inherent marks of a sovereign state.

You have, doubtless, noted that the 'Irish World' is booming in a very marked manner [for][2] Mr Doheny which may make him partial to this paper, especially, as the 'Gaelic American' is acrimoniously attacking him. It is unfortunate that the latter paper has assumed this attitude. It is a legacy of the strong antagonism to Doheny which originated at the time he gave his support to de Valera and the A.A.R.I.R. in the Pre-Treaty days, when much bitterness existed between these two organizations.

This hostility on part of the 'Gaelic American' is, unfortunately, too ingrained to induce it to adopt a reconciliatory attitude.

Mise, le meas,
[copy letter unsigned]

No. 211 NAI DT S1801E

T.M. Healy to J.H. Thomas (London)
(No. 152)
DUBLIN, 26 April 1924

Sir,
I have the honour to refer to previous correspondence on the subject of Article 12 of the Treaty, and in particular to your Despatch No. 232 of the 10th instant,[3] with special reference to paragraph 5 thereof.

[1] Charles Evans Hughes, United States Secretary of State (1921-25).
[2] Word missing.
[3] Not printed.

2. The Conference mentioned in the Despatches, which was attended by my Ministers on the invitation of His Majesty's Government, has terminated its sittings without arriving at any agreement.
3. My Ministers, therefore, request that His Majesty's Government will take immediate steps for the completion of the constitution of the Boundary Commission.

I have the honour to be,
Sir,
Your most obedient, humble Servant.
[stamped] T.M. HEALY

No. 212 NAI DFA GR 246

Timothy A. Smiddy to Desmond FitzGerald (Dublin)
(24/24)

WASHINGTON, 5 May 1924

My dear Minister:
I presume that you have obtained a rough idea of the general attitude of the principal newspapers of the United States towards the Irish Free State and towards its present Government; and as far as I can gather the newspapers which we peruse are fairly typical of the press of the U.S.A. as a whole.

During the last few months the Irish Free State got a good deal of favourable and sustained publicity; yet in a few instances, such as in the case of the New York Tribune, some publicity has been given[,] creative of an unfavourable atmosphere. This paper during the month of March published a series of articles under the name of Mr. Warre Wells, copies of which I sent you and on which I commented in my letter of March 26th.[1] To illustrate I again enclose a copy of an editorial of the 'New York Times' of March 25th and cutting on 'Ireland's Rising Revenue' of March 23rd.

Unfortunately, one unfavourable article is more injurious to the credit, trade, industry and world wide influence of the Irish Free State than many favourable ones, and they are certain to be affected by the impression formed in this and other countries by press reports.

To offset the unfavourable effect, if any, of the articles of the New York Tribune some influential friends of mine gave me a cordial introduction to Mr Oaks, chief stockholder of the New York Times, and Mr Wiley, General Manager. I had an interview with these gentlemen who had been notified by my friends of the object of my visit, viz. that I was anxious to discuss with them some true facts dealing with the constructive side of the Irish Free State in view of the unfavourable impression created by some articles that appeared in another New York paper. They listened with sympathetic interest to my remarks; introduced me to the principal editors of the paper with whom I discussed the subject in greater detail; and informed that they would instruct their Washington representative to keep in touch with me in matters affecting the Irish Free State.

[1] Not printed.

In view of the fact that many merchants are falsely representing goods of Irish origin (bacon, lace, poplin etc), I introduced Mr Lindsay Crawford to Mr Wiley. I expect that some good will result from these interviews and I shall maintain and improve the contact which has been made.

Everything possible has been done by this office to bring before the American public the stronger and more constructive elements in the Irish Free State's position. This has been effected, if in a somewhat haphazard way, by utilizing various avenues of publicity, viz. Publicity Department of the Department of Commerce of the U.S.A., Bankers Journal, banks, interviews, contacts with press representatives and circularizing many newspapers with the various publications we receive from the Government.

You, doubtless, will realise that, in consequence of the variety of work of this office, the area of the U.S.A. and the absence of any staff, except my secretary, – as Mr Slattery is wholly engaged on the work of the Republican Bond Certificates – it is absolutely impossible to attempt anything approaching an organized scheme of publicity. For the effective working of such a scheme a first class publicity man and a staff of two competent assistants would be required. A publicity man of first class standing and of editorial experience cannot be procured here under $10,000 per annum. And for this purpose a man acquainted with American publicity, methods and journalism is required. For instance, an institution such as the Catholic Welfare News Service pays its director of publicity $13,000. Similar salaries are paid by banks and business institutions to their publicity directors. I calculate that the outlay (in salaries, travelling, office expenses, and special articles) for an adequate publicity bureau attached to this office would be $25,000. Unless a competent staff of this character were established it would be better to content ourselves with the practice which obtains at present.

Perhaps, the financial exigencies of the Irish Free State may not permit this. However, *I simply wish to put on record the essentials of adequate publicity* for the constructive side of the Irish Free State as from time to time one hears criticisms, to the effect that it does not do a sufficient amount of publicity in the U.S.A. And these criticisms come from those who assume a spasmodic interest in the Irish Free State and who do not go to much trouble to acquaint themselves with its real conditions. Hence, I feel justified in claiming your esteemed and valuable consideration of what steps, if any, should be taken for comprehensive publicity in the United States.

I would again press upon you the great value of regular messages by Ministers to all representatives of the Foreign press in Ireland. Probably you have already considered some intermediary by which they can be kept in friendly contact with your Ministry.

I write this letter for you to consider, if, in the light of these comments, my previous reports and newspaper cuttings, the time has come for an organized and effective system of publicity based on the stable elements of the political, financial, agricultural, industrial, literary and artistic [life][1] of the Irish Free State.

[1] Word missing.

I am of opinion that any time, thought and money that can be spared for this purpose will be well spent, and confidence in the Irish Free State abroad cannot fail to have its bearing in assisting the settlement of problems at home. In the United States at present where there is so fertile a field for the creation of sentiment friendly or unfriendly everything possible should be done to place before the public the stronger and more constructive elements in the position of the Irish Free State.

I have already written to you suggesting the formation, and the lines on which it might be effected, of an Irish Press Association. I discussed the matter in some detail with Dr MacDonald when he was in New York.

At your convenience I shall be favoured with your comments on this memorandum.

Accept the renewed assurances of my highest consideration.

Mise, le meas,
[copy letter unsigned]

No. 213 NAI DT S1801P

Extracts from a letter from James McNeill to William T. Cosgrave (Dublin)
(Copy)

LONDON, 7 May 1924

My dear President,
Many thanks for your letter. I know how busy you are.
[Matter omitted]

I met Craig at a public dinner a few evenings ago. We exchanged civilities and mutual wishes that a peaceful solution would be found. I talked no detail. He said he felt sure you would like that and desired an assurance as to Kevin O'Higgins. I said the latter would be no opponent of a peaceful solution if that could be arranged.

I think the full report of K. O'H's speech in the 'Times' is useful. It is something that it is regarded as prudent to give the full report.

I have been asked by friendly inquirers if there was any risk that 'Republicans' would weaken instead of strengthening the firmness of our stand. I opined they would not. Could any of them be got to commend the Commission?

Yours sincerely,
(Signed) JAMES MCNEILL

No. 214 NAI DT S1801P

Kevin O'Higgins to William T. Cosgrave (Dublin)
(C. 1492) (Confidential)

DUBLIN, 7 May 1924

President,
I incline to the view that we cannot allow ourselves to be manoeuvred into a position in which an alleged ambiguity in Article 12 of the Treaty is to be left to the decision of the Boundary Commission, which, in effect, means to the

decision of a Chairman appointed by the British Government.

Our position, of course, is that we deny absolutely the existence of any such ambiguity, that the whole antecedents of the situation, together with the precise words of the Treaty, absolutely exclude the suggestion that such an ambiguity exists.

A British signatory and an ex-Lord Chancellor[1] has, however, come into the ring in favour of the assertion not merely that an ambiguity exists but that, in his view, the narrower construction, which is attempted to be placed on the provisos of Article 12, is the correct one. Such influential British newspapers as the 'Times', the 'Observer' and the 'Daily Chronicle' are in full cry on this note.

I believe that Lord Birkenhead's statement, as distinct from Press utterances, gives us an opportunity, which we ought to avail of, of taking up this matter with the British Government and asking them to declare plainly whether it is their opinion that any ambiguity of the kind exists in this particular Article of what is, after all, an international document.

Should they declare that it is their view that the Article is ambiguous then obviously we must have the ambiguity cleared up before the Boundary Commission sits, and the alleged ambiguity cannot be left to the tender mercies of the British nominee on the Commission.

If the British Government's interpretation of a particular Article of the Anglo-Irish Treaty conflicts with the view of the Irish Government – and we are entitled to know whether it does or does not – then some form of arbitration must be agreed upon, and such arbitration must take place before the Commission is set up. There must be no ambiguity or alleged ambiguity in the term of reference of the Commission.

As I am writing to you on this subject, I would like to add another suggestion. It is just possible that the North East, finding itself in a tight corner, would have resort to anarchy, in which event it would like very much to place the responsibility of precipitating such a state of affairs on us.

It might be well worth considering if not now, then at some later stage, whether we ought not to withdraw all our armed men a considerable distance from the border and announce publicly to the world that we had done so. A fool or an agent provocateur on either side of the existing Boundary might very easily cause an 'incident', and the British and North East Press might be relied upon to put their own interpretation on such 'incident' and to place the responsibility on us.

[signed] C. Ó hUIGÍN
Aire um Ghnóthaí Dúithche

[1] Lord Birkenhead.

No. 215 UCDA P4/414

Handwritten letter from Hugh Kennedy to William T. Cosgrave (Dublin)
DUBLIN, 9 May 1924

President.
The Boundary
1. I have read the enclosed minute from the Minister of Home Affairs[1] which I return herewith.
2. Hitherto it has been accepted both by the British Government and by ourselves (by us perhaps tacitly) (a) that the terms of reference of the Boundary Commission were set out in the Treaty in specific form; (b) that they do not call for, and are not to receive, any interpretation from either Government before the Commission is constituted; and (c) that it will be for the Commission to interpret its terms of reference when it proceeds to business. I think the position at least amounted to this that no question could properly arise until the Commission entered upon its work and moreover we on our part do not admit that any ambiguity exists or that any question of interpretation can arise. The British Government has not so far suggested that any ambiguity exists or that it favours an interpretation different from ours. The Northern Eastern people have raised the question but they refuse to take part in the Commission.
3. In these circumstances I doubt the wisdom of the proposal in the enclosed minute. In the first place, it is based on the assumption that there is some ambiguity which we have always denied and cannot now admit. In the second place, it proposes to arbitrate on the true interpretation of the terms of reference. Who are to be the parties to the arbitration? Three Governments or two Governments? But the British have not yet expressed any view. Who would choose the Arbitrator or Arbitrators? If the same parties as are to nominate the Boundary Commission, how are we any better off than we would be before the Commission?, while we would be worse off by having admitted ambiguity requiring determination. Lastly we would go into the Boundary Commission tied up by whatever construction the Arbitrator would have put upon the terms of reference.
4. If any question of interpretation arises at all, it will arise at the early stage of the proceedings of the Boundary Commission. If disagreement as to the meaning of the Terms of Reference should then appear, the question will be how that disagreement is to be solved. It would be open for the Commission in my opinion to refer back the Terms of Reference to the Governments concerned for further instructions on the matter in dispute. On the other hand, the British are committed to the line of allowing the Commission to determine such dispute themselves, while I rather think we are to some extent, I am not sure how far, committed to the same course.
5. It seems to me that there has been a settled policy of making us appear as having simply a clearcut demand for the Counties of Tyrone and Fermanagh. I feel that we should not allow ourselves to be pinned to this position. The area we claim cannot be so defined – hence the necessity for the Boundary

[1] No. 214 above.

Commission. We claim an area yet to be ascertained but to be determined by the wishes of the inhabitants subject to correction by economic and geographical considerations. I think we should never commit ourselves to any forecast as to what area the Commission will fix as transferable to us upon these considerations – the more open we keep it, the greater margin we have to work upon.

6. May I urge that Kevin O'Shiel be lent for the Boundary work as soon as possible.

H.K.
Príomh-Atúrnae

No. 216 NAI DT S1801P

James McNeill to William T. Cosgrave (Dublin)
(Copy)

LONDON, 13 May 1924

My dear President,

Cope[1] called today. He had just talked with Thomas. He did not say he was a messenger but I think he was. His object was to suggest that you should take an early opportunity of replying to Craig's speech. He referred generally to the 'Ulster' campaign and the general friendliness of the press here to their side. He thought you might state publicly that you had no objection to a *sincere* and *earnest*[2] conference to ascertain the wishes of the inhabitants concerned *in areas contiguous to the Boundary*[3] on the understanding that if unhappily an agreement cannot be arrived at Sir J.C. and his Government will do all needful to facilitate the operation of Article XII, the need for which the conference is designed to obviate. It would be an assumed condition that no interference with representation on local bodies would be practised during the continuance of the conference.

To summarise[,] the objects of the conference would be:

1. Do the work of the boundary conference, and enable Craig to recede gracefully from his speeches.[4]

2. If conference fails, the favourable effect of C's speeches and press campaign would be done away with.

3. Also in event of failure the help of the Six County Government in constituting the Commission is secured, though it is hoped that there will not be failure.

4. The I.F.S. case will get a much better British Press.

If some such speech could be quoted in House of Commons here and all parties commend conference on these terms then Thomas will be able to hold them all easily to Article XII.

Cope thought it might be necessary to make sure of party opinion and leaders of all parties in advance, and that if you could find an opportunity to speak

[1] Sir Andy Cope.
[2] (Marginal note) 'He accentuated these words'.
[3] (Marginal note) 'These are his words'.
[4] (Marginal note) 'No other work, and is unifying work suggested'.

over here valuable publicity would be gained. He would have the reasons underlying Article XII restated, and lay stress on the arbitrary nature of the 1920 division and the importance of conforming to the wishes of the people concerned.

I don't know that there is anything new in all this. I don't know that the British Press is going to be much affected. It is as likely to say that the conference had better continue.

In talk with an old journalistic friend recently I was told that Thomas said to my friend that he (Thomas) thought only line or adjustment of boundary was to be considered.

I'm told Borden[1] is a stupid man. I wonder if a Colonial is safer than an Englishman who is intelligent, straight and judicially minded.

I told Cope that the difficulty of a person who regarded himself as a trustee was to know just what definite advantage he could claim for delay when delay was on many grounds dangerous. It may be very speculative but it seems to me that the only thing real is the suggestion that it may find a way out for Craig as regards the appointment of a Commission, and that gives both time and relief here, which is much desired.

Yours sincerely,
(Signed) JAMES MCNEILL.

P.S.
Cope has just rung up to say that he is writing and will send letter through me tomorrow.

I can realise that the P.[rince] of W[ales]'s visit to Belfast might be inopportune if the Commission Question is acute.

No. 217 NAI DT S1983

T.M. Healy to J.H. Thomas (London)
(Confidential) (Copy)

DUBLIN, 16 May 1924

Sir,
I have the honour to refer to your Confidential Despatch of the 24th April[2] regarding the representation of the Irish Free State at Washington, and to state that it has received the careful consideration of my Ministers.

2. My Ministers are pleased to learn that His Majesty's Government will approach the Government of the United States with a view to the appointment at Washington of an Irish Minister Plenipotentiary with credentials from His Majesty and a letter of appointment from the Government of the Irish Free State.

3. My Ministers do not apprehend that the principle of Diplomatic Unity in the Commonwealth will be affected inasmuch as the proposed Irish Minister will represent the Irish Free State for the purposes of its particular interests only.

[1] Sir R.L. Borden, Prime Minister of Canada (1911-20), Secretary of State for External Affairs (1912-20).

[2] Not printed.

4. Questions which may arise regarding negotiation and signature of Treaties with the United States will be dealt with in accordance with the Resolutions of the Imperial Conference.
5. As the matter is extremely urgent and as presumably the Dominions have made no comments on your telegram of the 22nd April,[1] my Ministers will be very glad if action can be taken immediately at Washington for the purpose of having Professor Smiddy accepted in the capacity named.

I have the honour to be,
Sir,
Your most obedient, humble Servant,
[stamped] T.M. HEALY

No. 218 NAI DT S1801P

Statement by William T. Cosgrave relating to the Boundary Question
Undated, probably 24 May 1924

THE PRESIDENT'S STATEMENT.
I have read recently in the columns of the Press reports of several pronouncements made by Sir James Craig on the Boundary question. Whilst some of his statements appear to be contradictory I must frankly say, as one who has from the very beginning striven with all my might for the establishment of concord and harmony all over Ireland that I welcome with genuine pleasure the references to his willingness to make compromises for the sake of Irish peace.

If he has been reported correctly, he appears to be now prepared to alter his 'non possumus' attitude (which hitherto has made conference between us so difficult and fruitless) and meet us on the broad and general principle of 'the wishes of the inhabitants'. If I am interpreting his remarks aright I gather that he is not desirous of holding under his rule those portions of territory in the Northern area which are inhabited by majorities that are not in sympathy with his Government and are anxious for political reunion with the Free State.

On the [blank] May he is reported to have said:-

> 'If the South would only recognise how greatly a settlement by agreement between the two parties chiefly concerned would ultimately benefit Ireland as a whole and accept the Collins Pact which was freely entered into by the then leader of "Southern Ireland" and myself, they would find a generosity and accommodation on my part that would ensure an agreeable solution which would leave no sting behind'.

A little further on he defines expressly what he means by such a settlement:-

> 'A settlement by agreement means that those desirous of remaining in Ulster ... and those who desire to associate themselves with the Free State will be accommodated as far as it is possible to draw a line consistent with that realisation and the economic problems that accompanies it'.

This is, on the part of Sir James Craig a handsome statement and is in my opinion the most hopeful thing I have read for a long while on the Boundary dispute.

[1] Not printed.

I do not wish at this promising moment to harp back on the past but I think it right to remind the public that this has been all along and is still the attitude of my Government on the matter, bound as we are by the statutory force of Article XII[,] of which the words just quoted are an excellent paraphrase.

By Article XII of the Solemn Treaty Agreement Great Britain and ourselves are mutually pledged to see to it that a Boundary Commission 'shall determine in accordance with the wishes of the inhabitants so far as may be compatible with economic and geographic consideration the boundaries between Northern Ireland and the rest of Ireland, etc'.

It is clear from these terms of reference that economic considerations will play a part in determining the new boundary, *second only in importance* to 'the wishes of the inhabitants' which of course are paramount.

Whilst I welcome these recent responses of goodwill on the part of Sir James Craig I cannot too often repeat what our position on the Boundary matter is in view of the great deal of misunderstanding that still exists in that part of Ireland with regard to it.

Believe me, our objective is not that the North Eastern Province should be economically and politically brought to nought, but that a boundary in accordance with the wishes of the inhabitants should replace the present arbitrarily drawn line which gives satisfaction to no party or person, and which, as we all know, was passed through the House of Commons without the support of a single Irish member, North or South – a distinction unique in history!

Some have lately tried to claim for the Act that made this achievement that it is a contract, but, the fact is, that after its enactment the leaders of Sir James Craig's party again and again publicly repudiated all responsibility for the measure. It could hardly be a contract with a Government that did not exist, and it could not be a contract with the inhabitants as they were not consulted.

On the other hand there is no doubt as to the contractual nature of the Treaty. Not only is it a contract, but it is a contract of the most solemn character imposing on the signatories and their successors obligations which they can neither set aside nor alter and which they are legally bound to see carried through in every respect and particular.

Sir James Craig I am sure must realise that even if we so wished neither the British Government nor ourselves have the power to consent to any proceeding which either expressly or by implication would tend to defeat the provisions of Article XII, containing as it does the doubly binding force of a statute of the Parliament of Great Britain and of an Act of the Oireachtas of Saorstát Eireann.

In this matter we are not free agents to pick and choose at will. Governments, like individuals, are subject to the law and must perform their legal duties whether they wish to or not.

May I say here how much I have regretted that the Northern Government have hitherto thought proper to place difficulties in the way of the British Government carrying out its part of the Treaty. I must not be taken as criticising; no doubt they had their own reasons for such a course, but it has appeared to me [all] along to be very regrettable.

With those difficulties we are happily not directly concerned, but indirectly they have naturally not a good effect on the lawless elements in our midst. They are, however, small in comparison with the difficulties which we in the course of our duty have been obliged to meet and overcome. I have no doubt whatever that the British Government will also meet them and I am now completely confident that wiser counsels will prevail and that they will be cleared away by constitutional methods alone.

I come now to the most important parts of those pronouncements of Sir James Craig – those dealing with his offer to me to meet him as Irishman to Irishman and *to draw a new boundary line* which will be agreeable to all parties and which will leave no sting behind.

This I believe to be a sincere offer prompted by the highest motives, and in that spirit I have given it the most profound and earnest consideration.

I cannot, however, forget that since the tragic death of General Michael Collins in defence of our Bond with Great Britain, not yet two years ago, when I became head of the Saorstát Government, Sir James Craig and myself have met on no less than four occasions and discussed this matter earnestly and at length, but parted on every one of these occasions, not indeed with any personal bitterness, but without having found a way out of the deadlock.

Time after time since my accession to office I have stated, as General Collins stated before me, that if there must be a political frontier in this small country of ours it would be infinitely better to have that frontier drawn by consent than as the result of an international tribunal. So eager was I not to force the issue in the hope that a more friendly feeling would develop that, with great difficulty I got the people of the Saorstát, who feel very keenly on this matter, to agree to many lengthy postponements and this at the imminent risk of creating serious differences in our ranks. And I may say here in explanation that the discriminating legislation passed through the Northern Parliament during that time, inflicting unjust disabilities on Ulster Catholics, destroying popular control, suppressing County Councils and gerrymandering the Local Government areas in the Catholic districts, enormously increased the difficulties of my position by strengthening the desire of the people of those districts to rejoin the Saorstát.

However, since Sir James Craig has now met me in a generous spirit he will not find me less generous. As he has made concessions I also, for the sake of peace and in order to bring to a conclusion this troublesome matter, am prepared to make concessions. In spite of the great annoyance which further delay about setting up the Boundary Commission must cause amongst our people I am prepared to accept Sir James Craig's offer to draw a new boundary line in such a way, to use his own words, that 'those desirous to remain in Ulster and those who desire to associate themselves with the Free State will be accommodated as far as it is possible to draw a line consistent with that realisation and the economic problems that accompany it.' In other words we agree that the line will be drawn in accordance with the wishes of the inhabitants so far as it may be compatible with economic, and also I take it, geographic considerations.

On the important question as to what the unit of territory for ascertaining the wishes of the inhabitants is to be I am willing to make a sacrifice and meet Sir James Craig in as handsome a manner as he has met me. On this question he can make his own choice of any local government unit that was in existence prior to recent legislative alterations by the Northern Government. I do not care whether he decides on the County, the Rural District, the Poor Law Union, the County electoral Division or the Rural District electoral division (which is the smallest local government unit). I go further and say that he is at liberty to select even the non administrative parish or the townland if he so wishes.

I undertake in so far as my Government and myself are concerned to abide by this promise no matter how far into the Free State the selected Unit may go and no matter what the political risks may be personally to ourselves.

I make only one condition to this acceptance. It is this, that, should it unfortunately happen that this Conference will go the way of the rest and result in a fruitless deadlock, the Boundary Commission will be immediately set up and that everything possible will be done by the Northern Government to facilitate this in order to compensate us as far as possible for the delay caused by the Conference.

There is surely no great hardship in this condition as in the event of our agreeing at the Conference, we would eventually have to consent to an agreed Boundary Commission in order to comply with the statutory provisions of Article XII.

On hearing of Sir James Craig's acceptance I can arrange to meet him in either Belfast or Dublin at a suitable date, and I sincerely trust that as Irishman to Irishman, in our own land, we will be able to bring this cause of contention to a happy and successful conclusion that will leave no sting behind.

No. 219 NAI DT S1801P

Copy of interview given by William T. Cosgrave to the press

DUBLIN, 24 May 1924

From Sir James Craig's recent pronouncements, I take it to be admitted as a governing principle that the Boundary question is to be settled, so far as is geographically and economically practicable, in accordance with the wishes of the inhabitants.

On that basis, I see no reason why there should be any delay in proceeding with the business of the settlement. There is certainly not on my side any desire to prolong this controversy. If I am not mistaken, the great majority of the people in Great Britain as well as in Ireland expected and intended, as a result of the Treaty, that the affairs of each country should cease to be an intruding and disturbing factor in the life of the other. There is a relatively small minority in both countries, small but active and persistent and apparently with influential connections, who seem determined to maintain friction and controversy at the maximum, and whose minds, as General Smuts once said, are back in the seventh century. It is this minority which has been using every effort and every variety of argument to prevent the issue being decided in accordance with the wishes of the inhabitants, and thus to force it, if they can, as an international quarrel upon the public of both countries.

It is regrettable and disquieting that Sir James Craig, when he approaches this problem in a manner that seems to hold out hope of a better understanding, should find himself at the same time obliged to speak of his retirement being involved. The public must take this to mean that others will be in a position to disavow and nullify any agreement that does not please them, and the only result will be that they took Jonah and cast him into the sea, but the sea did not cease from raging. I would be without sincerity if I failed to keep to the point that we must seek to have this controversy ended not prolonged, and that it cannot be ended except in accordance with the wishes of the inhabitants of the areas concerned.

My Government holds itself bound by the terms of the Treaty to give effect to the wishes of the inhabitants in regard to the settlement of the Boundary. The British Government is equally so bound. I do not remember that anything so crude and indefensible as a claim to disregard and override the wishes of the people in the areas concerned has ever been put forward expressly on behalf of Sir James Craig's administration. But it did appear to me as implied from the various pleas and pronouncements that one read from time to time, that the wishes of the people of those areas were to be ignored. These people have natural rights in the matter, they have Treaty rights, and they have statutory rights. If Governments were to annul those rights, the people concerned would be entitled to seek every possible remedy in national and [in] international law. I am sure that they would prefer, as I would prefer, to see their right accorded without strife of any kind, and therefore I am glad to recognise – if I am right in recognising – that these elementary rights of theirs, which are also statutory rights and Treaty rights, are admitted to be the basis of a settlement. It will ease the situation when it is known that justice is not to be denied and is not to be delayed.

These people complain that they are at present governed by sheer force, that their franchises are annulled, that their majorities are converted by legislative devices into minorities, electoral districts being remodelled for the purpose on the principle of the jigsaw puzzle, and that their condition, for which British Government is still responsible, is intolerable. They are officially warned that there is worse still to come.

If such charges were brought against my Government, certain publicists and politicians, who think it good policy to keep up and stir up enmity between our country and theirs, would make the Press and the platform and the British Houses of Parliament resound with our iniquities.

I want to see and I think I am entitled to demand some earnest of good will and fair play in these matters.

I welcome every word of good will. Still more will I welcome actions that will bear out good words.

My willingness to enter into conference cannot be questioned, but I cannot be expected to take part in conferences that hold out chiefly the prospect of delay and consequent exasperation.

My Government has already asked that the Boundary Commission be set up without delay. When this is done, it will facilitate agreement. If then Sir James Craig and I, or any other two men or number of men duly representative, can come together and arrive at a settlement in due accord with the wishes of the inhabitants, we can present our agreement to the Commission for ratification in accordance with the Treaty and with the Statutes of both countries.

If a settlement is not to be reached in this way, what prospect is there of reaching it otherwise? In the event of a disagreement, the Commission would still be necessary – that is, unless the Treaty is to cease to operate. The establishment of the Commission in the first instance is the sole effective guarantee in sight for arriving at a settlement by consent or, failing that, for a settlement by procedure. I don't suppose that anybody imagines this issue will be settled by any amount of elaborate special pleading in newspapers, much of it directed to the opposite purpose.

No. 220 NAI DFA Letter Books (London 1924)

Extract from a letter from Joseph Walshe to James McNeill (London)
(E.A. 119/352)

DUBLIN, 27 May 1924

Dear High Commissioner,
[Matter omitted]
We invariably find that there is considerable delay in any matter in which the Foreign Office has to intervene and it is becoming more and more apparent that we have no friends there. They obviously believed that by holding up Professor Smiddy's appointment they would make it more difficult for us to get a distinct quota for the Free State. They did not know until it was too late for their purposes that Smiddy had been working behind the scenes all the time and had actually succeeded in getting the necessary modification into the Johnson Bill.
[Matter omitted]

Sincerely yours,
[copy letter unsigned]

No. 221 NAI DT S3716

Extract from a despatch from T.M. Healy to J.H. Thomas (London)
(No. 207)

DUBLIN, 28 May 1924

Sir,
I have the honour to refer to your Despatches, Dominions No. 89 of the 29th February and No. 141 of 3rd March, relating to the Treaty of Lausanne,[1] and to inform you that having studied the Treaty with attention my Ministers have not found that any general or particular interests of the Irish Free State are affected by its terms. This is presumably the reason why my Ministers were not given an opportunity of participating in the negotiations.
2. My Ministers while anxious that the state of war, in so far as it may be held to exist between the States of the Commonwealth and the Turkish people, should be brought to an end with the least possible delay, do not feel called upon to submit the Treaty itself to the Parliament of the Irish Free State with a view to ratification, more especially as the position of the Irish Free State as a party to the Treaty and in particular to Article 18 of the Straits Convention might involve her in action which would be inconsistent with Article 49 of the

[1] Neither document printed.

Constitution of the Irish Free State. In the circumstances, my Ministers do not wish the Treaty to be ratified on their behalf.

3. With regard to the Conventions annexed to the Treaty, my Ministers desire that the Irish Free State should be formally excluded from the Convention respecting conditions of Residence and Business, and from the Commercial Convention.

[Matter omitted]

I have the honour to be,
Sir,
Your most obedient, humble servant,
[stamped] T.M. HEALY

No. 222 NAI DT S1801G

William T. Cosgrave to Ramsay MacDonald (London)
(Copy)

DUBLIN, 28 May 1924

Dear Mr. Prime Minister

As I intimated by telegram to-day[1] I am willing to meet you and Sir James Craig immediately. I need hardly repeat what I said in the interview to which you refer, that if our meeting is to be fruitful, there should be agreement in the first instance to have the Commission constituted without delay. So long as the Commission is not in being, I fear it cannot be expected that other discussions will bring us any nearer to a settlement. On the other hand, if after the Commission has been constituted, we come to an agreement, or nearly so, the work of the Commission will be reduced to a minimum and the agreement or the settlement of the outstanding variance, through the action of the Commission, will have binding force forthwith, and nothing will remain but for the respective Governments to implement the Commission's decision as the Treaty requires.

We have a very heavy legislative programme on hands, besides more than normal administrative business, and you will understand that absence from Dublin is very difficult for me at this time.

Sincerely yours,
(signed) L.T. MAC COSGAIR

No. 223 NAI DT S1801H

T.M. Healy to J.H. Thomas (London)
(No. 217)

DUBLIN, 3 June 1924

Sir,

I have the honour to inform you that my Ministers note from your despatch No. 314 of the 23rd ultimo[2] that the Government of Northern Ireland have

[1] Not printed.
[2] Not printed.

declined to nominate a representative upon the Boundary Commission, and that arising out of the position thus created His Majesty's Government have requested the Judicial Committee of the Privy Council to advise them regarding the arrangements to be made by them in fulfilment of their obligations under Article 12 of the Treaty.

2. My Ministers deem it essential to make clear that, while they realise that His Majesty's Government are, no doubt, entitled to take advantage of the very high legal opinion available to them my Ministers cannot be regarded as being parties to the reference to the Judicial Committee or as being in any way committed to the acceptance of the opinions which may be obtained. They are gravely concerned, however, with the prospect of a further delay in the operation of the Boundary Commission which the seeking by His Majesty's Government of advice from the Judicial Committee appears to render possible and indeed most likely. They understand from the fifth paragraph of your despatch No. 232 of the 10th April[1] that His Majesty's Government had already considered the steps to be taken to complete the Commission, and they much regret that the contingency of a refusal by the Northern Government to appoint their representative, a course which Sir James Craig's public utterances indicated as likely, was not apparently among the matters so considered.

3. My Ministers feel that, in view of the extended time over which correspondence and Conference on this subject have now ranged, no further time should be lost in completing the work of the Commission, and they accordingly propose to His Majesty's Government that certain preliminaries should be put in hand forthwith. The requirement of the Treaty that the Boundary should be determined in accordance with the wishes of the inhabitants, subject to the other considerations therein mentioned, renders it necessary that the wishes of the inhabitants should first be ascertained, and there is no reason why this matter should not be undertaken forthwith by the Chairman of the Commission immediately on his appointment in conjunction with the representative of the Irish Free State (Dr. Eoin MacNeill). It merely involves the organisation of the requisite machinery and the collection of statistical information and raises no question of policy.

4. My Ministers would accordingly request His Majesty's Government to proceed with the immediate appointment of the Chairman of the Commission, so that this work may be begun without delay.

I have the honour to be,
Sir,
Your most obedient humble Servant,
[stamped] T.M. HEALY

[1] Not printed.

No. 224 NAI DT S1801H

William T. Cosgrave to Ramsay MacDonald (London)
(Copy)

DUBLIN, 4 June 1924

Dear Mr. Prime Minister,

1. I have given earnest consideration to your letter of yesterday[1] in which you express the opinion that the interval which will elapse before you receive a report from the Judicial Committee of the Privy Council might profitably be employed, with the assistance of the Chairman of the Boundary Commission, in examining the general aspect of the problem with a view to seeing how far an agreed settlement is possible. I regret that I cannot accept this view for the reasons which I gave you on Saturday, namely, that such a course would be bound to afford opportunities for suggestions from one quarter or other of a departure from strict impartiality on his part, which would be a source of serious embarrassment in the judicial task which he is to undertake.

2. The gravest apprehension is felt in Ireland regarding the manner in which Clause 12 of the Treaty has been canvassed. Since February last it would appear as if the terms of the Clause, viz., the wishes of the inhabitants[,] were to be subordinated to whims of persons in positions of authority and power. Further examination and approaches towards possible agreement in these circumstances would, of necessity, imply that the rights guaranteed by this Article are in jeopardy, and I have never had any authority to agree to any abrogation of the rights of the inhabitants as defined in the Article.

3. You mentioned in the course of the discussion on Saturday last that you were in a position to show me your signature appointing the Chairman. I must say that in the opinion of my Government – with which I concur – the appointment should be immediately announced. There is a large amount of preliminary work to be done which could be undertaken forthwith. It is evident that a census of the wishes of the inhabitants must be taken before the Commission can settle down to consider the problems which they will finally have to determine. This census is purely a matter of machinery for the ascertaining of facts and statistics, so that they may be available for the Commission to work upon. The collection of this information is in the opinion of my Government a duty which should be undertaken at once by the Chairman in conjunction with our representative, and we have addressed an official despatch to Mr. Thomas on these lines.[2]

4. I cannot conclude without urging upon you most earnestly that the delay which has occurred in the setting up of the Commission is causing very grave anxiety and unrest in this country. I realise that you desire to obtain the best legal advice possible as to the steps His Majesty's Government must take to implement Clause 12, and I understand that the reference to a Judicial Committee on which it is proposed to have the Chief Justice of Australia as a member must entail delay, but it will be represented here publicly and otherwise, and

[1] Not printed.
[2] See above No. 223.

will obtain some measure of credence, that the British Government must have known all along that Sir James Craig would decline to appoint his representative, and that the reference to the Judicial Committee is a device to cause further delay, and if possible to shelve the whole matter.

5. This is the type of criticism which is most pronounced here and it is strengthened by the daily references to Conferences and solutions in which it is implied that the wishes of the inhabitants are to be ignored. The situation is fast becoming critical and I shall find it necessary in the very near future to give a day for discussion in the Dáil of the whole problem. I am very much concerned at the prospect of such a discussion and its possible outcome, unless some definite progress towards the operation of the Commission can be shown. Mr. Thomas wrote me on the 10th April[1] that all the necessary steps had been worked out in advance. The position now is that delay follows delay, and if we point to the assurances which we have received we will be countered by an inquiry as to what tangible evidence of progress we can show. The immediate appointment of the Chairman and the starting of the work on the preliminaries would make matters much less difficult and would be regarded by our people as practical evidence that Article 12 is being fully carried out.

Yours sincerely,
[signed] L.T. MacCosgair

No. 225 NAI DE 2/301

Hugh Kennedy to William T. Cosgrave (Dublin)
(1229/24) (Strictly Confidential)

Dublin, 9 June 1924

A Uachtaráin, A Chara,

I have had for a considerable time a collection of papers in several files relating to the former unpleasantness that arose in relation to representatives in Germany.[2] You will remember that a lengthy correspondence took place during the regime of George Gavan Duffy, in which certain imputations were made on certain persons. Portion of the correspondence I think was before the Cabinet at one time and there was a good deal more of a most disagreeable character. Just before he resigned from office George Gavan Duffy brought me all the files containing what purported to be the entire original correspondence and

---

[1] Not printed.

[2] From January to September 1922 relations at the Irish office in Berlin were soured by a dispute between Charles Bewley (Irish Trade Representative) and John Chartres (Irish Diplomatic Representative) over their relative spheres of operation. Bewley had also acted offensively by insulting Robert Briscoe, a Sinn Féin supporter working as an arms purchaser in Germany, on his Jewish faith. Chartres came under suspicion in Dublin for appearing to support the anti-Treatyites in his propaganda activities in Germany. Chartres was transferred to the Department of Industry and Commerce in late 1922. Bewley took over the operation of the Berlin office but resigned in February 1923 and returned to Ireland. Cornelius Duane kept the Berlin office in operation for a time, but it was closed in the winter of 1923 for financial reasons. (See DIFP Vol I documents No. 224, 225, 229, 230, 243, 257, 258, 260, 263, 264, 286, 294, 302, 307, 313, 319, 323, 326 and Vol II documents Nos 149 and 162).

copies. He stated that he felt that before going out of office he must leave them with someone who would understand the matter. He had previously spoken to me about it on several occasions and assumed that I understood the whole thing. He asked me to keep the documents in the strictest confidence and to hold them until such time – if ever – as they might be called for, if the trouble developed after his resignation.

I do not feel that I can take these documents away with me now[1] and guard them against the day when some question arises. Moreover, the trouble to which they referred has, I believe, entirely blown over and it would be very improper that such papers should be held by me and possibly fall into other hands. I am in great doubt what to do with them, because I feel a responsibility and I do not feel that they should be open to all and sundry to read and gratify curiosity. I have come to the conclusion accordingly, that the proper course for me is to deliver them into your hands as custodian of State papers, and to ask you to be good enough to have them filed away amongst secret papers under your own charge. I therefore send them, strapped together in a parcel with this note.

Mise, do chara,
[signed] AODH UA CINNÉIDIGH
(Hugh Kennedy)

No. 226 NAI DT S1801H

Kevin O'Higgins to William T. Cosgrave (Dublin)
DUBLIN, 10 June 1924

President,

British Prime Minister's Letter 7th inst[2]

The gist of the matter is embodied in the last two paragraphs of the second page. In effect Mr. MacDonald puts up 'conciliation' as against the 'arbitration' which the Treaty provides for, and clings to the hope of an 'agreed settlement'. Who are to agree? Prime Ministers, Governments, Parliaments, or people? There *is* a real difference and a difference in principle between our proposal and that of the British Prime Minister. Our proposal involves the two members of the Commission who have been appointed occupying themselves with work which is an obvious preliminary to the operation of the Treaty Clause, while Mr. MacDonald's proposal seems to involve participation by a person nominated by a Government which has stated repeatedly and in all the moods and tenses that it will have nothing to do with the Treaty Clause. One proposal is within the Treaty and is preparatory to its enforcement, the other is outside the Treaty and would be interpreted on all sides, British, North East, Free State as well as abroad, as preparatory to its evasion, or as containing an implication, tacitly accepted by us, that a Boundary 'in accordance with the wishes of the inhabitants' is not within the sphere of practical politics.

[1] On his appointment as Chief Justice on 5 June 1924 Kennedy relinquished his Dáil seat and resigned as Attorney General.
[2] Not printed.

I suggest a reply briefly summarising the situation – existing Boundary purely arbitrary drawn in 1920 without the vote of a single Irish Representative. Failure of Buckingham Palace Conference. Treaty provided for no coercion of whatever area would be found to be homogeneously or predominantly Orange and Unionist. Equally it provided that wherever a majority of inhabitants desired inclusion in Free State Jurisdiction those wishes would be respected subject to any necessary correction by economic or geographic factors. We have found no willingness in Sir J. Craig or his Government to recognise that it is the wishes of the inhabitants themselves which must be the deciding factor. Open Conferences, without prejudice to the position of parties have repeatedly failed and hold no promise of future success. We can only confer for the purpose of devising the best means to settle this question by the simple democratic test of a census of the adult population and ascertainment of their choice of Jurisdiction.

C. Ó hUigín

No. 227 NAI DT S3176

Extract from minutes of a meeting of the Executive Council (C.2/104)

Dublin, 10 June 1924

LAUSANNE TREATY

It was agreed that a motion in the following terms may be laid before the DÁIL by the Min. for Ex. Affairs provided that the questions of Passports and Prof. Smiddy's appointment are settled with the British Govt:-

'That the Dáil, in order that the state of peace may be established beyond all reasonable doubt as between the Saorstát and the Turkish Republic, authorises the Executive Council to acquiesce in the ratification of the TREATY OF LAUSANNE provided that it be clearly understood that (unless the Oireachtas shall hereafter undertake such commitments by legislation) the Saorstát thereby incurs no commitments other than the definite establishment of peace'.

No. 228 NAI DT S1801H

William T. Cosgrave to Ramsay MacDonald (London)

Dublin, 17 June 1924

Dear Mr. Prime Minister,

1. A debate upon the Boundary Question which began on Friday is being resumed on Wednesday next, and I shall take the opportunity on that day to lay before the Dáil the text of the later correspondence between us on this subject.

2. There are a few points arising out of your letter of the 6th instant[1] which perhaps call for some observations from me. The most important is your view that there is scarcely any difference in principle between our proposal that the

[1] Not printed.

Chairman and Dr. Eoin MacNeill should proceed with the preliminary work of ascertaining the wishes of the inhabitants, and your suggestion that the Chairman with Dr. MacNeill and a representative from Sir James Craig should join in preliminary studies with a view to an agreed settlement being arrived at.

3. The major difference is that our proposal involves merely a question of setting up the necessary machinery for ascertaining facts and raises no point of policy. The other proposal postulates explorations for agreement which the principals have already failed, after repeated conferences, to reach. If agreement can be reached, it must be reached, not upon the basis of my views, or of Sir James Craig's views, but upon the basis laid down in Article 12 of respect for the wishes of the inhabitants of the area affected and for the economic and geographic conditions.

4. The possibility of agreement depends, therefore, upon considerations which have to be ascertained, and our proposal is that the work of ascertaining these considerations should be embarked upon at once. This work Dr. MacNeill is ready to operate in at a moment's notice.

5. As far as we are concerned, we will cordially co-operate in any action which will make for friendship between ourselves in these islands, but we are satisfied that any departure from the elementary democratic principle enshrined in Article 12 would not tend in that direction. We feel that it is essential for the maintenance of harmony between nations that the wishes of the inhabitants should be a primary consideration in any system of government, and we are prepared to translate this view into practice to secure not alone a spirit of brotherhood amongst ourselves, but, so far as it can be accomplished, amongst the whole human race.

6. This is the spirit in which I addressed the Assembly of the League of Nations last September.[1]

7. I cannot conclude without assuring you that I appreciate fully His Majesty's Government's desire to have the highest available opinion as to their course of procedure, under their Statutes, for giving effect to Treaty obligations entered into by them, and I also appreciate that the delay which is caused thereby may be to a certain extent inevitable. At the same time, I would urge upon His Majesty's Government that it is in the interests of all parties concerned that existing sources of possible irritation be removed at once, and accordingly that every effort should be made to have all outstanding matters in regard to the setting up of the Boundary Commission composed at the earliest possible date.

Sincerely yours,
(Sgd.) L. T. MacCosgair

[1] See No. 118 above.

No. 229 NAI DFA ES Box 29 File 191

Extract from a letter from Timothy A. Smiddy to Joseph P. Walshe (Dublin)
(Copy)

WASHINGTON, 17 June 1924

A Chara:

IMMIGRATION QUOTA.

I have just learned unofficially that there is disagreement among the members of the joint Committee of the Bureau of Immigration, the Department of Commerce and the State Department as to the assignment of a separate quota to the whole of Ireland or to the Irish Free State.

The Bureau of Immigration point out the following difficulties:-

administrative difficulties in allotting a separate quota to the 26 countier‡of the Irish Free State are very great, and will be still more so from July 1926 when racial origin will be the determining factor in the assignment of quotas;

there will be the possibility of intending immigrants of the six counties of Northern Ireland, when the British quota is full, coming under the Irish Free State quota, or vice-versa;

any quota for the Irish Free State at present would be unstable as the boundary separating the six Northeast counties from the Irish Free State is not yet finally settled.

It appears representatives of the Department of State favour a separate quota for the Irish Free State as it is more consonant with the terms of the Act – Northern Ireland being a political part of Great Britain and not being a self-governing dominion.

Yet, I am informed the opinion of the Bureau of Immigration is likely to prevail. Their real motive is to avoid the difficulties referred to which would entail investigations of a most complex character.

It was argued on the joint-committee of these departments that it is much more natural to put the six Northern counties with the Irish Free State with which they are geographically connected than with Great Britain from which they are separated by the natural boundary of the sea.

I regret there is this tendency to assign the quota to Ireland as a whole, and I shall endeavour – if I can – to have a separate quota assigned to the Irish Free State. It is a case in which diplomatic representation would be most helpful. [Matter omitted]

Mise, le meas,
[copy letter unsigned]

No. 230 NAI DT S1983

Notes of a meeting at the Colonial Office (London)
on the appointment of an Irish Minister at Washington
(Confidential) (Copy)

LONDON, 21 June 1924

Notes of Conversation at the Colonial Office on Saturday the 21st June 1924.

Present.

Mr. D. FitzGerald, T.D. (in the chair.)
Lord Arnold,
Sir C.J.B. Hurst, K.C.B., K.C.,
Sir C.T. Davis, K.C.M.G.,
Mr. L. Curtis,
Mr. E.J. Harding, C.M.G.,
Mr. Murphy,
Mr. C.W. Dixon.

It was made clear at the outset that, while the British Government had undertaken to approach the United States Government with a view to the appointment of a Free State Minister at Washington, and would use their best endeavours to obtain the concurrence of the United States Government, it was not possible to give any guarantee that the latter would accept the proposal. Mr. FitzGerald stated that this was fully understood.

As regards the status of the Free State Representative the following conclusions were reached:-

(1) While the Free State Minister would be the official channel of communication with the United States Government for dealing with matters exclusively affecting the Free State, the principles of the resolution of the Imperial Conference of 1923 as to the negotiation, signature and ratification of Treaties and in particular of that part of the Resolution which relates to the conduct of matters affecting more than one part of the Empire would apply generally to all questions with which he dealt, and the Ambassador would in the same way keep the Irish Free State Minister informed of any matters which might affect the Irish Free State. If any doubt should arise whether any particular question exclusively concerned the Free State, the point would, if possible, be settled by consultation between the Free State Minister and the British Ambassador. If the matter could not be settled by such consultation, it would be referred to the British Government and the Free State Govt.

(2) In order to meet the possibility that any particular question might in its initial stages be exclusively of concern to the Free State and might subsequently prove to be of concern to other parts of the Empire, the Free State Minister would keep in close contact with the British Ambassador.

(3) While the Free State Minister would not purport to deal with matters affecting the Empire as a whole, the assistance of the British Ambassador and the Embassy staff would always be at his disposal, if desired. The Ambassador would not, however, be in any way responsible for action taken by the Free

State Minister, nor would the latter be in any way subject to the Ambassador's control.

As regards the credentials to be issued (see Draft furnished to the Free State Government in the Secretary of State's Confidential Despatch of the 24th April[1]) Mr. FitzGerald asked for consideration of the following points.

Take another act of Parliament. Consultation with the other Dominions	(1) Whether in His Majesty's title in the heading to the draft credentials retention of the words 'United Kingdom of Great Britain and Ireland' was essential whilst the law remains as at present.
Omitted	(2) Whether some formula might be found in place of the words 'to attach him to our Embassy' in the first paragraph of the draft.
Omit counter-signature.	(3) Whether in view of the practice as regards certain documents relating to the negotiation, signature and ratification of Treaties, the counter-signature of the Secretary of State for Foreign Affairs was necessary.

Mr. FitzGerald agreed that it was desirable that a copy of the letter of instructions issued to the Free State Minister at Washington should be communicated to the British Government. Sir C.[ecil] Hurst expressed a similar opinion as regards any instructions sent to the British Ambassador.

As regards the method of raising the matter with the United States Government, Mr. FitzGerald stated that the Free State Government would prefer that a formal communication should be made to the United States Government without any preliminary informal enquiry.

It was agreed that the draft of the necessary communication to the United States Government should be prepared for consideration at a further meeting to be held on Monday the 23rd June at 5 p.m.

No. 231 NAI DFA 417/105

Diarmuid O'Hegarty to each member of the Executive Council, enclosing a letter from Alfred O'Rahilly to William T. Cosgrave concerning the registration of the Anglo-Irish Treaty at the League of Nations

DUBLIN, 23 June 1924

Urgent

To/

Each Member of the Executive Council.[2]

The President has asked me to circulate the accompanying copy of a letter which he received from Mr. Alfred O'Rahilly[3] regarding registration of the Treaty at Geneva.

[1] Not printed.

[2] Circulated also to Joseph Walshe (for information).

[3] TD for Cork (1922-24) and Professor of Mathematics at University College Cork.

The President is of opinion that application should be made for registration and he proposes to write Mr. FitzGerald, who is at present in London, accordingly.

He would be glad to have your views on the matter.

DIARMUID Ó HÉIGEARTAIGH
Rúnaí

[enclosure]

Geneva, 19th June 1924

Dear President,

You will be glad to see from a communication we have sent home that we have done exceedingly well so far out here. From being a sceptic I have already become a believer in the great political and social possibilities in our association with the League and the Labour Bureau. However, on all this matter I will write a full report.

I am writing now to you, personally and unofficially, to consider seriously (with the Executive Council if necessary) the immediate registration of the Treaty. I have not the slightest doubt that the vast majority of the Treaty supporters want this to be done. Even the Government apologises for the delay; witness Desmond FitzGerald's statement in the recent Dáil debate on Grattan Esmonde's motion. There is no difficulty whatever in having it registered; the matter is purely automatic, though it might be best done when certain people have left Geneva.

I quite realise that such an action may now seem rather a broad hint to Great Britain in connection with the Boundary Question. But we have now surely come to the stage when such reminders are useful. And certainly if any crisis occurs on the issue of the Boundary, the country will fix upon the present Executive Council a very heavy responsibility if it suddenly discovers that this step has not been taken.

I wish to place this view before you for your very serious consideration. If I can be of any assistance to you while I am here, my services are very wholeheartedly at your disposal.

Sincerely yours,
(Sgd) ALFRED O'RAHILLY

No. 232 NAI DT S3328

Letter from Joseph P. Walshe to Diarmuid O'Hegarty on the registration of the Anglo-Irish Treaty at the League of Nations
(42/116)

DUBLIN, 23 June 1924

REGISTRATION OF THE TREATY
Professor O'Rahilly's Letter

A Chara,

Professor O'Rahilly's letter does not touch the real difficulty, namely: the attitude of the British towards an attempt to register. If they object, the machinery of the Council is at their disposal for making their objection effective and for proclaiming to the world that the Treaty is a domestic arrangement.

It has always been the opinion of this Department that the disadvantages following rejection of our application would be far more serious than those accruing from mere inaction.

It was suggested in a Memo. from this Department addressed to you on the 1st October 1923[1] apropos of a Dáil question on the Registration issue that the intentions of Great Britain should be ascertained before any attempt was made to register.

Mr. MacWhite who is thoroughly well informed on all League matters has been unable to find out what would there and then happen if the Treaty were presented to the registering authorities. He declares that it would be 'highly improbable that the British would intervene after formal application', but it is eminently a case for dealing in certainties.

Professor O'Rahilly says 'the matter is purely automatic' but he takes care to add 'it might best be done when *certain* people have left Geneva.' When he knows Geneva a little better he will find that it is never completely abandoned by at least two or three very capable *certain* people.

If the President wishes I can wire the Minister in the morning to sound the British, or if the Minister has left, instructions can be sent immediately to the High Commissioner.

Le meas,
[signed] S.P. BREATHNACH
Rúnaí

[Handwritten postscript by Walshe] It may have some significance that Berriedale Keith[2] takes it for granted that the Treaty has been registered (See 'The Constitution, Administration and Laws of the Empire', p. 204, published in April of this year). It depends on the extent to which he represents the mentality of the F.O.
S.P.B.

No. 233 NAI DT S3328

John O'Byrne to William T. Cosgrave (Dublin)[3]
(1410/24)

DUBLIN, 23 June 1924

Re: *Registration of Treaty.*
It is impossible to exaggerate the importance of maintaining our position as based upon the Treaty and not on legislation. For this reason, it would be highly desirable that the Treaty should be registered, and I would be strongly in favour of registering same if I thought there would be no difficulty about the matter. The matter, however, is of such vital importance that I think careful enquiries should be made before we take any step with a view to registration. I do not suppose anybody would oppose our application – unless the British authorities

[1] Not printed.
[2] Arthur Berriedale Keith, a leading legal authority on Dominion status.
[3] Handwritten note at the foot of the letter by Diarmuid O'Hegarty dated 25 June 1924: 'Mr McDunphy. Please remind the Ministers of Finance, Industry and Commerce and Education'.

do so, but I have no knowledge as to what their attitude would probably be or as to the extent of their powers of blocking our application. If we applied and, through opposition from the British Authorities or otherwise, the application was unsuccessful, I think it would have a very disastrous effect upon our whole position. For this reason, I think the application should be made only after careful enquiry and consideration.

[signed] John O'Byrne
ATTORNEY-GENERAL

No. 234 NAI DT S1983

Desmond FitzGerald to Timothy A. Smiddy (Washington)
(Copy)

Dublin, 25 June 1924

A Chara,
The British Government has instructed H.M. Ambassador at Washington to present a formal request to the President of the United States to receive a Minister Plenipotentiary on behalf of the Irish Free State.

Should the American Government accede to this request, and agree to accept you in that capacity, Letters of Credence from His Majesty will be duly forwarded to you for presentation.

The Free State Minister will be the official channel of communication with the United States Government for matters exclusively affecting the interests of the Irish Free State.

RELATIONS WITH H.M. AMBASSADOR
The Free State Minister shall not purport to deal with matters affecting the whole Commonwealth.

H.M. Ambassador shall be in no way responsible for action taken by the Free State Minister.

The Free State Minister shall not be in any way subject to H.M. Ambassador's control.

Instructions are being forwarded to H.M. Ambassador requesting him to afford his assistance and that of his staff to the Free State Minister.

In all matters affecting, or likely to affect the other, or any other, States Members of the Commonwealth, the Irish Free State Minister shall consult with the Ambassador and inform him fully of the position.

If any doubt should arise as to whether any particular question exclusively concerned the Irish Free State the point should, if possible, be settled by consultation between the Irish Free State Minister and the British Ambassador. Failing settlement by such consultation it should be referred to the two Governments.

The Government desires that the frankest and most cordial relations should exist between the Free State Minister and H.M. Ambassador and all steps should be taken to avoid any possible misunderstanding. For this reason, the instructions given above as to consultation should be interpreted in their widest sense. It may well happen that matters which in their initial stages appear to be of exclusively Irish interest may subsequently prove to be of concern to other parts of the Commonwealth. It would be well therefore to make it a general rule that it is better to inform the Ambassador of matters of apparently purely Irish concern rather than that he should not be consulted in a matter which might later have general interest.

Mise, le meas,
[copy letter unsigned]
MINISTER FOR EXTERNAL AFFAIRS

No. 235 NAI DFA 417/105

Memorandum from Desmond FitzGerald to all members of the Executive Council on the registration of the Anglo-Irish Treaty at the League of Nations
DUBLIN, 26 June 1924

A chara,
With reference to Mr. Alfred O'Rahilly's letter[1] and the President's covering note re Registration of Treaty,[2] we endeavoured to ascertain through our Representative in Geneva if the Treaty would be accepted without question by the Secretariat. He was unable to get us the information on this subject, but last year, following on a statement of mine in the Dáil, the American Government asked a representative of theirs in Geneva named McCrew (?) to ascertain what the position was. I am informed that his report was that a High Authority in the League informed him that it would probably be regarded as 'a British Domestic matter.'

The procedure for registration of a Treaty is that it be handed in to the Secretariat for registration. If any question is raised about the matter there it is referred to the Legal Adviser to the Secretariat, Van Hamil, who is expecting a British decoration. If he decided that it was not a registrable treaty we would be informed so by the Secretary General. On our protesting against this it is presumable that we would be told that this matter must be settled between ourselves and England. If England disagreed with us in the matter we could claim to submit it to the Council. The Council must agree unanimously except where one member of the Council is a disputant. In such a case England would be a disputant and therefore English agreement would not be required, but at the same time if England objected strongly it is considered unlikely that the other members would agree unanimously against her.

The Members of the Council are: England, France, Japan and Italy, permanent members; Uruguay, Brazil, Belgium, Sweden, Czecho-Slovakia and Spain – non-permanent members.

If the Council decided in our favour England would have the right to appeal to, and if the Council decided against[,] we should have the right to appeal to:-

(1) The Assembly. Here it is decided by majority, but the majority must include all the Members of the Council other than the disputants, so that, if the Council had decided in our favour the chances are that the Assembly would

[1] See above No. 231.
[2] Not printed.

confirm their finding. If the Council had decided against us, the Assembly would decide against us; and,

(2) The Court of International Justice. Whatever the decision of the Court may be[,] it must be confirmed by the Council unanimously with the exception of the disputants.

It is therefore pretty apparent that if England decided to resist the registration of the Treaty she could succeed in preventing it. The question therefore arises, should we proceed to register the Treaty without sounding England. In the event of its being returned to us by the Secretariat we should then be able to decide whether we should or should not appeal to the Council. It is to be remembered that the League is the greatest centre of gossip in Europe, and that the return of the Treaty to us by the Secretariat would almost inevitably be public property. On the other hand we might sound England before taking steps for registration. I am agreeable to either course.

It seems possible that although England might object in their hearts to the registration of the Treaty, they might consider it impolitic to take any action against its registration in view of the fact that she has claimed for the Dominions the right to Membership of the League and the right to separate signature of Treaties etc., which she has had to maintain against the opposition of other Powers.

It should also be remembered that she might explain this away on the grounds that at the time the Treaty was signed Ireland was not a Dominion.

Another possibility is that on presentation of the Treaty, the Secretariat, without deciding that it was non-registrable, might inform us that there was a doubt as to whether or not it was registrable and say that it would be preferable that it should be presented jointly by us and Great Britain.

I think that in view of the explanation given above it would be well for each Minister to say if he thinks:-

(1) that the Treaty should be presented for registration without preliminaries; and

(2) if he thinks we should approach the British beforehand.

Mise, le meas,
[copy letter unsigned]
MINISTER FOR EXTERNAL AFFAIRS

[handwritten note by William T. Cosgrave] I favour no 1. L.T. MacC

No. 236 NAI DFA ES Box 29 File 191

Extract from a letter from Timothy A. Smiddy to Joseph P. Walshe (Dublin)
(No: 34/24)

WASHINGTON, 1 July 1924

A Chara:

PASSPORT VISAS

[Matter omitted]

The granting of visas in America by a Free State officer will remove a good deal of hostile criticism to the sovereignty of the Irish Free State. It will further emphasise with the rank and file the independent international status of the

Irish Free State. It is the necessary corollary of the appointment of a Minister at Washington; both will have the effect of winning over to the Irish Free State the face sympathisers with the Irregulars.
[Matter omitted]

No. 237 NAI DT S3328

Desmond FitzGerald to Michael MacWhite (Geneva)
(Strictly Confidential)

DUBLIN, 1 July 1924

A chara,
We are sending you herewith two copies of the Treaty certified by the President, to be handed in to the Registration Office at the League of Nations immediately for registration. This is to be done quietly and unostentatiously. There is to be no publicity whatever in the matter, and there is no need for other people to be told, even confidentially.

If the League people make any question about it[,] refer to us immediately by code telegram if feasible: otherwise by letter, and please keep us informed of everything relating to this matter. If for instance, after you have handed these documents in[,] information on the matter becomes known and you are questioned about the matter, please let us know nature of questions and the names of questioners.

I am sure you will realise fully how important it is that these instructions be carried out literally.

Mise, le meas,
[copy letter unsigned]
Minister for External Affairs

No. 238 NAI DFA GR 224

Extract from a letter from Joseph P. Walshe to James McNeill (London)
(224/421) (Copy)

DUBLIN, 2 July 1924

Dear High Commissioner,
I enclose the printed programme of the Itinerary of the Group of Irish Ex-Service Men and their friends (about 250 in number) who are going to Ypres via London for the unveiling of the Munster War Memorial. You will see that they are laying a wreath at the Cenotaph at 11-30 on Sunday. Mr. Jacobs, the Hon. Organiser has done his best to make the celebration an Irish one and we understand that they will carry the Irish Flag everywhere with them. They have asked us to send a special Government representative with them. This shows a new tendency and the Minister recognises that it should be encouraged until this element of our population is completely absorbed in the Saorstát and weaned altogether from its attachment to British Institutions.

In the circumstances, while the Minister does not wish to give any instructions he thinks it might help towards the process of absorption if you

attended the ceremony at the Cenotaph, though he wishes you to be guided by your own judgment.
[Matter omitted]

Sincerely yours,
[copy letter unsigned]

No. 239 NAI DFA 417/105

Michael MacWhite to Desmond FitzGerald (Dublin)
(N.S. 01/110)

GENEVA, 4 July 1924

A Chara,
I have the honour to acknowledge receipt of your letter of the 1st. instant referring to the Registration of the Treaty.[1]

In consequence thereof, I visited the Secretariat this morning, presented the Secretary-General with the two certified copies of the Treaty which you forwarded, and made a formal request that it be registered in accordance with Article 18 of the Covenant.

The Secretary-General who seemed to be a little surprised at first said he was thankful that we had taken the necessary steps to have the Treaty registered (This expression could hardly have any other signification than that of a simple courtesy.) He would like to know, however, if the British were informed of the fact that we were about to register it. I was not in a position to enlighten him on this point.

The Secretary-General then stated that the publication of our request would be likely to create a splash in the press but I hinted that so far as we were concerned we did not desire any undue publicity on the matter. Nevertheless, the League are likely to follow their usual procedure in this case as, according to Article 18 of the Covenant, any international agreement registered with the Secretariat shall as soon as possible be published by it.

I sent you a code telegram this morning immediately after leaving the League Secretariat giving you the gist of the foregoing.[2] I shall also keep you informed of further developments, if any.

Mise, le meas,
[signed] M. MACWHITE

No. 240 UCDA P4/415

William T. Cosgrave to Hugh Kennedy

DUBLIN, 5 July 1924

A Príomh-Bhreithimh, a Chara,
I enclose herewith as received copy of a despatch from the Governor General. I do not quite agree with his Excellency in the matter and shall put the matter

[1] Above No. 237. Handwritten note: 'Minister's file'. Handwritten note at the foot of the page reads: 'See copy attached to Banim's note of 15 August 1924' (Paul Banim, President's Office).
[2] Not printed.

before the A. Genl[1] as soon as possible. I should like to place it before him tomorrow at Midday (Sunday). Meanwhile as the subject is of paramount importance I trust you will not think it unreasonable for me to show it to you. I am now personally of opinion after two interviews with Mr. Justice Feetham that the rectificationist theory will be put into some practice. I gather from the conversation I have had with him that the Northern Gvt will take in the most unfriendly spirit any direction from the Privy Council at variance with this Boundary policy.[2]

I am of opinion that for us to enter the Privy Council proceedings with Counsel would destroy our letter to the B. Gvt which put it plainly that we did not subscribe to the submission.

Mr. Justice Feetham was here twice. If it were at all possible I do think that a conference with Jim[3] and the A.G. on the matter now be most advisable – but I presume there are technical professional ...[4] in that course.

Can I suggest that the A.G. or and Jim be in a position to inform me with any advance on the matter.

Mise,
le meas mór agat,
[signed] LIAM T. MACCOSGAIR

No. 241 NAI DT S1801I

Memorandum by William T. Cosgrave

DUBLIN, 6 July 1924

I saw Mr. Justice Feetham twice – once with Dr. MacNeill, who left shortly after the introduction, and secondly after his return from Belfast.

He asked for permission to see Sir James Craig on the matter of the British Prime Minister's paragraph relating to possible agreement between Sir James and myself.

I said I had no objection and pointed out that we had made no claim, that the rights of the people – guaranteed by the Article – were the matters which concerned us.

He said he had read that – but it was a matter which required some arrangement: viz., had we considered the areas which were to be investigated, what they were, area, extent, etc., and that it was more than possible that we should be able to arrange the parts which would require investigation. We had to arrive at some time at those areas etc. and at least those ought to be known. I said there was not much use in a meeting with Sir James. We found the maximum of difference between us, and the areas not in dispute had not been considered by us. He went on to speak of Procedure and interpretation of evidence before the Commission, and said he would like us to consider those points and also the matter of presenting the Case – possibly a written Case

[1] John O'Byrne.
[2] The text of the letter from this point is almost illegible. It has been reproduced as accurately as possible.
[3] Possibly James McNeill.
[4] Words illegible.

could be presented by Counsel. I said I was willing in very difficult circumstances to facilitate him, that Mr. Blythe was now ill and I had to take over the Ministry of Finance. He told me he was about going North. Subsequently I had a telephone message from him in Belfast asking for an interview on Friday. He came at 10 o'clock with the proposals in the attached papers.[1]

I said we had never admitted the possibility of losing any of our territory. He said he would be glad if I waived that point pre the Conference and made it in the Conference. I pointed out that McGilligan was away, Blythe was ill, and that there was not a quorum of the Executive Council. That so far as I was concerned I saw no hope of going to a Conference next week owing to congestion of business in the Dáil, Estimates, etc., and the following week was also a difficulty in the matter of public business. That I would require to have the statements made by me and the letters written examined so as to find out whether the proposed Conference would be in conflict with the undertakings given by me or the Government (Mr. O'Hegarty examined them subsequently and they are also furnished with a comment).[2]

I forget exactly whether he or I referred to the Judicial Committee of the Privy Council. I think I may have stated that once the Commission was set up we had no objection to conferences. He said that he believed (?) that a decision by the Judicial Committee which would clash with the stand taken by Sir James Craig's Government would make subsequent conferences as to possible agreements impossible. That such a decision would make for anything but a peaceful atmosphere, whereas there was an opportunity for finding out when there was agreement on any policy with regard to the whole matter or to certain points in the matter. He said he had his secretary, Mr. Porter, and had also at the Colonial Office [a man] named Bourdillon[3] – or some name like that – who had complete knowledge or particulars of boundaries on the Continent.

These conversations lasted for about three-quarters of an hour in the first instance and an hour in the second.

Further information as to the conversations may best be got out by question and answer; the main points are, I think, covered by this memo.

Decision is required in the matter of the two documents herewith, viz. the conference with Sir James and the second, which are both in the handwriting of Mr. Porter.[4]

Mr. Justice Feetham also said it might be necessary for him to make a statement and that he proposed saying that he was seeing me and Sir James on the lines of the Prime Minister's letter to me.[5] I said I had no objection to that.

I said I did not know if I could agree to the conference without informing the Dáil and of course affording an opportunity for a motion expressing want of confidence.

[1] Not printed.
[2] Not printed.
[3] F.B. Bourdillon, later Secretary to the Boundary Commission.
[4] Not printed.
[5] Not printed.

No. 242 NAI DT S3328

T.M. Healy to J.H. Thomas (London)
(No. 258)

DUBLIN, 8 July 1924

Sir,

I have the honour to inform you that in conformity with Article 18 of the Covenant of the League of Nations my Ministers have instructed their representative at Geneva to deposit for registration the Treaty concluded on the 6th December, 1921 between Ireland and Great Britain.

I have the honour to be,
Sir,
Your most obedient, humble Servant,
T.M. HEALY

No. 243 NAI DFIN 851/2

Joseph P. Walshe to Joseph Brennan (Dublin)
(A 50/212)

DUBLIN, 8 July 1924

Secretary,
Department of Finance.

I am directed by the Minister of External Affairs to refer to Department of Finance minutes No. 851/2[1] on the subject of expenditure on entertainment by this Department's Representatives abroad and to ask you to move the Minister of Finance to convey his sanction for the expenditure by the Representative at Paris of a sum not exceeding 8,000 Francs per annum.

The Representative at Paris in his relations with French Government Officials, Journalists, Publicists and Merchants, finds it necessary to be in a position to offer some small entertainment to persons with whom he is in negotiations in connection with official business. He is also frequently offered hospitality because he is the Representative of the Saorstát and it is obviously desirable to make some small return.

The Minister of Finance will be aware that the Representative at Paris devotes a considerable portion of his time to the collection of information for the Department of Industry & Commerce and in helping Irish Traders in France generally. To be successful in this it is often necessary to make indirect approaches and the medium of hospitality is the most obvious and follows the established custom on the Continent.

It is proposed that the method of vouching for entertainment expenditure should be a certificate each month certifying the amount spent on hospitality in connection with his official duties and giving the names and position of the persons entertained, nature of the business transacted and the amount spent on each occasion. In this way it is considered that a sufficient check may be maintained so as to ensure that the money is well spent.

S.P. BREATHNACH
Rúnaidhe

[1] Not printed.

No. 244 NAI DT S1983

T.M. Healy to J.H. Thomas (London)
(Confidential)

DUBLIN, 8 July 1924

Sir,
I have the honour to acknowledge receipt of your Confidential Despatch of the 28th June enclosing a copy of a telegram from His Majesty's Ambassador at Washington relative to the appointment of a Minister Plenipotentiary at Washington.

2. My Ministers note with pleasure that the American Government have agreed to accept a Minister Plenipotentiary from the Irish Free State. They will be glad if His Majesty's Ambassador is instructed by cable to ascertain from the American Government if they will accept Timothy Aloysius Smiddy in that capacity.

3. This Despatch confirms my telegram of 3rd July addressed to you.

I have the honour to be,
Sir,
Your most obedient, humble Servant,
T.M. HEALY

No. 245 NAI DFA D3904

Joseph P. Walshe to James McNeill (London)
(EA. 151)

DUBLIN, 9 July 1924

My dear High Commissioner,
We are enclosing you herewith documents relative to proposed preliminary conference which, as far as arrangements made up to present are concerned, is to take place in the House of Commons at 2. p.m. on Friday, 11th inst.

I confirm proposals I made yesterday as to line of action to be taken, namely, that unless we are directly represented at the Inter-Allied Conference with full powers we must regard any protocol embodying the decisions of that Conference as in no way concerning or affecting us and that consequently we cannot be signatories to such protocol.

It can be pointed out that prior to signature the protocol would have to be submitted to the Oireachtas which had only very reluctantly acquiesced in the ratification of the Liquor and Lausanne Treaties, to neither of which we have been negotiatory and signatory parties and that the Oireachtas is certainly not prepared to agree to a similar line of action again.

I take it from the Prime Minister of Canada's despatch, that his attitude is identical with ours. He insists that the terms of the Imperial Conference Resolution about Treaties shall be applied and that Canada shall be represented with full powers. Presumably as a corollary to that attitude they will take up the line indicated by us and refuse signature and refuse to accept liability for any commitments intended or implied in the protocol if they are not full negotiatory parties.

The difference between our attitude and that of Canada can be put this way. Canada presumes that as the Conference is to be held she must be represented directly by a plenipotentiary, whereas we may be said to consider ourselves as not officially aware of any such conference until we have received an invitation to assist with full powers.

If the Executive Council decides on any variation of or addition to this I shall append a note here or communicate with you immediately.

Yours sincerely,
JOSEPH WALSHE

No. 246 NAI DFA GR508

Memorandum by E.J. Riordan (Department of Industry and Commerce) on Free State trade representatives

DUBLIN, 9 July 1924

MEMORANDUM

The Representatives in New York, Brussels, Paris and Rotterdam have obtained a considerable amount of first class information concerning markets in their districts for goods produced in the Saorstát; information which has led to a decided improvement in Saorstát exports to these countries. In the first four months of the current year Saorstát direct exports to these countries were as follows:-

United States, America	£87,549	or approximately	£262,647	for the year
Belgium	48,985	" "	146,955	" " "
France	18,425	" "	55,275	" " "
Holland	6,314	" "	18,942	" " "

It should be borne in mind that these figures do not represent the total exports to the countries mentioned, but only those consigned direct.

They have also provided Irish manufacturers with information which has enabled them to procure raw materials from these countries at lower costs than might otherwise have been incurred.

They have been instrumental in preparing the ground for a considerable further increase in trade as soon as foreign exchanges become more settled. They have supplied the Ministry of Industry & Commerce with a valuable fund of commercial information which that Ministry has been able to pass on to interested persons in this country. They have, on a number of occasions, prevented firms here from suffering serious financial losses incidental to the trading with firms in foreign countries. They have also done very valuable work in checking the practice of unscrupulous firms advertising and selling non-Irish goods as Irish. They have brought representatives of Irish firms visiting their countries into immediate touch with reliable buyers and sellers in those countries, and, in a variety of other ways, have proved themselves an indispensable link between traders in Saorstát Éireann, and the countries they are attached to. The view taken by the Ministry of Industry and Commerce, which has had direct proof of their usefulness is, that not alone have they fully justified their appointment, but have demonstrated the necessity for the appointment of additional trade representatives in other important centres abroad.

[signed] E. J. Riordan

No. 247 NAI DT S1801I

T.M. Healy to the Registrar of the Privy Council (London)
(Copy)

Dublin, 10 July 1924

I am advised by my Ministers to acknowledge receipt of your letter of the 4th instant,[1] enclosing copy of an Order dated the 25th day of June, 1924,[2] whereby His Majesty referred to the Judicial Committee of the Privy Council, certain questions connected with the Articles of Agreement for a Treaty between Great Britain and Ireland, for the consideration and report of the Judicial Committee.

Considerable correspondence has already taken place between my Government and His Majesty's Government, in the course of which His Majesty's Government informed my Government that they proposed to submit to the Judicial Committee, under the Statute 3 & 4 William IV. Chap.41, the questions set out in His Majesty's Order. In doing so, His Majesty's Government made it quite clear that they were merely seeking advice from the Judicial Committee as to their legal and constitutional powers. My Ministers have at all times refused to be parties to the reference of these matters to the Judicial Committee, and do not recognise that they are in any way bound by its proceedings or decision, and His Majesty's Government are in complete agreement with them as to this.

My Ministers also desire me to say that in making the Order of the 25th day of June 1924, His Majesty did not act on the advice of my Ministers, in accordance with the constitutional practice applicable if it were intended that the determination of the questions set out therein should bind or affect the Irish Free State.

In the circumstances, my Ministers desire me to say, for the information of the members of the Judicial Committee, that they do not desire to attend, by counsel, before their Lordships, nor do they desire to submit any documents for the consideration of the Board.

[copy letter unsigned]

No. 248 NAI DT S1801I

William T. Cosgrave to Justice Richard Feetham (London)

Dublin, 10 July 1924

Dear Mr Justice Feetham
My Ministers and myself have given careful consideration to the suggestion made by you at our recent interview, namely, that an open conference should

[1] Not printed.
[2] Not printed.

take place between Sir James Craig and myself in your presence as to areas of consultation and methods of consultation on either side of the Boundary with a view to arriving at an agreement and to restricting the scope of the Commission to giving formal effect to any agreement so reached. Several conferences have already taken place, and my Government have shown the keenest desire to arrive at a friendly agreement, but I am compelled to say that not only has no agreement been arrived at, but no progress has been made in that direction. Great delay has already taken place in the carrying out of Article 12 of the Treaty, and this delay has already been the subject of discussion in the Dáil. My Government consider that any further conferences, such as you suggest, would only lead to further delay, and they are satisfied that neither the people nor the Dáil would approve or countenance any such delay.

We further consider that any such conferences would necessarily involve the raising and debate of various political questions, the discussion of which would certainly not assist you in the difficult judicial functions which you have to perform.

I may also point out that it is very questionable to what extent, if any, an agreement between Sir James Craig and myself or between the two Governments can control the provisions of Article 12 of the Treaty, which provides for the determination of the Boundary in accordance with the wishes of the inhabitants so far as may be compatible with economic and geographical conditions. The governing factor in the minds of those who negotiated the Treaty was that in the event of the address mentioned in Article 12 being presented, the inhabitants of those disputed areas should elect whether they would remain subject to the control of the Parliament and Government of Northern Ireland or would come under the jurisdiction of the Parliament and Government of the Irish Free State. The function of the Commission is to ascertain those wishes and determine the Boundary in accordance therewith, and it appears to us that no further delay should be allowed to take place in having the Commission set up for this purpose.

After the Commission has been constituted, my Government will carefully consider any suggestions made either by the Commission or by the Government of Northern Ireland with a view to reducing and facilitating the work of the Commission, but, pending the constitution of the Commission, they do not see their way to accept the proposal which you have made to me.

Sincerely yrs,
(signed) L.T. MacCosgair

No. 249 NAI DFA 417/105

Michael MacWhite to Desmond FitzGerald
(N.S. 01/119)

Geneva, 11 July 1924

A Chara,

I am forwarding you herewith a copy of a letter which I received this morning from the Director of the Legal Section of the League of Nations with reference to the registration of the Treaty.

In order to avoid any misinterpretation of this letter by us the Official who has to do with Registrations showed me copies of several letters of a like nature which were forwarded to other countries in corresponding cases. I have supplied the information asked for, and, as all the formalities have now been fulfilled, the formal Registration will take place at once. I expect to have official notice to that effect by Monday or Tuesday next.

It would seem that the League authorities spent three or four days discussing our demand for Registration and its various phases but, because of our Membership of the League, no valid objection could be raised against the steps we have taken in the matter.

Is mise, le meas,
[signed] M. MacWhite

[enclosure]

9 June 1924

Sir,
[Matter omitted]
The practice has become established of effecting registration of treaties and international engagements communicated to the Secretary-General on their coming into force, and it is a usual procedure to have a statement to this effect in hand at the time of registration. Would you be good enough, therefore, to inform me whether the Treaty which you communicated has been ratified in accordance with the provisions of its Article 18, as well as the date on which the Treaty came into force?

I have the honour to be,
Sir,
Your obedient Servant
for the Secretary-General
(signed) Van Hamil
Director of the Legal Section

No. 250 NAI DFA D3904

James McNeill to Desmond FitzGerald (Dublin)
London, 11 July 1924

My dear Minister,
As directed I attended the Conference at 2 p.m. in the Prime Minister's room in the House of Commons to-day. Present – The Prime Minister, Mr. Thomas, High Commissioners of Canada, New Zealand, and Australia, and Lord Olivier, Secretary of State for India. Sir Maurice Hankey and Mr. Harding also attended.

The Prime Minister briefly explained the European position and the need for a speedy understanding. Unless the Dawes Report could be put in operation without delay the present French Government would go under and Germany would collapse economically. As to representation the Prime Minister was sorry that there should be any trouble. He laid stress on the facts that the position remained as under the Versailles treaty, and that the decisions of the Conference in themselves would involve no military or economic commitment. He wanted the whole question of representation to be considered at an Imperial Conference in the near future, but meantime the gravity of the position necessitated special arrangements. The Allies and other conferring powers had not categorically objected to the full representation of Dominions, but as this would raise the British Commonwealth representation so greatly as compared with others mainly interested there was no hope of a speedy consent and delay would be disastrous.

The High Commissioners were asked to state their views. Each of the others expressed dissatisfaction with the position, though New Zealand took care to state that his Government assented. There was a sort of general discussion, in which I took no part, as to the possibility of some alternative to separate representation of each Dominion. Canada stated that his instructions were to the effect that Canada could not assent to secondary representation, as in the Canada premier's despatch, but was ready to consider and transmit suggestions. I said my instructions were definite and stated them briefly. I added that I was not authorised to depart from them or to express any opinion as to alternatives. There was some more discussion, not always pertinent, and a suggestion was made that the High Commissioners might jointly send a representation to their Governments. I explained that I could not join with the others in making a representation to my Government as I knew the latter would disapprove of my associating other views with my own or of addressing other Governments. Mr. Larkin[1] said he would have a similar difficulty. Apart from sending a communication there was some discussion as to whether in a telegram to be sent by the Prime Minister to the President and Premiers, it would be proper to state that the High Commissioners favoured any alternative. Again Mr. Larkin and I felt it necessary to state that our instructions forbade.

You will have received the Prime Minister's telegram.[2] It is the result of a long discussion of which the object was to ensure that the message contained nothing likely to cause complications in the dominions. I think some of the High Commissioners were eager to advise.

There was much discussion as to whether the Dominions could accept either the High Commissioner of Canada or the Colonial Secretary (Mr. Thomas) as a joint representative. My instructions again compelled me to state that I could not go beyond them. I could not undertake to commend any alternative.

The Prime Minister seemed to be genuinely sorry that any question as to representation should have to be raised. Briefly, he said that the exigencies of the European situation and the great danger of delay in seizing on the present chance of making a great change for the better, including the re-entrance of Germany into international politics, compelled him to ask the Dominions to agree to a proposal which ran contrary to his own views and could not become a precedent. He seemed to be really convinced that French adhesion to the Conference was secured with difficulty and that Poincaré and others would get the better of Herriot and the moderates if the Conference could not meet and arrive at decisions at once.[3]

[1] P.C. Larkin, Canadian High Commissioner in London (1922-30).
[2] Not printed.
[3] Raymond Poincaré (President of France) and Edouard Herriot (French Foreign Minister).

The suggested alternatives to direct representation were representation of Dominions jointly by one of three representatives assigned to the British Empire and the presence of delegations from Dominions with which the three representatives should be in constant communication.

I have written this hurriedly to catch the mail. I was to some extent pressed to commend to you the consideration of the alternatives. I said that my instructions were what they were and that I would report and that if I offered advice I did not think my doing so would be helpful to anyone.

Yours sincerely,
[signed] JAMES MCNEILL

No. 251 NAI DFA Minister's Office Files (1924-25)

Desmond FitzGerald to James McNeill (London)
(Copy)

DUBLIN, 12 July 1924

My dear High Commissioner,
In the matter of implementing Article 12 of the Treaty, the Ulsterior aim has been to represent the issue as one between two Governments fighting about territory, whereas the Article does not contemplate governmental claims at all, but makes 'the wishes of the inhabitants' the main factor.

'The inhabitants,' however, so far as they have found a voice, have practically acquiesced in the notion of a governmental tug-of-war. No body of them anywhere has come forward to claim a *locus standi*. They worry their respective Governments but they do not realise that the Treaty has invested them with rights, which are also statutory rights in virtue of the ratifying Acts. Their failure to understand this and to act upon it is now as much as ever fostering the notion that their *locus standi* can be ignored.

It is not at all necessary that all the inhabitants who desire a change of the boundary should act in common. In fact, any one of them or any group is competent to demand the fulfilment of the Treaty in his or their respect, to put forward a case, and to claim a hearing. Naturally, the case will be stronger the larger the number who unite in presenting it and the better they organise their action.

It would be a great mistake, however, to take no action until all could act together. That would mean a long delay, and the present muddled state of mind would lead to muddled action. The first body that moves in the right direction will be a nucleus round which the rest will rally and adhere.

It is highly needful that the first movers should move in the right direction, with their minds clear and their line understood. They need not lose themselves in trying to have everything settled to their pleasure at the outset – extent of zone, area of local plebiscite unit, plebiscite register, etc. They could easily tie themselves up in controversies on such points which might defeat their principal aim – and there are sure to be local statesmen who will want to show their form in this way.

The doctrinaire Republicans are already preaching against any action under the Treaty – that is, those of them who reside in the areas concerned. This is probably dictated from outside. They are doing this on the quiet. An organised move to obtain a *locus standi* for the inhabitants will force this policy to declare itself. The result will inevitably be a slump from the doctrinaires and discredit for them within and without. The longer the organised move is deferred, the more the doctrinaires will become crystallised, and in certain localities they might succeed in forming a considerable body of abstentionists.

Cahir Healy and Harbinson are the naturally suitable persons to take the lead in organising the inhabitants.[1] The process will no doubt begin with the formation of committees in the best centres. Care should be taken to have the work taken up in Derry and Newry as well as in Tyrone and Fermanagh. There should be no avoiding of publicity – rather the contrary, but not to the extent of mere trumpeting.

While a plan of organisation by localities should be in mind, there should be no waiting for simultaneous activity. The bodies organised should refrain from anything resembling party demonstrations and concentrate on one object, to secure that the wishes of the inhabitants in each locality shall be ascertained by plebiscite. The extent of the organisation will help to determine the extent of the plebiscite zone.

In some localities, it is reported, there is apathy. These should be left alone until the others are on the move – they will soon come into line. 'Left alone' does not mean 'ignored', only that formal organisation should wait until the movement is shaped elsewhere.

Perhaps you could see Cahir Healy and Harbinson, or in any case Cahir Healy, and put it to him that he might get a move on to get the people in the various areas to organise themselves to put forward their demands.

Yours sincerely,
[copy letter unsigned]
Minister for External Affairs

No. 252 NAI DFA D3904

Telegram from T.M. Healy to J.H. Thomas (London)
DUBLIN, 5.40 pm, 14 July 1924

With reference to your secret code telegram 11th July[2] it is impossible for the Irish Free State to participate other than by direct representative with full powers (stop) If such representation impossible it is necessary that Free State be specifically excluded from negotiations and resultant protocol.

[1] T.J.S. Harbinson, Nationalist MP for Tyrone.
[2] Not printed.

No. 253 NAI DFA D3904

James McNeill to Desmond FitzGerald (Dublin)
London, 15 July 1924

My dear Minister,

The High Commissioners were invited again to-day to the Colonial Office and Mr. Thomas stated that the British Delegation was to consist of the Prime Minister, Chancellor of the Exchequer, Mr. Thomas and Sir Eyre Crowe.[1] The French Government had intimated that they wished to have three ministerial delegates and the permanent head of the French Foreign Office. He was anxious to find out if some arrangement could not yet be made. The telegram dated 14th instant from the Prime Minister of Canada was read. I enclose a copy. It seemed doubtful whether this was or was not an assent to the panel system, under which full power delegates would be appointed in excess of the number admitted simultaneously to the session of the conference. Mr. Thomas sent to Canada from himself as Colonial Secretary a reply drafted at the meeting, acknowledging with thanks the assent which he took it to be to the panel system. Mr. Larkin is wiring for clear instructions. Mr. Thomas went on to say that if his interpretation proved correct he would cease to be a British representative and his place would be taken by a full power representative of each dominion in turn.

Please consider what our Government will do under these circumstances. If Canada accepts the panel system, i.e. appoints a full power representative (probably Senator Belcourt) who will be present at some sessions in his turn and always in touch, will the Irish Free State remain out unless represented at each session by an Irish Free State representative? Canada will reply to-night or to-morrow morning either assenting or dissenting clearly. I think the Canada telegram points to assent. I was told that the panel system was worked at Versailles.

If Canada dissents the conference will go on, constituted as above mentioned. The High Commissioners are invited to come to the Colonial Office and receive daily reports of transactions. The stenographic notes of each session will be supplied to them within a few hours of the close of the session, morning and afternoon.

Should Canada assent to the panel system and our Government agree to being represented in the same way you will have to name a representative. Probably the other High Commissioners will represent their several dominions on the panel. It would be better that our representative should be either yourself or failing you a member of the Dáil (Query – Professor O'Sullivan)[2] who could speak in the Dáil later. If neither you nor a member of the Dáil can come I should as High Commissioner be most suitable.

The position is now that South Africa does not wish to be represented separately, New Zealand agrees to Empire representation if that is more convenient. Canada's exact position is doubtful. If Canada accepts panel system

---

[1] Sir Eyre Crowe, British Permanent Under-Secretary at the Foreign Office (1920-25).
[2] Professor John Marcus O'Sullivan.

all Dominions (except South Africa) will be invited to accept panel and name a full power delegate who will remain in touch and attend a session in his turn, the order being fixed by ballot or some other method agreed upon. I think that our Government should agree if Canada does. I shall telephone as soon as I know to-morrow. If you have no other representative at once available you may appoint me without prejudice to my replacement at any time you wish during the conference. But it would be best to have you or, if you cannot come, a Dáil member. I don't think the duty in itself will be arduous, as I don't think the decisions arrived at will directly commit us to enforcement of sanctions of any kind.

A ground for accepting the arrangement, apart from Canada's assent, would be that the Prime Minister had undertaken to have the question of representation of dominions made the subject of a special conference in the near future. If Canada assents it would probably be impolitic to remain aloof. There would be no harm, I think, in assenting after Canada and being represented a day late.

During the meeting this morning Thomas interrupted Sir J. Cook who was talking rather generally and referring to the position in Canada and the Irish Free State, and stated inter alia there was as I (McNeill) knew a special trouble connected with the King's name. I said I knew only of the difficulty arising from the Dáil's objection to assent to agreements if there was no representative. It is a detail. I think Thomas meant partly to separate the two cases and partly to indicate that Cook was talking about things he didn't understand.

Yours sincerely,
JAMES MCNEILL

P.S. Should Canada dissent I see no harm in accepting invitation to go to the Colonial Office daily and get information from Colonial Secretary, if Canada High Commissioner also does so.

No. 254 NAI DFA D3904

James McNeill to Desmond FitzGerald (Dublin)
LONDON, 16 July 1924

My dear Minister,
I enclose for your information copy of two telegrams sent to Secretary of State for Colonies by Canada.[1]

I was told telephonically by Mr. Larkin this morning that a reply had been received. He read it as meaning adherence to abstention and the Colonial Office considered that it meant assent to panel. Senator Belcourt arrived this morning and Mr. Larkin had not seen him. A little later I went to Canada Office to see Mr. Larkin who had gone out. I saw the Secretary (Mr. Pacaud) and Senator Belcourt. They said the cable meant that Canada could not accept this panel system, that it was not as in Paris where Canada was continuously represented, though not by all her representatives, at each session. They never had less than one representative present at a session. Senator Belcourt said that the proposed

[1] Not printed.

system meant that he should represent Ireland one day and I Canada the next, an impossible arrangement. This talk took place during the interruption of our conversation, and while you were sending the rest of the telephone message interrupted. Mr. Larkin rang me up later and confirmed the interpretation. He will, as invited, go to the Colonial Office to-morrow morning to hear what the Colonial Secretary has to say. So shall I, unless forbidden. That commits no-one to anything. I shall express no opinions, but listen to anything that is said, making it clear as often as is necessary that my Government forbids anything that smacks of participation by expression of opinion or otherwise. I shall not go continuously if there are symptoms of an endeavour to keep us more or less attached. I think there can be no harm in accepting the first invitation to go and see Thomas.

Yours sincerely,
JAMES MCNEILL

No. 255 NAI DFA D3904

Joseph P. Walshe to James McNeill (London)
(Copy)

DUBLIN, 16 July 1924

Dear High Commissioner,
I am instructed by the Minister of External Affairs to confirm 'phone message of to-day as follows:-

'Representation proposed constitutes derogation from status of Dominions recognised at Versailles Conference. At Versailles Dominions had twofold representation. They were represented in the first place as separate nations on an equal footing with Belgium and in the second place as part of the British Empire delegation by means of the panel system. Representation as separate nations was claimed in December 1919 by Sir Robert Borden for Dominions and agreed to by Imperial War Cabinet. In the circumstances we find it impossible to agree to representation by panel system alone at the London Conference.'

and wire as follows: 'Consider better not attend Colonial Office[.] Writing.'

After the latter wire had been sent a cabled Despatch was received from Thomas stating that he would meet the High Commissioners to-morrow to report to-day's proceedings and to further consider question of representation.

In the new circumstances the following wire was sent:

'Since wiring[,] have learnt Conference arranged between Thomas and Commissioners to-morrow morning to report proceedings and further consider question of representation[.] Please attend and follow lines of to-day's 'phone message.'

The Minister regrets that you have had so much trouble about this Conference. Events have succeeded each other so rapidly that it has been difficult to keep the Ministers informed and to obtain their views.

The Minister will be glad to have result of to-morrow's discussion on representation by telephone or wire.

Sincerely yours,
[copy letter unsigned]

No. 256 NAI DFA 417/105

Joseph P. Walshe to Michael MacWhite (Geneva)

DUBLIN, 17 July 1924

A Chara,

I am directed to acknowledge receipt of your letters Nos: 110, 114, 119[1] and 120 with reference to the Registration of the Anglo-Irish Treaty with the Secretariat of the League of Nations.

The Minister wishes me to express his satisfaction at the manner in which you effected the Registration.

Le meas,
[copy letter unsigned]
Rúnaí

No. 257 NAI DFA Berne Embassy papers

Michael MacWhite to Timothy A. Smiddy (Washington)
(B.02/86) (Copy)

GENEVA, 28 July 1924

Dear Mr. Smiddy,

As I understand that the negotiations relative to your appointment as Minister Plenipotentiary at Washington are now completed and that you will formally present your credentials to the President in the course of a week or two, I hasten to send you my sincere congratulations.

Of all the other diplomatic posts in the United States Capital, yours will for some time to come, be the most difficult and it is possible that some interested persons may endeavour to lay pitfalls in your path. I hope, however, that our Ministry of External Affairs will always second you as up to the present it has not an enviable reputation in this respect. There is, I am glad to say, a little improvement lately.

The position of Representative accredited to the League of Nations at Geneva is becoming more and more important. Outside of the Saorstát about fourteen other countries are represented here directly. Brazil has an Ambassador and Poland and Austria have Ministers Plenipotentiary. There is also a question of transferring the seats of some of the diplomats accredited to the Confederation from Berne to Geneva. I meet Mr. Gibson, the United States Minister at Berne, frequently.

A few weeks ago I had the Anglo-Irish Treaty registered with the League. Our people expected some opposition but none was or could be forthcoming as, in the League, one Member is as good as another. They are, by force of circumstances, growing out of this timidity.

With best wishes
Very sincerely yours
[copy letter unsigned]

[1] Above No. 249.

No. 258 NAI DT S1801J

Extract from minutes of a meeting of the Executive Council (C.2/122)
DUBLIN, 1 August 1924[1]

BOUNDARY.
(a) Col. Office Despatch 'Secret' of the 31st ult. containing the text of a statement to be made by Mr. Thomas in the House of Commons on the 1st instant relative to the Report of the Judicial Committee of the Privy Council made to His Majesty was read and noted.[2]
(b) The position arising out of the Report was further considered and it was agreed:-

(1) That if legislation is to be passed by the British Parliament it must be introduced and passed at once.

(2) That it will have to be followed immediately by similar legislation in the Oireachtas.

(3) That the President should leave for London that evening to discuss the matter with the British Government.

No. 259 NAI DT S1801J

Secret memorandum of proceedings of Conference on the Boundary Commission
LONDON, 2 August 1924

The following were present at various stages of the Conference:

Representing the Irish Free State	–	1. President 2. Mr. John O'Byrne, K.C., Attorney General.
Representing the British Government	–	1. Mr. Ramsay MacDonald, Prime Minister. 2. Mr. J.H. Thomas, Secretary of State for the Colonies.
Representing the Northern Government	–	1. Lord Londonderry.[3] 2 Mr. Pollock, Minister for Finance.

[1] The date of this document has been changed here from 2 to 1 August. The original reads 'Friday, 2 August', but 2 August was a Saturday. The Council meeting took place between 11 am and 6.30 pm. Cosgrave was in attendance. On Saturday 2 August Cosgrave was in London at the Colonial Office at 10 am. Given paragraph (b)(3) of this document it is more likely the correct date is 1 August with Cosgrave travelling to London on the evening of 1 August to be there for 10 am on 2 August.
[2] Not printed.
[3] Northern Ireland Minister of Education.

Resumé of the Proceedings of Conference in London
2nd August 1924 regarding BOUNDARY QUESTION.

The President, on Mr Thomas' invitation attended at the Colonial Office at 10 a.m. on 2nd August 1924, and met the Secretary of State for the Colonies. Mr. Thomas explained that a new situation had been created by the report of the Judicial Committee of the Privy Council on the questions submitted for their advice in connection with Article 12 of the Treaty. It was evident that further legislation would be required to enable the Boundary Commission to be set up if the Northern Government persisted in their refusal to appoint a representative. The British Government proposed to introduce such legislation at once. The President pointed out the necessity for having the proposed legislation enacted before the British Parliamentary recess, indicated the distrust which would be occasioned by delay, and foreshadowed the possibility of an Irish Government coming into power which would denounce the Treaty. Mr. Thomas said they could get legislation passed in Commons but were not sure of Lords.

The President and Mr. Thomas then saw Mr. MacDonald, with whom the arguments were again gone over.

On their return to the Colonial Office Lord Londonderry and Mr. Pollock of the Northern Government were introduced, and Mr. John O'Byrne, Attorney General, was also called in. The determination of the British Government to see that the Treaty was carried out was reiterated to the Northern representatives. In the discussion which followed Lord Londonderry in response to a suggestion that the North having made their protest should now appoint their representative said this was impossible.

A suggestion made from the British side that the President should with Sir James Craig endeavour to work out an agreed boundary and that any matter on which they could not agree should be referred to (a) Mr. Justice Feetham, or (b) the Colonial Office, or (c) the Boundary Commission, was turned down by Lord Londonderry. He undertook however to consult some of his people as to whether any action to obviate the difficulty of new legislation could be suggested.

While awaiting the re-assembly of the Conference, Lord Londonderry indicated to the President that in his view the safest course for the Irish Free State and the Northern Government would be to let the proposed legislation be proceeded with.

Upon resumption the Prime Minister made a strong appeal upon the grounds of empire stability for the agreed boundary proposal. The method of giving effect to decisions so reached was mentioned, and, when it was obvious that it would necessitate legislation in both parliaments the proposal was dropped. The legislation to be introduced was then considered. A suggestion that the Commission might be constituted of the two Commissioners already appointed was dismissed on the President pointing out that this would lay Mr. Justice Feetham open to criticism on the grounds of partiality.

The Prime Minister explained that their Bill would provide that the British Government would appoint the third representative if the Government of Northern Ireland persisted in their refusal. He said that this was regarded by the British Government as a matter affecting the honour of the British people and hinted at the possibility of constitutional changes being rendered necessary if the House of Lords threw out the Bill. He asked Mr. Pollock if there was any influence in England which, if brought to bear upon the Government of Northern Ireland, could assist them in justifying to their people the appointment of a Commissioner. Mr. Pollock was unable to reply, but said vaguely it would require consideration.

The Prime Minister then asked, if the Bill were introduced on 6th August and further consideration deferred for fourteen days, whether he could get an assurance that the North would either appoint their Commissioner, or offer no serious opposition to the Bill. Lord Londonderry favoured deferring the remaining stages until the re-assembly of Parliament in the normal course, as otherwise the North would say that the matter was being rushed. The President could not agree to a postponement over the ordinary recess. His Cabinet were definite that the Bill should go through at once. He offered however to consult his colleagues as to the proposal to defer the final stages of the Bill to the resumption of Parliament provided the resumption was fixed for an earlier date and the British Prime Minister gave in writing a guarantee of the intentions of H.M. Government that the passage of the Bill would be made a matter of confidence. These conditions were agreed to by the Prime Minister and the Conference concluded.

Subsequently Messrs Curtis and Whiskard[1] visited the President and suggested that the Bills in both the British Parliament and in the Oireachtas should take the form of a confirmation by legislation of an agreement signed by the President on behalf of the Irish Government, and by the Prime Minister on behalf of the British Government. This course would prevent attempts at amending the agreement in Parliament. The President agreed and a draft was prepared in consultation with the Attorney General and Sir Francis Greer, as follows:-

In anticipation of the approval of the Executive Council the President signed two copies of the Agreement,[2] the signature not to be regarded as effective unless and until the approval of the Executive Council had been notified to the British Government. As soon as this has been done the Agreement will be signed by the Prime Minister and one copy forwarded to the President for record purposes.

During the course of the conversations it was stated by the Prime Minister that he had approved of the British Government undertaking to provide funds to migrate persons who were unwilling to remain in the jurisdiction within which their places of residence were located following the operations of the Boundary Commission.

It was also incidentally mentioned that the British Government were prepared to offer a lump sum in settlement of outstanding Compensation Claims in dispute.

[1] Lionel Curtis, Geoffrey Whiskard.
[2] See No. 262 below.

No. 260 NAI DT S1801J

Extract from minutes of a meeting of the Executive Council (C.2/123)
DUBLIN, 3 August 1924

BOUNDARY
The President submitted a report regarding his conference with representatives of the British Government in London on the 2nd inst. relative to Art.12 of the Treaty. During portions of the Conference representatives of the Northern Government had been present.

The following had represented the respective Governments:-
Representing the Irish Free State.
President Cosgrave.
Mr. J. O'Byrne – the Att. General.
Representing British Government.
Mr. R. McDonald, Prime Minister.
Mr. J.H. Thomas, Secy of State for the Colonies.
Representing Northern Government
Lord Londonderry and Mr. Pollock, Nthern.Min. for Finance.

Arising out of the situation created by the replies given by the Judicial Committee of the Privy Council to certain questions referred to them by His Majesty's Government relating to Art. 12 of the Treaty, that Government proposed to introduce legislation into the British Parliament – similar legislation being introduced into the Oireachtas – amending the Treaty so as to enable the British Govt. to appoint the Commissioner who under the Treaty should be appointed by the Nthern. Govt.

For this purpose a draft Agreement to be signed jointly by the President and the British Prime Minister and to be embodied by way of a Schedule in the respective Bills had been drawn up and had been approved by Mr. F. Greer and by the Irish Attorney General.

* * *

The draft Agreement, copy of which is appended was considered by the Executive Council and approved, and the President was authorised to affix his signature thereto jointly with the British Prime Minister for the purpose stated.[1]

The President mentioned that the Prime Minister proposed to introduce the necessary legislation into Parliament during the week and then to allow the House to adjourn in the usual course until late in October. On its reassembly the Bill would be taken up immediately and proceeded with to a finish.

This proposal was discussed at length by the Exec. Council and it was decided that the delay entailed thereby could not be entertained, and that the immediate passage of the Bill through the British Parliament before adjournment should be insisted on.

A letter to this effect to be signed by the President was drawn up and approved for issue.[2]

The corresponding Bill will be introduced into the Oireachtas immediately on its reassembly on the 12th instant.

[1] See below No. 262.
[2] See below No. 261.

No. 261 NAI DT S1801J

William T. Cosgrave to Ramsay MacDonald (London)

DUBLIN, 3 August 1924

Dear Mr. Prime Minister,

Immediately on my return this morning, I held a lengthy consultation with my colleagues regarding the matters which we discussed yesterday.[1]

The draft Agreement supplementing Article 12 of the Treaty was considered and meets with our approval. I was accordingly authorised to affix my signature to it on behalf of the Government of the Irish Free State. When the Dáil reassembles on the 12th inst., we will introduce the legislative measure necessary for its ratification, and press it to a conclusion.

My colleagues and I have given earnest consideration to the representations made to me that as the British Parliament would in the ordinary course adjourn this week it would meet the convenience of His Majesty's Government that the corresponding legislation in that Parliament, which you are introducing on Wednesday next, should await the reassembly of Parliament in October for the completion of its remaining stages. This course does not commend itself to us.

I have already in previous communications acquainted you of the grave apprehensions which have been aroused in this Country by the delays that have occurred in giving effect to Article 12 of the Treaty. Recent developments have not tended to allay these apprehensions. Suggestions have been made in the Dáil and elsewhere that faith is not being kept with our people, and my Government would fail in their duty were they to acquiesce in any proceeding which would tend to aggravate feeling of this nature. Any avoidable delay in dealing with the problem which now confronts His Majesty's Government would certainly increase dissatisfaction and foster distrust, and we accordingly urge most strongly upon you in the interests of both Countries that a prompt settlement of this matter is imperative.

I must therefore on behalf of my Government earnestly represent to you that it is essential that the legislation requisite on the part of His Majesty's Government to give effect to our Agreement shall be enacted before Parliament rises.

Sincerely Yours,
[signed] L.T. MACCOSGAIR

[1] See above No. 259.

No. 262 NAI DT S1801I

Agreement supplementing Article Twelve of the Articles of Agreement for a Treaty between Great Britain and Ireland to which the force of law was given by the Irish Free State (Agreement) Act, 1922, and by the Constitution of the Irish Free State (Saorstát Éireann) Act, 1922.

LONDON, 4 August 1924

WHEREAS the Commissioners to be appointed under the said Article Twelve by the Government of the Irish Free State and by the British Government respectively have been duly appointed by those respective Governments, but the Government of Northern Ireland has declined to appoint the Commissioner to be so appointed by that Government, and no provision is made by the said Articles for such a contingency:

NOW it is hereby agreed, subject to the confirmation of this Agreement by the British Parliament and the Oireachtas of the Irish Free State, that, if the Government of Northern Ireland does not before the date of the passing of the Act of the British Parliament or of the Act of the Oireachtas of the Irish Free State confirming this Agreement, whichever is the later date, appoint the Commissioner to be so appointed by that Government, the power of the Government of Northern Ireland to appoint such Commissioner shall thereupon be transferred to and exercised by the British Government, and that for the purposes of the said Article any Commissioner so appointed by the British Government shall be deemed to be a Commissioner appointed by the Government of Northern Ireland and that the said Articles of Agreement for a Treaty shall have effect accordingly.

Signed on behalf of the British Government:
J. RAMSAY MACDONALD

Signed on behalf of the Irish Free State Government:
LIAM T. MAC COSGAIR

No. 263 NAI DFA ES Brussels

Joseph P. Walshe to Count Gerald O'Kelly de Gallagh (Brussels)
(261/110) (Copy)

DUBLIN, 5 August 1924

A Chara,
I am directed to acknowledge receipt of your letter No: 570/E/24 of the 1st instant regarding the three Russian Students who desire to visit the Saorstát.

The reason for refusing admission is that it does not appear from the information at our disposal that these students have sufficient resources to maintain themselves during their proposed visit. Your telegram suggested that they might stay with the Christian Brothers and in your letter under reply you speak of friends of Sister Kavanagh. The attitude of the Department of Justice is that they cannot allow aliens to enter the Saorstát unless they are satisfied that the aliens will not become a charge on the public funds owing to lack of means. Unless you can guarantee that these students will be able to support themselves it is useless to ask the Department of Justice to re-consider their decision.

Le meas,
[copy letter unsigned]
t.c. Rúnaí

No. 264 UCDA P80/424

Extracts from a letter from Desmond FitzGerald to Senator N.A. Belcourt
DUBLIN, 13 August 1924

Dear Senator Belcourt,
I regret very much my long delay in answering your letters of the 25th July.[1] I have been hoping to be in a position to give you full information about the appointment of Professor Smiddy. That appointment is not yet completed; it was only the day before yesterday that we actually received word that the American Government were agreeable to the person of our appointment.
[Matter omitted]

With regard to the Washington appointment: perhaps I had better give you a little history of our proceedings. In the first place we wrote the British Government that we found it necessary to have a fully accredited representative in Washington, and we asked them to approach the American Government through their diplomatic channels to ascertain if the American Government would be willing to receive such a representative from us. In that despatch we also asked that if the American Government replied in the affirmative they should then be asked for their agreement with regard to Professor Smiddy as the person to be appointed, and if the American Government found Professor Smiddy persona grata we asked that His Majesty would forward to us a letter of Credence for us to transmit to Professor Smiddy.

The British Government notified this proposal to the other Dominions: Canada and South Africa approved: New Zealand disapproved and Australia thought the matter should be left for the next Imperial Conference. The British Government had made long delays, and as I impressed upon them that this matter was urgent[,] a conference was arranged in the Colonial Office. At that Conference it was agreed that the British Government would approach the American Government, and if America accepted the proposal the Free State Minister should be the official channel of communication with the United States Government for dealing with matters exclusively affecting the Free State. The principles of the resolution of the Imperial Conference of 1923 as to the negotiation, signature and ratification of Treaties, and in particular of that part of the Resolution which relates to the conduct of matters affecting more than one part of the Empire would apply generally to all questions with which he dealt, and the Ambassador would in the same way keep the Irish Free State Minister informed of any matters which might affect the Irish Free State. If any doubt should arise whether any particular question exclusively concerned the Free State, the point would, if possible, be settled by consultation between the

[1] Not printed.

Free State Minister and the British Ambassador. If the matter could not be settled by such consultation, it would be referred to the British Government and the Free State Government.

In order to meet the possibility that any particular question might in its initial stages be exclusively of concern to the Free State and might subsequently prove to be of concern to other parts of the Empire, the Free State Minister would keep in close contact with the British Ambassador.

While the Free State Minister would not purport to deal with matters affecting the Empire as a whole, the assistance of the British Ambassador and the Embassy staff would always be at his disposal, if desired. The Ambassador would not, however, be in any way responsible for action taken by the Free State Minister, nor would the latter be in any way subject to the Ambassador's control.

As regards credentials: the British Government had previously forwarded me a copy of the credentials which had been proposed for the Canadian Minister in 1920. There were three things in that document which were objectionable to us. In the first place the use of the term 'United Kingdom of Great Britain and Ireland' in His Majesty's title. In the second place the phrase 'to attach him to our Embassy,' and in the third place the counter-signature of the British Secretary for State.

With regard to the first point: as I was assured that steps were already being taken with a view to changing His Majesty's Title, I agreed that if the change could not be effected before the credentials were to be issued that I would agree to the Title in its present form.

With regard to the second point: the British agreed to eliminate the words 'to attach him to our Embassy.'

The third point I considered very important as it seemed to me that the counter-signature of the British Foreign Minister carried with it an implication that His Majesty could only act on the advice of the London ministers. Sir Cecil Hurst of the British Foreign Office agreed with me in this, and it was agreed that the counter-signature of the British Foreign Minister should not be included in this or in any similar documents in the future.

The British then showed me the telegram they proposed sending to their Ambassador. In due time we were informed that the American Government agreed to receive a Minister from us. We immediately asked the British to inquire if Professor Smiddy would be persona grata. They delayed doing this for a considerable time so that only two days ago did I get word that the American Government would accept Professor Smiddy. We have now asked the British Government to forward us Letter of Credence signed by His Majesty.

You will observe from above that the terms of the Letter of Credence were agreed to in conference between the British Government and me. I interpret the omission of the Foreign Secretary's counter-signature as meaning that His Majesty empowers Professor Smiddy directly on the advice of the Free State Government. We also shall forward to Professor Smiddy a letter of Authority, and the appointment of Professor Smiddy will be covered either by an Order by our Executive Council (which is our equivalent to an Order in Council), or by a Resolution of the Dáil.

As to the financial terms and conditions: Professor Smiddy's emoluments are: £2,750[.] This is subject to revision

I am unable to say so far what the full cost of our American Representation will be, but I shall be happy to forward this information as soon as I have some clear indication of it myself. We are very hopeful that as we have now arranged to have a passport control officer in New York that our receipts from visas to Americans travelling directly to the Irish Free State will go a long way to cover the cost of our American representation.

I am always most happy to give any information I have to you or to your Government. I shall write further as soon as I receive from the British Government documents I am now waiting for.

If you are likely to be in London during the next fortnight I hope to have the pleasure of calling upon you, and I can assure you that if you can see your way to come to Dublin we shall be very glad to welcome you.

Yours very sincerely,
[copy letter unsigned]
MINISTER FOR EXTERNAL AFFAIRS

No. 265 NAI DT S3328

William T. Cosgrave to Geoffrey Whiskard (London)
(Copy)[1]

DUBLIN, 14 August 1924

Dear Mr. Whiskard,

I have your letter of 13th.[2] I must say that it surprised me very much indeed. I understood you to say to me that there was no objection and would be none to the Registration of the Treaty but that a formal communication to this effect was not a matter which the Secretary of State would like to send. I may say that if I were to have inferred from you that there was a likelihood of objection to Registration I would not have undertaken the responsibility of moving the First Reading of the Bill on Tuesday.

Up to date of Mr. Henderson's[3] and Mr. Thomas's visit we had understood that the Treaty was duly registered without objections.

In accordance with Article 18 of the Covenant it was obviously our duty to register the Treaty as the Treaty regulated the relations between two States members of the League. We accordingly submitted the Treaty for Registration as we informed you on 5th July and we are informed the Treaty was duly registered on the 11th July.

Failure to register might rightly have been regarded as a breach of the Covenant.

I understood that I pointed out to you how much this matter affected us here[,] that the Treaty was a matter between two Nations and as such was regarded by those who supported it.

Yours sincerely.
(SD) L.T. MACCOSGAIR

[1] Handwritten note: 'original in President's handwriting'.
[2] Not printed.
[3] Arthur Henderson, the British Home Secretary.

No. 266 NAI DT S3920

Sean Lester to William T. Cosgrave and Joseph P. Walshe
DUBLIN, 20 August 1924

Secretary,
President.
The Irish State's participation in the League of Nations Assembly will again offer some scope for propaganda. The opportunities will not be as good as last year but several factors make it desirable that Irish participation this year should be emphasised, especially at home. The Irish newspapers are diffident about the necessary expenditure and I submit that anything we can do to make it possible for the Irish Press to obtain reports and photographs would be of considerable importance. This is particularly the case in view of impending bye-elections when the Treaty position will again be challenged, the fact that de Valera is free to embark on a campaign in various centres and while the Boundary situation is indefinite.

There are several ways in which, if considered desirable from the Government's point of view, publicity could be assisted. One would be to attach someone to the Delegation for the purpose of supplying Irish newspapers with reports and photographs. Another way would be for the Delegates to bear the whole situation in mind and use an occasional hour of leisure in supplying the necessary material. This does not seem feasible as the Delegates will be very preoccupied with the work of the Assembly, on the social side as well as otherwise. The third way would be to give special instructions to Mr. MacWhite with authority to spend a certain amount of money in obtaining photographs and, if the Irish Press are not directly represented, in supplying reports.

The last named method may be considered the most convenient. If it is so decided it would help very much if each of the Delegates felt the importance of publicity at home. Perhaps it would not be too much to ask that in this event the President's views should be conveyed to them.

[signed] SEAN LESTER
Director of Publicity

No. 267 NAI DT S3920

Osmond Grattan Esmonde to William T. Cosgrave (Dublin)
DUBLIN, 24 August 1924

Dear President,[1]
I write to urge most strongly that you should attend the Assembly of the League of Nations this year; if only for part of the time.

It would seem that not only MacDonald[2] and Herriot,[3] but also Mussolini,[4]

[1] Marginal note reads: 'Answered personally by the President 4/9/24'.
[2] Ramsay MacDonald.
[3] Edouard Herriot.
[4] Benito Mussolini.

will lead their respective Delegations; and several other Heads of Governments will be present.

In view of the comparative insignificance of the Dominion delegations, Mr MacDonald would be looked upon as the spokesman of the whole Empire. In your absence we would be reduced to a very subordinate position, at a moment when such is not advisable. Owing to the authority of the leading delegates, and the close connection between this year's proceedings and the recent London Conference, it will be the most important Assembly yet held.

The fact that it has already been published that you are not attending would give added significance to your visit. In any case it is quite obvious that nothing will happen at home during September, seeing that the Unionist Party have decided to allow the Boundary Bill through the Lords, and that Sir James has gone to the Baltic Sea!

Yours very sincerely,
[signed] O. GRATTAN ESMONDE

No. 268 NAI DT S3890

Memorandum by the Department of External Affairs on revision of the system of consultation between Britain and the Dominions with covering notes by Sean Murphy and Diarmuid O'Hegarty

DUBLIN, 2 September 1924

I herewith enclose memorandum on the above subject for the consideration of the Executive Council at its next Meeting.

SEÁN O'MURCHADHA
t.c. Rúnaí

Mr. McDunphy.
A copy of this memo is to be circulated to each Executive Minister, & arrgts. made whereby any such Minister who has not yet had an opportunity of seeing the entire correspondence should be given our file on loan for perusal.

DIARMUID Ó HÉIGEARTAIGH
3/9/24

MEMORANDUM ON SYSTEM OF CONSULTATION ON MATTERS OF FOREIGN POLICY AND GENERAL COMMONWEALTH INTERESTS.

The British Government in its telegram of the 23rd June point out that the present system of Consultation has two main defects.
1) Renders immediate action difficult, especially between Conferences,
2) Conclusions of Imperial Conferences are liable to reversal through change of Government.

It makes the following suggestions to meet these difficulties:-
1) In order to secure rapid decision on matters of foreign policy, a further examination of the Resolution on the Negotiation, etc., of Treaties, to consider how it can be supplemented and interpreted.
2) In order to make Imperial Conferences Resolutions effective suggests that future Conferences should not be confined to representatives of parties in Office.

This course might tend to hamper frank exchange of views on matters of foreign policy and defence. Another method might be to obtain parliamentary approval beforehand for policy to be adopted. This might tend to diminish flexibility of Conference procedure.

The final suggestion is to have a meeting for the preliminary examination of these problems. October is suggested as a suitable time. The British do not consider the time has come for a constitutional conference or a special meeting of the Imperial Conference.

The aim of the British Government is obviously to create some system which will enable it to control foreign policy and which will at the same time prevent difficulties like those caused by the Lausanne Treaty and recently by the Inter Allied Conference.

The question of representation at International Conferences is also to be discussed at the proposed Meeting.

The Saorstát is the only member of the Commonwealth that has not replied to British proposals.

The Australian Government has taken the attitude that the present system will become effective in time and that undue haste will attain nothing. It does not propose to send representatives to the Meeting but will give the question careful consideration. It suggests the establishment of a foreign office branch in the High Commissioner's Office in London to keep the Prime Minister informed on questions of foreign policy. It advocates the establishment of a General Imperial Secretariat in London to deal with all matters of General Empire interest, such as the carrying out of Imperial Conference Resolutions. It does not favour the representation of all political parties at Imperial Conferences.

The British Government has informed the Australian Government of the replies of the New Zealand and Canadian Governments and the Australian Government has agreed to be represented at a preliminary conference and recommends some time late in November as most suitable to it.

The New Zealand Government agrees generally with the British proposals but suggest that a Committee of men not necessarily politicians should examine the problems and prepare a report for the next Imperial Conference.

The Canadian Government is in favour of considering the possibilities of extending the Negotiation of Treaties Resolution. The Government is not in favour of having all parties represented at Imperial Conferences, as they are Conferences of Governments each responsible to Parliament and in no sense an Imperial Council. The Canadian Government favours preliminary examination of the question and the preparation of a report for further discussion.

The Government of South Africa regrets that it cannot see its way to take part in proposed conference, and is of opinion that preliminary conference is unlikely to prove of any advantage for coming to a final decision.

The Government of Newfoundland are not in favour of having all political parties represented at Imperial Conferences or of obtaining approval of parliament in advance. The Government agrees to send a representative to a preliminary conference.

The Minister of External Affairs is of opinion that the Saorstát should take part in the proposed Meeting for the following reasons:

1) It seems inevitable that for some time to come the British Government will control the foreign policy of the British Commonwealth of Nations and so it is desirable that the various members of the Commonwealth should have as much influence as possible on the moulding of that policy.
2) The proposed meeting will not be final and the participation of the Saorstát will not prejudice whatever attitude the Government may decide to take on the questions of foreign policy or Imperial Conferences. On the other hand, it will give an opportunity to the Government of ascertaining the views of the various Governments on these questions and also of influencing the proposals which result for the Conference.

No. 269 NAI DT S1932A

Extract from the Ministers and Secretaries Act (1924) dealing with the Department of External Affairs

DUBLIN, 4 September 1924

(*xi*) The Department of External Affairs which shall comprise the administration and business generally of public services in connection with communications and transactions between the Government of Saorstát Éireann and the Government of any other state or nation, diplomatic and consular representation of Saorstát Éireann in any country or place, international amenities, the granting of passports and of *visés* to passports, and all powers, duties and functions connected with the same, and of which Department the head shall be, and shall be styled, an t-Aire Gnóthaí Coigríche or (in English) the Minister for External Affairs.

No. 270 NAI DT S1983

Desmond FitzGerald to William T. Cosgrave (Dublin)

GENEVA, 12 September 1924

My dear President,
I have just received your note. The matter you speak of is one that has given me a good deal of concern, and I do not need to say that I am prepared to do anything in the matter.[1]

This occupied my mind so much that I talked it over with Judge Cohalan the day I left. I told him that I felt that it would be necessary for me to go across, and he recommended that quite earnestly, but he urged that it should not be before November, as it would be thought in America, if I went there before the election there, that my presence there had some political significance, in other words that I was trying to interfere in the election, or trying to use the circumstances of the election in order to get something for ourselves by party bargaining. Naturally, his advice in this matter had considerable weight with me. But if you think this matter so urgent that the consideration put forward

[1] The appointment of T.A. Smiddy as Irish Free State Minister Plenipotentiary to the United States provoked a campaign against the new minister amongst sections of the Irish-American community; FitzGerald was prepared to travel to America to counter this campaign.

by the Judge should be disregarded, I need not tell you that I shall return immediately on receiving a wire from you to that effect, and I should be ready to start within a week (allowing me a few days to get some extra clothes). Everything is going quite well here. The little hitch with the Marquess before we left has quite passed away, and has left nothing behind. Heffernan suffered from grievances a bit at the beginning, but I think he also is now quite mollified.

The big issue in the League is disarmament, which is a struggle between England and France. I should be inclined to think the gulf quite unbridgeable, but that in talking to the two delegations most concerned I find them most optimistic. I am told that in the League there will be agreement on one point, disagreement on another, that it will then go to the Conference which has been proposed, and that there things will be settled, mostly behind the scene.

Our delegation is very successful in its relations with others. Delegates from all countries seem to follow the boundary question more or less intelligently. They all refer to it in their conversations with us. Always with sympathy for our side.

As I have said above, on receipt of a wire from you I shall return immediately, but I think that we have to give some weight to the Judge's advice in the matter.[1]

I hope all is well at home, and particularly your own health,

Do chara,
D.[ESMOND] FITZGERALD

No. 271 NAI DT S1983

Telegram from William T. Cosgrave to Desmond FitzGerald (Geneva)[2]
(Copy)
DUBLIN, 15 September 1924

Received your letter am of opinion that you should return without delay

COSGRAVE[3]

No. 272 NAI DT S4084

Kevin O'Higgins to each member of the Executive Council, enclosing a memorandum on the Boundary Question
(C.1987/24) (Confidential)
DUBLIN, 25 September 1924

To each member of the Executive Council,
I send you herewith a memorandum on the boundary situation which has lately been given to me by a member of the North Eastern Bureau staff[4] acting in a more or less unofficial and free-lance way, and at my request.

The memorandum is closely reasoned and is in my opinion deserving of careful consideration.

[1] See below No. 275.
[2] Handwritten note on copy reads: 'Mr FitzGerald is returning on Saturday 20th inst.'
[3] See above No. 270.
[4] Probably Bolton C. Waller.

Personally, I am impressed by all the arguments leading up to the point at which the writer commences to deal with the kind of offer which in his opinion should be made.

My own state of mind at the moment is this. I agree with the writer that an offer should be made. I am inclined to think that he has named the right time for making it – after the Bill has become law and the Commission stands ready to function.

With regard to the possible offers sketched by the writer, I would agree with him in rejecting the Council of Ireland and also a return to Article 14. As to his plan marked 'B' on the third last page of the memorandum, I am of opinion that if we were to put it forward at all it should be with a statement that in our opinion it does not represent the best solution.

If this matter is discussed by the Executive Council I would like to outline an alternative scheme which might be considered worth putting forward if only for the sake of having it on record that such an offer was made.

[signed] CAOIMHGHIN Ó HUIGÍN
Aire Dlí agus Cirt

PRIVATE AND CONFIDENTIAL
NOTES ON POSSIBLE OFFER TO NORTHERN IRELAND

I. It seems plain that the nearer we get to the Commission the more doubtful the country is becoming as to the advantages to be gained from it. Signs of this are various articles in the 'Irish Statesman' and other papers, Devoy's and McCabe's letters, and the general feeling of apprehension which is noticeable. The way is thus being prepared for a different line of approach. The mistake made by most people is that they propose to drop the Boundary Commission as a preliminary, which is like throwing away your trumps before you play your hand. To come out with fresh proposals at the present moment would probably be disastrous. It would be put down to dread of the fate of the Bill in the British Parliament, and as a sign of weakness. It would probably be utilised as a reason for postponement of that measure, and leave everything in a state of uncertainty. (I put this view strongly to people in England.)

The psychological moment for a new offer seems to be immediately after the Bill is passed, or else immediately after the third Commissioner is appointed. We will then be in a position of strength. The way will be open for the Commission. We could then take the line that, while our right to the Commission is now absolutely acknowledged and its power to function plain, we want to make one more attempt to reach an agreed settlement. Such an offer at that particular moment would probably receive immense support both here and in Great Britain, and if it appeared reasonable great pressure from that side would be brought upon the North to secure acceptance.

It seems probable that in any case some new proposal of settlement will be made at that stage, by England if not by us. It seems altogether desirable that it should be made by us. We can take the line that this is a matter to be settled among Irishmen. We can get the discussion focussed on our proposals, and put on the other parties the responsibility for rejection or criticism. In the event of rejection we will have immensely strengthened our position in the eyes of the world, through having made an attempt to settle, while if a proposal put forward by England is not altogether acceptable we may seem just as responsible as the North for rejecting it. If eventually we must have recourse to the Commission, we will be able to go ahead with much greater confidence if we can always point back to an offer made by us and rejected by the other party, especially if the offer had won support in England.

II. Before the offer is made, however, it might be advantageous that there should be a better understanding among our own people of the disadvantages of the Commission solution and advantages of the other course, such as:

(a) we are entirely in the dark as to how the Commission will result, and its finding may prove much less favourable than most of us imagine. My own view of its likely result is that we should gain part of South Down (not including Belfast waterworks); a considerable part of South Armagh; most of that part of Fermanagh which lies South and West of the Lakes, but not including Enniskillen or the part lying just south of it; minor rectifications in the Belleek and Pettigo area; the Castlederg salient; while they are likely to gain some districts in the part of Donegal adjacent to Derry. I do not believe that the Commission will touch the large Nationalist population of central Tyrone, since this can be regarded as practically an island cut off by the preponderatingly Unionist populations of North Fermanagh and West Tyrone. This is of course a mere attempt to prophesy, but such a finding is likely enough, and would undoubtedly cause great disappointment. Also, it is probable that we could gain almost the same result by negotiations as by the Commission. While it could probably not be accepted in negotiations dealing with the Boundary alone, it might be taken as a sensible and moderate boundary alteration forming part of a general settlement.

(b) Any result of the Commission will leave a large number of Nationalists, probably the majority of those in the six Counties, still under the Northern Government.

(c) We will have lost our opportunity to alleviate their condition, by removing gerrymandering and other disabilities.

(d) There is an obvious and terrible risk of bloodshed during the course of the Commission and the carrying out of its findings. During all that time propaganda will be at work, passions will be rising, rumours will be flying about that this or that area is to be transferred. Even if both Governments were determined to maintain order, some hotheads on one side or other would probably start to shoot, and once that began it would spread. It would be a miracle if that did not happen.

(e) When the Commission has finished we may find union further off than ever. It is most improbable that it will so reduce the Northern area as to compel union. If not, it will have reduced the number of those who desire union, so that a larger turnover of present Unionist votes will be necessary to bring it about in future. A reduced Northern area may attach itself still more closely to England. Also if there is bitterness and bloodshed during the Commission's work this may immensely hamper union in the future. It is a very different thing to draw a Boundary in Upper Silesia between Germany and Poland which are to remain separate states, and to draw it between the two parts of a country which we hope will eventually be one. The way the present business is conducted may mean the difference between union in five years or in a hundred.

These things might be pointed out to the country, more explicitly than has yet been done, not of course by the Government, in order to prepare for the offer. Or else they could be said, in a modified form, along with the offer. Probably inspired articles could be written on these lines.

III. Any offer would have to take into consideration both Boundary alteration, and also general questions of the relations of North and South. I believe it to be impossible to get a settlement by negotiations on the former taken alone (since the opposition of interests of the two parties is plain), but possible when the Boundary is but one of a number of questions on many of which the interest of the two parties are akin (e.g. removal of Customs difficulties).

It is essential that the offer should be one which the North will be compelled at least to discuss, and if possible one which English opinion will back.

The difficulty of the proposal of a single Parliament, even when combined with financial and other advantages, seems to be that it can be at once depicted in the light of a demand upon the North to give up all they have stood for and to enter the Dublin Parliament which they dread. I fear we would have people not merely in the North but in England saying our only offer, apart from the Commission, was complete absorption, plus a suggestion to plunder the British taxpayer by eliminating Art. V. of the Treaty. Of course the Northerns are perfectly willing to plunder the British taxpayer, and do it habitually; but on this occasion it would suit them to take a high moral attitude and point to the wickedness of the proceeding. The suggestion of a single Parliament could, I think, come openly only from the Northerns themselves. Perhaps we could suggest it to them secretly, but as an open offer it would at once be turned down.

An offer on the following lines might be acceptable, and would be bound to get consideration.

(1) minor alterations of the Boundary by consent, to be ratified by the Commission in order to fulfil the Treaty.
Our definite suggestions, when it came to negotiations might be on the lines suggested above, or even less if we got fuller centralisation.

(2) Restoration of Proportional Representation, a reversal of gerrymandering in the Six Counties, disbandment of the Specials, release of prisoners and arrangement for return of expelled persons.

(3) Nationalists to enter the Northern Parliament, and to co-operate in local administration.
This they will do in any case when Boundary question is settled.

(4) Article V. to be waived (This would need to be tactfully put).

(5) A Customs arrangement, obviating some or all of the present difficulties.

(6) Some system of joint Government, giving an opportunity of advance to fuller Union later.
This is put last, though it is the most important, because it needs fuller consideration, and there are several possibilities.

(a) The least satisfactory is the revival of the Council of Ireland. Against this there are strong political objections, that is if the Council should consist of equal numbers from each area as formerly proposed, and should be so restricted in scope. Personally I would be for acceptance of it if nothing better was to be had, from a belief that if once we get even the smallest beginning of union we would find natural forces driving us further in that direction. I believe that a settlement which gained that, with the four other points above, would be immensely preferable to anything we can get from the Commission. But perhaps it could not be carried in the country, and it is not really a good settlement. In any case it would not be wise to start our offer with the Council, even if we were ready, as a last resort, to fall back on it.

(b) A better plan would be to have joint meetings of the Oireachtas and the Northern Parliament for matters of common concern. A scheme on these lines was worked out some months ago by the Boundary Bureau. There are many difficulties in detail but I believe it to be workable.

In general outline the plan would be to transfer to the joint body the reserved services which in respect of Northern Ireland are still retained by Great Britain, and the corresponding services in the Free State, together with such other services as the two parties agree to bring under central control. This would involve the centralisation of the main powers of taxation and finance, tariffs and defence, and very probably of various other matters which are now separate. The actual matters would be a subject for negotiation. In order to conciliate the North some special arrangements might be proposed, such as

(1) The joint body to meet alternatively in Dublin and Belfast.
(2) The Governor-General to be nominated alternately by the Northern and Free State Governments.
(3) Special Customs arrangements in the interests of Northern industries to be worked out as part of a general settlement.
(4) Financial safeguards, if required, as suggested in Article 14 of the Treaty.

(c) Reversal to plan of Article XIV of the Treaty. This I think is less satisfactory, as it leaves Northern Ireland in some respects in an unduly privileged position, with local parliament as well as representation in Oireachtas; and on the other hand leaves them subordinate, so that they could hardly expect ever to get representation in the National Executive Council. They could not long acquiesce in that position, as if they come in they will wish to have as full a right as anyone else to concern themselves with the larger national issues. (Probably the present relations of Northern Ireland with British Parliament are only tolerable because the Northern representation is such a very small part of the whole.)

A more detailed scheme would have to be worked out on one or other of these lines if a definite offer were to be made. But it would be a mistake to make it too detailed. The purpose should be to put forward a reasonable plan in general outline, on which negotiation would be bound to take place. It might be said expressly that this was only a general offer, and that modifications were expected. The great thing would be secure real negotiations, in Ireland, on the basis of our offer. Once negotiations began, on a scheme of union, it would probably be found that it was in the interests of both parties to make the union more close than the North will even admit, unless they are brought down to actual details.

IV. Politically, the advantages of such an offer seem to be:

(1) It would satisfy the general feeling of desire for unity, and for a peaceful settlement.
(2) It should be distinctly preferable to those Northern Nationalists (the majority) who will not be brought out by the Commission.
(3) It should appeal to business and commercial interests both in North and South.
(4) It would, if carried, be an immense strength to the Free State as against the de Valera Party, since they could obviously carry nothing of the kind.
(5) It would gain widespread support in England, which dreads the Commission.

As against this it would be attacked

(1) By border Nationalists, tho' in fact they will be the worst sufferers from a Commission if it leads to fighting.
(2) By the enemies of the Free State who want to make trouble, and will consider it a surrender of Treaty rights. They would have to be ignored, and are just as likely to make trouble if the Boundary Commission does take place.

23rd September, 1924

No. 273 NAI DFA Minister's Office files (1924-25)

James McNeill to Desmond FitzGerald (Dublin) enclosing copy of a statement made to journalists

LONDON, 26 September 1924[1]

My dear Minister,

You may like to have a copy of my statement to the journalists. I made a few remarks of welcome & then said I would read what I had to say to them. I expect I shall see myself as others see me in an hour or two. The atmosphere seemed friendly. Steed[2] worked[3] off a reference to his own proposals after I had answered a few questions. I hope you will think that the mountain air was nutritious.

Yours sincerely
JAMES McNEILL

I enclose a spare copy for K. O'H, & one for the Pres[iden]t. The newspapers may report it at length, but you may like to have just what I said.

[text of statement]

It seems to me that this question, this very controversial question, is being treated in some quarters here rather as a party question than an international

[1] This statement was occasioned by Lord Balfour publishing a 'secret' letter on 8 September 1924 sent to him by Lord Birkenhead on 3 March 1922 which interpreted Article XII as requiring the Boundary Commission merely to 'rectify' the Border. Lloyd George spoke publicly in the same sense a few days later and, on 26 September, *The Times* reported a speech by a third British signatory to the Treaty, Winston Churchill, claiming that Article XII intended only 'minor readjustments of boundary' – see Frank Gallagher, *The Indivisible Island: the History of the Partition of Ireland* (New York: The Citadel Press, 1937), pp 171-4.

[2] Wickham Steed, editor of *The Times* (1919-22), editor of *Review of Reviews* (1923-30).

[3] The word is difficult to read but may be 'worked' or 'cranked'.

question. The question at issue is a question as to what is just and honourable between two nations. The principles which are applied to its settlement should be such as to deserve recognition in any international settlement.

When the Treaty was made in 1921 the Irish Free State was not forthwith limited to 26 counties. Ireland was the unit and our representatives negotiated as the representatives of Ireland. By article 12 of the Treaty it was agreed that the Government of Northern Ireland could object to the inclusion in the Irish Free State, not of six counties, but of the areas of which the population preferred British to Irish Government, subject to economical and geographical considerations.

The right to opt for British Government was not recognised by Irishmen as an absolute right of any Irish minority, but it was recognised by the great majority as the surest as well as the most peaceful means of attaining Irish unity and ending hostility between Ireland and Great Britain. The unity might be delayed but would come by agreement in due course. We still have no doubt about that. The recognition of the right of a minority to adhere to an external Government has not as far as I know been imposed on any other people of which the national rights have been recognised by the League of Nations, and the resolutions of the Assembly of the League of Nations, which the representatives of Great Britain and the Dominions helped to frame, regard minorities as deserving of protection but not of segregation from the national unit. We in Ireland are, however, content that the minority should be segregated as the Treaty provides, because we are convinced that both sentiment and interest will lead to re-union. There is no doubt of the fact that some Irishmen now prefer to be governed from Westminster. It may seem to you to be stupid, but I think all will prefer hereafter to assist in governing Ireland. So the divergence from League of Nations ideals in the case of Ireland need not now be stressed.

The meaning of Article 12 of the Treaty seemed to us to be quite clear. We understood the words in their plain sense and in the sense in which the identical words were used in treaties made and carried into effect on the continent at the same time. We did not think and do not think that their meaning was to be gathered from the Berlin treaty which was, I think, made in Germany some time before the new world was called in to redress the balance of the old. We understood that the wishes of the people directly concerned were, as the words stated, of primary importance in this treaty as in the others. We did not think that the meaning of the words was to be ascertained by the perusal of subsequent correspondence between party politicians, which was doubtless for good reason marked 'Secret.' Was it the British people who could not be trusted to understand this secret doctrine in its fullness? Is there any other article of the Treaty of which the secret meaning is yet to be revealed? With all deference I request you British journalists to have this made clear. We shall have other agreements to enter into with British Governments and we should like to know all the secret interpretations of this first agreement. In any case there is nothing immoral, nothing offensive to modern political thought, in asking that when a country is being divided to satisfy a small minority of its citizens that human beings will not be treated like cattle. We are not looking outside our country for territory to rule. We are asking that areas in Ireland adjoining the Free State shall not be excluded from the Free State against the wishes of the majority of the inhabitants of those areas and be compelled to accept British Government against their will.

We have not asked that the principles recognised internationally in recent continental settlements should be applied in full to Ireland. We do ask that they should not be flouted, and we expect something else than threats of murder from your legislators in return for our moderation. So much for our interpretation of the Treaty. That interpretation needs no secret commentary to reconcile it with the text or with the principles which the League of Nations, of which Great Britain and the Dominions are members, has undertaken to maintain.

It has been urged as an obstacle to this interpretation that what was *granted* to 'Ulster' cannot be withdrawn. May I point out that the people placed under the Government of Northern Ireland are therefore under the Government of Great Britain, and that the fundamental issue is whether the British or Irish Governments should govern Irishmen in areas adjoining the Irish Free State who want to be governed by the Government of the Irish Free State. What is called the grant of territory to the subordinate Government of Northern Ireland cannot justify the inequitable segregation of Irishmen from the Irish Free State. As to the alleged grant of territory, no Irish member of Parliament voted for it, and more than three fourths of the Irish people were opposed to it. They regarded the arbitrary division as a hostile act. Its palpable injustice impelled large numbers of Irishmen to approve of *active* resistance to the British Government in Ireland.

It also stated that a pledge was given to 'Ulster' and that this induced Ulster to accept the 1920 Act. What does 'Ulster' mean in that connection? It certainly is not the people of the Nine Counties of the Irish province of Ulster, nor before 1920 could it be the Government of the Six Counties. 'Ulster' was obviously the Ulster Unionist Association, which accepted the political creed of British Unionists, and received financial support from that political association. Can such a party pledge or promise be regarded as a ground for casting aside a treaty?

English Unionists and 15 or 16 Irish Unionist members of the British Parliament agreed as to the division of Ireland for purposes of local self-Government. The Irish people were not consulted. That agreement, we are told, is to govern all the subsequent relations of Great Britain and Ireland. By labelling half of the Irish representatives of the Irish province of Ulster as Ulster, an internal party pledge is to override the terms of a treaty. This theory may satisfy those who are looking for reasons to justify a decision otherwise acceptable. It will satisfy no-one else in Ireland, in Great Britain or in any other country.

It has also been said that if the people were allowed to exercise a choice the area under the Government of Northern Ireland would be too small for practical administration by a subordinate Government. That cannot be taken seriously as a reason for breaking a treaty or forcing large numbers of Irishmen under the Government of Westminster. Nor is it a reason for preventing Irishmen who so desire from supporting an Irish Government, which is alleged to be in financial straits, compelling them to pay taxes to enable the English Government to reduce income tax in Great Britain.

I know that many other objections are alleged, including the objection that Irishmen in the border counties really prefer to escape Irish Government. Why then prevent the expression of their views directly by ballot? Under the Irish Government it has been shown that votes can be given freely. Under the British Government of the Six Counties is voting likely to be restricted while the gerrymandering of constituencies is unrestricted?

We are, however, willing, as the Treaty showed, that the Government of Northern Ireland should continue undisturbed within the Irish Free State. They would have the present population[,] area and jurisdiction, not as a matter of right but as a matter of good faith and good will. We recognise them as what they are, Irish, and we wish them both to prosper and to feel secure. The people who now wish to be governed by the Irish Free State, and not by the British Government would not then be compulsorily denationalised.

I am sorry to see that at least one member of the British House of Commons is already discussing the sending of armed men across the sea to resist violently any transfer of population of which the Government of Northern Ireland disapproves, even if the superior Government of Gt. Britain approves. Simultaneously we are asked by his colleagues to arrive at a settlement by consent. We have always been willing to discuss the terms of a friendly settlement and have assented to the postponement of arbitration in order that the possibilities of a friendly settlement should be examined. The arbitration procedure does not prevent a friendly settlement, and might expedite such a settlement. Threats of violence by British members of Parliament are not helpful. We are not appealing to force or violence but to reason and justice, and we ask that the settlement of the boundary be entrusted to an impartial arbitrator, to whom we offer no advice. What we want the British Government and the British people to do in this matter is simply to do as they would be done by. We assent to the temporary division of our country for the sake of peace. We think now as in 1919-1920, that the division should not have been made and we ask that, if a minority of Irishmen is to be withdrawn from the Government of the Free State and governed by Great Britain, that minority should not include a very large number who object to their forcible expatriation.

Those of us who have adhered to the Treaty and assented to the killing of our friends to maintain the Treaty, or even of our relatives, naturally regard with disfavour the visits of British legislators who threaten that we may expect more of our friends and relatives to be killed, as I think murdered, with their active assistance if we ask that Article 12 of the Treaty be interpreted honestly and put in force. I again repeat that the British people have to determine whether they will deny to large numbers of Irishmen living in areas adjoining the Free State the right of being included in the Free State. Are these people to be governed from Westminster against their will or from Dublin with their consent? I have always deprecated the unfairness of judging the British people by the utterances of extreme political partisans or of attributing to them a full and clear understanding of what was done in Ireland in their name. I have done so not merely because I have liked and respected many of your countrymen with whom I was thrown in contact, but because I believe the English people generally shrink from practising palpable injustice in cold blood. I believe the British people do not want to do dishonourable things, but I know they can be misled into doing things which they themselves regret. I ask you now to urge your countrymen to think seriously before they decide that the language of English treaties cannot be properly understood unless secret documents between party politicians are disclosed and read to the accompaniment of threats of the organised murder of dissenters. What the English people have to decide now is whether they are going to carry out the Treaty honourably or not, and if they decide to carry it out whether one of the British parties is or is not to be allowed to preach and practice murder in Ireland in order to deprive Irishmen of rights which they hold from God and which the British Government and people recognise.

I have expressed my views frankly. Like the rest of my countrymen I wish to end all disputes between Ireland and Great Britain, and to live in honourable friendship with the English people. If they stand honourably by the provisions of the treaty that simple act of good faith will not be forgotten.

Most Englishmen are weary of having to concern themselves with Irish affairs. If they honourably carry out the Treaty they will not only keep their good faith unsullied, but Irish political controversies will fade from the British political landscape. An arbitrary and inequitable division of Ireland must produce ill-will between our countries.

No. 274 NAI DT S4084

Memorandum by Kevin O'Higgins on the question of an offer to Northern Ireland, with covering letter by O'Higgins
(Confidential) (C. 1987/24)

DUBLIN, 29 September 1924

To each member of the Executive Council.

The memorandum which is circulated herewith is an elaboration of the one which I have previously circulated on the 25th instant[1] on the question of the advisability of making some public offer to the North if the Bill providing for the final constitution of the Boundary Commission becomes law.

In view of the possibility that the Bill will secure a fairly speedy passage into law I think that the Executive Council would need to come to an early decision on the question of whether such an offer ought in fact be made and we could then consider the occasion on which, and the form in which, it should be made public.

I feel that an approach by the British soon after the Bill becomes law is almost inevitable and it is a question whether we ought not to be first in the field with a reasonable offer calculated to command support in England and even to some extent in the North-east.

Perhaps this matter could be dealt with by the Executive Council at a meeting called for some day this week.

[copy letter unsigned]
Aire Dlí agus Cirt

[1] No. 272 above.

Draft outline of possible Offer to Northern Ireland.
N.B. This outline has been drawn up on the supposition that the Offer would be made in a speech or statement, immediately after the Agreement Bill has become Law in Great Britain.

I. The Government of Saorstát Éireann considers that with the successful passage of the Confirmation of Agreement Bill through the British Parliament the time has come for a further statement of its position with regard to Northern Ireland.

In the first place we must acknowledge that the British Government has kept faith, and has taken the necessary steps to implement the Treaty. The course is now plainly open to the Boundary Commission, and we believe that we can expect a fair deal from it. But before the Commission actually enters upon its work, we have thought it our duty to consider whether, in the interests of the country as a whole, the Commission does in fact provide the best method of dealing with the problem. In judging of this we have had several considerations in mind.

(a) The Boundary Commission has never been regarded by us as the most satisfactory method. This may be seen from

(1) The alternative put before Northern Ireland in Articles 14 and 15 of the Treaty.

(2) The Craig-Collins Pact.

(3) The appeal to Northern Ireland in a speech of President Cosgrave on the eve of their voting out.

(b) The Boundary Commission, while adequate to its own purposes of determining a new Boundary, cannot deal with other and more important matters such as the alleviation of the condition of those of our supporters (probably the majority) who would still be left in Northern Ireland, or the larger questions of the future relations between North and South.

(c) We, like the Northern Government, approach the Commission with a feeling of uncertainty as to its result, nor can either of us believe that a settlement imposed by an external arbitrator [will] be as satisfactory as one reached by agreement among Irishmen.

(d) While we cannot be deterred by threats of violence from asserting the just rights of our people, and while we do not believe that the operation of a statutory Commission gives any excuse for such violence, nevertheless we would do all in our power to avoid bitterness and ill-feeling and to ensure goodwill among all sections of Irishmen.

II. The Government has, therefore, decided to place all its cards on the table and to make a definite offer of an alternative form of settlement. We do this without prejudice to our rights (now fully acknowledged) to the Commission, to which we will have recourse should the alternative offer be rejected. But we put forward now what we believe to be a better way, in the interests of all Ireland, and we beg all the parties concerned to give it their most serious consideration.

We do not believe that the Boundary question, taken by itself alone, is a matter on which agreement by negotiation is likely. It must not be taken by itself alone, but in conjunction with other matters, which are really of greater importance, and on which it is an obvious interest of both parties to reach agreement. There will be a general consensus of opinion that the interest of the country demands two things:

(a) Not the shifting of the Boundary but the removal of the Boundary, or failing that the removal so far as possible of its disadvantages and inconveniences.

(Quote Craig's speech saying he wishes such a state of things that no one should care which side of the Boundary he was on.)

(b) Real peace and friendship between North and South, to be secured by the settlement of outstanding differences and by securing means of close co-operation for the future.

It is scarcely open to question that the economic results of a Boundary, especially a Customs Boundary, are disadvantageous to both parts of the country; nor that real peace and prosperity is possible so long as the two Governments remain so completely aloof as at present.

We do not propose to hark back to any of the plans formerly suggested, such as that contained in Articles 14 and 15 of the Treaty, nor the Council of Ireland, but to propound one which appears both sound and practicable.

III. With these ends in view we propose:

(a) An all-Ireland authority to be established, to consist of the Oireachtas and the Northern Parliament sitting together, [these to be elected on the same franchise, and][1] the number of members in each to be in proportion to population.

(b)The Powers retained by the British Parliament under the Act of 1920 to be transferred either to the all-Ireland authority or to the Northern Parliament as specified.

(c) The all-Ireland authority to control:

(1) External Affairs. Northerners could thus be among the representatives at League of Nations, Imperial Conference etc.

(2) Customs and Excise. (But see below (e)).

(3) Imposition of Income Tax etc. (to ensure uniformity), but not necessarily collection of such taxes.

(4) Such other matters as the two parties agree to transfer to central control. (It will probably be found that, if and when negotiations take place the desirability of centralisation will be plain in the case of e.g. Fisheries (as in Act of 1920), compilation of Census and other statistics, scientific research, etc.)

(d) The all-Ireland authority to meet alternately in Dublin and Belfast. The Governor-General to be appointed alternately on the recommendation of the Free State and Northern Governments.

(e) Abolition of the Customs barrier in Ireland, and collection of all Customs duties at the ports, under central authority. In order, however, to prevent any possible imposition of duties such as would injure Northern industries, a Customs Convention such as will suit those industries to be concluded as part

[1] A handwritten marginal note reads: 'suggested omission' and the square brackets are inserted by hand.

of the original agreement and to remain in force for a fixed term of years.

(This question of Customs will probably be the crux. In order to meet any possible objections an elaborate agreement may be necessary, corresponding to the Railway Agreement at the time of South African union.)

(f) Restoration of Proportional Representation in Northern Ireland, reversal of gerrymandering, and disbandment of Specials.

(g) Northern minority to enter the Northern Parliament.

(h) Minor alterations of the Boundary by agreement. Or, if thought preferable, Northern Ireland to consist of Nine Counties.

IV. These proposals are put forward as covering the main points at issue, and as giving the outline of a practicable scheme. Obviously they will require elaboration in detail, such as is impossible in one short statement. We do not ask for immediate acceptance or rejection of the proposals as they stand, but we ask for their acceptance as a basis of negotiation. We propose that such negotiations should take place between the two Governments, in Ireland, at the earliest convenient moment.

It may be well to recapitulate what is offered to the North:

(a) No cutting down of territory except by consent.

(b) Abolition of the drawbacks of the Boundary.

(c) Financial advantages through the transfer to them of powers retained by Westminster.

(d) Real peace and stability.

In return what we hope to gain:

(a) Fair treatment for our supporters in the North.

(b) Cooperation of the whole country in necessary work.

(c) Again, peace and stability.

No. 275 NAI DFA Minister's Office Files (1924)

Desmond FitzGerald to Timothy A. Smiddy (Washington)
(Confidential)

Dublin, 30 September 1924

Dear Professor,

I have to-day sent the following wire-

'SAORSTÁT, WASHINGTON: WRITING SUGGESTING YOU MAKE SHORT VISIT IRELAND WITH LEAST POSSIBLE DELAY. THIS WIRE CONFIDENTIAL YOU ALONE. IF FEASIBLE RETURN SAY YOU HAVE ASKED PERMISSION RETURN TO ATTEND PRIVATE AFFAIRS. LEAST POSSIBLE PUBLICITY. ESTERO.'

There was some thought of my going to America on a short visit, but as in view of the approaching Presidential elections my presence there might be represented as having a political significance it seems more feasible at the moment for you to make a short visit to Ireland, especially as possibly during the next month everybody there is pre-occupied with the Presidential election there may be less to demand your immediate attention there than after the election.

On your visit here we can go into the whole matter of the personnel of your new office and a dozen other matters that arise with the change created by your new status.

In my wire I suggest that the least possible publicity be given to your return and that by implying that the suggestion of the visit comes from you and not from here, and that you return for your personal business you prevent any significance being given to this visit. I do this because I have reason to believe that there are certain people over there working against you personally, and they might be glad to give the suggestion about that your being called back implies reprimand.

I may say that the reason I want you to come back is to put you *au fait* and on your guard. Regard this letter as personal from me to you.

Of course if it is not feasible for you to return[,] wire me to that effect and I will come out to see you as soon as it seems possible to do so without my visit being misconstrued.

You may look on this letter as from your friend D.F. and not from the minister.

[copy letter unsigned]

No. 276 UCDA P4/419

Handwritten letter from William T. Cosgrave to Hugh Kennedy
DUBLIN, 30 September 1924

A Chara Dhíl,
I enclose herewith for your comments a proposal[1] which has been made in connection with the Boundary.

It is in the strictest confidence that I am sending it & is with a view to getting your advice generally on the proposals.

There are some which appear to me to be unworkable but I prefer not to do more in the matter writing to you than to say that.

The general line – ultimate unity is good. It can come in many ways – it may come eventually if we have good government down here but good . . . . .[2] from a relatively poor country & from a people so long divorced from any respect for order.

I do not wish anyone to know that I have consulted you in the matter & perhaps to avoid any possible complication you might – if time permits – type any suggestions.

With many thanks in anticipation & of course a wish that the whole of the proposal be considered in its every respect. That is to say what you think of the proposal as a whole & in its parts.

Mise, le meas mór agat,
LIAM T. MACCOSGAIR

I would want an opinion by 10 AM – as the council meets at 11.

L.T. MACC

[1] Not identified, but possibly No. 274 above.
[2] There are four words here which are illegible.

No. 277 NAI DT S4084

Memorandum on Northern Ireland policy by Diarmuid O'Hegarty with covering letter

DUBLIN, 15 October 1924

1. In submitting the attached memorandum for the Committee's consideration, I realise that the proposals it contains are likely to be regarded as revolutionary, and I place on record that they are solely my personal views.
2. If they were accepted as the basis of an offer to Craig, the details would, naturally, not be divulged in the first instance.
3. An offer on this basis would be worded somewhat as follows:-
   1. The Irish Free State to embrace all Ireland and to be governed by a Federal Government and Legislature with two subordinate Governments and Legislatures.
   2. Federal legislature to consist of two houses – the lower house to be elected on proportional representation, and the constituencies to be determined on basis of population – the second chamber to have two electoral areas, viz., Southern Ireland and Northern Ireland with Northern representation in excess of due proportion. Powers of local parliaments to be somewhat as at present subject to financial arrangements in paragraph 6.
   3. A list of key industries to be prepared by each local legislature with approval of federal legislature. No increase in existing taxes on products of, or raw material for, these industries to be imposed without consent of local legislature concerned.
   4. Constitutional provisions to secure equal rights in proportion to population for candidates for public Federal appointments from each local area.
   5. All minorities to have a voice in legislation in proportion to their numbers.
   6. All taxation to be federal and uniform. Revenue to be attributed to local areas as follows:-
      (a) Indirect revenue on population basis
      (b) Direct revenue as collected.
      Expenditure on Federal administration to be attributed on population basis. Balance of revenue attributed to each area to be at the disposition of local parliament.
4. In the event of these proposals being agreed no difficulty arises about the settlement of the boundary. In fact, from the point of view of safeguarding minorities the allocation of nine counties to Northern Ireland would probably be a good bargain.

[Memorandum]

1. In order to consider any draft proposals which might be made to Craig after the third Commissioner has been appointed, it is necessary to form a clear idea of what the object of such proposals is to be. The object has been vaguely described as 'Union.' Union is conceivable on any one of three bases:-
   (a) Union on the basis of equality of citizenship;
   (b) Union with the 26 Counties predominant;
   (c) Union with the 6 Counties predominant.

Craig would in all probability accept (c), and reject (b). We would certainly reject (c) and accept (b). The only possibility of agreement is (a).

2. Various schemes for bringing about Union have been put forward. An application of the above test to these schemes will be instructive.

THE TREATY SCHEME provides an All-Ireland Parliament legislating in all respects for 26 Counties and in certain important matters for Northern Ireland, with a separate Parliament for other affairs in the latter territory. The Treaty, by the way, does not provide that the Northern Parliament would be subordinate to the All Ireland Parliament as it is at the moment subordinate to the British Parliament, although the All-Ireland Parliament from its control of Finance would be able to exert pressure upon it. Doubtless the relations between the Parliaments would have to be more closely defined in the Constitution, which would also contain machinery for securing the safeguards in Article 15. These safeguards would in fact be devices to prevent the All-Ireland Parliament from legislating for the Northern Area on certain vital matters such as Customs and Excise without the consent of the 6 Counties. Such an arrangement also connotes a similar veto on such legislation so far as the 26 Counties are concerned, because if there had been no opting out it is inconceivable that a Customs boundary would be set up, and hence Southern Customs duties would have to correspond with Northern Customs duties.

The Treaty Scheme is *unworkable*, because the senior Parliament would in effect be subject to the junior Parliament. To put it in another form, if the words of Article 15 were to be implemented, in a manner acceptable to Sir James Craig, the scheme would fall under head (c) and the majority here would certainly not agree to it.

THE COUNCIL OF IRELAND SCHEME as contained in the British memo. of 1st February, 1924,[1] is unworkable for the reasons stated in our memorandum – (a) the subjects for legislation are too limited, (b) the double majority brings the scheme under heading (c).

THE WALLER SCHEME[2] comes closer to fundamentals. It has certain obvious drawbacks. It gives a legislature without an Executive. It properly gives the All-Ireland legislature control of External Affairs, but on the other hand it gives the Executives of the subordinate parliaments alternately power to appoint the Governor-General who is the channel through which the most important external affairs are transacted. The same objectionable anomalies regarding Customs, etc. are retained, but in general the scheme comes under heading (b). I believe that the absence of provision for an Executive for the All-Ireland legislation apart from any other consideration vitiates the proposal.

[1] Not printed.
[2] See above No. 272.

3. If there is a genuine desire to achieve Union it can only be successful if it conforms generally to two conditions, viz:-

(a) that it accepts the principle outlined in *1* (a) that a Northern citizen is entitled to equal consideration with a Southern citizen, and vice versa;

(b) that it renders a majority incapable of infringing 'the rights' of a minority as distinct from 'the privileges of a minority'.

No scheme which creates or establishes a definitely privileged minority can ultimately be satisfactory. The very existence of such privileges provides a raison d'etre for a party to maintain them.

4. Any scheme based upon an All-Ireland Parliament legislating for the 26 Counties on all matters, and restricted in so far as the 6 Counties are concerned by a second, even though subordinate[,] parliament possessing complete legislative control over a very large number of important affairs establishes the 6 Counties in a privileged position. A party will always be able to exist for the maintenance of that privilege – to prevent in fact a complete fusion of interests.

5. It is quite evident that Northern Ireland will not consent to give up its legislature or its Executive as it is at present constituted. The problem then resolves itself into finding a solution which while it preserves intact the Northern Parliament and Government will at the same time deprive it of the privileged position which it occupies under Articles 14 and 15. I submit that the only possible solution is on federal lines. We must set off the Northern Parliament and Government by a Southern Parliament and Government co-equal in status, privileges and power. The Dominion of Ireland would then be governed in respect of all matters, exclusive of affairs of local importance, by a Federal Parliament. Matters of local importance would be dealt with by two co-equal local parliaments. A rough memorandum showing the relation of the three Parliaments is attached.[1]

6. One grave objection to this solution is that it opens the way for a separate dominion of Northern Ireland. I admit this, but I contend that this objection is applicable with equal force to all the other apparently less revolutionary proposals. The mildest is the British proposal of February, 1924, which transfers to the All-Ireland Authority control of Fisheries, Railways and Diseases of Animals legislation. Let us suppose for a moment that this Scheme were tried and found to fail. The All-Ireland Authority would in some manner or other resolve itself out of existence. Can anyone contend, in such event, that the body would recommend that its powers in relation to Northern Ireland should be re-transferred to Great Britain? Is it not inconceivable that Free State representatives would father such a suggestion as against a proposal to place them in the hands of Irishmen?

Whether we like it or not, the Irish Free State will ultimately find itself unable to continue to demand the retention by Great Britain of powers in respect of

[1] Not printed.

any portion of Ireland. Such a course may be within our powers under the Treaty – but once it has been established, if it is established, that a United Ireland is impracticable, it would be contrary to all our protestations to prevent the governed of say, for argument's sake, the Six Counties, from choosing the form of government under which they desire to live.

7. The most probable objection will be, however, on the grounds that such a proposal reduces the sovereignty of the Oireachtas. Of course it does, but so does every other proposal which has yet been made. The present Oireachtas will have to delegate powers to any All-Ireland body – even if that body is comprised of the present Oireachtas 'in toto' with additions from the Six Counties. This objection is based upon a desire for the Union of Ireland with the 26 Counties predominant which is, I believe, the correct exposition of the views of the majority of our people who talk about Unity.

8. The annexed memorandum on a Federal Ireland[1] contains very rough proposals for:

(a) The acquisition and subdivision of powers as between the three Parliaments.
(b) Constitutional safeguards for minorities.
(c) The establishment of a Federal Executive.

9. Behind the proposal is the hope that with the objective of privilege maintenance withdrawn, the All-Ireland Body will in time tend to restrict more and more the powers of the local Parliaments until their disappearance on the grounds of inutility will ultimately become a general popular demand. The proposal will in all probability be rejected by the North-East because it gives them no dominance. Undoubtedly they get a very big preference in the Seanad – the Unionists holding for twelve years from 1922 an equal voice with Nationalists, i.e. 15 of the nominated Southern members with 30 Northerns out of a total of 90. No effort has been made to go into details about the financial provisions or the Judiciary. These are matters which have many reactions and will require very careful consideration.

10. The only reasonable alternative is, in my opinion, to forego all thought of political union, to give full Dominion powers to the Six Counties subject to a Customs convention. This proposal is likely to be quite unacceptable in the Irish Free State, although it has, in justice, more to be said for it than the 'wart' solution which was originated by de Valera and has since been the basis of all the suggested solutions of the problem.

[signed] DIARMUID Ó HÉIGEARTAIGH

[1] Not printed.

No. 278 NAI DFA Letter Books Department of Justice 1923-25

Joseph P. Walshe to the Private Secretary to the Minister for Justice[1]
(Copy)

DUBLIN, 21 October 1924

YOUR REFERENCE C.2073/24
MR. O'HIGGINS'S OXFORD ADDRESS.

This Ministry has mainly concerned itself with work of a character preparatory to the gradual taking over of all our external relations.

Professor Smiddy's appointment as Minister in Washington establishes direct contact between us and the U.S.A. and completely eliminates the Foreign Office from the whole field of our relations with that country.

America is the only country with which our relations are entirely free and independent from any outside control. Mr O'Higgins may wish to emphasize the need for equally independent relations of the Dominions with all countries if the Commonwealth is to continue to exist. The entire trend of thought both conservative and liberal in Canada is in favour of complete control of all external relations.

As far as the broad lines of international policy are concerned, Ireland's geographical position will always oblige her to have a policy similar in all important respects to that of Great Britain so much so that Saorstát Diplomatic Representatives in the principal countries of the world should be welcomed by Great Britain as certain supporters in essential points.

Mr O'Higgins may wish to refer to League of Nations, International Conferences, power of making treaties, etc., or other matters connected with this Department. I shall be very happy to give you any information he requires on specific questions, but the main accomplishment in our external relations is the establishment of a Minister Plenipotentiary in Washington. Ireland is the first and only State of the Commonwealth so far to have such representation.

[copy letter unsigned]
Rúnaí

No. 279 UCDA P24/131

Report of the Committee appointed to consider an offer to Northern Ireland, with covering letter from Michael McDunphy to Ernest Blythe
(Secret) (S. 4048)

DUBLIN, 22 October 1924

To:
Minister for Finance
On the 1st October the Executive Council appointed a Committee, consisting of the following:-
(a) Mr. J.J. McElligott
(b) Mr. D. O'Hegarty
(c) Mr. E. Stephens

[1] See No. 281 below.

(d) Mr. B.C. Waller
(e) Mr. J.A. Costello
(f) Mr. George Murnaghan

to consider and to make recommendations to the Government as to the nature of an offer which could reasonably be made to the North East after the completion of the constitution of the Boundary Commission.

The Committee has now made its report and I enclose a copy for your information.

It will be observed that the report has been signed by the first four above mentioned members of the Committee. The other two, namely, Messrs Costello and Murnaghan, were not available when the report was completed, nor have they seen it in its final form, but their views have been embodied as far as possible.

[signed] M MacDonnchadha
a.s. Rúnaí

Report of Committee appointed to consider an Offer to the North-East.

The Committee appointed by the Executive Council has given careful attention to a number of plans which might form the basis of a union of Ireland, to be proposed in an offer to the North-East.

There are many possible forms which such a union might take, and each of them is open to many modifications in detail. In considering the Plans put forward the Committee has had in mind two main criteria, first their inherent desirability and workability, and second the likelihood or otherwise of their acceptance. Since these two considerations are often in conflict, and since it is impossible without knowledge of all the political factors to determine what weight is to be given to either, the Committee has felt it impossible to recommend any single scheme worked out in detail as that which should be offered. Five possible schemes are, therefore, set out below.

The Committee finds itself, however, very nearly in agreement as to the main features of any plan which can stand a chance of acceptance in both parts of the country. The principal points which such a plan should embody are the following:-

(1) The setting up of an all-Ireland Assembly to administer through its own Executive such of the powers at present exercised over Northern Ireland by the British or Northern Parliaments, and such corresponding powers exercised over the Free State by the Oireachtas, as may be assigned to it by agreement.
(2) The transfer to Northern Ireland of such of the services now under the control of the British Parliament as are not assigned to the all-Ireland Assembly.
(3) The following are the powers some or all of which might be assigned to the all-Ireland Assembly under (1):-

(a) Powers reserved to Great Britain under Sections 4 and 9 of the Government of Ireland Act, 1920.
(b) Council of Ireland Services under 1920 Act (Railways, Fisheries and Diseases of Animals).
(c) Certain services at present under the control of Northern Ireland, e.g. Agriculture, Registrar-General's Department (Registration of Births, Deaths

and Marriages, and Census), Scientific Research.

The number of these matters to be centralised would be the subject of negotiation, and would vary considerably according to whether a looser or a more complete form of union were adopted.

(4) The all-Ireland Assembly to be so constituted, either by way of special representation or by way of constitutional limitations, as to ensure that no legislation can become effective over the Northern Area which is detrimental to the interests of the majority of its inhabitants.

(5) A provision ensuring that minorities will have a due voice in legislation, if possible by the continuance of Proportional Representation, and at least by the repeal of legislation for gerrymandering constituencies. Minority rights should also be protected in regard to local bodies.

(6) A provision that a majority shall not exercise undue powers in the distribution of patronage.

(7) Representation of Northern Ireland at Westminster to cease.

(8) Financial arrangements in the interests of both parts of the country including the alteration or waiving of Article 5 of the Treaty.

(9) It would be desirable to make some effort towards securing uniformity in the level of taxation in the two areas, particularly in regard to Customs, so as to remove the present land boundary. It is also recognised as desirable that Excise and Inland Revenue Duties should be as far as possible identical. At present there is a considerable disparity between the two areas in regard to quite a number of duties and taxes which either do not exist in the North or are charged there at a lower level. The abolition and reduction of these duties and taxes in the Saorstát so as to produce uniformity with the North are apparently not quite feasible at the moment and may not be for some time to come. Customs uniformity so as to eliminate the boundary is, however, not beyond the reach of possibility, but it should be noted that difference in internal duties, even though inevitable, will have various undesirable reactions which need not be specified here. The North would probably ask for some special understanding in regard to the non-imposition of tariffs which would injuriously affect Northern industries. There would be no objection to the giving of such an undertaking.

In setting out these main features to be included in a settlement the Committee has had in view the following points. First, it must conform to the principle of equality of citizenship, regarding a Northern citizen as entitled to equal consideration with a Southern citizen, and vice-versa, and must not establish any section in a position of predominance. Second, it must render a majority incapable of infringing 'the rights of a minority' as distinct from 'the privileges of a minority.'

For these reasons it seems necessary to place the Governments and legislatures which deal with the local affairs of North and South on level terms, while placing under central control as many powers and services as possible. This implies two things which may be considered objectionable, first some diminution of the powers at present held by the Oireachtas and second a considerable increase of the powers of Northern Ireland.

As regards the first point it can be replied that while the Oireachtas as at present constituted will give up certain of its powers to a central body, yet this is no real loss to the country if it means that those powers will in future be exercised by one central body over the whole of Ireland. It is a step towards that union which is generally desired, and in fact is inevitable in any scheme of union short of the complete absorption or the subordination of the North.

As to the second, objection may be taken to any plan which makes possible, now or in the future, the obtaining of Dominion powers by Northern Ireland. This might come through a breakdown at some time of the union, and the reversion of the centralised powers not to Great Britain, as formerly, but to Northern Ireland. *The majority of the Committee hold*, however, that this is a risk which must be run if any union is to be attained, and are confident that subsequent developments will be in the opposite direction, not towards a new separation but towards further union. *Several members* also are of the opinion that in any case it would not be possible or indeed desirable for us to prevent the gradual acquisition of Dominion powers by the North once the Boundary question was settled, if such powers were desired; and that therefore it is better to offer such an extension of powers combined with some centralisation. Also there are indeed many reasons for holding that from our point of view it would be preferable that Northern Ireland should obtain Dominion powers and do away with its representation at Westminster, even if that was combined with no centralisation at first, rather than that it should continue in its present position.

Five Plans of union are given in some detail below.[1] They can here be briefly summarised, with the advantages and disadvantages which are considered to attach to each of them.

(A) *Federation.*
Legislatures for Southern and Northern Ireland with a Federal legislature. This is believed to be constitutionally sound and workable, and, if acceptable, would probably turn out the most satisfactory of the plans submitted. It would seem, however, to stand less chance of acceptance than some of the others, since it means a very large step towards complete union, and could be represented in the North as 'coming under a Dublin Parliament' and absorption in the Free State.

(B) *Subordinate Parliament in Northern Ireland.*
(As in Articles 14 and 15 of the Treaty).
This is held by one Member of the Committee to be the wisest and safest plan, as based definitely on the Treaty. The majority of the Committee, however, consider it offends against several of the principles laid down above, by placing the North in a position which is in some respects subordinate and in others privileged. Also since it has already been rejected, it seems very unlikely that it would be accepted if again put forward.

(C) *Joint Sittings of Free State and Northern Legislatures*, as one body with a responsible Executive. This bears a close resemblance to the Federal plan, attaining practically the same ends by different methods. It might prove more

[1] Not printed.

acceptable, as preserving more clearly the powers of the Northern Parliament. On the other hand it is objectionable as complicating the administrative and electoral machinery.

(D) *Central Council of Ireland.*
This, it should be noted, is not the Council provided for in the Act of 1920, but one formed on a different basis, partly by direct election, and partly by choice of the two legislatures. It gives less centralisation than the former plans and thus is less desirable, but perhaps more likely to be accepted for that very reason. Objection, has, however, been taken to it, as taking away from the powers of the Oireachtas and enabling the North to retain connection with Great Britain.

(E) *Central Assembly with safeguards.*
This provides for discussion in the Assembly of proposals affecting the whole country, but prevents their application to either area without its consent. The immediate centralisation would be of slight extent, but it would permit of easy development towards closer union. Because of its ample safeguards for the North it might prove more acceptable.

The Committee has given some consideration to the form in which an offer should be made. Should it present a detailed scheme of settlement, such as one of those outlined below; or should it be in more vague and general terms? The Committee are of opinion that it would be unwise to put forward too explicitly details of a scheme of future Government both because such details would be better worked out in the negotiations, and because much detail at present would mean presenting a bigger target for criticism, and would divert attention from the larger advantages held out in the offer. On the other hand the Committee believe that something more definite is required than a mere general proposal to discuss 'union,' and consider that the offer should embody most or all of the matters mentioned in the nine points suggested above. It would thus concentrate attention mainly on the objects which a scheme of union is designed to secure, rather than on the detailed machinery by which they are to be attained.

(Signed) J.J. McElligott
Diarmuid O'Hegarty
E.M. Stephens
B.C. Waller
21st October, 1924

No. 280 NAI DT S1801K

Eoin MacNeill to all members of the Executive Council
(Copy)

Dublin, 24 October 1924

It should be a cardinal point in regard of any offer of a settlement with 'Northern Ireland' that any such offer should not go beyond general terms sufficient to convey a notion of the character of the proposals to the ordinary public mind, and should not attempt to sketch out the working details.

It is valuable to consider the possible or probable details of any scheme of settlement as showing the merits of the plan, but the publication of any scheme in detail, however excellent, as a preliminary to conference, would be altogether fatal, unless the purpose was merely tactical, to put the other side in the wrong, which even as tactics is of no value to us.

The reasons against proposing a scheme in detail are quite conclusive:

The opponents of a settlement would have the opportunity of veiling their opposition to unity and concentrating on criticism of details, endeavouring to prove these bad or unworkable. It is obvious that if once agreement was reached on any general principle of unity, all difficulties on details could be overcome, but to proceed on the converse method would make agreement on a general principle or plan practically impossible.

The public mind, both in Ireland, Free State and Six Counties, and in Great Britain, would be easily confused about details, and even those most friendly to a national settlement would be led into endless controversies. In Ireland, especially, people delight in criticism and in propounding elaborate schemes in advance.

Hence, in any public offer, not a single word should be used that is not calculated to bring the two sides together in the hope of a friendly discussion.

(signed) EOIN MACNEILL

No. 281 NAI DFA P424

Extract from an address by Kevin O'Higgins to the Irish Society at Oxford University

OXFORD, 31 October 1924

[Matter omitted]

There followed three crowded years of unprecedented national effort, years in which practically the entire country rallied behind its proclaimed Dáil, with its subterranean Departments and its loose flung guerrilla territorial forces. It was a people at bay in defence of its native institutions which every proclamation served but to rivet in their hearts, while Dublin Castle fighting its grim battle for existence struck and struck again with all the ferocity and cunning it had learned through the centuries. Let no man attempt to pick his steps amidst that kind of welter[,] weighing with meticulous scales the rights and wrongs. The people fought as they could[,] remorselessly and desperately. The Castle gave measure for measure. When bullet, rope, bomb, mine[,] torch and thumb-screw had made in fierce crescendo their contributions to the controversy there came the truce, the negotiations and finally that which Miss MacSwiney and Lord Carson from their respective angles call 'The Great Surrender'.

Ireland secured by that 'surrender' a constitutional status equal to that of Canada. 'Canada' said the late Mr. Bonar Law 'is by the full admission of British statesmen equal in status to Great Britain and as free as Great Britain'. The constitutional status of Ireland, therefore, as determined by the Treaty of 1921 is a status of coequality with Britain within the British Commonwealth. The second Article of the Constitution of the Free State declares that 'All powers of Government and all authority legislative, executive and Judicial in Ireland are

derived from the people of Ireland.' Yet the right of the people of Ireland to found a State on that broad basis of Democracy was challenged more fiercely than Dublin Castle was challenged by many who had never challenged Dublin Castle and by methods that had not been adopted against Dublin Castle.
[Matter omitted]

No. 282 NAI DT S1801K

James McNeill to Desmond FitzGerald (Dublin)
LONDON, 31 October 1924

My dear Minister,
I enclose a note which I wrote in anticipation of election results, when the coming defeat of the Labour Government was certain. When asking for instructions I have ventured to place my own views before you. As Mr. O'Higgins was passing through when the note was ready for despatch I showed it to him. I don't know what his considered opinion will be as to the action to be taken but he agreed unreservedly as to the need for serious consideration at once.

Yours sincerely,
(signed) JAMES MCNEILL

[enclosure]

It seems desirable to consider now the need for obtaining from the new Conservative Government here a definite assurance as to its attitude towards the findings of the Boundary Commission. President Cosgrave has, on behalf of the Free State, stated that the findings of the Commission would be accepted. It ought to go without saying that the British Government would accept a division of Ireland settled by a Commission of which two out of three members were its own nominees. But it does not go without saying. The statements of Conservatives likely to be Ministers point to refusal to be honourably bound by any decision which the Six County Government would like to resist. Their conduct as regards Article 12 in the recent past is anything but a guarantee that they will not take advantage of any pretext for refusing to abide by the decision, and their attitude towards Ireland in the previous past must excite graver distrust. The seventy-one peers who resolved on the 8th instant that nothing but a mere readjustment of boundary could be enforced include men who would be in any conservative or coalition ministry. That explanatory resolution will now presumably rank as an honourable pledge published on this occasion to all the world.

When the new British Government comes into office our Government ought to be able to state at an early date that that Government has undertaken to abide by the decision. It may claim to be placed in that position as a matter of right. It owes it to its own people (not merely its sectional supporters) who accept the position that the decision binds both parties to have all reasonable doubts removed. It is needful to ensure that in any boundary discussions with Six County representatives it is recognised that the Free State's right to have the decision enforced cannot be evaded. Conferences in which the finality of the Commission's decisions is not regarded as undoubted, however distasteful that may be to the Northern Government, would be either useless or mischievous. If the British Government claims on grounds of 'equity' or fidelity to party pledges the right to abstain from preventing its subjects from violently resisting the decision, the fact should be elicited beforehand. We thought we knew what Conservative ministers meant by Article 12. We find that their later statements did not justify our belief.

If President Cosgrave is asked in Dáil Éireann whether the British Government has definitely undertaken loyally to abide by the Commission's award what will he say? Will he pledge his Government's credit for them and state that the 'honourable' party pledges given by Conservative ministers will be disregarded, even if a substantial area and population are removed from the jurisdiction of the Northern Government? Will he say he sees no reason to ask for a definite assurance?

Should there be no pronouncement from the new Government the organisers of fanaticism here and their dupes in Ulster will work up opposition in advance, and there will be murder and lawlessness not merely on the border but all over the six counties if the fanatics are disappointed as we believe they will be. If the British Government speaks out now there will be a great deal of furious talk both here and there for a time but little or no trouble later. Even the most elusive Conservative Unionist minister would find it hard to explain away a definite undertaking. He would not be allowed to do so by British, Colonial and American opinion. We should, I think, take pains to obviate a crop of McMahon cases and Cushendall cases, the crime of most of the new victims being a desire to be governed by their own countrymen after the British claim to govern them had been extinguished.

If the new Government is allowed to remain silent until the decision is announced they can then cast about for an excuse for honouring party pledges especially if the anti-Irish firebrands here and the fanatics in Ulster have been organising opposition. It is difficult to see what we can gain by delay in coming to a clear understanding or how we can pretend to have no uneasiness and no fear of another and much worse pogrom in the six counties. Possibly some Unionist elements in the Free State would think and speak more clearly if the point was settled at once.

The British Government might make the announcement in its own way provided it made it. Possibly its opponents will ask questions in Parliament. Should we leave the task of elucidation to Labour or Radical members of Parliament here? I think in similar circumstances Canada, Australia, etc., would do as I suggest.

I quite recognise that if our Government asks for a definite assurance and receives an unsatisfactory reply it may have to reconsider its whole attitude to the Commission. That would be most unpleasant but the Council have individually and collectively accepted unpleasant consequences before now. I don't know how the British Government will be constituted, or if there will be a coalition. But I cannot imagine any Government or party or combination which would not be rent asunder if it objected to giving an assurance. I think you will get a just view of balanced Imperialist, but not pro-Irish, opinion in an article on Ireland in the October Quarterly Review. No British Government could in cold blood refuse to be bound, and it is our business to see that the assurance is given in cold blood. I do not suggest that any menacing representation be made but I think it should be stated that our participation in the commission assumed unqualified acceptance of the Commission's decision. We should ask for an assurance of reciprocity. President Cosgrave's recognition of the good faith of previous Governments seems to provide a convenient peg for a new Ulster coat to be hung on.

Another consideration is that it would be well to obtain the assurance before Feetham's attitude was known or could be forecasted. Probably our Commissioner might like to know whether he should get down to real work before his Government was satisfied that the decision would be operative. Are the decisions to be final as against him only? Will the government behind his two colleagues be allowed to reserve a power of review of which his Government has publicly divested itself?

I suggest that the matter be considered without delay. You will understand that I am anxious to do what is right here. Am I to meet the new ministers on the basis of leaving it an open question whether they will accept or reject the decision? You will appreciate my need for precise instructions. The alternative is that on all occasions I speak only my own mind. I do not want to be in the position of talking my own mind when I can talk the mind of the Council and carry out its wishes.

For ready reference a short note is appended giving references to relevant parliamentary utterances of Conservative and other leaders.[1] Your publicity office will be able to locate other utterances, letters and speeches, in the British press during the last two months.

No. 283 NAI DFA 417/105

Michael MacWhite to Joseph P. Walshe (Dublin)
(N.S. 01/185)

GENEVA, 4 November 1924

A Chara,

Now that the Treaty (Confirmation of Agreement) Act for the purpose of supplementing the Treaty of 1921 has come into operation I think it advisable that it should be registered with the League of Nations, in accordance with Article 18 of the Covenant.

The registration of this Act will help to keep it in the public mind that all agreements arrived at between the Saorstát and Great Britain are of an international character and cannot be regarded as internal questions. Besides, the more the precedent created by the registration of the Anglo-Irish Treaty is followed the stronger will our position become in the eyes of the other Members of the League.

For registration purposes three copies of the document should be forwarded, of which one should be duly certified as true.

Is mise, le meas,
[signed] M. MACWHITE

[1] Not located.

No. 284 NAI DT S1801K

Extract from minutes of a meeting of the Executive Council (C.2/145)
DUBLIN, 10 November 1924

BOUNDARY COMMISSION. Letter from the High Commissioner
Consideration was given to a communication addressed by the High Commissioner in London to the Minister for External Affairs[1] in which he suggested the desirability of seeking from the new Conservative Government in Great Britain a definite assurance as to its attitude towards the findings of the Boundary Commission.

It was considered undesirable that any such assurance should be sought.

No. 285 NAI DFA Minister's Office files (1924-25)

Handwritten letter from James McNeill to Desmond FitzGerald (Dublin)
LONDON, 17 November 1924

My dear Minister,
Thanks for your letter regarding the Boundary question etc.[2]

I write this personally as I think I ought to be a model of discretion. The High Comm[issioner]s. were asked to meet Mr. Baldwin to-day at 10 D[ownin]g. St. We all went, the P.M., Mr. Austin Chamberlain, & Mr. Amery were also present. The P.M. said he had asked us to hear what the F.[oreign] Sec[retar]y. had to say. He did not quite say that this was definitely the beginning of a new system but it was, I think, implied. The H.[igh] C[ommissioner]s are apparently to be told what are the main things impending & what are the considerations regarded as most seriously affecting policy, & it was stated that they would use their own judgment as to what they passed on. Matters which were still the subject of consideration could be disclosed, the object being to obviate the need for asking the Dominion G[o]v[ernmen]ts. to assent to definite proposals about matters of which they had no previous knowledge.

Mr. Chamberlain mentioned the Geneva protocol. He said neither he nor the Cabinet had had time to give this full consideration. He had this morning discussed it with Mr. Ramsay MacDonald formally. The latter considered that it did not add to the Covenant of the League but gave more precise definition to the obligations incurred by members. There was a little discussion on this, the H.[igh] C.[ommissioner] for Australia referring to Japan's interpretation & the Japanese view regarding immigration. However, Mr. Chamberlain stated that he was still examining the question & that he had asked for a postponement of the League Council meeting in December to enable this G[o]v[ernmen]t. to consider the matter. France & Belgium had signed the protocol.

The position in Egypt was that Zaqhlul Pasha[3] was not content with the reservations made by Gt. Britain when Egyptian Independence was recognised.

---

[1] See above No. 282.
[2] Letter not located.
[3] Leader of the Wafd party and Egyptian Prime Minister.

The main reservations were the British right to defend the canal, the separation of the Sudan, & the retention of the Judicial Adviser whose presence was regarded as important while foreign nations were told that they would not be allowed to exercise direct pressure on behalf of their own nationals. It was thought that controversy might arise over the re-appointment of the Judicial Adviser, not because of the reservation itself but as a beginning of the anti-reservation campaign. Mr. Larkin[1] asked a few questions about this & indicated that he thought anything like serious trouble over this would not appeal to the man in the street. Mr C. said he did not know if trouble would arise or just what action could be taken but he wanted to let it be known that Zaqhlul would put up a fight on any question. It was added that the Egyptians in the Sudan public service were being urged to side with Zaqhlul's claim to the Sudan. The British Gvt. would adhere to its claim to control the Sudan & would oppose all modifications of the status quo unless Zaqhlul discussed as a basis of the [...][2] complete denial of all British claims.

I think that is a fairly accurate account of what passed, the Foreign Sec[retar]y's statement being at times broken by questions[,] remarks or even rather irrelevant conversations.

I do not know if we are to be asked frequently to such meetings. Mr. A.C. said that while he welcomed all means of informing the dominions he had no cut & dried plan to propose[,] he would almost certainly agree to any form of consultation which the H.[igh] C.[ommissioner]s agreed on. I think that was a very wise & a very safe statement.

As regards the matters mentioned no decision had as yet been reached by the British Gvt. & Mr. A.C. stated he was clearing his own mind. We met at 4.15 p.m. & the meeting lasted about 3/4 hour.

Just before going in I met in the hall Sir James Craig who introduced me to Mr. Pollock,[3] with whom I had a few words about my sister's death. Mr. P. knew my people well.

My taking pains to write privately does not mean that I have become a federalist. I am doing what as an Irishman I think is right.

Yours sincerely,
JAMES MCNEILL

P.S. (Wednesday morning)
To-day's Times suggests that certain topics were discussed. They were not even mentioned. Doubtless some topics had to be mentioned to satisfy public curiosity.

No. 286 NAI DT S1801I

Extract from minutes of a meeting of the Executive Council (C.2/146)
DUBLIN, 19 November 1924

BOUNDARY COMMISSION. Statement to be presented by the Irish Free State.
A statement prepared by the Attorney General for presentation by the Govern-

[1] Peter Larkin, Canadian High Commissioner in London (1922-1930).
[2] Word illegible.
[3] Hugh M. Pollock, Northern Ireland Minister of Finance.

ment of the Irish Free State to the Boundary Commission was approved subject to certain minor amendments. A copy of the statement as approved is attached.[1]

It was arranged that the Attorney General should see the President and discuss the statement with him.

The Secretary was directed to draft a covering letter to accompany the statement, in reply to the communication addressed by the Secretary of the Boundary Commission to the President under date of the 7th instant.

No. 287 NAI DT S1801L

Diarmuid O'Hegarty to F.B. Bourdillon (London)
(Copy)

DUBLIN, 20 November 1924

Sir,
I am directed by President Cosgrave to acknowledge the receipt of your letter of the 7th instant and in reply thereto to submit for the consideration of the Irish Boundary Commission the accompanying statement which sets forth the views of the Government of the Irish Free State in regard to the work with which the Commission are charged.[2] This statement is not intended to be comprehensive, and my Government propose from time to time, as the occasion arises and as the operations of the Commission proceed, to supplement it by further statements covering any considerations which, in their opinion, call for the attention of the Commission.

My Government desire to appear before the Commission by Counsel for the purpose of supplementing by oral exposition the statement now submitted, and they will be glad to be informed as to the procedure which the Commission propose to adopt at their sittings for the hearing of Counsel and the examination of witnesses. They will be represented by Messrs. John O'Byrne, K.C., Attorney General of the Irish Free State, Sergeant Hanna, K.C., Patrick Lynch, K.C. and Cecil Lavery, B.L., and these gentlemen will be ready to appear before the Commission at any date not earlier than the 2nd proximo which will suit the convenience of the Commission.

In regard to the submission of evidence to the Commission my Government find it difficult, in the absence of definite information as to the Commission's intended procedure, to decide at what stage and on what aspects of the matter it may be necessary or desirable for them to produce witnesses in support of their contentions.

I have the honour to be,
Sir,
Your obedient Servant,
[copy letter unsigned]
Secretary to the Executive Council

[1] See below No. 288.
[2] See below No. 288.

No. 288 NAI DT S1801L

Statement of the Irish Free State's case to the Boundary Commission[1]

DUBLIN, November 1924

The Government of the Irish Free State, believing that a just appreciation of the events leading up to and the circumstances surrounding the conclusion of the Treaty between Great Britain and Ireland entered into at London on the 6th December, 1921, will be of assistance to the Boundary Commission, places the following statement before them. In doing so, it has endeavoured to avoid all controversial matters and to confine the statement to facts which are either matters of history or else are evidenced by public statutes and Parliamentary records.

The Act of Union between Great Britain and Ireland was never approved of or accepted by the people of Ireland. It gave rise to great and continuous discontent, resulting from time to time in armed revolt against the Government established under that Act. There was at the same time a continued constitutional agitation carried on in the Parliament of the United Kingdom and throughout the country generally, having for its object the setting up in Ireland of a Parliament for Ireland and a Government responsible thereto. This agitation resulted, on the 18th day of September, 1914, in the passing of the Government of Ireland Act, 1914, (4 & 5 Geo. V. C. 90), but on the same day was passed the Suspensory Act, 1914 (4 & 5 Geo. V. C. 88) providing that the Government of Ireland Act should not be put into operation until the expiration of twelve months from the passing of the Act, or such later date (not being later than the end of the War) as might be fixed by Order in Council. The suspension of the Government of Ireland Act, 1914, accentuated the pre-existing discontent, and created the belief in Ireland that the British Government were not observing good faith with Ireland.

In these circumstances an election was proclaimed in December, 1918, for the election of members to the British House of Commons. The Act of 1914 was still on the Statute Book, but, owing to the Suspensory Act, had not been put into operation.

The election was held in December, 1918, and the new House of Commons met in January, 1919. Of 105 members elected to represent Irish constituencies only 32 attended that Parliament. The remaining Irish members met in Dublin and established the First Dáil Éireann, which claimed to act for the whole of Ireland. This assembly included three members who had been elected to represent constituencies in the six North-Eastern Counties, which now comprise 'Northern Ireland', namely, Mr. Arthur Griffith, who represented North-East Tyrone, Mr. Eoin MacNeill, who represented Derry City, and Mr. Sean O'Mahony, who represented South Fermanagh.

On the 25th day of February, 1920, a Bill was introduced into the British House of Commons for the Government of Ireland. It became law as the

[1] Original enclosed with Secretary's letter of 20 November 1924 (No. 287 above). The statement was heard by the Boundary Commission on 4 December (see No. 289).

Government of Ireland Act, 1920 (10 & 11 Geo. V. C. 67) on the 23rd day of December, 1920. No Irish member voted in favour of that Bill. The Government of Ireland Act, 1920 provided for the setting up of a Parliament for 'Northern Ireland', consisting of the parliamentary Counties of Antrim, Armagh, Down, Fermanagh, Londonderry, and Tyrone, and the parliamentary boroughs of Belfast and Londonderry, and another Parliament for 'Southern Ireland', consisting of so much of Ireland as was not comprised in 'Northern Ireland'.

Early in May, 1921, elections were proclaimed by the Lord Lieutenant for the House of Commons of 'Southern Ireland' and for the House of Commons of 'Northern Ireland'. The First Dáil Éireann, by resolution, agreed to dissolve and to accept the foregoing elections as elections for a new Dáil Éireann. The elections were held on the 24th day of May, 1921.

The Parliament of 'Southern Ireland' was summoned for the 17th day of June, 1921. Of the persons elected to represent constituencies in 'Southern Ireland' none attended save the members elected to represent Dublin University, and accordingly that Parliament was unable to function and never, in fact, did function.

The Parliament of 'Northern Ireland' was opened on the 22nd day of June, 1921, but 12 members elected for constituencies in 'Northern Ireland' refused to recognise the jurisdiction of that Parliament, and never participated in any of its functions. The said 12 members were distributed as follows:- namely, 4 were elected for the Counties of Fermanagh and Tyrone, 2 for the County of Armagh, 1 for the County of Antrim, 1 for West Belfast, 2 for the County of Down, and 2 for the County of Londonderry (including the Borough of Londonderry).

The new Dáil Éireann, known as the Second Dáil Éireann, met in Dublin on the 16th day of August, 1921. It comprised all the members elected to represent constituencies in 'Southern Ireland' (except the members for Dublin University), and certain members elected to represent constituencies in 'Northern Ireland'. The Second Dáil Éireann, like the First Dáil Éireann, claimed to represent and to act for the whole of Ireland.

On the 14th day of September, 1921, the Second Dáil Éireann appointed five plenipotentiaries to negotiate and conclude a Treaty of accommodation and peace with representatives of the British Government. The plenipotentiaries were Mr. Arthur Griffith, Mr. Michael Collins, Mr. Robert Barton, Mr. Eamon Duggan and Mr. George Gavan Duffy. Of these plenipotentiaries Mr. Arthur Griffith and Mr. Michael Collins had both been elected in May, 1921, to represent constituencies in 'Northern Ireland'. Mr. Griffith represented the Counties of Fermanagh and Tyrone and Mr. Collins the County of Armagh.

The Treaty was concluded and signed on the 6th day of December, 1921, and was subsequently duly ratified.

The Irish plenipotentiaries claimed to speak and act on behalf of Ireland, and were dealt with on that basis by the British representatives. The Treaty is a Treaty with the whole of Ireland and not with any part of it. Its first Article is:-

'1. Ireland shall have the same constitutional status in the Community of Nations known as the British Empire as the Dominion of Canada, the Commonwealth of Australia, the Dominion of New Zealand and the Union of South Africa, with a Parliament having powers to make laws

> for the peace, order and good government of Ireland and an executive responsible to that Parliament, and shall be styled and known as the Irish Free State'.

Though the Irish Free State, as set up by the Treaty, thus comprises the whole of Ireland, it was nevertheless recognised that a real problem existed in the North-Eastern corner of Ireland, and that special provisions were required to deal with that problem. The real difficulty of the problem arose from the fact that, whilst some of the inhabitants of that area were anxious to avail themselves of the advantages secured for them by the Treaty, others preferred to stand by the Act of 1920, and to maintain the position created by that Act. The wishes of the inhabitants of the area were recognised to be the dominant factor, and accordingly it was provided that the powers of the Parliament and Government of the Irish Free State should not be exercisable in 'Northern Ireland' for the period of one month, so as to give the people of that area, through their Houses of Parliament, the right of choosing between the alternatives comprised in Articles 12 and 14 respectively of the Treaty.

Article 14 was based upon the Houses of the Parliament of 'Northern Ireland' electing to remain under the jurisdiction of the Irish Free State. In such event, it was provided that the Parliament and Government of 'Northern Ireland' should continue to exercise, as regards the whole of 'Northern Ireland', the powers conferred on them by the Government of Ireland Act, 1920, but that the Parliament and Government of the Irish Free State should, in 'Northern Ireland', have the same powers as in the rest of Ireland, in relation to matters in respect of which the Parliament of 'Northern Ireland' had not power to make laws under the said Act of 1920. In the foregoing event, the boundaries of 'Northern Ireland' would have remained intact, but provision was made by Article 15 for safeguarding the rights of the minorities in 'Northern Ireland'.

Article 12 of the Treaty provided for the possibility of the Houses of Parliament of 'Northern Ireland' electing not to remain under the jurisdiction of the Parliament and Government of the Irish Free State. It provided that in such event the powers of the Parliament and Government of the Irish Free State should no longer extend to 'Northern Ireland', but that thereupon a Commission (being the Commission to whom this statement is addressed) should be set up to determine, in accordance with the wishes of the inhabitants, so far as might be compatible with economic and geographic conditions, the boundaries between 'Northern Ireland' and the rest of Ireland; and it was declared that, for the purposes of the Government of Ireland Act and of the Treaty, the boundary of 'Northern Ireland' should be such as might be determined by that Commission.

It is provided by the concluding words of Article 12 that 'for the purposes of the Government of Ireland Act, 1920, and of this instrument, the boundary of Northern Ireland shall be such as may be determined by such Commission'. That boundary has not yet been determined. The presentation of the address mentioned in Article 12 of the Treaty had the effect of staying for the moment, and pending the operations of the Boundary Commission, the powers of the Parliament and Government of the Irish Free State in 'Northern Ireland'; but it was not contemplated by the Treaty that any area within 'Northern Ireland' should have the right to withdraw permanently from the jurisdiction of the

Irish Free State, unless the majority of the inhabitants of such area were in favour of this course.

This Government considers that it is in the position of a trustee for such of the inhabitants of 'Northern Ireland' as wish to remain within the jurisdiction of the Irish Free State. It submits that the work of the Commission consists in ascertaining the wishes of the inhabitants of 'Northern Ireland', with a view to determining, in accordance with such wishes, so far as may be compatible with economic and geographic conditions, what portions of that area are entitled to withdraw permanently from the jurisdiction of the Irish Free State.

No. 289 NAI DT S1801L

Extract from minutes of a meeting of the Executive Council (C.2/148)

DUBLIN, 1 December 1924

BOUNDARY COMMISSION

(a) *Hearing of Counsel.*

It was reported by Dr. MacNeill that the Boundary Commission intended to visit certain districts in Ireland within the next few weeks, and the Minister for External Affairs[1] undertook to take up with the Revenue Commissioners and the Military and Police authorities the provision of customs facilities for the party in crossing the Border.

A letter from the Secretary to the Irish Boundary Commission[2] was read. It was noted that a sitting for the purposes of hearing Counsel would be held at 11 a.m. on the 4th instant. Consideration was given to the hope expressed by the Commission that Counsel will be in a position to inform the Commission of any suggestions which the Government of the Irish Free State may have to make as to the manner in which the wishes of inhabitants may be ascertained by the Commission.

It was decided to represent (*a*) that the wishes of the inhabitants should be ascertained by means of a plebiscite, (*b*) that the persons entitled to express their opinion should be residents who were 18 years of age in December, 1921, (*c*) that a register *ad hoc* of such persons will require to be prepared and (*d*) that the Unit should be the Poor Law Union.

On the question of the plebiscite area it was agreed that the Government might consent to the exclusion of Co. Antrim and Belfast City.

(b) *Irish Representative on the Secretarial Staff.*

Professor MacNeill reported that Mr. Justice Feetham had objected to the appointment of an Irish representative on the staff, and read a letter which he proposed to address to Mr. Justice Feetham on the subject.[3]

He will consult the Attorney General[4] as to the terms of the letter before sending it.

---

[1] Desmond FitzGerald.
[2] F.B. Bourdillon.
[3] Not printed.
[4] John O'Byrne.

No. 290 NAI DFA 417/105

Memorandum by Joseph P. Walshe to Desmond FitzGerald (Dublin) on the registration of the Anglo-Irish Treaty at the League of Nations

DUBLIN, 1 December 1924

THE REGISTRATION OF THE TREATY

To: The Minister of External Affairs

Events leading to the Despatch of 4th November

The Treaty was registered on the 11th July. On the 13th August Whiskard of the Colonial Office wrote to the President referring to a conversation of the previous week on the subject of the registration. The gist of Whiskard's letter is as follows:-

> In the opinion of the Colonial Secretary the action of the Irish Free State Government raised questions of very great constitutional importance as to the relations between the component parts of the Empire. In order to make their own position clear the British Government would feel bound to inform the Secretariat that the Treaty was not, in their view, an instrument proper to be registered under Article 18 of the Covenant.
>
> The President, Whiskard states, had taken the view that the matter was one for the Imperial Conference and should be left in abeyance for the present.

The President replied on the 14th August.[1] He had understood Whiskard's statement to mean that the British while acquiescing in the registration could not formally approve. If he had known there was any likelihood of real objection he would have refused to move the first reading of the Bill for supplementing the Treaty. For him the Treaty was a matter between two Nations and as such was regarded by those who supported it.

The Despatch of 4th November.

After acknowledging receipt of our Despatch of the 5th July notifying that our Representative had been instructed to register, continues:

> 'Since the Covenant of the League of Nations came into force, His Majesty's Government have consistently taken the view that neither it, nor any Convention concluded under the auspices of the League, are intended to govern the relations *inter se* of the various parts of the British Commonwealth. His Majesty's Government consider, therefore, that the terms of Article 18 of the Covenant are not applicable to the Articles of Agreement of 6th December, 1921, and are informing the Secretary-General of the League accordingly.'

The Despatch adds that copies of our Despatch of the 5th July and their reply are being sent to all the Dominions.

The British had obtained implicit recognition for their view about intra-Commonwealth relations at the Barcelona Transit Conference in March 1921, when the following article was inserted into each of the Conventions at their instance:

[1] See No. 265 above.

'It is understood that nothing in this Convention shall be interpreted as regulating rights and obligations *inter se* of territories forming part of, or placed under the protection of a single sovereign state whether these territories considered individually are, or are not, members of the League of Nations.'

The British obviously do not want to sacrifice their pet principle of the oneness of the sovereignty of the Commonwealth. They cannot allow two portions of the Commonwealth to bring a dispute before the League, the International Court or any other external body. If a single member of the Commonwealth brings a dispute with an outside state before the League, the fiction of the whole acting for the part will save the situation. The effort to maintain this fiction at all costs is at the bottom of the present ridiculous position of the Dominions in the League. They are actually members twice over and they have less power than the smallest State in the League. The Member of the League represented by the British Delegate is not the late United Kingdom, nor the United Kingdom plus Crown Colonies and Protectorates, but the British Empire in the most comprehensive sense of the term with the result that the signature of the British Delegate necessarily binds everyone of the Dominions unless there is an express reservation in each case excluding them.

The possibility of the Dominions being regarded as High Contracting Parties and independent Sovereign States was also faced at the Barcelona Conference and a remedy was sought in the division of the Conventions into two parts: a) A covering convention between High Contracting Parties, and b) An agreement between Contracting States. Sir Hubert Llewellyn Smith explained to the Conference that this was necessary because 'the League of Nations included a certain number of Members which are Dominions and not Sovereign States. In diplomatic language, they cannot properly be described, therefore, as High Contracting Parties.'

There was no Dominion represented at the Barcelona Conference to defend the individual sovereignty of the Commonwealth States, hence it seems to be taken for granted by League Members that the British Empire Delegation, as the British now call the combined delegations, is one for all effective international purposes. The League Members have not so far objected to the anomaly of plural representation by the British Empire. No really big issue involving jealousy between the big powers has been pushed to such a point at the League that a few votes one way or the other have made any matter. But at the Dawes Report Conference in London in July of this year France objected to the separate representation of the Dominions. The sop given to the Dominions was representation on the panel system which simply meant that the Dominion Representatives in turn acted as substitutes for one of the British Delegates.

There is no logic in the British position. In the League they follow the unity policy by manoeuvring the Dominions into agreeing to common ratification, into allowing themselves to be regarded as territories under the protection of a single Sovereign State, into letting themselves be called 'The British Empire Delegation'.

They refuse to recognise our passports unless we call ourselves British Subjects or describe ourselves as born within his Majesty's Dominions. On the other hand, Canada was allowed to make a Treaty with the U.S.A. (Halibut

Treaty, March 23) in complete independence of the British Representative. Ireland is allowed to have an independent representative who shall be her sole channel of communication with the American Government. The fact that he was deliberately made a Minister Plenipotentiary only in order that he should never take precedent of the British Chargé d'Affaires (who, henceforth, is to be a Minister Plenipotentiary and Envoy Extraordinary) does not take from the more important fact that his actual relations with the American Government are to be those of a Representative of a completely independent State.

The British refusal to recognise the registration of the Treaty simply because Great Britain has always held the view that the Covenant does not apply to intra-Commonwealth relations is the most barefaced explicit denial of equality of which we have an instance. Up to this they had confined themselves to little manoeuvres more or less subtle and difficult to combat.

At the moment I can only suggest that we should emphatically declare that we joined the League of Nations believing the Covenant to be of universal application to all members without exception. We accepted the obligations of the Covenant fully believing that we were getting all the rights of Member States.

If at the mere wish of Great Britain the League decides that the Covenant does not apply to our relations with that Member State, we can give notice that we intend withdrawing at an early date.

[signed] S.P. Breathnach
Secretary
Ministry of External Affairs

No. 291 NAI DFA 417/105

Joseph P. Walshe to Michael MacWhite (Geneva)
(Copy) (Personal)

Dublin, 1 December 1924

A Chara,
The Minister asks me to let you know that the British Government, in a despatch of a few weeks ago, declared that they did not recognise the Registration of the Treaty. Their view was, as the Despatch sets out, that neither the Covenant nor any convention made under the auspices of the League could in any way regulate or modify the relations between the component parts of the Commonwealth. They added that they were so informing the Secretary-General of the League. The Minister would be glad to have your opinion and Mr. Phelan's on the situation.

Sincerely yours,
[copy letter unsigned]

No. 292 NAI DFA 417/105

Michael MacWhite to Joseph P. Walshe (Dublin)

Geneva, 6 December 1924

A Chara,
The despatch from the British Government declaring that they did not recognise

the Registration of the Treaty does not modify in the least the fact that the Treaty has already been registered as an International engagement in accordance with Article 18 of the Covenant. This Article reads:-

> 'Every treaty or international engagement entered into hereafter by any Member of the League shall be forthwith registered with the Secretariat and shall, as soon as possible, be published by it. No such treaty shall be binding unless so registered.'

In this matter what applies to one Member equally applies to all and the Saorstát in the League is on the same footing as any other Member State.

In a memorandum approved by the Council of the League on the 19th. of May, 1920, it is laid down that the material to be registered, in accordance with the forementioned Article, 'comprises not only every formal Treaty of whatever character and every international Convention, but also every other international agreement or Act by which Nations or their Governments intend to establish legal obligations between themselves and another State, Nation or Government.' In view of this definition it would be idle to contend before an International Tribunal that the Anglo-Irish Treaty was not an Act intended to establish legal obligations between Great Britain and the Saorstát or between the British Government and the Irish Government. The League Secretariat who are acknowledged authorities on this subject have, after due consideration, given their decision and that decision must stand if the fundamental principles on which the League is founded are to be observed.

As the high officials of the League whom I could discreetly approach have gone to Rome for the meeting of the Council I have not yet been able to find out if the British note on this subject has arrived. Assuming, however, that such is the case it must have somewhat embarrassed the Secretary-General but it can take nothing from the validity of the Registration. Besides, if this note was anything else than an attempt to bluff the Saorstát Government it should be communicated to all the Members of the League. This is the usual procedure and it was adhered to in the case of the British declaration concerning Egypt which was forwarded to you a few days ago. Moreover, in our case, it is very improbable that the British would ask for publicity as that would be derogatory to the position of all the Dominions and raise the question of their Status as Members of the League.

In replying to the British note it may be well to emphasise the fact that, by her admission to Membership of the League, the Saorstát in accordance with Article 1 of the Covenant incurred certain international obligations which she did not intend to evade but at the same time she obtained certain international rights which she did not intend to forego. Firmness on this point would seem to be absolutely necessary at the present juncture as it is the evident intention of the present British Cabinet to endeavour to get back from the Dominions the control of Foreign Affairs which many of the latter have been exercising more or less independently for some time back.

So much for the Registration. But as regards the other phase of the question I have no doubt that the right of appeal to the League or to the Permanent Court of International Justice by the Saorstát remains intact, though it would to some extent be prejudiced by the publication of the British note. Article 34.Ch.ii. of the Statute of the Court reads:- 'Only States or Members of the

League of Nations can be parties in cases before the Court'; Art. 35 says 'The Court shall be open to Members of the League and also to States mentioned in the annex to the Covenant'. And Art. 36 'The jurisdiction of the Court comprises all cases which the parties refer to it and all matters specially provided for in Treaties and Conventions in force'. Besides, in framing the Barcelona Convention and later on that on Customs Formalities the British admitted the right of the Dominions to appeal to the League as against Great Britain or against one another in certain eventualities. In order to deprive them of this right in those two specific instances an Article was included which reads as follows:- 'It is understood that this Statute must not be interpreted as regulating in any way the rights and obligations *inter se* of territories forming part, or placed under the protection, of the same sovereign State, whether or not these territories are individually Members of the League of Nations'. If this right of appeal did not exist this Article would be superfluous.

In order that the hands of the Saorstát Government may be strengthened in League matters it is necessary that the Protocol of the Permanent Court and the Protocol for the Pacific Settlement of International Disputes should be signed as soon as conveniently possible. This step would be a pretty effective answer to the British declaration though personally I think the best answer, if circumstances permitted it, would be to hand it back to the Governor General, inviting him at the same time to take a holiday in London and informing him that his return would only be anticipated when the note was withdrawn.

Owing to his absence I have not been able to discuss the matter with Ph.[elan]. Since he came back I saw him for a few minutes when he promised to write a short memorandum which I hope to be able to forward you in the course of a day or two. I have no doubt but his opinions will coincide with mine on the subject. As soon as the sitting of the Council is over I expect to be able to get the views of the Legal Section of the Secretariat but as you may well understand a certain amount of discretion must be employed in the matter. To sum up, I don't think that the notification to the Secretariat changes anything. Had it been sent before the Treaty was registered then another situation would have been created to our detriment.

Is mise, le meas,
[signed] M. MacWhite

No. 293 NAI DFA 417/105

Michael MacWhite to Joseph P. Walshe (Dublin)
Enclosing a memorandum from Edward J. Phelan
Geneva, 9 December 1924

A Chara,
I enclose you herewith the memorandum which Phelan was good enough to write on the question of the Registration of the Treaty. As you can see he covers all the points that could be raised relating to the subject. The interpretation of Article 18 to which he refers was quoted in my letter.

It may be of interest to you to know that at the meeting of the League Council at Rome yesterday Chamberlain only employed the term 'British Empire' and corrected some one of his colleagues who referred to Great Britain. In dealing with the programme of the Health Commission he also gave his colleagues to understand that he was supporting the attitude of the Indian Delegation at the Opium Conference. By the way, this Conference will scarcely be able to finish before late in January.

Mise, le meas,
[signed] M. MacWhite

[enclosure]
Edward Phelan to Michael MacWhite (Geneva)
(Copy)

Geneva, 8 December 1924

Dear MacWhite,
With reference to our conversation on Saturday, I would submit to you the following observations on the registration of the Anglo-Irish Treaty:

I understand the registration may be contested.

Such contestation could only be made on two grounds – either that the Free State had neither the obligation nor the right to register the Treaty with the Secretariat in accordance with Article 18 of the Covenant, or that the Treaty was not a Treaty within the meaning of Article 18.

As regards the first of these possible objections, the Free State is a Member of the League. The terms of Article 18 are explicit. Any Member of the League is obliged to register every treaty or international engagement into which it enters. This obligation is binding as from the beginning of the existence of the League, i.e. from January 1920.

The Irish Free State is a Member of the League. Therefore the Irish Free State is not only entitled but obliged to register any Treaty or international engagement into which it may have entered since January 1920.

It may be argued that the Irish Free State was admitted to the League as a Dominion of the British Empire and that therefore arrangements between it and the Empire or parts of the Empire are not subject to the provisions of the Covenant.

To this it may be replied:-

(1) There are not different categories of Members of the League.

(2) All Members of the League have the same rights and are subject to the same obligations.

(3) A State on entering the League cannot, if it would, contract out of certain obligations – it is either admitted as a Member or not.

(4) The Assembly has no power to admit a State with rights or obligations differing from those of other Members. To do so would be equivalent to amending the Covenant and for that purpose a special procedure is provided by Article 26.

(5) It cannot be argued that a treaty or engagement between two parts of the Empire is excluded from the operation of Article 18 by Article 15, par.8, which refers to disputes within the domestic jurisdiction of one Member. Under Article 15 it is the Council which decides whether par.8 of Article 15 applies. To do so the Council would have to consider the relationship of the parties. The relationship cannot be regarded as settled a priori. Hence the rights of a Member

(even if a question such as registration of a treaty could be involved) remain unprejudiced until such time as the Council has pronounced. Therefore Article 15 cannot be invoked against Article 18.

(6) If the relationship of the Free State and Great Britain were such that the Free State could not register the Treaty, it would be in contradiction with Article 20, paragraph 2. As Great Britain supported the application of the Free State for Membership, she admitted that the Free State had undertaken no 'obligation inconsistent with the terms of the Covenant'. If the Free State cannot register the Treaty she should not have applied for Membership of the League and Great Britain should not have supported her application.

(7) The most conservative theorists in discussing the British Empire admit that within the limited sphere of the League of Nations the Dominions have the same powers and obligations as other Members of the League subject *perhaps* to Article 21 concerning regional understandings similar to the Monroe Doctrine 'for securing the maintenance of peace'. Whatever may be the effect of Article 21 as regards inter-Dominion relations under Articles X, XII, XIII or XV, it certainly cannot be held to derogate from their rights or obligations under other Articles of the Covenant. Keith[1] even goes so far as to state that disputes 'between different parts of the Empire can be brought to the cognisance of the League' and that the International Court of Justice is 'open to the Dominions' (The Constitution, Administration and Laws of the Empire, pages 33 and 51).

It may therefore be concluded that the Free State as a Member of the League has the same rights and obligations under Article 18 as the other Members of the League.

With regard to the second objection, namely that the Anglo-Irish Treaty is not a treaty or international engagement within the terms of Article 18, in addition to the above it may be argued that the official interpretation of Article 18 approved by the Council of the League, makes it clear that that Article applies not only to international treaties *stricto sensu* but to all international agreements, engagements or arrangements *lato sensu*. If the Anglo-Irish Treaty is a treaty – President Cosgrave on the admission of the Free State to the League referred to it as an 'international treaty' in the Assembly and the British Delegation did not challenge his description – it should be registered. Alternatively, if it is not a treaty *stricto sensu* but only an agreement between Governments, Article 18 still applies in accordance with the interpretation formally approved by the Council of the League at its Sixth (?) Session.

Finally, it may be noted that registration is not something which adds anything to the Treaty. Absence of registration might perhaps, very problematically, diminish something of its force but registration *as such* adds nothing. If the real objection, formulated as an objection to registration, is directed towards the possibility of an appeal to the League by the Free State concerning the non-observance of one or other Article of the Treaty, that is an entirely different question which is not relevant to the strict question of registration.

Article 18 was designed to secure publicity for International Agreements. As such its application was intended to be universal. But, while attempting to

[1] Arthur Berriedale Keith.

provide sanctions for non-registration, it does not provide for the enforcement of such agreements as may be registered. It was clearly the duty of the Free State to register the Treaty. It was equally clearly the duty of the Secretariat to carry out the registration. And it seems to me as impossible to challenge the registration, even supposing every point could be carried against the Treaty itself, as it would be to challenge the registration of a letter conveying prohibited matter through the post.

My personal impression is that if any protest has been made it is either in the nature of political bluff or it is a confused and unintelligent method of protesting against an appeal to the League concerning the application of the Treaty, which is quite another and a hypothetical matter.

The above is a very hurried summary of the arguments which may be used. I have not been able to add an accurate reference to the Council's interpretation of Article 18 as I have not my League documents. But I hope it will serve your purpose.

Yours very sincerely,
E.J. PHELAN

No. 294 NAI DT S3452

John O'Byrne to Desmond FitzGerald (Dublin)
(2862/24) (Copy)

DUBLIN, 11 December 1924

Re Amendment to Article 393 of the Treaty of Versailles

I have received your draft of the proposed reply to the Despatch from the Colonial Office of the 4th day of June, 1924.[1]

The original ratification of the Protocol without consultation with, and advice from, the Executive Council of the Irish Free State seems to me to have been wrong, and this is in substance admitted in the Despatch of the 22nd day of January, 1924.[2] The circumstances of the case, however, were exceptional and are not likely to occur again. This being so and there being really no question of principle involved, I see no good reason why the course suggested in paragraph 8 of the Despatch of the 22nd day of January, 1924, should not be adopted.

The alternative course is suggested in your draft despatch. That course will probably not be adopted by the British Government, and I do not think that any useful purpose would be served by asking for a separate ratification on behalf of the Irish Free State unless we are prepared, in the event of a refusal, to follow up the matter of repudiating, so far as the Irish Free State is concerned, the ratification that has already been made.

[copy letter unsigned]
PRÍOMH-ATÚRNAE

[1] Not printed.
[2] Not printed.

No. 295 NAI DFA 417/105

Michael MacWhite to Desmond FitzGerald (Dublin)
(N.S. 01/219)

GENEVA, 13 December 1924

A Chara,
So far, the British communication with reference to the Irish Treaty has not been given to the Press, in the usual way, by the Information Section of the Secretariat. Nevertheless, the editor of the 'Journal de Genève' got some inkling of it at Rome as you can see by the enclosed cutting in the article on 'M. Chamberlain et le Conseil de la S.D.N.'

It may be taken for granted that the writer of the foregoing article voices the opinions that are held in League circles and amongst the majority of the Members of the Council regarding the British pretensions as expounded in the Foreign Office letter. The claim that there are two kinds of Members of the League of Nations is regarded by everybody as inadmissible. It is incompatible with and contradictory to every Article of the Covenant.

The letter itself, as signed by Cadogan,[1] is a very clumsy production. From our point of view it could not be better drafted as it allows for a slashing reply which must make Chamberlain and his associates appear in a light which they can scarcely be expected to appreciate. I hope this reply will be forwarded to me without delay as every day lost will prejudice our situation in the League and our silence would have an ominous signification for our friends.

The British cannot contend that since the Covenant came into force their position has been as set forth in § 2 of Cadogan's letter. Had such been the case there was no need to insist on the insertion of the *inter se* Article in the Barcelona and subsequent Conventions. Besides, they did not inform the Saorstát Government that admission to the League was under those conditions and had such conditions existed prior to our admission they would certainly have been abrogated on the occasion of our admission by § 1 of Article 20 of the Covenant.

It is my opinion that if a reply is not forthcoming immediately after the publication of the letter the Government Party will be swamped at the forthcoming elections and the Saorstát will cease to be a subject of serious consideration abroad. On the other hand you will, by taking a definite stand on this matter, capture the support of many of those who believe that the Government is submissive to Britain and you will reinforce and consolidate our position as a Member of the League of Nations and as a factor in International diplomacy.

Is mise, le meas,
[signed] M. MACWHITE

[1] Alexander Cadogan (1884-1968), Head of the League of Nations Section of the Foreign Office, later Permanent Under-Secretary (1938-1946).

No. 296 NAI DT S3328

T.M. Healy to the Duke of Devonshire (London)
(No. 462)

DUBLIN, 16 December 1924

Sir,
I have the honour to refer to Mr. Thomas's despatch No. 628 of the 4th ultimo relative to the registration of the Treaty at the Secretariat of the League of Nations,[1] and to state that Article 18 of the Convention of the League clearly imposes upon States Members of the League an obligation to deposit for registration all Treaties and International engagements entered into by them.
2. Inasmuch as the Irish Free State is a member of the League and as the Treaty is the basis of the relations existing between the Irish Free State and the remaining members of the Commonwealth[,] also States Members of the League, my Ministers were and are convinced that, in pursuance of Article 18 of the Covenant, it was eminently their duty to deposit the Treaty for registration. Action to this effect was accordingly taken and the Treaty was duly registered on the 11th July of the present year.
3. As a condition of admission to membership of the League the Irish Free State gave guarantee of its sincere intention to observe its international obligations and to carry out all the obligations involved in membership of the League. In the opinion of my Ministers the view, expressed on behalf of the British Government in the despatch under reply, that the terms of Article 18 of the Covenant are not applicable to the Treaty, constitutes a disavowal of that Article of the Covenant and would, if accepted by my Ministers, involve a repudiation of their guarantees. My Ministers are, therefore, unable to accept that view.

I have the honour to be,
Sir,
Your most obedient humble Servant,
T.M. HEALY

No. 297 NAI DFA 417/105

Joseph P. Walshe to Michael MacWhite (Geneva)

DUBLIN, 18 December 1924

A Chara,
I am instructed by the Minister of External Affairs to request you to be good enough to hand the enclosed Note to Sir Eric Drummond immediately on receipt.

Le meas,
[copy letter unsigned]
Rúnaí

[1] Not printed.

P.S. It is presumed that the note will be circulated to all the Members of the League. Perhaps it would be well to make sure that no hitch will occur in that procedure on this occasion. The Minister would be glad to learn from you that the practice will be followed.

J.W.

[enclosure]

Joseph P. Walshe to Sir Eric Drummond (Geneva)

DUBLIN, 19 December 1924

Sir,

I am directed by the Minister for External Affairs to acknowledge the receipt of your communication of the 8th instant, enclosing copy of the letter addressed to you by the British Government concerning the Registration of the Treaty concluded between Great Britain and Ireland on the 6th December, 1921.[1]

The Government of the Irish Free State cannot see that any useful purpose would be served by the initiation of a controversy as to the intentions of any individual signatory to the Covenant. The obligations contained in Article 18 are, in their opinion, imposed in the most specific terms on every member of the League and they are unable to accept the contention that the clear and unequivocal language of that Article is susceptible of any interpretation compatible with the limitation which the British Government now seek to read into it.

They accordingly dissent from the view expressed by the British Government that the terms of Article 18 are not applicable to the Treaty of 6th December, 1921.

I have the honour to be,
Sir,
Your obedient Servant,
[signed] J.P. WALSHE
Secretary

No. 298 NAI DFA 417/105

Michael MacWhite to Joseph P. Walshe (Dublin)
(N.S. 01/224)

GENEVA, 18 December 1924

A Chara,

The highest officials at the Secretariat of the League are naturally somewhat reluctant to talk of the situation that has arisen as a result of the British note concerning the registration of the Anglo-Irish Treaty. Nevertheless, I have reason to know that they fully hold that the registration is well within the conditions laid down by Article 18 of the Covenant and is in accordance with the interpretation of the said Article, which was approved by the League Council at its Third Session at Rome in May 1920.

---

[1] Not printed.

It is generally felt, not only in League circles, but amongst the enlightened public, that the English Tory Government attempted to strike a blow at the prestige of the League and of the Saorstát at the same time, but that they will very likely be hoist on their own petard because of the energetic way in which the Irish Government took up the challenge and refused to be bullied in the matter. Your attitude meets with universal approval and sympathy and the League are afraid that you may eventually call on them to decide the issue which the British have raised.

The American Press will exploit the whole affair to the fullest. Fortunately all the principal news agencies were represented here because of the Opium Conference and, whilst remaining in the background, I was able to supply them with material which they used to advantage. Three of those agencies cabled between 2000 and 2400 words each. The New York World has requested its representatives in Canada, South Africa, Australia and New Zealand to obtain the views of those different Governments on the subject, so that you will probably have cognisance of them before this letter reaches you.

Is mise, le meas,
[signed] M. MacWhite

No. 299 NAI DFA 417/105

Michael MacWhite to Joseph P. Walshe (Dublin)
(N.S. 01/226)

Geneva, 23 December 1924

A Chara,

On receipt of your reply to the British note,[1] which arrived late yesterday afternoon, I had it presented to the Secretary General of the League, who felt somewhat relieved on finding that it was in accordance with his anticipations.

As I mentioned in my telegram to you last night,[2] your note will be circulated to the Members of the League to-day and distributed to the press tomorrow if they find it impossible to do so to-day.

In discussing the British note with the Secretary General he said: 'Between ourselves it was a most extraordinary step for the Foreign Office to take, as they have no ground to stand on.' This remark of his must, of course, be regarded as confidential. He also told me, though I do not know that he had any special reason for saying so, that he expected a protest from Canada against the British interpretation of Art. 18.

Is mise, le meas,
[signed] M. MacWhite

1 See above No. 297.
2 Not printed.

1925

No. 300 NAI DFA GR 246

Timothy A. Smiddy to Desmond FitzGerald (Dublin)
WASHINGTON, 2 January 1925

My dear Minister:
I have been much occupied since my return in endeavouring to bring up to date arrears of work, in interviews and in attending many official functions. I presume you have read the articles I gave the press on my arrival; they were afforded wide spread publicity throughout the U.S.A. I also gave an interview article to the New York Evening Sun, a copy of which has been sent you.

Extensive publicity was given both in U.S.A. and Canada to the Cablegrams I received with reference to the registration of the Anglo-Irish Treaty by the League of Nations; editorials appeared on the subject in most of the leading papers.

The articles by P.J. Kelly to the New York World are causing much interest here. It is regrettable that they are producing a pessimistic impression. I expect that the New York World will publish within a few days a special article which I have given them. The main point pressed by me in this article and interviews is the constructive work of the Government. I am booked for a number of lectures during the coming three months before some academic and other bodies which will provide a platform for placing a favourable interpretation before the American people on the work of the Government. The demands on my time in Washington compel me to refuse many other invitations to lecture.

Soon after my arrival Mr Frank O'Flannigan called on me in New York. In the course of the conversation he stated that some of the projects of Mr Howard Harrington were not feasible and that the men he got into contact with will not be very helpful. Among these schemes, which are not practical at present, is that of a free port in the South West of the Irish Free State. To any one with a knowledge of shipping and the geographical position in Ireland such an idea is at present mythical. Mr O'Flannigan further stated that he discussed with men such as Mr J.S. Cullinan the practical help that might be given to the successful exploitation of Irish resources by a man like the head engineer of the Panama Canal – Dr Goethals. If I am asked to submit my views on this idea and this man by the Minister of Industry & Commerce[1] I shall do so. The Minister of Industry & Commerce had already discussed with me a somewhat similar idea.

---

[1] Patrick McGilligan.

Subsequent to this conversation with Mr O'Flannigan I had a long interview with Mr Howard Harrington. He did not discuss his plan of a 'free port' but he informed me of efforts he was making to induce a Mr Lee (a successful building magnate in N.Y.) to build a few large hotels along the main tourist routes in the Irish Free State. He was not confident that he will succeed in his efforts. He is enthusiastic in his praise of the charms of the County Kerry and of its comparatively dry climate. This is news for me, I wonder if you can endorse it? At all events I must state that he is enthusiastic about Ireland.

Soon after my arrival in New York I left cards on Judge Cohalan and Mr William J. Shiefflein. The latter is a very wealthy man and well known for his civic performances. His house is quite palatial.

I have been entertained by Mr John S. Stewart at the lawyers club N.Y. I met there some very prominent lawyers and Judges who evinced much interest in the Irish Free State: a great number of them are of Irish origin. I have been asked to speak before the Governors of the club this month.

Sir Harry Gloster Armstrong[,] British Consul General[,] entertained to luncheon the Canadian Trade Commissioners, Representatives of the foreign press, the Collector and Assistant Collector of the port of New York; he had me as his guest of honour on the occasion. The speeches of the Canadian Representatives and Sir Harry Gloster Armstrong were very complimentary to the Irish Free State. In a private conversation I had with the Australian Commissioner (Mr Elder) he stated that religious issues were becoming much aggravated in Australia.

After the lunch I was asked to go to meet the senior partner of Mr J.P. Morgan, Mr Lamont. For an hour he discussed the conditions of Ireland especially the financial and economic. He told me that some time ago he met in London Mr Curtis (Colonial Office) and that the latter mentioned to him that one of these days the Irish Free State would borrow in the New York money market. Mr Lamont at the time gave as his opinion that the Irish Free State should and would be able to borrow what it needs for its Governmental and other requirements within the Free State. He said it had the means available for it. In spite of the various unfavourable reports that appear occasionally in the U.S.A. about the financial condition of the Irish Free State its financial administration has impressed Wall Street most favourably and its credit stands high in New York.

I entertained yesterday some prominent correspondents in Washington especially Mr Herbert Correy and Mr John Sinnot; also Admiral and Mrs Clark of the U.S. Navy[,] Mr Joseph Henry Bagley[,] Vice-President of the American Bank Note Company[,] Mr Howe[,] U.S.A. Naval Attaché at Rio.

Mr M.M. Mahoney, Canadian Representative at Washington, lunched with me a week ago. He informed me that he submitted to his Government an estimate of the staff and general requirements of the proposed Canadian Legation at Washington. He suggested a suite of twelve rooms or a small separate building for offices, leaving the Minister free to live where he pleases. The principal officers would be Counsellor, First[,] Second and Third Secretaries. It is proposed Mr Mahoney himself will act as first secretary whose chief function will be to direct the commercial and financial work of the Legation. However, as far as I can gather there is little likelihood of a Minister being appointed at an early date. There is much difficulty about getting a man to suit the various supporters of Mr MacKenzie King – especially Ontario and Quebec.

A Mr Wattawa and Mr John Walsh lunched with me last Wednesday; they are partners in the firm of Walsh, Spies & Wattawa – lawyers to Mr J.S. Cullinan. Mr F. O'Flannigan was entertained and taken care of by Mr Wattawa while in Washington. The latter has arranged a luncheon at the Capitol next Wednesday at which Senator Thomas Walsh is to meet me. You are doubtless aware that this is the Senator who conducted the onslaught on the Teapot Dome scandals and who was chairman of the Democratic Convention last July.

Yesterday there was the usual New Year's day reception by President and Mrs Coolidge at the White House. The affair was quite imposing; almost all the Diplomatic Corps turned up in brilliant uniforms. Subsequently, Secretary of State and Mrs Hughes were hosts to the members of the Diplomatic Corps at the Pan American Union. The British Embassy made a brilliant display both in numbers and appearance and were accompanied by Lord Robert Cecil.

Mr St. John Gaffney visits the office occasionally. He has just succeeded in getting paid his funds which had been tied up during the war in consequence of his remaining in Germany after America entered the war.

Yours very sincerely,
T.A. SMIDDY

No. 301 NAI DFA D3601

T.M. Healy to J.H. Thomas (London)
(No. 31)

DUBLIN, 22 January 1925

Sir,

With reference to Mr. Thomas' Despatch No. 607 of the 24th October last,[1] and previous correspondence concerning the recommendation of the Imperial Conference 1923 on the subject of the Negotiation, Signature and Ratification of Treaties, I have the honour to inform you that my Ministers accept the procedure set out therein as a working arrangement.

2. They desire me, however, to point out that they understand that the instrument of ratification will state in all cases the member or members of the Commonwealth on whose behalf it is made.

I have the honour to be,
Sir,
Your most obedient, humble servant,
(sgd) T.M. HEALY

[1] Not printed.

No. 302 NAI DFA ES Box 29 File 192

Timothy A. Smiddy to Desmond FitzGerald (Dublin)
(Confidential)
WASHINGTON, 6 February 1925

My dear Minister:
I have just learned unofficially at the Metropolitan Club, Washington, that the Department of State has settled the status of the Minister of the Irish Free State with relation to that of the Minister Plenipotentiary and Envoy Extraordinary resident in the British Embassy (Mr. Chilton) who will act as Chargé d'Affairs in the absence of the British Ambassador. According to this information the Irish Minister takes precedence of the British Chargé d'Affaires in state functions.

This confirms what has occurred in a recent reception at the White House where I preceded a Minister Plenipotentiary and Envoy Extraordinary who was appointed subsequently to me.

As soon as I have official verification of this I shall inform you.

If it is true, and I believe it is, it will furnish a refutation of the article by Sir Maurice Lowe which appeared in the Baltimore Sun of last November, a copy of which you have seen. In fact, Sir Maurice Lowe, in company with Mr. Lansing, former Secretary of State, were present when the above statement was made at the Club.

Yours sincerely,
[copy letter unsigned]

No. 303 NAI DFA Minister's Office Files (1925)

Timothy A. Smiddy to Desmond FitzGerald (Dublin)[1]
(Confidential)
WASHINGTON, 10 February 1925

Dear Minister:
In a conversation I had at lunch yesterday with Mr William Castle, Chief of the Western European Division, State Department, he referred to the proposal made by Congressman John J. Boylan to the Foreign Relations Committee to the effect that the U.S.A. Government should accredit a Minister Plenipotentiary to the Government of the Irish Free State. Mr Castle stated that he had one serious objection to such a proposal, viz., that political pressure would be brought to bear upon the U.S.A. President from various Irish organizations which may result in the appointment of one who might possibly voice, and work in, the interests of those opposed to the interests of the Irish Free State, and thereby cause embarrassments to both governments.

In a conversation he had with President Cosgrave last autumn he expressed this view.

It is interesting to note that Mr John J. Boylan pressed, last year, the House

[1] Handwritten note on letter: 'Copied and distributed at Cabinet meeting on 4/3/25'.

of Representatives to express themselves in favour of the release of Mr de Valera. As you have seen by the newspaper cuttings he has now been assailed by the followers of Mr de Valera in this country for suggesting a Minister from the U.S.A. to the Irish Free State.

Yours sincerely,
[copy letter unsigned]

No. 304 NAI DT S1801L

Note by William T. Cosgrave on matters relating to the Boundary Commission
DUBLIN, 18 February 1925

So far as the Government is aware, no demand has been made from our side of the Boundary for inclusion in Northern Ireland. It is, I think, on record that Sir James Craig once said there was an area in Donegal which would demand to be transferred to Northern Ireland. The answer to the paragraph is that the Commission has no authority under the Treaty – which is the basis of its authority so far as Saorstát Éireann is concerned – to transfer any part of our territory to Northern Ireland. In this connection it might be well to summarise, briefly and cogently, a reasoned argument, on paper, pointing out that in any case there has never been any movement or demand from our side of the Border for transfer to Northern Ireland so that the matter does not appear to be practical politics.

It is a matter for consideration whether, without prejudice to our position under the Treaty, the Government are prepared to put on record evidence that no representation or claim has been made upon the Government, or come to their knowledge, showing any desire on the part of citizens of Saorstát Éireann to secede to Northern Ireland and that that exhausts the evidence which can be offered on this particular matter, while the evidence in support of the claim of portion of the population of Northern Ireland for transfer to Saorstát Éireann is considerable.

It is a question for consideration whether there is not a danger in allowing the Boundary to be decided on a religious census, as it might possibly be considered whether a change on our side might not be made on the same basis. The religion of the people certainly does not disclose the wishes of the inhabitants.

No. 305 NAI DFA LN95

Diarmuid O'Hegarty to Desmond FitzGerald (Dublin)
(S. 4040)
DUBLIN, 19 February 1925

The Minister for External Affairs.
With reference to the various Colonial Office Despatches which have been received regarding the Protocol for the Pacific Settlement of International Disputes, I am directed by the President to inquire what progress has been made by you in the examination of this matter. He considers it very unfortunate that we appear to be the only one of the members of the Commonwealth which has not been able to reply to the British communications on the subject.

The President thinks, in view of the importance of the question, and of the extent of the documents which have to be gone through, that you should have a summary of the whole case prepared for the information of members of the Council. This summary should contain:-
(a) The important provisions of the Protocol and the arguments for and against these provisions.
(b) The action, if any, in which the adoption of the Protocol might involve us, and generally the effect which such adoption might have on our relations with other States.
(c) Our constitutional position in regard to its adoption and to any considerations set out under heading (b), with information as to whether any other States members of the League are similarly circumstanced.
(d) A draft of the reply which should be sent to the British Government on the subject (which should contain a suitable explanation of the delay which has occurred).

[signed] DIARMUID Ó HÉIGEARTAIGH
Rúnaí

No. 306 NAI DT S4040

Handwritten memorandum by William T. Cosgrave on the Protocol for the Pacific Settlement of International Disputes (Geneva Protocol)
DUBLIN, February 1925

The memorandum is reproduced in facsimile on pages 394 and 395.

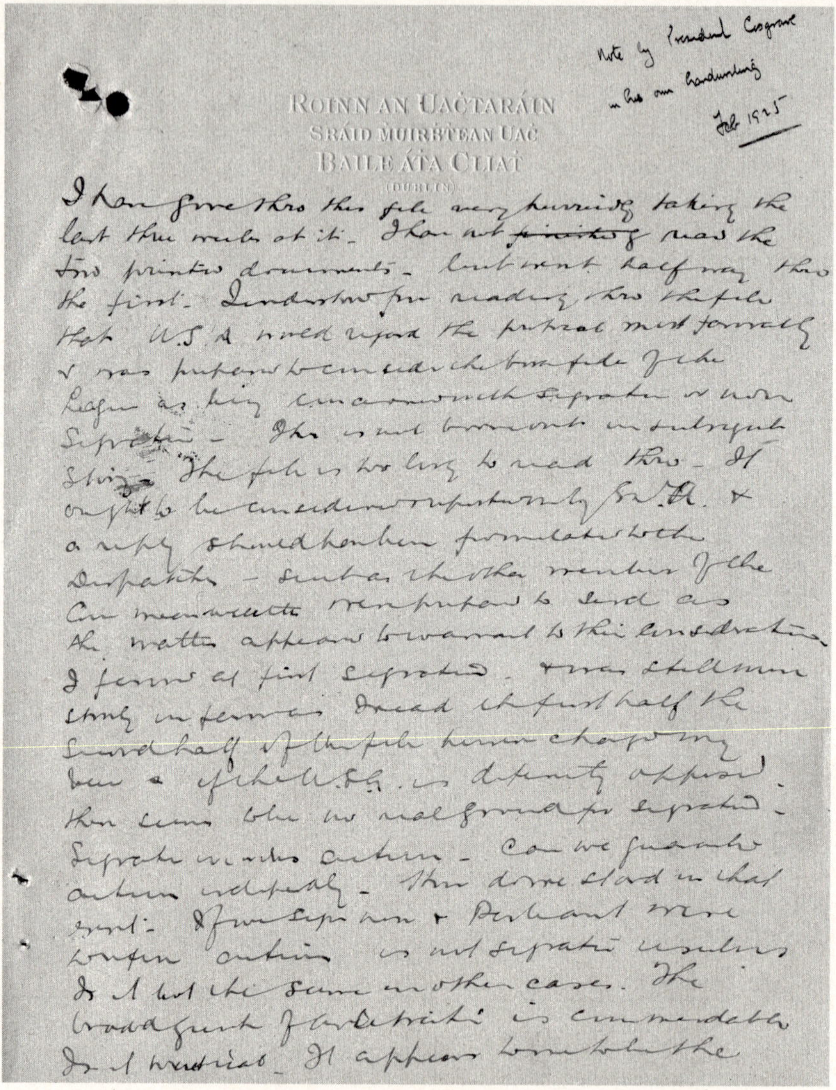

Note by President Cosgrave in his own handwriting Feb 1925

ROINN AN UAĊTARÁIN
SRÁID ṀUIRḂTEAN UAĊ
BAILE ÁTA CLIAṪ
(DUBLIN)

I have gone thro this file very hurriedly taking the last three weeks at it. I have not ~~finished~~ read the two printed documents – but went half way thro the first. I understood from reading thro the file that U.S.A. would regard the protocol most favorably & was prepared to consider the bona fide of the League as being Commonwealth separate or more separate. This is not borne out in subsequent stages. The file is too long to read thro. It ought to be considered [illegible] & a reply should have been formulated to the Dispatches – such as the other members of the Commonwealth were prepared to send as the matter appears to warrant to their consideration. I favoured at first separation & was still more strongly in favour as I read the first half. The second half of the file however changed my views & if the U.S.A. is definitely opposed there seems to be no real ground for separation. Separate [illegible] action – Can we guarantee action independently – [illegible] in that sort. If [illegible] & Parliament were [illegible] action is not separate [illegible] & I [illegible] the same in other cases. The broad grant of arbitration is commendable [illegible]. It appears to me that the

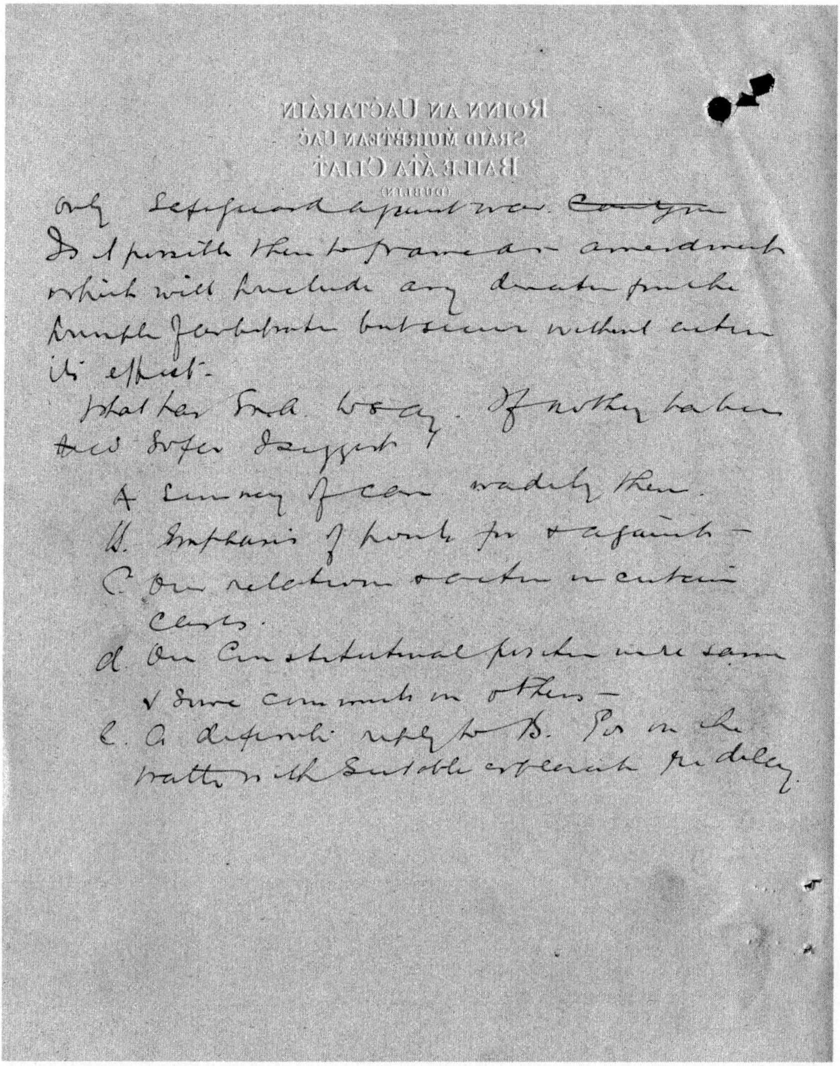

only safeguard against war. ~~Can you~~
Is it possible then to frame an amendment
which will preclude any deviation from the
principle of arbitration but secure without altering
its effect.
What has Sm.A. W.S. ay. If nothing has been
~~had~~ before I suggest
A. Summary of case made by them.
B. Emphasis of points for & against –
C. Our relations & action in certain
cases.
d. Our Constitutional position in the same
& some comments on others –
e. A definite reply to B. Por on the
matter with suitable explanation for delay.

No. 307 NAI DFA Minister's Office Files (1924-25)

Extracts from a letter from Thomas J. Kiernan to Sean Lester (Dublin)
(55a/25)

LONDON, 25 February 1925

In reply to your letter of 20th February,[1] 1925, I am to state that in the High Commissioner's opinion a good deal could be done here to promote tourist traffic in Ireland, but the methods proposed by the Irish Tourist Association seem to be inadequate.

The Tourist Agencies here are, generally speaking, not interested in sending tourists to Ireland. I think they find it directly profitable to commend Gleneagles, Strathpeffer, etc. Unless they have recently changed they prefer to send people elsewhere than to Ireland. Having heard complaints of this last year, a few visits were made to agency offices by members of this office staff, who inquired as potential tourists. In two of the cases the advice to those intending to travel to Ireland was an unqualified 'Don't'. There would be many more tourists to Ireland if travellers, especially from the U.S.A. and the Overseas Dominions, could obtain full information, book tickets, and reserve hotel accommodation through an Irish Tourist Agency. Space could be provided in this office for such an agency.

It would certainly be possible to arrange for the display of posters and leaflets inside the office and, with an addition of one to the personnel of the staff, to give information to inquiries. It is not known just what is meant by the fullest possible information about hotels, tariffs, etc. Presumably there would be a plan of each hotel, and a full list of charges, including the charge for each bedroom. If, however, a public servant is to give this information he should not, the High Commissioner thinks, be expected to express any opinion about the cleanliness or comfort of the accommodation or the efficiency of the service, unless his statements can be based on authoritative information. Furthermore, if a number of travellers who obtain information from this office later express their dissatisfaction with their treatment at any particular hotel, there must either be a reliable method of removing the cause of complaint or subsequent inquirers must be informed that dissatisfaction has been expressed. A public servant cannot for the pecuniary benefit of any person or body misstate or conceal facts from inquirers who are obviously entitled to get from him full and truthful replies to questions.

[Matter omitted]

The proposals as communicated suggest methods by which those financially benefiting by the tourist traffic could secure advantages at the taxpayer's expense, while there seems to be no guarantee that the public outlay will benefit anyone else, or that one of the main obstacles, if not actually the greatest, to the development of the tourist traffic will be removed. That obstacle is the dearness and discomfort of Irish hotels.

The High Commissioner thinks that help might perhaps be given by allowing a Tourist Agency to occupy a part of the premises at a nominal rent. If someone

[1] Not printed.

is employed to specialise in information about hotels, sailings, etc., the cost should be borne by the Tourist Association. If arrangements are made for the issue of tickets, doubtless a set-off would be made as regards the amount of any commission levied. The High Commissioner, through his Secretary, could, if desired, exercise effective control over any person who was formally or legally the servant of the Association.

[Matter omitted]

It is believed that the Department of Industry and Commerce are directly interested in promoting tourist traffic and in removing the obstacles to its development. You may think it well to let them have a copy of this letter.

[signed] T.J. KIERNAN
Secretary

No. 308 NAI DFA Letter Books Department of Justice (1923-25)

Joseph P. Walshe to Henry O'Friel[1] *(Dublin)*
DUBLIN, 12 March 1925

With reference to your Minute (H.4/179) of 10th inst. I am to point out that the arrangement made with regard to Saorstát Éireann visas for aliens coming here from the U.S.A. is, as you are aware, that the passports of all such aliens as embark at New York must bear the Saorstát visa. The Minister for External Affairs feels that you will appreciate the desirability of adhering strictly to this arrangement and not allowing any person sailing from the port of New York to disembark in Saorstát Éireann without the Saorstát visa.

It is not considered that persons travelling from New York with England as their destination should be permitted to land in An Saorstát because they have changed their minds en route. This would in effect mean that the Saortstát visa is superfluous, and that the British visa alone will in all cases suffice, which, as you doubtless will agree, would be a stultification of our whole position in the matter.

Although the Aliens Order contains no express provision as to visas it is in the view of this Department implicit that, having regard to the arrangement formally entered into between ourselves and the British, the passport of an alien sailing to An Saorstát direct from New York would not be valid for landing in this country unless it bore the Saorstát visa.

The Minister therefore requests that your Department may be good enough to instruct the Immigration Officers not to permit any alien coming direct from New York to land unless his passport has been duly visaed by our Passport Office in New York.

[copy letter unsigned]
t.c. Rúnaí

[1] Secretary, Department of Justice.

No. 309 NAI DT S4040

Memorandum on the Protocol for the Pacific Settlement of International Disputes (Geneva Protocol)
DUBLIN, undated, probably early March 1925

SUMMARY OF POINTS PARTICULARLY AFFECTING THE SAORSTÁT.

I. *THE PROTOCOL AND THE SOVEREIGNTY OF THE STATE.*
There is no provision made for consulting Parliament on a decision of the League Council.

Signatories are automatically bound to apply military, economic and naval sanctions against an aggressor state at the word of the Council. We have no representative on the Council and in two important contingencies decisions can be taken by a two-thirds majority which need not include Great Britain.

These decisions concern:

a) the establishment of an infraction of the undertakings set out in Art. 7 that no State will take any military or economic measures whatsoever during the consideration of a dispute which has arisen between it and another State.

b) the enjoining of an armistice and the fixing of its terms in the case of two states which have actually begun hostilities and in respect of which the Council is unable immediately to determine the aggressor.

On the other hand it requires a unanimous decision of the Council to call off the military and economic measures taken against an aggressor state at the request of the Council.

II. *NO ACTION IN PURSUANCE OF ITS OBLIGATIONS UNDER THE PROTOCOL COULD BE TAKEN BY THE SAORSTÁT INDEPENDENTLY OF GREAT BRITAIN.*
If Great Britain rejects the Protocol we cannot accept it because:

a) Economic measures taken by us against an aggressor state would be futile so long as Great Britain continued ordinary commercial intercourse with that state and military measures could not be taken in any case so long as the present Convention of the Commonwealth Constitution prevails that the Commonwealth is at war as a whole or not at all.

b) If Great Britain were the aggressor state it would be suicide to take any measures of either an economic or military nature against her.

It is clear therefore that for the purposes of the obligations assumed under the Protocol we are not in the position of an independent state and we have no choice but to act in solidarity with Great Britain.

No. 310 NAI DFA LN95

Memorandum by Joseph P. Walshe on the Protocol for the Pacific Settlement of International Disputes (Geneva Protocol)
DUBLIN, undated, probably early March 1925

Considerations particularly affecting the Saorstát
I We must either accept the Protocol with Britain or reject with her.
We could not carry out an Economic boycott of a state with which Britain

continues her ordinary commercial intercourse nor could we trade with a country with which our neighbour has severed all relations. The same principle applies to military cooperation.

Should Great Britain happen to be the aggressor state we should have no choice but to continue our ordinary relations with her no matter what obligations were imposed upon us by an international instrument. Any other course would be suicide in our present lopsided economic position.

According to our present conception no dominion can be in a state of war with another country unless the Empire as a whole is at war, and there is no possibility of changing that position except by a slow process of evolution.

Our attitude towards the Protocol, if it is to be realist must be the attitude of Great Britain.

II These arguments hold to a lesser extent in the case of the Covenant but the world has agreed to regard that document as having no serious value where really serious issues are concerned. Its sanctions are vague and all its provisions can be evaded by a quibble. Italy showed the way to treat the League in the Corfu incident, Poland when she seized Vilna. The protocol is more definitely a military and economic pact and was framed chiefly by France with a view to keeping down the Central powers. It has come much too early for the Saorstát which is not an independent state in so far as the purposes of the protocol are concerned. We can therefore reject it without having regard either to the motives of the framers or the advantages likely to accrue to them from it.

No. 311 NAI DFA LN87A

Extracts from a memorandum by Michael MacWhite on the 33rd Session of the Council of the League of Nations, with covering letter by MacWhite (M.L. 02/027)

GENEVA, 17 March 1925

A Chara,

I enclose you herewith a short memorandum on the work of the 33rd. Session of the Council of the League of Nations. From what transpired there, it would seem that the British are about to turn their back on the League and the fact that they have already agreed to assist at another disarmament Conference in Washington would lend colour to the idea. The Washington Conference is being called because the Geneva Protocol has been rejected and, consequently, the Conference which was proposed to take place next June under the auspices of the League of Nations for the purpose of limiting armaments has been indefinitely postponed.

Is mise, le meas,
[signed] M. MACWHITE

[enclosure]

MEMORANDUM ON THE WORK OF THE 33rd. SESSION OF THE COUNCIL OF THE LEAGUE OF NATIONS

The 33rd. Session of the Council of the League of Nations was opened at Geneva on the 9th. March under circumstances which may be described as dramatic from the standpoint of the Peace of Europe. If we leave aside some questions of a technical nature, its deliberations circled round the cardinal problem of European politics or, in other words, the question of the relations between France and Germany.

The political, moral and economic stability of Europe, and perhaps of the whole world, depends on the possibility of finding effective guarantees of peace. The solution of the problem of reparations was so far the biggest contribution in this respect. The regulation of the commercial relations between France and Germany, even though it be only of a provisional character, has produced a sensible reaction, but it is evident that nothing durable or lasting can be achieved before France has obtained guarantees of her security, which will satisfy French public opinion. This is the kernel of the whole question. In order to achieve this result, three methods of unequal value may be employed. The first is the disarmament of Germany, the second a pact of a limited nature such as the Germans themselves have proposed and the third a general pact of the nature of the Protocol of Geneva.

[Matter omitted]

The British declaration rejecting the Protocol, which was read by Mr. Chamberlain made a very bad impression. For the Representatives of the Middle European States who were present, it felt like the pronouncement of a death sentence. It was not couched in diplomatic language and the reference to the League attempting to regulate questions for which it had 'neither capacity nor competence' lead those present to believe that the moment has arrived when the League is considered by Great Britain to be more embarrassing than serviceable to her interests. As long as the League never questioned British policy and accepted without demur British proposals it was lauded to the skies, but now that many of its Members no longer see eye to eye with Britain and take the opportunity of voting against her as at the Opium Conference, it must be made to pay the price and be paraded before the world as a thing of no importance. When Mr. Chamberlain, in winding up his speech, stated that he was not in possession of the views of the Irish Free State on the question of the Protocol, there was a general murmur and everybody looked in my direction. The presumption was that the Saorstát Government held different views and the impression created was very favourable so far as we are concerned.

[Matter omitted]

[signed] M. MacWhite

No. 312 NAI DFA ES Box 29 File 192

Timothy A. Smiddy to Desmond FitzGerald (Dublin)
WASHINGTON, 26 March 1925

Dear Mr. Minister:
With further reference to my letter of February 6th[1], it is now definitely established that the Minister Plenipotentiary of the Irish Free State has the same official status as the Ministers Plenipotentiary and Envoys Extraordinary of other nations, and he takes precedence according to the date of his official recognition by the U.S.A. Government within the second grade of diplomatic representatives:- (b) Envoys Extraordinary and Ministers Plenipotentiary, etc.

In the Official Diplomatic List the Legation of the Irish Free State is now followed by those of Ecuador, Greece, Paraguay, and Haiti, the heads of which were appointed subsequent to your Minister and all of whom are Ministers Plenipotentiary and Envoys Extraordinary.

Yours sincerely,
[copy letter unsigned]

No. 313 NAI DFA GR509A

E.J. Riordan (Department of Industry and Commerce) to Joseph P. Walshe enclosing a memorandum on the work of Irish Free State Commercial Representatives
DUBLIN, 30 April 1925

Secretary,
Department of External Affairs.
In response to your telephone message of yesterday, I enclose herewith for the information of the Minister for External Affairs brief notes upon the work of the Commercial Representatives at New York, Brussels and Paris. This work consists in the main of a large number of enquiries made at the instance of Government Departments and traders at home or in the countries to which they are appointed, and of enquiries arising out of the general instructions which they have received from this Department. It is impossible to describe adequately this work within the compass of very brief notes as asked for.

There is considerable evidence in this Department that the services of the Commercial Representatives are being availed of to an increasing extent, and are much appreciated by the business community in An Saorstát.

E.J. RIORDAN

[enclosure]

COMMERCIAL REPRESENTATIVE AT NEW YORK (MR. LINDSAY CRAWFORD)

A considerable volume of important work on commercial matters has been dealt with through this office during the past 12 months.

[1] See above No. 302.

A number of disputes between Irish exporters and American importers concerning accounts due by the latter to the former have been amicably settled through the instrumentality of the Commercial Representative. Disputes of this kind are of very frequent occurrence especially in the fish trade.

A considerable amount of organising work has also been conducted by Mr Crawford in connection with the establishment of an Irish Fish Exchange and with the development of an export trade in Irish bacon to the United States. Other products which have received special attention in this respect are oatmeal, woollens, hosiery, lace and poplin, etc.

Steps have been taken at the instance of Mr Crawford and upon information supplied by him, to prevent American firms from mis-describing and mis-branding foreign goods as 'Irish'. Instances of such mis-description have arisen in connection with the sale of lace, poplin, ginger ale, bacon and hams, and woollens. Particulars of offences in regard to the mis-branding of lace, poplins, and bacon and hams have been brought to the notice of the Federal Trade Commission at Washington, and in the case of poplin a favourable decision has been obtained. Decisions in the other two cases have not yet been given.

Mr Crawford has also furnished specific information regarding the names and commercial repute of no fewer than 330 firms in the United States likely to be interested in the purchase of the products of An Saorstát (see accompanying list).[1]

A considerable amount of valuable information on the subject of tourist development, industrial assurance, trade marks, merchandise marks, exhibitions of various kinds, customs regulations and tariff changes has also been furnished through this office.

COMMERCIAL REPRESENTATIVE AT BRUSSELS
(Count Gerald O'Kelly de Gallagh)

The Commercial Representative at Brussels has been instrumental in promoting a new direct steamer service between Dublin and Antwerp and in arranging for some trial shipments of cattle to Belgium. He also succeeded in inducing the Belgian government to make a special concession in favour of Irish cattle which permitted the importation of such cattle without quarantine restrictions. The official Order of the Belgian government in the matter applied specifically to Irish cattle only.

Count O'Kelly has also furnished important data regarding the sugar beet industry in Belgium and he was instrumental in providing facilities for officials and others from An Saorstát who visited Belgium for the purpose of making enquiries in regard to the sugar beet, linen, and other industries. He has also had to deal with disputes between Irish and Belgian firms which had been referred to him for adjustment. He has devoted special attention to the marketing in Belgium of fish and wool and has besides furnished the names of as many as 270 Belgian firms likely to be interested in the purchase of a large range of Free State products (see list attached.)[2]

[1] Not printed.
[2] Not printed.

COMMERCIAL REPRESENTATIVE AT PARIS
(Mr Vaughan Dempsey)

Through the efforts of the Commercial Representative in Paris an Irish Chamber of Commerce has been established in that city. It is hoped that this Chamber will be instrumental in promoting the development of trade between the two countries. Mr Dempsey has also furnished valuable information regarding the sugar beet industry in France and in regard to markets there for a large range of Saorstát products. In addition, he has furnished lists of buyers likely to be interested in the purchase of such products (see list attached).[1] He has also furnished special reports upon exhibitions held in that country in which Irish manufacturers and exporters were, or might be, interested.

No. 314 NAI DT S3452

T.M. Healy to Leopold Amery (London)
(No. 145)

DUBLIN, 9 May 1925

Sir,
I have the honour to refer to Mr. Thomas's Despatch No. 342 of the 4th June last[2] and to previous correspondence regarding the ratification of the Protocol embodying an Amendment of Article 393 of the Treaty of Versailles and the corresponding Articles of the other Treaties of Peace.
2. My Ministers note that it is admitted that the Irish Free State cannot be bound by an agreement except with the expressed sanction of the Irish Free State Government. They regret that in the present instance the ratification was deposited without their knowledge and advice, but in the special circumstances and on the understanding that their prior sanction will be sought in all such matters henceforth, they agree to notify the League that the Irish Free State is included in the list of States Members of the International Labour Office which have accepted the Protocol. Steps are being taken to inform the Secretary General accordingly.
3. In order to avoid any confusion in future, my Ministers consider that every instrument of ratification purporting to include more than one member of the Commonwealth should set out nominatim the members on whose behalf the ratification is made.

I have the honour to be,
Sir,
Your most obedient, humble Servant,
(Sgd.) T.M. HEALY

[1] Not printed.
[2] Not printed.

No. 315 NAI DFA LN95

Dáil statement made by Desmond FitzGerald on the Protocol for the Pacific Settlement of International Disputes (Geneva Protocol)

DUBLIN, 13 May 1925

We have given earnest consideration to the Protocol for the Pacific Settlement of International Disputes drawn up at the Fifth Assembly of the League of Nations. We have approached the subject with due advertence to the admirable intentions which animated the authors of that document, and with which we are in complete accord, namely, that a basis should be found which would enable differences arising between Nations to be adjusted without recourse to arms, and thus remove from the sphere of international relations the menace of war.

For this country – a small nation with no aspirations to territorial aggrandisement and no interests other than the social and economic welfare of our people and the maintenance of cordial intercourse with all other nations – the attractions of a scheme which has for its objective the maintenance of international peace are manifest. In so far, therefore, as the Protocol constitutes a unanimous manifestation by the States Members of the League of their genuine desire to render recourse to war impossible, we welcome the opportunity which it has afforded for the study of measures devised for that purpose, and while on consideration of its details we find ourselves unable to recommend its acceptance, we wish to place on record that we are by no means of opinion that the object of the framers of the Protocol is beyond the realm of achievement.

The Covenant of the League of Nations, while it marked a notable advance in the direction of international peace, cannot be regarded as an instrument capable in all circumstances of preventing war. Its machinery for dealing with disputes is somewhat unwieldy, and the preponderance on its Council of the more powerful States tends to diminish its prestige amongst the smaller nations, who have less to gain and more to suffer by international strife. But it is our opinion that the place of the League of Nations in world civilisation is not to be gauged by the suitability of its machinery to arbitrate in disputes between Nations when they arise in acute form – rather is it to be measured by the efficacy of the intercourse between States to which it has given rise in resolving differences before they become acute by harmonious interchange of ideas and by mutual appreciation of national aspirations and national difficulties.

The Covenant of the League of Nations makes provisions for certain sanctions in the case of a State which resorts to war in disregard of its obligations. It has always appeared to us that the applications of these sanctions would present grave difficulties, and that the machinery for effecting them would in practice prove unworkable. It is true that sanctions could in all probability be effectively enforced against a relatively small State engaging in hostile operations for purposes of aggrandisement, where the verdict of the world-conscience would be unanimous in condemnation of the objects for which resort was had to war. But it appears equally evident that, in the case of aggressive acts by one or other of the greater Powers, and particularly where world opinion was divided as to the merits of the dispute, the sanctions could not be enforced. We are, accordingly, forced to the conclusion that, while the sanctions of the Covenant may prove a useful deterrent in the case of small and turbulent communities, they are quite powerless to prevent either the oppression by a larger power of small States or the occurrence of a war of world magnitude. It may also be observed that the application of sanctions implies the maintenance of armaments rather than their abolition, and in this respect is scarcely compatible with one of the primary objects of the Protocol, viz, disarmament. The portions of the Covenant, therefore, dealing with the imposition of sanctions appears to us to be the least valuable for the general purposes of the Covenant, and an extension of these provisions, such as is contemplated in the Protocol, the least profitable avenue of exploration towards improvement.

The expressed intention of the framers of the Protocol to exclude from the new system of pacific settlement any disputes which may arise regarding existing territorial divisions appears to us to detract considerably from the value of the instrument. Many existing frontiers were fixed by Treaties negotiated before the shadow of the Great War had receded and before the passions which the War aroused had subsided. The passage of years may prove these delimitations to be convenient and equitable; on the other hand, it may in time become apparent that present boundaries are in some cases unsuitable and provocative of ill will. We realise that the stability of the Continent of Europe, and the prevention of a renewed international race in armaments must depend largely on the extent to which the existing apprehensions of nations, whether well or ill-founded, regarding possible interference with their territorial integrity can be allayed. As long, however, as some of the more powerful States refrain from participation in the League of Nations the feeling of uneasiness and distrust will continue. The continued absence of certain of these States from the Councils of the League is in some degree admittedly attributable to their unwillingness to be called upon to take active measures to maintain for all time existing frontiers even though these should prove to have been inequitably drawn. We fear that the conclusion of an agreement which must to some extent appear to these Nations to partake of the nature of an alliance confined to States Members of the League emphasising by implication the immutability of these frontiers and imposing upon Members additional obligations, particularly by way of participation in disputes and in sanctions, is not calculated to induce them to accept the responsibilities of membership and is, therefore, likely to hinder rather than further the progress of world pacification and disarmament.

The Irish Free State, because of its geographical position, because its armed forces have been reduced to the minimum requisite for the maintenance of internal order, and because of its Constitution, which provides that, except in case of invasion, it can only be committed to participation in war with the consent of the Oireachtas, cannot be regarded as a material factor in the enforcement of sanctions. Consequently, the foregoing observations on the Protocol are not affected by any considerations especially affecting the Irish Free State, and are dictated solely by our genuine desire that the League of Nations should realise the aspirations of its founders by uniting all nations in the common interest of world peace.

If we might express an opinion upon the measures by which these aspirations may best be realised, and naturally we do so with the utmost diffidence, we would suggest that the solution is to be found not in an endeavour to close the fissures in the Covenant by elaborate definition or drastic sanction, but rather in an effort to enhance the moral influence of international conscience. An extension of the principle of Arbitration which serves to define and annunciate international judgment and which relies in the last resort on the moral pressure of world opinion and not upon the application of material sanctions appears to us to be the most effective feasible means of attaining, at least in a large measure[,] the objects which the Protocol has in view.

The League of Nations has justified its existence even if account is taken only of the immense scheme of social progress which it has initiated. The reconstruction of countries devastated by the Great War which has been accomplished under its aegis, the succour which has, through its machinery, been afforded to hundreds of thousands rendered homeless by international calamity, and the measures which have been adopted for the suppression of traffic in arms and of vice are achievements of which it may justly be proud.

It is not without significance that in this section of the activities of the League it has had the active cooperation and support of States which have not hitherto found it possible to accept obligations of membership, and perhaps it may not be too much to hope that the opportunities thus afforded for intercourse between member and non-member States may by the further development of these activities be instrumental in allaying the apprehensions and in removing the prejudices which hinder the full co-operation of those States in the efforts of the League for the maintenance of international peace.

No. 316 UCDA P4/424

Hugh Kennedy to William T. Cosgrave
(Strictly Confidential)

DUBLIN, 12 June 1925

A Uachtaráin, A Chara dhílis,
I saw in some paper the other day some reference to a claim by the Northerners that they are entitled to the whole of Lough Foyle. It occurred to me that I should drop you a line lest the question of territorial jurisdiction as regards water might be lost sight of. You will remember the point that was made that Northern Ireland consists of certain parliamentary counties and that the Free State consists of the rest of Ireland, so defined by the Government of Ireland Act, 1920; and you will remember that we have always contended that this definition gave us the whole sea shore surrounding the country, together with loughs upon which both Northern Ireland and ourselves abutted.

As far as I could make out – but I never could get anything definite upon it – this view was held in London in the early period of 1922, and was taken, I believe, by the first Law Officers who dealt with our business. Subsequently I was told, but only by hints, that later law officers had given a definite opinion the other way. I know that the Parliamentary Draftsmen were very shaky on the question and nervous about it until they got the later opinion.

Should it not be made clear at the Boundary Commission that we claim to have already in the Free State the whole of Ireland except the territory represented by the parliamentary areas of the Six Counties? The attempt to capture Lough Foyle would be very serious.

Mise do chara,
(HUGH KENNEDY)
Chief Justice

No. 317 NAI DFA ES Box 29 File 192

Timothy A. Smiddy to Desmond FitzGerald (Dublin)
(M/Sp. 135/25) (Copy)

WASHINGTON, 16 June 1925

My dear Minister:

Passport Visas.

With reference to cable of June 11th[1] advising your reconsideration of discontinuance of the endorsement: 'This visa does not entitle holder to disembark in the Irish Free State prior to landing in Great Britain,' I beg to state that this endorsement was prompted by the fact that:

(1) Some U.S.A. travellers who obtained visas from British Consuls other than the Consul-General at New York did not seek an Irish Free State visa, though they intended to land in the first instance at an Irish Free State port.

(2) Some travellers also felt that provided they had the visa of Great Britain – to whom they paid the fee – and the Free State they were free to change their minds on ship and disembark in the first instance at Cobh.

If this belief were to persist it will be likely to become sufficiently extensive to bring about a substantial decrease in the visa receipts because there would be no advantage in paying the visa fee to the Irish Free State if the traveller has in practice the choice while 'en route' to land either at an Irish Free State or a British port.

As custom is working in favour of the continuance of the British Visa for the Irish Free State – the necessity for an Irish Free State visa not being generally known to some intending travellers – the endorsement in question was devised to expedite its discontinuance and to ensure the payment of visa fees by all the U.S.A. travellers from the port of New York to the Irish Free State.

In this connection I wish to point out that everything possible has been done to give publicity to the existence of an Irish Free State Passport Control Office at New York and to the necessity for all U.S.A., and other aliens sailing from that port for the Irish Free State to have their passports visaed at that office.

I would again respectfully draw your attention to my previous correspondence on the necessity for the issue of Irish Free State passports;[2] and I would point out that if it is decided to issue them that power should be given to issue

[1] Not printed.
[2] Not printed.

them for applicants *in all parts of the U.S.A.*; this will avoid the incongruities that exist with regard to our ability to issue visas *only* to those sailing from the Port of New York. I am of opinion that the question of issuing visas to all suitable applicants in the U.S.A., it matters not from what port they sail, should have your esteemed consideration.

Yours sincerely,
[copy letter unsigned]

No. 318 NAI DFA ES Box 29 File 192

Extract from a letter from W.J.B. Macaulay[1] *to Joseph P. Walshe (Dublin)*
(M/Sp. 130/19/25)

WASHINGTON, 25 June 1925

A Chara:
[Matter omitted]
The Minister Plenipotentiary fears it is not fully appreciated that the work of the Legation is growing and that the position is entirely changed compared with this time last year when the Legation, as such, was not in existence. His Excellency begs to remind the Department that the scope of a legation and that of an unofficial representative is very different, not only vis a vis the State Department but the other Government Departments and Foreign Missions with which this Legation is in communication.

The Minister Plenipotentiary is fully aware of the need for economy and he has sought unceasingly to reduce to a minimum the expense of the Legation, nor would he now ask for sanction for this expenditure were he not convinced of its necessity.
[Matter omitted]

Mise, le meas,
[copy letter unsigned]

No. 319 UCDA P80/420

Extracts from a letter from William Craig Martin[2] *to Desmond FitzGerald (Dublin)*

SHANGHAI, 1 July 1925

Dear Desmond:
Hang your Excellency! and the devil take the whole damn Department of External Affairs! ! !

Have you still got writer's cramp, or has Annie McSweeney bitten off your right arm? How in thunder can one represent anyone whom one never hears from? You can tell Mabel[3] that I am very nearly converted to her point of view. After sitting like a cat on hot bricks for months and being blown up by every

[1] Secretary, Irish legation Washington (1925-29).
[2] Irish Free State Honorary Consul at Shanghai from January 1925 (See NAI DT S4256).
[3] FitzGerald's wife, Mabel, had republican sympathies.

holder of one of our passports all over the Continent of Asia I received a rag of a letter, signed by somebody called Sean Ó Murchadha,[1] magnanimously conferring upon me the most astounding powers in truly deliciously off-hand manner. Now, our dear friend, Sean, may be a most estimable young man, a right hand of our beloved Government. The only awkward thing is that no one here has ever heard of him and his chatty little letter was therefore a bit of a surprise. There is a rumour that the gentleman's name is Langford, but even I felt a trifle doubtful whether M-u-r-c-h-a-d-h-a is the correct Irish spelling for Langford!

Certainly he is a 't. c. Rúnaí'. None of my zoological dictionaries catalogue this animal, so I don't know whether it be dangerous or not. For Heaven's sake don't show him this letter or the next time he communicates with me he will be still more crushing. After reading his remark 'where the holder of a Free State Passport desires to have the protection of the British Consular Officers', I felt about an inch high and I do not think the British Legation in Peking, to whom I had to show the letter as my only authority was exactly pleased with the tone. Incidentally I might tell you that I am not a millionaire and that this whole arrangement has cost a pretty penny. It could not be put through here and I had to go to Peking, with the railways all upset this was a three day's journey by sea and it took ten days in Peking to settle. Altogether it cost me over £50, so tell friend Sean next time he writes to kindly enclose cheque, or the Imperial Authorities will be returning one honorary but destitute representative to his native heath.

By the way, I have asked you officially to give an authorization for my assistant, Mr. Thomas Murphy, to sign in case of my absence or sickness. Mr. T. Murphy, my assistant in business here, is a native of Macroom. You will understand that a passport may have to be attended to immediately and I might be out of town.

[Matter omitted]

I see in the Weekly Irish Times of June 6th. on page 9 that our Authorities in the United States have no power to issue passports. That all we can do is to vise passports and that even then the holder of such a passport must first disembark in England. This seems a most extraordinary state of affairs. Do find time, there's a dear fellow, and tell me what it means. I have been asked for an explanation from several Irishmen here.

I have sent you the papers with regard to the troubles here. They are worth reading. This situation is going to be a much bigger one than appears at first sight. Considering that we had two wars and a long riot since we returned in December things are going quite nicely.

[Matter omitted]

Yours ever,

C[RAIG] M[ARTIN]

[1] Sean Murphy, Assistant Secretary, Department of External Affairs.

No. 320 NAI DFA ES Box 29 File 192

Timothy A. Smiddy to Desmond FitzGerald (Dublin)
(MP/Sp.140/63/25)

WASHINGTON, 2 July 1925

Dear Minister:
May I submit the following suggestions for your and the President's consideration:

The time is now ripe when a visit either from you or the President, or both, or by the Vice-President and you to the United States would be very effective. In fact, few foreign notables would meet with as great a welcome. The advantages of such a visit are many.

Its publicity in favour of the Free State would outweigh the effects of any other kind incurred at much greater cost. Your pronouncements, interviews, etc., while here would occupy a prominent place in all the newspapers throughout the United States. It would be particularly helpful in further emphasizing your achievement in having a Minister Plenipotentiary in Washington, a step the significance of which is not yet fully understood or appreciated even among the Irish in this country.

Again, it would give you a first hand impression of conditions in this country with special reference to the problems of the Irish Free State such as no reports could convey.

Such a visit would be opportune in March when a public reception could be given by the Legation here on the 17th of March to which the diplomatic corps, members of the U.S.A. Cabinet, representative Senators and Congressmen would be invited.

I have no hesitation in saying that you or the President would be more than pleased with the results of your visit. It would expedite exceedingly the realization among all Americans of our real Constitutional status.

I respectfully commend my suggestions to your consideration.

Yours sincerely,
[copy letter unsigned]

No. 321 NAI DT S1801M

T.M. Healy to Leopold Amery (London)
(Confidential)

DUBLIN, 13 July 1925

Sir,
I have the honour to refer to your confidential despatch of the 4th instant[1] on the subject of the letter received from the Secretary of the Boundary Commission regarding the date upon which the determination of the Commission will take effect, and to state that my Ministers appreciate the necessity for a careful examination of the technical details of the administrative arrangements which

[1] Not printed.

will require to be made to enable the determination to take effect with the least possible inconvenience.

2. They are, however, of opinion that this examination would be much facilitated by a preliminary discussion between representatives of both Governments on the general lines which the arrangements should follow, and in view of the possibility that the work of the Commission may be completed by October, they would urge that a conference of this nature should take place if possible before the end of the present month.

3. In the meantime my Ministers are desirous that their reply to the Commission's letter should not be unduly delayed and they would be glad, therefore, to be favoured, in accordance with the terms of paragraph 4 of your despatch No. 243[1] of the 19th ultimo, with a copy of the draft of the reply which the British Government propose to send to the Commission,

I have the honour to be,
Sir,
Your most obedient humble Servant,
(sgd.) T.M. HEALY

No. 322 NAI DFA GR 459-9

Lindsay Crawford to Timothy A. Smiddy (Washington)
NEW YORK, 16 July 1925

IRISH TOURIST DEVELOPMENT

Traffic to An Saorstát since April 1st, 1925 shows a marked increase over past year. Agents generally regard the movement as most gratifying and look for still greater returns next season.

A conservative estimate of the number of Americans and Canadians visiting An Saorstát this tourist season would be at least 10,000. Taking $300 as a minimum expenditure per capita this tourist traffic means an influx of foreign capital in the neighbourhood of $3,000,000.

It will be seen, therefore, how important to An Saorstát is the development of this summer traffic, and how necessary it is that this valuable asset should be safeguarded and expanded by proper business organization and methods.

It is gratifying to report that a large proportion of the tourists to An Saorstát this year represent the highest types of Irish-American successful business and professional classes, many of whom are visiting Ireland for the first time. A large number of these sought an interview with the Trade Agent for the purpose of mapping out tours, enquiring as to hotels, etc. and looked forward with pleasurable anticipation to their Irish experiences. These travellers came from every State in the Union. It is interesting to record that a small proportion only of the tourists to Rome availed of the opportunity to include Ireland in their itinerary. In most cases this was due to failure of agents to include Ireland in their published Rome tour itineraries. Excuse may be found in the fact that Irish tourist literature was not available in time to attract attention. It is most

[1] Not printed.

important to bear in mind that all Irish tourist literature should be a season in advance. This was not possible this year, but an effort should be made to have fixed itineraries, as to railway time tables, hotel rates, etc. etc. in hands of American tourist agencies at latest by September preceding the summer tourist season.

Tourist Literature
There should be one Irish clearing house for the distribution of tourist literature. If this is undertaken by the Irish Tourist Association steps should be taken to simplify and condense the information needed in one pamphlet, attractively jacketed, and artistically reflecting the glamor and spirit of the country. The poster, 'See Ireland First', has been severely criticised by some American advertising men as lacking in artistic and advertising qualities. On this side national advertising is frequently promoted by competition amongst artists. It might be well to consider whether the Irish Tourist Association could be induced to advertise for competitive posters for use in U.S.A., giving a liberal award to the winner. Such posters should be framed and ready to hang. It is waste of money to send out sheet posters to this country.

Having decided upon a clearing house in Ireland that will undertake the work of collecting and preparing tourist literature – pamphlets and leaflets, etc. – for distribution in the United States, the next question to consider is a clearing house in New York.

In a previous report I suggested the use of the Irish Trade Office as an Irish Travel Bureau. As this met with no response I later suggested the establishment in this city of an Irish Travel Bureau under the control of the Irish Tourist Association or some Irish railway company.

Reviewing this question in the light of further experience, I have to report that, in my judgement, such an Irish Travel Bureau should be established as a department of the Irish Trade Office.

The reasons are as follows: (1) An Irish Travel Bureau outside Government jurisdiction might possibly lapse into a private concern as a ticket agency. In any case it might be open to the criticism of favoritism in its relations with the various tourist agencies and would not command the prestige that a Government bureau would in the eyes of rival shipping companies and agencies. It would be a mistake to substitute for this office a private office, to which the shipping companies would have to turn for all information regarding travel in An Saorstát.

(2) The name 'Irish Travel Bureau' would be a valuable business asset for any individual into whose hands the Bureau would fall and might easily be appropriated for purposes other than the original purposes for which it was established. I would suggest that this, or some equally striking name, be registered by the Government, at Washington.

If it is decided to establish an Irish Travel Bureau department in this office, no time should be lost in the work of organization. This Bureau should be in a position this autumn to make connections in person and by letter with the various tourist agencies throughout the country. Irish tourist literature in sufficient quantities should be sent to this Bureau not later than October 1st.

As the Passport Office work will fall away during the autumn and winter months, I would respectfully suggest that Mr. O'Farrell should concentrate on the tourist development work during this period; circularize agencies, make personal visits, distribute available literature and advertising leaflets and posters, and attend personally to the work of securing for An Saorstát a prominent place in all itineraries published by the tourist agencies. Mr. O'Farrell's previous experience and his personal knowledge of the personnel of the various shipping and tourist offices would be of great value in stimulating the tourist traffic to An Saortstát in the coming season and help to place the traffic on businesslike and permanent foundations.

[signed] LINDSAY CRAWFORD

No. 323 NAI DT S4541

Memorandum by the Council of Defence on Irish Defence Policy
(Secret)

DUBLIN, 22 July 1925

EACH MEMBER OF THE EXECUTIVE COUNCIL.
Re: DEFENCE POLICY.

We have the honour to invite your attention to the urgent and absolute necessity for placing us in possession of at least the outlines of the Defence Policy of the Government, and to bring under notice matters which we respectfully submit are factors in the Defence of the Country on which the members of the Executive Council should have the full and complete views of your responsible military chiefs.

NECESSITY FOR DEFINITION OF POLICY.

1. To point out the necessity for a Defence Policy in accordance with which we will organise the Defence of the Nation is to emphasize the obvious. Our Policy since the formation of the Army has been the establishment of forces for the suppression of the Irregulars and the education of our regular officers and men in the A B C of their profession.

2. The Government and the Taxpayers must be satisfied that the Nation will benefit as a result of the existence and functioning of an Army to such an extent as to justify the expenditure of the amount represented by the Army Vote. It follows that they must have in mind the particular functions which they expect the Army to perform. If they are to be performed they must be clearly defined by the Government with full knowledge of the implications and commitments involved.

3. In the absence of this definition of policy it is impossible to organise and equip the Forces to any very useful purpose. We must indicate to our officers the particular functions which they must be prepared to perform under various conditions and circumstances (as far as these can be foreseen) if they are to be in a position to meet these eventualities.

It is impossible to have the most effective organisation with a minimum of expense if the object in view is not clearly understood and if every man, organism or particle of material which does not contribute towards the achievement of that objective is not eliminated.

NECESSITY FOR APPRECIATION BY THE GOVERNMENT OF THE MILITARY FACTORS IN OUR DEFENCE POLICY AND FOR APPRECIATION BY MILITARY CHIEFS OF POLITICAL AND ECONOMIC FACTORS.

4. We of course appreciate the fact that the Executive Council collectively, and the Minister for Defence in particular, can alone pronounce authoritatively, fully and finally on this matter of Policy, and that the Military heads of the Army are merely concerned in implementing the Policy so given to them. We feel, however, that we would be lacking in our duty if we did not lay before you frankly our unanimous opinion on this most important and involved matter, even at the risk of going somewhat outside the scope of our responsibilities.

5. We will put before you in the following paragraphs considerations which we urge upon your attention as matters regarding which the Supreme Executive Authority must be fully informed and which we suggest demand the formulation and promulgation of a deliberate policy.

These are matters on which the complete Government attitude should be made clear (secretly) to those who like ourselves are charged with responsibility, of the weight of which we are duly conscious; and matters too upon which public pronouncement may be desirable according as may seem politic to you. We labour this point because we feel strongly that only when we and our immediate advisors are in possession of your views, and of the political, economic and other information which is available to you and not to us, can we be assured that we can lay before the Executive Council the full, reasoned and candid opinions and information which it is our duty to provide, and which is necessary to you for the proper conduct of the affairs of the Nation in regard to Defence. We feel bound to say that without this complete understanding our advice and assistance cannot be at all as useful or intimate as it should be. We would be in the invidious position of having to advise on matters which we might not have the spirit as well as the letter of the Government's intention, and of having to endeavour to meet its military needs without the fullest possible appreciation of those needs and an assurance that the Government understood fully the Military implications and commitments of its directions and the extent to which we could carry them into effect.

PROBABLE NATURE OF AGGRESSION AND IDENTITY OF AGGRESSORS AGAINST WHOM WE MUST DEFEND OUR COUNTRY.

6. The necessity for a Defence Policy and for an organisation to carry out that policy arises only from the obligation of preserving our country and our people from exploitation by nations or internal parties who may endeavour to enforce their will upon us. This being so we must attempt to visualize the nature and circumstances of the aggression and the identity of the aggressors before we can prepare our defence against them.

We may consider the matter as exhibiting two main aspects[,] which are External aggression and Internal aggression. In regard to the former the following facts and probabilities must be borne in mind.

7. The very recent development of warfare has been such as to make Aerial Forces, Submarines, Radio Telegraphy and Chemical warfare cardinal factors in war. These agencies in themselves are considered to be sufficient to completely defeat any adversary no matter how powerful, who does not get the

opponent in a vicelike grip in the opening stages of conflict. They are the weapons and agencies with which a powerful nation would endeavour to smash its enemy within a few weeks, or even days, of the declaration of war. They are essentially the weapons on which any power attacking England would rely. There are at least three, and probably four, great powers who could bring overwhelming forces of this nature into play without any appreciable delay. Developments in all these four agencies of combat and destruction are reported day by day.

8. Ireland by reason of her geographical position may be said to be the Aerial and Submarine key to England. For the operation of the four agencies mentioned above, either in attack or defence, England must consider Ireland as a dangerously vulnerable point and one of her most important lines of Defence. It is only natural that England's enemies would look upon this country in the same light, and while they would direct their main destructive efforts against the vital industrial and administrative centres in Britain, they would pay due attention to the destruction of British forces here. They would also consider very carefully the use of Ireland as a temporary base for Aerial raids on an immense scale, and probably find such a project feasible. They would of course attempt to exploit us to their advantage in every way possible.

9. We have the authority of several great figures on both sides in the recent great war, including Ludendorff, 'the brain of the German Armies', that propaganda was one of the most effective, if not the most effective weapon which the Western nations used against Germany. There is every reason to believe that it will play an equally important part in any great war which may come upon us. The great Irish populations abroad make it a weapon of importance to us. It could be used to bring us into war against our will, and it could be used with even greater effect in our defence.

10. The fact that Ireland supplies in a great measure England's imported food, and that our imports of food and other necessities are carried in English bottoms would be a vital matter during a war in which she became involved.

11. Our Defence Forces such as they are depend entirely for their existence on supplies of war material from England.

12. They are not capable, as at present constituted, of taking any really effective part in the Defence of the country against a modern army, navy or air force.

13. In view of all these and many similar and relative factors, Ireland is as likely to become a cockpit for the belligerents in a war between England and any other power, as Belgium was before the Great War, if not to the same extent.

14. In any such eventuality, British troops, the British Air Force and the British Navy would assume control of the country. They would insist on unity of command. That means that any troops we put in the field would be under the orders of the Imperial General Staff from 'Somewhere in England', instead of the Irish Government, and would be supplied with material only when and how that Staff pleased.

15. Happily our people have not experienced the horrors of modern war. They do not, therefore, appreciate the appalling destruction with which we would be almost certain to be visited if England went to war with any first class power. Their slight experience has, however, made them alive to the blessings of peace and the necessity for taking effective steps to maintain our neutrality.

16. Apart entirely from the case of a war in which England is involved, we must consider the possibility of a war between the U.S.A. and France, Germany or Russia, or any war in which the belligerents would have vital interests or communication by Sea, Aeroplane, Airship or Wireless in or around Ireland, or in which they would endeavour to exploit Irish resources and populations in their individual interests. In such an eventuality there would be several matters which might involve us in serious international complications, if not in war, if the Nations have not reason to respect our ability to maintain our neutrality, or if our weapons of defence are not sufficiently organised to prevent exploitation by interested parties.

17. The second or Internal aspect of Defence is one with which we are all familiar and we need not dwell upon it longer than to say that we have to consider the following three possibilities:

(a) Serious disturbances in the North East.

(b) An outbreak by the Irregulars.

(c) A serious riot or disturbance by any body such as the Association of ex-Army men, The Communists, etc.

We must, we presume, have machinery to protect the State against these and similar disturbances.

THE POSSIBLE ALTERNATIVES AND SOME FUNDAMENTAL PRINCIPLES AND FACTS IN WAR AND DEFENCE.

18. There appear to be three alternative policies which might possibly be pursued by the Government in the matter of Defence. They are:

(a) The development of our individuality as a Nation; the gradual assumption of responsibility for Defence, and the development and organisation of our resources into a complete Defensive machine.

(b) The organisation and maintenance of Defence Forces which would be an integral part of the British Imperial forces and would, in the event of war, be controlled by the Imperial General Staff.[1]

and

(c) The abandonment to England of responsibility for Defence against external enemies, and the formation of a force to deal with internal disorders.[2]

19. It is axiomatic that the Defence Policy of the State should conform with its general position and development, and more particularly with its Foreign, Agricultural, Industrial and Commercial policies and development.

20. It is also axiomatic that expenditure on National Defence should be so applied as to contribute to the greatest possible extent to the general well being, the cultural, industrial and economic good of the country, and that the expenditure which does not bring some direct return in those respects should be mainly on the organization of our resources in men and material, and the training of the men who[,] should the necessity arise, will control and direct this organisation in the prosecution of war or the preservation of neutrality.

---

[1] Handwritten note by Cosgrave referring to paragraphs (a) and (b): 'Combine: Independent organisation capable of complete co-operation with British forces'.

[2] Handwritten note by Cosgrave: 'No'.

21. In National security more than in any other matter, efficiency must be paramount. It would be much better to have no Defence Organisation than to have an inefficient one.
22. Modern war is not a war of Armies; it is a conflict of peoples. The Nation as a whole, our industrial, administrative and agricultural activities, and our unarmed citizens are as much subject to attack as our Defence Forces if such attack suits the ends of our opponents, and our Defence must be the Defence of the entire population and our vital activities. If the occasion demands we must be prepared to employ all our resources in our Defence. Defence as thus visualized is more than actual combat; it is the struggle for the continuance of the National life, the preservation of our populations, our resources, our institutions and our international position.
23. The maintenance and effective preservation of the National life side by side with the exertion of the necessary force (it may be the maximum force of which we are capable) necessitates the establishment of an organisation that can utilise all our resources and power to this end. This organisation must be subject to one authority, the Minister for Defence. One of the fundamental principles in the successful conduct of war is unity of command.

THE POLICY OF INDEPENDENCE IN THE DEFENCE OF IRELAND.
24. It would be foolish for Ireland to endeavour to become a Military force or to indulge in militaristic adventures as the ally of England or any other power. On the other hand it is obvious that we will be used by powerful nations because of our unique geographical position if those nations find it profitable to so use us.
25. It would certainly be possible to organize our defence in such a manner that it would not be profitable for any power to interfere with us in any way. Without being aggressive we can be sufficient of a hornet's nest to any outsider to make him keep his hands off in his own interests. It would not be worth the while of France or any nation attacking England to use this country if such a step involved the commitment of any considerable amount of force and energy against us. Similarly England will be quite content to know that we will keep out her enemies, and she will be secure in the knowledge that it would not be in our interest to attack her.
26. In our general relations England will be more circumspect if she finds that she cannot control us militarily without an expenditure of force which would not be worth the result.
27. As previously mentioned, our Defence Policy is an integral part of the general policy of the State, is dependent on our economic position and is bound up with our Foreign, Industrial, Commercial and Agricultural policies. Therefore, if the policy dealt with in these paragraphs is adopted the aims should be

(a) to develop our individuality as a Nation;

(b) to establish friendly and intimate relations with U.S.A., France and Germany, all of whose interests would be served by an independent Ireland.[1]

[1] Handwritten note by Cosgrave: 'Do not visualise anything but alliance with G.B.'.

(c) to make the country as self-supporting as possible, particularly in the matter of food and other necessaries of life;

(d) to develop and foster those industrial resources which would enable us to equip ourselves in our defence;

(e) to organise our weapons of defence and offence with a view to ensuring that the people of this country would suffer as little as possible in the event of a war in which England would be involved and in which we might find it desirable to join her (We are of course assuming that we will not or could not take part in a big war otherwise) and with a view to being sufficiently dangerous to possible aggressors that we will be able to maintain our neutrality at will.

28. Our weapons of Defence and Offence appear to be:

(a) Propaganda and Diplomacy. The Irish in America and elsewhere make these particularly powerful weapons for such a small State, always provided that there is a united front at home.

The adroit use of these weapons will help to prevent either England or any other Nation from encroaching on our rights or liberties.

(b) An Irish Air Force, which could be built up by the development of Civil aviation so as to provide a maximum number of Airmen and Machines which would perform commercial and other work in peace time and be formed into a fighting force by organisation as a reserve. Our geographical position as a suitable and likely European base for a transatlantic Air Service should compensate for other drawbacks in the development of aviation in this country.

(c) A Chemical Warfare Service which could be organised and developed in conjunction with Medical, Industrial and Agricultural research. Our State laboratories, educational establishments and laboratories connected with industrial concerns should all be subject to the co-ordinating and animating influence of the Defence Council.

As in the case of our Air Force, a reserve corps of officers could be formed which would perform the ordinary duties of their calling in peace time and be available for service in war with the experience, discipline, understanding and esprit de corps necessary to success in Army organisation.

(d) A Coastal Defence System built up in the progress of the years by the development of our fishing industry and Irish Mercantile Marine, and Dockyards for the repair, and, as far as possible, the construction of surface craft.

By close attention on the part of the Defence Council our nautical activities could be brought in line with our Defence Scheme and our seafaring population organised into a branch of the reserve.

The construction of Submarines is not feasible in the immediate future but there is no reason why we should not keep the matter in mind.

Defence against surface craft and submarines could be organised by nets, sunken ships, mines, etc.

The question of the Coast Defences in the hands of the British Government, which is due to come up for consideration next year, is a matter for consideration in the light of this aspect of our Defence Policy.

(e) Attack by means of mining operations on enemy nerve centres, such as Dockyards, Railway termini, Aerodromes, Industrial Plant, etc. etc. This could be effected by the organisation of Irish populations which exist in almost every country and could be considered for execution by way of reprisal or otherwise. Our activities during the Anglo-Irish war, and those of Germany and England during the world war, furnish a headline, and

(f) A standing Army of Infantry supported by Artillery, Armoured cars, Tanks, Mounted Infantry, Engineers, etc., strong enough to form the nucleus of a force to be raised in war and so highly organized as to be able to train a very much larger reserve or territorial force.

The available man power of the country not otherwise absorbed into the Defence Scheme, i.e. those not earmarked for employment in activities mentioned in (a) to (e) above, or not engaged in work vital to the life of the Nation, should be organised into a reserve or territorial unit of the Army and trained as far as possible in their warlike duties.

In the preceding paragraphs we have dealt with Defence Policy in regard to foreign aggression as we think it should develop if the form now under consideration be adopted. We recognise of course that this is a matter for Government decision and definition, and we also recognise that the immediate need is to concentrate on those means of Defence which are at hand and which are not likely to involve us in international or Imperial difficulties.

The production at home of sufficient food and other essentials to enable the nation to exist through a period of blockade; the production at home of weapons and materials of defence including mechanical transport, wireless apparatus, clothing, power alcohol, etc. etc., and the planning of an organisation that will control and co-ordinate all vital national activities in time of war to whatever degree is found necessary, are three big questions of National Defence which should command immediate attention.

The organisation and development of each weapon of offence and defence can at least be begun. Our Army, the most important weapon, can be organised with due regard to the fact that it is only one of a number of weapons of defence and organised so as to harmonise with each other weapon in the whole scheme.

We must also keep before us the relative strengths of ourselves and other countries, the position of Switzerland, Belgium and Denmark, in regard to defence matters; the development of warfare and the tendencies towards alliances or towards a spirit of enmity of States in whose actions we are interested. It is also most important that we fully realise the extent of our comparative weakness.

DEFENCE AS A PART OF THE DEFENCE SCHEME OF THE BRITISH EMPIRE.

29. If the policy of organising forces dependent upon England for the supplies vital to their existence and capable only of acting in conjunction with England is adopted, we should, in order to conform to the principles of economy and efficiency, face the implications of this policy squarely and carry it into effect as thoroughly as possible.

30. Our whole Defence organisation should be complementary to the Imperial Forces. We should be trained, equipped, organised, etc. in accordance with the Imperial scheme. Our position would not, in the carrying into effect of this policy, be that of Canada, but more nearly related to that of the British Territorial Army in relation to the Imperial General staff. Money spent on Defence would largely be spent in England on war material. We should conform to the methods

and standards of Britain; our officers should be educated by British Staff officers either in England or here; the spirit of the British Army should and would pervade our forces.

31. We cannot go into the manner in which this policy could or should be adopted, as we have no information regarding the decisions taken at the Imperial Defence Conference held some years ago, and we have not had any opportunity of being in touch with the communications, if any, which have passed between our Government and the British on the subject of Defence.

32. We must, however, remark that the forces created in accordance with this policy would not be effective in the suppression of internal disorders.

From the military point of view we have also to put on record the fact that this policy would not, in our opinion, be the most effective means of economically organising our resources for defence purposes. As mentioned above, but in other words, the only effective Army is that which is the expression of the Nation's fighting capabilities. The morale of the Army is a most vital matter, and it would be difficult to maintain a high state of morale under the conditions which the adoption of this policy would create. These and other matters could not be as satisfactorily dealt with in accordance with the policy now under consideration as they could be by adopting a national policy which would have for its primary objective the general well being of the State.

THE POLICY OF ABANDONING TO ENGLAND RESPONSIBILITY FOR THE DEFENCE OF IRELAND.

34.[1] The only other Policy which appears open to the Government is that of entrusting the entire responsibility for our Defence to the British Government. This is the policy adopted in Northern Ireland, and could be put into effect here in a similar manner.

35. If it is considered necessary to maintain home forces for the suppression of internal disorders this end could be best achieved by the abolition of the Defence Forces as at present constituted, and the formation of a special Constabulary on the model of North East Ulster, with the augmentation of the Detective Division of the Police, somewhat after the manner of the Danish precedent.

36. Our present Army is not by any means an economical or effective machine for the suppression of internal disorders, and there does not appear to be any justification for its existence in its present form if this is its only function.

NORTH EAST ULSTER

37. We have avoided any reference to the position created by partition for two reasons:

(a) The fact that we have no information on the National position in this respect other than that which we obtain through Army machinery, and what is available to the ordinary man in the street, makes it impossible for us to deal adequately with a matter which is the subject of very delicate political negotiations and which in view of the functioning of the Boundary Commission, may be said to be sub judice.

[1] The document contains no paragraph numbered 33.

(b) The Ulster position does not affect the matter at issue from a military point of view, i.e. the selection of one of the three alternative policies mentioned above. The inherent weakness of partition in regard to security is recognised, but this does not affect the necessity for taking the best possible steps to secure the Defence of the Area under the jurisdiction of our Government.

In conclusion we wish to observe that we have only laid the outlines of the alternative schemes of Defence before you, that we will be happy to elaborate any particular suggestion or observation, and that the necessity for an early decision is most acutely felt.

PEADAR Ó HAODHA, Minister for Defence
S[EOIRSE] MAC NIOCAILL, Parliamentary Sec. Department of Defence
PEADAR MAC MATHGHAMHNA, Lieut. Genl. Chief of Staff
AODH MAC NÉIL, Major Genl. Adjutant General
F.[ELIX] CRONIN, Major Genl. Quartermaster General

No. 324 NAI DT S1801L

T.M. Healy to Leopold Amery (London)
(Confidential)

DUBLIN, 23 July 1925

Sir,
I have the honour to acknowledge the receipt of your confidential despatch of the 20th instant[1] regarding the date upon which the determination of the Boundary Commission will take effect, and to state that my Ministers concur generally in the terms of the reply which the British Government propose to make to the Commission's memorandum on the subject. My Ministers, however, for reasons which they will advance at the forthcoming preliminary discussion, are of opinion that it may not be found possible to hold the further conference referred to in the 4th paragraph of your despatch before October, and they would suggest that the reply to the Commission should be altered accordingly.
2. A copy of the draft of the reply which my Ministers propose to address to the Secretary of the Boundary Commission, and which is couched in similar terms to the draft which accompanied your despatch, is sent herewith.
3. My Ministers agree that Tuesday the 28th instant will be a suitable date for the preliminary discussion between representatives of both Governments of the general lines which the arrangements to enable the determination of the Commission to take effect with the least possible inconvenience should follow, and the Minister for Justice, the Minister for Finance and the Attorney General, accompanied by the High Commissioner, will accordingly be in attendance at the Dominions Office at 11 a.m. on that date.

I have the honour to be,
Sir,
Your most obedient humble Servant,
(Sgd.) T.M. HEALY

[1] Not printed.

No. 325 NAI DT S1801N

Diarmuid O'Hegarty to F.B. Bourdillon (London)
(Confidential)

DUBLIN, 27 July 1925

Sir,
I am directed by the Executive Council to refer to your letter of the 8th June[1] last enclosing a memorandum drawn up by the Boundary Commission on the subject of the taking effect of the Commission's decision when reached and to acquaint you for the information of the Commission, that my Government are advised that the Commission have no power under the terms of Article 12 of the Treaty between Great Britain and Ireland to postpone the effect of their determination and that, once the determination has been made, the Boundary, as so determined, becomes automatically the Boundary between Northern Ireland and the rest of Ireland for the purposes of the Government of Ireland Act and of the Treaty. It is understood that the British Government concur in this view.

It is proposed that a Conference should take place not later than October next between representatives of the two Governments for the purpose of considering the administrative and other arrangements which it may be necessary to make in order to enable the determination of the Commission to take effect with the least possible inconvenience to the public, and in the meantime the technical details of such arrangements are receiving a careful preliminary examination in the various departments concerned. A further communication will be addressed to you on this subject after the proposed Conference has taken place.

A copy of this letter is being sent to the Secretary of State for Dominion Affairs for the information of the British Government.

I am, Sir,
Your obedient Servant,
[initialled] D O'H

No. 326 UCDA P4/424

Handwritten letter from William T. Cosgrave to Hugh Kennedy

DUBLIN, undated (but late August 1925)

Do d'Uasal Cinnéide
Príomh-Bhreitheamh

A chara Dhíl,
The last phase of the Boundary hearing took place this week. The A. Genl and P. Lynch were heard mainly on the issue that it was not open to the Boundary Cmn. to take any territory or area from us. We have heard from Murnaghan that the Atty Genl was not at his best and that Lynch was weak – very weak.

[1] Not printed.

I suggested that MacNeill should put in a caveat or some similar instrument giving if possible stronger reasons & also mentioned that I was sure if I approached you any assistance [page or more missing in original] I only met him once – at Beechpark at a Garden Party – or perhaps you would not like me to do anything in that connection.

I am sure MacNeill would be available at any time you are in a position to see him.

Mis[e],
[signed] L.T. MacCosgair

No. 327 NAI DT S4596

Michael MacDunphy to Joseph P. Walshe (Dublin)
(S4430)

Dublin, 24 August 1925

A chara,

As you are aware a delegation consisting of the following persons will be setting out for America about the middle of next month to attend the Congress of the Inter-Parliamentary Union at Washington during the first half of October:-

Professor Hayes,[1] Ceann Chomairle,
General Mulcahy, T.D.,
T. Johnson,[2] T.D.

The Minister for Industry and Commerce[3] will also be in the United States and Canada about the same time on a mission connected with the work of his Department.

2. Subject to the observations contained in paragraph 4 (four) hereof, the President considers it desirable that each of the persons concerned should be provided with material in compact form which will enable him to answer enquiries, and, if necessary, to speak at Receptions &c., on matters of interest relating to the Irish Free State, whether political, commercial, social or otherwise, including among other things the Shannon Scheme and the Sugar Beet project. The question of Medical Registration which is now occupying so much space in the Press may also possibly claim attention. Statistics relating to Industry, Unemployment, crime &c., showing the rise or fall in recent years and the comparison with other States, would be useful.

3. The President desires therefore, that you will kindly arrange immediately with the various departments concerned to prepare the necessary material in the form of brief notes and readily available statistics, which when ready should be collated and assembled by your Department in convenient form for use of the Delegates.

4. The position of Mr. Johnson, who is not a member of the Government or of the Parliamentary Party, with which it is associated[,] is somewhat different

[1] Professor Michael Hayes (1889-1976), Ceann Comhairle (Speaker) of the Dáil (1922-32).
[2] Thomas Johnson (1872-1963), Leader of the Irish Labour Party.
[3] Patrick McGilligan.

from that of the other persons named, but he should certainly be made aware of the existence of, and have at his disposal, in case he desires to avail himself of it, the material which is being provided for them.

5. The President considers that the time has come for breaking down the tradition of subscription-seeking with which Ireland has so long been associated in American minds. This condition of things, which in the past was more or less inevitable owing to our political circumstances, is no longer defensible, at least on the scale which has hitherto obtained, and is certainly not in accord with our dignity as a State. He thinks that good pioneer work could be done by the delegation in regard to this matter, by bringing it home to friendly Americans that the time is past when the appearance of persons or delegations representing the Irish Free State in America was tantamount to call for subscriptions for some charitable or political object. If the friendly feeling which undoubtedly exists and which has hitherto expressed itself in the form of generous support for every collection organised for the benefit of Irish or pseudo-Irish interests could be diverted to the much more useful and dignified channel of contribution to the economic development of this country by supporting our industries, very valuable work will have been done both for our prestige and for our prosperity.

6. The accepted tradition of a race of starving peasants and needy politicians must be replaced by the realisation of a self-reliant Ireland with great potentialities of prosperity, governing herself with dignity and efficiency, taking her natural place in the commercial arenas of the world, asking no favours, but ready and willing to trade her products, the quality of which is famed throughout the world. It should be made clear to our friends in the United States that the use of articles of Irish manufacture or production is much more serviceable to our interests and much more acceptable to our national sensibility, than subscriptions to various causes, deserving or otherwise, in regard to which they have shown themselves to be so generous in the past. As a small beginning it might be suggested that Irish goods should be used as far as possible in connection with the various public and semi-public ceremonies which are such a feature of Irish American life, and that a demand for their use should be fostered as far as possible, with a view to developing and expanding Irish Trade.

7. Undoubtedly there will occur cases in which we will find it necessary or desirable to seek financial aid from our friends in the United States, but cases of this nature can always be vouched for by our Minister Plenipotentiary at Washington.

8. The President desires me to add that he has not been approached by any of the delegates in regard to the above matters, but he feels personally that they urgently call for attention.

Mise, le meas,
[initialled] M MacD
a.s. Rúnaí

No. 328 UCDA P80/420

Extracts from a letter from Desmond FitzGerald to William Craig Martin (Shanghai)

Dublin, 29 August 1925

Dear Craig Martin,

Mea culpa, mea culpa, mea modified culpa! Yes, I have not been a very brilliant correspondent. When I want to write a long letter I postpone it until I have leisure, and leisure that one could call leisure never comes along.

Your official letter of July 1st is being answered through the office, and I am sending you the authorisation you require.

We have been very worried about you since we began getting news of trouble in China. The good-humoured irritability of your letter helps to re-assure me. I do hope things are not too bad out there, or at least their reactions don't affect you.

I am very sorry you had the expense of that long journey. This business is very complicated. Breaking new ground is a very slow process. All Dominions before our advent described their Nationals on their passports as British Subjects. Our people naturally objected to that which is quite unnecessary, and to some extent misleading, and as the British objected to anything that has not precedent they refused to be helpful in the matter. I think that would easily be settled if there were anything in the nature of an Imperial Conference, but any change for which there is no precedent is difficult in the absence of an Imperial Conference.

None of our representatives abroad issue passports, again for the same reason that it is not being done by other Dominion representatives, and again I think this matter will be settleable with a Conference.

We broke new ground by issuing visas in the United States. I wanted to see how that would work before pushing ahead with the issue of passports. The statement you saw in the 'Weekly Irish Times' was correct in as far as the issue of passports is concerned, incorrect in the other part. When we made the arrangement for the issue of visas we had to recognise the fact that there was no passport arrangement between here and England, and it would cause a good deal of inconvenience if we demanded passports between the two countries. Therefore it was obvious that anybody landing in Ireland from America could proceed to England and anybody landing in England could come on to Ireland. The arrangement I made was that when a person was coming to Ireland they should apply to our office in New York for a visa and pay us ten dollars. If they wished also to visit England they should go to the British Consul who would give a visa for nothing. And when a person proposed landing in England he should go first to the British Consul, pay ten dollars for visa and we would give visa free for coming to Ireland.

In order to encourage the people to put the ten dollars in our pocket we indicated that unless they had one of our ten dollar visas they could not land direct in Ireland. The argument about the matter came from the fact that through laziness, stupidity, etc. people who proposed coming here first didn't bother doing what they were instructed to do, went to the British Consul, paid ten dollars for a visa, and either came or did not come to our office in New York for a free visa. These got British visas and embarked not intending to come to Ireland and then on the journey changed their mind and decided to land at Cobh, and were annoyed when we raised the question about their lack of Irish visa. As a matter of fact we have told the agents at Cobh to allow the people to land but to explain to them that we are merely overlooking their lack of ten dollar visa on that one occasion to encourage them in future to put the money in our pocket as we need it.

I shall if possible move on to have our offices issue passports and have some of our representatives made fully exequatured consuls. I cannot guarantee that I shall succeed but I think I shall. Neither can I guarantee to do it quickly. [Matter omitted]

A whole lot of things have been happening since you went away, but the most recent thing has been the Horse Show and all the social events associated with it. Dublin for that time was quite a gay City; bigger crowds than ever and all sorts of amusement in the way of theatres, dances and a cabaret. Also there was an American flag-ship here which induced social events. The result was that for that period one hardly got any sleep. The whole events of that time were a sort of interpretation or re-action to the political history of this year. The big batch of bye-elections early in the year in which the Government Party succeeded rather brilliantly had a very reassuring effect on people.

Then the Budget with its two million pound reduction in taxation cheered them. That was followed up by the pushing ahead of the Shannon Scheme (the actual construction works on this are now beginning); the beet sugar and other schemes which have stirred peoples' imaginations and brought a tone of optimism. So that the Horse Show period came along as though to interpret the general cheerfulness and optimism of the country.

Naturally we[,] seated in this thoroughly stable well-established and progressive country[,] feel very worried about you over there. I hope we are about as wrong-headed as say the English people who a year ago thought that if one came to Dublin one was pretty certain to be disintegrated by a bomb.
[Matter omitted]

No. 329 NAI DFA EA198

Timothy A. Smiddy to Desmond FitzGerald (Dublin)
WASHINGTON, 7 September 1925

CONFERENCE OF THE BRITISH COMMONWEALTH OF NATIONS
WILLIAMSTOWN, MASS., AUGUST, 1925.

1. At the above conference I spoke, August 3rd, on the general subject of the relation of the British Dominions and the Irish Free State to Great Britain and the Imperial Crown with special reference to the Status of the Irish Free State as defined by the Anglo-Irish Treaty of December, 1921.
2. Mr. Lionel Curtis preceded me by outlining the History of Ireland up to the time of the Ulster trouble, 1922. From this time to date I dealt with the more important events and with the military, legal and economic achievements of the Government. I had no manuscript for this part of my address, but I enclose

a copy of the manuscript which treated of the constitutional status of the Irish Free State.[1]

3. This latter formed the text for a general discussion on August 17th on the constitutional status of the nations forming the British Commonwealth of Nations in which Sir Robert Borden[2] and Professor Duncan McArthur (Professor in Queen's University, Kingston, Ontario) were the principal speakers. Cuttings from the press have already been sent to you giving extracts from their speeches.

4. Sir Robert Borden prefaced his speech by stating: 'I am in substantial agreement with Professor Smiddy and differ from him only in the following assertions:-

'(a) The League of Nations and its Membership weaken the ties which unite the nations which form the British Commonwealth.

(b) The unity of the Commonwealth is very largely formal.

(c) Hasty bellicose action on the part of Great Britain is thereby much lessened – as a result of the co-equality of nations forming the British Commonwealth.'

5. I wound up the debate in which I replied to Sir Robert's disagreement on these points. As regards (a): The divergence of views which has already manifested itself in non-essential matters does give rise to a belief in the weakening of the ties which unite the nations forming the British Commonwealth. Keith in his recent work, 'The Constitution, Administration and Laws of the Empire', states, 'The unit of the Empire preserved *generally* in diplomatic relations is largely lost in the part assigned to it in the League of Nations.' In the main I agreed that in essentials such unity is not likely to be lost as the fourth sentence of the second last paragraph in enclosed copy of my address indicates.

6. As regards (b): Sir Robert stated: 'In all essentials there must be real unity' and 'This unity is not diminished by the right of the Dominions to negotiate treaties regarding "purely domestic affairs".' In my written address I endeavoured to indicate what I consider the nature of this unity and in the subsequent discussion I further developed my idea of its implications. I pointed out that the whole British Constitution rested on the concept of constitutional rights; and while the Imperial Crown and Parliament had always the legal power to act in opposition to such constitutional rights – such as a veto of the Crown – yet it would be revolutionary of either to do so. Such legal power was merely a symbol of unity, and, hence, had only a *formal* validity: it did not work. In fact, Mr. Lionel Curtis went even further in this direction on the following day, August 18th, when he said 'The Crown is only a registering body and the King was only a hereditary president.'

7. Further, in this connection Sir Robert said there was no innovation in the signing [of] the Halibut Treaty, 1923, by the Canadian Minister without the concurrence of the British Ambassador. I expressed the view there was a real innovation as appeared evident from the correspondence that took place between the Canadian Government and the British Foreign Office. This Treaty is another illustration of the point that the diplomatic unity of the nations

---

[1] Not printed.

[2] Prime Minister of Canada (1911-20), delegate of Canada to the Washington Conference (1922), and to the League of Nations (1930).

forming the British Commonwealth tends to become more formal.
8. With regard to (c), he said he did not anticipate any such hasty bellicose action on the part of Great Britain as I had thought. I replied that it was not very probable but it was possible as exemplified by the Chanak affair when Lloyd George was checked by the protests of Australia and the other Dominions. General Sir Frederick Maurice, who also took part in the debate, made a statement not calculated to raise the prestige of British Diplomacy, viz., 'that Mr. Lloyd George simply endeavoured to *bluff* the Turks and that he had no intention of fighting.'
9. Sir Robert made the statement that, in order to insure unanimity of action on the part of the nations forming the British Commonwealth on essential matters, their representatives should meet in London beforehand and agree on common action. Mr. Curtis was much perturbed at this statement because it would furnish a strong weapon in the hands of the opponents of the League of Nations in this country, who frequently assert that the British Empire has seven votes to the one the U.S.A. would have in the event of her joining the League, a view which Professor Rappard strongly contested on the following day.
10. In ultimate analysis there was substantial agreement in the views expressed by me, Sir Robert Borden, Professor McArthur and Mr. Lionel Curtis. To illustrate further the evolutionary character of the British Commonwealth and the extent to which it depends on the 'will' of its constituent units, Sir Robert stated 'that Canada could attain the status of an absolutely separate nation to-morrow if her people so desired; but such a desire is wholly wanting.' On this statement the New York Sun, August 21st, in an editorial, comments:

> 'The implication … is that the present status exists *not at the pleasure* of the British Empire but at that of its constituent States. The question therefore is not what the Imperial Government ought to concede to them but what they will insist upon taking as their right from the Imperial Government.'

11. Sir Robert also emphasized the point that Great Britain herself was only a constituent State co-equal with the other States of the Commonwealth and that she will, in actual practice, have to accept that position.
12. In the discussion that was opened the following day, August 18th, on the League of Nations Mr. Curtis expressed himself fully on his conception of the status of the nations forming the British Commonwealth in which he gave the most liberal interpretation possible to its recent developments and its further tendencies. He went as far as he could short of admitting that each nation in the Commonwealth was a completely separate political entity. He referred to the Constitution of the Irish Free State as being the first instrument in which is written some of the conventions of the British Constitution, and stated that the logical mind of the Irish demanded this, but that it was entirely contrary to British political tradition and to British temperament. With reference to this point Professor Rappard said such unwritten conventions were very well for a powerful nation like Great Britain which prefers the vague and undefined so that they could give words and conventions a meaning that would suit their own interests. Throughout the conference the attitude of Mr. Curtis was one of strongly marked sympathy with the Irish Free State, and I took the opportunity, at the end of the debate, to pay a tribute to his good work for the Irish Free

State during the years 1922-23.
13. With reference to the discussion on the League of Nations, I simply made a reference to the registration of the Treaty and to the statement current at the time that the final settlement of the boundary between the Irish Free State and the counties under the jurisdiction of the Northern Parliament might be taken before the League and that the registration of the Treaty was made in view of this emergency; further, that the principle of submitting disputes among the nations of the British Commonwealth to the League was involved in this issue. Speaking from a personal point of view I took up the attitude similar to that recently adopted by Minister Blythe when he stated that prosperity, tolerance and the prestige of the Irish Free State would in time abolish any boundary that would be set up.
14. The audience at Williamstown was a very representative one and of the type that will diffuse knowledge of these problems throughout the country. Wide publicity was given to the addresses and the discussions by every newspaper in the U.S.A. and Canada.

[signed] T.A. Smiddy

No. 330 NAI DFA ES Box 29 File 192

William J.B. Macaulay to Joseph P. Walshe (Dublin)
(M. Spl. 135/4/25)
Washington, 9 September 1925

A Chara,
I am directed by the Minister Plenipotentiary to acknowledge the receipt of your letter of 18th August, 275/300,[1] and to state that in his opinion the number of persons still shewn on the Black List solely on account of their support of the pre-Saorstát movement is exceedingly small, if any.

It will be found on an examination of the Irish names on the list that probably all of these individuals are primarily Bolshevists or Anarchists and while they may have made speeches or otherwise lent their aid in support of the Irish movement, such support was merely incidental and secondary to their real purpose of Bolshevist or anarchical propaganda. Nearing's is a case in point. This man is a notorious anarchist, and the Minister for External Affairs will no doubt agree that any Irish sympathies he may have displayed do not entitle him to claim to be regarded as one proscribed on that account alone. Mr Murphy states that Quinlan was on the list only on account of his republican activities. This has not yet been verified but he certainly has not the infamous reputation which Nearing enjoys in this country.

The British Authorities have always been found to be entirely agreeable to the removal from the Black List of the name of any person whose inclusion thereon could reasonably be regarded as solely due to his support of the pre-Saorstát movement.

The British Embassy, like every other Embassy and Legation save this one, has been in its summer quarters since June and will not return to Washington

[1] Not printed.

until the end of September. Upon its return His Excellency will take up the matter of the Black List directly with the Ambassador, obtain a list of Irish names and endeavour to ascertain whether any of these is included solely on account of the individuals pre-Saorstát activities. There will be no difficulty in having such names removed. It should however be noted that the Embassy is not furnished with full details of the reasons for the inclusion of names on the list; this information is in the Foreign Office and fuller information could be obtained therefrom direct by your Department.

From an examination of the Black List in New York the Minister Plenipotentiary does not consider that it is out of date. The London Passport Officer's list is, of course, quite different since it governs the issuance of passports and the British Foreign Office will not issue passports to residents of Saorstát Éireann since your Department does that. A British Subject requires no visa and none but the names of aliens appears on the Black List.

His Excellency proposes, as a rule, not to allow a visa to be given in cases where persons although known to have supported the pre-Saorstát movement are in fact Bolshevists and who used the Republican movement here merely as a means for gaining publicity and as a side issue in their real activity. The Minister is aware that there are many of this type and he does not think they should be allowed to capitalize any support they may have given to the Irish movement which they utilized, not on its merits, nor for a genuine desire to serve it, but merely as a stepping stone or a convenient instrument in an agitation with which the Republican movement had nothing in common.

Mise, le meas,
[copy letter unsigned]

No. 331 UCDA P4/424

Memorandum on the Boundary Question
(Probably by Hugh Kennedy)

19 September 1925

QUESTION – Can the Boundary Commission transfer any part of the area now within the jurisdiction of the Government of the Saorstát and add such part to the area under the joint jurisdiction of the Government of Great Britain and the Government of Northern Ireland?

1. It appears pretty clearly from the remarks of Mr. Justice Feetham made during the course of the recent hearing in London (25th August, 1925) that, applying certain principles of construction to the Treaty, he is of opinion that the answer to the above question is 'Yes,' that is to say that the Commission has power to determine that territory now governed by the Government and Parliament of the Saorstát shall pass from it and be governed by the Governments and Parliaments of Great Britain and Northern Ireland in their respective spheres of jurisdiction under the Government of Ireland Act, 1920.

2. Mr. Justice Feetham arrives at this opinion by applying a canon of construction which he states as follows:-

'Our business is to look at the Treaty, and then if we find difficulties or ambiguities or have trouble in identifying the subjects dealt with we are entitled to look outside to clear up those difficulties. But our first business is to look at the language of the Treaty and where such language does not admit of doubt other extraneous facts will not assist us. It is only when we are in difficulties about the language that we ought to look at extraneous facts' (page 27 of the transcript of proceedings sent me).

3. If this principle is to be rigorously applied by the Commission and the *litera scripta* of the Treaty is alone to be looked at (unless what are called 'patent ambiguities' appear upon reading the *litera scripta*), then there would be a strong case for the Judge's interpretation of the document as giving to the Commission power to fix a boundary for Northern Ireland which would include territory now outside that boundary. Therefore the first question to be considered is whether the Judge's canon of construction is sound and is applicable to the document (the Treaty).

4. It is to be observed that the Counsel for the Saorstát, in reply to a direct question from Judge Feetham, said he agreed with the rule of construction as stated by the Judge but subject to the qualification that you must have regard to the facts and the parties at the time you *signed the contract*, that is to say the rule as stated, but with the qualification mentioned, applies to the interpretation of *contracts inter partes*, and so applies to the Treaty, implying that the Treaty is, as a matter of law, to be construed as if it were an ordinary private contract between two private persons.

5. There is no doubt that Mr. Justice Feetham was, in the passage I have quoted (paragraph 2 above), stating his conception of the rule of English Law to be followed in construing English contracts, and it is evident that he supposes himself bound to apply to the interpretation of the Treaty the rules of English law and practice governing the interpretation of ordinary contracts between private parties, rules which I may mention are noted for their much greater strictness and more rigid adherence to the *litera scripta* than the principles favoured by other, especially Latin, countries.

6. In my opinion, even from the point of view of a private contract, the rule as stated by Judge Feetham cannot be accepted as an accurate statement of the canon of construction according to English law. The strict rule is certainly that the intention of the parties is to be sought in the written instrument. Parties are taken to intend what they express in writing, not simply in isolated clauses or passages read separately but in the instrument read as a whole and each clause or passage in its context. The instrument itself however is not to be read as an isolated fact. It is to be read in its context, i.e. in the surrounding circumstances, and the plain ordinary meaning of the bare words used is subject to be controlled by reference to the subject matter dealt with and to the surrounding circumstances at the date when it was made and the facts or matters in relation to which it is to operate. A contract is therefore to be interpreted in the light of these matters and so read the intention of the parties is to be ascertained from the actual terms of the instrument. External evidence of intention different from what can be so ascertained is not permissible except in a case where,

upon such reading of the instrument, there is found to be a hidden or 'latent' ambiguity (i.e. an ambiguity not apparent merely upon the written word but shown in the circumstances to exist) and in that case extrinsic evidence of intention may be admitted to solve the ambiguity, or as it is sometimes expressed 'to resolve the equivocation.' This is a somewhat compressed (but I think accurate) statement of the relevant English law upon the interpretation of ordinary private contracts, law which is also the law in force in the Saorstát. Judge Feetham's statement will therefore be seen to be a far too narrow statement of a very narrow and strict rule of English law.

7. But I find that Judge Feetham appears to feel himself bound to apply to the interpretation of the Treaty these narrow and rigid principles governing the interpretation of English private contracts (principles which, on the occasion referred to already, he did not, in my opinion, state with accuracy). I do not know why he should feel so bound in dealing with an international instrument. There is no well-recognised code of rules for the interpretation of Treaties though there are some few generally accepted rules. But even the leading English text-writers on International Law admit that the rules of English law governing the interpretation of private contracts are not capable of application to the interpretation of Treaties. See for example, PITT-COBBETT, 'Leading Cases on International Law' (4th Edition, 1922, Volume I, page 344):-

> 'On the question of the interpretation of Treaties, it seems that both international tribunals and municipal courts will, in construing international compacts, adopt a more liberal construction than that which would ordinarily be applied, at any rate in the English and American courts, to the construction of private instruments and agreements. This arises from the fact that the prime aim of all interpretation must be to get at the real intention of the parties; and that in determining this regard must be had at once to the nature and subject-matter of the compact, and the circumstances under which it was arrived at. Applying these considerations to Treaties, we find that such compacts are usually made by diplomatists, and not by lawyers; that they commonly deal with large national interests; and that they are often concluded in circumstances which render it impossible to settle all minor points or to provide for every conceivable contingency.' (See also page 346.)

WESTLAKE, International Law, Part I (1910) at page 293, says:-

> 'The important point is to get at the real intention of the parties, and that enquiry is not to be shackled by any rule of interpretation which may exist in a particular national jurisprudence but is not generally accepted in the civilised world. On the whole we incline to think that the interpretation of international contracts is and ought to be less literal than that usually given in English courts of law to private contracts and acts of parliament.'

HALL, International Law, (7th Edition, 1917), tries to draw up a set of rules for the interpretation of treaties which he thinks might meet with acceptance, but he says in a footnote at page 349 – 'There is no place for the refinements of the courts in the rough jurisprudence of nations.' In my opinion, the Boundary Commission is not to regard itself as fettered by the narrow rules of English law as to the construction of private contracts when they approach the interpretation of the Treaty.

8. One further consideration of this matter is to be noted. In their considered opinion, given to the Crown on 31st July, 1924, the British Privy Council advised, in answer to the Supplemental (the 5th) Question submitted to them, that the finding of a majority of the Boundary Commission would rule on the ground that it was not a private arbitration but a body entrusted with matters of a general nature and of public concern. The findings on the earlier questions support the view of the international character of the Treaty and of the Commission, and exclude the notion that the instrument is in the nature of a private contract.

9. I have laboured this aspect of the Question because I gather from the transcript of the shorthand note that here lies the real and fundamental difficulty with Judge Feetham. Acting on what I believe to be an erroneous view of his legal position as member of the Boundary Commission, he refuses to look outside the four corners of the written instrument. In my opinion he is wrong in this even from the narrow point of view of an English contract, but much more so from the point of view proper to the interpretation of an international agreement or treaty. I will now discuss the question on the assumption that the considerations I have offered are accepted and that my conclusion is accordingly assented to.

10. Assuming then that we are entitled to look outside the Treaty document itself and consider the surrounding circumstances, the context of fact, at the time it was made, for the purpose,

(a) as limited by English rules of construction of private contracts, of truly interpreting the express words and terms actually used, the *litera scripta*, of the document; or

(b) as more liberally permitted in construing public international documents, of ascertaining the real intention of the parties, what they were at and what they intended to agree, even though not adequately or aptly expressed by the words and terms actually used.

I will refer shortly to such of those facts and circumstances as appear to me to stand out as relevant to and decisive of the question under consideration. They are comparatively few but impressive.

11. The first fact is the existence of an Irish minority concentrated in the North-East corner forming an almost homogeneous population in four counties and at some points beyond the boundaries of those four counties. That population, politically organised as the Ulster Unionists, opposed the realisation in any measure of Irish national aspirations. This minority with the advantage of local concentration claimed separate treatment in any settlement of the Irish question by way of self-government in Ireland, when some such settlement became inevitable, but, being a minority even in the Province of Ulster, they made it clear by resolution of the Ulster Unionist Council (10th March, 1920) that they would not have separate treatment for the whole Province. They demanded the Six Counties now known as Northern Ireland as far back as 1916 (resolution of the Ulster Unionist Council 12th June, 1916) and that demand was conceded

by Great Britain in the Government of Ireland Act, 1920, passed after the Irish representation had been withdrawn from Westminster, and in the teeth of the hostility of the majority of the population in two of the counties.

12. The Six-County area was the high-water mark of the Ulster Unionist demand. It was conceded by the British Government without any authority from Ireland, opposed by the majority of the Irish people, bitterly opposed by the populations of large areas who were not in harmony with the political or religious creeds of the homogeneous population already referred to. Moreover, the British Government knew well from the breakdown of the Buckingham Palace conference that no political leaders in Ireland could stand for a settlement which consigned the populations in Tyrone and Fermanagh to the rule of the Ulster Unionists. The rest of the country would not agree to the sacrifice and these people would not submit to be alienated from those to whom they were bound by every tie.

13. When the Treaty came to be negotiated, the Irish delegates were appointed by the Dáil which spoke for the whole of Ireland and included representatives from the Six Counties. The delegation was appointed to negotiate an all-Ireland settlement. Two of the delegates represented Northern Ireland constituencies, viz. President Griffith (Tyrone and Fermanagh) and General Collins (Armagh) and were in an especial manner concerned with the interests of their constituents who had been coerced into the ambit of Ulster Unionist authority in Northern Ireland.

14. An all-Ireland settlement was arrived at. The British Government had committed itself to a policy of 'no coercion for Ulster,' meaning by the term 'Ulster' the homogeneous population of the North-East corner who owned the political leadership of the Ulster Unionist party. Accordingly the British on their side imposed one qualification, namely, a qualification which would enable the British Government to honour its pledge that the Ulster Unionist population would not be coerced to accept an all-Ireland Government if they should persist in rejecting it. But such rejection would raise anew the problem of the nationalist populations collected against their will into Northern Ireland – the problem which had broken up the Buckingham Palace conference, the problem which was necessarily a very live question for President Griffith and General Collins directly representing the populations affected, the problem which would block any settlement providing no solution for it. The Boundary Commission was the solution agreed to for that problem in the event of the all-Ireland settlement being defeated by the Ulster Unionist politicians.

15. To sum up the outstanding facts of the circumstances surrounding the making of the Treaty, relevant to the question under consideration, we have:-

1. The effective revolt of the Irish people against British rule, leading inevitably to the withdrawal of British rule and the recognition of an Irish Government:
2. The existence of a dissident minority, consisting of a homogeneous population concentrated in the North-East corner of the country, speaking through the Ulster Unionist leaders:
3. Pledges given by British political leaders to that minority that they would not be forced to accept the rule of an Irish Government:

4. A hasty attempt by British politicians to secure fulfilment of the pledge behind the backs of the Irish people by setting up the Government of Northern Ireland over the Six Counties:
5. A new problem caused by coercion of Nationalist populations, separated from those with whom they have everything in common, put against their will under the Ulster Unionist Government, converted from being part of an effective majority into a helpless minority under a hostile authority:
6. A truce in the Anglo-Irish war to permit of negotiations for an all-Ireland settlement:
7. An all-Ireland settlement agreed subject to a reservation saving the British position consequent on the pledge given to the Ulster Unionist people of the North-East corner:
8. The reservation required by the British pledge necessarily qualified by a provision to be made for the problem of the Nationalist populations in Northern Ireland in case the British pledge should be insisted upon:
9. Agreement that this ultimate problem, if it should arise, be left to a Commission who should solve it according to the wishes of the inhabitants so far as economic and geographic conditions would not be incompatible with the fulfilment of those wishes:
10. No demand or claim ever made by the people of the Six Counties or by any of their political leaders for the inclusion of any part of the area of the twenty-six counties in the area of Northern Ireland:
11. Northern Ireland constituted as a Province of Great Britain with limited local government and representation in the parliament of Great Britain, which remains the undisputed supreme government and ruling authority in Northern Ireland:

16. From all that I have said there emerges the vital fact, the key to the situation, namely, that there was but one problem of area to be solved, and that was the problem of that portion of the area snatched into Northern Ireland whose inhabitants demanded that they should be in political association with the rest of Ireland and as to whom the people of the rest of Ireland demanded that they should continue in the National fold. There never was any other problem facing the delegates of the two nations. There was no claim for the transfer to Northern Ireland of any other part of the area of Ireland, 'not an inch,' consequently no such question arose for solution. The area of Northern Ireland alone was in dispute, and that only on the happening of the contingency of the Northern Government electing to stand out of the settlement. Once the facts are recalled, the intention of the parties to the negotiations becomes clear. The intention in agreeing to set up a Boundary Commission was to provide a settlement for the one big national question which would remain for settlement as a consequence of the obstinacy of the Ulster Unionist politicians. Such is the context of fact in which the boundary provisions of the Treaty are to be read. Such was the actual intention of the agreement for a Boundary Commission. I now come to the instrument itself and consider what is expressly set down in writing.

17. Let me repeat that in arriving at the effect of a particular provision of a written instrument, the whole document is to be taken into consideration (unless forbidden by the document itself which is not the case here). In my opinion,

the intention of the parties as found upon the examination of the history of the transaction which I have made in the foregoing paragraphs, is to be found clearly expressed in the Treaty read in the light of the facts.

18. We begin with Article I. of the Treaty which contains the fundamental agreement resulting from the negotiations, that is to say, (a) Dominion status is agreed as the constitutional and political form of the settlement; and (b) the settlement is an all-Ireland settlement. The Dominion recognised under the name of the Irish Free State is to comprise the whole of Ireland.

19. But the pledge given to the North Eastern Unionists by the British political leaders is to be honoured. Accordingly machinery is provided by Article XII. whereby, if they so elect, the people to whom that pledge was given can secede from the Dominion of Ireland and pass back again as a province under the Government of Great Britain.

20. But, again, the people who have no interest in the British pledge to the North Eastern Unionists, who do not form part of the homogeneous population covered by that pledge, are not to be coerced to pass out of the Dominion with the provincial fragment. It is therefore agreed and the Treaty provides by the proviso to Article XII. that they are to be relieved from any coercion save the coercion of economic and geographic conditions.

21. To read into the proviso to Article XII. a provision for transferring any part of the twenty-six counties into the area of Northern Ireland, is to read into it something which is not there in express terms, and is not there for the very good reason that no such question arose before the signing of the Treaty, no such operation had to be considered in the absence of any demand for it, the negotiations were not concerned with it, and it was not within the contemplation or intention of the parties.

22. The history of the transaction as I have examined it, establishes that the meaning and intention of the Proviso to Article XII. was, as indeed it reads, to qualify the power of 'opting out of' the Free State given by the Article, by saving as far as possible from its operation those who wished to remain in the Free State. Hence this Proviso is engrafted upon the 'opting-out' provision, modifying and qualifying that provision and none other. Hence the declaration at the end of the proviso speaking only of the boundary (i.e. the area) of Northern Ireland, the one matter in dispute and before the minds of the signatories as arising upon the event of an 'opting-out' – the boundary which called for correction to meet the demand of one of the two negotiating parties that coercion and injustice should not be inflicted on the Nationalist population then within that boundary in the process of securing freedom from coercion for the Unionist people of Northern Ireland. The boundary of Northern Ireland only is dealt with in the clause because no similar case had been made in respect of the area comprised in the twenty-six counties. To provide for the transfer of any part of that area to Northern Ireland would have been to penalise the new Dominion for the act of the Northern Ireland Government in seceding contrary to the agreement and intention of both negotiating parties to have an all-Ireland settlement if possible.

23. It is, therefore, I think, clear upon the face of it that –
(a) The Proviso to Article XII. of the Treaty is a modification or qualification upon the right given by that Article to the Parliament of Northern Ireland to 'opt-out-of' the Irish Free State:
(b) The Proviso limits the area which may be carried out of the Free State by the operation of 'opting-out':
(c) The Proviso does not refer to, and is in no way concerned with the area comprising twenty-six counties theretofore styled by the British under the Government of Ireland Act, 1920 as 'Southern Ireland,' an area not the subject of dispute between the negotiating parties in the settlement at which they had arrived:

24. While I think the matter is sufficiently clear on Article XII. as I have explained it in preceding paragraphs, I look for corroboration elsewhere in the document. Such corroboration is not far to seek.

25. Article XI. in my opinion fully corroborates the position I have stated. The Dominion is established by the first Article for the whole of Ireland. It came into immediate effect and operation throughout the whole undisputed area of the twenty-six counties. The exercise of its powers of government is suspended in the disputed area of Northern Ireland. It is clear that the settlement effected by the Treaty is regarded as final and complete so far as the twenty-six counties are concerned, while the way is kept clear for the operation of Article XII. in respect of the six counties then comprised in Northern Ireland. In face of that state of affairs, the Boundary Commission have no power or authority to reopen the completed operative settlement made and in full force and effect in the twenty-six counties.

26. Again, the whole of Ireland being comprised in the Dominion of the Free State and its governmental authority being merely suspended in the Six Counties, so much of Northern Ireland as is excluded by the Boundary Commission from the 'opting-out' area comes automatically under the authority of the Government and Parliament of the Free State and no legal or constitutional difficulty arises. But the Government and Parliament of the Dominion of the Free State are now in full operative authority by virtue of the Treaty and the ratifying legislation, throughout the twenty-six counties. The Dominion is in a very different constitutional position from that of Northern Ireland which is constitutionally a subordinate province of Great Britain. The Dominion being completely established in the twenty-six counties and now operative in that area, does the Commission propose to ask for legislation of the Parliament of the Free State transferring territory to the Parliaments of Great Britain and Northern Ireland, the only way such transfer can now be effected? Is it not thus apparent that the Commission has no powers or functions in relation to the area of the twenty-six counties.

27. The case then is that –
1. The intention in fact was that the Commission set up under the proviso to Article XII. was to deal only with the disputed area then included in Northern Ireland:

2. The intention actually expressed by the clause as explained by the surrounding circumstances is in accord with the intention in fact:
3. The frame of the Treaty, in particular Articles I. and XI., confirms the interpretation of Article XII. in consonance with the intention in fact.

No. 332 NAI DFA ES Box 29 File 192

William J.B. Macaulay to Desmond FitzGerald (Dublin)
(M/Sp.145/2/25)

24 September 1925

Philadelphia Exposition.

A Chara:
With reference to Mr. Lester's letter of 28th August (457/313) I am directed by the Minister Plenipotentiary to state it appears that this Exposition is of some importance, but whether an immediate return to the exhibitors would follow depends almost entirely on whether they have already exhausted the potential market for their goods in this country; that is to say, whether the present demand is met and whether an increased demand could be supplied.

The Minister considers that possibly the installation of a small tourist bureau in some kind of a small kiosk building might be favourably considered and if this were well fitted out and supplied with a large quantity of attractive booklets, photographs and if possible kinematograph films of Irish beauty spots or other features of Ireland or Irish life, considerable interest would be created and the tourist industry would undoubtedly benefit. This is perhaps a matter for the Tourist Development Association but in view of the terms of your letter and the views of the Department of Industry and Commerce it appears it would be the only form in which the Saorstát could be a participant, either officially or unofficially.

Mr. Crawford has suggested that the Irish Army Band might be sent to Philadelphia but in the Minister's view this is an idea which is open to serious criticism and His Excellency does not consider it likely that this idea is practicable from the point of view of the Army authorities, in which case it is hardly necessary to discuss the proposition from its American aspect.

Mise, le meas,
[copy letter unsigned]

No. 333 NAI DT S4541

Department of the President to each member of the Executive Council enclosing schedule on Defence Policy (Secret)

DUBLIN, 28 October 1925

DEFENCE POLICY

A chara,
With reference to the Secret document of the 22nd July last[1] on the above subject,

[1] See No. 323.

circulated to each member of the Executive Council, with Form F. 1. Cabinet, on 27th idem, and considered by the Council on the 17th August, I am directed by the President to transmit herewith for consideration by the Council a draft memo based on notes of the discussion and decision at the meeting in question.

The memo purports to be a statement of the Government's Defence Policy, and is intended, if approved, for transmission to the Department of Defence for the guidance of the Army Authorities.

Mise, le meas,
[copy letter unsigned]
a.s. Rúnaí

SCHEDULE I.[1]

DEFENCE POLICY.

The policy of the Executive Council with regard to the Military Forces of the State may be summed up as follows:-

(a) The size of the standing Army to be retained in normal times should not exceed 10,000 to 12,000 all ranks.

(b) The organisation of this force should be such that it would be capable of rapid and efficient expansion in time of need to the maximum strength of the country's manpower. This will necessitate the training of all ranks in duties of a more advanced nature than those normally associated with each rank.

(c) The Army must be an independent national Force capable of assuming responsibility for the defence of the territory of Saorstát Éireann against invasion, or internal disruptive agencies; but it must also be so organised, trained and equipped as to render it capable, should the necessity arise, of full and complete co-ordination with the forces of the British Government in the defence of Saorstát territory whether against actual hostilities or against violation of neutrality on the part of a common enemy.

In laying down this policy for the Army, the Executive Council are conscious that expenditure on the Army is bound to be subjected year after year to very critical examination. In times of peace, there is a tendency to overlook the necessity for the maintenance of a force trained in arms which will be ready to repel attack. The present international situation does not, in the opinion of the Council, justify the hope that recourse to arms will in future be rendered impossible. The internal situation on the other hand which renders it necessary to keep in existence a force which will act as a deterrent to the disaffected element in the community does not justify the substitution of the present Army by a militia force. The Council is of opinion that a standing Army 10,000 to 12,000 strong should suffice both as a deterrent against internal disorder and as the nucleus of a defensive force against external attack.

It is impossible to forecast what international combinations may from time to time develop or what disturbances may arise between Nations. Events which at the time of occurrence may appear trivial have been the occasion of wars of world magnitude. The earnest desire of the Executive Council is to avoid participation in any international struggle, but it might happen that the occasion

[1] Handwritten note: 'approved by the Executive Council 13 Nov. 1925 – (2/225)'.

would arise when by reason of an attempt by some foreign Power to utilise our geographical position either as a base for an offensive against Great Britain or against sea-borne traffic between ports in Saorstát Éireann and other countries, we would be forced into taking action. At the moment the defence by sea of both Great Britain and Ireland is undertaken by British Forces. The Article of the Treaty which contains this provision is due to be reviewed towards the close of 1926 with a view to our undertaking a share of our own coastal defence. Until this review has taken place it is not practicable to take any special steps other than to ensure that if co-operation with British Forces should become necessary at any time, the personnel of the Irish Army would be capable of efficient co-operative action, and that our officers would be capable of assuming control, if necessary, of mixed forces of all arms when operating in Irish Territory.

In general the Executive Council consider that the equipment and training of the Army should be directed towards the defence of Irish territory which involves specialised preparation of plans to resist invasion from any quarter – a study of likely landing places and of the tactical problems which would arise in offering resistance to Forces attempting to land or effecting a landing at such points.

In so far as the international aspect of the matter is concerned, the Minister for Defence in his capacity as a Member of the Executive Council, will be kept in touch with situations as they arise by the Minister for External Affairs and the policy in each particular emergency will be decided by the Council as a whole.

No. 334 NAI DFA Minister's Office Files (1924-25)

Handwritten letter from James McNeill to Desmond FitzGerald (Dublin)
LONDON, 2 November 1925

Dear D.[esmond] F.[itzGerald]
I think I ought to tell you that I am good for, at most, one year more of exile. I hope you will think that four years is long enough. I thought I had ended my nomadic life ten years ago. By this time next year the boundary excitement should be over and any trouble incidental to the swopping of remote houses[1] will not exist. I am giving long notice because you will probably wish to have reasonable time for finding the next H.C.

I am anxious to get back to Ireland & have another try at settling down. I don't want to grumble unduly but life here is not for me exactly a succession of thrills.

Of course if it suits you to detach me earlier I can have no grievance. This is not a letter of grievance in any sense but a dutiful notice. Good luck.

Yours sincerely,
JAMES MCNEILL

[1] Word unclear, could be 'horses', perhaps a reference of some kind to the Boundary Commission.

No. 335 NAI DFA Minister's Office Files (1924-25)

Desmond FitzGerald to James McNeill (London)

DUBLIN, 6 November 1925

My dear High Commissioner,

I have received your private note of the 2nd,[1] and read its contents without any marked degree of cheerfulness. The consoling feature about it is that it is a year hence and not sooner. If I were an optimist I might say to myself that with a year's grace one has plenty of time to look for somebody to take your place, but, the last few years have knocked any optimism I ever had out of me. Of course I knew that if we announced to-morrow that we needed a High Commissioner we would have applicants enough to run a dozen Shannon Schemes, all of them able to prove that they were born for the job. But – well you know there are a dozen buts. I might say that it is not a High Commissioner we want but a James McNeill, and where to begin looking for one I haven't the remotest notion. Of course I know that as the proverb says 'a good beginning is half the work' and we began well any way, and we can afford to drop a little, but there is a margin for that drop. And I imagine that we shall be hard put to it to get somebody who reaches even the lower end of that margin.

I am not saying this to flatter you. You know it is true as well as I do. I am saying it merely because it may serve as a basis for argument with you, if we do have to try to persuade you to postpone it even a little longer. Of course I shall only do that if it is absolutely necessary. I know that you took on that most uncomfortable job merely to assist, and I quite understand and sympathise with your feeling that four years has been a fairly long period.

I have only mentioned the matter to Blythe[2] so far. I shall mention it to the others the first Cabinet meeting, and we can all be having it in mind and looking round for a successor. You might also think about it yourself. You know what is needed better than I do, but the one quality that of automatically taking the right line – the right line being of course the line that the Government would desire to be taken – is rather hard to find.

This Foreign Representative question is very difficult. You were obviously the one man for London. Paddy MacGilligan, who is probably with you now, has sent me a note confirming my own idea that Professor Smiddy is eminently successful in Washington. Count O'Kelly certainly seems to do well in Brussels. But if all three of you resigned to-morrow I don't know where we would get anybody to fill even one of these posts. As it is I am quite dissatisfied with Paris but have nobody on hand to send there. And if we decide to have a place in Berlin I don't know who would be suitable.

But I mustn't continue in this doleful strain. I think we were lucky to have you for those four years, and you have every reason to feel yourself justified in giving up a position that you never asked for.

When I began this letter I merely meant to try to convey to you how much I appreciate the good fortune we had in having you there in London, and to

[1] See No. 334 above.

[2] Ernest Blythe, Minister for Finance.

thank you for that and for the timely warning you are giving us. I will do my best to find somebody during the next year and of course I always have the consolation of knowing that I may be eliminated from my own post before the time arrives.

We can talk the matter over a bit when I see you next. Meanwhile best wishes to you and to Madame[1] and to Paddy if he is there with you.

Yours sincerely,
[copy letter unsigned]
Minister for External Affairs

No. 336 NAI DT S1801O

Extract from minutes of a meeting of the Executive Council (C.2/224)
DUBLIN, 10 November 1925

BOUNDARY COMMISSION.

The President reported on interviews which he, the Minister for Justice and the Minister for Finance[2] had with certain members of the Party and also with a deputation from East Donegal regarding the forecasts of the Boundary report which had been published in the Press.[3]

Consideration was given to a letter received from the Secretary of the Boundary Commission inviting a representative of the Government to a Conference on the 19th instant,[4] to discuss certain matters arising out of the imminence of the publication of the Commission's report, as well as to a letter from Mr. Cahir Healy, M.P., asking to be informed whether the Executive Council and representatives of the areas concerned would be consulted before the report was signed.

It was decided:-

(a) that so far as signature of the report is concerned it is a matter for Dr. MacNeill's sole discretion,

and

(b) that, accordingly, the Council does not require to be kept informed of the proposed line beforehand.

A letter is to be sent to Mr. Healy on the basis of these decisions.[5]

---

[1] Josephine McNeill.

[2] Kevin O'Higgins, Ernest Blythe.

[3] On 7 November 1925 the pro-Tory *Morning Post* newspaper published a leaked map of the proposed revisions to the Irish border that would be recommended by the Boundary Commission. The map indicated that there would be no major changes to the border and that the Irish Free State would in fact cede land to Northern Ireland. The Irish Free State authorities had never envisaged such an outcome. They had expected that the Commission would only recommend large transfers of land to the Irish Free State. Though the source of the leak was never revealed, evidence pointed towards J.R. Fisher, the British nominee as Northern Ireland representative on the Commission, who was known to have Ulster Unionist connections. The leaked map effectively sealed the fate of the Boundary Commission. It led to a political crisis in the Irish Free State and the resignation of Eoin MacNeill as Irish Free State Boundary Commissioner.

[4] Not printed.

[5] Not printed.

It was agreed that the Attorney General should represent the Government at the proposed Conference with the Boundary Commission on 19th instant, and that he should press for a copy of the full records of the Commission to be given to this Government. He was authorised to state that this Govt. favours the immediate publication of all evidence given before the Commission.

No. 337 NAI DT S1801O

Extract from minutes of a meeting of the Executive Council (C.2/225)
DUBLIN, 13 November 1925

BOUNDARY:
Consideration was given to

(a) a letter from the Secretary of the Boundary Commission[1] stating that the Commission were desirous of conferring with a representative of this Government and a representative of the British Government on certain matters relating to the publication of the award of the Commission and to the publication and custody of certain documents, and suggesting as a suitable date, Thursday the 19th instant, and

(b) a secret despatch from the British Government dated 11th instant[2] stating that a similar letter had been received by them from the Boundary Commission, and that they proposed to accept the invitation to the Conference, and to ask the Commission whether they would have any objection to the British Government's being represented by a maximum of six persons. The despatch suggested also that the British and Irish representatives should meet beforehand to discuss the matters which were to be the subject of discussion at the Conference.

Having regard to the fact that the estimates of the Department of Education would probably detain the Minister for Education – who was the Irish Free State Representative on the Boundary Commission – in Dublin on Tuesday and Wednesday of next week, it was considered unlikely that the conference could be held on the date suggested. It was decided therefore to

(1) suggest to the Commission that the Conference be postponed until Tuesday the 24th instant, and

(2) to notify the British Government accordingly, to suggest that the prior meeting of the representatives of both Governments should be held on Monday the 23rd instant, and to inquire whether it was intended that the British delegation to the Conference should consist of Ministers or of officials.

Letters drafted to this effect were submitted to the Executive Council and approved.

[1] Not printed.
[2] Not printed.

No. 338 NAI DT S1801O

Extract from minutes of a meeting of the Executive Council (C.2/226)
DUBLIN, 18 November 1925

(a) *Boundary – Conference at Dominions Office, 29th Oct. 1925.*
The Secretary reported that he had received from the British Government and circulated to the Executive Council copies of a note of a meeting held at the Dominions Office on October 29th between representatives of the British Government and of this Government, to discuss matters relating to the examination of the areas to be transferred under the findings of the Boundary Commission.

It was decided that the Ministers and the Attorney General should examine the note with a view to correction if and where necessary.

(b) *Proposed Conference with the Boundary Commission 24th Novr. 1925.*
On the assumption that the Commission would agree to the British Government's proposals that both Governments should be represented by more than one delegate at the Conference with the Commission which had originally been fixed for 19th instant, but had now been postponed to the 24th instant, the following were appointed to represent the Government of Saorstát Éireann at the Conference in question:-

Mr. K. O'Higgins, Vice President & Minister for Justice,
Mr. E. Blythe, Minister for Finance,
Mr. J. O'Byrne, K.C. Attorney General,
Mr. Jas McNeill, High Commissioner,
Mr. D. O'Hegarty, Secretary to the Executive Council.

In the event of the Commission's adhering to their original proposal that only one representative of each Government should be present, this Government would be represented by the Attorney General alone as already decided.

The Secretary was instructed to notify the Boundary Commission and the British Government accordingly and to inform the latter that the Irish representatives would be prepared to meet the British Representatives in prior consultation as desired on Monday the 23rd instant at the Dominions Office.

No. 339 NAI DT S1801O

Telegram from James McNeill to Dublin
LONDON, undated, late November (probably 20) 1925

My brother definitely withdrew from B.C. to-day. He will be in Dublin tomorrow morning.

No. 340 NAI DT S1801O

Eoin MacNeill to William T. Cosgrave
DUBLIN, 21 November 1925

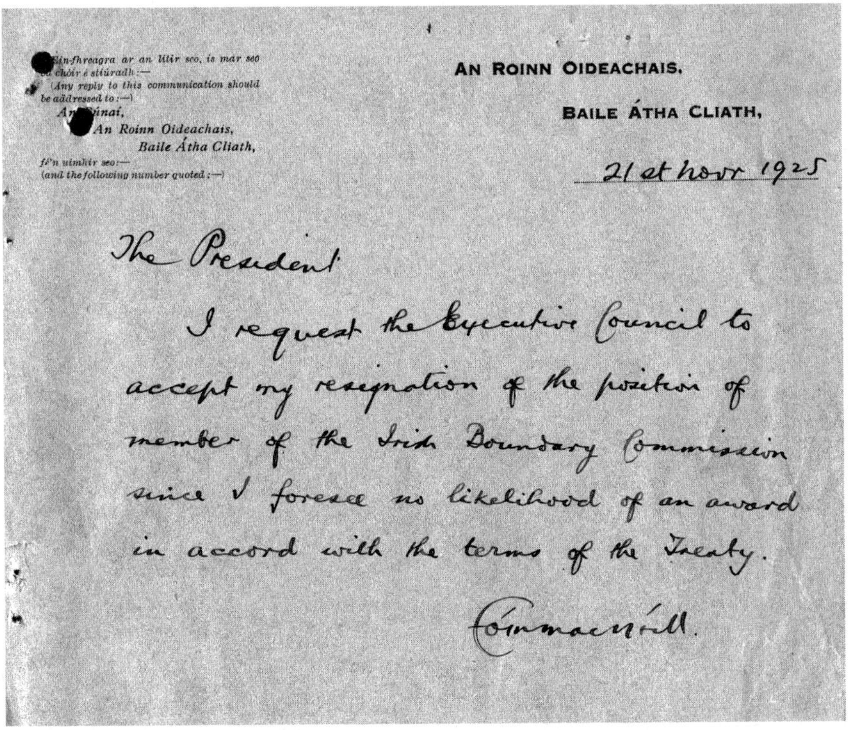

Éin-fhreagra ar an litir seo, is mar seo ba chóir é stiúradh:—
(Any reply to this communication should be addressed to:—)
An [illegible]ínaí,
An Roinn Oideachais,
Baile Átha Cliath,
fé'n uimhir seo:—
(and the following number quoted:—)

AN ROINN OIDEACHAIS,
BAILE ÁTHA CLIATH,

21st Novr 1925

The President

I request the Executive Council to accept my resignation of the position of member of the Irish Boundary Commission since I foresee no likelihood of an award in accord with the terms of the Treaty.

Eoin MacNéill.

No. 341 NAI DT S1801O

Extract from minutes of a meeting of the Executive Council (C.2/227)
DUBLIN, 21 November 1925

BOUNDARY.
Dr. MacNeill tendered to the Executive Council his resignation as a member of the Irish Boundary Commission in the following terms:-

'21st November, 1925,[1]
President.
I request the Executive Council to accept my resignation of my position as Irish member of the Irish Boundary Commission as I foresee no likelihood of an award in the terms of the Treaty'.
(sd) EOIN MACNEILL'.

After a full statement from Dr. MacNeill of the reasons for his action his resignation from the Commission was approved:-

'Dr. MacNeill has tendered to the Executive Council his resignation as a member of the Irish Boundary Commission. The resignation has been accepted.'

No. 342 NAI DT S1801O

Diarmuid O'Hegarty to F.B. Bourdillon (London)
DUBLIN, 21 November 1925

Sir,
I have to acknowledge receipt of your letter of the 20th instant[2] regarding the Conference which it was proposed should take place at the Commission's Offices on the 24th instant.

I am to state that Dr. MacNeill has tendered to my Government his resignation as a member of the Commission. This being so, a Conference with the Commission is obviously impossible.

In order to avoid inconvenience the High Commissioner of the Irish Free State at London was requested by telephone this morning to acquaint you of the acceptance of Dr. MacNeill's resignation and of the consequent cancellation of the Conference.

I have the honour to be, Sir,
Your obedient Servant,
[copy letter unsigned]
Secretary to the Executive Council

No. 343 NAI DT S1801O

Resumé of a statement by Eoin MacNeill at a meeting of the Executive Council
DUBLIN, 21 November 1925

On Friday morning the 20th November he, Dr. MacNeill, went to the High Commissioner's Office and 'phoned to the Secretary of the Boundary Commis-

[1] This version of MacNeill's letter of resignation contains a number of differences and additions to the original reproduced above in facsimile (No. 340). MacNeill's original text is here conflated with that in the Executive Council Minutes. Additions to the original letter are in **bold** and excisions in *italics*:

'I request the Executive Council to accept my resignation of *the* **(my)** position *of* **(as) (Irish)** member of the Irish Boundary Commission *since* **(as)** I foresee no likelihood of an award in *accord with* the terms of the Treaty.'

[2] Not printed.

sion asking whether any time had been fixed for the meeting of the Commission that day.

The meeting having been fixed for 11-45 a.m. Dr. MacNeill attended at that hour and found Feetham and Bourdillon present. Fisher arrived almost immediately.

The minutes of the previous meeting having been read, they were proceeding to deal with the Agenda, when Dr. MacNeill asked leave to make a statement.

He said that a situation of extreme gravity had arisen in Ireland consequent on the Morning Post *Revelations*. He emphasised the word *Revelations*.

Feetham replied that the Morning Post statement was not accurate, but admitted, in response to a question from Dr. MacNeill, that it was substantially correct.

Dr. MacNeill continued that he had been in touch with representative persons of all kinds in Ireland and that the unanimous opinion of all classes was that the fixing of a boundary line such as that indicated as in the Morning Post would be a *violation* of the Treaty.

He himself would not go so far as to say that such a line would endanger the Treaty but it would certainly endanger the common objects of the Treaty, that it would seriously injure the friendly and existing sound relations between the two countries.

Dr. MacNeill developed his argument on these lines, and finished by stating that under the circumstances he had come to the conclusion that it was his duty to withdraw from the Commission and to place his resignation immediately in the hands of his Government.

Fisher who all through the proceedings of the Commission has been impassive and had left all to Feetham, made no comment which Dr. MacNeill could remember.

Feetham said that this was a very serious step to take and asked that it be not taken without very full consideration, suggested that Dr. MacNeill should wait to hear what the other members had to say, and enlarged at length on the results which would follow on the taking of this step.

Dr. MacNeill replied that he had given the matter full consideration, that none of the aspects covered by Mr. Feetham had failed to be considered by him, and that he had made up his mind accordingly.

Mr. Feetham seeing that Dr. MacNeill had definitely made up his mind to withdraw, passed to other considerations and tried to induce him to take some time to consider the matter, even to postpone action until the afternoon.

Dr. MacNeill stated he was acting on an existing state of things and he could not foresee that anything was likely to arise which would justify an alteration of his decision.

Feetham asked then whether this decision was construed by Dr. MacNeill as releasing him from the obligation to secrecy imposed on [and undertaken by] the members of the Commission and Dr. MacNeill replied that that was his opinion.

Immediately – though it is not clear that this has any significance – Bourdillon turned up the entry in the minutes imposing this obligation, as if this step on the part of Dr. MacNeill had not been unexpected.

Feetham then suggested, obviously with a view to playing for time, that it was desirable that Dr. MacNeill should be in possession of everything necessary to enable him to make a full and accurate statement on the whole matter and that he would require maps, documents, etc. It was obvious that he was anxious to gain time so as to consult with some one outside the Commission.

Dr. MacNeill replied that the facts in his memory were sufficient for the explanation which he intended to make to the Executive Council and that he required no documentary aids.

Finally after discussion lasting about an hour Feetham saw that Dr. MacNeill had made up his mind and the matter dropped.

Dr. MacNeill then turned to Bourdillon who had charge of his papers and keys to arrange for their future custody, and *immediately* Feetham interjected:- 'Oh, by the way, I have your copy of that memorandum'.

In explanation of the reference to the memorandum Dr. MacNeill mentioned that after the compilation of evidence, Feetham drew up a memorandum setting out his view of the interpretation and application of Article 12 of the Treaty. He handed copies of this to the other two members and stated that he did not think that it need be discussed or replied to by a formal memo. from them. It was drawn up simply to show the state of his mind on the subject.

Dr. MacNeill read it and stated his objections to it in detail, having, for his own information, summarised the various points by way of brief outspoken marginal notes entered on his copy of the memorandum.

Feetham borrowed this copy on the plea that he had lost his own copy, apparently for the purpose of fortifying himself against Dr. MacNeill's arguments.

When the question of custody of Dr. MacNeill's documents arose, Feetham had to explain the absence of this memo from Dr. MacNeill's papers.

Dr. MacNeill offered no objection to his retaining it.

Before the meeting dispersed it was clearly understood that Dr. MacNeill was free to make any statement he liked.

Papers which are duplicates of the Commission's documents are to be retained by the Commission. Personal papers of Dr. MacNeill are to be forwarded to the office of the High Commissioner.

No. 344 NAI DT S1801O

Telegram from T.M. Healy to Leopold Amery (London)
DUBLIN, 12.40 pm, 22 November 1925

Secretary of State for Dominions.
My ministers have just received and accepted the resignation of their representative on the Boundary Commission. The situation thus created will require to be carefully considered by them and in the meantime they feel that the proposed conferences on Monday and Tuesday next cannot be held. They are communicating with the Secretary of the Boundary Commission to a similar effect.

No. 345 NAI DT S1801C

Speech by William T. Cosgrave at Emyvale, Co Monaghan
EMYVALE, 22 November 1925

I have come here to-day uninvited and unexpected, but I have come because I have a statement to make to you and through you to the people of Monaghan and to the people of Ireland. It is that Dr. MacNeill, the Representative of the Irish Free State on the Boundary Commission has tendered to the Executive Council his resignation from membership of that Commission and that the Executive Council has accepted his resignation. For many months the Boundary Commission have been sitting, shrouded in an atmosphere of secrecy; all their sittings have been held in private; all their deliberations have been conducted behind closed doors; the Commissioners had bound themselves to each other to maintain the most profound confidence in regard to their progress. As a consequence neither I nor any other Minister, with the exception of course of Dr. MacNeill, had any knowledge of what was taking place. We knew the representations which we ourselves had placed before the Commission; we knew the arguments which we had advanced in support of those representations; we knew also that very complete evidence had been tendered to the Commission regarding the wishes of the inhabitants by those of our fellow-countrymen who had against their will been handed over to Northern Ireland by the Partition Act of 1920; we were aware of representations made by small and isolated bodies in Saorstát Éireann for their transfer to the Six County area, and we were thoroughly appreciative of the futility of the arguments contained in those representations. Beyond this we knew nothing. All else was hidden as by a November fog. I do not want to be taken as saying that this was altogether unwise and unjustifiable. I know that the conditions under which Nationalists lived in the Six County Area were such that it was by no means easy for them to give testimony of their desire to be included in our territory. I merely state the fact that so far as the work of the Boundary Commission was concerned, it was a closed book to us, and it was equally, if guarantees were of any avail, a closed book to everyone else.

On the 7th of this month, however, the 'Morning Post', an English newspaper which has been consistently and fiercely hostile to Irish nationality, to Irish sentiment, and to Irish existence generally, published what it assured its readers was an accurate forecast of the Commission's report. Now the only thing we knew about the Commission's report at that moment was that it did not exist. It does not yet exist. Where then did this forecast come from? Was it in fact an indication of the mind of Mr. Justice Feetham, or of Mr. Fisher or of Dr. MacNeill or of any two of them or of all of them conveyed in some mysterious manner to this favoured journal, or was it what it seemed to be, a line drawn for propagandist purposes by a hostile organ with a view to influencing the ultimate decision of the Commission? Whichever it was, however it was conveyed, it was sufficiently detailed and sufficiently unjust to give rise to a feeling of disquiet which has manifested itself in the various deputations which I have received since its publication and in the debate which took place in the Dáil on Thursday last. On that occasion I said that it was inconceivable to me that any body of men respecting the terms of reference placed in their hands by Article 12 of the Treaty, recognising their functions as a judicial authority, and setting upon their reputation for impartiality and honour the value which honest men place upon those things, could lend their names to such a decision. I reiterate those words to-day, and I do so in the light of the fuller knowledge which I now possess. That fuller knowledge is the resignation of Dr. MacNeill from the Commission.

Dr. MacNeill has come to the Executive Council[1] and has told us that during the course of the last meetings of the Commission he has been completely and amply satisfied that there was no likelihood that the work of the Commission would result in a report based upon the terms of reference provided for it by the solemn international engagement under which the Commission was created. The Terms of Reference are set out with great clarity in Article 12 of the Treaty. The Boundary was to be determined in accordance with the wishes of the inhabitants subject to possible rectifications by economic and geographic considerations.

The Treaty settlement was intended by all parties to mark the end of coercion in Ireland and to substitute the principle of democratic government based on the consent of the governed. No other interpretation of Article 12 could possibly accord with the general spirit of the Treaty. It was clearly intended, in the event of Northern Ireland deciding to secede from the Irish Free State, to bring relief to the Nationalist inhabitants of the Six Counties who would otherwise be held under a Government not acceptable to them.

On the very day following the signing of the Treaty this fact was publicly recognised by Lord Birkenhead in a speech explaining the arrangement which had been made with regard to Northern Ireland. Referring to the suppression of the County Council of Tyrone, he stated that the Boundary Commission had been agreed to with a view to rendering impossible such an incident as that of a few days before in which popularly elected bodies of one or two districts were excluded from their habitations by representatives of the Northern Parliament. Clearly Lord Birkenhead was then under the impression that County Tyrone or a substantial portion of it might properly be transferred to the Irish Free State.

Mr. Lloyd George, who was, at the time of the signing of the Treaty, Prime Minister of Great Britain, and Chairman of the British Delegation, speaking in the British House of Commons a week after the Treaty was signed said:- 'There is no doubt, certainly since the Act of 1920, that the majority of the people of the two counties prefer being with their Southern neighbours to being in the Northern Parliament. Take it either by constituency or by Poor Law Unions, or, if you like, by counting heads, and you will find that the majority in those two counties prefer to be with their Southern neighbours. What does that mean? If Ulster is to remain a separate community you can only by means of coercion keep them there, and although I am against the coercion of Ulster, I do not believe in Ulster coercing other units.' These are the words not of members of the Irish Delegation but of British Signatories spoken while the events leading up to the Treaty were still fresh in their minds.

[1] See above No. 343.

I am aware that at a later date other views were expressed and other explanations were attempted. I do not set myself to ascribe the motives for these later utterances, but their effect can only have been to exert an improper influence upon the minds of the British nominees on the Boundary Commission.

I pointed out in the Dáil last Thursday that the contention of the Executive Council has always been that the Commission has no right to take away any Free State territory. I go further and say that if the terms of reference contained in the Treaty were properly interpreted and effect given to the wishes of the inhabitants, this question could never arise. No boundary line could possibly be drawn, consonant with the terms of reference, which would infringe Free State territory, even if in the abstract such power did in fact exist.

I venture to say that at the time of the Treaty nobody had any doubt as to the work which the Boundary Commission was intended to perform. It was arranged by the Treaty that in the event of Northern Ireland remaining under the jurisdiction of the Parliament of the Free State provision should be made for the protection of the nationalist minority in that area. No such provision was to be made in the event of the Northern Parliament exercising its right of continuing its association with Westminster. In that event the Boundary Commission was to bring the minority relief by returning them to the Government of their choice. What has happened since the signing of the Treaty to throw doubt on so clear a proposition? How does it come about that a judicial Commission provided with ample evidence on all the aspects of its enquiry comes to be regarded by one of its Members as unlikely to produce an award based on its terms of reference or in accordance with the evidence. This lamentable result can only be explained by the persistent and unscrupulous use of threats of violence and political pressure. From the moment that the Boundary Commission was in course of formation threats have been circulated, emphasised and encouraged by an influential section of the British Press.

This section of the Press, while giving the most unstinted hospitality to the unconstitutional threats of the North, practically closed its columns to any reasoned arguments for the honest carrying out of an international engagement, supported by the law both of Great Britain and the Free State.

British politicians lent their influence to this unscrupulous movement. Public men in the highest positions lent themselves, without hesitation, to the campaign of whittling away, by misrepresentation, the rights which a large number of Irishmen had acquired by Treaty and Statute, to be returned to the Government of their choice. This campaign had the express purpose of prejudicing the Commission in their interpretation of their terms of reference. Through how many channels, through what secret organisations must this campaign have been carried on?

I said on Thursday last that I would prefer to wait for better proof than the publication in the 'Morning Post' before coming to the conclusion that the members of the Commission were men who did not place a value on impartial justice, who did not respect the considerations which had been laid down for their guidance and direction, and who were prepared to allow themselves to be swayed from the path of judicial rectitude by outside considerations. Dr. MacNeill, as an honourable man, has left the Commission and has proved that, so far as he was concerned, our confidence in him was not misplaced.

It has come then to this. Our Representative has lost faith in the other Members of the Commission, and has felt himself in honour bound to dissociate himself from them.

I must say that I also have lost faith in the other members of the Commission and am forced to the conclusion that they have allowed themselves to be swayed in the discharge of their judicial duty by the threats and political influences which have been brought to bear upon them. Dr. MacNeill left not because we were not getting all we asked for, but because justice was not being done, because the rights of our people in the North that were enshrined in Article 12 were being shamefully flouted and their destinies being made the plaything of hostile prejudice.

The grave situation which has occurred calls for the most careful consideration by your Government. It calls for the serious consideration of the British Government who have appointed the two remaining members of the Commission and who cannot escape moral responsibility for any act of injustice which may be inflicted through the agency of their nominees. I have no doubt that it will receive that consideration from them. It will certainly receive it from us.

But it calls for more than that. It calls for the exercise of restraint and dignity by all the people of Ireland and particularly by those most closely and most directly affected. A new and grave situation has undoubtedly arisen but good citizenship dictates that no heated words or foolish acts should render our task more difficult. The serious nature of that task we fully realise. We are under no misapprehensions as to the magnitude of the problem with which we are confronted. We will consider it with the utmost care and we will take such steps as appear to our considered judgment to be the most suitable and the most effective to prevent the infliction of injustice upon our people.

No. 346 NAI DT S1801O

James McNeill to Desmond FitzGerald (Dublin)[1]

(Copy)

LONDON, 24 November 1925

My dear Minister,

Mr. McDunphy arrived this morning. I went, as usual, to the Dominions office and saw Mr. Amery and the other High Commissioners. We did not discuss Irish matters during the meeting which was at 10.30 and not 11 o'clock as Mr. Amery was going to meet the Boundary Commission at 11 o'clock. We both expressed regret that matters had taken such a grave turn. When leaving I said that I knew he would have to arrive at a decision in this matter and that I hoped he would realise the grave consequences. He thought it was especially regrettable that the existing position should arise when the Commission were on the point of coming to an agreed decision which would have been generally satisfactory.

[1] Handwritten marginal note by Michael MacDunphy: 'seen by all members of the Executive Council 25/11'.

About 12 o'clock I got a message asking me to call on him at 5.15 this afternoon. I anticipate a stiff communication but of course don't know. Whatever it is it will be received by me as my Government's agent. I propose to indulge in no technical arguments on my own account. I shall say that while I have had no instructions I am sure my Government acted in the interests of peace, and that it had not foreseen the possibility of a transfer of Free State people to Northern Ireland.

When coming away from the meeting at the Dominions office I walked back with Mr. Larkin. He was friendly as usual but his reticence as regards this trouble showed that he had nothing consoling to say. He deplored that the world was full of trouble. We did not refer to the details.

I shall try to see Sir A. Cope.

I write now (3 o'clock) so as to have time to add whatever arises in my talk with Amery.

I have just heard of my brother John's[1] resignation from the Executive Council. I think that was unavoidable, and I hope it will be helpful. General opinion here seems to be against us. I cannot hear as much as usual directly because my brother's action is of course censured. The publication of the statement by the other two Commissioners has stiffened people here, and I think you may take the ' Times' as expressing considered views in its article to-day.

While I do not know what Mr. Amery will say, I fancy it will require patient hearing. With the average man disposed to take the 'Times' view and the Die-Hards ready to back any policy injurious to us I don't know that I can lightly take the 'Irish Times' view, viz. that the safety of the Free State depends on getting some compromise.

I am sorry that you are still having to face such trouble. May I, with deference, suggest that personalities and bitter words be discouraged. I think that with my brother's resignation opinion in Ireland will be mollified and that sensible people will realise that you must be helped and not injured or weakened. Opinion here though hard will possibly be less hostile if new cause of hostility is not created.

LATER.

I saw Mr. Amery and he told me he had gone with Mr. Joynson-Hicks[2] to the Boundary Commission to-day. He was told that the report was practically ready and that the two Commissioners thought it would be published by the 1st December. The Commissioners had expressly asked them to come as, they stated, they had asked both Governments to send Ministers originally and wished to meet the British ministers though the Irish ministers were not going to attend. Mr. Amery and Mr. Joynson-Hicks were told the general result of the award but did not see the map as Mr. Amery thought that, however little difference that might make, the map should be disclosed simultaneously to representatives of both Governments. He referred to the despatch of a letter[3]

[1] John is the English for Eoin. MacNeill had resigned as Minister for Education on 24 November, following his resignation as Boundary Commissioner on 20 November.

[2] Original reads 'Jackson-Hicks'.

[3] Not printed.

which you will have got[,] sent this afternoon by the Secretary of the Boundary Commission to your Government.

The British Government hoped that the Free State Government would send [a] Minister to meet Ministers to discuss privately the carrying out of the terms of the award. Mr. Amery hoped that my brother's resignation would be regarded merely as an unfortunate incident and that in the interests of both north and south the Free State Government would have this boundary question settled in accordance with the award in friendly co-operation.

I said that I had no instructions from my Government and know no details. As regards their action I was satisfied that they had considered that what they had done was necessary to obviate serious danger, and that the proposed award, which I understood differed only slightly from the 'Morning Post' account, surprised my Government utterly. They had, I presumed, to take account of the political fact that in the south as well as in the north there would be strong feeling at the suggested transfer of any people to Northern Ireland. He said the same might be said of the Northern Ireland people. I told him that without wishing to raise over again the boundary controversy I thought it was a different thing to remove people from their own Government and to alter the boundaries of a local government.

He hoped that either a Minister would come or that I should be authorised to attend Thursday's meeting at the Boundary Commission office. I said the time was very short and that very little time was given to my Government to decide on a very serious question. He explained that this would not be a publication of the award but only a preliminary communication. The date of publication would be later. As regards the date of publication that would rest with the commission. I cannot remember his words but he implied that the Commission might not insist on immediate publication. He dwelt at some length on the legal validity of the award, and quoted the Quebec judgment. He also said that he relied on Northern Ireland to ensure peaceful transfer and hoped that the Free State Government would realise that acceptance of the award by our people would expedite ultimate unification, to which no one here was opposed, and the British Government would benevolently further.

His general attitude was rather friendly. He referred to the President's reference to people in high positions acting improperly as if the British Ministers were referred to. I said that I did not understand the references in that way; that as far as I knew both in words and in mind President Cosgrave recognised the correctness and willingness to help on the part of the Ministry. I added that I thought they referred to members of the House of Lords and others, and that I did so because I should have personally denounced their conduct.

I said I would convey what he said.

Yours sincerely,
(signed) JAMES MCNEILL

No. 347 NAI DT S1801O

Telegram from T.M. Healy to Leopold Amery (London)
DUBLIN, 2.15 pm, 25 November 1925

Secretary of State for Dominions.
Following from President of Executive Council for Prime Minister: I feel it my duty to let you know that the proposed issue of an award by the Boundary Commission has created a difficult and very anxious situation. My colleagues and I view with the gravest concern and apprehension the intense feeling which has been gradually growing here. We are convinced that the situation calls for a conference between the two governments with a view to seeing how far it is possible to arrive at some settlement of this matter less likely to afford grounds for serious discontent and possible disorder.

An invitation has been received to be represented at a conference with the Boundary Commission on tomorrow Thursday, but it would seem desirable, if my suggestion commends itself to you, that the conference between ministers should take place first. As we should answer the invitation today, I shall be much obliged if you will let me have a reply by telegraph.

Governor General

No. 348 NAI DFA Minister's Office Files (1924-25)

James McNeill to Desmond FitzGerald (Dublin)
LONDON, 25 November 1925

My dear Minister,
I telephoned to you to-day a message advising that the Council should insist on being given time to consider the situation created by my brother's resignation and your knowledge of the draft award. I am convinced that, while the Commission is in law entitled to make its award at its own time, neither the Commission nor the British Government would wish that it should be published under conditions which rendered any attempt to enforce it likely to lead to (1) active and prolonged resistance on the part of persons directly affected and those in sympathy with them, and (2) deep feeling in Ireland against the British Government and the Treaty position.

In my talk with Cope last night we discussed the whole matter at length. I agreed with him that it would be easiest to let the award go on if it were possible, but as that was impossible it was necessary to consider alternatives. The alternative of preserving the status quo would obviate immediate trouble but would retain a state of friction and unsettlement and would put the Six-Counties in a state of defensive anxiety which would render conferences as to unification either impossible or fruitless, while it would enable the Ulster Separatists to keep their ranks united and prevent internal dissatisfaction with their militant regime. The third possible course seemed to be to press the British Government to induce the Northern Government to come to an agreed compromise to be adopted as an award. I thought that the East Donegal portion must be retained in the Free State if trouble was to be avoided. Cope thought it might be worth proposing that a greater population elsewhere, otherwise likely to be included in the proposed transfer to the Free State, were to remain in the six counties, and some compensation paid on either side to people who left any jurisdiction because of the change. I agreed that it would probably be less troublesome to let some people stay in Northern Ireland than to eject any from the Free State. I explained that what was possible in any way depended on the effect on our people, which I could not estimate here.

Taking the position as it stands at the moment I think that it would be best to push the third proposal hard, and try to see Sir James Craig here as well as ministers of the British Government.

While Mr. Amery urged the need for proceeding with the award I simply do not believe that any Government here would determine to rush you into compliance and risk violent and continued resistance to the introduction of a new Government in East Donegal. The legal and constitutional position is with them but the political fact is that we have been treated with gross unfairness by their nominee. We may be unable to redress the greater part of the evil but we must I think put it up to them that no Irish Government could hope to secure the peaceful application of such an award or prevent the re-opening of the whole Treaty position. This Government could not, in my opinion, refuse to join with you in a request to the Commission to hold over the award for a few weeks and the arbitrators could not reject such a request.

I expect every moment to hear from Cope who was going to try to see Mr. Churchill and possibly either Mr. Baldwin or the latter's Private Secretary. Whatever he may learn I think we must demand time in everyone's interest. If Sir James Craig could be moved to assent to the omission of the East Donegal area, not impossible if his action was recognised and in some fitting way commended, it would be a way out of a bad business. I think that if the President and Vice-President saw the Prime Minister, Amery and Joynson-Hicks and frankly said it was that or a speedy change from growing national friendliness to a steady anti-British movement accompanied by prolonged resistance to the Northern Ireland Government in the portion transferred with the active sympathy of their neighbours and their kindred overseas. Against all arguments about the validity of the award you can urge its palpable unjustness.

If Ministers come over I think they should not meet the Boundary Commissioners.

The Secretary of the Boundary Commission sent me a copy of his letter to our Government[1] about Thursday's meeting and added in his letter that I might telephone its contents if I thought fit. I thought that I had better not assist in any expediting procedure. One advantage of delay is that the legal and constitutional technicalities of the case seem less important and the political meaning and consequences of the award as generally outlined will move public opinion here and everywhere towards us. Though analogies are dangerous I

[1] Not printed.

think we are at least as much entitled to political redress for a serious wrong under judicial forms as the Scottish Churchmen whose endowments were judicially taken away and legislatively restored. If we assail the award as grossly unjust and stick to the need for substantial compromise we must win.

As I finished this Cope rang me up and told me in language which could not be understood by listeners that he had seen people and that an invitation to come over would be sent to Ministers if it was likely to be accepted. I hope this will be done, avoiding of course all contact with the Commission. I feel sure that if the manifest wrong of the decision is sufficiently assailed at least some, perhaps much, improvement will be effected. Cope hoped a moderate reply was sent to the Commission's letter. He suggests that moderation of tone (not matter) be practised in all things. I am to let him know early to-morrow.

Can Thomas Johnson[1] say nothing which will strengthen the Council in bettering our position?

You will realise that in suggesting demands to be made as to compromise I am trying to estimate the minimum on the assumption that you could not escape refusal to take any responsibility if less is conceded. To get the minimum it may be desirable not to set forth or even hint what it is until you must. You may well get more than a minimum as estimated by me on slender knowledge.

Yours sincerely,
[signed] JAMES MCNEILL

No. 349 NAI DT S4720A

Handwritten text of telegram from James McNeill to Dublin
LONDON, 4.52 pm, 25 November 1925

Talked with Cope[2] last night. I explained that position grave and that Council must have time to consider, one of three courses must be taken, acceptance of award or maintenance of present boundary or agreement for modification of terms of award before final publication. He promised to go House of Commons last night and let me know today. He hoped to see ministers and others.

I wait for his news.

Meanwhile I urge you send courteous but firm request for time to consider position both Government and Commission.

SAORSTÁT[3]

---

[1] Leader of the Labour Party.
[2] This telegram synopsises No. 348 above.
[3] Telegraphic code for Irish High Commissioner's Office in London.

No. 350 NAI DT S4720A

Rough handwritten note by Joseph P. Walshe of two coded messages received from James McNeill in London

DUBLIN, 25 November 1925

Two code messages received from H.C. Wed[nes]d[a]y Ev[enin]g.[1]

1. (by phone)
Please reply immediately if invitation be sent to me or two of our Ministers to meet one or two Ministers here for frank discussion of situation, invitation will be accepted by the government. Cope & I recommend acceptance.

2. (by wire)[2]

No. 351 NAI DT S4720A

Rough notes of meeting with British Ministers by Diarmuid O'Hegarty

LONDON, 26 November 1925

The notes are reproduced in facsimile on pages 459-472 inclusive.

[1] Handwritten note by Nicolás Ó Nualláin (Secretary, Department of the Taoiseach), 31 May 1950: 'Apparently Wednesday evening, 25th November, 1925'.

[2] The second coded message is not reproduced.

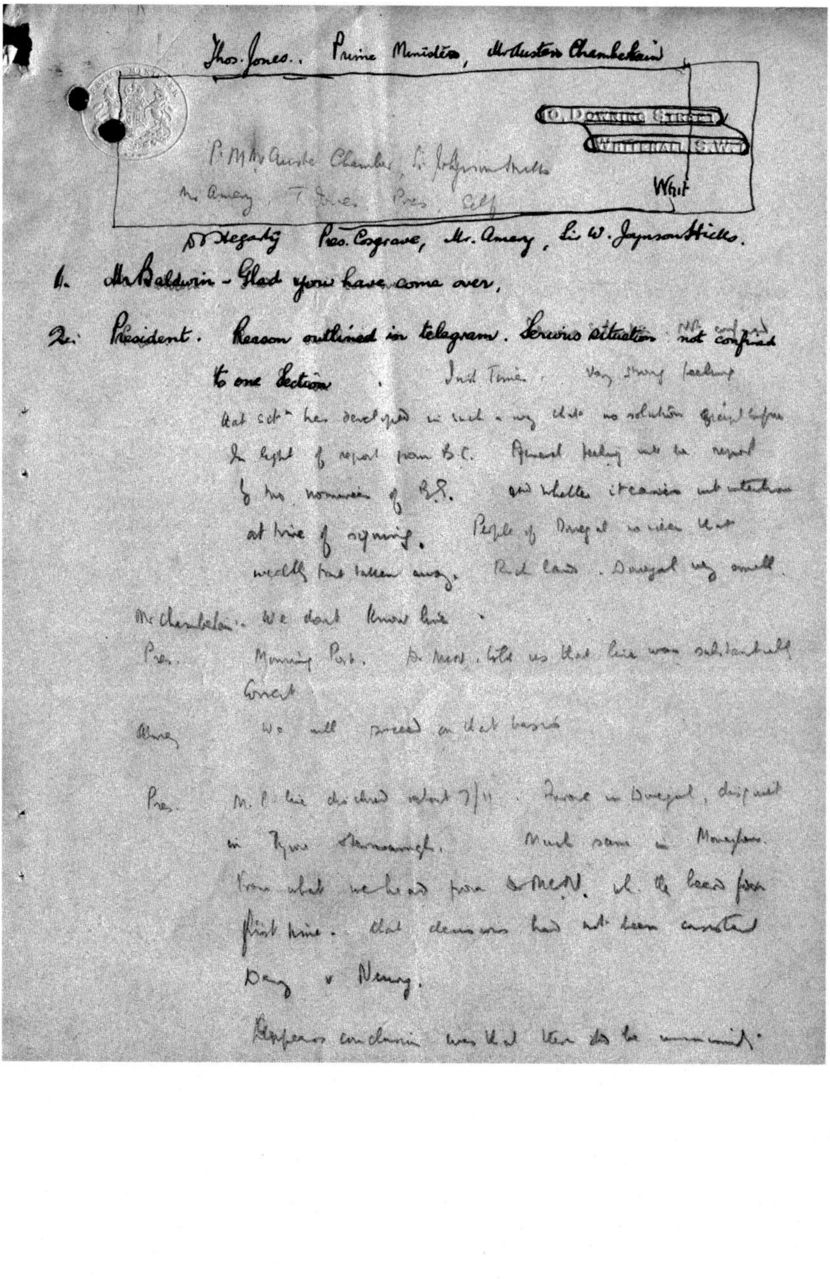
Thos. Jones. Prime Minister, Mr Austen Chamberlain

10, DOWNING STREET
WHITEHALL, S.W.1

Whit

Dr Hegarty Pres. Cosgrave, Mr. Amery, Sir W. Joynson Hicks.

1. Mr Baldwin – Glad you have come over.

2. President. Reason outlined in telegram. Serious situation not confined to one Section.

Mr Chamberlain. We don't know line.

Pres. Morning Post.

Amery We will proceed on that basis

Pres.

Derry v Newry.

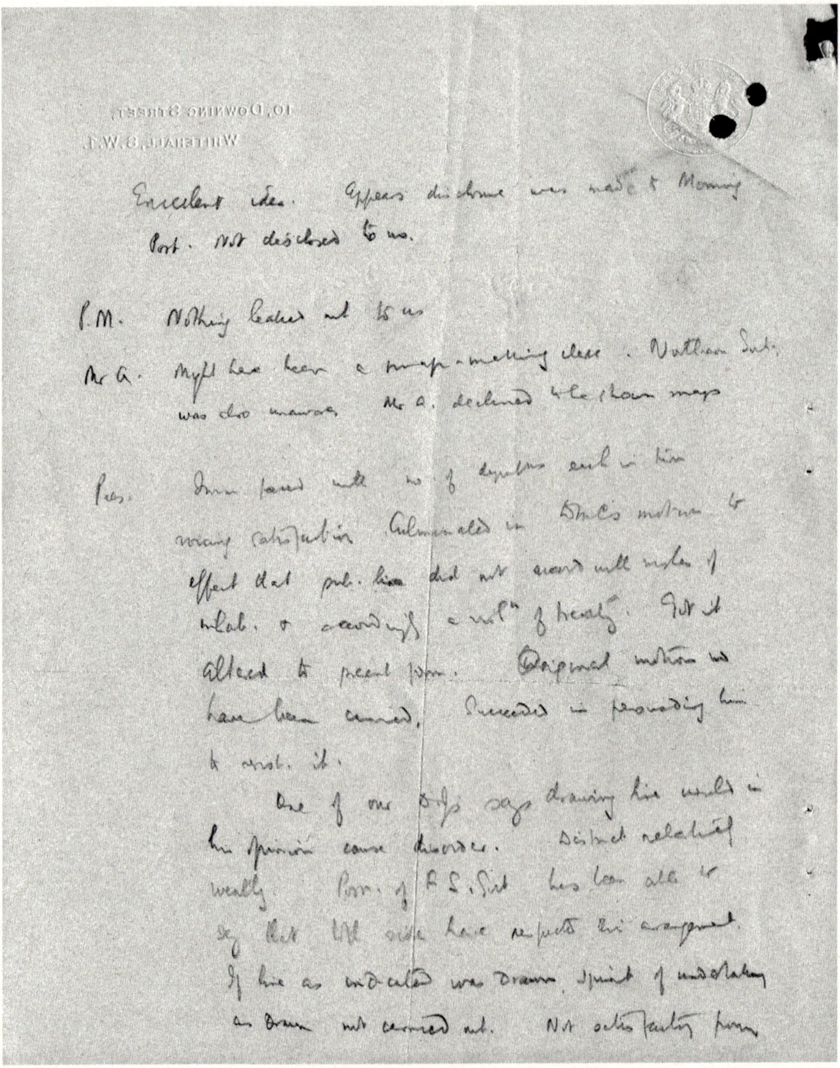

10, Downing Street,
Whitehall, S.W.1.

Excellent idea. Appears disclosure was made to Morning Post. Not disclosed to us.

P.M. Nothing leaked out to us

Mr A. Might have been a map-making clerk. Northern Govt. was also aware. Mr A. declined to be shown maps

Pres. Been faced with no. of deputations each in turn voicing satisfaction. Culminated in [illegible] motion to effect that pub. line did not accord with wishes of inhab. & accordingly a viol[n] of treaty. Got it altered to present form. Original motion w[oul]d have been carried. Succeeded in persuading him to [illegible] it.

One of our B[ishop]s says drawing line would in his opinion cause disorder. District relatively wealthy. Pos. of F.S. Govt has been able to say that UK side have respected the arrangement. If line as indicated was drawn, spirit of undertaking as drawn not carried out. Not satisfactory from

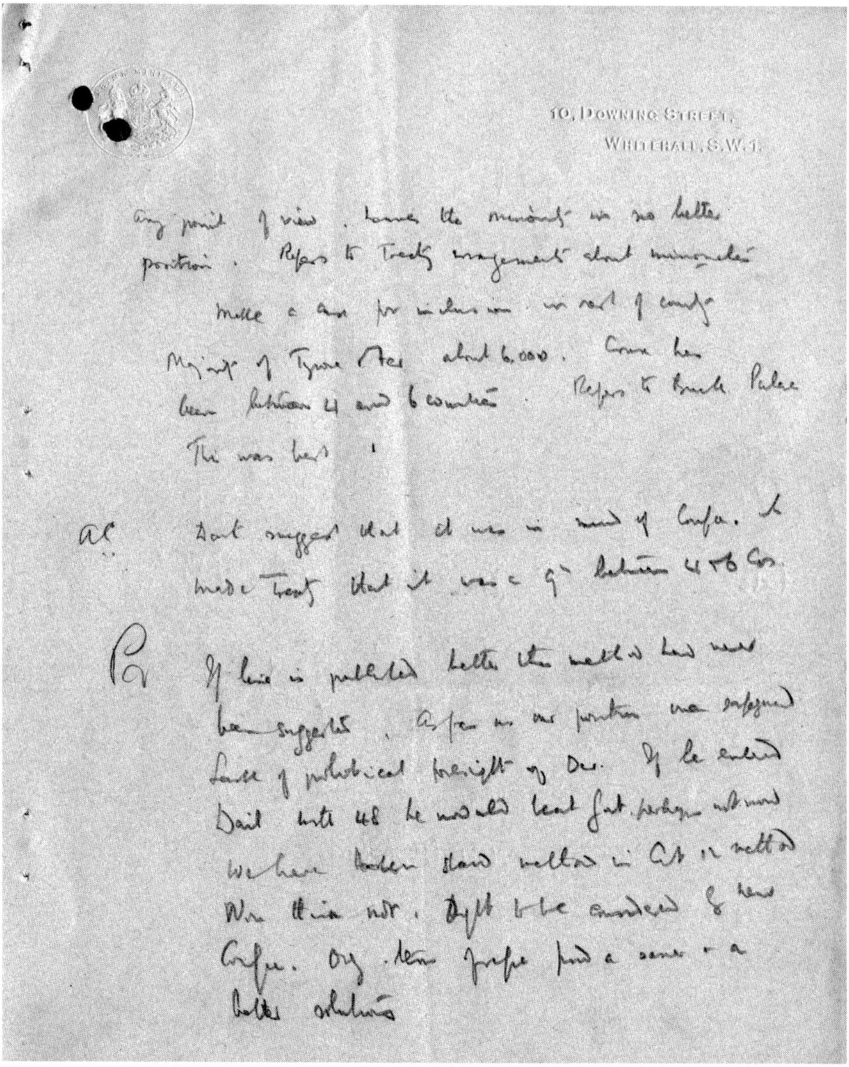
10, Downing Street,
Whitehall, S.W.1.

any point of view. Leaves the minority in no better position. Refers to Treaty arrangement about minorities

Make a case for inclusion in rest of county

Majority of Tyrone & Fer about 6,000. Crown has been between 4 and 6 counties. Refers to Buck. Palace

This was best!

AC Don't suggest that it was in mind of Confce. He made Treaty that it was a qn between 4 & 6 Cos.

PM If line is published better that matter had never been suggested. As far as our position was safeguarded Loss of political foresight of Dev. If he entered Dail with 48 he would have beat Govt. perhaps not now

We have broken through matters in Ct. is matter

Now think not. Ought to be considered by new Confce. Only terms propose find a same or a better solution

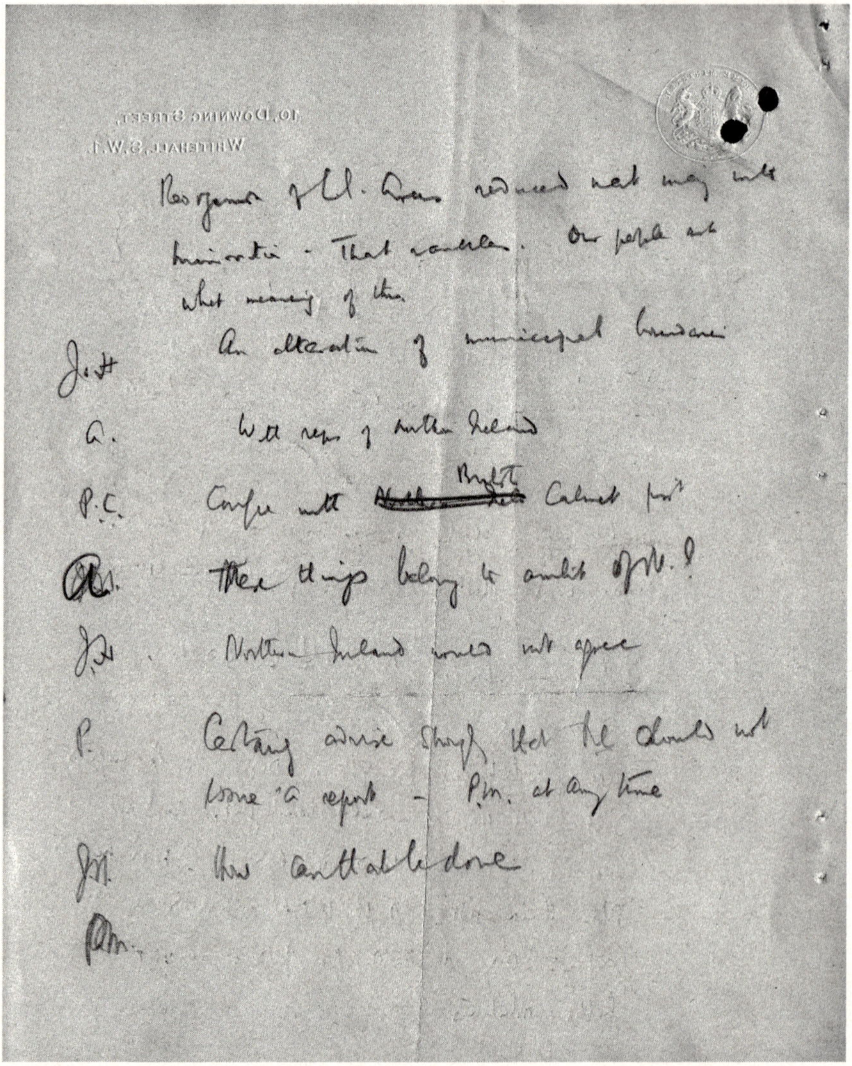
Reorganisation of Cl. Areas reduced next may with minorities - That cancelled. Our people ask what meaning of this

J.H. An alteration of municipal boundaries

A. With regard of Northern Ireland

P.C. Confer with ~~[illegible]~~ Bright Cabinet first

[illegible]. These things belong to ambit of N.I.

J.H. Northern Ireland would not agree

P. Certainly advise strongly that we should not issue a report - P.M. at any time

J.H. How can that be done

P.M.

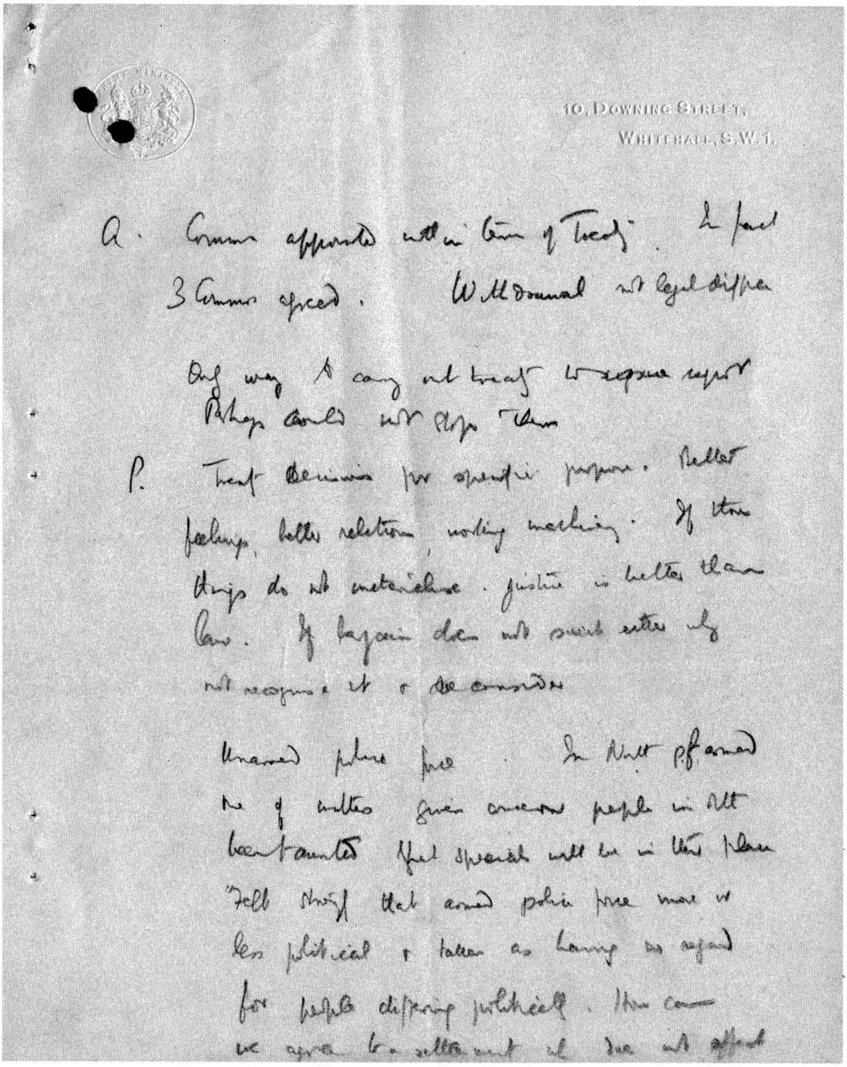
10, Downing Street,
Whitehall, S.W.1.

Q. Commn appointed within terms of Treaty. In fact 3 Commrs agreed. Withdrawal not legal differ[illegible]

Only way to carry out treaty to require report
Perhaps could not stop them

P. Treaty decisions for specific purposes. Better feelings, better relations, working machinery. If these things do not materialise. justice is better than law. If bargain does not suit either why not recognise it & reconsider

Unarmed police force. In Ulster P.F. armed [illegible] of matters given concern people in Ult[illegible] [illegible] Special would be in their place. Felt strongly that armed police force more or less political & taken as having no regard for people differing politically. How can we agree to a settlement which does not affect

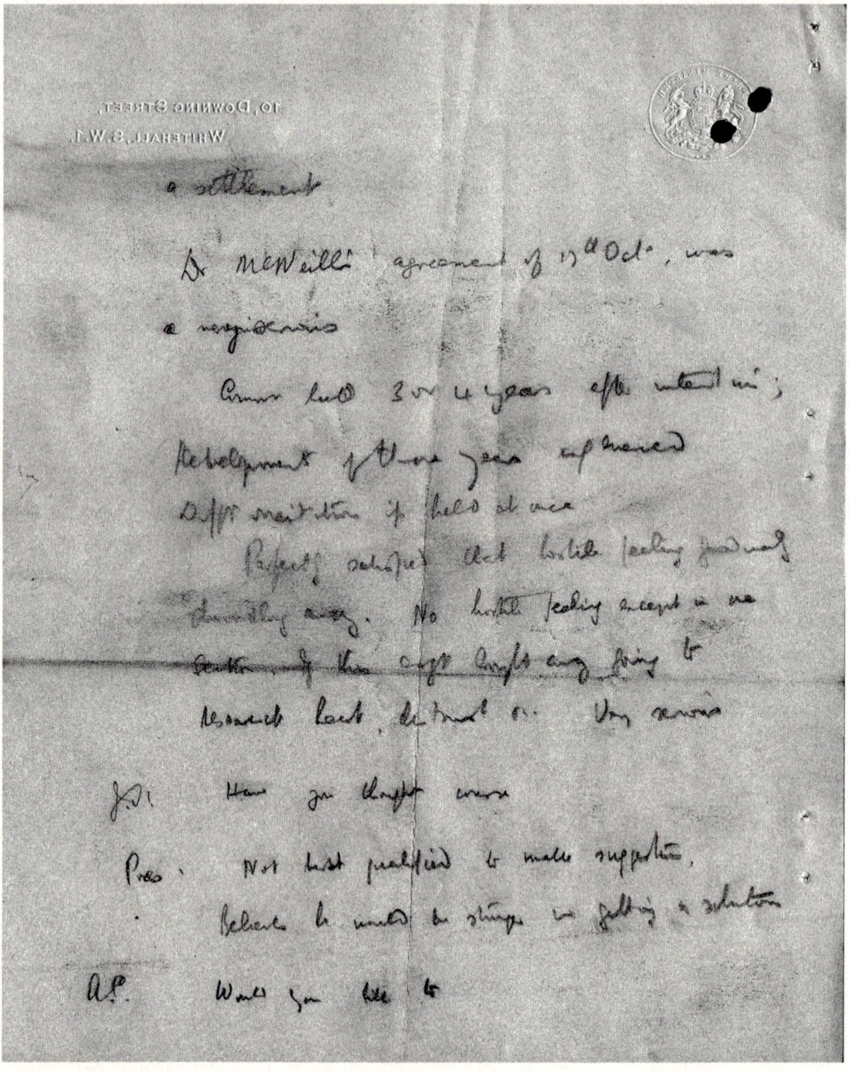
a settlement

Dr McNeill's agreement of 17th Oct., was

a [illegible]

[illegible] held 3 or 4 years after [illegible]

Development of those years [illegible]

[illegible] if held at once

Perfectly satisfied that hostile feeling gradually

dwindling away. No hostile feeling except in one

section. If there [illegible] going to

[illegible] [illegible]. Very serious

[illegible] Have you thought course

Pres. Not best qualified to make suggestions.

Believe he would be [illegible] in getting a solution

A.C. Would you like to

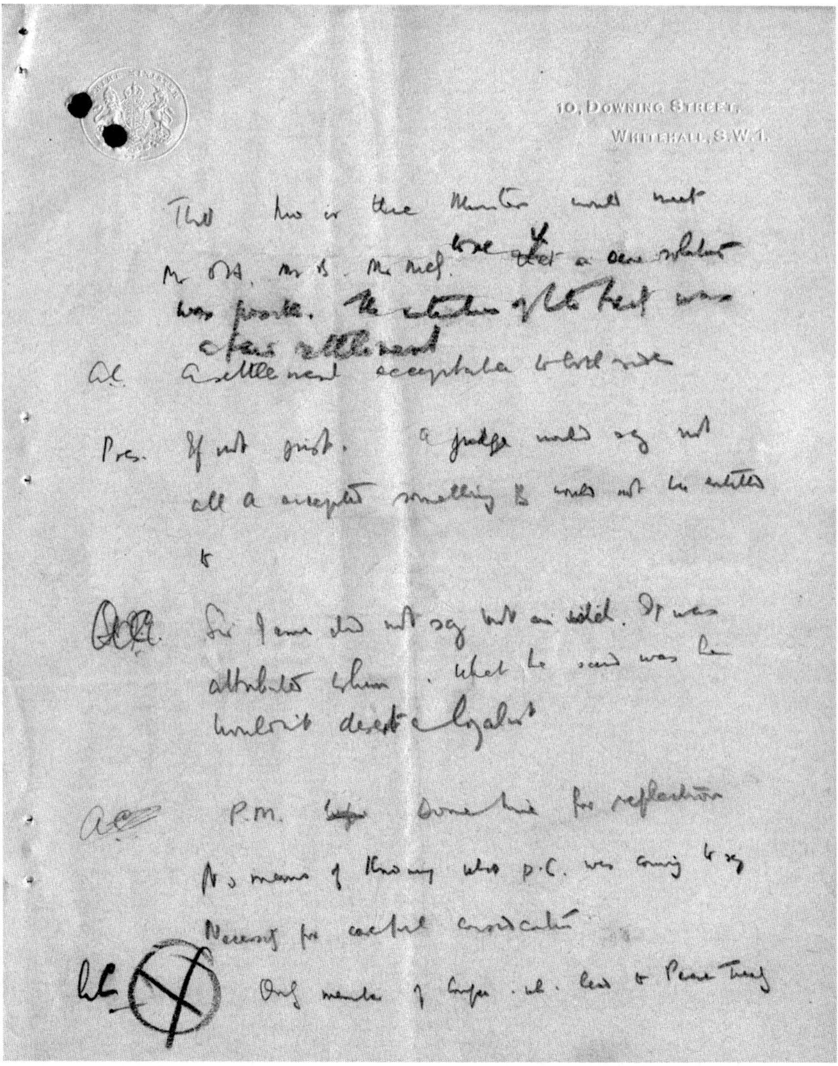
10, Downing Street,
Whitehall, S.W.1.

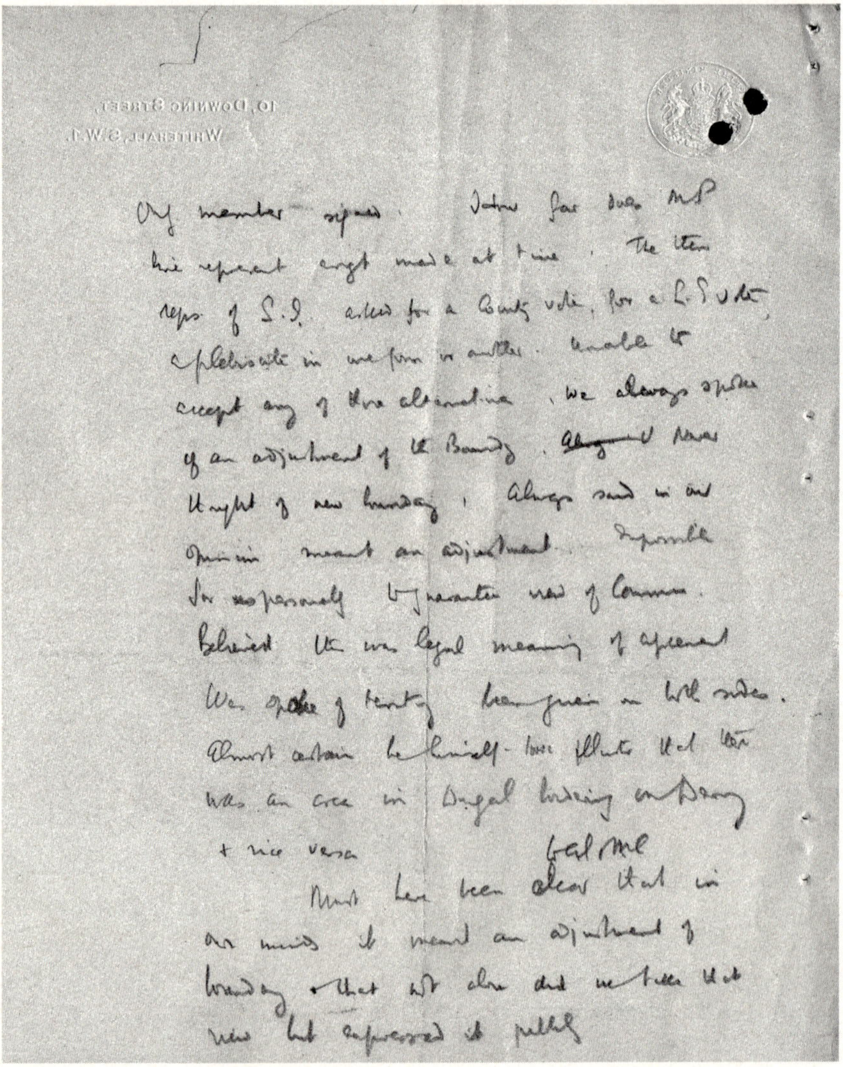

Only member [illegible]. [illegible] M.P.
[illegible] agreement ought made at time. The then
reps of S.I. asked for a County vote, for a P.S. vote,
a plebiscite in one form or another. Unable to
accept any of these alternatives. We always spoke
of an adjustment of the Boundary. ~~Alleged~~ Never
thought of new boundary. Always said in our
opinion meant an adjustment. Impossible
for us personally to guarantee view of Commission.
Believed that was legal meaning of agreement
We spoke of territory being given on both sides.
Almost certain he himself knew perfectly that there
was an area in Donegal looking on Derry
+ vice versa [illegible]
Must have been clear that in
our minds it meant an adjustment of
boundary + that not alone did we take that
view but expressed it publicly

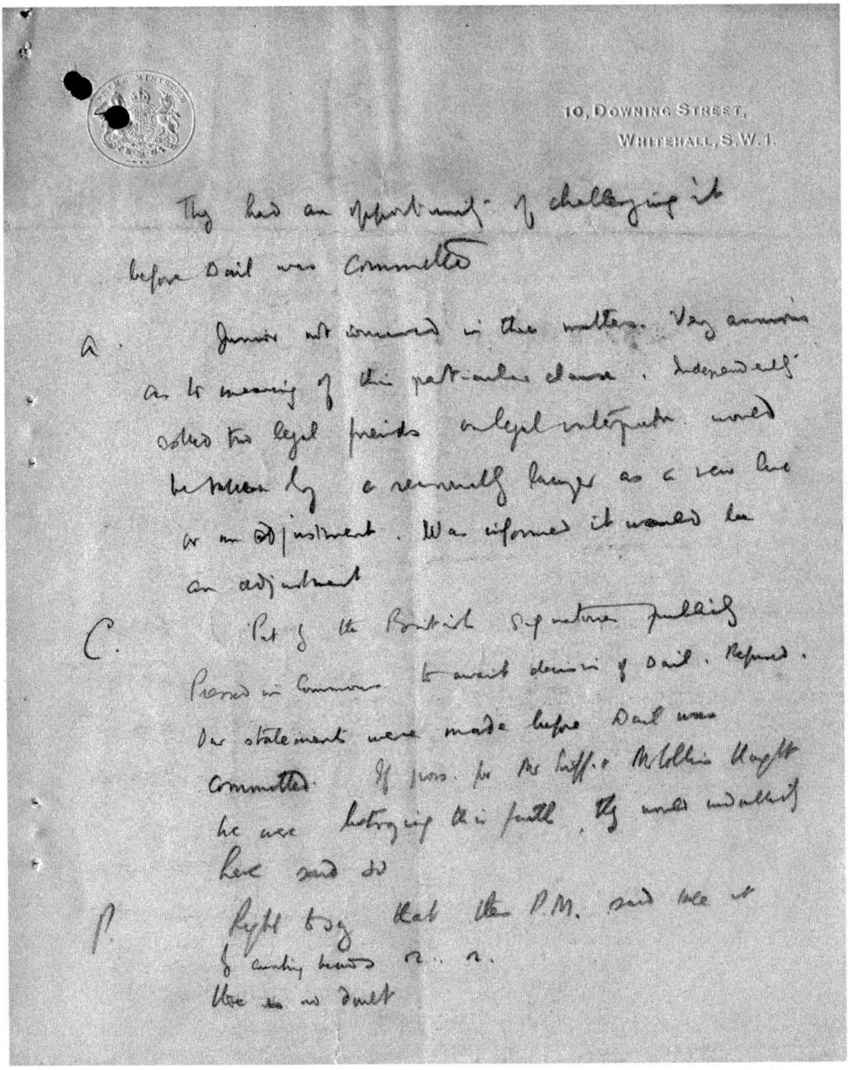

10, Downing Street,
Whitehall, S.W.1.

They had an opportunity of challenging it
before Dail was Committed

A. Junior not concerned in these matters. Very anxious
as to meaning of this particular clause. Independently
asked two legal friends on legal interpretation would
be taken by a reasonably [illegible] as a new line
or an adjustment. Was informed it would be
an adjustment

C. Put of the British signatures publicly
Pressed in Commons to await decision of Dail. Refused.
Our statements were made before Dail was
Committed. If poss. for Mr Griffith & McCollins thought
we were betraying their faith, they would undoubtedly
have said so

D. Right to say that the P.M. said [illegible]
of [illegible] [illegible]
there was no doubt

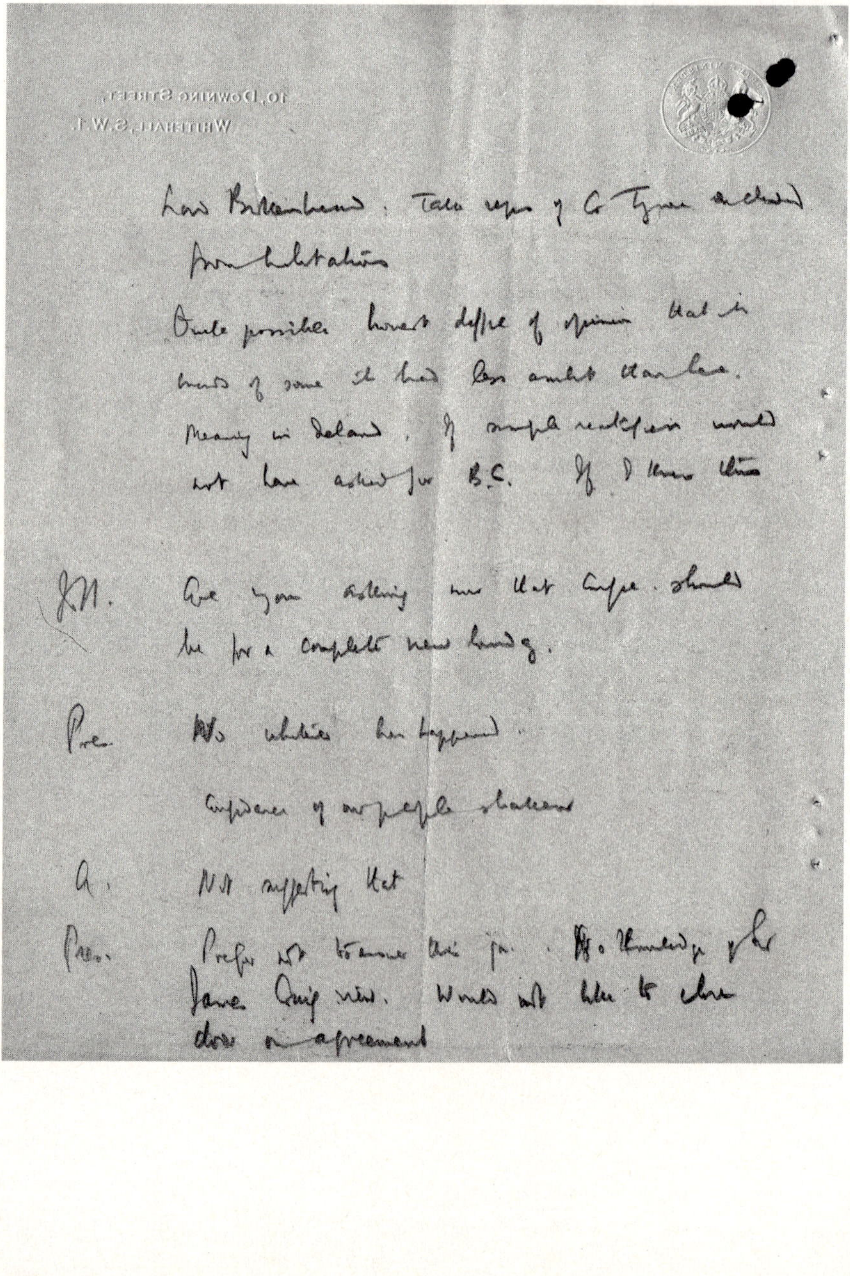

Lord Birkenhead. Take case of Co Tyrone excluded from [illegible]

Quite possible honest differ of opinion that in view of some it had less ambit than [illegible].

Meaning in Ireland. If simple readjustment would not have asked for B.C. If I knew this

J.M. Are you asking me that Cosgrave should be for a complete new boundary.

Pres. Not whatever has happened.

Confidence of our people shaken

A. Not suggesting that

Pres. Prefer not to answer this q. No knowledge of Sir James Craig view. Would not like to close door on agreement

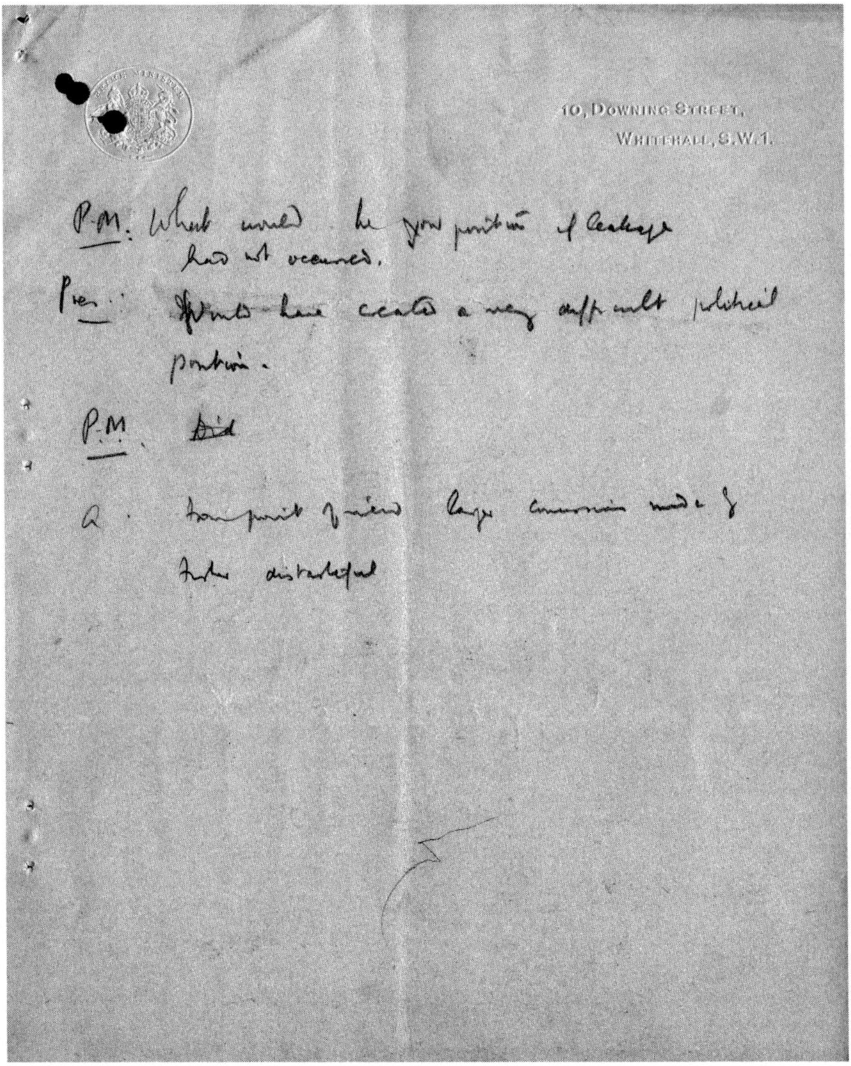
10, DOWNING STREET,
WHITEHALL, S.W.1.

P.M.: What would be your position if leakage had not occurred.

Pres.: It would have created a very difficult political position.

P.M. ~~Did~~

Q. From point of view large concession made & further distasteful

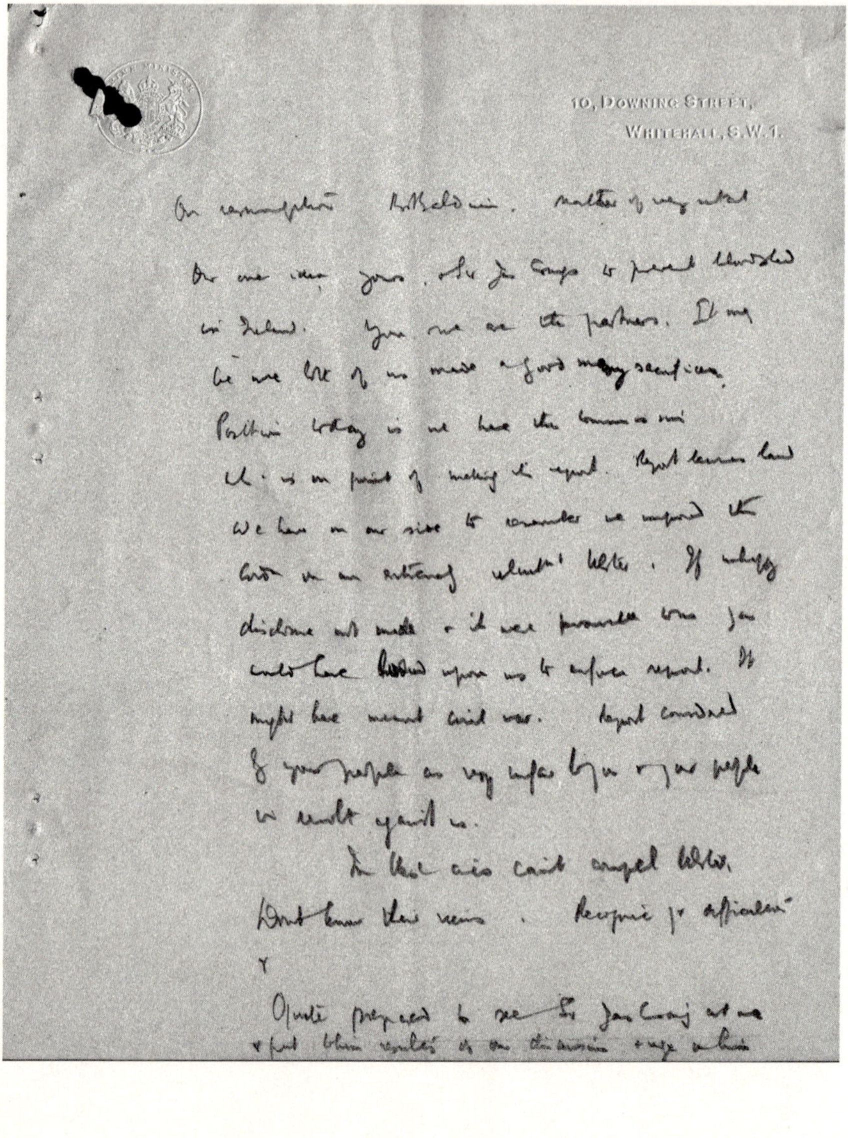
10, Downing Street,
Whitehall, S.W.1.
Position today [illegible]
[illegible] might have meant civil war. [illegible]
Quite prepared to see Sir James Craig [illegible]

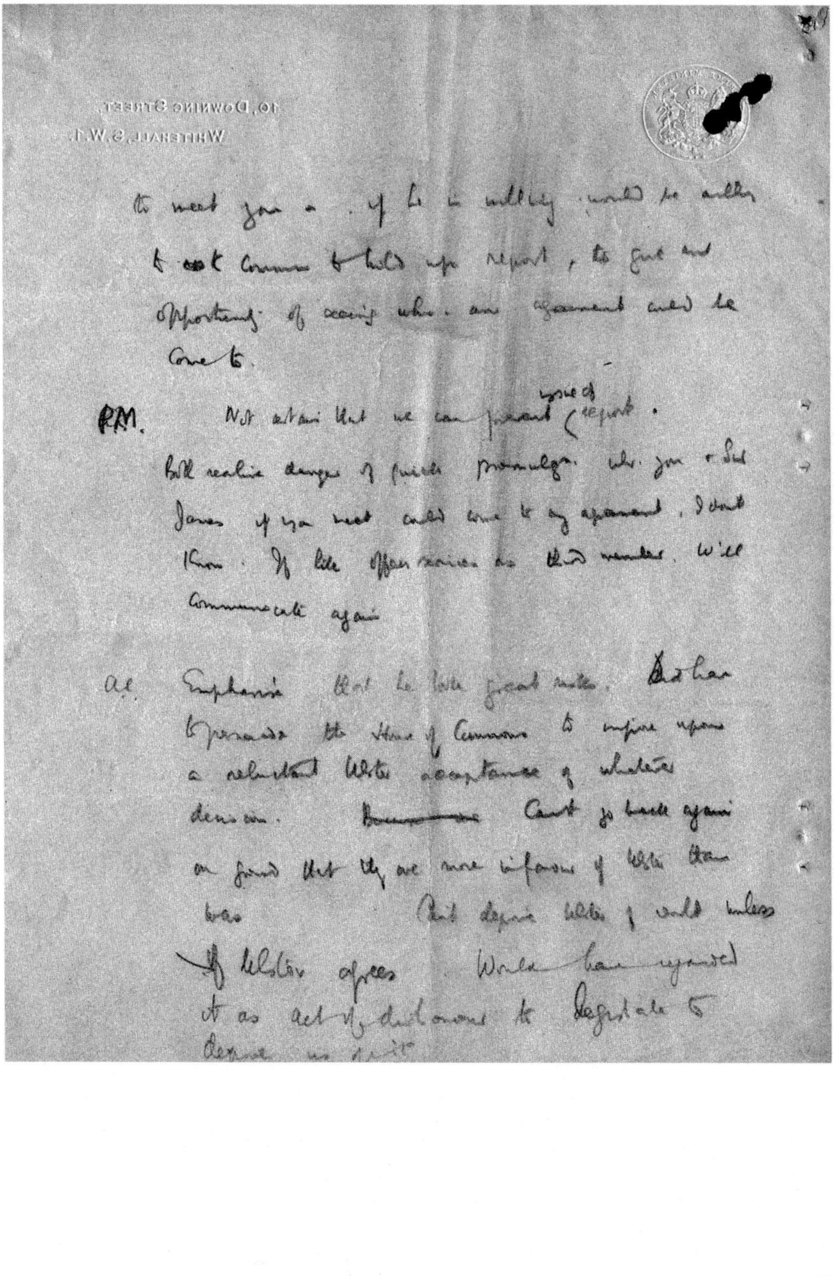

to meet you & . If he is willing would be willing
to ask Commission to hold up report, to give an
opportunity of seeing whether any agreement could be
come to.

RM. Not certain that we can prevent issue of report.
Both realise danger of publication. Whether you & Sir
James if you meet could come to any agreement, I don't
know. If like offer services as third member. Will
communicate again

AC. Emphasise that he took great risks. And had
to persuade the House of Commons to impose upon
a reluctant Ulster acceptance of whatever
decision. ~~[illegible]~~ Can't go back again
on ground that they are more in favour of Ulster than
was Can't deprive Ulster of [illegible] unless
If Ulster agrees. Would have regarded
it as act of dishonour to legislate to
deprive us [illegible]

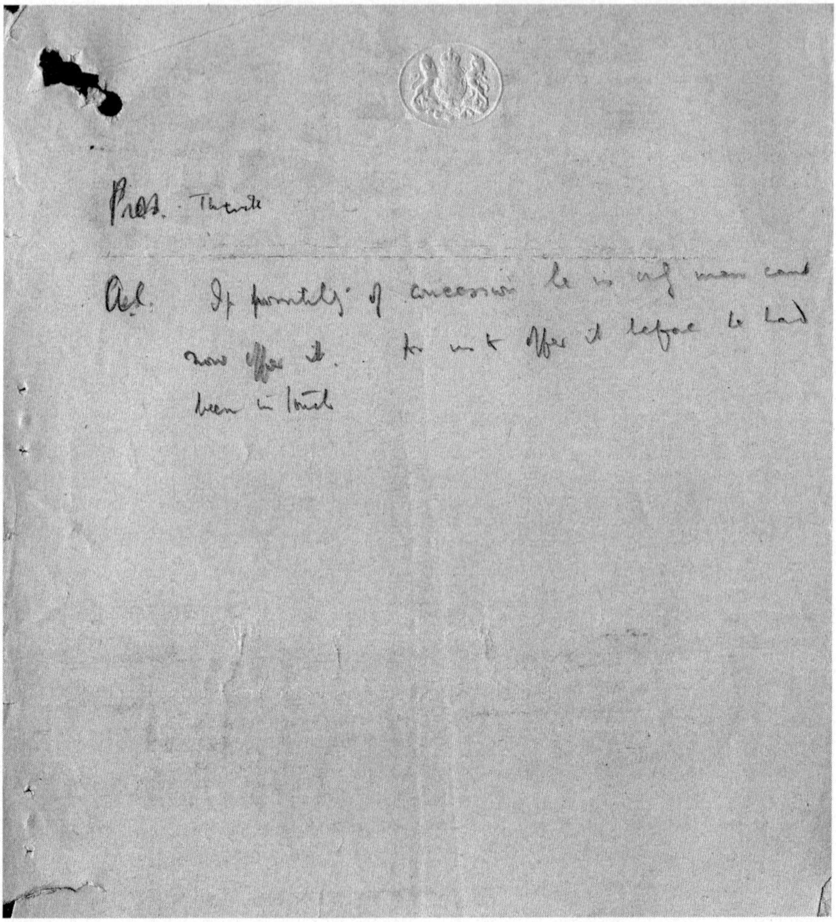

Pres. [illegible]

Ack. If possibility of concession he is only man could now offer it. [illegible] not offer it before he had been in touch

No. 352 NAI DT S4720A

Draft Notes of a Conference held at No. 10 Downing Street, S.W./1 (Secret) (CA/H/48 1st meeting)

LONDON, 11.00 am, 26 November 1925

Present.

Great Britain.
The Right Hon. Stanley Baldwin, M.P., Prime Minister. (In the Chair)
The Right Hon. Austen Chamberlain, M.P., Secretary of State for Foreign Affairs.
The Right Hon. Sir William Joynson-Hicks, Bart., M.P., Secretary of State for Home Affairs.
The Right Hon. L.S. Amery, M.P., Secretary of State for Dominion Affairs.

Irish Free State.
Mr. W.T. Cosgrave, T.D., President of the Executive Council, Irish Free State.

Secretaries.
Mr. T. Jones, Deputy Secretary, Cabinet Secretariat.

Mr. D. O'Hegarty, Secretary to the Executive Council, Irish Free State.

MR. COSGRAVE said that a very serious and difficult situation had arisen in the Irish Free State. It was not confined to any one section, but it affected all, as was evident from the position taken up by the '*Irish Times*'. There was a strong feeling amongst them that the situation had developed in such a way that he could see no solution except by means of a Conference. A report issued by the Boundary Commission at the present moment would be felt to be that of two nominees of the British Government who have not interpreted the situation as it was at the time of the Treaty. There is already an acute situation in Donegal where it is understood a rich portion is to be taken away and transferred to Ulster.

MR. CHAMBERLAIN, intervening, said that the British representatives had no information as to the new boundary line proposed. The Boundary Commission would have been willing to communicate the information, but the British representatives had preferred to wait until the Irish representatives could attend the Commission with them.

MR. COSGRAVE said he was referring to the line which had appeared in the 'Morning Post', and which he understood from Mr. MacNeill to be substantially correct. This line had been disclosed in the 'Morning Post' about November 7th. Its publication created a furore in Donegal and disquiet in Tyrone and Fermanagh; feeling was much the same in Monaghan. There had been a reasonable expectation of additions to the Free State from the first two counties. Notwithstanding the disclosure in the '*Morning Post*' Mr. MacNeill had made no statement to the Executive Council until the end of last week.[1] With the publication of the forecast in the 'Morning Post', the confidence reposed in the Commission had broken down. It had been learnt that whereas in the case of Derry a sector of Donegal had been taken from the Irish Free State to help Derry, a quite different procedure had been adopted in the case of Newry.

MR. AMERY said that the Northern Government had similarly no information as to what the line was going to be, and the British representatives had declined to look at the map prepared by the Commission.

MR. COSGRAVE, continuing, said that in any event there had been a leakage, and his Government were immediately faced with deputations from the various border areas. One of the Dáil members for Donegal had handed in a motion to the effect that the published line did not conform to the wishes of the inhabitants, and was therefore a breach of the Treaty. He (Mr. Cosgrave) contrived to have this modified to indicate approval of the representations made to the Boundary Commission by the Executive Council that no transfer should take place from the South to the North. Had the original motion been put, it would have been carried. Since the debate in the Dáil, representations have continued to be made, and one of the Justices had reported that if the line proposed were adopted, there would certainly be disorder, especially in the relatively wealthy district of Donegal to which he had referred. Up to the present the position of the Free State Government had been that they could say with truth that both sides had carried out the spirit of the Treaty, but the Free State Government felt that the proposed line went against the spirit of the undertaking embodied in the Treaty. It was not satisfactory from any point of view as it left the minority in no better position.

Under Article 12, it had been open to Northern Ireland to opt out or to come in. If they came in then certain safeguards were to be inserted in the interests of Sir James Craig's supporters. If they opted out, it was for the Nationalist minority to make a case for inclusion in the rest of the country. That seemed to have gone by the board. There was a majority in Tyrone and Fermanagh of some six thousand in favour of inclusion in the South. The crux of the matter had been the question of six counties or four, and it was on that issue that the Buckingham Palace Conference had broken down.

MR. CHAMBERLAIN said that it had never been in the mind of the Treaty Conference that the question of four or six counties was to be referred to the Boundary Commission.

MR. COSGRAVE agreed. Nevertheless, Article 12 had been drawn up to solve the situation and if the line now proposed were adopted, it would have been better never to have suggested Article 12. In his view, the question ought to be considered anew by a Conference which should have for its terms of reference the finding of a saner and better solution. Since 1921, certain local Government areas in Northern Ireland had been reorganised in such a way as to do violence

[1] See above No. 343.

to the feelings of the Nationalists. That was a matter which should receive attention and ought to be capable of appeasement. He thought that a Conference between representatives of the Cabinet and the Executive Council should take place.

SIR W. JOYNSON-HICKS said it was most improbable that the Government of Northern Ireland would consent at the suggestion of outsiders to change their local boundaries or even to discuss such a proposal.

MR. COSGRAVE said that at least an effort could be made in that direction and that he thought it would be preferable to hold a preliminary meeting of representatives of the Cabinet and Executive Council. He strongly urged that the Boundary Commission should not issue their award either now or at any time.

MR. AMERY reminded Mr. Cosgrave that the Commission had been appointed in accordance with the Treaty and that he was not sure that they were not absolutely entitled to issue their award, and could only be prevented by fresh legislation.

MR. COSGRAVE replied that the whole object of the Conference which terminated in the Treaty, was to arrive at better relations and to devise workable machinery to that end. If it were now found that this purpose was about to be defeated even although the law might technically stand in the way, there was a justice above the law. Why should not the bargain be reconsidered if it were now found to suit neither party?

The Irish Free State had an unarmed police force which, all things considered, had functioned very well. In the North the forces were armed. He was concerned with the position which would arise if the line were drawn, and the Northern 'Specials' were put in the transferred area. In the one area would be an unarmed police force, in the other, an armed force, and this armed force was regarded by many in the South as a political force. That was one of the gravest difficulties. How could they justify a settlement which did not in fact effect a settlement? He admitted that the fact of Mr. McNeill's agreement on the 17th October was a difficult point. Had Mr. McNeill been in touch with border or Free State feeling, he could scarcely have been a party to that agreement. He had resigned; it was a deplorable situation, but it did not affect the judgment of the other Commissioners. The Commission had been held three or four years after the signing of the Treaty, and the situation which had developed since the signing of the Treaty was in their minds. That was not fair. Had the Commission been held immediately after the Treaty, there would have been a different orientation. In the meantime, the hostile feeling between the countries had been dwindling away; there was only one hostile section which was politically biased and losing influence. If the award of the Commission were to go forth, it would resurrect the heat and hate which had been dying away in the last few years.

SIR W. JOYNSON-HICKS asked if Mr. Cosgrave had thought out a course of procedure.

MR. COSGRAVE replied that he would rather not make suggestions himself.

MR. CHAMBERLAIN: You would prefer a suggestion from us?

MR. COSGRAVE assented. He had in mind that two or three of his Ministers should meet two or three members of the British Cabinet and confer. His position was that Article 12 had failed in its purpose. A settlement might be found which would be just; one which a judge could commend. Even if it did not give all that A wanted, B could accept.

MR. CHAMBERLAIN said that it was important that there should be time for careful reflection by the British members on the statement made by Mr. Cosgrave. He did not propose at that moment to speak on the substance of what had just been said, but as the only member of the Irish Treaty Conference present, he would like to make one or two observations of a historical character. It was important to recall some of the features of that Conference in their bearing on the question of a Boundary.

The representatives of Southern Ireland asked for a vote by Counties or by local Government areas, or for a plebiscite in some form or other. We said we were unable to accept any of these. On our side we always spoke of an adjustment. We excluded the drawing of a new boundary apart from and independent of the existing boundary. In all our subsequent public speeches we explained that, whilst we were not entitled to prejudge the Commissioners' decision in the matter, we believed that to be the legal interpretation of the Article we had signed. Every British signatory spoke of territory being given not only by Ulster to the Free State, but by the Free State to Ulster. He himself was almost certain that he had taken as an illustration the case of a homogeneous area in Donegal bordering on Derry that might be attributed to Ulster, whilst more to the South were homogeneous areas which might go to the Free State. It must have been clear to Mr. Griffith and Mr. Collins that this was an adjustment of an existing boundary implying some cession of territory from each side to the other. That was the position we took up in the House of Commons at a time when had they regarded it as improper Mr. Griffith and Mr. Collins could have challenged it in the Dáil.

MR. AMERY said that at that time he was a junior member of the Government and very anxious as to the meaning of Article 12. In order to satisfy himself, he had privately consulted legal friends as to its interpretation. They were agreed that no lawyer would regard it as meaning other than an adjustment, and armed with these opinions, he had voted for the Treaty.

MR. CHAMBERLAIN said that perhaps even more important than what had passed in the Conference itself was the interpretation put by the signatories publicly in the House of Commons. It should be remembered that the British Government were pressed to await the decision of the Dáil, but we took the line that we ought to find out whether Parliament would ratify the Treaty before the Dáil considered it. Had it been possible for Mr. Griffith and Mr. Collins to suggest that we were betraying the faith we had pledged, they would have protested at once, and would have refused to go to the Dáil till the misconception was cleared up.

MR. COSGRAVE said that the then British Prime Minister had referred to county and local areas as within the ambit of the discussion of the boundary. He could not emphasise too strongly what had been the real impression of the Irish people. Had it been mere rectification, they would not have asked for a Boundary Commission with all the trouble and delay involved. It would have been much simpler for Sir James Craig and himself to have met and endeavoured to settle matters together.

SIR W. JOYNSON-HICKS asked whether Mr. Cosgrave was now asking for a Conference charged with the task of drawing a new boundary line.

MR. COSGRAVE said that was not his suggestion. Whatever had happened it was clear that the intention of Article 12 had not been carried out. The people had lost confidence in it, and some new arrangement should be explored.

MR. AMERY asked Mr. Cosgrave whether he was suggesting the drawing of a new boundary other than the existing one and other than that proposed by the Commission.

MR. COSGRAVE replied that he would rather not answer that question as he had no knowledge of the views of Sir James Craig. If it transpired that there could be an agreement not contemplated by the Boundary Commission, and not necessarily coinciding with the present line, he would not close the door.

THE PRIME MINISTER asked what would the position have been had there been no leakage through the 'Morning Post', and had the award been signed.

MR. COSGRAVE replied that the leakage had made the political situation extremely difficult, and had led to the resignation of Mr. MacNeill, who had somehow got out of touch with the people of Ireland on the question.

At this stage THE PRIME MINISTER suggested that he would like to confer with his colleagues and consider the statement which Mr. Cosgrave had made to him.

MR. COSGRAVE and MR. O'HEGARTY withdrew.

On their being recalled at 12.10 p.m., the PRIME MINISTER addressing Mr. Cosgrave, said:

> 'Our one idea, the idea of all three Governments, would be to prevent bloodshed in Ireland. You and we are partners in the Treaty. Both of us may have made sacrifices when that Treaty was concluded. The position to-day is that we have a Commission on the point of making a report which becomes law when made. We have to remember that we imposed this Commission on an extremely reluctant Ulster. If this unhappy disclosure had not been made, and had the report been favourable to you, you would have expected us to impose it on Ulster.'

MR. COSGRAVE: Yes.

THE PRIME MINISTER: It might have been such as to lead to Civil War. Now it looks as if the report, in the view of your people, is unfavourable to you, and they are in revolt against it. We cannot compel Ulster in any direction. We have no means of doing so. I have not been in communication with Ulster. We recognise your difficulty and I am prepared to see Sir James Craig before lunch, and put to him the result of our talk and to urge him to meet you on this matter. I would be willing to ask the Commissioners to hold up their promulgation in the hope that in a short interval, some agreement could be reached. We shall have to find some way of holding up the award.

MR. CHAMBERLAIN: That would probably mean legislation; they are under a statutory obligation.

THE PRIME MINISTER: We both realise the danger of an immediate promulgation. Whether you and Sir James Craig, having regard to the grave dangers of the situation, can come to an agreement, I do not know; but if I can help and you both wish it, I am willing to join you. All I can say at the moment is that I am willing to see him.

MR. CHAMBERLAIN: I should like to emphasise one more point as one of the Ministers who had to secure the assent of the House of Commons to the Treaty. In my Party, I took great risks in the confidence that Mr. Griffith and Mr. Collins having set their hands to the Treaty would carry it through. We had to vote down Ulster – to impose upon a reluctant Ulster acceptance of the verdict of this Commission whatever it might be. It is impossible for me or any man who signed that Treaty now that the verdict is alleged to be unduly and unexpectedly favourable to Ulster to put my hand to any agreement which would deprive Ulster of the Commission's findings except with the consent of Ulster. You have recognised that had the verdict been unexpectedly favourable to you, you would have regarded it as an act of dishonour to deprive you of it.

MR. COSGRAVE: Yes. You think it better to have a Conference now with Sir James Craig? I am still of opinion that it would be better if we had the Conference I suggested between the two Governments.

MR. CHAMBERLAIN: If a compromise is possible, he can make it: we cannot offer it. For us to offer it before we had consulted with him would make any compromise impossible.

MR. COSGRAVE then agreed to meet Sir James Craig later in the day if the Prime Minister found himself able to arrange the Conference.

No. 353 NAI DT S4720A

Notes of a meeting at Chequers
(Secret) (C.P. 500 (25))

CHEQUERS, 28 November 1925

The Prime Minister to-day at Chequers saw Mr. O'Higgins (Vice-President of the Executive Council), Mr. McGilligan (Minister of Commerce and Industry) and Mr. O'Byrne (Attorney-General) in compliance with a telegraphic request made by Mr. Cosgrave on the evening of Friday, 27th November. The Prime Minister had with him Sir John Anderson, Mr. Thomas Jones and Mr. C.P. Duff. The Irish Representatives arrived for lunch, and the discussion began at 2-45 p.m.

Earlier in the morning the Boundary Commission had indicated that they regarded it as so important that the parties should be cognisant of their award that they were despatching the Secretary of the Commission (Mr. Bourdillon) with all the necessary papers to Chequers. The Secretary was requested to delay setting out for Chequers until the Prime Minister had an opportunity of mentioning the matter to Mr. O'Higgins. On his arrival the Prime Minister informed Mr. O'Higgins of this; and, as Mr. O'Higgins agreed that it would be well for the Secretary with the award to be on the spot, even if they did not avail themselves of his information, arrangements were made for Mr. Bourdillon to arrive at Chequers at 4-30 p.m.

The Prime Minister having referred to this arrangement Mr. O'Higgins then explained the situation which had arisen on Mr. Cosgrave's return to Ireland after his meetings in London on November 25th[1] [handwritten marginal note: '26th?'].

At 4-0 p.m. the Prime Minister withdrew and conferred with Sir John Anderson and Mr. Jones. At 4-20 p.m. the Prime Minister saw the Irish Representatives alone, and informed them that Sir John Anderson would see Sir James Craig that evening.

At 5-o'clock, after an interval for tea, the Prime Minister very briefly summarised the position reached in the earlier discussion. He said that there emerged two alternatives, each presenting very serious political difficulties. The one was to accept the existing boundary. That, in the view of the Free State Representatives, would only be possible if it were accompanied by important and far-reaching concessions on the part of Northern Ireland. They asked, not only that prisoners should be liberated, but that the Catholic population in Ulster should have their civic rights completely restored.

Failing to obtain these concessions there remained the second course – to impose the award of the Boundary Commission. If this were done, and while the Free State Representatives might formally accept it, the political reactions would be grave and would undoubtedly involve the fall of the present Free State Government.

The Prime Minister undertook to invite Sir James Craig to Chequers and the Free State Representatives agreed to return to Chequers with a view to meeting Sir James Craig at noon tomorrow, Sunday, 29th November.

It was agreed to issue a notice to the Press to the effect that conversations were proceeding.

The representative of the Boundary Commission arrived at 4-30 p.m. Although the Irish Representatives were not disposed themselves to see him or to peruse the documents he brought, they informed the Prime Minister that it would be with their concurrence that he should do so after their departure that evening.

About 5-15 p.m. the Free State Representatives returned to town. At 5-30 p.m. the Prime Minister received the Secretary of the Boundary Commission. Mr. Bourdillon handed to the Prime Minister the following documents in duplicate:-

[1] See above No. 352.

(1) Letter from the Chairman of the Commission covering a Resolution adopted by the Boundary Commission today (circulated herewith).
(2) A printed Memorandum entitled 'Sketch of the General Character of the Boundary Line as about to be determined by the Commission.[1]
(3) An advance proof of a Chapter of the Commission's Report dealing with the general principles forming the basis of the Award.[2]
(4) A quarter-inch scale map showing the line as about to be determined by the Commission.[3]

[enclosure]
COPY OF A LETTER FROM THE CHAIRMAN OF THE IRISH BOUNDARY COMMISSION TO THE PRIME MINISTER
28th November, 1925.

Sir,
As you will be aware the Irish Boundary Commission, at its interview with representatives of the British Government on Tuesday, November 24th, raised the question as to the giving of preliminary information in advance to the Governments concerned as to the general character of the award about to be delivered, and expressed the view that it was desirable that any such preliminary information should be given simultaneously to both the British Government and the Government of the Irish Free State.

It was suggested that in the first instance the information should be given by means of an inspection of maps at a meeting to be arranged between the representatives of the two Governments and the Commission; the date suggested for this meeting was Thursday, 26th November. A letter was despatched on 24th November conveying this suggestion to the Government of the Irish Free State, and a copy of that letter was forwarded to the British Government. Neither Government was able to accept the invitation for Thursday, the 26th, and the Commission has been expecting to hear further with regard to this matter, but has not yet received from either Government any definite suggestion as to a date for the proposed meeting.

In the circumstances that have arisen it appears to the Commission to be desirable that the Governments concerned should without further delay have before them definite preliminary information as to the nature of the award which is being prepared for delivery, embodying the line agreed upon by the Commission. The general features of this line were approved by the Commission and fully recorded with illustrative tracings in the Minutes of the Commission of the 17th October: certain minor detail adjustments were approved at a further meeting of the Commission held on the 4th November. It was estimated by the Commission's advisors that the preparation of a full detailed description with three sets of the necessary maps on a six inch scale would take six weeks from the 17th October: the work of preparing this description and the maps is now nearly completed.

Under authority of a resolution of the Commission adopted to-day, copy of which is attached, I forward herewith for the confidential information of the

[1] Not printed.
[2] Not printed.
[3] Not printed.

British Government and the Government of Northern Ireland the Memorandum referred to in the resolution, which I have initialled. I also enclose under authority of the same resolution:-

(1) A quarter inch scale map showing the line as about to be determined by the Commission;

(2) An advance proof of a chapter of the Commission's Report dealing with the general principles forming the basis of the award which is to be delivered. This proof has not yet actually been corrected for the printer, but may be taken as substantially correct.

Owing to the position created by Doctor MacNeill's withdrawal from the Commission it has been necessary to prepare a report in some detail for presentation with the award. This course had not previously been contemplated. In order to allow time for the completion and printing of this report a few further days are required. The Commission now proposes to complete and deliver its award on Monday, the 7th December. The Commission contemplates that it may be desirable in the public interest to publish the information contained in the memorandum at an earlier date, but on this point the Commission will be glad to consider the views of the Governments concerned.

No. 354 NAI DT S4720A

Minutes of a meeting between Stanley Baldwin, Kevin O'Higgins, Patrick McGilligan and John O'Byrne
(Secret) (I.A. (25) 6)

CHEQUERS, 2.45 pm, 28 November 1925

PRIME MINISTER: Just before you came we had a message from the Boundary Commission. They said it was important that we should be aware of their proposals and they intended accordingly to send a Secretary down with documents, maps, etc. I have of course had no previous indication of the Commission's findings. In a short conversation with me before this meeting Mr. O'Higgins has agreed that the Secretary of the Commission should come and be on the spot here although we need not necessarily see him. At any rate we are talking in the air till we have seen the Commission's Report: we are going now on the Morning Post report which may be inaccurate.

MR. O'HIGGINS: The Morning Post report is, we understand, inaccurate.

PRIME MINISTER: Whatever the report is, when it is published it becomes law. That is the situation we have to meet. We must discuss how we can delay the report or postpone indefinitely its publication.

MR. O'HIGGINS: What I have to say is contained in Mr. Cosgrave's letter (which had been handed to the Prime Minister before the Meeting commenced). When Cosgrave met the Executive Council on his return from England we discussed the situation most thoroughly and after the most careful consideration it was the general feeling that no one on the Council could recommend the proposals to the Dáil. We could not carry our own party and would run into certain defeat. The situation in Ireland is so fluid that this is a prospect we could not face: it is emphatically the case that no party but ourselves is ready or able to carry on against those who oppose the Treaty. I do not anticipate that the country would give an explicit mandate to the Republicans if Cosgrave were defeated; but it would mean such a degree of chaos that ultimately a negative victory for the Republicans, i.e. the smashing of the Free State, must be the upshot. In fact there is no other Parliamentary group capable of forming a Government which could withstand the elements menacing the Treaty. These latter had been divided and without money; everything had pointed to disintegration among the opponents to the Treaty: but now we have a crisis which may be the defeat of Cosgrave and lead, if not directly then eventually, to a break-up of the State based on the Treaty. If we face the Dáil on the basis of the old line with a few concessions from Craig (e.g. prisoners) our own Party would scout us: they would vote in a negative way against the Government without any alternative policy but thinking that anything, even chaos, would be better than this Government. If it only meant our political extinction we should not worry, but we feel that you should know that these are the reactions we anticipate and that England will have to cope with these reactions. It is fruitless to elaborate our views on the Commission's Report. Everyone in Ireland regarded the Commission as set up merely to see how much of existing Northern Ireland should not fall into the Free State, and to delimit more fairly than the 1920 Act how much of Northern Ireland wanted no communication with the Free State. We thought that the British signatories held the same view – Lord Birkenhead expressed it on December 7th and Lloyd George on December 14th in the House of Commons, what they said is on record in Hansard, but e.g. Lloyd George's words were 'If Ulster desired to live isolated, only by coercion can Fermanagh and Tyrone be kept in Ulster.' I suggest that Fermanagh and Tyrone have in fact had that coercion by police and restrictive acts; and Ireland thought that this Commission was going to rescue them. If Cosgrave, in the face of this, was to say that the best he could achieve was that the old line should remain and a few prisoners be released, he would have the entire Dáil against him, and anyone who took his place could not long survive the anti-Treaty element.

THE PRIME MINISTER: We must look at the facts of the case. The Commission was set up under the Treaty; they got to a certain point where the judgment about to be given had the assent of all three parties. Then one party resigned, and we are at the stage where the Commission is about to report with the consequences we know. As signatory of the Treaty England wants to do her best to get Ireland over her difficulties. There are three courses open and trouble, in the nature of the case, attends any of them. The first alternative – Let the Boundary Commission deliver judgment. The second alternative – Accept the existing boundary. The third alternative – The delimitation of a boundary to be agreed between the two Governments. This last seemed impossible and Cosgrave and Craig had so regarded it. As an outsider I cannot see how even an angel could devise a boundary which would be agreed, so we are thrown back on one or two. Can you see any other?

MR. O'HIGGINS: I must advert to what you said on the subject of MacNeill. Up to a point an award was taking shape which met with the approval of all parties.

At an early stage Mr. MacNeill agreed in the abstract with his colleagues that if the award was not going to make matters worse it should be signed by all three but that this should not imply that there was no disagreement on details. Sector by sector they worked their way down the line, McNeill fighting all the way: they began at Derry and finished at Newry. It would have been better if they had begun the other way as Newry is nationalist up to 75 per cent: the economic hinterland is nationalist and I cannot understand how the award could leave Newry out. The same arguments for leaving Newry out of the Free State were used against putting Eastern Donegal into Northern Ireland and applied in full – or fuller – force. The award took shape sector by sector and it came before the Commission for consideration as a whole on October 17th. Soon after the Morning Post came out with its forecast of the award. MacNeill saw that the motive which had made him give his undertaking to his colleagues to sign with them (i.e. that the award was likely to have a peaceful issue) was not going to be realised. The Free State Government told him that any award like that envisaged in the Morning Post would be disastrous and that he should withdraw from the Commission. For a month he had felt that he ought to stand to the undertaking given in advance that he would sign with his colleagues and during that period he was vacillating while the unhappy tendency of the report was becoming more apparent to him.

If that award is delivered no man or woman in the Free State could get up and say that it is in accordance with the wish of the people subject to geographic and economic conditions: it cannot lead to anything but hate and the starting of the old fires which the Treaty had laid. The growing friendship between the peoples would be quenched and on every platform it would be said 'We have been tricked again; see how your Treaty works when it comes to hard facts.' We cannot stand up to these statements and say that they are not true because we believe that they are true and that the award does not fulfil the intention of the Treaty. If the award is made public we would formally accept it: we would vacate the transferred areas and take over the administration of the new ones; but we could not pretend to the people that the Treaty had been fulfilled and though we might try to avoid direct action the people would expect some safety valve for their feeling to be provided. They might have to consider whether Ireland's membership of the League of Nations opened up any course for them to take. We could go to the Dáil with the proposals made to Mr. Cosgrave on Thursday but we should be riding for a certain fall.

PRIME MINISTER: Look at our position for a moment. It is a pity the question was not allowed to sleep. However, a Commission was set up and the Labour Party chose a Chairman while we stood by not knowing what the Commission's findings would be. Had their award been satisfactory to the South and unsatisfactory to the North, the South would have expected us to carry it through even by force of arms. We cannot say that this Commission is unsatisfactory, so we will set up another: any award of any Commission will cause trouble. We want to-day so far as we can to help you in a difficult domestic position. I asked Craig to meet Cosgrave as between the two you are all Ireland so that as far as possible you could both agree what should be done. Craig said that so far as he could keep his more advanced elements quiet he would fall in with either alternative and he did not press either point of view. Cosgrave seemed to think there were less difficulties in the way of sticking on the present boundary than in putting the award into effect. If it were me I should have said that we cannot get a boundary that does not cause trouble: let us stay as we are and set up a small Commission from all Ireland to see if we can get in course of time some agreement and alleviation of our differences.

MR. O'HIGGINS: Craig always met us straightly and he defined his position frankly. He said 'I stand pat on the Act of 1920, and I will have none of anything else.' To the South of Ireland the existing boundary with a few prisoners as a makeweight is an impossible offer without in addition some substantial alleviation for the Nationalists of the North-East. If we could say that these Nationalists are not getting all that we expected in the Treaty but the Special Police are to go and other restrictions, political and local, are to be abandoned, there might be a chance for us to carry the Dáil with us. These Nationalists have had no proper representation under the Northern Government either in Parliament or in local administration; the constituencies have been faked to deprive them of representation. They are politically impotent and are kept down by an army of Special Constables paid and maintained by the British Government. We have to face the taunt that they have been maintained *ad hoc* – to influence and perilise the Boundary Commission, to impress its members with an idea of terrible things to happen if they acted strictly and fairly on their Terms of Reference.

The Commission took the line of least resistance; where the special police were thick in the North the Commission sheered away. This is what from all her supporters members of the Free State Government hear, that the Commission has been influenced by 'specials' standing with their finger on the trigger. It is no good in these circumstances getting up in the Dáil and saying 'We are very sorry but the old line shall stand and in return Sir James Craig will give up 24 prisoners.' I do not know whether there is anything to be hoped from a tri-partite conference and asking Craig to give 'Catholic emancipation' in the North-East.

MR. McGILLIGAN: I have not anything to add to Mr. O'Higgins' presentation of the case except this. He indicated that after proposing the offer which Cosgrave brought back, we might survive to consider whether the League of Nations might offer a remedy. My conviction is that from the moment that we appear before the Dáil with Thursday's proposal we disappear politically.

PRIME MINISTER: Of the two alternatives, which is the worse? Is it less difficult to carry out the award of the Commission?

MR. O'HIGGINS: We might try to do it but we should not last.

MR. TOM JONES: Do I understand this correctly? If, with the present boundary you could get substantial relaxation for the Catholics in the North-East, you might be able to ride the storm?

MR. O'HIGGINS: We might if we had far-reaching concessions and recognition that for three years past they have had very unfair and harsh treatment. The men who could never have got out under a boundary award from living too far North to be affected, would feel happier, and the satisfaction of those people would be some set-off against the disappointment of people who had been hoping that the award would get them out.

No. 355 NAI DT S4720A

Summary of proceedings at Chequers
(Secret) (C.P. 501(25))

CHEQUERS, 29 November 1925

Sir James Craig, Mr. Kevin O'Higgins, Mr. McGilligan, Mr. O'Byrne, and Sir John Anderson arrived shortly before noon.

The Prime Minister read to Sir James Craig a letter which he had received from Mr. Cosgrave. Sir James Craig said that the re-adjustment of frontier would mean some re-shuffling in the six counties, and in the re-adjustment he would try to treat the Roman Catholics with as much consideration as possible.

At 12.30 p.m. the Prime Minister conferred with the Free State representatives, and asked them did they wish to see the documents which had been received from the Boundary Commission. Mr. O'Higgins stated that he had refused to accept the documents on the previous evening, but he had no objection to hearing a summary of the figures dealing with the persons and the areas affected. The Prime Minister accordingly read a brief summary.

At 12.40 Sir James Craig entered, and the summary of the proposed transfer of land and people was again read by the Prime Minister. Mr. O'Higgins then made a full statement of the Free State position in regard to the present and the proposed boundary, and directed the attention of Sir James Craig in particular to the disabilities of the Nationalist minority in Northern Ireland.

At 1.20 p.m. Sir James Craig began his reply to Mr. O'Higgins.

At 1.25 p.m. the discussion was adjourned for luncheon.

At 2.30 p.m. the discussion was resumed by Sir James Craig and Mr. O'Higgins alone, and shortly after 3.0 p.m. Sir James Craig saw the Prime Minister with Sir John Anderson and Mr. Jones. Sir James Craig indicated that Mr. O'Higgins had raised the question of Article 5 of the Treaty.

At 4.0 p.m. Sir James Craig saw the three Free State representatives alone.

At 5.0 p.m. it was agreed that Mr. McGilligan should return to Dublin that evening and indicate to the Executive Council the course of the day's discussion. He is to invite Mr. Cosgrave to come to London to meet the Prime Minister and Sir James Craig at a Conference on Tuesday next.

It was agreed to issue the following Press Notice:-

'Conversations in regard to the Irish Boundary were continued at Chequers to-day. In addition to the Irish Free State representatives, Sir James Craig was also at Chequers in consultation with the Prime Minister.'

No. 356 NAI DT S4720A

Summary of statements made at meetings on morning of Sunday 29 November at Chequers between Stanley Baldwin, Kevin O'Higgins, Patrick McGilligan, John O'Byrne and Sir James Craig
(Secret) (I.A.(25)-7)

CHEQUERS, 29 November 1925

The Prime Minister accompanied by Sir John Anderson, Mr. Thomas Jones and Mr. C.P. Duff, met the representatives of the Free State alone at 12.30. He stated that he would report to them what happened after they had left the previous evening and would then propose to call in Sir James Craig. Between them and Sir James Craig they comprised all Ireland and they must therefore discuss together the situation that confronted them. There were two possibilities; either to maintain the boundary as it is or, if they could reach no agreement on that, then the boundary as it would be by putting the Award into force. Many of the things that Mr. O'Higgins had said yesterday he would do well to state direct to Sir James Craig. After they had left last night the Secretary of the Boundary Commission had brought to the Prime Minister a letter from the Chairman of the Boundary Commission, a Resolution of the Commission, maps showing the line given by the Award and a chapter from the Commission's Report showing the basis on which their Award had been framed. Had the Irish Representatives received these documents? Mr. O'Higgins said, 'No'. Had Mr. Bourdillon called on them last night bringing the documents? Mr. O'Higgins said, 'Yes'. The Prime Minister continuing, observed that the line in the Award is not the same as that given in the Morning Post map. To anyone maintaining the view that alterations of the boundary should only take place in one direction the Award might not be satisfactory: but if there is to be any give and take the Free State under the Award have the best of it. If the discussion was to be of practical value, it would be much better to base it on the real Award and not on the Morning Post's representation: and he had the figures here and the other relevant documents.

Mr. O'Higgins replied that trifling inaccuracies in the Morning Post's indication of the Award did not affect them. An Award leaving Newry and its economic hinterland within Northern jurisdiction could not be an award based on the evidence before the Commission. Newry is the acid test of the Commissioners' desire to act on their Terms of Reference undeterred by considerations outside those terms.

The Prime Minister enquired whether Mr. O'Higgins would still prefer not to know exactly what the terms of the proposed Award are? Did he think it better for the Award to be published and become law without his having seen it?

Mr. O'Higgins replied that they had had a message from Mr. Bourdillon saying that he was sending a courier to Dublin as he had not been given an opportunity to deliver the papers personally. Their position was that Professor McNeill had come away seeing no likelihood of the Report being in accordance with the Terms of Reference or the evidence. In those circumstances the less contact they had with the Commission the better.

The Prime Minister said, 'Shall I give you the figures of the area and population transferred in either direction before we talk?'

Mr. O'Higgins replied that he knew the figures presented a contrast and that more population came to them than to Northern Ireland. He did not object to the exact figures being stated here but their position fundamentally was this, that they regarded the Commission as influenced by the truculent utterances of Northern Ministers and the tyranny of the special constables; and that in their Award they had followed, not the wishes of the inhabitants, but the line of what seemed, at the time, the least resistance.

The Prime Minister said 'Would you like the figures?' to which Mr. O'Higgins replied, 'I have no objection to your stating them'.

The Prime Minister then read the following:-

Summary of transfers to Irish Free State.
183,290 acres, 31,319 persons, of whom 27,843 are Roman Catholics and 3,476 of other Denominations.

Summary of transfers to Northern Ireland.
49,242 acres, 7,594 persons of whom 2,764 are Roman Catholics and 4,830 of other Denominations.

The gains of the Free State under the Award exceed those of Northern Ireland by 134,048 acres and 23,725 persons.

Mr. Jones added that the boundary was also shortened by 51 miles.

At this point it was decided to invite Sir James Craig to come in. While waiting for him, the Prime Minister observed that English opinion, at any rate, would be disposed to regard the Award as fair.

Mr. O'Higgins replied that an irrelevant factor had influenced the Commission in as much as the starting off point of their Award was the preservation of the political entity of Northern Ireland as given form to in the 1920 Act. This was a political factor which should have been outside the consideration of the Commission. When the Treaty was being made the price which Northern Ireland knew she was to pay for contracting out was a substantial alteration of her position. The North knew that a Commission was to be set up for the express purpose of determining how much of Northern Ireland was to be allowed to remain outside the Free State.

At this point Sir James Craig entered.

The Prime Minister explained to Sir James Craig that the Irish representatives had not seen the actual figures or any of the Commission's documents but had just heard from him a summary of the figures. On Sir James Craig replying that he also had heard nothing, the Prime Minister read the summary set out on a previous page. He added that what they had to consider was how to get through the present situation without damage to Ireland as a whole. What would be the effect if the issue of the Award were avoided and the Free State Government found themselves able to recommend that the existing boundary should be stabilised? Mr. O'Higgins had yesterday given his view of the difficulties of that course and it would be best for him to put that view to Sir James Craig and indicate what he thought Northern Ireland could do to minimise those difficulties.

Mr. O'Higgins replied that some of what he had to say must be distasteful to his hearers, to which Sir James Craig answered that if their discussions were to be of any value all the cards must be on the table, and each must say exactly what was in his mind.

Mr. O'Higgins stated that Sir James Craig was familiar with the Free State conception of Article 12. Michael Collins had told him long ago and Sir James Craig was surprised on hearing it then. The difference at that interview had lasted ever since in full force. It was always understood by the Irish Signatories of the Treaty that the Northern Government were faced with the alternatives provided by Article 14 or by Article 12. When the course provided by Article 14 was abandoned and Article 12 became operative by the presentation of an Address to His Majesty for the North of Ireland to be excluded from the Free State the North acted with their eyes open and realised that a Commission would be set up, whose duties it would be to determine how much of the country known as Northern Ireland under the 1920 Act would remain a political entity. This conception of the Commission had remained in the Free State since 1920 and they had been confirmed in their view by the utterances of British Signatories, notably that of Lord Birkenhead on the 7th December, the day after the Treaty, and Mr. Lloyd George on the 14th December in the House of Commons. They understood then from what he said that Lord Birkenhead had in mind that, by the agency of the Commission, either Tyrone was going to the Free State or such a portion of it going that what was left would be predominantly non-Nationalist. Mr. Lloyd George's words 'If Ulster is to remain a separate unit, only by coercion can Tyrone and Fermanagh remain there' show that he obviously at the time thought Tyrone and Fermanagh could not remain part and parcel of political Ulster.

Sir James Craig had always objected to the Commission touching anything arranged by the 1920 Act: and they understood his point of view. The Free State had never shared the view which had emerged in England under Parliamentary pressure, as he regarded it, that this Boundary was a small and innocent thing, just a dinge here and a bulge there along the existing line. It might be said that when utterances were made in the British House of Commons which clashed with the Free State view of the Treaty, the Free State should have protested officially: but at the time they were in the middle of a Civil War. The Free State had always regarded the Commission as set up for no other purpose but to see how much of Northern Ireland was entitled to be excluded from the rest of Ireland. Sir James Craig's attitude had always been consistent. He had refused to nominate a member to the Commission and the Free State were entitled to say that unless the Commission were set up the Treaty was broken. After meetings with the British Government of the day[,] a Bill was passed setting up the Commission and the British Government took on the duty of nominating a commissioner for Northern Ireland. Although the Commission was for the purpose of ascertaining the wishes of the people the Free State raised no objection against the action of the Commission in not taking a plebiscite. They realised that legislation might be necessary to give the Commission the requisite powers and this would have caused delay: but, in addition, the resolution passed by the House of Lords, which was a flagrant and deliberate attempt to influence the Commission in its findings, they regarded as indicating that any further Bill for the purpose of holding a plebiscite would on that analogy be resisted. The Free State agreed with the Chairman of the Commission in taking the 1911 census as providing a fair basis for their deliberations and in regarding 95% or 97% of nationalists as wanting to go into the Free State and 95% or 97% non-nationalists as wanting to go to Northern Ireland. This was a rough and ready method but the Free State agreed it. The Commission moved on and whatever mutual confidences were given among the commissioners were observed by Dr. MacNeill. But the Morning Post article appeared: a flow of deputations poured into Dublin and an agitation broke out which led to Professor MacNeill's withdrawal. An award approximating to the Morning Post account was obviously going to lead to no harmony: so MacNeill felt that he ought to go, albeit that he had previously felt that the Award ought to be presented over the signatures of all the members without prejudice to their disagreement on the details. Professor MacNeill's attitude of giving agreement in the abstract and yet fighting his colleagues sector by sector was incomprehensible to his colleagues on the Executive Council: but finally when the Press exposure came and it was clear that the motive for his original undertaking no longer existed he retracted his engagement and handed in his resignation on the grounds that there was no likelihood of the Award being in accordance either with the Terms of the Commission's Reference or with the evidence before them.

The Award is practically ready and there is no one of any class or political creed in the Free State who could get up and defend it. It is not a fulfilment of the Treaty. The Free State Government are faced with a serious position: they do not mean to fly in the face of the legal position which they realise the Award would create, and they would have to do the administrative acts that would result from their formal acceptance. But in their public utterances they would have to say that the Treaty was not fulfilled. If they could hope to keep the controversy away from conflict on the physical plane and direct action they would have to direct the minds of their constituents to some other course: possibly the Free State's membership of the League of Nations might provide a resource. The Free State Government would have to say that, while giving formal assent to the legal position created by the Award, they believed that the Commission had been terrorised by the consideration of the armed forces of special constables backed up by a Government ready to resist and with the moral support given by the House of Lords Resolution.

The President had come home a few days before with the proposal that the existing boundary should stand, and that Sir James Craig would release a few prisoners who had already served four years of their ten years imprisonment. On such proposals the Free State Government would fall at once; they would not live a day: and any Unionist with political sense would confirm that view. The position in the Free State is too fluid for the Government to regard the prospect of their defeat without apprehension. This is on no personal grounds, but simply because there is no Party ready to carry on the State as based on the Treaty. The present Free State Government would be defeated on the question of British goodwill: in the face of the award no one could carry on against the anti-Treaty elements who would have derived new support from the trend of events. The President now shares this view: and no member of the Executive Council considers that they could face the Dáil or keep a majority even in their own party. He had been asked yesterday if he had any suggestions: he could say that if the award were delivered a legal position would be created and that would be better than confronting their people with the existing boundary merely set off with the addition of a few prisoners. If the Free State Government could point to some substantial improvement in the lot of the minority in Sir James Craig's area – a radical improvement and emancipation – they might survive when recommending the *status quo* to their people. The disabilities of the minority are these: they live at the mercy of the special police: Tyrone and Fermanagh are coerced: 45,000 'specials' in a six counties state shows that only coercion keeps the national majority of Tyrone and Fermanagh there. The present system of representation would have to be abolished and the conditions in the constituencies of the North East which deprive nationalists of their due representation must be changed. The position of Catholics in the North is not equal to that of Catholics elsewhere: if the Free State Government could say that the Catholics' lot would be improved and they would cease to be 'hewers of wood and drawers of water' then they might survive. Without all the alleviations he had indicated the nationalists of the North East who expected relief from the Commission would raise an outcry which would find an echo in every nationalist breast in the twenty six counties. The country would vote against the Government in a negative sense, without, that is, giving an explicit mandate for a republic: but with this new impetus against them no new Government could withstand the anti-Treaty elements.

SIR JAMES CRAIG said that Mr. O'Higgins had very accurately traversed the ground as regards the historical part of his review. The only comment he had to make on that part of the review was to exonerate himself and his colleagues from the charge of ever having done anything else but emphasise to the Free State that they were living in a fool's paradise as to what the outcome of the Commission would be.

MR. O'HIGGINS replied that Sir James had boycotted the Commission and they accordingly were confirmed in their view that the findings of the Commission could only advantage the South.

SIR JAMES CRAIG observed that he had stated to Michael Collins 'Supposing the findings of the Commission are of an in-and-out character, will you not be worse off in the end?' Collins had taken that view and had considered it better in the circumstances to substitute the method of a round table conference between Sir James Craig and himself. After Collins returned to Dublin, however, Sir James visited him there and this arrangement broke down: but at that time and later Sir James kept on asking what the position would be in regard to the transfer of areas from the South of Ireland to the North. The only reply he could get from the Free State was that they held other views and would not discuss such a contingency. He had told Ramsay MacDonald at the time of the setting up of the Commission that great harm was being done in the South by the people there being brought up to believe that they would get great advantages from the Commission.

At this point the Prime Minister observed that as it was now lunch time it would be well for Sir James Craig to resume his observations after the adjournment.

No. 357 NAI DT S4720A

Kevin O'Higgins to Stanley Baldwin (London)
(Copy)
HOTEL VICTORIA, LONDON, 30 November 1925

Dear Mr. Baldwin,
I wish to suggest to you the desirability of having a joint request made on behalf of your Government and ours to the Boundary Commissioners with reference to the publication of their award. We are engaged at present in anxiously considering whether an agreement can be arrived at, and one possible result of our discussions might be that the publication of any award would be neither necessary nor desirable. If the Boundary Commissioners are not definitely informed of this fact and proceed as a body entirely independent of the Governments concerned with the peaceful settlement of this matter the result may be deplorable. The 'Times' of today is responsible for the definite statement that in the opinion of your Government it is for the Commission alone to decide whether publication of the award should or should not be postponed. It is undoubted that the Commission may legally arrive at a decision in this matter without reference to the wishes of either or both Governments. But I am confident that they would agree to postpone publication if both our Governments requested them to do so in the interests of all parties. The Irish Free State Government has no desire needlessly to prolong the discussions which are now taking place, but these are hampered rather than assisted by having it either recognised or asserted that they may be terminated at any time by independent action of the Boundary Commissioners. You will, I think, agree with me that if our discussions were so terminated merely owing to an omission to intimate our views to the Boundary Commissioners such omission would be gravely criticised by all those who share our desire to find a peaceful and durable solution of our present difficulties.

Yours sincerely,
(Sgd.) KEVIN O'HIGGINS

No. 358 NAI DT S4730A

Memorandum by Joseph Brennan on Article 5 of the Anglo-Irish Treaty
DUBLIN, 30 November 1925

(*Important Note.* The following comments do not pretend to be anything more than a very hasty, rough and partial statement of some of the leading points which should probably be used in an argument on behalf of the case of the Irish Free State in the event of an arbitration taking place on Article 5. Until data and arguments have been collected and sifted much further than has been possible up to the present, it is unsafe to assume that the best ultimate presentation of our case should necessarily follow the lines indicated by the preliminary ideas set out below. If, therefore, the case of Article 5 is to be discussed at the present stage with the British Government formally as a financial problem, it would be undesirable that the arguments given below under the various heads should be put on record in any way as a considered and final exposition of the Free State contention. If, however, references at the present stage to our position under Article 5 are merely incidental to the discussion of other political problems, some of the points below can perhaps be used in a loose way with advantage, but in that case it would be preferable that the written statement should not be put in British hands and that it should be clearly understood that such arguments as were being advanced were mentioned entirely without prejudice).

1. The British claim under Article 5 as formulated in April 1923 gave figures of £7,840 millions and £850 millions for the capital amount of public debt and war pensions respectively as at the date of the Treaty. On the basis of the comparative yield of direct taxes in the two countries the British claim that we were liable for 1.5 per cent. of these amounts, that is, for £117½ millions in respect of public debt and £12¾ millions in respect of war pensions. They proposed to add a further amount of £27½ millions as compound interest on these amounts at 5 per cent. during the four years following the Treaty. Thus the actual total of the British claim is £157¾ millions. A claim was also made in respect of certain other matters not mentioned in Article 5 but subsequently agreed to be dealt with as part of the ultimate financial settlement. The main items in the latter category were liability for bonus and Excess Land Stock and Liability for charges under the Irish Railway (Settlement of Claims) Act, 1921.
2. Of the debt figure mentioned an amount of more than £2,000 millions was incurred for the purpose of making advances to Dominion and Allied Governments and those Governments are under a corresponding liability for repayment. The chief items of this nature were as follows:-
(Circa December 1921) –

	£
Dominions	150,000,000
France	584,000,000
Russia	655,000,000
Italy	503,000,000.

There is not the least reason why the Irish Free State should be expected to bear a burden in order to relieve other British Dominions in this connection and it is obviously very much a matter of question how far the Free State should be expected to accept a burden by reason of any default that may occur on the part of any of the Allied Governments. A settlement for repayment of the French debt has already been approved in principle by the French Government and it appears to be expected that a settlement on a similar basis is about to be effected in respect of the Italian debt. The Russian item will, no doubt, be irrecoverable at least to a large extent.

If the £2,000 millions here referred to is deducted from the total figure put forward by the British Government under the head of public debt, the latter

becomes reduced to £5,840 millions and the resulting British claim against us becomes reduced from 157 ¾ millions to £121 ½ millions.
3. In considering the proportions in which a given debt charge should be allocated between two different territories one of the factors requiring special attention is the extent to which the securities representing the debt are held in the two areas. It is evident that the debt charge on the people of either territory taken in itself and as a whole will be lighter or heavier according as citizens of that territory do or do not hold a high proportion of the securities. The great bulk of the public debt for the present purpose is represented by securities owned by citizens of Great Britain. The payment of the debt charge in the main, therefore, represents a mere transfer by the process of taxation of income from some members of the British community, who pay taxes, to others who receive the dividends. Diminution of the British National Income as a whole is not involved. Assuming that citizens of the Free State in proportion to their number do not possess as large holdings of British Government securities as British citizens, it will be found that a charge met by the Free State in respect of British public debt, while set off to some extent by dividends on British Government securities held in the Free State, will to a large extent not be set off in this way but will constitute a definite drain from Free State income to meet a foreign charge. The Free State is entitled to claim credit in this connection either by modification of the total debt figure for the purpose of calculating our fraction thereof or by modification in our favour of the fraction itself in so far as the method of computing the fraction may not already have allowed for this consideration.
4. It is certain that the pressure of taxation upon the National Income of the Irish Free State is at present so severe that any increase of this burden is likely to have serious economic consequences for the country. This applies more particularly to any increase that would be necessary for the purpose of meeting a British claim under Article 5, as a foreign drain would thereby be involved. The exchange position of this country has already begun to disclose very disquieting symptoms and we can confidently urge that this factor must play a large part in determining the measure of what is fair and equitable for the purpose of Article 5.

Some indication of the trend of the exchange position can be gleaned from recent statistics of the imports and exports of the Irish Free State, which may be summarised as follows:-

	Full year 1924	First seven months 1924	First seven months 1925
	£.	£.	£.
Imports	65,811,406	38,387,000	35,579,000
Exports & re-exports	49,752,313	26,470,000	22,430,000
Adverse Trade balance	16,059,093	11,917,000	13,149,000

After making full allowance for correction to some extent of the deficits here revealed by a favourable balance, probably of small amount, in respect of 'invisible factors' of a normal kind, there remains a final adverse trend of serious extent in our general exchange position in recent times. Evidence of a drain of capital is found in the fact that whereas the holdings of cash and British Government securities by eight banks doing business in the Irish Free State amounted to £124 ½ millions at the end of 1922 the corresponding figure at the end of 1924 was lower by £12 millions. During the same two years a sum of £4 ½ millions was withdrawn by individuals in the Free State from the British Savings Bank or British Savings Certificates.

The heavy payments (nearly £3 ¼ millions per annum) being made by the Free State to Great Britain in respect of Land Purchase Annuities are already a serious factor in our exchange position and this probably applies also to a large portion of the heavy annual charge of £1 ¼ millions borne by the Free State in respect of R.I.C. pensions.

5. The British test of relative yield of direct taxes as a standard of relative taxable capacity for the present purpose is unquestionably fallacious. There are not many tests of taxable capacity which have received any general measure of assent and the whole subject bristles with difficulty and controversy but it is at least well recognised that one cannot determine in the abstract a quantitative measure of taxable capacity for any country without enquiring at the same time into the nature of the purposes for which the taxation is applied. It is quite obvious that a country might bear extremely heavy taxes for certain purposes more easily than a much lighter scale of taxation for different purposes, e.g., in particular when the latter purposes involve payments abroad.

6. The primary factor in this connection is the excess of national income over the subsistence provision necessary to produce such income and scarcely of less importance is the manner of distribution of national income between individual citizens. The immensely greater taxable capacity of Great Britain relatively to the Free State in the light of these considerations requires no argument. There is one point, however, peculiarly affecting the Free State in this connection which it is important not to overlook. British income is derived largely from an immense and varied trade both with a large internal population and with all the great countries of the world. Different branches of this trade have their ups and downs from time to time but on the whole the Nation enjoys a large steady income which has been increasing for generations and is likely to continue doing so in the future. In the Free State, on the other hand, the national income is of a much more precarious kind and is largely derived from agriculture. Owing to its dependence upon the weather etc., the income from agriculture is a decidedly unstable quantity and this consideration has to be guarded against in measuring any important State charge which would entail a burden over a period of years.

7. The actual figure of 1.5% used by the British in their claim is, apart from its basis, clearly excessive from other points of view. The figure represents almost exactly the proportion in which Southern Ireland should have made an Imperial contribution under the Government of Ireland Act according to the calculation in the British White Papers used as the basis of that Act. Even for that purpose the figure was grossly excessive and the corresponding figure for Northern Ireland has since been reduced drastically. Moreover, the figure was based upon revenue figures of a period when war profits had put an unusual amount of

money into circulation in Ireland and when consequently the yield of taxes was heavier and the burden of them proportionately much lighter than at the present time.

In addition, however, the fundamental position under the Act of 1920 was very much different from that of the present case seeing that the Act of 1920 contemplated that the Land Purchase Annuities collected in Southern Ireland would not be payable to Great Britain but would pass as revenue to the Irish Exchequer. In this light the present payments of Land Purchase Annuities to Great Britain can be said to take the place of a net contribution under Article 5.

8. It may be urged again that after the introduction of Old Age Pensions in 1908, Ireland, according to the Treasury, ceased to have any surplus of revenue over expenditure and became a definite net charge on the Imperial Exchequer. It was not until the heavy war taxation began to produce its effect that Irish revenue again began to exceed expenditure. There is little doubt that if there had been no Government of Ireland Act nor Treaty this country would now again be well on the way, if it had not already reached that stage, of becoming a financial burden on the British Government. It would, therefore, be in the nature of a windfall for the British Government if they were now to effect an arrangement under Article 5 which would assure them of a future profit at the cost of the Irish Free State. In this connection it should be noted that according to the general economic trend up to the time of the Treaty it was quite clear that our taxable capacity was steadily diminishing in comparison with that of Great Britain. Our population was falling steadily throughout the Nineteenth Century, the figure for the whole of Ireland representing 32½% of that of the United Kingdom in 1821 and only 9.51% by 1914. The same tendency was indicated in many of the other figures by which the relative economic progress of countries is usually measured. Even as between Northern Ireland and the Free State the same trend was evident. Taking, for example, the valuation of hereditaments other than agricultural land, we find that between 1864 and 1925 the figure for the Free State had increased from £2,714,287 to £4,218,835, that is 55.4%, whereas in Northern Ireland the figures were £1,009,209 in 1864 and £3,159,238 in 1925, showing an increase of 187.4%. This result is all the more remarkable seeing that Dublin was revalued as recently as 1916.

9. In determining what contribution, if any, the Free State could in future reasonably pay to Great Britain it is necessary to make allowance for the fact that the events leading up to the Treaty and attending its enforcement made it necessary for this country to incur large compensation and military charges, the meeting of which constitutes an obligation of somewhat similar character to any that would arise under Article 5. This obligation however, must in the circumstances take priority over any British claim. A similar point arises as regards the external and internal Dáil Loans which will probably entail an eventual charge of at least £2½ millions.

10. Analyses of the British claim in the light of the foregoing arguments and after making due allowance for the minimum necessary expenditure of the Irish Free State in the future might well result in persuading a neutral tribunal that it would not be fair or equitable to impose any contribution on the Free State in respect of public debt and war tax. Nothing, however, has yet been allowed in respect of possible items of counter claim and when this is taken

into account it appears to be quite clear that the British cannot hope to get anything from us. Leaving aside matters which do not easily lend themselves to quantitative measurement, there is one counter claim of considerable weight to which the labours of the Childers Commission have given a claim to recognition, namely, the counter claim in respect of over taxation. There is one point at least on which such a counter claim on our part would appear to be fairly entitled to acceptance. It is now generally recognised that the principle of graduation is one of the necessary features of an equitable fiscal system. This principle is capable of application only in the case of direct taxes. During the Nineteenth Century taxation was very largely indirect and it necessarily followed that the poorer members of the community bore an undue share of the public burdens. It followed, of course, that any given area of the United Kingdom which had a greater proportion of poor people than the remaining area bore as a whole an unfair share of taxation and it is obvious that the area of the Irish Free State was in that position. In this respect it will be seen that there is a radical fallacy in the argument sometimes put forward that an indiscriminate system of taxation applied to two countries is fair as between the two countries.

[initialled] S. ÓB

No. 359 NAI DT S4720A

Draft notes of a conference held in the Board Room,
Treasury, Whitehall, London
(Secret) (C.A./H./48 – 2nd Minutes)
LONDON, 12.00 noon, 1 December 1925

Present.

Great Britain.

The Right Hon. W.S. Churchill, C.H., M.P., Chancellor of the Exchequer. (In the Chair)

The Most Hon. The Marquess of Salisbury, K.G., G.C.V.O., C.B., Lord Privy Seal.

The Right Hon. The Earl of Birkenhead, Secretary of State for India.

The Right Hon. Sir John Anderson, G.C.B., Permanent Under Secretary of State, Home Office.

Mr. G.G. Whiskard, C.B., Assistant Secretary, Dominions Office.

Mr. P.J. Grigg, Treasury.

Irish Free State.

Mr. W.T. Cosgrave, T.D., President of the Executive Council.

Mr. Kevin O'Higgins, T.D., Vice-President of the Executive Council.

Mr. J. O'Byrne, K.C., T.D., Attorney-General.

Secretaries.

Mr. T. Jones, Deputy Secretary, Cabinet Secretariat.

Mr. A.F. Hemming, C.B.E.

Mr. D. O'Hegarty, Secretary to the Executive Council.

MR. CHURCHILL said that the present meeting was the result of the wish of the British Cabinet to meet the desire of Irish Ministers who, it was understood, desired to discuss the financial position between the two countries.

MR. COSGRAVE pointed out the great difference between the financial position today in the Irish Free State and that which had obtained in 1922. Conditions had greatly worsened during these two years. In 1922 there were British securities amounting to £124,500,000 held in the Free State. At the present time these securities had been reduced by £12 millions, while £4½ millions had been withdrawn from the British Savings Bank and British Savings Certificates. There were moreover considerable payments amounting to £3¼ millions in respect of Land Purchase Annuities.

The Import and Export position showed that in 1924 imports amounted to £65 millions, and exports to £49 millions, there being an adverse balance of £16 millions. In the first seven months of that year imports amounted to £38,387,000, and exports to £26,470,000, leaving an adverse balance of approximately £12 millions (£11,917,000). During the corresponding seven months in 1925 the figures for imports were £35,579,000, and for exports £22,430,000; the adverse balance was therefore £13,149,000.

In the Free State it was important to remember that there are 250,000 occupiers of uneconomic holdings, i.e., holdings of less value than £10 per annum: this represents approximately one-third of the whole people. There were in addition 212,000 agricultural labourers whose position could also be regarded as uneconomic. Where the whole of their wages were paid in cash, they amounted to 25/- or 26/- a week, while when they lived in house, their wages in cash did not exceed more than £25 per annum.

As another example, the progressive increase of value of hereditaments from 1864-1925 could be cited. The value in the 26 counties had increased during that period by £2,714,000 to £4,218,000, being a percentage of 55.4%. In the six North Eastern counties during the same period it had increased from £1,009,000 to £3,159,000, an increase of 187.4%.

As regards taxation, there was a heavier tax on beer in the Free State than in this country: this amounted to 20/- a barrel. It was true that there was no tax on tea, but the amount of revenue that the tea tax would have yielded was fully off-set by the Free State imposition on clothing and boots.

As regards social services, the Old Age Pensions Scheme in the Free State provided a smaller maximum pension by 1/- a week. Moreover, the Free State Government had not been able to fund their Unemployment Insurance.

MR. CHURCHILL asked Mr. Cosgrave whether he was still decided in his former attitude in regard to the boundary. Did he still wish to maintain the existing boundary rather than adopt the new one?

MR. COSGRAVE replied that he did so. Since his return to Dublin after the discussions of last week he had received something in the nature of an Ultimatum from the tail of the party which normally supported the Government in the Dáil. It was clear that exception would be taken to any agreement, if made, by which Article 12 of the Treaty would be rendered inoperative.

MR. CHURCHILL enquired whether he considered it possible to prevent the publication of the Award by the Boundary Commission.

MR. O'HIGGINS referred to the conversations that had taken place at Chequers with the Prime Minister during the week-end. He then said that the Free State Government could survive on the basis of the territorial *status quo* if they got compensation in one of two directions. It was necessary for them either to secure an amelioration of the conditions under which the Nationalists were at present living in North-East Ireland or to obtain some form of concession by which they would be able to deaden in the 26 counties the echo of the outcry of the Catholics in North-East Ireland. He would personally greatly prefer to secure the first of these alternatives and he had discussed the question with Sir James Craig. He had pointed out the disabilities attaching to the minority in the six counties. In that area there were not only a substantial force of Royal Ulster Constabulary and British soldiery but 45,000 armed 'specials', while in the remaining 26 counties of Ireland there were only 6,000 unarmed civic guards and 15,000 soldiers. The second disabilities attaching to the Northern Catholics was that proportional representation which had been imposed by the Act of 1920 on the six counties had since been repealed to the disadvantage of the Catholic minority. There had, moreover, been a scientific re-distribution of electoral areas that amounted, in effect, to gerrymandering. The result of this was that the minority had suffered further injury both in their Parliamentary representation and in local government.

The position of the minority in the Free State presented a strikingly different picture. Protestant Bishops in the 26 counties had borne witness to the impartiality of the Free State administration, and even Grand Masters of Orange Lodges in the three excluded counties of Ulster had declared publicly, even on the 12th July, their satisfaction with the fairness of the Free State rule. It would be impossible to find a Catholic in Northern Ireland who would say the same of that Government.

If, however, it was impossible to secure any form of alleviation for the Nationalists in the six counties, would it be possible for the Free State Government to obtain compensation in some other form? It was necessary for them to consider the position not only of those who might have had a chance of entering the Free State under the award of the Commission, but also of those who never had such a chance owing to being too far North. If it were possible to improve the position of the latter, it might go some way to cut at the dissatisfaction of the former.

He had, however, succeeded in making no headway on these lines in his discussions with Sir James Craig. The latter had stated definitely that he could not re-enact what he had repealed, nor repeal what he had enacted. He could offer nothing that would enable the Free State Government to maintain their political existence on the basis of the territorial *status quo*. It was clear, therefore, that the Free State Government would fall if they were to attempt to proceed on the basis of last Thursday's discussion. Their fall would have serious reactions in the Free State where the political position was of a most fluid character. There was no coherent party ready to carry on the Government in the event of their resignation. They would probably be followed by a weak coalition who would be unable to withstand the forces of those who were endeavouring to obtain a mandate against the Treaty.

He had informed the Prime Minister of the negative result of his conversation with Sir James Craig, and he had asked the Prime Minister whether he could make a contribution beyond the meagre offer of Sir James Craig in regard to the release of political prisoners. The Prime Minister had enquired what form such a contribution could take, and he had suggested that it might lie in the direction of a modification of Article 5 of the Treaty. He had made this suggestion, but he did not consider that it was the most desirable line. He would have preferred to secure amelioration for the Catholics in Northern Ireland.

LORD BIRKENHEAD was anxious to be clear on the points raised by Irish Ministers. There were in substance really two matters to which they attached importance: (a) the undue number of armed special Constabulary maintained by the Northern Government and (b) the re-distribution of Constituencies in Northern Ireland in so partial a manner as to be unfair to the minority.

MR. O'HIGGINS agreed, adding that an additional point on which they were concerned had been the abolition of proportional representation by the Northern Government.

Turning to Article 5 the position was that the Free State Minister of Finance maintained that financially there was nothing in that Article from the point of view of Great Britain. The Free State Treasury held, that with the legitimate 'set-offs' and what might be called the Colwyn considerations in regard to taxable capacity and necessary expenditure, the result would be that the contribution, if any, would be negligible.

If this was the correct view might there not result very favourable political reactions, not only in the Free State but also in Northern Ireland and in Great Britain, if the determination under Article 5 were anticipated?

There was at present intense discontent and alarm in the Free State at the published forecast of the Award of the Boundary Commission. There was no prospect of that Award being accepted as a fulfilment of the Treaty. It was true that a Free State Government might succeed in keeping the controversy off the physical plane of direct action but they could only do so if they could point to some other form of alleviation. It was essential to supply the people with some safety valve.

Any Government in the Free State trying to restrain the people would be forced to consider whether any way out of their difficulties lay through their membership of the League of Nations. The whole matter had been considered with the greatest anxiety by the Executive Council of the Free State and the result of these deliberations he had communicated to the Prime Minister. They were now convinced that the proposals of last Thursday were politically impossible for them as a Government.

MR. CHURCHILL suggested that it would be convenient if at this stage he were to state the views of the British Government in regard to Article 5. The British Government had throughout strictly adhered to the Treaty and when eighteen months ago great difficulties had arisen they had, none the less, carried legislation appointing the Boundary Commission over the head of Ulster's objections. The British Parliament had thus rigidly carried out the conditions of Article 12. There then followed the protracted labours of the Commission and the position now was that Free State Ministers were disappointed at what they understood to be that Commission's finding. He was bound to say that having now seen the map prepared by the Commission (which he had not seen when he had last seen Mr. Cosgrave) he could truly say that the result of the Commission's labours was very much what he had expected and meant when he signed the Treaty. The British Government felt that they had done everything to carry out the letter of the Treaty, and as regards the spirit of it their conscience was quite clear. They had from the beginning stated that they anticipated a finding of this character.

As regards Article 5 the Treaty was perfectly clear. When Article 12 had been disposed of, it followed under the Treaty that discussion on Article 5 should begin. It was impossible to forecast the result of the arbitration under that Article, though each side naturally had confidence in its case. The view of the British Treasury, after a full examination, was that an arbitrator might reasonably be expected to award Great Britain the sum of 155¾ million and if that sum were paid over a period of 60 years it would mean an annual annuity of £8¼ millions at 5%. If, however, following the analogy of recent International agreements the rate of interest were reduced to 3½%, the annuity for the same period would be 6¼ millions. It would be a very serious step for a British Government to renounce on behalf of the British taxpayer so substantial a claim, especially at a time like the present when economy in every field of national expenditure was being rigidly carried out. Retrenchments were being pressed in education, health services, unemployment allowances and the armed forces of the Crown. Such economies naturally created dissatisfaction and all those affected would certainly attack the Government if the latter were to forego what they regarded as important claims of the British Government under this Article. There was not only this to be considered but there were also possible reactions to be borne in mind on the Northern Irish contribution. There was very little doubt that the waiving of Article 5 would strengthen the movement in Ulster to reduce or abolish the Northern Irish contribution. There were also reactions in the other Dominions to be feared. Large repayments were now being made, for example by Australia, of money borrowed during the war for war purposes. Finally, there was the position of the loyalists in Southern Ireland who were very discontented at their position. They would certainly object to any waiving of British rights while the damages they had sustained had, in their view, only been met to an inconsiderable extent.

The British Government had considered this question on Monday afternoon and they took a grave and adverse view of the consequences of waiving Article 5. The British Ministers at the present meeting were not authorised to do more than open discussion and to exchange views. It would be their duty to report their discussion to the Cabinet. It was important in considering the financial position of Great Britain to remember not only the internal debt, the service of which more than covered the yield of income tax and super-tax, but also the unexampled payments amounting to £34 million per annum which were being made to the United States. The interest charged by the United States would in

1933 be increased by $^{1}/_{2}$ with a consequent annual increase of £4,400,000, in the annuities to be paid[1]. With this prospect in view it was essential that all the resources at the disposal of the British Government should be husbanded. There would, he believed, be an explosion of public opinion if the British Government were to abandon Article 5 although they had carried out to the letter the terms of Article 12.

MR. COSGRAVE reminded the Conference that the Treaty had been signed for two purposes. In the first place it was to make peace between the South of Ireland and Great Britain and in the second place to secure peace in Ireland itself. Article 12 and the proposed Award under it gave no satisfaction either in Northern Ireland or in the Free State. He had gathered that Sir James Craig was prepared to allow Article 12 to drop. The trouble had been of twelve or fourteen years standing and had been the cause of much bitterness. Peace over the whole of Ireland as the result of agreement between Northern Ireland and the Free State was, he believed, possible. Such peace would be of importance to the British Government also.

As regards the sum of £150 (odd) million, this was based upon a total figure of £7,840 million for national debt, but of this £2,000 million were due from the Dominions and foreign countries. On this account the figure of £150 (odd) million should be at once reduced to £120 million. Assuming, however, for a moment that the arbitrator decided that an annuity of £6 millions was due by the Free State how could they possibly pay such a sum? They had not succeeded in existing circumstances in balancing their budget and they would not be able even to maintain services at the figure estimated in this year's Budget. The British Government surely did not wish to see the Free State bankrupt. They had great difficulties to face and were handicapped by having no substantial industries; they had moreover recently undergone a civil war and they had at their credit no large investments. They had faced their considerable financial burdens and they were trying to rectify the position in regard to Irish trade, but it would be a long process.

As regards the Southern loyalists they had suffered no disability from Free State legislation. They could only make complaint in regard to one matter and that was the refusal of compensation for consequential losses. Compensation in such cases had in a few instances been granted under the Malicious Injuries Acts but these decisions had been set aside by the late Lord Chancellor (Sir John Ross).

It was, however, fair to point out that this decision did not fall on the loyalists alone. It was equally true of other sections of the community including the supporters of the Free State Government. Incidentally he did not consider the House of Lords plan for dealing with this question satisfactory, but the problem did not appear to him to be incapable of solution. If the present difficulties were overcome, it might be possible – he could not, of course, pledge himself – to consider what flat rate of addition might be added.

MR. CHURCHILL asked whether he attached most importance to the amelioration of the treatment of Roman Catholics in the six County area.

[1] This sentence is handwritten in the original.

MR. O'HIGGINS replied that the intention of the Treaty by the proviso to Article 12, was to determine how much of Northern Ireland, as fixed by the 1920 Act, should have the right of remaining outside the Free State and to continue a separate political existence. Sir James Craig had referred to the abstention from the Northern Parliament of the Nationalists' members. The reason for this was, of course, in regard to the boundary. They felt that the position of their constituents might be prejudiced if they entered the Northern Parliament before the boundary question was settled.

Free State Ministers had always thought that they had seen confirmation of their view of Article 12 in the statements by the British Signatories to the Treaty. He referred to speeches by Lord Birkenhead and Mr. Lloyd George in December, 1921. It was impossible to mince matters, and he felt it right to say that the proposed Award was regarded in the Free State as a grotesque travesty of the Proviso to Article 12. The Free State Government were politically bankrupt and they were earnestly searching for a way out with a sincere desire for peace. They could, however, only say that the Treaty had broken down in this respect. The elements which always challenged the Treaty would in this way have at least a negative victory.

LORD BIRKENHEAD enquired when in point of time the Free State crisis would come. When was their Debate in the Dáil?

MR. O'HIGGINS replied that Mr. Johnson, the Leader of the Labour Party, had challenged a Debate last week. The Dáil expected to meet tomorrow (Wednesday) but it could perhaps be put off, though only for a short time. A definite line must be taken by the Free State Government within the next few days.

LORD SALISBURY said that the British Government took a rigid view of the obligations of Article 5, but he fully understood, and indeed sympathised with the Free State anxiety in regard to the position of Roman Catholics in Northern Ireland. He saw, however, a very great difficulty in correlating this attitude with the desire for relief under Article 5. Indeed he thought it a dangerous position to occupy.

MR. O'HIGGINS admitted that the Free State Government would be open to the taunt of having sold the Roman Catholics in Northern Ireland, but such an argument would only be a half truth. The fact was that the Proviso to Article 12 of the Treaty had completely broken down. The proposed Award touched the fringes of Northern Ireland only; it did not comply with the Free State conception of that Article of the Treaty. Free State Ministers had discussed the possibility of maintaining the Territorial *status quo*, and they believed that they could face the position which this would create if they could obtain substantial alleviations for the Roman Catholics of the six counties *or* if they could secure the elimination of Article 5. In the former case the outbreak of feeling might not be great. He had personally tried with Sir James Craig to secure a settlement on these lines, but he had failed. There would no doubt be an outcry from the Roman Catholics who would get no relief, but could not the Free State Government get some form of concession to prevent that outcry finding an echo in every one of the twenty-six counties in the Free State. The position would no doubt be invidious, but the Roman Catholics in the North would[,] it seemed, be let down in any case. The position was that the proposed Award was impossible, and that even the territorial *status quo* would be impossible unless the Free State got something in addition. It was clear that the forecasted line was not based on the wishes of the inhabitants, but was in fact the line of least resistance and had been adopted as such by the Commission, who saw on the one hand a large force of Special Constabulary and a truculent Government in the North, while in the Free State there was only an unarmed civic guard.

The actual promulgation of the Award, if made, would no doubt create a definite legal position in the face of which it would be the height of folly for the Free State Government to fly, and it would be the duty of the Free State Government as far as possible to restrain the feelings of their people but they could not do so on the ground that the Treaty had been fulfilled because through such an Award they did not consider that it had.

The Free State Government could ride the storm on the basis of the territorial *status quo* if they could get Article 5 waived. It was important in this connection to bear in mind the recent statement by de Valera in which he had pointed to the proposed Award of the Boundary Commission under Article 12 and had urged the people to brace themselves to meet a similar shock when arbitration took place under Article 5. Until recently the republicans had been divided but the way in which Article 12 had worked would be looked upon as a forecast of the way in which Article 5 would operate.

MR. COSGRAVE referred to another suggestion which had been made, viz. that the Oath should be made optional by modification of Article 4. Those in favour of such a course would argue that owing to the breakdown of Clause 12, by which it had been hoped to bring in more members to the Dáil, the only other way of strengthening that body would be to let in the 48 republican Deputies. Such a course, if adopted, would give poor chances of stability for the State and it would moreover make the republicans a political entity which they were not at present. Great benefits might be hoped to follow if agreement were reached with Sir James Craig. Indeed, there was already a change of atmosphere for the better.

MR. CHURCHILL suggested that the Conference should meet again at 4 p.m., and added that in the meanwhile he would confer with the Prime Minister. It was clear that definite conclusions could not be reached today and he expressed the hope that Mr. Cosgrave and his colleagues would be able to stay in London to continue discussion on the following day.

MR. COSGRAVE undertook to alter his plans and to remain in London for the night.

MR. O'HIGGINS said that there were other reasons apart from those already advanced in favour of waiving Article 5. The Irish Free State had been challenged in its infancy by civil war. In the first year of its life it had to pay £7 millions for its army; in the second year £10$^1/2$ millions and subsequently £4 millions. A great amount of material destruction had resulted from the civil war and the compensation that followed was an added burden in no way contemplated at the time of the Treaty. The Irish signatories to the Treaty had stood by their bond. Two of them had indeed died in that service. Due weight should be given to these considerations in discussing the method of dealing with this Article of the Treaty.

The Conference then adjourned until 4 p.m.

No. 360 NAI DT S4720A

Draft notes of a conference held in the Board Room,
Treasury, Whitehall, London
(Secret) (C.A./H./48 – 3rd Minutes)

LONDON, 4.00 pm, 1 December 1925

PRESENT:-

Great Britain.
The Right Hon. W.S. Churchill, C.H., M.P., Chancellor of the Exchequer. (In the Chair)
The Most Hon. The Marquess of Salisbury, K.G., G.C.V.O., C.B., Lord Privy Seal.
The Right Hon. The Earl of Birkenhead, Secretary of State for India.
Mr. P.J. Grigg, Treasury.

Irish Free State.
Mr. W.T. Cosgrave, T.D., President of the Executive Council.
Mr. Kevin O'Higgins, T.D., Vice-President of the Executive Council.
Mr. J. O'Byrne, K.C., T.D., Attorney-General.

Secretaries.
Mr. T. Jones, Deputy Secretary, Cabinet Secretariat.
Mr. A.F. Hemming, C.B.E.

Mr. D. O'Hegarty, Secretary to the Executive Council.

LORD BIRKENHEAD at the outset referred to the counter-claim which had been handed in by the Irish Delegation at the Treaty Conference. The British Government were advised by their experts that the claim was untenable.

If it were assumed that for a period of 10 or 15 years, or any considerable period, the Irish Government would be unable to pay. If as a result the present Irish Government were defeated, it would create a serious situation. At the same time, these conditions might change, and an alternative Irish Government might be possible at a later date. So far as the British Government was concerned, insuperable difficulties presented themselves.

LORD BIRKENHEAD then referred to the economies which the British Government had to make in its endeavour to balance its Budget. If at that moment the British Government were to face the British people with the statement that not only would they allow the Free State a respite in financial difficulties, but that they were wiping out Article 5 altogether, then they would create grave political difficulties for themselves. He had no authority to make any offer to Irish Ministers, but he was anxious to know whether a considerable moratorium, say for x years, would be of assistance. Such an arrangement would leave the rights of the parties to be determined subsequently by arbitration. Would discussion on such lines prove useful to Irish Ministers?

LORD SALISBURY deprecated any actual figures being mentioned. The whole Government, almost without exception, were unanimous that this potential debt could not be wholly wiped out. The reason for this was obvious. They were merely trustees in this regard for the British public, and as such, had no right to sign any agreement by which the British people gave up this claim. He was, however, sympathetic to the suggestion that further time should be given to the Free State under this article, but he thought that as a condition there should be a general clearing up of the many ragged ends which still remained as a result of the Treaty (which he personally had never supported). If the British Government could say that they had laid all these outstanding questions at rest, it might be possible that they would be able to persuade the public that notwithstanding the grave political situation indicated by Lord Birkenhead, it would be well to agree to give further time for the financial settlement between this country and the Free State. The points he had in mind had relation to the Irish adherents of the old regime, double Income Tax, and questions arising out of land purchase.

LORD BIRKENHEAD agreed that the British Government were trustees for this claim, but in view of other recent debt transactions, it might be well for them in the interests of those for whom they were trustees, to strike a bargain with the Free State.

MR. CHURCHILL thought that it [might be] desirable to consider the question not only strictly from the financial point of view. It might be possible in that regard for the British Government to go some distance, but not as far as the Free State desired. Sir James Craig for his part might also be able to do something, but not as much as the Free State wished. A combination of the two lines of solution, namely, amelioration of the lot of the Catholics in Northern Ireland, and easement of Free State finance in relation to Article 5, might be to the interest of the Free State. He was anxious to know what ideas Free State ministers held as to the lines that assistance could take. The Prime Minister had agreed that he should discuss the question further with Sir James Craig, and for his part, he thought that this course might be more fruitful than direct negotiations between Northern Ireland and Free State Ministers.

As regards proportional representation, there were many obvious objections, and it might well be that other more satisfactory means could be devised for protecting the Catholic minority in the North, e.g. (though he had no authority to make such a suggestion) an arrangement might be made whereby additional members were nominated to the Northern Parliament to secure better representations of the minority.

MR. O'HIGGINS said that so far as proportional representation was concerned, strong objections would be raised by representatives, such as Major Bryan Cooper,[1] of Southern Irish minorities if the Free State Government were to propose its abolition. Moreover, these representatives of minorities had had a

[1] Independent Unionist TD and later Cumann na nGaedheal TD for Dublin County (1923-30).

stabilising effect in the Dáil. Any effort to remove proportional representation, by which alone such representatives could be elected, would be open to strong objection. Free State Ministers considered that proportional representation was required by the peculiar circumstances in the North Eastern area where there was the sharpest conflict of opinion between the majority and the minority. It had been an unreasonable step to repeal that system which had given fair representation to the minority in the six counties. The best evidence of goodwill that Sir James Craig could give towards his minorities would be to restore proportional representation.

MR. CHURCHILL enquired, therefore, whether the restoration of proportional representation would be the first point at which the Free State Ministers would aim.

MR. O'HIGGINS said that perhaps the Catholics in Northern Ireland would not regard it as more important than the disbandment of the special constables.

MR. CHURCHILL said that so far as that force was concerned, he had always understood that it was to be disbanded as soon as the boundary question was disposed of.

MR. O'HIGGINS replied that on that point Sir James Craig had told him on Sunday that he was not in a position to make any immediate contribution except in regard to certain prisoners.

MR. CHURCHILL said that he did not anticipate any great difficulty regarding the disbandment of the special constables, but the re-enactment of proportional representation might be a greater difficulty.

LORD SALISBURY enquired whether there was any actual oppression of Roman Catholics as such in Northern Ireland to-day.

MR. O'HIGGINS replied that it was a question of degree. They were allowed to earn their living if they could, but they had no part in the administrative life of the country. Appointments, for instance, to judgeships and magistracies, were practically closed to them, and the number of Catholics in the R.U.C. was small. This constituted a great contrast in the position of the Free State where the majority of the judges were non-Catholics, as were a large number of the Senators and many of the Deputies in the Dáil.

MR. COSGRAVE said that so far as appointments in the Free State were concerned, individual merit was the only consideration to which regard was paid. The question of religion was not allowed to arise in that connection. In his view, the re-distribution of electoral areas in Northern Ireland was of even greater importance than the re-enactment of proportional representation. Under the scheme brought in by the Northern Government, larger numbers of Catholics had secured smaller representation, while relatively smaller numbers of Protestants had secured larger representation.

The Irish signatories of the Treaty had never contemplated the possibility of such a situation. At that time, proportional representation was in operation both in the North and in the South, under the Act of 1920. When the Irish signatories agreed to Article 5 they did so in the perspective of Articles 12 - 15. Without those latter articles, the other Article would not have been accepted. Article 12 proved to be unworkable, and he believed there was no possible method of solving that particular problem. The aim he had in view was by surrendering some immediate advantage to obtain something of far greater value in, say, 20 years, and that was a better feeling between the North and South, by eliminating the disputes and distrusts that existed to-day. In this way, he hoped for the possibility in the future of their becoming one country with the same political outlook.

MR. CHURCHILL said that this was his hope, and it had, he believed, been that of all those who had signed the Treaty. From that point of view, the maintenance of the existing boundary was in every way preferable to the marking out of a new boundary by the Imperial Commissioners. Such an arrangement would only stereotype existing differences.

MR. COSGRAVE said that the old boundary was more satisfactory from the point of view of Sir James Craig.

MR. CHURCHILL enquired whether the Free State Ministers were not afraid of the position with which they would be faced in the event of the award being made public. Would they not be confronted with serious criticisms from their own supporters when it became apparent that they had refused to accept an arrangement which had added increased acres and larger population to the Free State. It would, he believed, be very difficult, to keep the terms of the award secret. Indeed, the Commissioners might desire that it should be made public in view of the criticisms to which they had been subject.

MR. COSGRAVE said that if the terms of the award were published, both the Northern and the Free State Governments would be faced with the utmost pressure from persons who under the award would be transferred to the areas to which they wanted to go. The question of immediate relief would over-ride the question of the ultimate good of the community as a whole. Speaking as an Irishman, and not as a Minister, he admitted that he viewed with distrust and disfavour an arrangement whereby the Catholic minority in the North would be still further weakened. That minority had to-day only a small voice with which to support its interests, and under such a scheme it would be still further weakened.

MR. CHURCHILL thought that Irish Ministers would run a grave risk if they were to assume that the report of the Commission would not become known. The Commission had been much attacked on account of their anticipated award; he did not know their views but he thought it possible that they would wish to publish their finding. Indeed, he thought it a strong probability.

MR. O'BYRNE took the view that publication of an unauthorised award differed materially from an official statement by the Commission. Surely the Commission would hold its hand if a joint request were made by the British and Irish Governments?

MR. CHURCHILL thought that this might be so, but it was not safe to assume it.

The Commissioners were, he knew, pressing to see the Prime Minister, and while publication would not be the same as an actual promulgation by the Commission, its possible effects must be considered. Would the publication of the award affect the views at present held by the Irish Ministers?

MR. COSGRAVE replied that it would not, but he would much prefer that there should be no publication.

MR. CHURCHILL said that Sir James Craig was seeing him at 5.0 p.m. and he suggested a resumption of the present meeting at 6.0 or 6.30. Were there any other points that Irish Ministers would like to put to him before he saw Sir James Craig?

MR. COSGRAVE briefly reviewed the position from the point of view of Irish Ministers. At the time of the Treaty, the revenue of Ireland was £50 millions per annum, but in the year following it had dropped to less than half. In the month that the Treaty had been signed, the price of cattle had fallen from 112/- to 56/-: they had considered it a passing phase, but the price had never since risen above 60/- to 65/-. The system of Government which they found in operation was a system suited to the needs of a country of much greater financial resources. Education services amounted to £5 millions per annum: Old Age Pensions, £3 millions, and pensions under Article 10 amounted to £2 millions. These three services reached therefore a total of £10 millions per annum. From the point of view of Ireland, a postponement of financial settlement from the present bankrupt to a future solvent period would mean that Ireland would thus surrender factors which at present would be of value in determining that settlement.

MR. CHURCHILL pointed to the tremendous payments that this country was called upon to make to America. These payments would increase in 1933. If, however, the attitude of the United States were to become less rigid, the atmosphere would be easier for this country, and it would thus place us in a position to deal more generously.

In reply to a question by LORD BIRKENHEAD, MR. COSGRAVE said that if he were to accept a moratorium on the lines proposed, his action would be riddled with criticisms. He would much prefer to secure improved conditions for the Roman Catholics in Northern Ireland, but failing this he looked for more than a moratorium of the provisions of Article 5.

MR. O'HIGGINS said that in order to ride the political storm, it was essential to have regard to the feeling of the electorate in the 26 counties. The Government could only survive if one or other of the two conditions to which he had referred were secured, either the improvement of the position of the Northern Catholics, or the elimination of Article 5. He believed that the Government could maintain their position if they were to stand on the territorial *status quo*, were to secure the release of the prisoners to which Sir James Craig had agreed, and if Article 5 were to disappear.

The Meeting then adjourned till 6 p.m.

No. 361 NAI DT S4720A

Draft notes of a conference held in the Board Room,
Treasury, Whitehall, London
(Secret) (C.A./H./48 – 4th Minutes)

LONDON, 6.15 pm, 1 December 1925

PRESENT:-

Great Britain.
The Right Hon. W.S. Churchill, C.H., M.P., Chancellor of the Exchequer (In the Chair)
The Most Hon. The Marquess of Salisbury, K.G., G.C.V.O., C.B., Lord Privy Seal.
The Right Hon. Sir John Anderson, G.C.B., Permanent Under Secretary of State, Home Office.
Mr. G.G. Whiskard, C.B., Assistant Secretary, Dominions Office.
Mr. P.J. Grigg, Treasury

Irish Free State.
Mr. W.T. Cosgrave, T.D., President of the Executive Council.
Mr. Kevin O'Higgins, T.D., Vice-President of the Executive Council.
Mr. J. O'Byrne, K.C., Attorney-General.

Northern Ireland.
The Right Hon. Sir James Craig, Bart., M.P., Prime Minister.
Mr. C.H. Blackmore, C.B.E., Assistant Secretary to the Cabinet.

Secretaries.
Mr. T. Jones, Deputy Secretary, Cabinet Secretariat.
Mr. A.F. Hemming, C.B.E.

Mr. D. O'Hegarty, Secretary to the Executive Council.

LORD SALISBURY said he felt it his duty to say at once that the British Government could not entertain a proposal for writing off Article 5. It would be impossible to persuade the Cabinet or the public to accept such a course. The Government were, however, prepared to consider proposals for postponing payment under that Article. He and his colleagues had been much impressed by the feeling in the Free State, however unaccepted that feeling might be in North-East Ireland, that the Roman Catholics in the six Counties were not receiving fair treatment. Whether this was the case or not, the mere fact that such a feeling existed did great harm to the interests of good government. It was essential that people should not only be well treated, but to think that they were well treated. He personally could not see that proposals for the improvement of the position of the Northern Roman Catholics on the one hand and proposals for the modification of Article 5 on the other were in *pari materie*. He agreed, however, that fair treatment of all members of the community was essential and indeed it was a fundamental consideration of British policy. He and his colleagues had accordingly asked Sir James Craig whether any steps could be taken to improve the position of Catholics in Northern Ireland. They were anxious not only to eliminate injustice, which was not, of course, admitted, but to destroy the feeling that injustice existed.

SIR JAMES CRAIG said that he was most anxious that a belief in justice should become general among the people in Northern Ireland. His difficulty was that many unfounded criticisms had been circulated against his administration before the two Nationalists members had entered the Belfast House of Commons. Since that time many illusions had been dissipated. For example, the fact that at least one-third of the Royal Ulster Constabulary were to be Catholics had now become more generally known. As regards the Judiciary there had, it is true, been a recent difficulty in appointing a Catholic, but so far as the stipendaries were concerned he had recently appointed a Catholic. Monies voted by the Northern Parliament in relief of unemployment were strictly allocated on the basis of population, namely two-thirds for the relief of Protestants and one-third for the relief of Catholics. The questions asked by nationalist members of the Ulster Parliament had done much to destroy old misconceptions. The widows and orphans pension Scheme was being administered with absolute impartiality between Protestants and Catholics and much had been done to break down the old difficulties of the Catholics working in the shipyards. If only those in Northern Ireland were left alone by mischief-makers they would win through successfully. If any practical suggestion were made to him he would do his best to meet it. For his part he was willing to make a suggestion that the two Governments of Ireland should meet together for joint consideration at an early date. If charges were made against either Government let those who made them substantiate their case before the joint Cabinet meeting.

MR. CHURCHILL said that in his view the proposal for the joint meeting of the two Irish Executives was a matter of enormous importance. The Executive Officers of both parts of Ireland had a vital interest in achieving success. This proposal was, however, only a fraction of the task with which the British and Irish Governments were faced to-day.

MR. COSGRAVE enquired what business could be transacted by a joint meeting of the two Irish Cabinets. He foresaw great difficulties if it were to act by (say) a majority vote.

MR. CHURCHILL agreed that to achieve success mutual agreement was essential. He was anxious to know whether Sir James Craig's suggestion would be valued in the Free State.

MR. COSGRAVE thought that joint meetings would in themselves be excellent, but if they were brought forward at this stage as a contribution to the present discussions they would certainly be regarded as a piece of eye-wash.

LORD SALISBURY said that the essential thing was to restore confidence. The Free State had relied on obtaining from the Boundary Commission a relatively large territorial extension embracing a substantial number of Roman Catholics.

It was clear that this anticipation would not now be realised. The present suggestion was therefore that the existing border should be maintained. Under such an arrangement the Free State Ministers would have lost the chance, for which they had hoped, of looking after the interests of the Roman Catholics on the border. Would not good result by the appointment of an official liaison officer, appointed (say) by the Roman Catholics and Nationalists in North-East Ireland? Would they not feel increased confidence if they had their own official representative to put forward their grievances? Such a representative would, he contemplated, be on close terms of confidence with Sir James Craig and would have direct access to the Northern Irish Cabinet. The appointment of such an Officer would form part of the terms of arrangement whereby the Free State definitely abandoned their hopes of assisting the Catholics on the boundary. It would, in fact, be a substitute for their former ambitions.

MR. COSGRAVE thought that it would be a mistake to define a proposal to this end in the form of a definite agreement. It would be better to allow it to be the natural outcome of a growing improvement of mutual understanding.

MR. CHURCHILL said that for his part he was most anxious to see joint action by the two Irish executives. The practical question was, however, to meet the immediate emergency. He suggested that the Free State Government might make its stand on the following points. (i) Article 12 had been abrogated. (ii) As regards Article 5, a Moratorium had been agreed to for x years. (iii) A responsible liaison Officer had been appointed by the Catholics in Northern Ireland to represent them and to defend their interests. (iv) Agreement had been reached for periodical joint consultation between the two Irish Governments. Such a scheme in his view was a general proposition that was worthy of consideration. All were agreed that unity in Ireland was the goal to be aimed at and that the results of partition were bad. A definite declaration on the part of the Irish Governments that they would meet in joint Council from time to time might do good to the cause of unity.

SIR JAMES CRAIG feared that such a proposal might in the present circumstances be a source of embarrassment to Mr. Cosgrave.

MR. O'HIGGINS enquired whether this proposal was put forward in substitution for what he had indicated, namely the restoration of proportional representation in North-East Ireland? That system had been specially devised for the protection of minorities and had been imposed by the British Parliament in the Act of 1920, both on what was now the Free State and on North-East Ireland for the specific purpose of securing adequate representation for minorities. That safeguard had since been abolished by the action of the Northern Parliament.

SIR JAMES CRAIG took the view that the proper place for dealing with the grievances of minorities was the Ulster House of Commons. He personally considered that proportional representation had been a failure in every country that had adopted it. Many foreign countries were now reverting to the British system. In view of the results of the Free State Senate Elections he believed that the Free State Government would themselves have to abolish it.

MR. O'HIGGINS said no objection had been made against proportional representation so far as elections to the Dáil were concerned. Had it not been for it[,] representatives such as Major Bryan Cooper of the minority in the South would never have been elected. A strong protest would be raised if the Free State proposed to abolish this system. In his view the real criticism of the Senate Election lay in the fact that the whole country was merged in a single constituency and that there were 76 candidates for 19 vacancies.

MR. COSGRAVE said that people in Southern Ireland took the view that proportional representation was a security for minorities. It was, in his view, a fair method, but the objection to it was that parties were apt to be so evenly divided that[,] in order to form a Government[,] coalitions were necessary.

MR. CHURCHILL suggested that the questions at issue should be further considered to-morrow when he hoped it would be possible to reach a definite agreement. He accordingly suggested that the present meeting should be resumed at 12 noon. He would himself see Sir James Craig at 11 a.m.

The Conference then adjourned.

No. 362 NAI DT S4720A

Draft notes of a conference held in the Board Room,
Treasury, Whitehall, London
(Secret) (C.A. (H) 48.– 5th minutes)
LONDON, 12.15 pm, 2 December 1925

PRESENT.

Great Britain.

The Right Hon. W.S. Churchill, C.H., M.P., Chancellor of the Exchequer.
The Most Hon. The Marquess of Salisbury, K.G., G.C.V.O., C.B., Lord Privy Seal.
The Right Hon. The Earl of Birkenhead, Secretary of State for India.
Mr. G.C. Upcott, C.B., Deputy Controller of Establishments, Treasury.
Mr. F.W. Leith Ross, C.B., Deputy Controller of Finance, Treasury.
Mr. G.G. Whiskard, C.B., Assistant Secretary, Dominions Office.
Mr. P.J. Grigg, Principal Private Secretary to the Chancellor of the Exchequer.

Irish Free State.

Mr. W.T. Cosgrave, T.D., President of the Executive Council.
Mr. K. O'Higgins, T.D., Vice-President of the Executive Council.
Mr. J. O'Byrne, K.C., Attorney-General.

Secretaries.

Mr. T. Jones, Deputy Secretary, Cabinet Secretariat
Mr A.F. Hemming, C.B.E.

Mr. D. O'Hegarty, Secretary to the Executive Council

MR. CHURCHILL read to the Conference the reply[1] which had been received the previous evening from the Boundary Commission in answer to a letter despatched earlier in the day expressing the hope on behalf of His Majesty's Government and the Government of the Irish Free State that the Commission would be prepared to postpone the issue of their determination until a further communication was addressed to them by or on behalf of both Governments. (The full text of the Boundary Commission's reply is contained in C.P. 512 (25)).[2]

In that letter the Commission agreed to take no steps either to issue its Award or to publish its Report without previously communicating further with both Governments.

MR. CHURCHILL thought that it was clear from the terms of this letter that the Boundary Commission would insist on their Award ultimately being made public. He then read to the Conference the following Question of which Private Notice had been given to the Prime Minister for answer in the House of Commons that afternoon:-

> 'To ask the Prime Minister whether the findings of the Irish Boundary Commission will be put into effect in the absence of the signature of the Free State Commissioner?'

He had suggested to the Prime Minister that the reply might be as follows:-

> 'After consultation with Mr. Cosgrave, I have communicated with the Boundary Commission, and, in deference to our wishes, the Commission has agreed temporarily to postpone publication of their Report and Award.'

MR. COSGRAVE indicated that he concurred in the terms of the proposed reply.

MR. CHURCHILL stated that he had had that morning a conversation with Sir James Craig who had informed him that he had satisfied the Free State Ministers in regard to the position of Roman Catholics in Northern Ireland. He understood therefore that the Free State Ministers had now no requests on this score to make to Sir James Craig.

MR. COSGRAVE said that the arguments that he and his colleagues had previously put forward had failed to convince Sir James Craig. Politically an agreement with Sir James Craig would not be of value to the Free State Government. Under existing conditions he did not believe that the Nationalist members for Tyrone and Fermanagh would enter the Northern Parliament. He had, however, been forced to abandon his claims against the Northern Government because he saw that it was impossible to obtain their acceptance. He added that even if he had succeeded in his efforts he would not have made any real progress and would in fact have done nothing more than revert to the position of the time of the abortive Collins-Craig agreement. He was satisfied that Sir James Craig could not at the present time 'deliver the goods'.

In reply to a question by MR. CHURCHILL, MR. COSGRAVE said that a paper

---

[1] Not printed.
[2] Not printed.

agreement with Northern Ireland would under existing conditions be useless to the Free State.

MR. CHURCHILL said that in that case the only question remaining to be discussed was that of finance. He and his colleagues had received from Sir James Craig a framework on which an agreement might be built. He then read the following document which he had received from Sir James Craig:

> '*Article 5.*
> Representatives of the Free State and of the British Treasury having discussed the question of the amount involved under Article 5 reached an Agreement this morning that £_____ is due by the Free State and that this debt shall be funded on the same terms as were agreed in the case of the British debt to the United States of America. It was further agreed that the whole financial position shall be brought under review in1933 by the Joint Exchequer Board on which two Members shall be appointed by the Free State Government in substitution for the Representatives of Northern Ireland.
> *Compensation.* (For private circulation only.)
> In addition, the Free State Government undertake to increase the amount available for post-truce compensation by a sum not exceeding 10% over and above the amounts awarded by the Courts.'

MR. CHURCHILL said that the British Government were not opposed in principle to an immediate financial agreement in substitution of arbitration. He enquired whether Sir James Craig's proposals outlined in the document he had read were acceptable to the Free State.

MR. COSGRAVE said that while he had discussed the question with Sir James Craig, he had not been able to go so far as to agree terms such as those outlined in the statement that had just been read to the Conference.

MR. CHURCHILL suggested that they might, however, serve as a basis of discussion for direct settlement.

LORD BIRKENHEAD thought that as the settlement had not been agreed, it would be better to approach the question *de novo*. He thought the most hopeful line of advance lay in the direction of a financial agreement in lieu of Article 5.

MR. COSGRAVE shared this view. It was true that Sir James Craig had mentioned a figure (£20 millions) the previous evening. He had, however, told Sir James that such a figure was impossible from the Free State point of view.

MR. CHURCHILL referred to the terms of Article 5 of the Agreement of the 6th December 1921 which provided that:-

> 'The Irish Free State shall assume liability for the service of the Public Debt of the United Kingdom as existing at the date hereof and towards the payment of war pensions as existing at that date in such proportion as may be fair and equitable, having regard to any just claims on the part of Ireland by way of set off or counterclaim, the amount of such sums being determined in default of agreement by the arbitration of one or more independent persons being citizens of the British Empire.'

MR. COSGRAVE considered that this obligation was limited by the capacity of the Irish Free State Government to pay. He referred in particular to the words 'fair and equitable'.

LORD BIRKENHEAD said that in his view these words had reference to legal or quasi legal claims and that the expression 'fair and equitable' was governed by the subsequent words 'having regard to any just claims on the part of Ireland by way of set off or counterclaim'.

MR. O'HIGGINS referred to the so-called Colwyn principles which he considered should apply to the interpretation of this Article.

MR. CHURCHILL said that in his view such principles had no application in this case.

MR. O'HIGGINS pressed his argument that the applications of such principles should be regarded as implicit in the Article unless it was sought to impose on Ireland a hopeless burden of phantom millions.

MR. CHURCHILL thought that the question could most conveniently be dealt with in two stages. In the first place, it was necessary to determine the amount due, and in the second place, the capacity of the debtor to pay. He cited the example of the Italian debt to the United States. In that case there was no dispute whatever in regard to the actual sum due. The question at issue, however, was how much they were able to pay to the United States.

MR. COSGRAVE suggested that while Article 5 might not admit an arbitrator to have regard to such considerations, the fact that Ireland was a poor country must necessarily result in weight being given to arguments of this kind.

MR. CHURCHILL pointed out that no state in Europe was at the present time paying less than 10% of its Budget in the service of public debt. If those conditions obtained in Ireland, the Irish Free State would be paying £2.6 millions a year for debt charges out of a total revenue of £26 millions.

LORD BIRKENHEAD enquired whether the Free State Ministers had considered the question of spreading the payment of the debt over a long period.

MR. COSGRAVE said that this point had been considered by his colleagues and himself.

MR. CHURCHILL assured the Free State Ministers that they would not find any difficulties raised on that aspect of the question. He again cited the example of the Italian debt where payment was to be spread over an immense period of years. He reminded the Conference that the British Government were paying nearly 50% of their Budget in the service of debt.

MR. COSGRAVE drew a distinction between payment of foreign debt and the payment of interest on sinking fund in respect of internal debt.

MR. CHURCHILL agreed that this was so, but pointed out the onerous character of the British debt payments to the United States.

MR. COSGRAVE referred to the payments amounting to £3 ¼ millions per annum being paid by the Free State mainly to persons not living in that country in respect of land purchase. No other example could be cited of a country paying such large sums for its land.

LORD BIRKENHEAD referred to the case of Northern Ireland whose income was small in relation to the amount of their financial contribution to this country.

MR. CHURCHILL said that this contribution had, for various reasons, been reduced from £8 millions to about £1 million per annum. The British Government expected that this figure would be substantially increased when the Special Constabulary had been disbanded and the Northern Ireland Parliament House had been built. He expected ultimately that the contribution would amount to £3 millions per annum.

In reply to a question by MR. CHURCHILL, MR. LEITH ROSS explained that the position in regard to Austria was that 16% of the total Budget was devoted to the service of public debt notwithstanding the fact that there was a moratorium on a special debt amounting to £30 millions. France was paying as much as 55% on its debt services.

MR. COSGRAVE said that the Free State did not want a mere paper arrangement. As regards the foreign countries, such as France, it should be remembered that they had had the advantages, such as they were, of a successful war. The Irish Free State had not had any such advantages, and were faced with the fact that 250,000 persons in the Free State occupied uneconomic holdings of less value than £10 per annum and that in addition, there were 212,000 agricultural labourers whose position could only be regarded as uneconomic. Nine counties in the Free State had moreover been scheduled as Congested counties. It would be impossible for the Free State to make debt payments in proportion to foreign countries except by a Poll tax or a tax on food.

MR. CHURCHILL suggested that the question of capacity to pay did not arise until after the actual amount of debt due had been agreed. In the present instance there could be no question of coercion, but the Free State could not fail to be sensible of the advantages to their credit that would follow a debt settlement. It was considerations of this kind that had led France and Italy to change their ideas and to cause them within the last year to attempt to settle their foreign debts. The British and Free State Governments were not in the same position as, say, Italy and the United States, because they had already agreed to the terms embodied in Article 5 of the Treaty. The British Government could not compel the Free State to carry out that Agreement, but there was the self compulsion of their own feelings. The British Government in dealing with debt questions were always ready to take a much lower figure than their paper claim. The British settlement of the American debt whereby the whole amount was to be repaid stood alone in such transactions. The British Government were anxious for a statesmanlike settlement of the present difficulties. Irish interests were dear to them, but if there was to be an agreement, it must take the form of a real and not a derisory settlement. If Free State Ministers felt in a position to make any suggestion, he would at once consult his colleagues in the Cabinet.

LORD BIRKENHEAD said that ever since the Treaty, he had watched anxiously the fortunes of the Irish Free State, and he entreated the Free State Ministers to put forward for discussion a figure of a character that the British Government would have some chance of successfully defending. It would not be necessary to put forward at the present time a binding figure, but merely a figure as a basis of discussion. He suggested that Irish Ministers might care to consider this question among themselves.

MR. CHURCHILL said that the British Government were in a position to offer a moratorium to the Free State, but if this was of no use to them, there remained the alternative of a definite figure on which to reach a settlement. If Free State Ministers would put forward such a figure, he and his colleagues would at once consider it and then set to work in regard to devising a method of payment. The debt settlement terms exacted from Great Britain by the United States were severe, and there was no need to take that transaction as a model. If a figure could be fixed as the total amount of the debt, he did not anticipate any difficulty in regard to the period of payment.

LORD BIRKENHEAD suggested as an alternative that it might be possible to grant a moratorium for a period of x years unless agreement was reached at any period in the meanwhile.

MR. O'HIGGINS said that politically a moratorium offered no advantage to the Free State. It would indeed only serve to make Article 5 a more sinister reality to the people than ever before. The experience they had had in regard to Article 12 would constantly be held before them as an indication of what they might expect under an arbitration at the conclusion of the moratorium period. Postponement of a decision would redouble the fears at present entertained on this score.

LORD SALISBURY said that His Majesty's Government were anxious to settle this question by agreement, but if that could not be achieved, it must be borne in mind that the Award of the Boundary Commission would inevitably become operative.

MR. COSGRAVE observed that the Free State would not be the only country that would bear the disadvantages attaching to that course.

LORD SALISBURY suggested that possible agreement might be reached by combining the principles of a moratorium and of an agreed figure as to the total amount of the debt due by the Free State. Under such an arrangement no payments in respect of the debt so agreed would be made before a certain date. Such an arrangement would have the advantage of refuting the alarmist forecasts by people such as de Valera regarding the total amount of the debt, and would also relieve the Free State Government from immediate financial pressure. In considering such a solution, it was necessary to bear in mind that the British Government were not in a position to accept a derisory figure.

MR. O'HIGGINS referred to the possibility mentioned by Lord Salisbury of the Boundary Commission's Award becoming operative. The publication of that Award would no doubt create a legal position, but it was impossible to forecast the consequences that would flow from the position so created. It was safe, however, to say that no good would come to the British Government or the Free State Government or the Government of Northern Ireland from such a situation. If the Free State Ministers were to return to Dublin without having reached a settlement, and being in consequence politically bankrupt, the primary responsibility for the conduct of affairs in the Free State would inevitably, within a short period, pass to others. He would regard such a result as a grave misfortune both for Ireland and for Great Britain. There was, he believed, at the present time, an opportunity of obtaining durable peace between Northern Ireland and the Free State. Was that opportunity to be lost because the British Government were not willing to make a contribution to a settlement by agreeing to forego phantom millions of money that they could never hope to obtain?

MR. CHURCHILL said that the public that the British Government would have to convince would not admit the accuracy of this view.

MR. COSGRAVE argued that the soundness of this contention was borne out by a comparison between the situation of Northern Ireland and of the Free State. Northern Ireland had a balance of revenue over expenditure and it was for this reason that they were able to make a contribution to the British Exchequer. The Free State Government had no such balance from which to make payments in respect of debt. There was, moreover, an immense disparity between North East Ireland and the Free State in regard to the proportion of the population that must be regarded as uneconomic. In the Free State the number of persons dependent on uneconomic holdings represented approximately one-third of the whole people. The Free State had not only been unable to balance their Budget, but had been forced to maintain the tax on beer and postal charges at a higher level than that in Great Britain, while their old age pension services were on a less generous scale. Northern Ireland paid no higher taxes than, and enjoyed as generous scale of social services as, Great Britain, but even so had been able to balance their Budget.

The Free State had moreover a national debt of £18 millions, and were paying annually in land purchase annuities a sum of £3 ¼ millions, the bulk of which left the country. They were also bearing a burden of £2 millions in respect of pensions[,] much of which also was paid out of the country. If Old Age Pensions were added, the total charges in respect of pensions amounted to no less than £5 millions. No one ever expected that the Free State would be called upon to bear higher taxes and receive less advantages than they had prior to the Treaty of 1921.

MR. CHURCHILL said that for long periods of time there was a surplus of exports over imports in Ireland.

MR. COSGRAVE believed there had only been a surplus during the war period. In the 17 years since 1909 when Old Age Pensions began, there had been an adverse balance for 10 years. If the Treaty had never been signed, Ireland would have been a liability and not an asset to England.

MR. CHURCHILL did not believe that this was a permanent condition, and he anticipated that future years would show a surplus. As regards the fixing of a figure at which the debt should be settled, the most important point to consider was the amount to be paid per annum. This was a more practical way of approaching the question than attempting to fix a capital sum, the size of which might look alarming. All that he asked the Free State Ministers to put forward in the first instance was an impression of a figure; it was not necessary for them to make an offer.

The Meeting then (1.15 p.m.) adjourned for Lunch.

No. 363 NAI DT S4720A

Draft notes of a conference held in the Board Room, Treasury Chambers, Whitehall, London
(Secret) (C.A./H./48 – 6th Minutes)
LONDON, 3.50 pm, 2 December 1925

PRESENT.

Great Britain.
The Right Hon. Winston S. Churchill, C.H., M.P., Chancellor of the Exchequer. (In the Chair)
The Most Hon. The Marquess of Salisbury, K.G., G.C.V.O., C.B., Lord Privy Seal. (Left early)
The Rt. Hon. The Earl of Birkenhead, Secretary of State for India. (Arrived late).

Irish Free State.
Mr. W.T. Cosgrave, T.D., President of the Executive Council, Irish Free State.
Mr. Kevin O'Higgins, T.D., Vice-President of the Executive Council, Irish Free State.
Mr. J. O'Byrne, K.C., Attorney-General.

Secretaries.
Mr. T. Jones, Deputy Secretary, Cabinet Secretariat.
Mr. D. O'Hegarty, Secretary to the Executive Council, Irish Free State

At 3.30 p.m. when the meeting was about to begin, Mr. Cosgrave stated that he saw no basis for a proposal from his side. Neither he nor Mr. O'Higgins were expert financiers. He was satisfied that Sir James Craig would not meet them with adequate concessions. He then indicated that he desired a private conversation with the Chancellor of the Exchequer. They adjourned to the room of the Financial Secretary to the Treasury and returned about 3.50 p.m.

On their return, the Chancellor of the Exchequer said that two alternative proposals had been suggested by Mr. Cosgrave:

(a) The debt of the Free State should be fixed at £6 millions, the payment spread over an agreed period, or

(b) Article 5 should be waived and the Free State should repay the British Government moneys paid for compensation since 1921 plus 10 per cent on the awards made by the Courts under the Damage to Property Act 1923.

LORD SALISBURY, who had to leave at this point for the House of Lords, said that as then advised he was unable to accept either of these proposals.

THE CHANCELLOR OF THE EXCHEQUER emphasised that outside these payments there were others which would not be affected and he referred specifically to the importance of reaching agreement on the payment of income tax deducted by the Free State from the Land Purchase Annuities.

THE CHANCELLOR OF THE EXCHEQUER undertook to place the Free State proposals before the Cabinet at a special meeting which had been summoned for six o'clock that evening.

After the Free State representatives had withdrawn, LORD BIRKENHEAD called attention to the unfortunate economic situation of the Free State and to the undesirability of fixing payments which they could not possibly hope to discharge.

After the meeting, Mr. Cosgrave dictated to Mr. Jones the following as roughly embodying the proposals which he had in mind:-

Proposed Agreement under Article V.
In 1921 when Treaty was made about £10 millions had been decreed in the Courts for damage to property. The Wood Renton Commission was set up to review these awards and apportion the liability to each Government. Our proposal is that we take over and repay to British Government sums they have paid under these awards. The Irish Free State undertakes to pay also 10 per cent of the total sums awarded by the Courts under the Damage to Property Act, 1923, in 5% compensation bonds.

Or -

As an alternative the Irish Free State will pay subject to allowances in respect of a moratorium £250,000 a year for 60 years.

No. 364 NAI DT S4720A

Draft notes of a conference held in the Board Room, Treasury Chambers, Whitehall, London
(Secret) (C.A./H./48 – 7th Minutes)
LONDON, 7.45 pm, 2 December 1925

PRESENT.

Great Britain.
The Right Hon. Winston S. Churchill, C.H., M.P., Chancellor of the Exchequer. (In the Chair)
The Right Hon. Sir John Anderson, Permanent Under Secretary of State for Home Affairs.
Mr. P.J. Grigg, Principal Private Secretary to the Chancellor of the Exchequer.

Irish Free State.
Mr. W.T. Cosgrave, T.D., President of the Executive Council, Irish Free State.
Mr. Kevin O'Higgins, T.D., Vice-President of the Executive Council, Irish Free State.
Mr. J. O'Byrne, K.C., Attorney General.

Secretaries.

Mr. T. Jones, Deputy Secretary, Cabinet Secretariat.

Mr. D. O'Hegarty, Secretary to the Executive Council, Irish Free State.

THE CHANCELLOR OF THE EXCHEQUER stated that he had explained to the Cabinet the alternative proposals made earlier that day by the Free State representatives. The Cabinet had carefully considered them and had accepted them in principle. They had done so in order to give one more manifestation of their desire to make the Treaty policy a permanent success. There were certain outstanding matters apart from Article 5 which it was desirable should be settled now once for all. He suggested that the Free State Minister of Finance[1] and his advisers should be summoned to London at the earliest moment. The Cabinet preferred the alternative proposal which was based on compensation. It would be necessary to define it in more detail than had been possible that day and to agree a method of payment.

He wished to repeat the expression of his satisfaction in making this announcement of the Cabinet's agreement to the representatives of the Free State and to have been authorised to make it in the most friendly and generous temper.

MR. COSGRAVE agreed that his Finance Minister should be summoned immediately and that among the outstanding matters to be fixed up should be the Income Tax deductions on Land Purchase Annuity payments.

MR. COSGRAVE (continuing) said that he most gladly welcomed the action of the British Cabinet. It would go far to cement the friendship of the two peoples. He appreciated fully the great care the question had received at the hands of His Majesty's Government and from the Chancellor personally. He knew something of the financial troubles which weighed upon him. His own Irish burdens were colossal. The arrangement now proposed showed a spirit of neighbourly comradeship which had never before been revealed. The active cooperation of Sir James Craig in promoting this spirit was also most welcome.

THE CHANCELLOR OF THE EXCHEQUER said that he understood the two alternative proposals were to be regarded as roughly equivalent in respect of the payment to be made. The details could be arranged on the next day. It would be a triple arrangement involving the acceptance of the present boundary, the waiving of Article 5, and the recognition that the burden of compensation would be assumed by the Free State.

MR. O'HIGGINS said that the Cabinet had chosen the form of payment which would be the better, politically, for the Executive Council. It would enable them to say that they were prepared to shoulder their own burdens arising out of the disturbances in Ireland.

THE CHANCELLOR OF THE EXCHEQUER said that he had informed the Cabinet of Sir James Craig's concurrence in the proposed arrangement so far as Northern Ireland was concerned.

[1] Ernest Blythe.

MR. COSGRAVE said that while Sir James Craig would be able to announce that he had given nothing away it was clearly understood between them that every effort would be made to promote goodwill between North and South.

MR. O'HIGGINS promised that what seven men could do to clothe the agreement with the spirit of friendship should be done, and they would also use what influence they possessed to induce the Nationalist members in Ulster to take their place in the Northern Parliament.

After MR. COSGRAVE had again expressed his gratitude for the generosity of the terms proposed and his recognition of the courage and resource of the Chancellor, the conference adjourned until 10.30 a.m. on Thursday, December 3rd.

No. 365 NAI DT S4720A

Draft notes of a conference held in the Board Room, Treasury Chambers, Whitehall, London
(Secret) (C.A./H./48 – 8th Minutes)
LONDON, 10.45 am, 3 December 1925

Present.

Great Britain

The Right Hon. Winston S. Churchill, C.H., M.P., Chancellor of the Exchequer. (In the Chair).
The Right Hon. Sir John Anderson, Permanent Under Secretary of State for Home Affairs.
Sir Frederick Liddell, K.C.B., Parliamentary Counsel.
Mr. G.C. Upcott, C.B., Deputy Controller of Establishments.
Mr. G.G. Whiskard, C.B., Assistant Secretary, Colonial Office.
Mr. P.J. Grigg, Private Secretary to the Chancellor of the Exchequer.
Mr. E.H. Marsh, C.B., C.M.G., C.V.O., Private Secretary to the Chancellor of the Exchequer.

Irish Free State.

Mr. W.T. Cosgrave, T.D., President of the Executive Council, Irish Free State.
Mr. Kevin O'Higgins, T.D., Vice-President of the Executive Council, Irish Free State.
Mr. J. O'Byrne, K.C., T.D., Attorney General, Irish Free State.

Secretaries.

Mr. T. Jones, Deputy Secretary, Cabinet Secretariat.
Mr. A.F. Hemming, Cabinet Secretariat.

Mr. D. O'Hegarty, Secretary to the Executive Council, Irish Free State.

THE CHANCELLOR OF THE EXCHEQUER stated that in his view the amount of payment to be fixed should cover the Wood Renton awards and personal injuries and the proposal for a ten per cent addition should be dropped. The effect of adding ten per cent would be to swell the claims on the fund. He would prefer to meet the hard cases needing further assistance in another way.

In the course of that day it would be necessary to draw up an agreement which could be signed by the three Prime Ministers and possibly be published in the press immediately. He had prepared a first draft of a suitable preamble which he would read to the Conference (Appendix).[1] It would not be necessary to include the question of political prisoners in the Agreement.

MR. COSGRAVE approved generally the terms of the draft preamble.

MR. O'HIGGINS asked whether it might be possible to add a paragraph on the following lines:

> 'In the event of the Government of the Irish Free State and the Government of Northern Ireland at any time entering into an agreement for the political union of all Ireland the British Government and the Government of the Irish Free State will respectively promote such legislation and take such steps as may be necessary to give effect to such agreement.'

Its inclusion would have a sentimental and political value.

THE CHANCELLOR OF THE EXCHEQUER was doubtful of the wisdom of incorporating this addition in view of the possible opposition of eminent Ministers. But he would consider the point.

MR. COSGRAVE agreed that if it were found difficult the point should not be pressed.

THE CHANCELLOR OF THE EXCHEQUER raised the question of the Prime Minister seeing the members of the Boundary Commission with a view to asking them to suppress or postpone the issue of their Report and Award. He proposed that in the first instance the Prime Minister should see the Commission and that later, if agreeable to the Commission, the three Prime Ministers should meet the Commission and make a formal application to them to suppress the Award. It could be published later as a matter of historical interest.

Some discussion took place as to the time when legislation should be introduced in the British and Free State Parliaments to give effect to the Agreement. MR. COSGRAVE'S view that there should be no unavoidable delay and that action should be taken if possible in the course of the next week was generally shared by those present.

The Conference agreed –

(1) That the Prime Minister should be asked to invite the Boundary Commission to meet him that afternoon and that he should inform the members of the position reached by the three Governments. If they indicated a willingness to suppress the Award, a meeting with them should be held later in the day at which the three Prime Ministers should present a joint address asking that the Award should be withheld.

(2) That a Committee should meet at once to prepare the Agreement for signature by the Prime Ministers, the Committee to consist of:-

[1] Not printed.

Sir John Anderson.	Mr. O'Higgins.
Sir Frederick Liddell.	Mr. O'Byrne.
Mr. Hemming. (Secretary).	

(3) That a Committee should meet to agree and record the details of the financial settlement between the two countries, the Committee to consist of:-

Sir John Anderson.	Mr. Cosgrave.
Mr. Upcott.	
Mr. Whiskard.	
Mr. O'Hegarty. (Secretary).	

No. 366 NAI DT S4730

Draft note of proceedings of a meeting in 11 Downing Street
LONDON, 11 am, 3 December 1925

Present.

Right Hon. Sir John Anderson.	Mr. Cosgrave.
Mr. Upcott.	Mr. O'Hegarty.
Mr. Whiskard.	
Mr. Waterfield.	

The principle having been already agreed that the Free State Government should accept liability for payment for all material damage done in the Irish Free State, and Mr. Cosgrave having offered an annuity of £250,000 for 60 years in settlement of this liability, the Conference considered what relation this offer bore to the total amount of liability undertaken.

Mr. Upcott said that the present capital value of the said annuity, calculated at 3 ½% interest, was £6,236,000. The liabilities which the British Government had already incurred, or would have to incur under existing agreements, on account of damage to property in the Irish Free State, were as follows (the calculation being necessarily provisional and approximate):

	£.
British share of Pre-truce awards of Compensation (I.) Comm. (prior to 1st July, 1924).	3,720,500
British share of defended Decrees.	178,500
War Compensation awards and ex-gratia payments.	20,000
British share of Reinstatement awards outstanding (before 1/7/24).	375,000
Balance outstanding under £900,000 Agreement.	524,800
	£4,868,800[1]

The total thus fell short of the capital liability which the Free State had offered to assume, by about £1,500,000, and the British representatives suggested that, in order to square the account, the Free State Government should be deemed to have undertaken to repay the second moiety (£1,500,000) of the compensation

[1] The total as originally printed is incorrect.

payable to the Irish Railways under the Irish Railways Settlement Act, 1922, which might be regarded as within the scope of the undertaking. Mr. Cosgrave, however, could not see his way to accept this suggestion. He preferred that the Free State should be regarded as having assumed liability for repayment of the above sums, together with interest at 5% on the amounts already paid by the British Government to 31st December, 1925 (subsequently ascertained to be £268,174), making a total of approximately £5,100,000.

The discussion then turned on the offer of the Free State Government to increase all payments made by them on foot of post-truce claims (including cases 'reported' as well as cases in which awards were given) by 10%. Mr. Whiskard pointed out that the British Government had been obliged to promise a measure of additional compensation to those 'loyalists' in Southern Ireland who had suffered really exceptional hardship, which could not be brought within the scope of the Damage to Property Compensation Acts, and though the cost of this undertaking could not yet be calculated, it would certainly exceed the 10% increase offered by the Free State Government in such cases. The British Government would prefer that the Free State should place a lump sum at their disposal to meet these exceptional cases, instead of paying a flat-rate increase of 10% on all awards, which would be much more expensive to the Free State. Mr. Cosgrave, however, preferred to adhere to the 10% increase, but offered to discharge the capital liability to be issued by the Free State as above mentioned by an immediate payment of £150,000, to be followed by the proposed annuity of £250,000 a year for 60 years commencing on 1st April, 1926. If these payments were capitalised at 4¾%, the resultant figure of present value would be approximately equivalent to the capital liability referred to above. While some objection might be taken to this method of computation, Mr. Cosgrave felt that he could justify it to the Dáil more easily than any other which could be suggested.

The British representatives agreed to recommend the Chancellor of the Exchequer to accept this proposal.

It was agreed that payments should be made as follows:

£150,000 on the 1st January, 1926, and the first payment of the annuity on the 1st April, 1926, and the second and succeeding payments on the 1st April in each subsequent year up to 1985.

That the initial payments as they fall due from the Irish Free State under this Agreement should be set off against the outstanding liability of the British Government under existing agreements, which would henceforward cease to be payable in cash.

An explanatory account being rendered by the British Government as soon as possible after the 1st January next and periodically thereafter.

No. 367 NAI DT S4720A

Notes of a conference with the Irish Boundary Commission held in Stanley Baldwin's Room, House of Commons (Secret) (C.P.503(25))

LONDON, 5.15 pm, 3 December 1925

PRESENT:-

The Rt. Hon. Stanley Baldwin, M.P. British Prime Minister.
The Rt. Hon. W.S. Churchill, C.H., M.P., British Chancellor of the Exchequer.
Mr. W.T. Cosgrave, T.D., President of the Executive Council, Irish Free State.
The Rt. Hon. Sir James Craig, Bart., Prime Minister of Northern Ireland.
Mr. Justice Feetham, Chairman, Irish Boundary Commission.
Mr. J.R. Fisher, Member, Irish Boundary Commission.

Secretaries:-

Mr. T. Jones, Deputy Secretary, Cabinet Secretariat.
Mr. F.B. Bourdillon, Secretary, Irish Boundary Commission.

THE PRIME MINISTER stated that he had just had a short conversation with Mr. Justice Feetham and Mr. Fisher, and had given to them a brief résumé of the happenings of the last few days. He had indicated to them that a settlement was about to be reached which was agreeable to the three Governments, and he had explained that if the Agreement were ratified, it would supersede the Commissioners' Report. A difficult situation had arisen, but he was sure that all would wish to help each other. He invited Mr. Justice Feetham to address the Conference.

MR. JUSTICE FEETHAM said that he wished to make the following points on behalf of Mr. Fisher and himself. The terms of the proposed Award had been agreed in October. The Commission had studied the matter carefully, had heard everybody, and while the Award would disappoint many, it would also meet the wishes of many on the Border, and remove difficulties which were severely felt. The present Border was an accident. The grievances found at particular places were serious.

MR. JUSTICE FEETHAM proceeded to quote the following examples of drawbacks attaching to the present line:-

(a) the difficulties of the farmers who lived in County Donegal for whom Derry was the market town;
(b) the difficulties caused by the present frontier at Pettigo;
(c) the complicated situation as regards the roads at Belleek;
(d) the position of Drummully and the Clones area.

Continuing, he said that the new Boundary as proposed would produce great improvement on both sides. While the Governments had to decide their action on larger and broader grounds than the Commissioners, he hoped that their findings would not be entirely disregarded, and that a way would be kept open for the removal of the more acute anomalies revealed by the enquiry.

In the second place, while the Commissioners recognised that the paramount interest was to secure peace and goodwill, and that it must overwhelm smaller issues, it was most important to remove from the public mind the idea that the Award was based on a betrayal of the interests of the Free State. In the circumstances which had developed, the Award had been debated with great vigour and condemned in the absence of accurate information as to its real character. The Report ought therefore to be published, so that the public should not be left permanently under a delusion. The good faith of the Tribunal was at stake. So was the method of arbitration which had been adopted. The Governments were charged with having influenced the Tribunal improperly, and it would be a bad service to the profession which he represented if he allowed it to be thought that he had betrayed his trust. He urged most strongly that the Governments should not attempt to muzzle the Commissioners, and that the Report should be brought before the public in the last resort. The Agreement about to be signed ought not to be based on the idea that the Commissioners had betrayed the interests entrusted to them.

MR. COSGRAVE said that it had been his deliberate opinion all through that there was bound to be dissensions whatever the verdict; that it would leave bitterness behind. The Award involved the transfer of a considerable number of people from one area to another. He had not seen the proposed Award, but he understood that x persons were to be removed from the Free State to Ulster, and y persons from Ulster to the Free State.

MR. JUSTICE FEETHAM: 'We sent you the particulars of our Report'.

MR. COSGRAVE said that he had not seen them. In the present conditions x persons would have a cause of complaint against himself, and y persons against Sir James, and no amount of explanation would satisfy them. He had made up his mind that if good relations with Ulster were to be secured, they had better come by voluntary growth, and that any cast-iron agreement would be thwarted by the supporters of Sir James and by his own. It was important to avoid providing a rallying ground for agitation. If the demobilisation of the Specials took place naturally, that would be avoided. Every Government has its opponents, and if thousands of the supporters of Sir James Craig objected to the new line, and similarly thousands of his own supporters objected, that would not lead to stable and peaceful relations.

MR. JUSTICE FEETHAM pointed out that at present everyone had his own misleading figures.

MR. COSGRAVE replied that they were problematical. He did not wish to speak disrespectfully, but he believed that it would be in the interests of Irish peace that the Report should be burned or buried, because another set of circumstances had arrived, and a bigger settlement had been reached beyond any that the Award of the Commission could achieve.

SIR JAMES CRAIG said that the matter divided itself in two. If the settlement succeeded it would be a great dis-service to Ireland, North and South, to have a map produced showing what would have been the position of the persons on the Border had the Award been made. If the settlement came off and nothing was published, no-one would know what would have been his fate. He himself had not seen the map of the proposed new Boundary. When he returned home he would be questioned on the subject and he preferred to be able to say that he did not know the terms of the proposed Award. He was certain that it would be better that no-one should ever know accurately what their position would have been.

In the second place he wished to say that he felt strongly for the Tribunal and regretted the charges which had been made against them; made no doubt in the heat of the moment. Would it not be possible to apologise? If the settlement were made in the right spirit it ought to be possible to satisfy Mr. Justice Feetham and Mr. Fisher that no foundation existed for the charges made. All of them had said hot things in their time. In the case of the Commission he had been rather an onlooker, but he hoped that Mr. Cosgrave out of the largeness of his heart would be able to say that the Commissioners had conducted their proceedings on the basis of strict justice.

MR. COSGRAVE replied that he would undertake to devote a paragraph of the speech he was about to make to this aspect of the subject. His statement would be conceived in the hope of giving satisfaction. He was of the same view as Sir James Craig in regard to examining the map, but on the general question he would be prepared to say that when an examination of this problem was made various judgments became possible and it did not follow that they were not honestly made.

MR. FISHER said that he was sure that Dr. MacNeill would admit that no word of bitterness had passed between them. They had worked closely together and he had never complained.

MR. COSGRAVE undertook to submit the paragraph of his speech to Dr. MacNeill so that he could see that he was dealing justly with the matter.

MR. FISHER said that he was sure there were a number of difficult points on the Border on which the findings of the Commission would be valuable to Sir James Craig and Mr Cosgrave if they could together consider them later.

MR. COSGRAVE welcomed the suggestion and addressing Sir James Craig added 'One of us no doubt will hear from the other?'

MR. JUSTICE FEETHAM said that the Report ought to be completed and presented to the British Government and some part of it ought to be published, especially the part dealing with questions of interpretation. Unless that were done it would be difficult for the public to understand why the interpretation adopted by the Commission could not possibly have the effect desired in the Free State.

THE PRIME MINISTER said that publication might have very different effects in Ireland and in this country. Sir James Craig and Mr. Cosgrave could speak for

Ireland. It was the fortunes of Ireland which were at stake. He was most anxious to meet the wishes of the Commission if possible. At the moment the important thing was that the matter should be hung up until the Agreement became an accomplished fact. The situation might present a different aspect in a week or two after the discussions in Parliament.

MR. FEETHAM pointed out that the question of publication would undoubtedly arise in the course of the Debate in Parliament.

MR. CHURCHILL said that he had been mixed up with Irish negotiations since 1910. It was this very question of Tyrone and Fermanagh which had throughout been found most insoluble. Even when we were on the verge of Civil War and confronted with a situation which had no parallel for generations, the Buckingham Palace Conference broke down. Then came the Great War in the course of which Empires disappeared, and after the War a controversy about these same parishes emerged again and nothing would induce the two Governments to agree. The Bill of 1920 was nearly wrecked on this issue and it had so nearly wrecked the settlement reached in the Treaty that the question was left uncleared, one side understanding one thing and the other side another. It was inherent in the circumstances of the case and inevitable that it should be left in a certain vagueness. Then came the labours of the Boundary Commission, and now suddenly the two Parties have settled the matter out of Court. The issue is finished, and so is the work of the Commission. The work of the Commission had led to this settlement. Neither he nor the Prime Minister had met Mr. Justice Feetham before that day. The only question that could possibly be in the minds of right thinking people was the peace of Ireland. It was a great sacrifice that this admirable report should not be published. Over the whole area of the Empire it will be felt that something has happened which has brought peace, and it will be recognised that these secret labours of the Commission have profoundly helped that peace. The withholding of publication was therefore a sacrifice that in the circumstances the Commissioners might properly make. Not the slightest slur on their integrity would rest on them.

THE PRIME MINISTER said he was satisfied that a solution would never have been reached without the Commission.

MR. CHURCHILL, continuing, said he would beg the Commission to leave their reputation in the hands of the three Governments. Let them make their report to the British Government and leave it to their discretion. As a historical document it might some day appear. At present it was absolutely in the public interest to merge it in the happier prospect, although it had been the vehicle and agency by which the miracle of peace had come about.

MR. JUSTICE FEETHAM said that he wished to put no obstacle in the way of the Government. On the other hand, he did not wish the public to be deluded. The position was not as described by Mr. Churchill. The view which prevailed among the public was that the Commission had prepared a report which was thoroughly discreditable to them, and therefore it had better not be published. That impression had to be removed.

Testimonials from Sir James Craig or Mr. Cosgrave could not be of much value as they had not seen the report. The Commission were being judged on the basis of forecasts. He could not deceive himself into believing that an Agreement if reached would redound to the credit of the Commission. It would be said that the Commission had made a mess of their business. He did not read the newspapers, but he understood it was suggested that they had acted under improper influences. The Report ought to be presented and received by the British Government.

THE PRIME MINISTER said that he agreed that the Report ought to be received by his Government, and he had some sympathy with the suggestion that the principles which had guided the Commission in dealing with Article 12 should be broadly stated and published.

MR. JUSTICE FEETHAM said the Commissioners could indicate the portions of the Report suitable for publication, without any reference to areas.

MR. CHURCHILL suggested that the Report could be presented and that it might be accompanied by a letter addressed to the Prime Minister, and this letter might be published. The letter might run:-

> 'We are informed that the three Governments have come to an Agreement, and in these circumstances we do not propose to publish our Award, but we wish to place on record the principles which have guided us in the discharge of our task. The Report itself will be presented to the British Government and will be available should it be deemed desirable to make it public at some future date.'

MR. JUSTICE FEETHAM agreed that the Report should be completed and presented. It would state principles and go into the full details underlying the Award. After that had been done the Commissioners could discuss with the Prime Minister what portions would be suitable for publication.

THE PRIME MINISTER agreed, and said it might be possible to meet later to examine the form of any communication to be made to the public.

MR. COSGRAVE said that he and Sir James Craig were bound to be careful to avoid mistakes in handling their own people. If any portions of the actual Report were published, they would not be discussed on their merits. The critics would not be a judicial tribunal. The Commissioners based themselves on law and evidence, but if the public were given extracts, enquiries and controversy would be set in motion, fruitful of harm.

SIR JAMES CRAIG thought the demand of Mr. Justice Feetham was reasonable, and he was willing to leave it to the Prime Minister and Mr. Justice Feetham to agree on what should be published.

THE PRIME MINISTER asked whether the Commissioners had any idea of the date at which publication should take place, if it were decided to publish anything.

MR. JUSTICE FEETHAM replied that it should be without undue delay but that they did not wish a moment chosen which would embarrass the Government.

MR. CHURCHILL repeated that he thought the proper course would be for the Commissioners to complete and present their Report, and to arrange for a covering letter embodying the reasons which vindicate the principles which had guided the Commissioners.

MR. JUSTICE FEETHAM said he could not undertake not to use in such letter some of the language used in the Report.

SIR JAMES CRAIG asked whether it would be any use associating the Commission in some way with the Agreement, but this suggestion did not find favour.

MR. JUSTICE FEETHAM said he understood the Commission would be formally asked not to issue their Award at all. That would be a good reason for holding their hand. They wanted to help in any way.

THE PRIME MINISTER asked Mr. Justice Feetham to let him have a proof of what he would like published at some later date.

MR. JUSTICE FEETHAM said that expectations had been aroused in connection with the Treaty which were bound to be disappointed.

THE PRIME MINISTER said that no one could draw a boundary on which all would agree.

MR. COSGRAVE said that no possible boundary could have been drawn which would not give rise to discontent, and he would say that when he next spoke on the subject.

MR. JUSTICE FEETHAM said that the Commissioners would state that Article 12 could not have the effect which the people of the Free State had been led to expect. The instrument in which the Free State trusted had broken in their hands. Article 12 had not been expressed so as to bear the interpretation put on it by the Free State. The Free State would be put in the position that the Court had decided against them for very good reasons. The Free State was the only Government which had come before the Commission and it had naturally tried to put its case in the strongest possible manner. The Commissioners, desirous of reaching the right conclusion, had rejected the main contention of the Free State.

THE PRIME MINISTER said that he recognised the independent position in which the Commissioners stood, and he fully appreciated the anxiety of Mr. Justice Feetham to justify himself in the eyes of the judicial fraternity, and to show that the motives which had guided him were worthy of the high traditions of his profession.

MR. JUSTICE FEETHAM said he was also anxious that arbitration as a method of procedure should not be damaged in the eyes of the public.

MR. CHURCHILL said he was convinced that the best way would be for the Commissioners to embody in a separate communication the judicial principles on which they had acted, bringing in a reference to the Articles of Agreement and stating their decision not to publish the report. The letter might be published some weeks hence at a time when it would cause no trouble.

MR. COSGRAVE said the moment chosen would be an important factor.

THE PRIME MINISTER said he would be glad to fall in with the course suggested, and when he came to speak on the subject in the House of Commons he would take the line that the British Government and the Free State Government had hoped to reach a settlement by arbitration; the facts had been too strong for them; no settlement of that kind could give satisfaction; this they have now recognised for the first time and they have agreed to stand on the present Boundary.

MR. CHURCHILL suggested that the Prime Minister when speaking on the Bill should vindicate the Tribunal.

THE PRIME MINISTER said he would go at length into that and would trace its effect in Ireland. The Irish menaced with an imminent judgment had come together. The Governments owed an immense debt of gratitude to the Commission. They were an independent body and could issue their report tomorrow if they so desired, but after over a year of intense work, smarting, as all who were not politicians must smart, under unfair attacks; seeing the gravity of the situation they had welcomed the larger solution. It was very fine of them.

MR. COSGRAVE said he would like to add his appreciation of the way in which the Commission had met them. It would be at least of some satisfaction to them that it was through their agency that he and Sir James Craig had come together and made peace.

SIR JAMES CRAIG endorsed what Mr. Cosgrave had said. The Commission had done splendidly.

MR. JUSTICE FEETHAM said that he and his colleagues recognised that peace was the better way and all they desired was to avert any danger which might arise from the covering up of the report. He asked how soon it was hoped to conclude the Agreement.

MR. CHURCHILL said he hoped it would be signed that evening and would be announced in the newspapers on the following day.

MR. JUSTICE FEETHAM then read a press announcement,[1] which the Commissioners had prepared with a view to removing the wrong impressions under which the public were labouring, impressions which had received a quasi confirmation from speeches in Ireland. He recognised, however, that a new situation had arisen and that publication at this moment would be undesirable.

[1] Not printed.

No. 368 NAI DT S4720A

Agreement Amending and Supplementing the Articles of Agreement for a Treaty between Great Britain and Ireland to which the force of law was given by the Irish Free State (Agreement) Act, 1922, and by the Constitution of the Irish Free State (Saorstát Éireann) Act, 1922

LONDON, 3 December 1925

WHEREAS on the 6th day of December, nineteen hundred and twenty-one, Articles of Agreement for a Treaty between Great Britain and Ireland were entered into:

AND WHEREAS the said Articles of Agreement were duly ratified and given the force of law by the Irish Free State (Agreement) Act, 1922, and by the Constitution of the Irish Free State (Saorstát Éireann) Act, 1922:

AND WHEREAS the progress of events and the improved relations now subsisting between the British Government, the Government of the Irish Free State and the Government of Northern Ireland and their respective peoples make it desirable to amend and supplement the said Articles of Agreement, so as to avoid any causes of friction which might mar or retard the further growth of friendly relations between the said Governments and peoples:

AND WHEREAS the British Government and the Government of the Irish Free State being united in amity in this undertaking with the Government of Northern Ireland, and being resolved mutually to aid one another in a spirit of neighbourly comradeship, hereby agree as follows:—

1.—The powers conferred by the proviso to Article 12 of the said Articles of Agreement on the Commission therein mentioned are hereby revoked, and the extent of Northern Ireland for the purposes of the Government of Ireland Act, 1920, and of the said Articles of Agreement shall be such as was fixed by sub-section (2) of section one of that Act.

2.—The Irish Free State is hereby released from the obligation under Article 5 of the said Articles of Agreement to assume the liability therein mentioned.

3.—The Irish Free State hereby assumes all liability undertaken by the British Government in respect of malicious damage done since the Twenty-first day of January, Nineteen hundred and nineteen to property in the area now under the jurisdiction of the Parliament and Government of the Irish Free State, and the Government of the Irish Free State shall repay to the British Government at such time or times and in such manner as may be agreed upon moneys already paid by the British Government in respect of such damage or liable to be so paid under obligations already incurred.

4.—The Government of the Irish Free State hereby agrees to promote legislation increasing by Ten per cent. the measure of compensation under the Damage to Property (Compensation) Act, 1923, in respect of malicious damage to property done in the area now under the jurisdiction of the Parliament and Government of the Irish Free State between the Eleventh day of July, Nineteen hundred and twenty-one and the Twelfth day of May, Nineteen hundred and twenty-three, and providing for the payment of such additional compensation by the issue of Five per cent. Compensation Stock or Bonds.

5.—The powers in relation to Northern Ireland which by the Government of Ireland Act, 1920, are made powers of the Council of Ireland shall be and are hereby transferred to and shall become powers of the Parliament and the Government of Northern Ireland; and the Governments of the Irish Free State and of Northern Ireland shall meet together as and when necessary for the purpose of considering matters of common interest arising out of or connected with the exercise and administration of the said powers.

6.—This Agreement is subject to confirmation by the British Parliament and by the Oireachtas of the Irish Free State, and the Act of the British Parliament confirming this Agreement shall fix the date as from which the transfer of the powers of the Council of Ireland under this Agreement is to take effect.

Dated this 3rd day of December, 1925.

Signed on behalf of the British Government:	Signed on behalf of the Government of the Irish Free State:	Signed on behalf of the Government of Northern Ireland:
STANLEY BALDWIN.	LIAM T. MAC COSGAIR.	JAMES CRAIG.
WINSTON S. CHURCHILL.	KEVIN O'HIGGINS.	CHARLES H. BLACKMORE.
W. JOYNSON-HICKS.	EARNÁN DE BLAGHD.	Secretary to the Cabinet of Northern Ireland.
BIRKENHEAD.		
L.S. AMERY.		

No. 369 NAI DT S4720A

Statement by William T. Cosgrave and Kevin O'Higgins to the Editors of the Irish Times *and the* Irish Independent

3 December 1925

To-day we have sown the seeds of peace. The problem with which we were confronted is not new. It has baffled two generations. We faced it in circumstances fraught with the gravest possibilities. We bring back an instrument solemnly executed by the representatives of three Governments – an instrument which provides a sane and constructive solution. Born of a generous desire for peace and friendship, this agreement, accepted in the spirit in which it was negotiated and signed provides the basis of a sure and lasting peace. We confidently recommend it to the Irish people.

(Sgd)
COSGRAVE,
O'HIGGINS

No. 370 NAI DFA ES Box 29 File 192

Timothy A. Smiddy to Desmond FitzGerald (Dublin)
(MP/Sp.165/21/25)
WASHINGTON, 15 December 1925

Dear Mr. Minister:

Publicity

I enclose copy of the subjects covered in a series of pictures by the Fox Film Corporation which were recently taken in Ireland. At the invitation of the Fox Film Corporation I attended a private screening of these pictures and was very favourably impressed by their elevated character. At the request of the Company I chose those which in my opinion would be most suitable for publication. They will undoubtedly produce on American audiences an impression of Ireland quite different to that which many of them have. They give such an alluring character to Irish scenery and Irish life as to tempt many people who visit Europe to pass through Ireland either on their eastward or westward bound trip.

The Managing Director of this Company is Mr. Sheehan, a nephew of the late Bishop of Waterford.

Mr. Meighan's picture, 'Irish Luck' has met with an unusually good reception in New York and in Washington. Nothing is more calculated to advertise good features of Ireland than publicity of this character.

In addition you will be also glad to learn that some books have been recently published describing Irish scenery and presenting many interesting aspects of Irish life, the most recent of which is 'Ireland Beautiful', by Wallace Nuthing, Old America Company, Framingham, Massachusetts.

Yours sincerely,
[copy letter unsigned]

[enclosure]

IRELAND TODAY

FOX FILM CORPORATION WELCOMES YOU to a private screening of Eight Reels of pictures just made in various parts of IRELAND. These pictures are shown to you without titles. Since it will be necessary to eliminate parts of these pictures before they go out for feature distribution, we have asked you to see them in their entirety believing that you will find interest in every scene that is projected.

The subjects covered in the various reels are, briefly, as follows:

REEL ONE
Kilkenny Castle at Kilkenny; Tramore Beach; Reginald's Tower; Port of Wexford; Sheep and cows in streets at Waterford; Church at Waterford; Woollen mills at Cork; Yarn and Thread Machines; Harbor in Cork; a Brewery; Factory in Cork; Scenes about the city; Killarney Lakes; Torc Waterfalls; Dunloe Castle at Dunloe.

REEL TWO
Dunloe Castle; Scenes in Kenmare; More scenes of Dunloe Castle; Farm scenes near Kenmare; A fair in Kenmare; Road to Glengarriff; Street scene in Cork;

Cobh Harbor; Looking up the harbor towards Queenstown; The River Suir at Clonmel, Tipperary; the Rock of Cashel; the Shannon at Limerick.

REEL THREE
Senator Gogarty's Garden Party in Dublin; Mr. Harrington, Mr. Gogarty and Mrs. Harrington; Countess of Fingall, Gov. General Healy of Ireland; Lady Lavery; Closeup of Governor General Healy; President Cosgrave of the Free State and Governor General Healy; Town scenes; John McCormick; Bank of Ireland. City Hall; Police Force of the Free State; Staff: O'Carroll; MacCarthy and Gantley; General Eoin O'Duffy, Chief of Police; Scenes in Dublin; Gate to the Governor General's Home; The River Liffey; Shelton Abbey, residence of Lord Wicklow at Bray; John McCormick with friends at his home near Dublin.

REEL FOUR
Bacon Factory at Limerick; Cliff at Kilkee; Cliffs of Moher; Salmon stream at Galway River; Lynch Castle; Cladagh Village for Fishermen; Woollen Mill at Athlone; The Shannon at Athlone.

REEL FIVE
Government Building in Dublin; Residential Section; Pipe Factory showing methods of manufacture; Free State Army in battle practice; Keep Fit; The Air Force.

REEL SIX
Aeroplane shots over Dublin; Guinness's Brewery; Government building and other shots; Horses leaving the famous brewery; Scenes of the brewery; Loading boats for shipment on River Liffey; Dublin Harbor looking towards the sea; Kingstown in background.

REEL SEVEN
Scenes along the sea coast showing how the sand is piled in great heaps by the force of the winds.

REEL EIGHT
Blarney Castle; Cutting peat in the bogs; Ross Castle; Thatching straw roof; Muckross Abbey; River Shannon; Killarney Lakes; Birr Castle; Limerick Castle; Cave of Port Coon and Kerry.

No. 371 NAI DT S4730A

William T. Cosgrave to Winston Churchill (London)
DUBLIN, 21 December 1925

Dear Mr. Churchill,
I am sorry that there has been such delay in answering your letter of the 8th[1] instant, but we were so busy in getting the Parliamentary business through that I was unable to get a chance of discussing the matter with Mr. Blythe. I have just now had a conversation with him on the subject, and I gather that his representatives were over in London discussing with your Inland Revenue

[1] Not printed.

Authorities the settlement of the Double Income Tax along the lines of adopting residence as the future basis of assessment and that they only returned here on Friday last.

Mr. Blythe will lose no time in considering the report of their discussion and he hopes to be able to let you have his views at the latest by the first week of January when he will also deal with the other suggestions put forward in the Treasury Memorandum. I may say that he is not quite happy in regard to some of these suggestions but I have no doubt that at the further meeting in London which will be necessary these can all be settled in a spirit of mutual accommodation.

May I take the opportunity of thanking you for the very valuable contribution you personally made towards the solution of the problems which confronted us in our recent Conferences and of congratulating you on the successful issue which will I trust, redound to the mutual advantage of Gt. Britain and Ireland alike.

Yours sincerely,
(sgd) Liam T. MacCosgair

No. 372 UCDA LAI/H/126

William T. Cosgrave to Eoin MacNeill
Dublin, 22 December 1925

My Dear Professor,
I wished to write you during the past few weeks to convey my own personal thanks & acknowledgments for the many services you rendered to the State & to me for many years. I think I ought to have done so earlier – but perhaps it is better that the immediate circumstances of the past month should have passed before I wrote.

I wish to repeat what I said in the Dáil that the task set the Boundary Commission was to secure a Divine Solution by human agency. I have not much inside information about the work of the Boundary Commission – most of what I have being Mr Feetham's contribution to the discussion which took place in the Prime Minister's Room in the House of Commons when the P.M. Sir James Craig & myself met Messrs Feetham & Fisher.[1]

I am personally satisfied that you did what was possible in most difficult circumstances. If it be not irrelevant I should say that the best thing possible was done in our negotiations which ended by the Treaty Amendment Agreement. In the end it will I believe & hope be the best solution – but time must be allowed to enable its full benefit to be derived.

I regret your loss to the Ex[ecutive] Council. I believe that regret is shared by the other members. I am grateful for the help which you always afforded us in Council – & I shall always treasure the memory of our long association during most difficult times – and the heroic fortitude you displayed when called upon to make a big sacrifice for the decision you took in supporting the Treaty.

Believe me sincerely yours
Liam T. MacCosgair

[1] No. 367 above.

1926

No. 373 NAI DT S5985

William T. Cosgrave to Edward J. Phelan (Geneva)
DUBLIN, undated

I am much obliged for your letter of 21st January and also for the copy of the article you wrote for 'STUDIES'[1] – which was most interesting. I think the article will do much good here as the functions of the International Labour Office may not be quite well understood and it is possible that the concluding sentences - in fact the last paragraph – will serve as a corrective to the view which may be prevalent regarding the International Labour Organisation. I think it was an excellent idea of yours to get 'Studies' to publish the article, as it is unquestionably the finest periodical in Ireland. May I take the opportunity of congratulating you on the work of the office as well as the article.

I am glad of your references to the Agreement of December last. We discovered that Article XII did not solve what it had generally been believed it was designed to solve. As a matter of fact it made a solution of our difficulties with our Northern fellow-countrymen almost impossible. The settlement has, I believe, a much better effect than even we had supposed. The fever had to be abated. Already I am told there is a distinct sign of normal conditions appearing. A more cordial political understanding will come more slowly but I am certain more surely by reason of the settlement [than anything else].[2] It is the fact that Sir James won easily so far as territory goes. I am better satisfied, however, with the result than I believe he could be. And the financial settlement is eminently satisfactory. It was a great tribute to British statesmanship. What I feared more than anything was an appeal to the League. Putting myself in the position of, say, France or Spain, or even one of the South American members, my inclination would be to say go home and solve your domestic difficulties - that the League had more than enough to do to solve international problems. [There was an attempt to place the problem on an international basis.] It was originally an international question. But I am afraid the five years that elapsed made it no longer a question to be solved between the British and ourselves: it developed into a difficulty for solution between Irishmen. It is a good job that the matter has ended without any disorder. It is a good matter to be rid of Article V. It may not find immediate satisfaction to the people of the North who had been looking for political emancipation for five years. But if the seeds of ultimate unity have been sown, they have a better soil to grow in and fructify

[1] Edward J. Phelan, 'The International Labour Organisation', *STUDIES*, Vol. 14 (1925).
[2] Square brackets (here and below) inserted by hand in original.

and in that sense as well as others it is the best possible arrangement for our Northern friends.

With kindest regards and best wishes for the New Year.

[copy letter unsigned]

No. 374 NAI DT S4743A

E.M. Stephens to Diarmuid O'Hegarty

DUBLIN, 12 January 1926

A chara,

You asked me for notes on the work which was being done by this Office[1] and which should be continued under the altered conditions produced by the Boundary settlement.

I take it that the Government's policy under the agreement will be to maintain the unity of the country as far as is possible by co-operation with the Northern Government. There is no doubt that co-operation of this kind would be worked by both parties with a view to using the associations which it entails to further their respective political objectives so far as they concern the future government of the country as a whole.

The Free State Government would naturally develop its policy in such a way as to lead towards a united Ireland with Dominion status. The Northern Government would naturally endeavour to use the associations with us in order to draw us, if possible, nearer to the British system. This tendency is very plain even at this early stage. The Northern politicians have engaged in a regular propaganda, led by Mr. Pollock, Minister for Finance, in favour of a zollverein of the British Isles.

Under the altered conditions the tendency to use the North as a means of preventing divergence between us and Great Britain will undoubtedly increase. It seems essential that all our dealings with the North should be carefully watched with a view to preventing a tendency of this kind manifesting itself in subtle ways, gaining advantage before it is detected.

It has been part of the work of this office to collect for the Government's information, all available information which would throw light on political activity in the North. This involves, in the first place, a careful scrutiny of the press and the classification of all published material on such subjects as finance, police, local government and gerrymandering. It is difficult to see how co-operation could be managed unless the Government was kept fully informed on all such matters.

The financial position of Northern Ireland, both as a self-governing unit, and in its relations with the British Treasury, are also matters on which first hand and up to date information is necessary. I have been in the habit of collecting and examining all white papers, financial statements, and such documents as the Report of the Special Arbitration Committee, and reporting on them where necessary.

Some special avenue of contact with the Northern Nationalists also seems

[1] The North-Eastern Boundary Bureau.

necessary. This has hitherto been afforded by the Boundary Bureau. At present the Northern Nationalists are alienated by the recent agreement, of which they disapprove, but there is little doubt that as new conditions tend to harden, co-operation will again be possible.

As Departmental dealings develop between the Free State and Northern Ireland, questions will be raised and political tendencies disclosed, of which it would not be the ordinary duty of the Departments concerned to take cognizance. A tendency, partly disclosed by the work of one Department, would be confirmed by the work of another. If there is nobody with a full knowledge of the Government's policy towards the North to co-ordinate this information and point out its general effects, unforeseen political results might easily be produced by what at first seemed ordinary Departmental dealings.

There is a large body of political opinion in the Free State which will always demand an active Northern policy. The Government have committed themselves to an active policy of friendly co-operation. New subject matter for such co-operation will have to be constantly found. All statements made in the Dáil on such matters will have to be very carefully considered, as they will have a political effect, not only in the Free State, but in Northern Ireland.

All these matters are in their nature outside the scope of ordinary departmental activity. They are probably sufficiently important to justify the appointment of a representative in Belfast if there were not political arguments against dealing with the matter in this way. It is possible that this may be the ultimate solution, but in the meanwhile it is, I think, a matter of urgent necessity to secure continuity for the portion of our work which did not deal with the boundary itself.

You asked me to estimate the amount of my time which would have to be devoted to work of this kind if I am to continue responsibility under different conditions. The answer to this question depends on certain unknown factors. If there is to be continuous activity in relation to Northern matters, my whole time would probably be occupied. Our experience so far has been that the Northern question was like a volcano, subject to erratic eruptions. When it was active it required undivided attention, and at other times such careful watching that, I think, in future fifty per cent of my time could profitably be devoted to Northern matters at times when no particular issue was engaging the attention of the Government. It may be necessary to enlarge the work of record which we have been doing, and to review in detail the ever increasing differences in legislation and administration between the two areas. If this is to be done[,] still more of my time would be occupied.

Mise, le meas,
[signed] E.M. STEPHENS
Rúnaidhe

No. 375 NAI DFA EA 231/1/29

Extract from a letter from Timothy A. Smiddy to Desmond FitzGerald (Dublin)
WASHINGTON, 4 February 1926

Dear Mr Minister:
I have just returned from the Middle-West where I gave a series of lectures and

talks on the Irish Free State: its economic, financial, agricultural, conditions and problems; achievement of its Government; some of the High Lights of Irish History; comments on the Constitution of the Irish Free State; International Status and its political relation to Great Britain and the Dominions.

I lectured at the following:

1. The University of Michigan. This university has ten thousand full-time students on its roll. I was entertained by the President – Mr Little – and members of the Faculties who were subsequently present at my lecture.
2. The North-western University, Evanston, Illinois; it has fourteen thousand registered students. The President – Mr Walter Dill Scott – many professors, students and public were present.
3. The University Club, Evanston. The audience was composed of graduates of the North-western University and other universities who are resident in Evanston. President Scott was present as also the Mayor of Evanston. Subsequent to the lectures many questions were asked. Such questions showed an interest in the Gaelicization of Irish education and its philosophy; in the Constitution; in our universities and educational standards.

I think some surprise was occasioned by the knowledge of the liberal attitude of the Government towards non-catholics as illustrated by the personnel of the High Court and Supreme Court.

The North-western University is the centre of Methodist education in the U.S.A.
4. Reception at Evanston by the Ancient Order of Hibernians at which the State Secretary and National Secretary of the Order were present as also the Mayor of Evanston who made a very appropriate talk on the Irish Free State.
5. Reception by and address to the Catholic Ladies' Club of Evanston. Evanston is the best residential suburb of Chicago.
6. Reception by and address to the Irish Fellowship Club at the Palmer Court Hotel, Chicago. It was a distinguished gathering of 465 people. The Mayor of Chicago, Mr Dever, was among the guests and made a laudatory short speech on the Irish Free State. The members of the Supreme Court were much in evidence. Among the general audience were people representative of different views and attitudes towards Irish affairs, from the indifferent to men like John McGarry, Joseph O'Donnell and two old Fenians, a Mr Byrne and Mr O'Callaghan: the latter travelled forty five miles for the occasion, and their ages are respectively eighty five and eighty six.
7. Reception by and address to the Mid-day Club of Springfield, Illinois, which is the State Capital. The Mayor of Springfield and State Senator Hay made appropriate speeches. I visited the shrine of Abraham Lincoln[,] laid a wreath on behalf of the Government and said a few words suitable to the occasion.
8. On my return to New York I attended the reception and banquet given by Sir James and Lady Elder (Commissioner to the U.S.A. from Australia). In my capacity as Minister Plenipotentiary I was guest of honour. Six hundred were present. I was one of the speakers. The gist of my remarks was the international status of the Irish Free State; the existence of seven sovereign entities within the British Commonwealth of Nations was a stabilizer of peace, to the maintenance of which none would contribute more by her moral influence than the Irish Free State.

The outstanding impression derived from the reaction to my addresses, questions and conversations with the various types of people I met was their surprise to learn of the 'sovereign status' of the Irish Free State and that its Minister at Washington had the same diplomatic status as that of any other sovereign nation, and that he was in no way subservient to the British Embassy in so far as purely affairs of the Irish Free State were concerned. Even among many real sympathizers of the Irish Free State I have already witnessed this ignorance of our real status. In fact, they cannot realize that the Irish Free State could possibly have attained to the international status which the presence of its Minister at Washington indicates; and were under the impression that an Irish Free State Minister must be somewhat of a fiction or minister 'in air'. Even this belief existed in the minds of many in Washington until recently, when in consequence of the publicity afforded by lectures, talks, etc., our status is now fully appreciated.

It may be of interest to know that at a recent reception given by the President to the members of the diplomatic, myself and the staff of the Legation took precedence of fourteen other legations whose chiefs of mission were appointed subsequently to me. Further, as the Ambassador of Great Britain was absent the British Legation was preceded by the legations whose chiefs of mission were present. This bears out what I pointed out in a previous communication that the British Chargé d'Affaires, though a Minister Plenipotentiary and Envoy Extraordinary, is regarded by the U.S.A. State Department only as a Minister 'in air' and cannot function as a real Minister.

You might remember an article written by Sir Maurice F. Lowe, correspondent for the Morning Post, in the Baltimore Sun, November, 1924, in which he emphasized the steps adopted by the British Foreign Office to ensure that the British Embassy would at no time 'take the dust' from the feet of the Minister of the Irish Free State.

From the above you can see that his statement did not come true.

During the last few years I have observed the increasing sympathy of Americans, especially those from whom the governing classes are derived, with Great Britain. In the leading universities the vast majority of all the teaching staff are strongly pro-British both politically and socially, and very active in their endeavours to promote the entrance of the U.S.A. into the League of Nations. The same remarks apply to the influential press except the Hearst, and even the latter quite recently remarked that Great Britain gave a moral lesson to the world by the way in which she honoured her bond. Great Britain is regarded by them as the power on which the stability of Europe depends, and there is the feeling, which is freely expressed, that an 'entente cordiale' – though informal – between the peoples of the U.S.A. and Great Britain is the best guarantor of world peace.

[Matter omitted]

Yours sincerely,
[signed] T.A. SMIDDY

No. 376 NAI DFA ES Brussels

Count Gerald O'Kelly de Gallagh to Desmond FitzGerald (Dublin)
(Confidential)

BRUSSELS, 10 February 1926

A Chara,

You will remember when I was in Ireland last Spring, after lunching with the Governor General, I asked you for a document certifying that both myself and my wife had been officially presented. This document was necessary before we could be presented at the Belgian Court. Well, a Court ball took place last week and you will be interested to hear that at last the presentation in question was achieved. The application was in the first instance put in by Sir George Graham, who was very pleasant over the whole thing, though rather worried as to what uniform I should wear. When I told him that our official uniform was just plain evening dress, he appeared to be quite satisfied – Indeed he could not well have been anything else, insofar as the matter could hardly be said to be a direct concern of his – but that was not the end of the matter. When I received the official invitation from the Grand Maréchal de la Cour, this invitation was sent through the Embassy and bore on it the legend 'Uniforme ou habit de cour'. In a moment of friendly zeal on my behalf, which I believe to have been genuine (since our interview last month we are now figuratively all over each other) Sir George immediately sent down the first secretary to the office of the Grand Maréchal to point out that in the case in question, my uniform is merely evening dress. He told me over the telephone that he did this so as to make sure that I should have no difficulty in being admitted in the event of my coming in evening dress. The Grand Maréchal was absent, but his No. 2, the Comte Guy d'Oultremont, was very emphatic in stating that evening dress could not be recognised as uniform for anybody other than a member of the corps diplomatique. He advanced many cogent reasons for this ruling, all of them based on the sanctity of tradition. When the first secretary returned to the British Embassy, Sir George rang me up, told me of the conversation with d'Oultremont and suggested that if I had not a court suit available, I should compromise by wearing a military uniform, had I still possessed one as a relic of my British Army days. I thanked him for his efforts on my behalf and accepted his suggestion that I should make any demarches I wished myself with the Palace authorities. I need not tell you that the suggestion of appearing at the Court ball in British uniform appealed more to my sense of the ridiculous than of the fitting. The whole thing appeared to me to be a storm in a tea-cup, but still when you are in Rome you must do as Rome does. Fortunately the Court ball was put off from the 27th of January to the 2nd of February, owing to the death of Cardinal Mercier and this gave me time to get my bearings. Knowing the democratic tendency at present in control of the Affaires Etrangères, I took the opportunity of mentioning the case to Rolin, the chef de cabinet. As I expected he jumped saying: 'Qui vous a dit ca? Mais c'est parfaitement idiot!' He then prepared to attack the Palace authorities by telephone, but in the meantime, not having the smallest confidence in the outcome of the intervention, I made my own arrangements and was finally presented in full court dress. I confess that this dress is such that apart from the court hat which I had to my credit and the striped waistcoat which my butler has to his, it would be hard to tell one from the other.

A very noticeable feature in the Court ball was the fact that none of the Socialist ministers was present. In all there were about 3000 guests and I think I met there everybody whom I knew. The invitations were for 8.15. Presentations did not take place until, I should say about 9.30 and at 11 o'clock both myself and my wife were very glad to get home.

The entertainment is of a very national nature in this sense that all phases of public life, with the notable exception of the socialists, are represented. The entire corps diplomatique attend in full regalia. Most of the official world is there, from heads of the Departments down to comparatively junior officials, while of course, the noblesse, the bar, finance, the army and the universities are much in evidence.

Personally I am of opinion that the abstention of the socialist element is in the nature of a sop to the extreme doctrinaire element in the party, because, as I have stated, the Bal de la Cour appears to foreigners at all events as an extremely democratic festival.

The local temperament is fond of display and if there were a republican regime in force to-morrow, I am perfectly convinced that there would soon be found a suitable substitute for the Bal de la Cour which would probably be christened 'Bal du Président'.

To come back to the personal question, I am very glad indeed that we went and were seen there, because many persons could not understand why we were not there before and seemed to consider that the British Embassy were keeping us out.

On the 5th of the month, we went to a reception of the American Embassy. It is always good to be seen at the American receptions, because particularly since they have acquired the Palais d'Assche for an Embassy, the American prestige and influence here both socially and officially is considerably increased. This is also largely due to the personality of the present Ambassador and his wife, who recently showed us several unmistakable signs of friendliness.

A couple of days afterwards, I was present at a reception by Madame Jules Destrée. Her salon usually assembles politicians and intellectuals of the liberal and socialist colours. Her husband was once Minister of Education here and was formerly Minister in Petersburg. He is one of the leading intellectual lights of the socialist party. At the same time his relations are fairly catholic and one meets all shades in his house. Funnily enough, the first person who came up to me there and asked to be introduced is the new Chef du Protocole at the Affaires Etrangères, Monsieur Papeians de Morchoven. I am to see him again one of these days for a longer informal chat. I told him that his Department had probably been worried by my existence, in the past, but it is significant that when taking over control, he should go out of his way to approach me personally.

Last Friday night, I attended a lecture at the Gaulois given by Monsieur Maurice Despret, President of the Banque de Bruxelles. Taxation has been drawn very high in Belgium recently, partly owing to its weight and partly to what Despret claims to be its inequitable incidence, a good deal of feeling has been roused in financial, commercial and industrial circles, that is to say, in about half the population of Belgium and Monsieur Despret has launched a campaign for the institution of what would correspond to a Geddes Committee for reform of Belgian finances, as well as for the reduction of current expenditure. He has been carrying the firey cross around various towns in Belgium recently and his lecture at the Gaulois obtained a full house. Various Government Committees have been set up from time to time to study questions of national economy, but they have all had more or less a party colour and Despret is out for a non-party committee consisting of at the most five men who could justly be described as national figures in the worlds of finance, industry, commerce, cooperation and officialdom. He claims that such a committee should be given full authority to hear evidence and not only to study possibilities of Departmental economy, but also to study reforms in the whole method of raising revenue. He claims that the report of such a committee could not be ignored by either the Government or Parliament and cites as an example the operation of the Geddes Committee in England. He is founding a Ligue de l'Intérêt Public for which he is inviting membership. This Ligue is at present being boosted in a number of papers and is intended to serve as the medium whereby the public can keep contact with the Committee in question. Despret's lecture achieved a great success in the Gaulois, as indeed his lectures achieved a great success wherever he has delivered them. At the same time, I am not prepared to state as yet what is the general opinion in the country concerning the necessity for such a Ligue or the efficacity of Mr. Despret's remedy for the admittedly bad condition of Belgian finance. Nine tenths of the audience, in the Gaulois at all events[,] were of the higher bourgeoisie and military elements. Industry and finance and the liberal professions were strongly represented as well as the Belgian fascist committee. Under the circumstances it is not surprising that any manifestation which could be used as a stick to belabour the present coalition Government would be welcome. The military and the fascist element are particularly aggrieved with the Government's army policy at the moment, which is one of retrenchment. Yesterday several regiments were disbanded and their standards solemnly handed in to the Musée de l'Armée. In this the policy of the Belgian Government is similar to that of practically all European Governments since the war. There is no doubt that there was a good deal of popular sentiment aroused by the sight of the passing of these troops, but at the same time, I do not believe that there would be any popular demand against the disbanding of the troops, though the occasion yesterday was seized upon by certain groups to manifest against the prime minister, the Vicomte Poullet, who is a catholic, but who is accused of having sold the Catholic party to the socialists. The anti-Poullet manifestation went to the extent of his being spat upon by the crowd, but it is hard to tell how far this reflects more than a party attitude.

There has been a crisis in the Ministère de la Défense Nationale for some time past, because, owing to the programme of reforms sanctioned by the coalition cabinet, it had been determined to reduce the period of service of the conscripts to six months. The Minister for War, the General Kestens, resigned a couple of weeks ago and it was popularly stated in the conservative press that he resigned because of his opposition to this measure. At the same time, there seems to be no doubt that the motive which he gives himself for his resignation is the application of the six months service to the 1926 recruits instead of to the 1928. His resignation was followed by that of the chief of the staff and in the meantime the prime minister has taken over ad interim the Ministry of Defence. That is the situation as it stands and I confess that I do not anticipate any immediate trouble.

The Government are confronted with an imperative necessity to effect economies and that they should cut down the army in the circumstances, particularly with a semi socialist Government in power was perfectly obvious.

On reading through the latter part of this letter I find myself rubbing my eyes and wondering if I have been writing to you about Belgium, or if you have been writing to me about Ireland within the last couple of years. If fellow feelings have the value that is usually ascribed to them the 'relations' between Belgium and Ireland ought to be very cordial.

Mise, do chara,
[copy letter unsigned]

No. 377 NAI DFA LN1-4

Michael MacWhite to Desmond FitzGerald (Dublin)
(M.L. 03/019)

GENEVA, 13 February 1926

A Chara,

The Council of the League of Nations met yesterday, February 12th in a special Session in order to deal with the application of Germany for Membership of the League. The Members of the Council were of the unanimous opinion that the Assembly should be convened in extraordinary Session on the 8th of March at 3 o'clock in the afternoon to deal with the matter.

The Agenda of the extraordinary Assembly, which has been approved by the Council, will comprise four questions:-

(1) The admission of Germany,

(2) Consideration by the Assembly of proposals made by the Council concerning the application of Article 4 of the Covenant,

(3) Budget questions,

(4) Building of an Assembly Hall.

From the Agenda it may be inferred that only two Commissions - the Sixth and the Fourth - will be constituted by the Assembly. The Sixth will naturally deal with the formalities connected with the admission of Germany to Membership of the League as well as her election to a permanent seat on the Council. The Fourth Commission will fix the German contribution to the expenses of the League and decide how it is to be expended. It will also have to deal with the Architects' reports on the proposed construction of an Assembly Hall and examine this question from the commencement, as the decision arrived at by the last Assembly on this matter has been upset owing to the fact that no offer has been received for the present Secretariat Buildings.

It is thus anticipated that the Members of the League will be represented at the forthcoming Assembly by two delegates each. The big powers will very likely have larger delegations and the small and distant States will probably send only their local Representative or their Minister at Berne or at Paris.

The first question on the Agenda will not give rise to any particular difficulties, but the second item dealing with the composition of the Council is much more delicate. In view of the Locarno Agreements nobody is likely to contest the right of Germany to a Permanent Seat on the Council, but the debate can scarcely be limited there, as the composition of the Council is one of the most difficult of the constitutional questions which the League has to face, and carries with it germs of innumerable complications. Other States besides Germany have already posed their candidature for a Permanent Seat on the Council and amongst those may be cited in particular the Republic of Poland. But neither Spain nor Brazil will accept an increase in the number of Permanent Seats, outside of that accorded to Germany, unless they also fall within the same category. In order to facilitate her own candidature Poland proposes that Spain and Brazil be also given permanent representation on the Council. This proposition has the support of France and the Petite Entente, but it seems to be opposed by Great Britain and Sweden. According to the rules of procedure, a permanent seat on the Council is accorded to a Member of the League only on the unanimous recommendation of the Council and by a two-thirds majority of the Assembly.

Even if the Extraordinary Assembly is called upon to pronounce on the question of enlarging the number of permanent seats, the great problem of the composition of the Council will not be resolved, because the creation of new permanent seats would take away from the non-permanent Members, or the small countries, the numerical superiority which they, at present, enjoy. Nowadays, the latter are in the proportion of six to four. After the admission of Germany, they will be only six to five. Any further change would upset the equilibrium, which would mean that the Permanent Members of the Council would have all the organisation of the League between their hands. This, in my opinion, would create an intolerable situation, which would be incompatible with the democratic principles on which the Covenant is based and constitute a menace to the small States.

Is mise, le meas,
[signed] M. MacWhite

No. 378 NAI DFA LN 1-4

Michael MacWhite to Desmond FitzGerald (Dublin)
(M.L. 03/023)

Geneva, 19 February 1926

A Chara,
As far as I can gather the Extraordinary Assembly is likely to sit for four or five days. It will meet on the afternoon of March 8th, when two Commissions will be constituted – one Financial and the other Constitutional.

In addition to allocating Germany's portion of the expenses, the Financial Commission will have to deal with the question of the new buildings and the creation of several new posts in the Secretariat. Discussion on those matters will last for at least two days. The Commission on Constitutional questions will, as soon as it meets, appoint a sub-committee to examine the German demand for admission. This sub-committee will sit in private and satisfy itself that the application conforms to Article I of the Covenant. It is likely that the Members of the Sub-Committee will put many questions to the German delegates concerning their military, naval and air forces, and also as to the manner in which Germany has carried out the clauses of the Treaty of Versailles. As soon as the Sub-Committee presents its Report, a Plenary Meeting will be held, when Germany will be admitted to Membership. This will probably take two or three days.

Immediately after Germany's admission the Council of the League will sit and decide that Germany is to have a Permanent seat on the Council. This decision will be communicated to the Constitutional Commission and afterwards to the Assembly, where no opposition is anticipated. In any case a majority vote of the Assembly will decide.

In the meantime, Poland is pushing her candidature with all the means at her command. In this, she is being strongly backed by France and Belgium. Several other Members of the Council are also supposed to be favourable to Poland's claim, but Sweden seems to be completely antagonistic to it. The attitude of Great Britain is doubtful, but I have reason to believe that when Chamberlain and Briand discussed the matter at Paris a few weeks ago the former was in no way hostile.

It is probable that once Germany gets her permanent seat on the Council, somebody will propose that the claims of the other candidates be only examined at the ordinary Assembly in September, but Poland is likely to object, as she believes that once Germany is in possession there is little chance of the Council arriving at a unanimous decision on the matter afterwards. Brazil is withdrawing her candidature on condition that, in future, three non permanent seats be allotted to Latin America, instead of two as at present. Spain, of course, still holds the field, but Quinones de Leon is not likely to press his claim, in view of Poland's attitude.

Outside of the permanent seats, there is a likelihood that one or two non permanent seats may be created. In that case, I am assured that Canada will be a candidate and her chances are not at all bad, as the Dominions represent greater interests and larger resources than either the Little Entente or the Baltic Groupe. Canada would hold the seat by turns with the other Dominions. I cannot say whether this idea originated in London or in Ottawa, but I know that at the last Assembly the aspirations of Senator Dandurand[1] did not at all exclude the possibility of Canada being a Member of the Council at no distant date.

In case you are to assist at the special Assembly, it would be wise to calculate that it will last from March 8th to March 13th. It is quite impossible at the moment to form a correct estimate of the time it will last.

Is mise, le meas,
[signed] M. MacWhite

[1] Raoul Dandurand, Canadian first delegate to the League of Nations assembly (1924-27).

No. 379 DT S4834A

Joseph P. Walshe to Diarmuid O'Hegarty (Dublin)
(L.N. 1/4/23)

DUBLIN, 25 February 1926

The Secretary,
EXECUTIVE COUNCIL.
The Extraordinary Assembly of the League of Nations for the admission of Germany to Membership of the League will begin on the 8th March. For nearly two weeks after Germany's request for admission had been sent to the Secretariat, the European press was full of speculation as to the possibility of Poland seeking a permanent seat on the Council as a set off to Germany who was to become a Permanent Member as a matter of course. Claims were also made for permanent membership on behalf of Spain and Brazil. No formal official action has however been taken by these three countries to lay their claims before the League, and it seems now fairly clear that the Assembly will not be asked to discuss any changes in the Constitution of the Council beyond the admission of Germany to a permanent seat. The action of Sweden – an elected member of the Council – in declaring herself definitely opposed at this juncture to the claims of Poland, Spain and Brazil has definitely excluded their case from serious discussion, as no new permanent member can be elected without a unanimous vote. Should any dispute on this matter arise, the Minister, with the approval of the Executive Council, *will support those States – probably the majority – which adopt the attitude that the question of the reconstitution of the Council should be postponed to the ordinary General Assembly.*

Canada will be represented by Senator Dandurand, the High Commissioner in London, the High Commissioner in Paris and the Canadian Representative at the League.

The Minister considers that the Saorstát should send a delegation to the Extraordinary Assembly and he accordingly requests that an early opportunity of obtaining the sanction of the Executive Council for that purpose may be given to him.[1]

[signed] S.P. BREATHNACH
Rúnaí

No. 380 NAI DT S4743

Final Report of the North-Eastern Boundary Bureau
E.M. Stephens to Kevin O'Higgins (Dublin)

DUBLIN, 26 February 1926

Minister for Justice:
The North-Eastern Boundary Bureau was set up on the authority of a Minute of the Provisional Government dated 2nd October, 1922,[2] authorising Mr. Kevin O'Shiel, then Assistant Law Adviser, to take all necessary steps for the collection

[1] See No. 381 below.
[2] See Nos 1, 2 and 3 above.

and compilation of data in connection with the Boundary Commission. Mr. O'Shiel remained Director of the Bureau until his appointment to the Irish Land Commission in November, 1923.

The Bureau was not only assigned the duty of collecting and compiling data for the Commission, but also of collecting information on Northern matters generally, of acting as a channel of communication between the Government and the Northern Nationalists for whom they were acting, and also of carrying on a publicity campaign so that public opinion might be informed as to the true implications of Article 12 of the Treaty.

The Offices of the North-Eastern Boundary Bureau were opened at 16, Kildare Street, on the 12th October, 1922. These premises had been in the occupation of the Constitution Committee, which had completed its labours, and the members of the staff of that Committee then remaining were transferred to the Bureau. On the 21st February, 1923, the Bureau moved to Offices in the College of Science, and on the 26th September, 1924, moved to Offices in Government Buildings, which it has since occupied.

At the time the North-Eastern Boundary Bureau was set up the Treaty had not been fully ratified, and consequently no formal decision had been taken by the Belfast Parliament to dissociate itself from the Free State. This decision was, however, anticipated, and the anticipation justified by the event on the 7th December, 1922. The decision of the Northern Government to remain under the jurisdiction of Westminster brought the provision for the setting up of the Boundary Commission, in Article 12 of the Treaty, into legal operation. It was only when the recent agreement between representatives of the Governments of Great Britain, the Irish Free State and Northern Ireland received the force of law, that the proviso of Article 12 ceased to have legal effect, and that the work of this Office reached its conclusion.

While the closest co-operation between all members of the Staff was necessary in carrying out the work assigned to us, it was, at the same time, found convenient at the beginning of our operations to divide the work as far as possible into sections for which different members of the Staff were primarily responsible. The statistical, historical and economic sections, a section dealing with international precedents and procedure, and a publicity section, were organised. Contact with the Nationalist population in the North was established by the appointment of legal agents, one of whom was in Belfast and the others in districts that would be affected by the Boundary Commission. With this system in operation the position of the Free State in relation to Northern Ireland created by the Treaty was reviewed in all its aspects. The facts were analysed, the information required by the Government was furnished in the form of memoranda, and the material suitable for publication furnished to the press by means of leaflets, pamphlets, the Weekly Bulletin, and letters.

For the statistical and mapping section of our work, Mr. George A. Ruth, of the Registrar General's Department, was primarily responsible. Mr. D. St. P. Murphy, B.L., took charge of the historical research work, which subsequently proved comparatively unimportant. Mr. Joseph Johnston, F.T.C.D., Lecturer on Economics, was appointed Economic Adviser, and Mr. Lionel Smith Gordon, then Manager of the National Land Bank Limited, kindly agreed to act as voluntary adviser on financial matters. Mr. B.C. Waller dealt with international precedents and procedure in connection with Boundary Commissions, and other kindred matters. Mr. Hugh A. MacCartan, on loan from the National Health Insurance Commission, took charge of the publicity section. With these sections of the work I will deal in detail later.

The following were the legal agents appointed:-

Mr.	P.J. Agnew,	Solicitor,	Magherafelt,
"	J.H. Collins,	do.	Newry,
"	Alex Donnelly,	do.	Omagh,
"	T.J. Harbison,	do.	Cookstown,
"	P. Lavery,	do.	Armagh,
"	W.P. Maguire,	do.	Enniskillen,
"	G. Martin,	do.	Belfast,
"	J. Tracy,	do.	Derry.

It was the duty of these agents, with the exception of Mr. Martin, to furnish the Bureau with the case for inclusion in the Free State of their respective areas, in brief form, setting out all local facts and circumstances. Mr. G. Martin, Belfast, could not of course, prepare a case of this kind. He was assigned the duty of preparing the case of the Belfast Catholics against their treatment by the Northern Government.

When the North-Eastern Boundary Bureau was inaugurated the method of procedure before the Boundary Commission had not been determined. It was not prescribed by the Treaty, and, as the Boundary Commission itself was not in existence, there was no authority to prescribe the procedure by which the claim of the Northern Nationalists was to be presented. It was at this time thought that, in accordance with certain continental precedents, the claim might be put forward by the Government of the Irish Free State for a specified area and facts and figures produced to the Commission to substantiate this claim. It was, moreover, desirable that the effect of the application of Article 12 to the local circumstances should be examined in detail. The first work of the Office was accordingly to prepare maps showing possible boundary lines and accompanying reports showing the effect of such suggested lines in respect of the transfer of inhabitants and the economic and geographical conditions of the neighbourhoods concerned.

These maps and reports were considered by the Government, and it was eventually decided that as the Government were trustees for persons unascertained, no specific claim should be made for a definite area, but that the area to be assigned to the Free State should be regarded as a matter for the Commission to decide on evidence provided by the people themselves. On this view the Commission subsequently acted, hearing Counsel for the State on matters of law and interpretation, and making enquiries on the spot as to the wishes of the inhabitants and the economic and geographical conditions affecting the disputed areas.

In order to facilitate the inhabitants of areas in Northern Ireland who sought inclusion in the Free State, and to make available for publication the salient facts of the case, the Handbook of the Ulster Question was compiled and issued by this Office. It served both purposes well. It was furnished to leading papers in Ireland, Great Britain, and America. It was supplied free to statesmen and politicians likely to be interested or influential in the matters with which it dealt, and was placed on sale for the information of the general public. When the inhabitants of the different areas came to formulate their cases for the Commission the Handbook served in all districts as a book of reference, and as an indication of the form in which the cases should be presented.

Some delay was occasioned in the appointment of the Free State representative on the Boundary Commission by the disordered state of the country in the spring of 1923. It was not until the 19th July that Dr. MacNeill's appointment was communicated to the British Government accompanied by a request that the personnel of the Commission should be completed. It was not, however, until the 6th June, 1924, that the announcement of Mr. Justice Feetham's appointment as the Chairman of the Commission was made by the British Government, and the personnel of the Commission was not completed by the appointment of Mr. Fisher by the British Government to represent Northern Ireland until the 29th October, 1924.

This long delay in the constitution of the Commission was occasioned in the first place by the obstructive policy of the Northern Government. It was delayed in the second place by General Elections both in the Free State and Great Britain.

The period which intervened was availed of by the Northern Government and its supporters to create a situation which would render it as difficult as possible for the British Government to carry out its obligations under Article 12 of the Treaty. The principal method adopted was a gigantic press campaign conducted for the most part through influential newspapers favourable to the Northern Government in Great Britain. This course was adopted in the hope of obtaining political support in Great Britain for the 'not an inch' policy adopted in direct defiance of the Treaty.

During this period a large part of our work was devoted to combating this publicity campaign and to correcting mis-statements which were constantly appearing. In order to do this it was necessary that every public statement made by the supporters of the Northern policy should be examined and the facts it alleged analysed. Such public statements dealt with every phase of the Northern question; the interpretation of the Treaty, the financial position of Northern Ireland, the position of trading centres such as Derry, and other matters too numerous to mention in detail. In order to meet the campaign in the British press it was found necessary to send Mr. MacCartan to London to carry on his publicity work in the High Commissioner's Office, where during part of the campaign Mr. MacCartan had the assistance of other members of the staff.

As mentioned above the Boundary Commission was fully constituted on the 29th October 1924, and preparations had at once to be made for the presentation of their cases for inclusion in the Free State by the Nationalists of Northern Ireland. On the 4th December the Commission heard Counsel on behalf of the Free State Government who laid before the Commission all such considerations as might be regarded as generally applicable to the case of the Northern Nationalists as a whole and their position under the Treaty. When this hearing had concluded the Commission proceeded to Ireland and made an informal tour of the border counties. When this had been done the Commission advertised the fact that they were anxious to receive representations from any parties affected by the re-drawing of the Boundary, containing any claim which they wished to put forward for investigation. The Commission received a large number of representations of various kinds, of which the principal Nationalist representations were submitted on behalf of districts in which our legal agents had been working, and dealt separately with the districts assigned to the respective agents. When all these representations had been received the Boundary Commission arranged its sittings for hearing of evidence in support of representations from those on whose behalf they had been submitted. The method of presenting the case for any locality was left entirely to the discretion of the inhabitants or those authorised by them to act on their behalf. This Office was at the same time put entirely at their disposal for advice and assistance of which Northern Nationalists gladly availed themselves.

Preliminary meetings of witnesses were held at the different centres which I was usually asked to address. When the Boundary Commission sat to hear evidence I attended the sittings at the request of those conducting the case in each locality and reviewed the evidence with each witness before he made his statement to the Commission.

While the Boundary Commission was sitting this Office acted as an information bureau for those giving evidence. In the two principal distributing centres, Newry and Derry, Mr. Johnston, Economic Adviser, gave evidence on the economic conditions, producing figures and statistics, derived from customs and railway returns and other sources which would not have been accessible to local witnesses.

After the evidence had been heard the Commission again heard Counsel for the Free State and then held private sittings in London and prepared a report which was about to be made public when the proceedings of the Commission were arrested by the resignation of the Free State representative and the negotiations which followed, terminating, as they did, in the agreement which has become law, thus concluding the work of the North-Eastern Boundary Bureau.

Having briefly reviewed the scope of operations and the work done by this Office I now turn to the manner in which the work was carried out. As mentioned above the Office was as far as possible divided into sections which have already been enumerated. With the work of these sections I will now deal in greater detail.

From the nature of the circumstances the statistical and mapping section, of which Mr. Ruth was in charge, was the first called upon to outline the problem with which we had to deal. The religious census was taken as a basis which would indicate the political complexion of the population in the districts under consideration. Maps were prepared of new boundaries based on the wishes of the inhabitants as shown by the census. These maps were submitted to the Executive Council, accompanied by reports showing the effect of drawing such proposed boundaries in terms of the transfer of willing and unwilling citizens.

When this work was done the statistical section of the Handbook was prepared for publication. This contained maps and diagrams showing the wishes of the inhabitants and detailed tables setting out the population figures for each administrative area and District Electoral Division. A statistical map, showing, in coloured squares, the distribution of the population and its political complexion by District Electoral Divisions, was prepared for printing by the Ordnance Survey Office. Copies of this map were enclosed in a folder at the end of the Handbook. The statistical tables and this map were in constant use among those presenting the case for the Boundary Commission for the different districts in Northern Ireland during the preparation of the case and the hearing of evidence.

Our statistical section was always at the disposal of the Northern Nationalists and its services were constantly availed of both for the checking of figures and for research.

During our publicity campaign figures dealing with population, finance, and elections, were prepared for publication. A number of maps were prepared during this campaign, some of which were published in pamphlet form, and some furnished to the press.

Maps illustrating the contention made in the presentation of the case on behalf of the Government of the Free State before the Commission that the Poor Law Union, with its principal town as a market centre, should be taken as a unit for transfer, were prepared and furnished to Mr. George Murnaghan, Solicitor, acting for the Irish Free State.

Through the activities of this section a body of statistical evidence was placed on the records of the Boundary Commission which, had the terms of reference been interpreted in the sense in which they were understood by the signatories of the Treaty, must have resulted in the transfer of a considerable area now in Northern Ireland to the jurisdiction of the Free State.

At the beginning of our work we carried out an historical investigation of the Northern Question. Of this work Mr. D. St. P. Murphy took charge. This work was undertaken partly because it was necessary to be fully informed on all matters which might have a bearing on the boundary question, but chiefly because, as mentioned above, the question of procedure had not at that time been determined, and had it been thought advisable for the Government to present a printed case for a specific area, the historical argument would have assumed a much greater importance than it did under the procedure which was eventually adopted. Historical material was collected in connection with the Plantation of Ulster, and portions of Bohn's history of this subject translated from the German. An historical and political section was prepared for publication in the Handbook of the Ulster Question, to which Dr. MacNeill, Mr. J. Good, and Mr. MacCartan, contributed. Mr. Murphy resigned at the end of August 1923, and Miss Kathleen Sullivan, who was at that time appointed to our staff, continued any necessary research work in connection with modern political events.

Mr. Joseph Johnston, F.T.C.D., was appointed Economic Adviser and worked as a part time officer. It was Mr. Johnston's duty to consider and, when necessary, to report upon the financial position of different districts in the North, as affected by the boundary, and to forecast the possible economic effects of possible boundary lines. He also was concerned with the general financial position of Northern Ireland, and in this connection had to advise on the contents of financial White Papers or other such information which we were able to obtain. Many complicated questions arose, particularly at the time of the setting up of the customs frontier, and Mr. Johnston was on several occasions sent to the

North to make special reports on difficulties which had arisen.

The work of reviewing political proposals of a financial nature made by Northern leaders belonged to our economic section. Mr. Johnston was responsible for the preparation of the economic section of our Handbook, to which Captain Henry Harrison also contributed.

During the course of the preparation of the local claims for inclusion in the Free State and during their hearing before the Boundary Commission, our economic work proved particularly important. The general survey of the economic conditions which had been made, enabled me to assist the witnesses, who represented different business interests in the North, in relating the facts of their individual experience to the general question of the boundary line. At the request of Mr. J.H. Collins, who was conducting the case for Newry, and of Mr. J. Tracy, who was conducting the case for Derry, Mr. Johnston gave evidence before the Boundary Commission in both these centres.

In order to supply the material for Mr. Johnston's work, and for his evidence before the Boundary Commission, we had to collect a very large mass of statistics, showing the distribution, by land and by sea, of different classes of goods, and particularly of dutiable goods. Statistics of this kind were supplied by the courtesy of the Great Northern Railway, and also by the courtesy of the Commissioners of Revenue and the Department of Statistics. Besides these sources, to which we were indebted for a large body of information, we had many sources of local information from which statistics of this kind were derived. Mr. Johnston handed in, both in Newry and Derry, memoranda outlining his evidence, accompanied in both cases by an epitome of statistics on which he relied. His memorandum, handed to the Commission in Derry, entitled 'A Statistical Determination of Derry's Hinterland,' contained very detailed and conclusive proof that the economic life of the city was chiefly dependent on Free State trade.

The section of our work which dealt with international precedents and procedure in connection with Boundary Commissions was in charge of Mr. B.C. Waller. Mr. Waller was first employed as a part time Officer, but it was soon found necessary to arrange that he should become a whole time member of the staff. Mr. Waller's first duty was research. It was necessary to investigate all the difficulties presented by the drawing of international boundaries, particularly those which were drawn in post war territorial settlements. In this connection the terms of reference of the Boundary Commissions, their mode of interpretation, methods of voting, political effects, and the international relations involved, had to be examined. These investigations were rendered difficult by the fact that much of the material required was not readily available. It was found necessary to send Mr. Waller to London in order to make investigations direct from persons who had been involved in conducting proceedings for Boundary Commissions, and by consulting documents of which it was impossible to obtain copies here. Mr. Waller was in a position to accomplish this work as he had acted as Secretary of the Peace with Ireland Council in London prior to the Truce, and was consequently in touch with a circle of people who were anxious to give all assistance possible with the work on which he was engaged. Mr. Waller also dealt with the relation of the League of Nations to Boundary disputes, a subject on which, as an expert on the League, his advice was particularly valuable. He contributed to the Handbook the section entitled 'Analogous Problems in Other Countries.'

Mr. Waller also assisted in the general work of the Office, and particularly in the publicity section, in which he assisted Mr. MacCartan both here and in London. While still a member of the Staff Mr. Waller won the Filene Prize of £1,000 for the best plan for securing world peace. At the end of November, 1924, as Mr. Waller's work was completed, and the Boundary Commission was about to begin its sittings, Mr. Waller resigned, in order to devote his whole time to literary work in connection with international affairs.

Our publicity section, in charge of Mr. H.A. MacCartan, had a very arduous task to perform. During the whole Boundary Commission controversy it was essential to keep the public, both in this country, and, as far as possible, in Great Britain, informed as to the facts and real difficulties of the situation. There was certain material suitable for publication derived from other branches of our work which it was the duty of the publicity section to issue in suitable form for the particular public for which it was intended.

The first work which the publicity section had to undertake was in connection with the British General Election of 1922. For this election leaflets were prepared for circulation and their distribution was arranged in different centres in Great Britain where the Irish vote was considerable. In order to focus public opinion at home on the important features of the boundary trouble small paragraphs were prepared, each stating some important point. These the press published, in leaded type, framed, on the front page.

From November, 1922 until the British Government invited a conference on the Northern question, a weekly bulletin was issued to the press, which dealt with current controversy on the boundary or partition questions. It analysed the facts or financial statements which might be relevant to this issue. In this and all other publications which were issued from the Bureau, all acrimonious arguments were omitted. Our literature was specially designed to remove the Northern question as far as possible from the realm of heated controversy, and make it a matter of reasoned political argument. The Bulletin was greatly appreciated by the press. The material it contained was often used, as was intended, in an unacknowledged form, while some papers frequently published the bulletin in full.

Copies of the bulletin, in addition to being sent to the press, were also sent to the Consuls, our agents in the north, and other persons likely to be interested. When it was considered wise to discontinue the bulletin, owing to the change in circumstances, a press analysis was prepared each week for the Executive Council, which was continued during the time that the setting up of the Boundary Commission was a matter of public controversy.

Northern politicians, and their supporters in Great Britain, carried on a publicity campaign on a gigantic scale, in order to deflect public sympathy from the Free State case for the transfer of Nationalist areas under the provisions of the Treaty. This campaign was made easy for the supporters of the Northern Government, not only because of the large sums of money at their disposal, and their numerous individual supporters throughout Great Britain, but also because most of the influential newspapers in Great Britain were definitely pro-North in sympathy. Our counter campaign had, in consequence, to be carried on against overwhelming odds. In the February of 1924 it was arranged that our publicity work in Great Britain should be conducted from the High Commissioner's Office, and Mr. MacCartan went to London to take charge of this work.

It was impossible to obtain publication for much of our material in the hostile British press, but by taking part in newspaper controversy Mr. MacCartan was able to obtain publication of hundreds of letters in both the London and the provincial newspapers, and by continually contradicting misstatements of facts he was able to restrict the efforts of the Belfast propagandists. In order to obtain the co-operation of the Irish in England, Mr. MacCartan got in touch with the Irish organisers there, and invited correspondence. He compiled lists of organisers and sympathisers, to whom were distributed thousands of leaflets by post.

Mr. MacCartan contributed to portion of the historical section of the Handbook. He was in charge of the record of current events which was compiled from the Press. In order to obtain material for his publicity work Mr. MacCartan visited the north on several occasions, in order that he might by personal observation, give a more exact account of northern conditions. He also assisted in the preliminary organisation in the Cookstown-Dungannon area, before the sitting of the Boundary Commission.

While the work of the Office was, as far as possible, divided into the sections described, in practice many matters could not be classified under any one section. For publicity purposes it was necessary to draw on the information collected under all the other headings from time to time. This necessitated close co-operation between the different members of the staff. It was indeed only through their very willing and loyal co-operation that our work was carried out successfully.

When the Boundary Commission had been fully constituted and preparations were being made for its sitting, the assistance of this Office in the work of organising the presentation of the claims presented by the different areas in the North, was invited by those who were appointed by the inhabitants locally of the different districts represented before the Commission. This assistance was very willingly given. I took charge, personally, of the work in the North which this arrangement entailed. The representative men in charge in different districts called meetings of witnesses, which they invited me to address. Meetings of this kind were held in Armagh, Newry, Enniskillen and Omagh. In Derry no meeting was called, but it was arranged that the witnesses should meet me at the Offices of Mr. Tracey, Solicitor, where I was accompanied by Mr. Johnston.

When the sittings of the Boundary Commission itself took place, I attended in the witnesses' room, and reviewed the evidence of each witness separately, before he presented himself for examination before the Boundary Commission.

During the sittings of the Boundary Commission, as the evidence proceeded, the questions which the witnesses were asked, and the representations made to the Commission on behalf of those who wished to remain in Northern Ireland, made the lines of argument more definite. All matters on which further research was required were referred to this Office, which, as mentioned above, acted as an information bureau during the sittings of the Commission.

The case presented to the Commission by the representatives appointed for the different areas, and supported by large numbers of witnesses for each district, when taken together, constituted a very remarkable statement of the case of the Northern Nationalists for inclusion under the authority of the national Government. The case was ably presented and was enthusiastically supported by the individual witnesses. The arguments in support of the case were clear, and quite free from acrimony. I feel sure that the way in which the case was presented and the facts concerning the minority in the north, and the interdependence, for trade purposes, of north and south, which the evidence disclosed, did much to render possible the recent agreement. It is a matter of deep personal disappointment for everybody engaged on the presentation of the Nationalists' case to the Commission, that those on behalf of whom the case was made were not returned, by the Commission, to the Government of their choice. In the altered circumstances, however, it may prove that the work of investigating the relations between Northern Ireland and the rest of Ireland, and of investigating the effect of a customs barrier in Ireland, wherever drawn, may, in the end, instead of resulting in improved partition, contribute something to the case of ultimate union.

[signed] E.M. STEPHENS
Secretary

No. 381 NAI DT S4834

Extract from minutes of a meeting of the Executive Council (C. 2/247)
DUBLIN, 2 March 1926

LEAGUE OF NATIONS.
It was decided that the Minister for External Affairs should attend the Extraordinary Assembly of the League of Nations commencing on the 8th instant, which had been convened in connection with the admission of Germany to membership of the League and to permanent membership of the Council.

Arising out of the possibility that application would be made by Poland and probably by Spain and Brazil, for permanent seats on the Council, the Minister's proposal that he should support those States which adopt the attitude that the question of the re-constitution of the Council should be postponed to the ordinary general assembly in September was approved.

No. 382 NAI DFA ES Box 30 File 193

Timothy A. Smiddy to Desmond FitzGerald (Dublin)
WASHINGTON, 12 March 1926

Dear Mr Minister:
I trust you will excuse my bringing to your notice a personal matter and my asking you to give it your sympathetic consideration.

I enclose a memorandum which I received from the Secretary of your Department with reference to my rent allowance.

1. The principle stated by Mr Boland[1] in the last paragraph thereof is against all diplomatic precedent. All Chiefs of Missions in Washington and other countries are given residence allowances without any condition other than that vouchers must be submitted for the rents actually paid. This principle is adhered to in Mr Crawford's case who, I note, is to be allowed a rent allowance which is to have effect as from October 1st, 1924.
2. Again, there is no such proviso in the letter sent to me on December 18th, 1924, which authorises a rent allowance not to exceed £1,000 per annum.
3. The rent I have already paid is much larger than a person with my salary would be normally expected to pay – roughly a third of my net salary. My rent will be at least three times more than this as soon as my family arrives. The rent of my house at Foxrock is £144 per annum: an adequate amount for a salary of £1,500, less income tax. Hence, on Mr Boland's own principle – *a principle which I do not admit* – I should get a refund of two-thirds of rent *already* paid.
4. Mr Boland, in his memorandum, refers to a 'suite of rooms' and to the absence of a residence. This is quite an inaccurate description and I would point out that Mr Boland is not acquainted with one of the normal modes of residence in this country. I reside in a large Apartment Hotel which practically means a group of residences within one building, each of which is a self-contained flat – kitchens, halls, etc. The majority of Senators, Secretaries of the Government Departments, many Ministers, live in such Apartments. For instance, in the Apartment Hotel in which I live there reside Secretary of Labour Davis, Secretary of the Department of Justice, the Chief of the Inland Revenue, and the following Chiefs of Mission:- the Minister of Portugal – Dean of the Ministers–, the Minister of Bolivia, the Minister of Nicaragua, the Minister of Paraguay, the Minister of the Dominican Republic and upwards of fifty Secretaries of Legations.

Many members of the U.S.A. Cabinet, such as Secretary Mellon – worth over two hundred million dollars – and the others referred to above reside in apartments. Hence, Mr Boland's conception of what an apartment and suite of rooms are is inaccurate: it is a customary method of residence in this city, and the one I have is worthy of the dignity of the Irish Free State.
5. When I procure a larger apartment as soon as my family arrives my rent will be equal to the amount of my net salary – $525.00 per month. Unless I receive rent allowance to the full amount of £1,000 per annum it will be impossible for me to maintain, even frugally, the dignity of the Irish Free State.
6. I have considered carefully the feasibility of a house and visited several houses and find that the cost of a staff alone would be $600.00 or £120 per *month*: this in addition to the lowest rent at which a suitable furnished house can be acquired – $600.00 per month – makes such a proposition untenable: it would leave little available for entertainment or representation.
7. I am sure Mr Boland does not realize the amount of expenditure a Minister has to incur – as also Secretaries – on necessary entertainment. Dinners, luncheons, receptions are tendered by diplomats and members and heads of the Government and their Departments which have to be returned – twice and

[1] H.P. Boland, Assistant Secretary in charge of Establishment Division in the Department of Finance.

three times a week one is obliged to entertain in some form. It is a necessary part and an inevitable consequence of the presence of a Minister and Legation here.

8. In view of the above I am sure the Minister of Finance will agree to refund in full the rent already paid by me and pay in future £1,000 per annum as rent allowance, provided that that sum or more has been expended in rent: this is in accordance with the practice of all Governments which give a rent allowance irrespective of the condition laid down by Mr Boland.

9. On account of the financial embarrassment occasioned by withholding my rent allowance with the consequent reduction of my standard of living to a degree out of keeping with the dignity of my position, I trust, Mr Minister you will give my request your sympathetic support and inform me of the result at your earliest convenience – if possible by cable.

With the assurance of my highest esteem,
Your sincerely,
(Sgd) T.A. Smiddy

No. 383 NAI DFA ES Box 22 File 250

Joseph P. Walshe to Count Gerald O'Kelly de Gallagh (Brussels)
(Confidential) (Copy)

Dublin, 12 March 1926

A Chara,

We realise very clearly in this Department that a proper system of information for our Foreign Representatives as to our relations with all External Countries should be established. At the moment the only country with which we have continuous relations is Great Britain and these are of such a purely administrative and routine nature that it would add nothing to the efficiency of our Foreign Representatives to be made aware of them. The Privy Council and the Boundary issues are the only two examples in recent times of unusual interest. Both were as clearly and as fully set out in the Press as in Despatches. In fact the Privy Council question was never mentioned at all in a Despatch.

The Treaty with France is under consideration, but the first definite step will be the visit of O'Riordan[1] to Paris some time next month.

Very probably Monsieur Goor[2] has been talking to his Government about the advantages of a Treaty with this country and he has no doubt spoken about it here, but if we were to take note of every nebulous project and broadcast it to our Representatives we should certainly not be doing them a good turn. The real situation with regard to commercial treaties is full of doubt. Why make commercial treaties with foreign countries before a definite need arises and especially before re-organising our trade with Great Britain?

Mise, le meas,
[copy letter unsigned]

[1] E.J. Riordan, Department of Industry and Commerce, Dublin.
[2] Belgian Minister in Dublin.

No. 384 NAI DT S4834

Handwritten memorandum by Joseph P. Walshe on the admission of Germany to the League and associated questions
DUBLIN, 16 March 1926

Comment
The proposed solution inclusive of (4) has the following advantages:
1. Germany will be a member of the Council before any change takes place in its constitution.
2. The entire changes proposed depend on a *free* vote of the Assembly which may reject them all including the election of Poland to a *non*-permanent seat.
3. (4) has the particular advantage of excluding Poland for an indefinite period from permanent membership.
4. The political balance would be fairly well maintained by the interchange of Poland & Norway for Sweden & Czechoslavakia.
The main point is that Germany agrees.

I think the Minister should be left a free hand to do as he thinks fit after consultation with Canada.

[initialled] J.W.

No. 385 NAI DT S4730A

Heads of the Ultimate Financial Settlement between the British government and the government of the Irish Free State
LONDON, 19 March 1926

1. The Government of the Irish Free State undertake to pay to the British Government at agreed intervals the full amount of the annuities accruing due from time to time under the Irish Land Acts, 1891-1909, without any deduction whatsoever whether on account of Income Tax or otherwise.
2. The Government of the Irish Free State agree to pay to the British Government prior to March 31st 1926, the sum of approximately £550,000, being the amount hitherto withheld by them in respect of income tax on annuities payable under the above-mentioned Acts.
3. The British Government accept liability for the provision out of monies provided by Parliament of the cost of the interest and sinking fund on bonus and excess stock under the above-mentioned Acts subject to a contribution by the Irish Free State Government of the sum of £160,000 in the year 1926-27 and at the rate of £134,500 per annum thereafter.
4. It is agreed between the two Governments that the question of double income tax shall be settled generally on the residence basis as elaborated in the scheme which has already been provisionally agreed between the Revenue Departments of the two Governments. The two Governments agree to promote any legislation necessary for this purpose to take effect from the beginning of the financial year 1926-27.
5. The Irish Free State Government agree to discharge their liability outstanding on 1st April, 1926, in respect of the Local Loans Fund by the payment of an

annuity payable half-yearly of £600,000 to the Fund for a period of 20 years payable on the 1st January and the 1st July in each year, the first half-yearly payment being payable on the 1st July, 1926.

6. Subject to the provisions of this Agreement the British Government undertake to make no further claim in respect of any portion of the value of property taken over by the Irish Free State belonging to British Government Departments whose administration and powers were under Article 9 of the Provisional Government (Transfer of Functions) Order in Council of 1st April, 1922, excluded from transfer to the Irish Free State Government.

Provided that—

(*a*) This paragraph shall not be held to affect the position in regard to the Kilmainham Hospital, the Royal Hibernian School and the Tully Stud Farm.

(*b*) Nothing in this paragraph shall prejudice the right of the British Government to be indemnified under paragraph 8 of the despatch from the Colonial Office of the 13th October, 1924.[1]

7. The Irish Free State Government agree to pay to the British Government the sum of £275,000 in full and final discharge of all claims made to the Compensation (Ireland) Commission in respect of damage done prior to July 11th, 1921, to property belonging to any of the British Government Departments mentioned in the last preceding paragraph:

Provided that this paragraph shall not be held to affect the liability of the Irish Free State Government to satisfy awards of the Compensation (Ireland) Commission made in respect of claims preferred by British Government Departments on behalf of private individuals or the Government of Northern Ireland.

8. The British Government waive all claims against the Government of the Irish Free State for the refund of any portion of the sums paid by them under Section 1 of the Irish Railways (Settlement of Claims) Act, 1921.

9. The Government of the Irish Free State agree to pay to the British Government so much of the deficit of the Unemployment Fund of the United Kingdom as may be attributable to the Irish Free State on the basis of the relative proportions of the insured populations of the two countries as at 31st March, 1922, with interest thereon from that date.

10. The Irish Free State Government agree to make no claim in respect of any of the assets of the Consolidated Fund of the United Kingdom including *inter alia* the Civil Contingency Fund and receipts on account of Reparations and Inter-Allied Debts.

11. The Irish Free State Government agree to repay to the British Government 75 per cent. of the pensions and compensation allowances payable to ex-

[1] [Footnote in original] This despatch deals generally with an agreement (the effect of which is set forth in the report of the Comptroller and Auditor-General on the Appropriation Accounts for 1924-25 in connection with the Property Losses Compensation Vote) between the Government of Saorstát Éireann and the British Government concerning the allocation of compensation charges between the Governments; and in paragraph 8 of the despatch is set out an undertaking by the Government of Saorstát Éireann to indemnify the British Government, its servants or agents, against all claims, actions, suits, damages, costs and expenses which might be brought against or incurred by the British Government, its servants or agents, arising out of or in connection with any claim or demand for the settlement of which the Government of Saorstát Éireann, as part of the agreement, assumed responsibility.

members of the Royal Irish Constabulary under the Constabulary Acts, subject to the exception mentioned in Article 10 of the Articles of Agreement for a Treaty between Great Britain and Ireland.

12. For the purposes of any previous agreements between the two Governments, this Agreement shall be deemed to be the ultimate financial settlement mentioned therein.

(Signed) WINSTON S. CHURCHILL
(Signed) EARNAN DE BLAGHD

Appendix 1

Months of the year in Irish and English

Irish	*English*
Eanair	January
Feabhra	February
Márta	March
Aibreán	April
Bealtaine	May
Meitheamh	June
Iúil	July
Lúnasa	August
Meán Fómhair	September
Deireadh Fómhair	October
Samhain	November
Mí na Nollag	December

Appendix 2

Glossary of Irish words and phrases

This list was compiled with the help of Dr Eamon O hÓgain, Stiúrthóir of the Royal Irish Academy's Foclóir na nua-Ghaeilge project. Details of the editorial conventions on the reproduction of Irish language material are given in the introduction (page xvii).

Aire	Minister
Aire Dlí agus Cirt	Minister for Home Affairs
Aire um Ghnóthaí Dúithche	Minister for Home Affairs
Ard-Aturnae/Príomh-Aturnae	Attorney General
Ard-Fheis	National Convention
A chara	Dear Sir/Dear Madam
A chara dhílis	Dear Sir/Dear Madam
a.s. Rúnaí (ar son Rúnaí)	on behalf of the Secretary (p.p. Secretary)
Comhairle Ceanntair	district council (direct translation)
Do chara/Mise, do Chara	Yours sincerely
Dáil Éireann/Dáil	the Lower House of the Irish parliament
A (X) dhil/A (X) dhílis	Dear (X)
Gníomh Rúnaí	Acting Secretary
Le mórmheas/le meas mór	Yours sincerely
Is Mise, le meas/Mise, le meas	With respect
Príomh-Bhreitheamh	Chief Justice
Rúnaí/Rúnaidhe	Secretary
Saorstát	Free State
Saorstát Éireann, An Saorstát	Irish Free State
Sinn Féin	Sinn Féin (political party) (literally: 'Ourselves')
t.c. Rúnaí (thar ceann Rúnaí)	On behalf of the Secretary
Teachta Dála (TD)	Dáil Deputy
Uachtarán	President

Appendix 3

The Anglo-Irish Treaty (6 December 1921)

DE 2/304/1

Final text of the Articles of Agreement for a Treaty between Great Britain and Ireland as signed.

LONDON, 6 December 1921

1. Ireland shall have the same constitutional status in the Community of Nations known as the British Empire as the Dominion of Canada, the Commonwealth of Australia, the Dominion of New Zealand, and the Union of South Africa with a Parliament having powers to make laws for the peace, order and good government of Ireland and an Executive responsible to that Parliament, and shall be styled and known as the Irish Free State.

2. Subject to the provisions hereinafter set out the position of the Irish Free State in relation to the Imperial Parliament and Government and otherwise shall be that of the Dominion of Canada, and the law, practice and constitutional usage governing the relationship of the Crown or the representative of the Crown and of the Imperial Parliament to the Dominion of Canada shall govern their relationship to the Irish Free State.

3. The representative of the Crown in Ireland shall be appointed in like manner as the Governor-General of Canada and in accordance with the practice observed in the making of such appointments.

4. The oath to be taken by Members of the Parliament of the Irish Free State shall be in the following form:-

I .... do solemnly swear true faith and allegiance to the Constitution of the Irish Free State as by law established and that I will be faithful to H.M. King George V., his heirs and successors by law, in virtue of the common citizenship of Ireland with Great Britain and her adherence to and membership of the group of nations forming the British Commonwealth of Nations.

5. The Irish Free State shall assume liability for the service of the Public Debt of the United Kingdom as existing at the date hereof and towards the payment of War Pensions as existing at that date in such proportion as may be fair and equitable, having regard to any just claim on the part of Ireland by way of set-off or counter-claim, the amount of such sums being determined in default of agreement by the arbitration of one or more independent persons being citizens of the British Empire

6. Until an arrangement has been made between the British and Irish Governments whereby the Irish Free State undertakes her own coastal defence, the defence by sea of Great Britain and Ireland shall be undertaken by His Majesty's Imperial Forces, but this shall not prevent the construction or maintenance by the Government of the Irish Free State of such vessels as are necessary for the protection of the Revenue or the Fisheries. The foregoing provisions of this article shall be reviewed at a conference of Representatives

of the British and Irish governments, to be held at the expiration of five years from the date hereof with a view to the undertaking by Ireland of a share in her own coastal defence.

7. The Government of the Irish Free State shall afford to His Majesty's Imperial Forces

(a) In time of peace such harbour and other facilities as are indicated in the Annex hereto, or such other facilities as may from time to time be agreed between the British Government and the Government of the Irish Free State; and

(b) In time of war or of strained relations with a Foreign Power such harbour and other facilities as the British Government may require for the purposes of such defence as aforesaid.

8. With a view to securing the observance of the principle of international limitation of armaments, if the Government of the Irish Free State establishes and maintains a military defence force, the establishments thereof shall not exceed in size such proportion of the military establishments maintained in Great Britain as that which the population of Ireland bears to the population of Great Britain.

9. The ports of Great Britain and the Irish Free State shall be freely open to the ships of the other country on payment of the customary port and other dues.

10. The Government of the Irish Free State agrees to pay fair compensation on terms not less favourable than those accorded by the Act of 1920 to judges, officials, members of Police Forces and other Public Servants who are discharged by it or who retire in consequence of the change of government effected in pursuance hereof.

Provided that this agreement shall not apply to members of the Auxiliary Police Force or to persons recruited in Great Britain for the Royal Irish Constabulary during the two years next preceding the date hereof. The British Government will assume responsibility for such compensation or pensions as may be payable to any of these excepted persons.

11. Until the expiration of one month from the passing of the Act of Parliament for the ratification of this instrument, the powers of the Parliament and the Government of the Irish Free State shall not be exercisable as respects Northern Ireland, and the provisions of the Government of Ireland Act 1920, shall, so far as they relate to Northern Ireland, remain of full force and effect, and no election shall be held for the return of members to serve in the Parliament of the Irish Free State for constituencies in Northern Ireland, unless a resolution is passed by both Houses of the Parliament of Northern Ireland in favour of the holding of such elections before the end of the said month.

12. If before the expiration of the said month, an address is presented to His Majesty by both Houses of the Parliament of Northern Ireland to that effect, the powers of the Parliament and the Government of the Irish Free State shall no longer extend to Northern Ireland, and the provisions of the Government of Ireland Act, 1920, (including those relating to the Council of Ireland) shall so far as they relate to Northern Ireland, continue to be of full force and effect, and this instrument shall have effect subject to the necessary modifications.

Provided that if such an address is so presented a Commission consisting of three persons, one to be appointed by the Government of the Irish Free State, one to be appointed by the Government of Northern Ireland, and one who shall be Chairman to be appointed by the British Government shall determine in accordance with the wishes of the inhabitants, so far as may be compatible with economic and geographic conditions, the boundaries between Northern Ireland and the rest of Ireland, and for the purposes of the Government of Ireland Act, 1920, and of this instrument, the boundary of Northern Ireland shall be such as may be determined by such Commission.

13. For the purpose of the last foregoing article, the powers of the Parliament of Southern Ireland under the Government of Ireland Act, 1920, to elect members of the Council of Ireland shall after the Parliament of the Irish Free State is constituted be exercised by that Parliament.

14. After the expiration of the said month, if no such address as is mentioned in Article 12 hereof is presented, the Parliament and Government of Northern Ireland shall continue to exercise as respects Northern Ireland the powers conferred on them by the Government of Ireland Act, 1920, but the Parliament and Government of the Irish Free State shall in Northern Ireland have in relation to matters in respect of which the Parliament of Northern Ireland has not power to make laws under the Act (including matters which under the said Act are within the jurisdiction of the Council of Ireland) the same powers as in the rest of Ireland, subject to such other provisions as may be agreed in manner hereinafter appearing.

15. At any time after the date hereof the Government of Northern Ireland and the provisional Government of Southern Ireland hereinafter constituted may meet for the purpose of discussing the provisions subject to which the last foregoing Article is to operate in the event of no such address as is therein mentioned being presented and those provisions may include:-

(a) Safeguards with regard to patronage in Northern Ireland.

(b) Safeguards with regard to the collection of revenue in Northern Ireland.

(c) Safeguards with regard to import and export duties affecting the trade or industry of Northern Ireland.

(d) Safeguards for minorities in Northern Ireland.

(e) The settlement of the financial relations between Northern Ireland and the Irish Free State.

(f) The establishment and powers of a local militia in Northern Ireland and the relation of the Defence Forces of the Irish Free State and of Northern Ireland respectively, and if at any such meeting provisions are agreed to, the same shall have effect as if they were included amongst the provisions subject to which the powers of the Parliament and the Government of the Irish Free State are to be exercisable in Northern Ireland under Article 14 hereof.

16. Neither the Parliament of the Irish Free State nor the Parliament of Northern Ireland shall make any law so as either directly or indirectly to endow any religion or prohibit or restrict the free exercise thereof or give any preference or impose any disability on account of religious belief or religious status or affect prejudicially the right of any child to attend a school receiving public money without attending the religious instruction at the school or make any discrimination as respects State aid between schools under the management of different religious denominations or divert from any religious denomination or any educational institution any of its property except for public utility

purposes and on payment of compensation.

17. By way of provisional arrangement for the administration of Southern Ireland during the interval which must elapse between the date hereof and the constitution of a Parliament and Government of the Irish Free State in accordance therewith, steps shall be taken forthwith for summoning a meeting of members of Parliament elected for constituencies in Southern Ireland since the passing of the Government of Ireland Act, 1920, and for constituting a provisional Government, and the British Government shall take the steps necessary to transfer to such provisional Government the powers and machinery requisite for the discharge of its duties, provided that every member of such provisional Government shall have signified in writing his or her acceptance of this instrument. But this arrangement shall not continue in force beyond the expiration of twelve months from the date hereof.

18. This instrument shall be submitted forthwith by His Majesty's Government for the approval of Parliament and by the Irish signatories to a meeting summoned for the purpose of the members elected to sit in the House of Commons of Southern Ireland and if approved shall be ratified by the necessary legislation.

(Signed)

On behalf of the British Delegation,
D. LLOYD GEORGE.
AUSTEN CHAMBERLAIN.
BIRKENHEAD.
WINSTON S. CHURCHILL.
L. WORTHINGTON-EVANS.
HAMAR GREENWOOD.
GORDON HEWART.

On behalf of the Irish Delegation.
ART Ó GRIOBHTHA.
MICHEÁL Ó COILEAIN.
RIOBÁRD BARTÚN
E. S. Ó DUGAIN.
SEÓRSA GHABHÁIN UÍ DHUBHTHAIGH

6th December, 1921.

ANNEX.

1. The following are the specific facilities required:-

Dockyard Port at Berehaven.

(a) Admiralty property and rights to be retained as at the date hereof. Harbour defences to remain in charge of British care and maintenance parties.

Queenstown.

(b) Harbour defences to remain in charge of British care and maintenance parties. Certain mooring buoys to be retained for use of His Majesty's ships.

Belfast Lough.

(c) Harbour defences to remain in charge of British care and maintenance parties.

Lough Swilly.

(d) Harbour defences to remain in charge of British care and maintenance parties.

AVIATION.

(e) Facilities in the neighbourhood of the above ports for coastal defence by air.

OIL FUEL STORAGE.

(f) Haulbowline [and] Rathmullen[:] To be offered for sale to commercial companies under guarantee that purchasers shall maintain a certain minimum stock for Admiralty purposes.

2. A Convention shall be made between the British Government and the Government of the Irish Free State to give effect to the following conditions :-

(a) That submarine cables shall not be landed or wireless stations for communication with places outside Ireland be established except by agreement with the British Government; that the existing cable landing rights and wireless concessions shall not be withdrawn except by agreement with the British Government; and that the British Government shall be entitled to land additional submarine cables or establish additional wireless stations for communication with places outside Ireland.

(b) That lighthouses, buoys, beacons, and any navigational marks or navigational aids shall be maintained by the Government of the Irish Free State as at the date hereof and shall not be removed or added to except by agreement with the British Government.

(c) That war signal stations shall be closed down and left in charge of care and maintenance parties, the Government of the Irish Free State being offered the option of taking them over and working them for commercial purposes subject to Admiralty inspection, and guaranteeing the upkeep of existing telegraphic communication therewith.

3. A Convention shall be made between the same Governments for the regulation of Civil Communication by Air.

Appendix 4
Calendars for years 1922, 1923, 1924, 1925, 1926

1922

January

Su	Mo	Tu	We	Th	Fr	Sa
1	2	3	4	5	6	7
8	9	10	11	12	13	14
15	16	17	18	19	20	21
22	23	24	25	26	27	28
29	30	31				

February

Su	Mo	Tu	We	Th	Fr	Sa
			1	2	3	4
5	6	7	8	9	10	11
12	13	14	15	16	17	18
19	20	21	22	23	24	25
26	27	28				

March

Su	Mo	Tu	We	Th	Fr	Sa
			1	2	3	4
5	6	7	8	9	10	11
12	13	14	15	16	17	18
19	20	21	22	23	24	25
26	27	28	29	30	31	

April

Su	Mo	Tu	We	Th	Fr	Sa
						1
2	3	4	5	6	7	8
9	10	11	12	13	14	15
16	17	18	19	20	21	22
23	24	25	26	27	28	29
30						

May

Su	Mo	Tu	We	Th	Fr	Sa
	1	2	3	4	5	6
7	8	9	10	11	12	13
14	15	16	17	18	19	20
21	22	23	24	25	26	27
28	29	30	31			

June

Su	Mo	Tu	We	Th	Fr	Sa
				1	2	3
4	5	6	7	8	9	10
11	12	13	14	15	16	17
18	19	20	21	22	23	24
25	26	27	28	29	30	

July

Su	Mo	Tu	We	Th	Fr	Sa
						1
2	3	4	5	6	7	8
9	10	11	12	13	14	15
16	17	18	19	20	21	22
23	24	25	26	27	28	29
30	31					

August

Su	Mo	Tu	We	Th	Fr	Sa
		1	2	3	4	5
6	7	8	9	10	11	12
13	14	15	16	17	18	19
20	21	22	23	24	25	26
27	28	29	30	31		

September

Su	Mo	Tu	We	Th	Fr	Sa
					1	2
3	4	5	6	7	8	9
10	11	12	13	14	15	16
17	18	19	20	21	22	23
24	25	26	27	28	29	30

October

Su	Mo	Tu	We	Th	Fr	Sa
1	2	3	4	5	6	7
8	9	10	11	12	13	14
15	16	17	18	19	20	21
22	23	24	25	26	27	28
29	30	31				

November

Su	Mo	Tu	We	Th	Fr	Sa
			1	2	3	4
5	6	7	8	9	10	11
12	13	14	15	16	17	18
19	20	21	22	23	24	25
26	27	28	29	30		

December

Su	Mo	Tu	We	Th	Fr	Sa
					1	2
3	4	5	6	7	8	9
10	11	12	13	14	15	16
17	18	19	20	21	22	23
24	25	26	27	28	29	30
31						

1923

January

Su	Mo	Tu	We	Th	Fr	Sa
	1	2	3	4	5	6
7	8	9	10	11	12	13
14	15	16	17	18	19	20
21	22	23	23	25	26	27
28	29	30	31			

February

Su	Mo	Tu	We	Th	Fr	Sa
				1	2	3
4	5	6	7	8	9	10
11	12	13	14	15	16	17
18	19	20	21	22	23	24
25	26	27	28			

March

Su	Mo	Tu	We	Th	Fr	Sa
				1	2	3
4	5	6	7	8	9	10
11	12	13	14	15	16	17
18	19	20	21	22	23	24
25	26	27	28	29	30	31

April

Su	Mo	Tu	We	Th	Fr	Sa
1	2	3	4	5	6	7
8	9	10	11	12	13	14
15	16	17	18	19	20	21
22	23	24	25	26	27	28
29	30					

May

Su	Mo	Tu	We	Th	Fr	Sa
		1	2	3	4	5
6	7	8	9	10	11	12
13	14	15	16	17	18	19
20	21	22	23	24	25	26
27	28	29	30	31		

June

Su	Mo	Tu	We	Th	Fr	Sa
					1	2
3	4	5	6	7	8	9
10	11	12	13	14	15	16
17	18	19	20	21	22	23
24	25	26	27	28	29	30

July

Su	Mo	Tu	We	Th	Fr	Sa
1	2	3	4	5	6	7
8	9	10	11	12	13	14
15	16	17	18	19	20	21
22	23	24	25	26	27	28
29	30	31				

August

Su	Mo	Tu	We	Th	Fr	Sa
			1	2	3	4
5	6	7	8	9	10	11
12	13	14	15	16	17	18
19	20	21	22	23	24	25
26	27	28	29	30	31	

September

Su	Mo	Tu	We	Th	Fr	Sa
						1
2	3	4	5	6	7	8
9	10	11	12	13	14	15
16	17	18	19	20	21	22
23	24	25	26	27	28	29
30						

October

Su	Mo	Tu	We	Th	Fr	Sa
	1	2	3	4	5	6
7	8	9	10	11	12	13
14	15	16	17	18	19	20
21	22	23	24	25	26	27
28	29	30	31			

November

Su	Mo	Tu	We	Th	Fr	Sa
				1	2	3
4	5	6	7	8	9	10
11	12	13	14	15	16	17
18	19	20	21	22	23	24
25	26	27	28	29	30	

December

Su	Mo	Tu	We	Th	Fr	Sa
						1
2	3	4	5	6	7	8
9	10	11	12	13	14	15
16	17	18	19	20	21	22
23	24	25	26	27	28	29
30	31					

1924

January

Su	Mo	Tu	We	Th	Fr	Sa
		1	2	3	4	5
6	7	8	9	10	11	12
13	14	15	16	17	18	19
20	21	22	23	24	25	26
27	28	29	30	31		

February

Su	Mo	Tu	We	Th	Fr	Sa
					1	2
3	4	5	6	7	8	9
10	11	12	13	14	15	16
17	18	19	20	21	22	23
24	25	26	27	28	29	

March

Su	Mo	Tu	We	Th	Fr	Sa
						1
2	3	4	5	6	7	8
9	10	11	12	13	14	15
16	17	18	19	20	21	22
23	24	25	26	27	28	29
30	31					

April

Su	Mo	Tu	We	Th	Fr	Sa
		1	2	3	4	5
6	7	8	9	10	11	12
13	14	15	16	17	18	19
20	21	22	23	24	25	26
27	28	29	30			

May

Su	Mo	Tu	We	Th	Fr	Sa
				1	2	3
4	5	6	7	8	9	10
11	12	13	14	15	16	17
18	19	20	21	22	23	24
25	26	27	28	29	30	31

June

Su	Mo	Tu	We	Th	Fr	Sa
1	2	3	4	5	6	7
8	9	10	11	12	13	14
15	16	17	18	19	20	21
22	23	24	25	26	27	28
29	30					

July

Su	Mo	Tu	We	Th	Fr	Sa
		1	2	3	4	5
6	7	8	9	10	11	12
13	14	15	16	17	18	19
20	21	22	23	24	25	26
27	28	29	30	31		

August

Su	Mo	Tu	We	Th	Fr	Sa
					1	2
3	4	5	6	7	8	9
10	11	12	13	14	15	16
17	18	19	20	21	22	23
24	25	26	27	28	29	30
31						

September

Su	Mo	Tu	We	Th	Fr	Sa
	1	2	3	4	5	6
7	8	9	10	11	12	13
14	15	16	17	18	19	20
21	22	23	24	25	26	27
28	29	30				

October

Su	Mo	Tu	We	Th	Fr	Sa
			1	2	3	4
5	6	7	8	9	10	11
12	13	14	15	16	17	18
19	20	21	22	23	24	25
26	27	28	29	30	31	

November

Su	Mo	Tu	We	Th	Fr	Sa
						1
2	3	4	5	6	7	8
9	10	11	12	13	14	15
16	17	18	19	20	21	22
23	24	25	26	27	28	29
30						

December

Su	Mo	Tu	We	Th	Fr	Sa
	1	2	3	4	5	6
7	8	9	10	11	12	13
14	15	16	17	18	19	20
21	22	23	24	25	26	27
28	29	30	31			

1925

January

Su	Mo	Tu	We	Th	Fr	Sa
				1	2	3
4	5	6	7	8	9	10
11	12	13	14	15	16	17
18	19	20	21	22	23	24
25	26	27	28	29	30	31

February

Su	Mo	Tu	We	Th	Fr	Sa
1	2	3	4	5	6	7
8	9	10	11	12	13	14
15	16	17	18	19	20	21
22	23	24	25	26	27	28

March

Su	Mo	Tu	We	Th	Fr	Sa
1	2	3	4	5	6	7
8	9	10	11	12	13	14
15	16	17	18	19	20	21
22	23	24	25	26	27	28
29	30	31				

April

Su	Mo	Tu	We	Th	Fr	Sa
			1	2	3	4
5	6	7	8	9	10	11
12	13	14	15	16	17	18
19	20	21	22	23	24	25
26	27	28	29	30		

May

Su	Mo	Tu	We	Th	Fr	Sa
					1	2
3	4	5	6	7	8	9
10	11	12	13	14	15	16
17	18	19	20	21	22	23
24	25	26	27	28	29	30
31						

June

Su	Mo	Tu	We	Th	Fr	Sa
	1	2	3	4	5	6
7	8	9	10	11	12	13
14	15	16	17	18	19	20
21	22	23	24	25	26	27
28	29	30				

July

Su	Mo	Tu	We	Th	Fr	Sa
			1	2	3	4
5	6	7	8	9	10	11
12	13	14	15	16	17	18
19	20	21	22	23	24	25
26	27	28	29	30	31	

August

Su	Mo	Tu	We	Th	Fr	Sa
						1
2	3	4	5	6	7	8
9	10	11	12	13	14	15
16	17	18	19	20	21	22
23	24	25	26	27	28	29
30	31					

September

Su	Mo	Tu	We	Th	Fr	Sa
		1	2	3	4	5
6	7	8	9	10	11	12
13	14	15	16	17	18	19
20	21	22	23	24	25	26
27	28	29	30			

October

Su	Mo	Tu	We	Th	Fr	Sa
				1	2	3
4	5	6	7	8	9	10
11	12	13	14	15	16	17
18	19	20	21	22	23	24
25	26	27	28	39	30	31

November

Su	Mo	Tu	We	Th	Fr	Sa
1	2	3	4	5	6	7
8	9	10	11	12	13	14
15	16	17	18	19	20	21
22	23	24	25	26	27	28
29	30					

December

Su	Mo	Tu	We	Th	Fr	Sa
		1	2	3	4	5
6	7	8	9	10	11	12
13	14	15	16	17	18	19
20	21	22	23	24	25	26
27	28	29	30	31		

1926

January

Su	Mo	Tu	We	Th	Fr	Sa
					1	2
3	4	5	6	7	8	9
10	11	12	13	14	15	16
17	18	19	20	21	22	23
24	25	26	27	28	29	30
31						

February

Su	Mo	Tu	We	Th	Fr	Sa
	1	2	3	4	5	6
7	8	9	10	11	12	13
14	15	16	17	18	19	20
21	22	23	24	25	26	27
28						

March

Su	Mo	Tu	We	Th	Fr	Sa
	1	2	3	4	5	6
7	8	9	10	11	12	13
14	15	16	17	18	19	20
21	22	23	24	25	26	27
28	29	30	31			

April

Su	Mo	Tu	We	Th	Fr	Sa
				1	2	3
4	5	6	7	8	9	10
11	12	13	14	15	16	17
18	19	20	21	22	23	24
25	26	27	28	29	30	

May

Su	Mo	Tu	We	Th	Fr	Sa
						1
2	3	4	5	6	7	8
9	10	11	12	13	14	15
16	17	18	19	20	21	22
23	24	25	26	27	28	29
30	31					

June

Su	Mo	Tu	We	Th	Fr	Sa
		1	2	3	4	5
6	7	8	9	10	11	12
13	14	15	16	17	18	19
20	21	22	23	24	25	26
27	28	29	30			

July

Su	Mo	Tu	We	Th	Fr	Sa
				1	2	3
4	5	6	7	8	9	10
11	12	13	14	15	16	17
18	19	20	21	22	23	24
25	26	27	28	29	30	31

August

Su	Mo	Tu	We	Th	Fr	Sa
1	2	3	4	5	6	7
8	9	10	11	12	13	14
15	16	17	18	19	20	21
22	23	24	25	26	27	28
29	30	31				

September

Su	Mo	Tu	We	Th	Fr	Sa
			1	2	3	4
5	6	7	8	9	10	11
12	13	14	15	16	17	18
19	20	21	22	23	24	25
26	27	28	29	30		

October

Su	Mo	Tu	We	Th	Fr	Sa
					1	2
3	4	5	6	7	8	9
10	11	12	13	14	15	16
17	18	19	20	21	22	23
24	25	26	27	28	29	30
31						

November

Su	Mo	Tu	We	Th	Fr	Sa
	1	2	3	4	5	6
7	8	9	10	11	12	13
14	15	16	17	18	19	20
21	22	23	24	25	26	27
28	29	30				

December

Su	Mo	Tu	We	Th	Fr	Sa
			1	2	3	4
5	6	7	8	9	10	11
12	13	14	15	16	17	18
19	20	21	22	23	24	25
26	27	28	29	30	31	

Index

This volume is indexed by page number and should be used in conjunction with the list of documents reproduced (pp. xxvi-xlv).

Abbreviations used in index

IFS	Irish Free State	NEBB	North Eastern Boundary Bureau
LGB	Local Government Board	NI	Northern Ireland

C

F